Economic Complexity and Evolution

Research on the dynamics and evolution of economies and their subsystems has increasingly attracted attention during the past three decades. Micro-level activities related to innovation, imitation, adoption and adaptation are sources of often important impulses for abrupt as well as continuous, local as well as generic, systemic as well as modular changes in mesoeconomic and macroeconomic structures. These changes driven by selection and co-evolution, by path-dependencies and lock-ins as well as by transitions and jumps in turn feedback to the system's microeconomic units. Out of this a highly interconnected system of interaction between agents, subsystems and levels of aggregation emerges and confronts researchers with the challenges to grasp, reduce and understand the complexity and her dynamics involved. The series "Economic Complexity and Evolution" addresses this wide field of economic and social phenomena and attempts to publish work which comprehensively discusses special topics therein allowing for a broad spectrum of different methodological viewpoints and approaches.

All titles in this series are peer-reviewed.
This book series is indexed in Scopus.

More information about this series at http://www.springer.com/series/11583

Andreas Pyka • Keun Lee
Editors

Innovation, Catch-up and Sustainable Development

A Schumpeterian Perspective

Springer

Editors
Andreas Pyka
Department of Innovation Economics
University of Hohenheim
Stuttgart, Germany

Keun Lee
Department of Economics
Seoul National University
Seoul, Korea (Republic of)

ISSN 2199-3173 ISSN 2199-3181 (electronic)
Economic Complexity and Evolution
ISBN 978-3-030-84930-6 ISBN 978-3-030-84931-3 (eBook)
https://doi.org/10.1007/978-3-030-84931-3

Spin-off from the Journal of Evolutionary Economics, Volume 30, Issue 4, 2020

This Springer imprint is published by the registered company Springer Nature Switzerland AG.
The registered company address is: Gewerbestrasse 11, 6330 Cham, Switzerland

Contents

Innovation, Catch-Up, and Sustainable Development: Introduction to the Proceedings from the 2018 ISS Conference

Andreas Pyka and Keun Lee

1 Conference Summary

It is great to launch these conference proceedings from the ISS 2018 conference held in Seoul, July 2–4, Korea. The theme of the ISS 2018 was "Innovation, Catch-up, and Sustainable Development. Keun Lee, one of the guest editors of this volume, served as the President of the Society (2016–2018) and also as the main host or Chairman of the Organizing Committee, for the Seoul conference. Actually, it took 26 years to return to Asia: the last ISS conference in Asia was held in Kyoto, Japan, in 1992. And it turned out to be a good decision for the International Schumpeter Society to return to Asia: About 380 papers were presented out of the 469 initial submissions from more than 50 nations around the world. Among these 380 presentations, there were about 90 papers presented by young scholars who are either graduate students or new Ph.D. students.

At the conference, keynote speakers included the long-standing Schumpeterian scholars as well as those scholars whose research subject is related to the theme of the conference. In the opening session, Bengt-Åke Lundvall gave a speech on Transformative Innovation Policy and Global Challenges: a System's Perspective, and Sr. David Sainsbury talked about New Economic Thinking: A Dynamic-Capability Theory of Economic Growth.

Other notable scholars gave their talks in special sessions on the following topics: creative destruction and capitalism, innovation policies and strategies, productivity slow-down, issues in east Asian economies, Schumpeterian economics, frontiers of

A. Pyka (✉)
University of Hohenheim, Stuttgart, Germany
e-mail: a.pyka@uni-hohenheim.de

K. Lee
Department of Economics, Seoul National University, Seoul, Republic of South Korea
e-mail: kenneth@snu.ac.kr

A. Pyka, K. Lee (eds.), *Innovation, Catch-up and Sustainable Development*, Economic Complexity and Evolution, https://doi.org/10.1007/978-3-030-84931-3_1

innovation studies, and finally, a session in honor of Luigi Orsenigo. Some of their names are as follows, in the order of the days and time of their presentation: Massimo Egidi, Horst Hanusch, Mike Gregory, Chen Jin, João Carlos Ferraz, Slavo Radosevic, Giovanni Dosi, Justin Yifu Lin, Hiroyuki Odagiri, Jang-Hee Yoo, John Mathews, Bjørn T. Asheim, Bo Carlsson, Yoshinori Shiozawa, Ben Martin, Uwe Canter, Franco Malerba, William Maloney, Andrea Pyka, John Walsh, Kazuyuki Motohashi, Cesar Hidalgo, Xiaobo Wu, and Mei-Chih Hu.

In the meantime, the Schumpeter Prize of the ISS 2018 went to two eminent scholars in the field. Professor John Mathews and Michael Best shared the prize for their book on "Global Green Shift" (Anthem Press, 2017) and "How Growth Really Happens" (Princeton University Press 2017), respectively. John Mathews has also contributed a chapter to this proceedings volume on a theme related to his prize-winning book, that is, Schumpeterian economic dynamics of greening.

The fifteen chapters in this conference proceedings volume were selected by our reviewers and then by the editors to reflect the state-of-the-art Schumpeterian economics dedicated to the three conference topics innovation, catch-up, and sustainability. Innovation is driving catch-up processes and is the condition for a transformation towards higher degrees of sustainability. Therefore, Schumpeterian economics has to play a key role in these most challenging fields of human societies' development in the twenty-first century. And therefore, the three topics are well suited to capture the great variety of topics, which very likely have the potential to shape the scientific discussion in economics and related disciplines in the years to come.

2 Innovation

Our proceedings begin with an important tradition in Schumpeterian economics, namely the history of innovation. Keiichiro Suenaga analyzes the historical emergence of the British steelmaking industry, which surprisingly so far was not closely connected to scientific advances. Despite the outstanding role of this industry in the early decades of industrialization, only the innovation part is well analyzed and not the early origins of new knowledge stemming from scientific insights and inventions. Suenaga's chapter closes this gap with an informed contribution of the early scientific knowledge sources relevant to the steelmaking industry.

The chapter by Hạnh Luong La and Rudie Bekkers entitled Science and technology relatedness: the case of DNA nanoscience and DNA nanotechnology also deals with a classical Schumpeterian topic, namely knowledge analysis in order to gain new insights into the generation of new technological opportunities, this time placing central very recent science-based industries. The authors deal with the relation between the science and technology domain, which for so-called science-based industries, is the main artery for new opportunities and knowledge-triggered development. Their insights concerning the technological relatedness between the knowledge bases allow for new targets in innovation policy design, in particular when commercialization of science-based knowledge needs to surpass critical thresholds to be applied in innovation processes on the industry level.

Krzysztof Szczygielskia, Wojciech Grabowskib and Richard Woodward address innovation strategies and their focus on internal and external knowledge in an empirical study analyzing data from the Community Innovation Survey. Their econometric model evidences the importance of external determinants for innovation success despite predictions from other studies which emphasized the dominant importance of firms' internal line-ups.

The end of the first and beginning of the second decade in the twenty-first century gives an intensive foretaste of what might be expected: New industries based on digitization are emerging, and the artificial intelligence and machine learning sectors are widely believed to be only the forerunners of a development which will encompass broader manufacturing sectors and also mergers with service sectors. Junguo Shi and Bert M. Sadowski refer to the work of an outstanding colleague who we remembered very much during the conference in Seoul: Luigi Orsenigo. Luigi's oeuvre is the backbone of industrial dynamics theory which helps us to understand the complex process of birth, life, and death of industries by combining the concepts of appropriability, opportunity, and cumulativeness. The contribution of Shi and Sadowski demonstrates that we will keep Luigi Orsenigo and his intellectual heritage forever and can gain important new insights into industry dynamics now and in the future.

3 Catching Up

The President of the Society, Keun Lee, followed the custom of the ISS to deliver the presidential address. The topic of his address was "the Art of Economic Catch-up: barriers, detours, and leapfrogging in innovation systems," and a part of his presentation was about the measurement and analysis of national innovation systems. That part has become the basis for his contribution entitled "National innovation system, economic complexity and economic growth," which opens these conference proceedings. The chapter develops a composite NIS index and shows that it is a powerful predictor of economic growth, more robust than other measures of economic complexity. The online-first version of this paper has been awarded the Kapp Prize by the EAEPE (European Association for Evolutionary Political Economy).

Whereas there are many researches measuring national innovation system (NIS), which is a key theoretical concept in Schumpeterian economics, they often use too many variables from heterogenous sources, which make the measurement very demanding, less comparable and less coherent. This article, co-authored by Keun Lee and Jongho Lee, develops a new, coherent, and less-demanding way of measuring NIS of nations around the world, using five variables all made up from patent citation data which show the way how knowledge is created, diffused, and used in each nation. Each of the five variables represents different aspects of innovations in the different economies, such as concentration, diversification, localization, originality of innovations as well as cycle time of innovations. These five variables are also combined into one composite NIS index, so that we may compare and rank countries around the world using this index at a time and also investigate their change over time. Thus, it also helps policy makers to find out weak or strong aspects of each nation's innovation systems.

Fang Wang's contribution also takes up the topic of the conference. Fang Wang empirically analyzes the relationship of regulation on product innovation in the Chinese economy in 2012, a year when China was about to accomplish the target to catch up to the world technology frontier. In the analysis, a trade-off relation between opportunities generated by regulations and potential resource misallocation due to increasing transaction costs is identified, which leads to an inverted U-relationship between regulation and product innovation in the Chinese case. The increasing difficulties to benefit from regulation come from both sides, the administration and the regulated companies, and indicate problems of rent-seeking behavior as well as inflexibilities when confronted with high complexities of innovation processes.

The following chapter by Alexander Gerybadze and Helen Mengis deals with catching up, leapfrogging, forging ahead and re-catching up processes due to changing technological leadership from an innovation systems perspective. The chapter is an industry case study in the field of Lithium-Ion batteries, which originally were invented in Europe before mass production in Japanese and South Korean firms took over the pool position in this industry. In the meantime, technology transfer has changed direction again, and European companies are potentially swinging back to the fast lane in the wind of electrical vehicle supporting policies.

Foreign direct investment might be considered as one of the variables which foster, at least support, catching-up processes of industries. Nejla Yacoub and Hajer Souei investigate the case of the Chinese pharmaceutical industry, which managed to massively attract foreign direct investment despite the Chinese reputation of fiercely imitating western technologies in the last four decades. The authors identified Chinese patent protection of new medical compounds to be so strong that despite potential involuntary knowledge spillovers, the Chinese market for western pharmaceuticals is so attractive that their investment activities are not distorted by losing control of proprietary knowledge generated in their home countries.

Cristiano Antonelli and Christophe Feder return to the conference's catch-up topic with their contribution entitled "Total Factor Productivity, Catch-up and Technological Congruence in Italy, 1861–2010." So far, the focus of most investigations of catch-up processes was on the rate of catching up and not on the direction of technological change. Cristiano Antonelli and Christophe Feder present an innovative approach to measure also the effects of the direction. Their most interesting empirical case is Italy's economic development from the mid of the nineteenth century until the present day.

The contribution "Acting as an innovation niche seeder: how can the reverse salient of Southeastern Asian economies be overcome?" by Hsien-Chen Lo, Ching-Yan Wu and Mei-Chih Hu deals with a typical (co-)evolutionary problem of catching up processes. It is most likely that the speed of development of single system components is differing and that the success of any system transformation critically depends on the slowest system component. The authors highlight this co-evolutionary relation in the catching up of South East Asian economies and analyze in a case study the development in Taiwan.

The following chapter by Giorgio Prodi, Francesco Nicolli and Federico Frattini is also focusing on catching-up processes in Asia. This time a regional perspective is applied to Chinese prefectures. In their contribution "Embeddedness and local patterns of innovation: evidence from Chinese prefectural cities" the authors find evidence for a strong explanatory meaning of the time regions are exposed to innovation determining how structures are aligned to innovation dynamics for varying innovation performance in Chinese prefectural cities for a period of 30 years and of the twentieth and the beginning twenty-first century.

Intellectual property rights are always used as an explanatory variable for economic growth and development. Gokay Canberk Bulus and Ibrahim Barkitas frame their research in this tradition and investigate the role of patent rights for macro-economic growth and micro-economic firm performance. Empirically they focus on the case of Turkey and illustrate the difficulties of the Turkish companies to benefit from intellectual property rights.

4 Sustainability

The next contribution to this volume, authored by the 2018 Schumpeter Prize winner, John Mathews, is entitled as "Schumpeterian economic dynamics of greening: propagation of green eco-platforms," and takes up the issue of sustainable development from the conference theme. John Mathews' approach applies fundamental Schumpeterian principles of economic development, like increasing returns, learning curve effects and emerging innovation and production networks which contrasts sharply with the negative perspective of degrowth and zero-growth approaches, which got stuck in the quantitative view of the economic mainstream and therefore are not capable to understand the economic opportunities which emerge from the overcoming of the lock-in in fossil-based technologies.

The chapter by Marlene O'Sullivan touches on the sustainable development topic of the conference. The author analyzes, with a remarkable database, global developments in the renewable energy sector over the last 25 years. In particular, she highlights the developments in the wind energy sector and applies concepts from industry dynamics, namely the idea of industry life cycles. It is most interesting to see that in a comparative analysis of various international and national developments, the global development is derived from aggregating national developments. While innovation processes in the wind energy industry are global, the dynamics of the national industry development are dominantly following national patterns.

The last contribution to this volume is also dedicated to the sustainability topic of the Seoul conference and focuses on the importance of the precautionary principle for sustainability. Although written more than 2 years before the Corona pandemic, the insights are most relevant today when we can observe that companies having implemented sustainability thinking in their business strategies get through the crisis much better than traditional fossil-resources-based companies. The two authors Shyama V. Ramani and Mhamed-Ali El-Aroui apply their ideas on the seed industry in their contribution "On application of the Precautionary Principle to Ban GMVs: An Evolutionary Model of New Seed Technology Integration" and model in a game the conditions for varying outcomes. It is by far not self-evident that the precautionary principle becomes dominant in particular if different time horizons influence the decisions of the agents. For sustainability, however, it is required that our decisions are not tightly calculated but offer scope for adaption to allow for resilience.

5 Conclusion and a Personal Note

Once again, like in all conference proceedings appearing biannually since the 1980s, the chapters selected for the conference proceedings of the 17th Schumpeter conference show the broadness and high standard of Schumpeterian analysis. The ideas of dynamics, heterogeneity, novelty, and innovation as well as transformation are the most attractive fields in economics today and offer the most prolific interdisciplinary connections now and for the years to come when humankind, our global society, has to master the transition towards sustainable economic systems by solving the grand challenges and wicked problems with which we are confronted today.

With the publishing of this conference volume following the 2018 Seoul conference, the 12 years' term of Andreas Pyka as editor of the International Schumpeter Society ends. Having edited the proceedings from Rio de Janeiro in 2008, Aalborg in 2010, Brisbane in 2012, Jena in 2014, Montreal in 2016 and Seoul in 2018, always cooperating closely with the distinguished Presidents of the Society as co-editors, I want to thank the members of the society for their trust, and most importantly, for the intellectual delicacies, which helped me, more than a decade to develop an understanding for the broadness of evolutionary economics and to escape of the tiny box of my own field within this wide, diversified, and exciting intellectual landscape.

Part I
Innovation

The Influence of Science and "Industrial Enlightenment" on Steelmaking, 1786–1856

Keiichiro Suenaga

Abstract Scientific knowledge is crucial to opening up new possibilities for major technological advances. However, the role of science has not been regarded as important in the innovations leading to modern steelmaking. In addition, how did science begin to play an important role? Mokyr focuses on the "Industrial Enlightenment," which has its origins in the Baconian program of the seventeenth century. This paper examines the process through which modern steelmaking emerged and clarifies the role of science and "Industrial Enlightenment." When much time elapses between scientific and technological advances, the role of science is often not regarded as important and sensational innovations such as the Bessemer process are emphasized. However, this is not a proper evaluation. The role of "Industrial Enlightenment" on the supply side must also be recognized as significant in the emergence of modern steelmaking technology.

Keywords Steel · Science and technology · Industrial enlightenment · Bessemer process · Modern chemistry · Innovation diagram

JEL Classification B52 · N73 · O12 · O31

1 Introduction

Science's influence on economic development has long been discussed (e.g., Smith, 1920; Kuznets, 1966; Dosi, 1988b; Mokyr, 2002, 2009; Stephan, 2010). Dosi (1988a) points out that scientific knowledge is crucial to opening up new possibilities for major technological advances and that in the twentieth century, the emergence of major new technological paradigms has often been directly dependent on, and associated with, major scientific breakthroughs. "It is nowadays apparent that

K. Suenaga (✉)
School of Political Science and Economics, Meiji University, Tokyo, Japan
e-mail: suenaga@meiji.ac.jp

A. Pyka, K. Lee (eds.), *Innovation, Catch-up and Sustainable Development*, Economic Complexity and Evolution, https://doi.org/10.1007/978-3-030-84931-3_2

the development of science provides much of the basis for future industrial development. These connections, however, have been present from the creation of science as an organized activity in the 17th century" (Etzkowitz & Leydesdorff, 2000, p. 117).[1]

When did science become important for economic development? According to Kuznets (1966, p. 10), the steam engine was the earliest major science-based invention. It dominated much of the first century of modern economic growth. As Dickinson (1958) states, "an important step leading to the invention of the steam engine was the discovery of the pressure of the atmosphere. The discovery suggested the possibility of using atmospheric pressure to do work on a piston beneath which a vacuum could be created [and this] culminated in the invention of the steam-engine" (pp. 168–170). Cardwell also observes that "combining the expansive properties of steam with the recently discovered pressure of the atmosphere" (1972, p. 56) made the steam engine feasible. Lipsey et al. (2005) also describe its emergence and insist that 'clearly, science played an important role in the development of the steam engine" (p. 253). (See also Suenaga (2019a) on steam (heat) engines.)

Conversely, the role of science has not been regarded as important in the innovations leading to modern steelmaking, including the development of Bessemer's converter, Siemens's open hearth and Thomas's basic lining. For example, Smith (1961) insists that "[t]he innovations which marked the discontinuous stages of growth of the iron and steel industry – the introduction of the blast furnace and finery, of puddling, and of the Bessemer and open-hearth steel-making processes – all owed almost nothing to the direct influence of science" (p. 363). Mowery and Rosenberg (1989) agree, saying that "Bessemer had developed his process without the benefit of any training in the chemistry of his day. Neither he nor his contemporaries had a very precise idea of the chemical transformations that

[1]Kuznets (1966) places importance on the application of science to economic production as the main characteristic of modern economic growth, but does not suggest that modern technological innovation is triggered by scientific discovery. Rosenberg (1982) also insists that technological knowledge has preceded scientific knowledge, and that, even in industries founded on scientific research, practical experience with new technology often precedes scientific knowledge.

It is particularly important, however, to mention that the relationship varies, subject to the stage of industrial development. The role of science is more important in its initial stages. Although at least the first ten years of the history of the semiconductor industry were characterized by a crucial interrelationship between science and technology, the distance between the two has increased since the 1960s. Basic semiconductor technology has become established and its development path no longer needs a direct "coupling" with "Big Science" (Dosi, 1984, p. 28). In addition, technological paradigms are driven by the main scientific advances and the interval between scientific discovery and innovations in some cases is more than 50 years (Coccia, 2015, p. 30).

Although there are many arguments about the relationship between science and technology, a chain linking science and technology forms an evolutionary system and the hierarchical evolution of the chain generates industrial and economic development. In addition, "science and technology were both endogenous to a third set of factors that determined the direction and intensity of the intellectual pursuits that led to advances in both" (Mokyr, 2005, p. 290). See Suenaga (2015b) in detail. In Suenaga (2015b), the relationship between science and technology is classified into four models: the Price, Bush (linear), Rosenberg and Dosi models.

occurred inside the converter.... None of the three great technological innovations in ferrous metallurgy in the second half of the nineteenth century ... drew on anything but elementary chemical knowledge that had already been available for a long time. Indeed, only Siemens had had the benefit of a university education" (pp. 28–31). In the same vein, Bernal (1953) states the following: "In considering these three contributions to the nineteenth-century revolution in metallurgy, the first striking point is their independence of any organized scientific movement. Of the three inventors only Siemens had a university education, and none of them received any material assistance or more than a little advice from academic, scientific or governmental sources" (p. 109). Harris (1998) even insists that "[t]he real scientific breakthrough of Monge, Vandermonde and Berthollet in 1786 may itself have been a misleading incentive to make industrial progress depend on more scientific investigation, for it had no useful technological spin-off" (pp. 219–220).

How did science begin to play an important role? Mokyr (2005, 2009) focuses on the "Industrial Enlightenment," which has its origins in the Baconian program of the seventeenth century. Evans and Withey (2012) state that "[t]he Industrial Enlightenment, we contend, cannot account for technological change in the steel trades. There is little evidence that the circulation and codification of "useful knowledge" among artisans (a key feature in Mokyr's formulation) had a discernible effect on the ways in which steel goods were made. The nature of demand, in other words, was the key determinant, not the cognitive conditions of supply. In this sense, there was an enlightenment in steel, but it manifested itself in the design and marketing of goods rather than their manufacture' (p. 534). Furthermore, Allen (2009) insists that "metals were striking for the absence of much connection to the Enlightenment" (p. 250).

On the contrary, Mokyr (1999, 2002, 2009, 2010) emphasizes the importance of scientific knowledge on the invention of the Bessemer process and insists "the growth of the epistemic base in the preceding half-century was pivotal to the development of the process" (2002: p. 86). However, although he focuses on some of the key factors, he has does not analyze the relationships between science and technology in detail.

This paper examines the process through which modern steelmaking emerged and clarifies the role of science and "Industrial Enlightenment." This discussion is also important in determining how to view the role of science in economic development and in considering "the Great Divergence" (Pomeranz, 2000) and "the Great Knowledge Transcendence" (Jin, 2016). In addition, the examination of this paper will show how to create radical innovations that are completely different from existing paradigms and how to create new technological paradigms to overcome difficulties such as the recent Covid-19 pandemic and environmental problems. In the process of emergence of these new paradigms, new combinations of science and technology and the "fields" that create such new connections play a very significant role.[2] The composition of this paper is as follows. Section 2 examines the history of

[2]See also Fox et al. (2020), Lyu et al. (2020) and Suenaga (2012, 2015a, 2015b, 2019a).

steelmaking, focusing on advances in science and technology. Section 3 highlights some steelmaking issues and examines the role of science and "Industrial Enlightenment." Finally, Sect. 4 concludes the article and raises some theoretical and strategic implications.

Although Suenaga (2015a, 2019a, 2019b) analyzes the Paleolithic Age, heat engines, semiconductors, etc. and clarifies the relationship between science and technology in the technological paradigms and the emerging process of industry (the basic model is presented in simplified form in Sect. 2), does this model apply to other industries? Suenaga (2020) conducts a descriptive analysis of modern steelmaking methods, but in the current paper, based on the previous one, a more explicit and detailed analysis is performed using the model in Sect. 2. Section 3 discusses the development of science and technology related to steelmaking, and Sect. 4 clarifies the importance of science and "Industrial Enlightenment" in the invention process of modern steelmaking. Section 5 introduces the concept of hierarchy into the model of Sect. 2 and conducts a structural and qualitative analysis of the technological paradigm of modern steelmaking. In addition, Sect. 6 adds an analysis of the "field" in which scientific and technological knowledge is combined, enabling such knowledge transcendence.

2 Innovation Diagram, Technological Paradigms and Hierarchy[3]

Figure 1 illustrates Dosi's "technological paradigms" and "technological trajectories" (1982), based on the innovation diagram of Yamaguchi (2006). In Yamaguchi's diagram, existing scientific knowledge (S) advances through scientific research ($S_1 \rightarrow S_2$). Advances in scientific knowledge are indicated by a rightward arrow in the soil because they are not valued economically. Existing technological knowledge (T) advances through technological development, etc. ($T_1 \rightarrow T_1$'). This is illustrated as the upward arrow above the soil. That they are valued economically means they achieve success as goods in the market.

With regard to Dosi's (1982) definitions, this paper defines "technological paradigms" as "a 'model' and a 'pattern' of a solution to *selected* technological problems, based on *selected* scientific knowledge," and defines "technological trajectories" as "the progress process of technological knowledge, based on a technological paradigm." In Fig. 1, technological paradigms are expressed as a dotted line, and technological trajectories are illustrated as upward arrows within the technological paradigms. Although Dosi, given the stock of scientific knowledge, discusses the process whereby technology is selected from existing scientific knowledge, scientific progress such as progress from S_1 to S_2 is illustrated in this figure. Advanced scientific knowledge, S_2, may induce new technological knowledge, T_2, or may be

[3] About this section, see Suenaga (2015b).

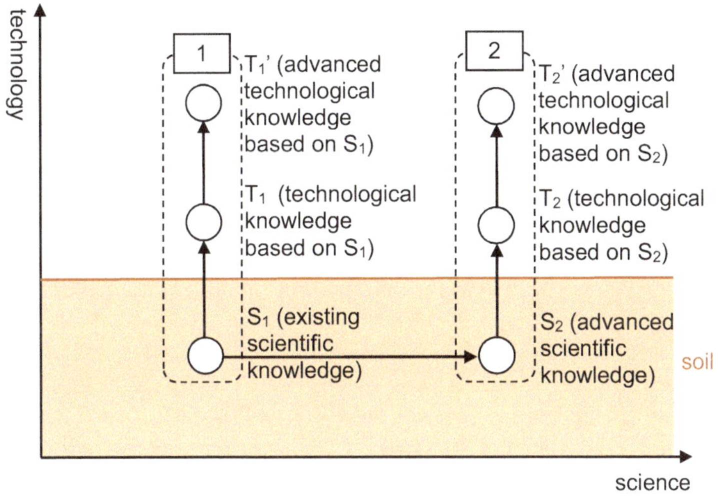

Fig. 1 Technological paradigms and technological trajectories, based on innovation diagram. Source: Suenaga (2015b), Fig. 4). Note: This figure illustrates the view of Dosi (1982), based on Yamaguchi's innovation diagram (2006)

triggered by existing technological knowledge, T_2. Therefore, Fig. 1 includes both cases. Whether these advances are improvements along a technological trajectory or a paradigm shift causing new technological trajectories to emerge depends on whether or not the "selected scientific knowledge" as the basis of the technological trajectory is new (regardless of whether scientific knowledge precedes technological knowledge or vice versa).

In addition, although advances in scientific knowledge have been located in the soil up to this point, the soil itself contains numerous layers. For example, while the academic framework itself changed, advances also occurred in science within the academic framework. With regard to the diagram above, advances in the academic framework are depicted as being located in the deeper layer of soil (referred to here as the third layer), whereas smaller advances such as connection methods are considered as being produced in a shallower soil layer (referred to here as the first layer). Advances in scientific knowledge arising in the third layer form more extensive technological paradigms, and advances in scientific knowledge occurring in the first layer form smaller technological paradigms. Advances in scientific knowledge in the second layer are not as extensive as those occurring in the third layer but are more extensive than those arising in the first layer. As a result, a hierarchy is also formed in technological paradigms when a hierarchy of scientific knowledge exists. In addition, the hierarchical development of scientific knowledge and technological paradigms results in industrial and economic development.

3 Relationship between the Science and Technology of Steelmaking

It is said that the production of iron began in western Asia. After that, the technology diffused to other regions, and steel production became widespread. Although the origin of steelmaking is ambiguous, steel was probably produced by the bloomery process by 1200 BC and carburizing and quenching were practiced in the Near East by 800 BC (Barraclough, 1984, p. 13). Bai (2005, p. 43 and 142) states that in China, carburizing began in the late Western Zhou era (about eighth century BC), and de-carburizing began in the early Warring States era (about fourth century BC). Although it is still not known when Indian wootz steel was developed, it is said to be at least a few centuries before the third century AD (Feuerbach, 2006, p. 49).[4]

Although there are various views on steel's technological diffusion between Asia and Europe (e.g., Needham, 1964; Wagner, 2008), natural steels were made in the Weald by fining cast iron in 1509, and the cementation process was recorded in Nuremberg in 1601 and patented in England in 1613 (Barraclough, 1984, p. 13). René Réaumur tried to introduce carburizing to France and used tensile tests and microscopy to analyze the process. Although he used the term "sulphur and salt" instead of "carbon," he clarified how wrought iron, steel, and cast iron differ and clarified carburizing methods (Réaumur, 1722). Because the quality of steel made by carburization was not stable, Benjamin Huntsman, who was a clockmaker, developed a crucible process to stabilize its quality by smelting carburizing steel in about 1735.

While these steels were also produced in India, Torbern Olof Bergman in Sweden was interested in Indian wootz. Referring to Réaumur's studies, Bergman used wet chemical analysis with acid and balances for quantitative analysis and was able to extract the source of the differences among wrought iron, steel, and cast iron (Bergman, 1781), although he based his work on phlogiston theory.[5] Carl Wilhelm Scheele in Sweden, who studied with Bergman, discovered oxygen using wet chemical analysis. Joseph Priestley in England also found the same element independently. Antoine Lavoisier in France denied the theory of phlogiston and built the basis of modern chemistry on such studies about various elements. In these processes, the chemical analysis of steel and the development of modern chemistry were closely intertwined.[6] Vandermonde, Berthollet and Monge, who studied with Lavoisier in the Parisian Science Academy, stated that 'the theory of phlogiston is no longer tenable after the latest discoveries on the calcination of metals and on the

[4]See also Bronson (1986) for steel in the Muslim medieval world.

[5]Réaumur also acquired and verified wootz (Réaumur, 1722, p. 176), and Heath (1839, pp. 391–393) also described in detail the manufacturing method (the crucible process) of wootz. Ranganathan and Srinivasan (2006) states the following: "Modern metallurgy and materials science rest on the foundation built by the study of this steel during the past three centuries" (p. 67).

[6]Smith also insists that "[t]his knowledge arose out of and contributed to the Chemical Revolution in an intimate way" (1964, p. 150).

decomposition and reconstitution of water’ (1786; 1968, p. 307) and identified carbon as the most important element based on the modern chemistry of Lavoisier instead of the phlogiston theory.

Wootz, which had an effect on Bergman’s studies, also came to be of interest in England. Joseph Banks, the president of the Royal Society of London, ordered some cakes of Indian wootz and let James Stodart and George Pearson investigate them. Pearson identified manganese’s significant role in the production of wootz ‘as the fine experiments of Professor Gadolin, made under the direction of Bergman, have demonstrated’ (Pearson, 1795, p.342). (Scheele and Johan Gottlieb Gahn, who studied with Berman, discovered manganese in 1774). Pearson had been influenced by the scientific knowledge of Bergman and Berthollet, and Stodart was an ingenious artist (Pearson, 1795). In addition, Stodart was the first to measure the temperatures corresponding to colors associated with the tempering of steel (Srinivasan & Ranganathan, 2004, p. 53). William Reynolds, who operated iron works with the Darby family, was a pupil of Dr. Joseph Black, Professor of Chemistry at the University of Edinburgh. He was, as were James Watt, Josiah Wedgewood, and James Keir, adept in both the laboratory and the workshop as Ashton (1948, p. 16) states. He gained a patent for steelmaking using manganese in 1799. ‘This patent of Mr. Reynolds’ started a host of imitators, who all laid claim to improve iron for steelmaking, or to improve steel when made by alloying it with manganese’ (Bessemer, 1905, p. 258).

Wootz further influenced scientists and technologists. David Mushet, who took out a patent for combining iron with carbon for steelmaking through a direct process in 1800,[7] received cakes of wootz from Sir Joseph Banks and also showed that wootz involved a large amount of carbon (Mushet, 1805). D. Mushet had a profound knowledge of the works of French chemists of the Lavoisierian ‘oxidation’ school and of the works of mineralogists such as Bergman and Kirwan, as pointed out by Musson and Robinson (1969, p. 185). He also published a paper about steel and manganese in 1816 (Mushet, 1816).[8] Moreover, the above-mentioned Stodart studied wootz and alloys of steel with Michael Faraday of the Royal Institution of London (Stodart & Faraday, 1820, 1822).

Josiah Marshall Heath, who served in the East India Company, imported a considerable quantity of wootz and had it assayed by D. Mushet. Heath, being affected by the experiments of Faraday and Stodart, got a patent for steelmaking using manganese in 1839.[9] Heath (1839) states the following about D. Mushet: “That iron could be converted into cast-steel by fusing it in a close vessel in contact

[7] See Percy (1864), Ashton (1939, p. 48) and Feuerbach (2006).

[8] See also Mushet (1805) for the influences of Bergman and Reynolds on D. Mushet.

[9] ‘With this view, he returned to England, and placed himself in the chemical school of Dr. E. Turner, of the University of London, one of the most accomplished professors of that day, here he was permitted to erect a furnace of his own, and assisted by Dr. Ure and by the late David Mushett, the most distinguished of modern British authors and workers in this class of subjects, he became familiar with the most approved means of chemical analysis and manipulation’ (Webster, 1856, p. vii). See also Gill (1828) for further information about Heath.

with carbon, was a discovery made by Mr. D. Mushet about the year 1800. This was undoubtedly the original idea of a man of talent, following the light thrown on the theory of steel-making by the discoveries of modern chemistry" (p. 396).[10] As Clow and Clow (1952, p. 352) insist, D. Mushet's work led directly to Heath's Process.

Bessemer made a presentation for a revolutionary steelmaking method in 1856. In his process, molten cast iron changes to steel by only blasting air into it. Moreover, Robert Mushet, a son of D. Mushet, played a role in improving the Bessemer process using manganese (see also Osborn (1952) for the personal relationship between the Mushet family and Heath). Although the Bessemer process was only applied to ores containing little phosphorus, Sidney Gilchrist Thomas invented a new process (the Thomas process) using basic firebrick based on a study by Professor Louis Emmanuel Gruner. (In addition, Scheele, who is mentioned above, identified phosphorus as a factor causing cold-shortness in 1785). Thus, the Bessemer process came to be applied to a variety of ores and has been a mainstream process in steelmaking since the invention of the Linz-Donawitz (LD) process in 1951, although Siemens's open-hearth process was also used in many countries.[11]

4 The Influence of Science and "Industrial Enlightenment" on Steelmaking

In the previous section, we considered the relationships between science and technology of steelmaking. In this section, we discuss some issues in modern chemistry and steelmaking technology and deepen our understanding.

First, even if scientific and technological knowledge was not transcendent from 1790 to 1850, a variety of advances in knowledge were underway. D. Mushet advanced scientific and technological knowledge about steel and carbon. Pearson, Reynolds, Mushet and Heath published many papers and took out many patents related to steel and manganese, and greatly contributed to the evolution of steelmaking (see Sect. 3).

The important thing is how to understand the time lag between advances in scientific knowledge such as those clarified in Vandermonde et al. (1786) and advances in technological knowledge like the development of the Bessemer process (1856). Sometimes there is almost no lag between scientific discovery and technological application, while in other cases, it takes a long time (decades or more) (Suenaga, 2015b, p. 221). Even if scientific knowledge is potentially useful, it may

[10]Furthermore, Wertime (1962) describes that "[p]ractical students of cementation and cast steel quickly learned that the carbide-forming qualities of manganese made it an ideal "regulator" in iron (however not in quantities to produce brittleness): and this knowledge was made the basis of important improvements in English cast-steel manufacture by William Reynolds and Josiah Heath" (p. 279).

[11]See Poznanski (1986) for the rise and fall of each technology.

not be possible to apply it as technology due to the lack of other technologies.[12] In the case of steelmaking, the technology for achieving high temperatures and for making furnaces capable of working at these temperatures had become an obstacle, and the mechanism for financing such development had also been premature. Just because there is a long lag between advances in science and technology, we should not regard science as unimportant.

Next, we revisit the insistence of Evans and Withey (2012) recounted in Sect. 1, but taking the science to technology time lag into consideration. Because no one was able to develop modern steelmaking technology right after the chemical revolution fully, it might seem that the demand for 'enlightened practitioners' such as physicians and anatomists influenced the incremental improvement of pre-modern steelmaking technology as Evans and Withey insist. However, if we allow for an indeterminate time lag, the "Industrial Enlightenment" and science of Lavoisier, Stodart, Pearson, Banks and Mushet can be seen as having gradually contributed to modern steelmaking technology over an extended period of time. That is, the "Industrial Enlightenment," on the supply side, played a significant role in the modern steel industry. In this process, as discussed by Jacob (1997), the prevalence of 'scientific culture' in society had a significant impact.[13]

In addition, Allen (2009) "put together a database of seventy-nine important inventors in the seventeenth and eighteenth centuries. Concentration on this time period ... reflects my view of technological development as a path-dependent process" (pp. 242–243) and insisted that "[i]n the cases of metals ... [s]cience and technology were separate spheres with little interaction" (p. 251). Furthermore, he defined macro-inventions as follows: "Macro-inventions are characterized by a radical change in factor proportions" (p. 151). However, what is important when considering the role of science and the "Industrial Enlightenmen"' is not the important inventors that influenced radical changes in factor proportions, nor the path-dependent process of technological development (technological trajectory), but the relationship between science and technology in the process of emergence of the technology paradigm. Although Allen insisted that "elaboration [of the macro-inventions of the eighteenth century] drove the British economy forward through much of the nineteenth century" (p. 243), it goes without saying that inventions such as the Bessemer process in the nineteenth century were not merely elaboration of the inventions in the eighteenth century.

According to Mowery and Rosenberg, "Bessemer had developed his process without the benefit of any training in the chemistry of his day" (1989, pp. 28–29). Bernal adds that he had not "received any material assistance or more than a little advice from academic, scientific or governmental sources" (1953, p.109). However,

[12]See also Suenaga (2019a) on the time lag from Huygens' invention of the internal combustion engine to its commercialization in forms such as Newcomen's engine.

[13]Jacob and Stewart (2004, p.63) insist that "The scientific revolution thus entered a distinctly new phase characterized by the public disputes of the eighteenth-century Enlightenment." In addition, Jacob (1997, p.113) emphasizes that "English science in the form of Newtonian mechanics directly fostered industrialization."

it is not important whether he directly benefitted from a university education and academic sources. Whether he used the knowledge that had accumulated regarding steelmaking, however, is significant. From the text of a presentation Bessemer gave at the British Association for the Advancement of Science in 1856, it is clear that he benefitted from modern chemistry.[14] Bessemer (1856) said the following:

> On this new field of inquiry I set out with the assumption that crude iron contains about 5%. of carbon; that carbon cannot exist at a white heat in the presence of oxygen without uniting therewith and producing combustion; that such combustion would proceed with a rapidity dependent on the amount of surface of carbon exposed; and, lastly, that the temperature which the metal would acquire would be also dependent on the rapidity with which the oxygen and carbon were made to combine, and consequently that it was only necessary to bring the oxygen and carbon together in such a manner that a vast surface should be exposed to their mutual action, in order to produce a temperature hitherto unattainable in our largest furnaces.

Bessemer's father was a member of the Parisian Royal Academy of Sciences, and Bessemer himself received advice from Andrew Ure, a fellow of the Royal Society of London and author of The Dictionary of Mining and Technology (Bessemer, 1905).[15] As Schürmann (1956) says, Bessemer was well acquainted with chemical processes, for example, through his reading of specialized literature.

Bessemer's invention came about following a long accumulation of scientific and technological knowledge since the chemical revolution, rather than being triggered by scientific knowledge in a linear manner as in the Bush model depicted in Suenaga (2015b). Smith (1961) insisted that "[a]lthough Bessemer remarked in his 1856 paper that he built his first converter with a view of testing practically a theory involving the reaction of carbon and oxygen, from his autobiography it is clear that his work was precipitated simply because he happened to note an unmelted shell on a pig of iron that had been superficially oxidized" (p. 363). However, we need to pay attention to the "chain of science and technology" rather than discussing whether science precedes technology or not.[16] There was a chain of science and technology tying the endless endeavors of scientists and technologists to the completion of the Bessemer process. Thus, as the functions of elements such as oxygen, carbon, manganese, and phosphorus were clarified based on Lavoisier's modern chemistry, a new technological paradigm, the modern blasting process (the Bessemer process), was approaching completion. Although the announcement of the Bessemer process in 1856 received sensational attention, we should not regard the preceding chain of evolution in science and technology as unimportant. Furthermore, the accumulation of scientific and technological knowledge made the improvements by R. Mushet and Thomas possible. Thus, in the analysis of the modern blasting process, we should

---

[14] Mokyr (2002) also insists that 'Bessemer knew enough chemistry to realize that his process had succeeded and similar experiments by others had failed' (p. 86).

[15] See also footnote 9 of this paper for the relationship between Ure and Heath.

[16] The term, "chain of science and technology," is not just synonymous with "co-evolution." Science and technology are not a unified evolutionary system, but a chain of their actions forms an evolutionary system. See also Yamaguchi (2006) and Suenaga (2015b) for discussion.

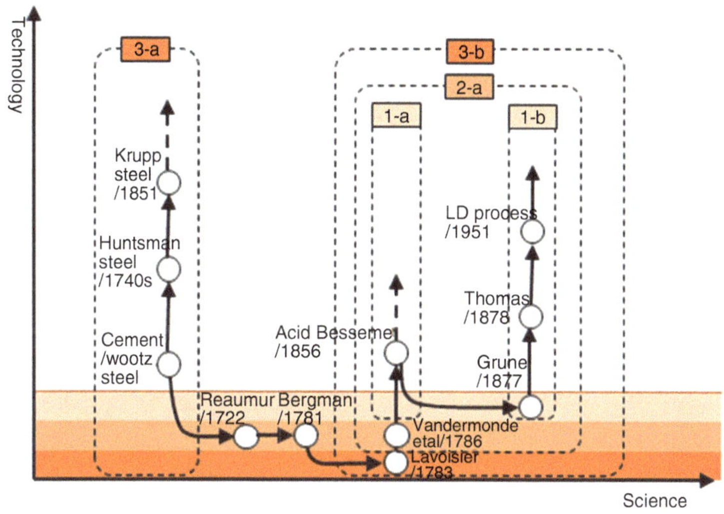

Fig. 2 Innovation diagram: steelmaking and chemistry

emphasize the chained evolution of science and technology over a long time rather than one technologist, Bessemer.

5 Hierarchical Development of Scientific Knowledge and Technological Paradigms

How can we illustrate the relationship between modern chemistry and steelmaking by using the innovation diagram presented in Sect. 2? Although Yamaguchi (2008), in the diagram below, depicts the innovation of the iron industry from wider viewpoints, including the time of Henry VIII and uses for military purposes, this paper conducts a more detailed analysis of the process before and after the emergence of modern steelmaking technology and introduces the concept of hierarchy. Figure 2 illustrates the chained evolution of scientific and technological knowledge in modern chemistry and steelmaking, and the hierarchy (see also Table 1).

As we have already discussed, the modern steelmaking technology, although not directly produced by Lavoisier's modern chemistry, had a very close relationship with it, forming a technological paradigm (3-b). The production of steel before modern chemistry was, in a sense, the result of craftsmanship, not of understanding the working process theoretically. In this article, the term "alchemy" is used in a broad sense, including not only converting base metals into precious metals but also converting iron into harder steel. It can be said that the production of steel before modern chemistry was, in a sense, alchemical (3-a). However, it was far from 'science' in the modern sense, and the scientific understanding of steel production was very vague. Under the scientific system of modern chemistry, the existence and

Table 1 Technological paradigms/scientific knowledge: Steelmaking and chemistry

1st layer: Methods of connections		(1-a) Bessemer/ Acid	(1-b) Thomas/ Basic	(1-a)' Martin/ Acid	(1-b)' 'Thomas'/ Basic
2nd layer: Operating principles		(2-a) Blowing/ Oxygen and carbon		(2-b) 'Co-fusion'/ Carbon content	
3rd layer: Academic frameworks	(3-a) Cementation/ 'Alchemy'	(3-b) Modern steel/ Modern chemistry			

functions of elements such as oxygen and carbon were understood, and the Bessemer method was realized based on this understanding. The working principle of the blasting method was a technological paradigm (2-a) that formed the basis of modern steelmaking. The original Bessemer method used acid refractory materials (1-a), but Dr. Gruner's research on basic refractory materials greatly contributed to the realization of Thomas' basic Bessemer method (1-b).

Apart from the Bessemer method, the Siemens = Martin method is a technological paradigm (2-b) that uses the operating principle of the "co-fusion method" under the technological paradigm of modern steelmaking (3-b). Although this co-fusion method was a technology already used in China in the fourth century AD (Needham, 1964), this principle was scientifically proposed by the French scientist Réaumur (1722), who clarified the difference in carbon content between wrought iron, steel, and cast iron. It is theoretically easy to make intermediate steel by mixing wrought iron with low carbon content and cast iron with high content, but it was very difficult to realize a high temperature for melting it and to develop a refractory material that can withstand the high temperature. In addition, a century and a half later, it became possible to melt cast simultaneously and wrought iron with the heat storage method (1856) devised by Siemens and the Siemens = Martin method (1-a)' was put into practical use (1864). Then, the realization of the basic Siemens = Martin method (1-b)', which was an application of Thomas' basic refractory material, became the mainstream of the steelmaking method (although the Siemens and Martin open-hearth process was replaced by the LD converter process).[17]

[17] Due to its complexity, Figure 2 does not show the 2-b technological paradigm.

6 The Emergence of a Technological Paradigm and the Field of Combining Science and Technology

In addition, the field of knowledge creation in which scientists and technologists collaborate played a significant role in the emergence process of technological paradigms such as those described above. Deeper layers of knowledge creation, whether scientific or technological, require unpredictable and discontinuous processes (Suenaga, 2015b). Although Mokyr (2005) points out that the Parisian Science Academy and the Royal Society of London became institutional factors that reduced access costs to knowledge, great knowledge transcendence often occurs as an unexpected result of a new combination of scientific and technological knowledge. Such a combination often results from collaborative research between scientists and technologists rather than occurring naturally when the cost of access to knowledge decreases. This process requires scientists and technologists facing the limitations of the existing paradigm to return to the underlying knowledge that forms the existing paradigm (T_1 to S_1, or T_2 to S_2, as shown in Fig. 1) and achieve knowledge transcendence (in Fig. 1, the rightward arrow from S_1 to S_2).[18]

The Parisian Science Academy, which created an important impetus in the formation process of the new technological paradigm for steelmaking, was an organization that sought not only science but also technology.[19] Réaumur conducted a study of steelmaking in this academy and identified the factors that create the differences among wrought iron, steel, and cast iron. Réaumur's study also had a major impact on Sweden, where the iron industry and the scientific analysis were active (Beck, 1884). In Sweden, for the iron industry, the Board of Mines and the chair of chemistry at Uppsala University had been set up, both of which had led to advances in Swedish chemistry (Fors, 2008, p.32). Then, the Royal Swedish Academy of Sciences was established as a manifestation of utilitarianism and commercialism (Lundgren, 1988, p. 146) and had a close relationship with the progress of Swedish chemistry. In addition, Wässtrom's paper, reporting on an attempt to imitate a Damascus barrel in a Swedish factory, was sent to the Royal Swedish Academy to inspire Rinman, and Rinman's research in turn inspired Bergman at Uppsala University (Smith, 1960, p. 30). Moreover, the relationship between the theorist Bergman at Uppsala University and the practitioner Scheele, a pharmacist who worked at a pharmacy in Uppsala, also played an important role in the subsequent development of the steelmaking process (see Sect. 3 of this paper).

Furthermore, Lavoisier's chemical revolution, which played the most important role in transforming the steelmaking paradigm, was realized at the Parisian Science Academy, where Réaumur worked. In the process, British and Swedish research and methods had various influences, but Lavoisier recognized the limitations of phlogiston theory and proposed a new paradigm. Based on this new paradigm, the

[18] See also Yamaguchi (2006) regarding this point.

[19] See also Suenaga (2019a) for the Parisian Science Academy.

existence and function of various elements involved in the steelmaking process were better understood. This new paradigm was not immediately accepted in Britain (Priestley and Cavendish) and Sweden (Bergman and Scheele), but Vandermonde and Berthollet, who had shared tacit knowledge with Lavoisier in the same field (the Parisian Science Academy), accepted the new paradigm immediately. Then, the fundamental element of steel that Bergman had grasped based on Phrogiston's theory was correctly understood as "carbon" based on the new paradigm. Here too, Monge, who focused on cannon production, and Berthollet, a well-known technologist, played significant roles.

Moreover, various scientific and technological advances had also been realized using the new chemical paradigm in the UK. Although Joseph Banks of the Royal Society of London provided Studart, Pearson, D. Mushet and others to study Indian wootz and found that they were rich in carbon and manganese (Pearson, 1795; Mushet, 1805), it is reasonable to think that these studies influenced W. Reynolds' patents for manganese-based steelmaking in 1799 and D. Mushet's patent of the wootz process in 1800. Furthermore, Stodart's research with Faraday of the Royal Institute and the relationship between the Lunar Society and researchers such as Banks, Priestley and Reynolds played a major role in the development of the steelmaking process. Although some researchers emphasize the impact of technologists on scientists in these processes (e.g., Evans & Withey, 2012), it is more appropriate to see the relationship as a chained evolution of science and technology rather than as a one-way street.

7 Conclusions and Implications[20]

As shown in Sect. 2, the innovation diagram of Yamaguchi (2006) was developed from a neo-Schumpeterian viewpoint, and the concept of hierarchy was introduced. The revised version of Yamaguchi's innovation diagram then clarified that a chained evolution (co-evolution) of science and technology generates a new technological paradigm and new industry, and the hierarchical evolution results in economic development. Kuznets (1966) indicates the importance of applying science to economic production as the main characteristic of modern economic growth. However, almost all theories of economic development, like that of Schumpeter (1934), treat science as an exogenous factor. Nevertheless, a true theory of economic development can be constructed by endogenizing advances in science. The hierarchical evolution of a chain of scientific and technological knowledge generates economic development. The chained evolution of science and technology has also occurred in the process of steelmaking development.

[20] See also Suenaga (2015b; 2019) about theoretical, political, and strategical implications in this paper.

Many of the advances in science and technology in the period, from Lavoisier's chemical revolution to Bessemer's steelmaking revolution, were described in Sect. 3. Section 4 touched on how our view of the role of science in the emergence of modern steelmaking technology can change depending on how a 70-year time lag between scientific discovery and technological development is regarded. It is more useful to frame the emergence of technological paradigms as a chained process of science and technology than to discuss whether science precedes technology or not. When much time elapses between scientific and technological advances, the role of science is often not regarded as important and sensational innovations such as the Bessemer process are emphasized. However, this is not a proper evaluation. The role of "Industrial Enlightenment" on the supply side must also be recognized as significant in the emergence of modern steelmaking technology.

In addition, in Sect. 5, we analyzed the chained evolution of science and technology using the innovation diagram discussed in Sect. 2. There is a hierarchy in the new technological paradigm based on new scientific knowledge, and there are hierarchical features in the scientific knowledge of each hierarchy. In Sect. 6, we analyzed the 'field' in the process of creating such a new paradigm. Especially in the field of creating a new paradigm in the deep layer, the collaboration between scientists and technologists played a major role.

Chained evolution is also observed in the cases of heat engines (Suenaga, 2019) and semiconductors (Suenaga, 2015a).[21] In the future, more industries will need to be analyzed, but it is interesting that the characteristics of each layer of the technological paradigm are similar in some industries. In the case of steelmaking, as in the case of heat engines and semiconductors, a hierarchy of scientific knowledge exists in which the third layer is an academic framework, the second layer represents the operating principles, and the first layer contains methods of connection. Each layer's characteristics may differ in other industries. However, the most important point is the existence of a hierarchy of scientific knowledge as well as the existence of a hierarchy of technological paradigms based on the hierarchy of scientific knowledge.

Another factor that should be recognized is that organizations like the Parisian Science Academy and the Royal Society of London, which pursue both science and technology, played an important role in the emergence of modern steelmaking. This is similar to the case of heat engines and even semiconductors, where Bell Laboratories played a significant role. Organizations that focus on technological development can be important in promoting advances along a technological trajectory. However, there can also be significant differences between the advances along a technological trajectory and changes in technological paradigms, irrespective of whether scientific knowledge or technological know-how comes first. A field that straddles science and technology often plays a significant role in the emergence of technological paradigms.[22]

---

[21] Needless to say, science's degree of importance differs depending on the characteristics of the industry in question.

[22] See also Etzkowitz and Leydesdorff (2000), Siedlok et al. (2015) and Perry et al. (2016).

On the emergence of technological paradigms, demand plays a certain role, but the role of "Industrial Enlightenment" and attitudes in trying to apply science to technology is significant (this is also applicable to recent cases, such as semiconductors).[23] Factors such as these are the reason why technological leaders, such as China and India 500 years ago, could not develop modern steelmaking technologies.[24]

Acknowledgments Work on this paper was funded by the Institute of Social Sciences, Meiji University. The author is grateful for the valuable comments and suggestions of all participants at "The Research forum for Technology and History of Iron, ISIJ" and at a session of the 17th International Schumpeter Society at the Seoul National University. The comments of anonymous referees are also gratefully acknowledged. I am especially indebted to Fumitaka Nakamura for his profound advice. All remaining errors are my own.

Conflict of Interests: The author declares that I have no conflict of interest.

References

Allen, R. C. (2009). *The British industrial revolution in global perspective*. Cambridge University Press.

Allen, R. C. (2011). *Global economic history: A very short introduction*. Oxford University Press.

Ashton, T. S. (1939). *An eighteenth-century industrialist: Peter stubs of Warrington 1756–1806*. Manchester University Press.

Ashton, T. S. (1948). *The industrial revolution, 1760–1830*. Oxford University Press.

Bai, Y. X. (2005). *Archaeological study on iron works before 3rd Century A.D. in China*. Science Press. (in Chinese).

Barraclough, K. C. (1984). *Steelmaking before Bessemer: Volume 1, Blister Steel: The birth of an industry*. The Metals Society.

Beck, L. (1884). *Die Geschichte des Eisens in Technischer und Kulturgeschichtlicher Beziehung*. Fr. Vieweg.

Bergman, T. (1781). *De Analysi Ferri, Upsala. English translation by J. P. Hickey and C. S. Smith in sources for the history of the science of steel 1532–1786* (Vol. 1968). M. I. T. Press.

Bernal, J. D. (1953). *Science and industry in the nineteenth century*. Routledge & Kegan Paul Ltd..

Bessemer, H. (1856, August 14). *On the manufacture of malleable iron and steel without fuel*. The Times.

Bessemer, H. (1905). *An autobiography: With a concluding chapter*. Institute of Metals.

Bronson, B. (1986). The making and selling of Wootz, a crucible steel of India. *Archeomaterials, 1*, 13–51.

Cardwell, D. S. L. (1972). *Technology, science and history*. Heinemann Educational Books.

[23] See also Van den Ende and Dolfsma (2005) regarding to the role of demand on the emergence of technological paradigms.

[24] The discussions of Allen (2011), Clark (2007) and Pomeranz (2000) are interesting, but the discussion in this paper is similar to that of Mokyr (2002, 2005). However, Mokyr (2002) emphasizes the reduction of the cost of access to knowledge as a result of the ICT revolution, while Suenaga (2015a) analyses the chained evolution of science and technology as generating the ICT revolution as in this paper. In addition, Jin (2016) emphasizes the existence of 'artificial skepticism' as a factor that prevented China and India from developing modern steelmaking technology.

Clark, G. (2007). *A farewell to alms*. Princeton University Press.

Clow, A., & Clow, N. L. (1952). *The chemical revolution: A contribution to social technology*. Books for Libraries Press.

Coccia, M. (2015). Technological paradigms and trajectories as determinants of the R&D corporate change in drug discovery industry. *International Journal of Knowledge and Learning, 10*(1), 29–43.

Dickinson, H. W., 1958, "The steam-engine to 1830 Charles Singer, et al., A history of technology, IV, : Clarendon Press, 168–198. Chpter 6

Dosi, G. (1982). Technological paradigms and technological trajectories. *Research Policy, 11*, 147–162.

Dosi, G. (1984). *Technical change and industrial transformation: The theory and an application to the semiconductor industry*. Macmillan Press.

Dosi, G. (1988a). Sources, procedures, and microeconomic effects of innovation. *Journal of Economic Literature, 26*, 1120–1171.

Dosi, G. (1988b). The nature of the innovation process. In G. Dosi et al. (Eds.), *Technical change and economic theory, ch.10* (pp. 221–238). Pinter.

Etzkowitz, H., & Leydesdorff, L. (2000). The dynamics of innovation: From National Systems and "mode 2" to a triple Helix of university–industry–government relations. *Research Policy, 29*, 109–123.

Evans, C., & Withey, A. (2012). An enlightenment in steel? Innovation in the steel trades of eighteenth-century Britain. *Technology and Culture, 53*, 533–560.

Feuerbach, A. (2006). Crucible Damascus steel: A fascination for almost 2,000 years. *COM, 58*(5), 48–50.

Fox, S., Griffy-Brown, C., & Dabic, M. (2020). From socio-technical systems to biosocial technical systems: New themes and new guidance for the field of Technology in Society. *Technology in Society, 62*, 101291.

Gill, T. (1828). *Gill's technological repository; or, discoveries and improvements in the useful arts, being a continuation of his technical repository* (Vol. II). W. Spiers.

Harris, J. R. (1998). *Industrial espionage and technology transfer: Britain and France in the eighteenth century*. Ashgate.

Heath, J. M. (1839). *On Indian Iron and steel; in a letter addressed to the secretary to the Royal Asiatic Society of Great Britain and Ireland.*

Jacob, M. C. (1997). *Scientific culture and the making of the industrial west*. Oxford University Press.

Jacob, M., & Stewart, L. (2004). *Practical matter: Newton's science in the Service of Industry and Empire, 1687–1851*. Harvard University Press.

Jin, D. (2016). *The great knowledge transcendence: The rise of Western science and technology reframed*. Palgrave Macmillan.

Kuznets, S. (1966). *Modern economic growth: Rate, structure and spread*. Yale University Press.

Lipsey, R. G., Carlaw, K. I., & Bekar, C. T. (2005). *Economic transformations: General purpose technologies and long-term economic growth*. Oxford University Press.

Lundgren, A. (1988). The new chemistry in Sweden: The debate that wasn't. *Osiris, 4*, 146–168.

Lyu, Y., Zhu, Y., Han, S., He, B., & Bao, L. (2020). Open innovation and innovation 'radicalness': The moderating effect of network embeddedness. *Technology in Society, 62*, 101292.

Mokyr, J. (1999). La seconda rivoluzione industriale (1870–1914). In V. Castronovo (Ed.), *Storia dell'economia Mondiale*. Laterza Publishing.

Mokyr, J. (2002). *The gifts of Athena: Historical origins of the knowledge economy*. Princeton University Press.

Mokyr, J. (2005). The intellectual origins of modern economic growth. *Journal of Economic History, 65*, 285–351.

Mokyr, J. (2009). *The enlightened economy: An economic history of Britain 1700–1850*. Yale University Press.

Mokyr, J. (2010). The contribution of economic history to the study of innovation and technical change: 1750–1914. In B. H. Hall & N. Rosenberg (Eds.), *Handbook of the economics of innovation, ch. 2* (pp. 11–50). Elsevier.
Mowery, D., & Rosenberg, N. (1989). *Technology and the pursuit of economic growth*. Cambridge University Press.
Mushet, D. (1805). Experiments on Wootz. *Philosophical Transactions of the Royal Society of London, 95*, 163–175.
Mushet, D. (1816). On cast Iron and steel: With experiments to ascertain whether manganese may be alloyed with Iron. *Philosophical Magazine, 48*, 295–300.
Musson, A. E., & Robinson, E. (1969). *Science and technology in the industrial revolution*. Manchester University Press.
Needham, J. (1964). *The development of Iron and steel Technology in China*. W. Heffer & Sons.
Osborn, F. M. (1952). *The story of the Mushets*. London.
Pearson, G. (1795). Experiments and observations to investigate the nature of a kind of steel, manufactured at Bombay, and there called Wootz: With remarks on the properties and composition of the different states of Iron. *Philosophical Transactions of Royal Society of London, 85*, 322–346.
Percy, J. (1864). *Metallurgy: Iron and steel*. Murray.
Perry, S. J., Hunter, E. M., & Currall, S. C. (2016). Managing the innovators: Organizational and professional commitment among scientists and engineers. *Research Policy, 45*, 1247–1262.
Pomeranz, K. (2000). *The great divergence*. Princeton University Press.
Poznanski, K. (1986). The extinguishing process: A case study of steel Technologies in the World Industry. *Technovation, 4*, 297–316.
Ranganathan, S., & Srinivasan, S. (2006, June). A tale of wootz steel. *Resonance, 11*, 67–77.
Réaumur, R. A. (1722). *L'art de Convertir le Fer Forgé en Acier, et L'art D'adoucir le Fer Fondu*. Brunet. (English translation by Anneliese a. Sisco and Cyril Stanley Smith. Chicago: University of Chicago Press, 1956).
Rosenberg, N. (1982). *Inside the black box: Technology and economics*. Cambridge University Press.
Schumpeter, J. A. (1934). *The theory of economic development*. Oxford University Press.
Schürmann, V. E. (1956). Der metallurge henry bessemer. *Stahl und Eisen, 76*, 1013–1020.
Siedlok, F., Hibbert, P., & Sillince, J. (2015). From practice to collaborative community in interdisciplinary research contexts. *Research Policy, 44*, 96–107.
Smith, A. (1920 [1776]). *An inquiry into the nature and causes of the wealth of nations*. Methuen.
Smith, C. S. (1960). *A history of metallography: The development of ideas on the structure of metals before 1890*. University of Chicago Press.
Smith, C. S. (1961). The interaction of science and practice in the history of metallurgy. *Technology and Culture, 2*(4), 357–367.
Smith, C. S. (1964). The discovery of carbon in steel. *Technology and Culture, 5*(2), 149–175.
Srinivasan, S., & Ranganathan, S. (2004). *India's legendary 'Wootz' steel: An advanced material of the ancient world*. National Institute of Advanced Studies.
Stephan, P. E. (2010). The economics of science. In B. H. Hall & N. Rosenberg (Eds.), *Handbook of the economics of innovation, vol. 1, ch.5* (pp. 217–273).
Stodart, J., & Faraday, M. (1820). Experiments on the alloys of steel, made with a view to its improvement. *The Quarterly Journal of Science, Literature, and the Arts, 9*, 319–330.
Stodart, J., & Faraday, M. (1822). On the alloys of steel. *Philosophical Transactions of the Royal Society of London, 112*, 253–270.
Suenaga, K. (2012). The role of local government in an era of open innovation: An analysis based on the example of a Flemish government-funded NPO. *Journal of Urban Management and Local Government Research, 27*(2), 1–10.
Suenaga, K. (2015a). The hierarchy of technological paradigms: A case study of semiconductor industry. *Josai University Bulletin, The Department of Economics, 33*, 1–13. (in Japanese).

Suenaga, K. (2015b). The emergence of technological paradigms: The evolutionary process of science and technology in economic development. In A. Pyka & J. Foster (Eds.), *The evolution of economic and innovation systems* (pp. 211–227). Springer.

Suenaga, K. (2019a). The emergence of technological paradigms: The case of heat engines. *Technology in Society, 57*, 135–141.

Suenaga, K. (2019b). The theory of knowledge Progress in the quaternary period: The new combinations of anthropology, archaeology and economics. In *The 73rd Annual Meeting of the Anthropological Society of Nippon*, Saga, Japan.

Suenaga, K. (2020). The 'industrial enlightenment' and technological paradigms of the modern steel industry. *Technology in Society, 63*, 101375.

Van den Ende, J., & Dolfsma, W. (2005). Technology-push, demand-pull and the shaping of technological paradigms: Patterns in the development of computing technology. *Journal of Evolutionary Economics, 15*, 83–99.

Vandermonde, C. A., Berthollet, C. L., & Monge, G (1786). "Mémoire sur le fer consideré dans ses différens états métalliques," from the Mémoires de l'Académie Royale des Sciences, pp. 132–200. (Translated by Anne S. Denman and C. S. Smith, "On the Different Metallic States of Iron," in Cyril Stanley Smith ed., Sources for the History of the Science of Steel 1532–1786, The M. I. T. Press, Ch. 10, pp. 284–348.)

Wagner, D. B. (2008). *Science and civilisation in china, volume 5, chemistry and chemical technology, part 11, "ferrous metallurgy,"*. Cambridge University Press.

Webster, T. (1856). *The case of Josiah Marshall Heath, the inventor and introducer of the manufacture of welding case steel from British Iron*. W. Benning &.

Wertime, T. A. (1962). *The coming of the age of steel*. University of Chicago Press.

Yamaguchi, Eiichi, 2006, Innovation: Paradigm disruptions and fields of resonance, NTT publishing., (in Japanese).

Yamaguchi, E. (2008). Industrial revolution as paradigm disruptive innovations. *Organizational Science, 42*(1), 37–47. (in Japanese).

Science and Technology Relatedness: The Case of DNA Nanoscience and DNA Nanotechnology

Hanh Luong La and Rudi Bekkers

Abstract The relatedness between knowledge components within the science domain is widely discussed in the economic, innovation, and management literature. The same is true for the technology domain. Yet, the relatedness between knowledge components across these knowledge domains has received considerably less attention. This chapter aims to introduce the concept of knowledge relatedness between science and technology (S&T), which have been disentangled as two distinct corpora. We approach S&T relatedness from two perspectives: content relatedness (with four indicators: similarity, complementarity, commonality, difference) and temporal relatedness. We then test our ideas with novel empirical material from the field of DNA nanoscience and DNA nanotechnology. We find that the relatedness between S&T scores relatively low, which may explain the relative lack of commercial activity in this field. In light of their indirect complementarity, we recommend that funding "bridging areas" could lead to simultaneous progress in S&T.

Keywords Science and technology relatedness · Knowledge relatedness · Knowledge complementarity · Concept approach · Text-mining · DNA nanotechnology

JEL Code O33

H. L. La (✉)
UNU-MERIT, Maastricht University, Maastricht, The Netherlands

Faculty of Economics, Academy of Finance, Ha Noi, Viet Nam

School of Innovation Sciences, Eindhoven University of Technology, Eindhoven, The Netherlands
e-mail: la@merit.unu.edu; krasplanet@gmail.com

R. Bekkers
School of Innovation Sciences, Eindhoven University of Technology, Eindhoven, The Netherlands

A. Pyka, K. Lee (eds.), *Innovation, Catch-up and Sustainable Development*, Economic Complexity and Evolution, https://doi.org/10.1007/978-3-030-84931-3_3

1 Introduction

The relation between science and technology (S&T), two knowledge domains that are believed to be main sources for innovation and economic growth,[1] is a broad and fascinating topic for evolutionary economists and science-technology-innovation (STI) policymakers. It is widely accepted that S&T are interacting, interdependent, and interconnected entities (Breschi & Catalini, 2010; Meyer, 2000; Wang & Li, 2018), especially in science-based technologies. The nature of S&T relationship, therefore, can be investigated in a narrower sense via S&T interaction. Such interaction, for instance, between the public science sector and the private sector, is a crucial factor shaping the competitiveness of firms, regions, and countries (Nomaler & Verspagen, 2008). However, S&T interaction cannot easily be observed directly. Most empirical literature studies S&T interaction by looking at similarities (e.g., patent-paper pairs[2]) and at linkages (scientific non-patent literature[3]). Possible complementarities between these domains have received relatively little attention.

Addressing the gap in both theory and empirics, this chapter introduces the concept of "S&T relatedness" as a proxy for S&T interaction. It is an umbrella concept encompassing both similarities and complementarities across the domains. We theorize that the higher the S&T relatedness (but not only S&T similarities), the more economically one can further develop both domains, given the scarcity of resources, including funding R&D projects. A higher S&T relatedness also means a higher probability that a scientist in the field reaches out of her specialization towards technology-oriented activities, or a higher probability that an inventor in the field engages in more science-based activities. Via measuring S&T relatedness empirically, we aim to find which knowledge areas in both domains should deserve more attention. Choosing a text-mining and keyword analysis approach, we aim to identify the most important knowledge areas and their relatedness across S&T domains.

We tested our concept on the case of DNA nanoscience and DNA nanotechnology (to which we will from now on refer to as DNA-Nano). We found this field is growing in science, and promises many emerging technological applications (e.g., in electronics, molecular and cellular biophysics, biomimetic systems, energy transfer and photonics, and in diagnostics and therapeutics for human health, Pinheiro et al., 2011). However, actual industrial applications are lagging behind, and there has been little marketable activity (Dunn, 2020). We suspect if there was due to too little S&T interaction, or a significant technology lag in comparison to science. We asked ourselves: "How closely related is the knowledge in both S&T regarding this specific field?", "How can one enhance the growth of both S&T economically?", and

[1] See the discussion on neo-classical and evolutionary theories in Nelson and Winter (1974) and concerns raised by Dosi (1982), Suenaga (2015), and others about uncertainties related to S&T that may cause new technological paradigms.

[2] We later refer to these as PPPs.

[3] We later refer to it as NPL.

Table 1 Four quadrants of research on S&T relationship with examples

	Literature that considers S&T as two distinct entities	Literature that focuses on S&T convergence
Theoretical	I	II
	Dosi (1982), Pavitt (1987), Price (1965)	Arthur (2009), Layton (1974), Nordmann (2008)
Empirical	IV	III
	Mina et al. (2007), Zhao and Guan (2013)	Breschi and Catalini (2010), Murray (2002)

"Which knowledge areas in S&T should deserve more priorities for funding and development"?

The remainder of the chapter is structured as follows: we start by discussing the current literature on the S&T relationship, S&T interactions, and on knowledge relatedness in Sect. 2, as well as introducing our research questions. Then, Sect. 3 presents our research methods, including the selection of S&T domains and the measurement of S&T relatedness. We measure S&T relatedness in two dimensions: content relatedness and temporal relatedness. In Sect. 3, we also present an overview of our empirical data. Section 4 discusses our results, while Sect. 5 offers discussion and conclusion.

2 Literature Review: From the S&T Relationship to S&T Relatedness

2.1 S&T Relationship and Interaction

The S&T relationship and interaction is a recurring and fascinating topic in the economic and innovation literature. It can be considered an interrelationship, because multiple knowledge components in science are connected to multiple knowledge components in technology, and we encounter variations across these S&T domains. We discuss the theoretical and the empirical literature that focuses on observable patterns in the development of S&T. We conclude the section by raising our research questions.

Since S&T are very much interrelated, numerous works have focused on comparing their knowledge developments. While both domains encompass research activities, their objectives are different. Science aims to discover, describe phenomena, and build theories (Drexler, 2013, p 116; Kuhn, 1970, p 60). Technology aims to find solutions for problems and is more concerned with design and production (Dosi, 1982; Drexler, 2013, p 117).

Table 1 shows selected literature on comparing knowledge development between S&T. Basically, there are two main streams, and both acknowledge the interaction between the two domains. However, the first stream (Quadrant I and IV) considers

S&T as two separate entities, whereas the second stream (Quadrant II and III) regards them as two converging entities.

Quadrant I comprises the theoretical literature that considers S&T as two separate entities, typically characterized by similarities and complementarities. Examples of scholars who followed this approach are Price (1965), Dosi (1982), and Pavitt (1987). The work by Price (1965) is considered one of the earliest seminal studies on the S&T relationship and interaction. It refers to Toynbee's "pair of dancers" as a metaphor for the relationship between S&T. Price implies that S&T are two (parallel) co-evolving, cumulative, and autonomous structures/entities. Although the dancers could be men or women, with *differences* in attitude and structure, they move to the *same* music. In the view of Price, the "S&T dancers" typically have "infrequent interaction," a "separate cumulating structure" and more interestingly, are considered to be *complementary*. Two decades later, Dosi (1982) describes the two domains in terms of scientific and technological paradigms, and scientific and technological trajectories. He reiterates Thomas Kuhn's (1970) view of a scientific paradigm as a model, a pattern, and a set of problems of inquiry. In an analogy of Kuhn's scientific paradigm, Dosi defines the technological paradigm as a "model, a pattern of solution of selected technological problems, based on selected principles derived from natural sciences and on selected material technologies." In this sense, the *similarities* between scientific and technological paradigms lie in the mechanism and procedure of both S&T. Pavitt (1987) strongly argues that the efficiency of the whole field is not inevitably an outcome of creating more similarities between S&T. He emphasized that policymaking should consider the *complementarity* between S&T, which "varies considerably among sectors of application, in terms of the direct usefulness of academic research results, and the relative importance attached to such results and to training."

Quadrant IV comprises empirical studies that consider S&T as two separate entities, and is, compared to the other quadrants, understudied. Mina et al. (2007) study the evolution of scientific and technological knowledge on the treatment of coronary artery disease by comparing the two *top main paths*[4] of its scientific and technological citation networks and found them somewhat similar. From a different perspective, Zhao and Guan (2013) introduce a model characterizing the relationship between S&T based on their classification of S&T styles and the changes in producing publications and patents. While their approach is novel, their dataset (on nanotechnology) was limited to publications and patents at selected universities only. Their work thus ignores the role of industry in publishing and patenting.

Quadrant II comprises theoretical contributions investigating the S&T knowledge relationship via the integration or overlap between these domains. Layton (1974) explains how transforming a set of technological rules became a new entity

[4]The main path approach is a network analysis tool introduced in the late 1980s to investigate networks of scientific publications, and later to study patent networks (see Verspagen, 2007; Bekkers & Martinelli, 2012). The top main path is considered as representing the most important developments in citation networks.

of science: "technological science" or "engineering science." In a similar vein, Arthur (2009) further articulates that S&T are "deeply interwoven." In fact, in the field of nanoscience and nanotechnology, some scholars articulate the term "nanotechnoscience" (Nordmann, 2008; Patra, 2011). Such terms reflect the belief in a true integration of S&T, a context in which we cannot simply distinguish between S&T, or between basic and applied research (Nordmann, 2008).

Quadrant III comprises empirical contributions that examine the S&T knowledge relationship via the convergence or overlap between scientific and technological networks. Scholars in this quadrant emphasize similarities, rather than complementarities, making the differences between S&T appear insignificant (Meyer, 2000). Since Narin et al. (1997), a large body of quantitative literature used NPL references as a direct proxy for S&T interaction including Meyer (2000), Verbeek et al. (2002). Other studies, such as those of Murray (2002) and Chang et al. (2017), investigate S&T interaction via patent-paper pairs (PPPs), based on the assumption that a single idea is described in both a patent and a paper. From such pairs, networks of co-authoring and co-patenting can form the basis for further analysis. Murray's work (2002) forms the basis for Boyack and Klavans (2008), Breschi and Catalini (2010), who trace the link between scientific and technological networks via their gatekeepers: inventors-authors. Perhaps, the emerging topics around these gatekeepers are just the tip of the iceberg, reflecting only the part of both networks where the similarities are the strongest and most visible. Arguably, the S&T interaction may occur in certain other places than just where direct citation links, PPPs or inventors-authors exist, and the largest share of knowledge is through work by non-author inventors and non-inventor authors. If this is true, then it would be good to look at the S&T interaction also from a broader perspective, through various patterns of interaction (e.g., complementarities), rather than only based on similarities. We also note that observing citations links has inherent limitations: while patents do at some rate refer to scientific publications (NPL), scientific publications rarely refer to knowledge contained in patents, even if granted patents, by mere definition, must be novel.

2.2 From Knowledge Relatedness to S&T Relatedness

The literature on knowledge relatedness is fragmented and not well-established. The S&T relatedness and knowledge relatedness between two domains have not been discussed in any literature. In this sub-section we will discuss the "relatedness" as a "universal" concept, and then in different contexts, ranging from computational linguistics, management studies to economic geography, then explain why we need this concept in explaining S&T interaction.

Most of the literature refers to "relatedness" as the measure of proximity—or distance—between two entities, activities, or components, generally within one domain (in one corpus, in science or in technology, in one region, or in one sector, etc.). Originating from one domain, these entities normally are not identical but sharing some commonalities. The relatedness between two entities is often measured by the overlap (via co-classification or co-occurrences) between them. Therefore, knowledge relatedness has been mostly equated with knowledge similarity, which just reflects part of the whole picture of all possible patterns of relatedness. In computational linguistics, semantic relatedness is often used interchangeably with semantic similarity, which is the distance between two-word vectors (measured by the cosine of the angle between vectors, Euclidean distance, or Spearman rank correlation coefficient, etc.).

Economic geographers and innovation economists see technology relatedness as the extent to which the variety of technologies being used in a region is related (Boschma & Frenken, 2009). Scientific relatedness refers to the cognitive distance between a new potential scientific topic and a set of specialized topics (Boschma et al., 2014). These concepts of relatedness are often employed to study how specialization and diversity influence firms' performance or regional economic growth.

Makri et al. (2010) investigate science similarity and complementarity, technology similarity and complementarity, but only at a firm level. In this study, they conceptualized knowledge relatedness as knowledge similarity and complementarity. They argued that technological overlap can proxy the similarity of technological assets but cannot capture possible technological complementarities. Even 10 years after their publication, knowledge complementarity is still under-researched in different contexts.

As far as we are concerned, knowledge production is an interactive, path-dependent, and cumulative process (Boschma et al., 2014; Dosi, 1982). The extent to which knowledge entities are related can also reflect the interaction between agents. According to Tripodi et al. (2020), knowledge relatedness increases the probability of a scientist reaching out of her own specialization. Looking at our context of S&T relationship, S&T relatedness could indicate the probability of a scientist engaging in more technology-oriented activities or an inventor engaging in more science-based activities. It could also reflect the interactive learning process between scientists and inventors, in short S&T interaction.

In summary, the literature on the S&T relationship and interaction, and knowledge relatedness discusses both similarities and complementarities. The empirical literature, however, mostly focuses on similarities, sometimes on differences, and hardly focuses on complementarities. Empirical works on S&T similarities mainly use PPPs, as a proxy for S&T interaction. But we think there might be more room to discuss the S&T interaction in a more systematic manner, because PPPs just reflect the similarities in an incomplete extent.[5] The players in both S&T can interact (or learn from each other) in multiple ways[6] (for instance, reading and referring to others' work, but also being co-funded in the same project, or sharing the same

[5]In a similar vein, Heinisch et al. (2016) used co-location as a proxy for direct knowledge interaction.

[6]Both directly and indirectly.

equipment), which contribute to the similarities and complementarities. Moreover, empirical work on S&T relatedness, including S&T complementarity, remains a research gap in S&T studies and knowledge relatedness across domains. For these reasons, our study aims to introduce the concept "S&T relatedness," its dimensions and measurement. In this chapter, we test it empirically on the case of DNA-Nano S&T. Thus, we aim to investigate empirically to what extent the knowledge contents in DNA Nanoscience and DNA Nanotechnology are related; more specifically, how they are similar, complementary, or different, over time. Additionally, we also look at the temporal relatedness of these domains, based on the gap between the emergence of knowledge areas in each domain.

3 Methods and Data

To study S&T relatedness, we consider these two domains as two corpora, i.e. bodies of text. In text-based methodologies, science is often proxied by academic publications,[7] whereas technology is often proxied by patents. By combining our relatedness metrics with text-mining publications and patents, we aim to discover narrative information within and across the two interrelated domains. Such a method is useful not only in information retrieval but also in the evaluation of research and funding, future complementary qualitative research, STI studies, and policymaking.

Accordingly, we extract publications (mainly journal articles) and patents systematically from two database platforms (Web of Science, provided by Clarivate Analytics and PATSTAT by the European Patent Office), which provide extensive search and retrieval facilities within their meta-data. Accordingly, we employ text-mining techniques to convert unstructured data (raw text) into structured data, namely "knowledge areas" represented by the most "significant" terms[8] (a smaller unit of analysis[9]).

In a nutshell, our methodology is four-fold: assembling two corpora, one for science and one for technology, by retrieving relevant documents from the respective databases, using our concept approach (Sect. 3.1), text-mining methods that extract key terms with their occurrences and co-occurrences from each corpus and can proxy the respective knowledge base underlying the two knowledge domains (Sect. 3.2), measuring the content relatedness between S&T by several indicators: commonality, similarity, complementarity (direct, indirect), and difference (Sect. 3.3), and measuring the temporal relatedness between S&T based on the emergence of knowledge areas (Sect. 3.4). In Sect. 3.5, we provide a description of our data.

[7]Note that while we use the term "academic publications," such publications can also be authored by people working for firms. Likewise, university staff can also apply for patents.

[8]They are "term groups," which consist of synonyms, abbreviations...which have the same meaning.

[9]We used two levels of analysis: domain level, and term level.

3.1 Selecting S&T Domains: The Concept Approach

For both publications and patents, the most common search/selection strategies are keyword search and classification search (Benson & Magee, 2013), or the combination of both. The keyword search typically employs search terms in combination with Boolean operators. The classification search is applicable when publications are classified in research areas (e.g., Web of Science categories), or when patents are hierarchically classified according to technology/application areas (e.g., IPC or CPC codes). More sophisticated approaches for keyword search use structured text-mining software and expert inputs to identify key terms (see Arora et al., 2013). Other approaches for classification search include the Classification Overlap Method, which splits the definition of a technology into two components, a functional or "artifact" component and a "knowledge" one (Benson & Magee, 2015).

The selection procedure to build the datasets of publications and patents is a critical step, and we evaluate our selection using two criteria: recall and precision. Recall is defined as the proportion of all relevant records retrieved, whereas precision is the proportion of retrieved records that are relevant. Both in practice and (information retrieval) theory, it is hard for any query to achieve perfect recall and precision at the same time, because of the inherent trade-off between the two. Search strategies can increase recall (e.g., using synonyms, wild-flags, and OR operators) at the expense of lower precision. Alternatively, search strategies can increase precision (e.g., using AND operators together with highly specific search terms) typically imply lower recall. The true challenge is to find an appropriate balance between recall and precision in a given context. The achievable levels of recall and precision also depend on the subject area and the novelty of the field. In emerging fields, tracking patents and publications is often challenging (Huang et al., 2015). Data might be poorly defined, and terminology may change over time. Classifications systems for publications/journals and for patents may not yet offer specific classes for emerging fields. The researchers often face the challenges of either low recall or low precision or the imbalance in the sub-areas of the emerging field (*ibid.*).

It is worth noting that for data retrieval in emerging fields, the requirement for precision is often considered to be not as important as in well-established fields. Porter et al. (2008) argue that for a vast domain like nanotechnology, there is no absolute standard for recall and precision. Huang et al. (2015) suggest that a search with high recall and satisfactory precision is useful in emerging technology studies. We think Huang et al. (2015)'s suggestion above is quite reasonable and applicable in our case, because for an emerging field like DNA-Nano, it is harder to achieve precision than recall. While we can define and estimate recall by counting the presence of relevant contributions by key individuals in DNA-Nano, defining and estimating precision is a daunting and infeasible task. Among other things, this is because the boundaries of an emerging field with its adjacent fields have not yet been precisely defined.[10] Moreover, each individual expert in the field works within

[10]This may due to the fact there is no fixed perfect definition for a new field.

his/her narrow area of expertise and is not fully aware of the knowledge development and recombination in the entire field. The growth of the field now has much gone beyond what Seeman—the pioneer of DNA-Nano, and his first-generation students ever imagined. Based on the above considerations, for this study, we choose to prioritize recall over precision.

Our initial exercises with keyword search and classification search strategies for DNA-Nano (a field we will describe later) revealed low levels of recall and precision. Most likely, this was because it is an emerging, complex technology field, whose boundaries with other knowledge fields (e.g., bio-nanotechnology, biochemistry, biophysics) are fuzzy and still developing. Classification codes are not yet available for this specific complex field, because DNA-Nano's scope does not certainly fall within even one or more traditional classifications such as nanotechnology or biochemistry. Keywords that can precisely distinguish DNA-Nano from adjacent fields are hard to find.

Finally, we adopted an approach that we learned through intensive interaction with technology and business intelligence units in the industry that work on patent landscaping and patent text-mining. Unsatisfied with traditional patent selection methods (specifically based on keywords and IPC codes), these industry experts pioneered their own approach and found it useful for capturing patents in emerging fields. To the best of our knowledge, the method they developed is new to scholarly studies, and we will refer to it as the "concept approach." In short, it works as follows: First, one operationalizes the definition of a *knowledge field* into a minimum number of independent concepts (often 3 or 4), each representing an indispensable element of the field in question. For each concept, one performs an inclusive search, aiming at a (much) high recall rather than precision (for instance, using all known synonyms related to the concept, combined with the OR operator). As a second step, one selects only the intersection of all concept groups, resulting in a much smaller set. Precision is achieved at this second stage. The concepts approach is an iterative process, whereby the results of each step are monitored in terms of achieved levels of recall and precision,[11] and search queries are refined until no further improvement can be reached, and the sought level of recall and precision is achieved. While originally developed for patents, this approach can be equally used for publication retrieval.

We applied this concept approach on the knowledge field of "DNA Nanotechnology" (terminology often used in both publications and patents), and "DNA Nanoscience," by which we mean the scientific domain of DNA Nanotechnology (see Douglas, 2016, for a more elaborate discussion on the concept of DNA Nanoscience). The journal Nature Research (2018) defines DNA Nanotechnology as "*a branch of nanotechnology concerned with the design, study and application of*

[11] Precision can be estimated by taking a random sample of the set, and manually investigating whether all the records indeed belong to the sought field. Recall can be estimated by independently creating a set of records that are known to belong to the sought set (e.g., by asking an independent expert in the field, or selecting the relevant patents or publications of key contributors) and then testing whether these records are present in the set.

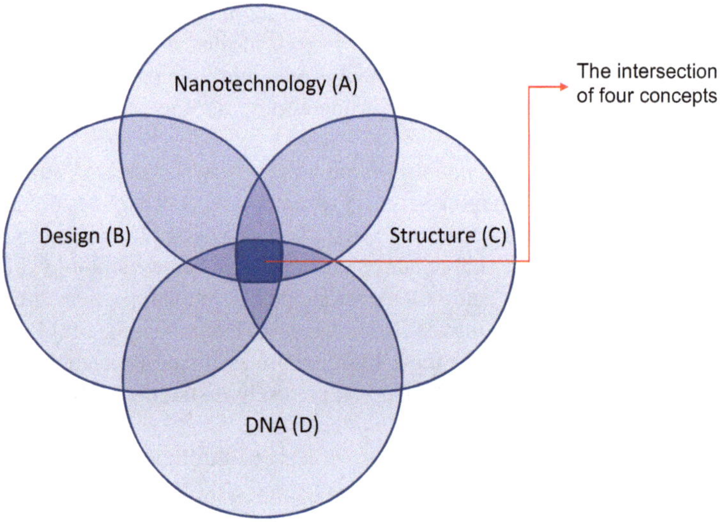

Fig. 1 Illustrating the concept approach to DNA nanotechnology

synthetic structures based on DNA. DNA Nanotechnology takes advantage of the physical and chemical properties of DNA rather than the genetic information it carries." Based on a literature review and on consultation with active researchers in DNA-Nano we met at conferences, we derived four[12] independent concepts to use in our concept approach. These are Nanotechnology (A), Design (B), Structure (C), and DNA (D), as illustrated in Fig. 1 (see also Annex). For each concept, we developed search queries that used all relevant keywords and known synonyms, which were collected exhaustively from multiple sources.[13] Ideally, we want to apply the same query for publications and patents, as being described in our previous work (La & Bekkers, 2018). However, investigating the relevant publications and patents of known scientists and inventors in this field, we learned that the language in publications is different from that in patents. The language in publications tends to be broader, while the language of patents is narrower and more precise. Consequently, we had to adapt our queries to the different language use in publications and patents, in order to achieve both high recall and satisfactory precision. Consequently, we employed a set of queries to collect publications, and another set of queries to

[12]We found that, in our context, four was the number of concepts allowing us to reach the best balance between recall and precision. With three concepts, the level of precision reduced significantly. With five concepts, the concepts started to lose their initial independence, and the level of recall dropped.

[13]Information sources include materials and notes taken at technical conferences on DNA-Nano, communication with experts by email and Skype, and publications and news items in the field of DNA-Nano.

collect patents. We involved two experts[14] to validate that queries included appropriate keywords. Subsequently, for each dataset, we selected the records satisfying all four concept groups. To improve the precision of each dataset, we imposed two lists of exclusion terms, one to remove the irrelevant records from the titles, and the other to remove irrelevant records from titles, abstracts, and keywords. We found these exclusion terms by reading the irrelevant records retrieved from the overlap of the four concept groups. After a number of iterative steps of improvement and refinement,[15] we created our final datasets. Because the patent dataset was much smaller than the publication dataset (there are considerably fewer patents than publications in this area), we complemented the identified patent data with their forward citations. This step further increases recall, while testing confirmed there was no notable drop in precision. (The publication set was already sufficiently large, so we did not have to take such a step). Annex provides details on the concepts we used, as well as our final search queries.

3.2 *Selecting Knowledge Areas Within S&T*

An important next step was to identify distinct knowledge areas in the field of DNA-Nano. The text from the title and abstract of papers and patents offers opportunities to do so, but also poses several challenges:

1. Technical terms often consist of combinations of words, rather than a single word (Nakagawa, 2000). The field we study is not an exception to that. Single words appearing with high frequencies[16] (e.g., "DNA," "temperature") are insufficient to describe a new concept or authors' main contributions. High-frequency single words can become meaningful, descriptive terms if they are combined with other single words to form compound nouns (e.g., "DNA origami," "temperature control"). We addressed this challenge by using the automatic Term Recognition algorithm proposed by Nakagawa (2000). In this algorithm, a Term Extract score is computed based on how many compound nouns have a simple noun N included as an element. In other words, the more frequently a simple noun is integrated with other compound nouns, the higher its score. Our tokenization

[14] Sungi Kim, PhD candidate at Seoul National University, validated the queries for collecting publications. Jürgen Schmied, CEO of Gattaquant, a company working in the field of DNA Nanotechnology, validated the queries for collecting patents.

[15] We improved recall by checking whether the authors and inventors whom we know are present in our search results. If not, we included more keywords from their publications/patents. We improved precision by sampling 20 records each time and checking if any record is irrelevant. Then we identified the keywords that distinguish DNA-Nano from other fields in that record, and put them in the exclusion terms.

[16] And even those with high term frequency-inverse document frequency (tf*idf).

process considers bigrams and trigrams, as long as they appear in the Term Extract list with a score.
2. Frequently occurring compound nouns can still be non-technical or non-descriptive,[17] or may fall outside our field of interest. As no software or algorithm can solve this in a fully automated way, we addressed this challenge through extensive manual checking and exclusion. As part of this manual checking, we excluded POS (Part of Speech) words and other generic biological terms such as "DNA," "RNA," "protein," and "acid amine."
3. Certain terms can be written in more than one way. Techniques such as stemming (cutting ends off words, e.g., from "saying" to "say") or lemmatization (finding the original form of a word, e.g., from "said" to "say") may be helpful for some words (especially verbs), but will not work for others, such as synonyms and abbreviations. To address this challenge, we manually harmonized terms (such as grouping synonyms, abbreviations) into term groups,[18] which represent knowledge areas. For example, we harmonized "3D structure" into "three-dimensional structure," "control of temperature" into "temperature control," and "Au nanoparticle" into "gold nanoparticle."
4. We counted the document frequency[19] (the number of documents where a term occurs at least once) of extracted and harmonized terms (resulting from the above steps) in our datasets across years and periods.

3.3 Measuring S&T Relatedness

As argued above, in the literature, knowledge relatedness has mostly been discussed within the realm of one single domain—science or technology. To investigate the evolving knowledge base of S&T related to a specific new field, we believe it is important to develop cross-domain measures. When analyzing S&T as two separate text corpora, one would not have to describe the interaction between them via conventional channels such as NPL references, PPPs. In this chapter, we use the S&T relatedness as a proxy for S&T interaction. More specifically, we need to clarify different types/indicators of knowledge relatedness as proxies for the extent and content of the knowledge interaction between the two domains.

Because we follow the approach of breaking down each of the two domains into smaller units—knowledge areas represented by terms, we will first discuss four indicators of cross-domain relatedness at the level of knowledge area[20]: similarity, commonality, complementarity, difference. *Knowledge similarity,* the most stringent measure of cross-domain relatedness, *occurs when the same narrowly defined*

[17] For instance, "this study," "this invention."

[18] We ended up with 109 cross-domain term groups, which have been harmonized from 400 technical terms extracted with highest scores by the automatic Term Recognition algorithm.

[19] We used Higuchi Koichi's KH coder text-mining software (Version 3a12d).

[20] A sub-domain unit of analysis.

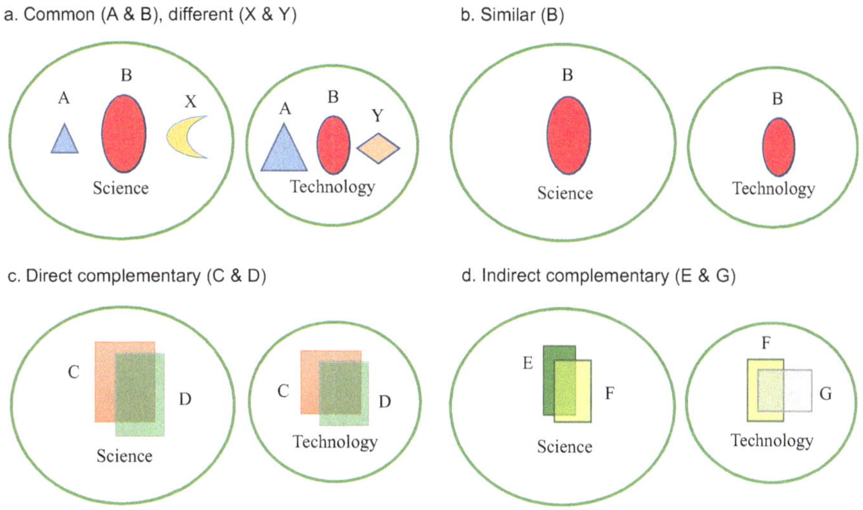

Fig. 2 Types of S&T content relatedness: commonality, similarity, complementarity (direct and indirect), and difference. (**a**) Common (A&B), different (X&Y). (**b**) Similar (B). (**c**) Direct complementary (C&D). (**d**) Indirect complementary (E&G)

knowledge area appears in both domains with similar relative frequency (example B in Fig. 2b). Similar knowledge areas are per definition common ones, but not the other way around. *Knowledge commonality occurs when the same narrowly defined knowledge area appears in both domains regardless of their relative frequency in each domain* (examples A and B in Fig. 2a). It means that the same knowledge area is used in both S&T, even if the extent of use is different. While *knowledge similarity* may indicate the highest intensity of S&T interaction, *knowledge commonality* may indicate it at a somewhat lower level. However, this is potentially useful, as a pair of common knowledge areas like C and D co-occurring in both publications and patents could strengthen the knowledge base of both S&T; a common knowledge area like F can help to bridge S&T in the case of indirect complementarity between E and G (Fig. 2d).

We furthermore distinguish two forms of knowledge complementarity in the absence of knowledge similarity. We talk of *direct knowledge* complementarity when two knowledge areas strongly co-occur in both S&T (in Fig. 2c, C and D are directly complementary). In this case, C and D are certainly common knowledge areas. However, they indicate a weaker intensity of knowledge flows between the two domains. It means that this combination frequently occurs in publications but also in patents. This should reflect the combinatory nature of each domain in an evolutionary vein. *In this case, technology relatedness coincides with science relatedness.*

In addition, we theorize *indirect knowledge complementarity* between two knowledge areas, when each of them co-occurs strongly with a third knowledge area, called a bridging knowledge area, which appears in both domains (in Fig. 2d, E and G are directly complementary, and F is the bridging area connecting them). Identifying and promoting bridging knowledge areas could help to stimulate the continuous progress of both domains economically.

Finally, knowledge areas are *different* if they only exist in one domain, not in the other (examples X and Y in Fig. 2a). This case indicates the absence of relatedness between two domains.

The above definitions relate to the individual term level. To compare two domains, the result needs to be aggregated to the domain level. We did so for the full time period of the sample, but also for three subperiods separately (see Sect. 4.2). Regarding *knowledge commonality*, we tried to identify all distinct knowledge areas (represented by terms) that two domains have in common in different subperiods, regardless of their extent. To measure *knowledge similarity*, we aimed to check if those common knowledge areas appear at a closely similar relative extent in both domains. From the list of common terms, we performed the Chi-square test for corpus similarity to assess whether both domains consist of terms drawn randomly from some larger domain (for this test, see Evert, 2005; Kilgarriff, 2001).[21] We considered the domains to be similar (i.e., belonging to some larger population) in respect of each term if the outcome is significant at 5% confidence level.

To our knowledge, no standard cross-domain measure of either *direct* or *indirect complementarity* exists. So, we propose two tests that can, in principle, be applied to any two knowledge domains. Both tests are based on the co-occurrences of terms. The first test measures the direct complementarity between two knowledge areas (represented by two terms). It is calculated as follows:

$$J_{\text{direct}} = \sqrt{J_i \times J_j}$$

where J_i is the Jaccard index of the co-occurrence of the two terms in the Science domain, and J_j is the Jaccard index of the co-occurrence of the two terms in the Technology domain. Thus, our measure of *direct complementarity* J_{direct} is high when the terms in question frequently co-occur in both domains. Our second test measures *indirect complementarity* between two knowledge areas (represented by two terms). It derives from the co-occurrences of the two terms of interest with a third term, the bridging term. It is calculated as follows:

$$J_{\text{indirect}} = \sqrt{J_{im} \times J_{jn}}$$

where J_{im} is the Jaccard index of the co-occurrence of the first term and the bridging term in the Science domain, and J_{jn} is the Jaccard index of the second term and the bridging term in the Technology domain.

[21] We used Stephan Evert's R package "corpora" for this specific Chi-square test.

Our empirical exercise for both types of knowledge complementarity involves three steps. Firstly, we reduced the co-occurrence networks of 109 terms[22] to smaller networks with only edges with a Jaccard index greater than 0.01.[23] Secondly, we matched common pairs between S&T, calculated the Joint Jaccard index,[24] then sorted and compared the lists of direct and indirect complementarity. Thirdly, we discussed our results with experts in the field (see Sect. 4.2).

3.4 Measuring the Temporal Relatedness Between S&T

Our second research question concerns the measurement of the temporal distance/ relatedness between S&T. Our basic assumption here is that in modern age, what emerges at approximately the same time could be strongly related to each other.[25] We traced our list of knowledge areas, represented by the most significant terms to check if the time lag is insignificant (less than 5 years) or significant (more or equal to 5 years). We base our 5-year-threshold on the observations of Daim et al. (2007) and Finardi (2011) that a usual time lag between S&T is 3–4 years. A short time lag implies a high degree of temporal S&T relatedness. When the time lag is long, it suggests a low degree of S&T relatedness.

Note that we do not aim to determine causality here, but rather a measure of temporal relatedness. Those terms appear simultaneously in S&T could reflect the similarity between S&T, or the highest level of interaction between S&T. An inventor can file a patent first and submit a publication on the same matter right afterward. Or, scientists doing experiments in the same lab might share their collegues' work. As long as one's contribution is published or filed as a patent, other teammates can cite that contribution right away. Moreover, terms that appear with a short time lag across the S&T domains could show complementarity. There might be a hidden knowledge area in the other domain, which triggers the use of focal knowledge in one domain. In contrast, those terms appear at a longer time lag could reflect difference. In the end, we will compare with the results of our earlier analysis.

For each individual knowledge area (as represented by a term), we determined the moment it first appears (emerges) in the science domain, and when it first appears in the technology domain. While our time lag threshold of 5 years is by definition somewhat arbitrary, we believe it is appropriate to the distinction we aim to make.

---

[22]We explained how we selected 109 term groups in Sect. 3.2. For the actual analysis of S&T relatedness, we called them "terms" for convenience.

[23]This first step resulted in 538 pairs in Science and 391 pairs in Technology.

[24]This second step resulted in 133 pairs of direct complementarity and 10,525 pairs of indirect complementarity.

[25]In earlier ages, however, the temporal relatedness between S&T could happen in 2000 years (Johns, 2020).

Moreover, we carried out robustness checks which showed that variations to this threshold do not lead to substantially different results.[26]

To determine the exact moment of a term emerging the science or the technology domain, we consider the year of publication and the patent filing year, respectively. However, we aim to prevent our determination of these moments from being merely driven by an early, single, and isolated occurrence of that term. Therefore, we want to observe a certain critical mass, reflecting that knowledge has started to develop in the domain in question, rather than a one-time or incidental use of the term. For that reason, we applied a threshold: we consider the emergence of a term to be when that term hits 5% of its cumulative frequency over the full period. For most of our terms, this 5% threshold is met at the approximate value of 100 documents. Figure 3 presents an example of the time lag and threshold we applied. In our publication dataset, the term "liquid crystal" is first mentioned in 1990. Already in the same year, it reached 5% of the total cumulative frequency in 26 years. In our patent dataset, the term does not reach the 5% threshold until 1994. Therefore, the time lag between S&T regarding this specific knowledge area is 4 years. However, based on our previously mentioned criteria, we determined the time lag in this case is insignificant.

3.5 *Data*

Using the search queries based on our concept approach discussed above, we created a scientific publication dataset using the Web of Science (WoS) database, and a patent dataset using the Autumn 2016 version of PATSTAT. While a title of a publication or a patent is usually a set of words carefully selected by the author, it is the abstract that often mentions the relevant concepts and the contribution of authors or inventors; therefore, our queries used the text appearing in both titles and abstracts. We found 135,055 publications and 11,226 patents, dated between 1947 and 2015. However, because the WoS data on academic publications prior to 1990 often lack abstracts, we truncated both our datasets to the period between 1990 and 2015. After removing duplicates and incomplete records (e.g., publications without titles), our final datasets comprised 123,929 publications and 10,476 patents. After applying our text-mining techniques (see Sect. 3.2), we identified 109 harmonized terms that appear either solely or simultaneously in our two corpora.

To investigate the S&T relatedness over time, we further divided this 26-year time span of data into three subperiods: Subperiod 1 from 1990 to 1997, Subperiod 2 from 1998 to 2005, and Subperiod 3 from 2006 to 2015. The breaking point between Subperiods 2 and 3 is based on a ground-breaking contribution by a Caltech researcher Paul Rothemund, published in 2006 in Nature, which by September 2021 received over 4000 citations (Rothemund, 2006). The first patent for this invention

[26]These robustness checks are available upon demand from the authors.

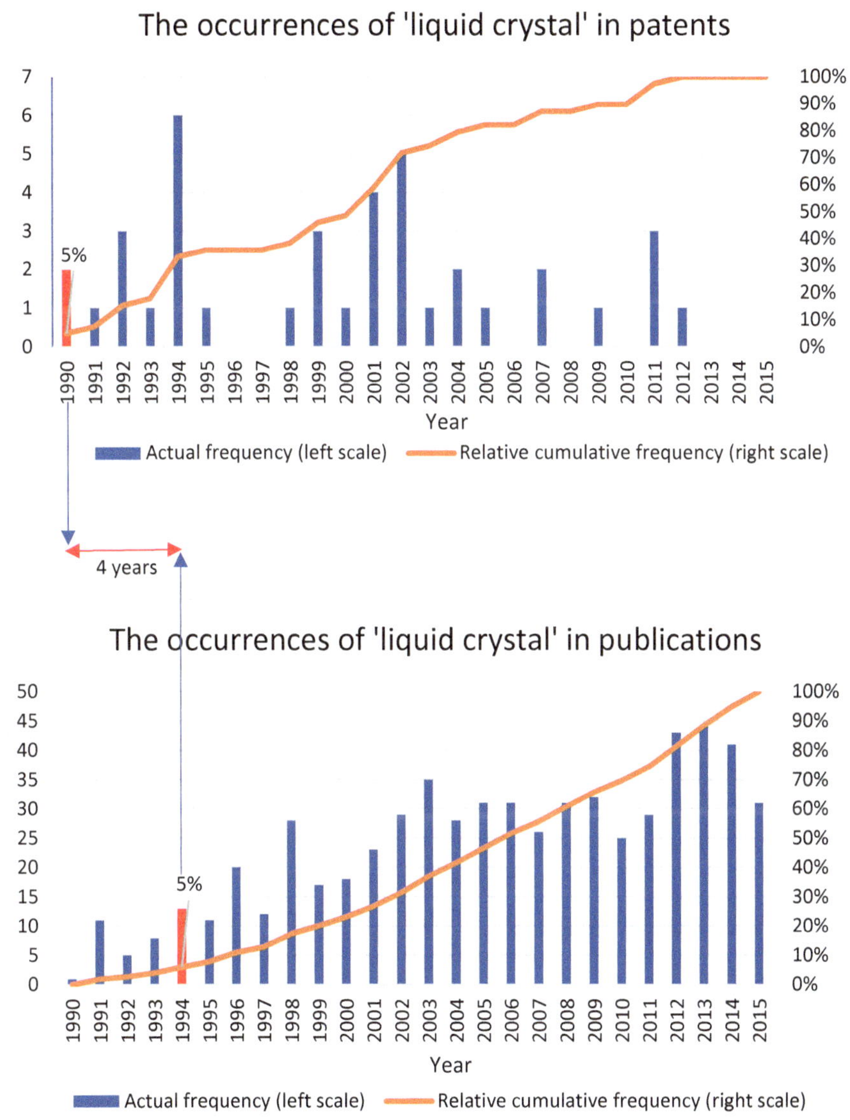

Fig. 3 The time lag of the term "liquid crystal" between S&T (represented as a red arrow)

was filed in 2005. Before and after 2006, no such compelling breaking point existed, so we chose subperiods 1 and 2 of equal length. Note that Subperiod 3 is 2 years longer than subperiods 1 and 2, which might somehow affect the data and impact the comparability. Yet, we do not expect a significant change in the number of publications, patents, and document frequencies per period due to this division. We believe that our choice of breaks between periods, based on Rothemund's breakthrough, is better than just dividing it into three equally long subperiods and ignoring this breakthrough's timing.

4 Empirical Analysis and Results

This section presents our analysis and the results we found with relation to our two main research questions (see at the end of Sect. 2.2), using the methodology described in the Sects. 3.3 and 3.4.

4.1 Descriptive Statistics of Two Corpora

Table 2 provides the descriptive statistics of our data in more details. The publication corpus is larger than the patent corpus almost 12 times in terms of the number of documents, 22 times in terms of the number of tokens, and 19 times in terms of the types of tokens. The mean of document frequency of those tokens in the publication corpus is 20, which is higher than 15 of the patent corpus. Regarding the dispersion, the standard deviation of the document frequency of the publication corpus is much higher than that of the patent corpus (371 and 81). Therefore, the publication corpus seems to be richer and more heterogeneous.

We can observe a consistent growth of the publication corpus during the full period (1990–2015), but an inconsistent growth of the patent corpus with a decline in Subperiod 3 regarding all metrics. As mentioned earlier, Paul Rothemund introduced

Table 2 Descriptive statistics of two corpora

1. Publication corpus	Full period (1990–2015)	Subperiod 1 (1990–1997)	Subperiod 2 (1998–2005)	Subperiod 3 (2006–2015)
Number of documents	123,929	22,222	37,915	63,792
Tokens in use	12,128,976	2,261,737	3,695,122	6,273,821
Types of token in use	414,234 (100%)	123,448 (100%)	178,681 (100%)	248,822 (100%)
Types of token occurring less than 5 times	359,792 (87%)	105,688 (86%)	153,728 (86%)	214,804 (86%)
Mean of document frequency	20	12	14	17
Standard deviation of document frequency	371	368	173	250
2. Patent corpus	**Full period (1990–2015)**	**Subperiod 1 (1990–1997)**	**Subperiod 2 (1998–2005)**	**Subperiod 3 (2006–2015)**
Number of documents	10,476	1679	5784	3013
Tokens in use	540,992	94,285	302,308	144,412
Types of token in use	21,741 (100%)	8125 (100%)	14,939 (100%)	9972 (100%)
Types of token occurring less than 5 times	16,414 (76%)	6221 (77%)	11,225 (75%)	7571 (76%)
Mean of document frequency	15	7	12	9
Standard deviation of document frequency	81	29	72	44

DNA origami technique in late 2005 (as a patent) and in early 2006 (as a scientific article). His contribution receives a huge number of forward citations in WoS (over 3700), but a much lower number of forward citations in PATSTAT (28). His invention is quite impactful in science, but not yet so in technology. Despite promising applications described in scientific literature, perhaps finding its way to real technological industrial applications is not so easy.

In our sample of 109 cross-domain term groups, the mean document frequency within the publication corpus is 1336, in within the patent corpus is 77. The standard deviation in the publication corpus is 1788, in the patent corpus 164.

4.2 S&T Content Relatedness

We now investigate the extent to which knowledge content in S&T domains is similar, complementary, or different, and how this evolves over time. Table 3 presents our findings, using our novel dataset and the methodologies outlined in Sect. 3.4. Examples of *similar* terms are "liquid crystal," "mass spectrometry," and "carbon nanotube"; they appear in the full period in both corpora. Examples of *complementary* terms are "cancer diagnosis" paired with "cancer cell," as well as "therapeutic agent" paired with "drug delivery." Table 3 also shows examples of differences. For instance, in Subperiod 1, the term "microfluidic device" only appears in patents, while the term "crystal structure" only appears in publications.

Table 4 presents our findings about the degrees of commonality, similarity, complementarity, and differences in the full period and in the three subperiods. The fluctuating commonality, stable and low similarity, and increasing complementarity between the two domains suggest that the S&T domains of DNA-Nano evolve in different ways, yet achieve a higher degree of relatedness in Subperiod 3. This may be down to differences in purposes of S&T, or various knowledge recombination processes going on in each domain. Even when, using Price's analogy, these "dancers infrequently move to the same music" (low similarity), their interaction could be estimated from their increasing complementarity.

Row 1 in Table 4 presents the results of our quantitative analysis of commonality. To prevent accidental occurrences of terms in both corpora, we removed all terms with frequencies lower than five (see the discussion about common and similar knowledge areas in Sect. 3.3). This step also helps us to achieve reliable results from our Chi-square test for similarities (Rayson & Garside, 2000). We see that the degree of commonality in the whole period is high 82.6% (91 out of 109 terms appear in both domains). Looking at the subperiods, we observed that the commonality is lowest in Subperiod 1 (at 43.3%), increased in Subperiod 2 (to 80%), and started to decline in Subperiod 3 (down to 73.3%).

Row 2 in Table 4 shows the results of our similarity test for common terms that have the same relative frequency (for the Chi-square test used here, see Sect. 3.3). We found that the similarity over the whole period is only 14.4% (13 out of 90 terms have similar relative frequencies). Yet, if we consider the subperiods 1 and 3, the

Table 3 Examples of similarity, complementarity (We report pairs of complementary term in square brackets.), and difference

		Full period	Subperiod 1 (1990–1997)	Subperiod 2 (1998–2005)	Subperiod 3 (2006–2015)
1	Similar	Liquid crystal, mass spectrometry, living cell, carbon nanotube, biological material	Self-assembly, mass spectrometry, molecular structure, binding affinity, polymer synthesis	Mass spectrometry, polymerase chain reaction, synthetic DNA, polymer synthesis, physical properties, nucleic acid structure	DNA origami, DNA synthesis, carbon nanotube, drug delivery, hairpin structure, programmability, living cell
2	Directly complementary	[Therapeutic agent, drug delivery], [therapeutic agent, cancer treatment], [X-ray crystallography, protein structure]	[Functionalization, drug delivery], [DNA sequencing, DNA fragment], [structural analysis, atomic force microscope]	[Living cell, in vivo], [structural analysis, molecular structure], [magnetic resonance imaging, magnetic properties]	[DNA origami, atomic force microscope], [gold nanoparticle, DNA origami], [self-assembly, functionalization]
3	Indirectly complementary	[Supermolecule, X-ray crystallography]	[Gold nanoparticle, carbon nanotube]	[Cancer treatment, DNA amplification]	[Cancer treatment, cancer diagnosis]
4	Bridging area	Electron microscope	Functionalization	Cancer cell	Cancer cell
5	Different (only in publications)	Natural DNA, g-quadruplex DNA, two-dimensional structure	Cryoelectron microscope, transmission electron microscope, crystal structure, carbon nanotube, structural stability, gold nanoparticle	Cryoelectron microscope, molecular machine, molecular dynamic simulation, RNA detection, g-quadruplex DNA,	Scanning tunneling microscope, nuclear magnetic resonance, natural nucleic acid, g-quadruplex DNA
6	Different (only in patents)		Microfluidic device	Hybridization chain reaction	Nucleic acid array
7	Absent in both domains		DNA origami, hybridization change reaction, short hairpin RNA, bio stability, RNA interference, semiconductor device		

Table 4 Overview of S&T relatedness indicators

	Number of terms	Full period	Subperiod 1 (1990–1997)	Subperiod 2 (1998–2005)	Subperiod 3 (2006–2015)
1	Common terms[a]	90/109 (82.6%)	39/90 (43.3%)	72/90 (80%)	66/90 (73.3%)
2	Similar terms[a]	13/90 (14.4%)	9/39 (23.1%)	14/72 (19.4%)	16/66 (24.2%)
3	Directly complementary pairs of terms[b]	133	85	127	133
4	Indirectly complementary pairs of terms	10,525	n/a	n/a	n/a
5	Different terms, only in publications	18/109	50/109	31/109	42/109
6	Different terms, only in patents	1/109	3/109	4/109	1/109
7	Absent in both domains	0/109	17/109	2/109	0/109

[a]Excluding terms with fewer than 5 occurrences
[b]Data are cumulative (up to and including the listed period)

similarity level is higher (23–34%). Subperiod 2 has lowest similarity (19.4%), which might be an indirect cause of the drop of the number of patents in Subperiod 3. The similar terms seemed to be established knowledge areas in both domains, such as liquid crystal and biological material.

For the full period, we identified 133 pairs of direct complementary terms. For the three subperiods, that number increased from 85 to 133. By definition, indirect complementary terms can occur in much higher numbers and we identified no fewer than 10,525 of these. Because of computational limitations, we did not analyze indirectly complementary terms for the different subperiods. Some similar and complementary knowledge areas form the mainstream of DNA-Nano.[27]

Table 4 also provides the result from the absolute differences (unrelatedness) between the two corpora. The level of difference is low (19 out of 109 terms are different) in the full period (as the reflection of the high commonality in the full period), is highest in Subperiod 1, and drops almost by a half in Subperiod 2 and slightly increases in Subperiod 3. The number of terms showing up only in publications is higher than terms showing up only in patents. This may trigger a thought that there are still many promising applications, which discovered by scientists but not yet materialized into real applications.

To have our findings validated by experts in the field, we asked six experts attending a major conference in DNA Nanotechnology.[28] One was Nadrian Seeman, whom we already mentioned as the founding father of this field. When we presented the similar terms we found, these experts indeed recognized them as similarities

[27]This does not happen with knowledge areas that are neither similar nor complementary.

[28]We did so at the third workshop on Functional DNA Nanotechnology (6–8 June 2018, Rome, Italy).

between S&T and believed they were the result of S&T interaction. Regarding complementarity, the experts agreed on 98% of our pairs of direct complementary terms (133).[29] However, because our list of indirectly complementary terms is so long (10,525 terms), we could neither ask the experts to check them all nor suggest any priority of importance. Perhaps future research can find ways to identify the most prominent indirect complementary terms.

4.3 Temporal Relatedness Between S&T

We measured the time difference between the emergence of knowledge areas (represented by terms) in S&T, as the proxy for S&T temporal relatedness. As we can only observe such time differences if a term appears in both domains, we excluded the 19 terms (out of 109 original terms in our datasets) that do not appear in both domains or have a frequency of only 5 documents or less. This left us with 90 terms for which we measured time lags.

From these 90 terms, 72 (80%) emerged with insignificant time lags between S&T (Group 1, examples in Box 1), which implies a strong temporal relatedness. A total of 18 terms (19.8%) emerged with significant time lags between S&T (Group 2), which implies a weak temporal relatedness: 7 emerged in science significantly earlier than in technology (Group 2a, Table 5), and 11 terms emerged in technology significantly earlier than in science (Group 2b, Table 6). These numbers could show signals of technology leads, in comparison to science.

Box 1. Examples of Terms with Insignificant Time Lags Between S&T (Group 1)
DNA origami, DNA synthesis, cancer diagnosis, self-assembly, carbon nanotube, mass spectrometry, atomic force microscope, therapeutic agent, supermolecule, RNA synthesis, DNA fragment, resonance energy transfer, temperature control

For a better understanding of types of knowledge areas emerged with a strong or weak temporal relatedness, we looked at the terms in more detail. Terms in Group 1 (e.g., DNA origami, DNA synthesis, self-assembly, etc.) represent the knowledge areas where knowledge in S&T emerged and developed almost simultaneously. Scientific and technological knowledge might originate from the same place, the same person, or be the result of a co-creation process by scientists and inventors

Table 5 shows the list of 7 terms (Group 2a), which emerged significantly earlier in science than in technology. These 7 terms represent the knowledge areas with a

[29] We explained the concepts of direct and indirect complementarity, and gave them the list of 133 pairs of terms. Some experts reacted right away, others responded later by email.

Table 5 List of terms with significant time lags (Group 2a)

	Term	When threshold was 5% total frequency of each term in publications (1)	When threshold was 5% total frequency of each term in patents (2)	Time lag between (1) and (2)
1	X-ray crystallography	1993	2004	–11
2	Crystal structure	1994	2002	–8
3	E-coli	1992	1999	–7
4	Raman spectroscopy	1994	2001	–7
5	High stability	1995	2002	–7
6	DNA structure	1993	1999	–6
7	Molecular biology	1992	1997	–5

Table 6 List of terms with significant time lags (Group 2b)

	Term	When threshold reached 5% total frequency of each term in publications (1)	When threshold reached 5% total frequency of each term in patents (2)	Time lag between (1) and (2)
1	Hybridization chain reaction	2010	1998	12
2	Functionalization	2001	1994	7
3	Liquid phase	1997	1990	7
4	Programmability	2001	1994	7
5	Biosensor	1999	1993	6
6	DNA detection	2001	1996	5
7	DNA hybridization	1999	1994	5
8	Drug delivery	2001	1996	5
9	Magnetic resonance imaging	1998	1993	5
10	Mechanical properties	1999	1994	5
11	Nucleic acid amplification	2001	1996	5

weak temporal relatedness between S&T. This could happen when scientific development occurred much earlier, but only after a long period it can be realized into real manipulations/applications in technology. This is the case of "DNA structure," for which Seeman constructed the theoretical foundation, however, realized into real structures only much later. Seeman and his followers encountered many practical challenges before Rothemund stepped into this field in late 2005, early 2006. Sometimes, it could be the case that innovation development (starting from R&D projects) could not pass the valley of death, or not become successful commercially (e.g., "Raman spectroscopy"). Sometimes, it could be some knowledge areas inherited from other science fields ("X-ray crystallography," "crystal structure," "molecular biology"), but turned out not to find much use in technology.

Table 6 presents the list of terms that emerged in technology significantly earlier than in science (Group 2b). These 11 terms also represent the knowledge areas with a weak temporal relatedness between S&T. Among the 11 terms found, "hybridization chain reaction" is the one with the longest time gap between technology and science. Not only driven by techniques (DNA hybridization, DNA detection, magnetic resonance imaging) and applications (biosensor, drug delivery), technology also took the lead in "programmability" and "functionalization," which turn structures into devices. To build machines at the nanoscale, technology signaled what it needed from science: "mechanical properties."

The 11 terms in Table 6 are knowledge areas where science indeed lagged behind technology. We note that some are closely linked to medical healthcare, such as biosensor and magnetic resonance imaging. The long investment process required by firms and other actors in those areas may have resulted in patented inventions, whose diffusion to academia took time. These may be the areas where scientists needed time to recognize the relevance to their work, time to set up collaborations with industry, then use them in the context of their own research on DNA-Nano. Especially where "science of the artificial" is concerned, technology comes first in the form of workable structures, devices, and artifacts, which later become the subject of scientific research. It is also important to bear in mind that laboratory works always involve equipment, some of which may have been patented several years earlier. Traditional enabling techniques, methods used in long-existing knowledge fields (such as molecular biology and biotechnology), are still usable/recombined in emerging DNA Nanoscience.

5 Summary, Discussion, and Conclusion

While the economic, innovation, and management literature extensively discusses knowledge development and relateness in both the science and in the technology domain, few studies look at the interaction and knowledge relatedness across these domains. This study proposes a systematic way of measuring such cross-domain S&T interaction relations. Starting from the concept of S&T relatedness (both over content and time), we introduce five novel indicators of knowledge relatedness across S&T, as shown in Table 7 (in decreasing level of S&T interaction). Following a text-mining approach, we provide the actual degrees of relatedness across DNA-Nano S&T according to the five above indicators and detect important knowledge areas across S&T, which is helpful for research evaluation, funding, and policy recommendations.

Applying our measures to the case of DNA-Nano, a research field that has delivered interesting developments in both S&T, we summarize our observations on the above indicators in Fig. 2. We find that the level of knowledge similarity, the

Table 7 Indicators for knowledge relatedness across the S&T domains

Knowledge similarity	Share of narrowly defined knowledge areas that appear in both domains with similar relative frequency
Knowledge commonality	Share of narrowly defined knowledge areas that appear in both domains regardless of their relative frequency in within each domain
Knowledge complementarity (direct)	Share of narrowly defined knowledge areas that strongly co-occur with each other in both S&T
Knowledge complementarity (indirect)	Share of narrowly defined knowledge areas that strongly co-occur with a "bridging knowledge area" that appears in both domains
Knowledge differences	Share of narrowly defined knowledge areas that exist in one domain but not in the other

most stringent measure of cross-domain relatedness, is relatively low: only 14.4% of the narrowly defined knowledge areas (represented by compound noun terms) we distinguish in our case qualify as similar. This indicator remains relatively stable over time (see Fig. 4). Yet, knowledge similarities only reflect a part of the whole picture of S&T relatedness. The commonality measure delivers a more interesting trend. Over the three subperiods, it grows from 43.3 to 80% and falls back slightly to 73.3%. Direct knowledge complementarity also goes up over time, without a fallback.[30] Differences in knowledge drop considerably from subperiod 1 to subperiod 2, but grow slightly towards subperiod 3.

The overall low degree of similarity and the increasing complementarity may indicate that although S&T interaction in this knowledge field started low, it increased and then stabilized. We may expect more industrial applications in the coming period (after Subperiod 3). Altogether, we believe this case illustrates how our proposed measures provide a sophisticated view on the development of knowledge relatedness across S&T.

While S&T similarity is the form of knowledge relatedness most discussed in the existing literature, this measurement seems mostly limited to the field's mainstream, where S&T have overlapped, intertwined, and most strongly related. Our empirical results show that we get a much more complete picture if we also measure S&T complementarity. Taking Price's analogy of a pair of dancers, S&T do not need to be identical and too close to each other. It is challenging for dancers to move if they appear to be too close to each other. While their similarities help with their sustainable and incremental movement, their complementarities encourage more knowledge recombination and learning between them. In the future, they could take more innovative, and breakthrough steps resulted from their current learning and interaction process. Without including the measure of temporal relatedness, one may not be

[30]For reasons indicated in Sect. 4.2, we did not measure indirect complementarity over the different subperiods.

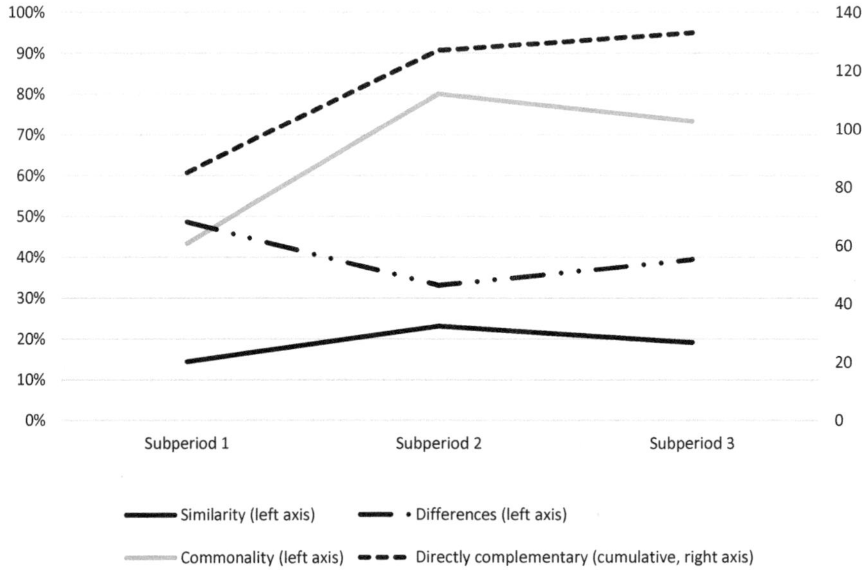

Fig. 4 Knowledge relatedness (The number of possible complimentary pairs is a very high number, and therefore the measurement of direct complementary cannot be plotted in a relative scale. See Sect. 4.2 for more details.) across the S&T domains in DNA-Nano

able to see the leading role of either science or technology, and that they grow together, hand in hand!

The S&T complementarity is our second important indicator of S&T relatedness, which has been neglected in previous empirical literature (possibly because it is much harder to measure). In practice, S&T complementarity is harder to be recognized as a form/indicator of S&T interaction. This could originate from academic-university partnerships, which facilitate knowledge exchange, equipment sharing, or star scientists' collaborations in industrial projects. Identifying complementary knowledge areas across S&T could help establish future crucial partnerships, co-authorships, co-patenting, co-location, co-creation of potential innovations, and promote technology transfer from university to industry. Funding "bridging knowledge areas," e.g., "electron microscope," "functionalization," "cancer cell," from public investment might provide a necessity for S&T's future development economically. Knowledge complementarity might reveal the combination and recombination process within each domain and the matching capabilities across these essential domains. These processes would help generate synergies, reduce R&D costs, promise the growth of more emerging science-based technologies, technology transfer in the future.

The knowledge difference indicator reflects the knowledge areas which have not yet been developed in one of the two domains. When the time lag of knowledge areas between S&T (e.g., "hybridization chain reaction") is too long, it could result in a different knowledge area. However, it is not always the case. Some knowledge areas only show up in one domain in the end of one subperiod could also appear in both domains in the early subsequent subperiod. This is the case of different knowledge areas per period but with insignificant time lags. The analysis of the relatedness per year could show a better picture of knowledge evolution. However, our statistical tests may not be implemented because of low or zero frequencies of some terms in some years, especially in the patent corpus.

The specific approach we chose for our studies also has limitations. Among other things, it does not observe a direct link between the S&T domains. Subsequent research could further explore the interaction between these domains by direct linkages such as NPL citations and PPPs and provide more insights into the knowledge recombination processes within each domain. Future studies could also apply our measures to a wider range of fields, and perhaps generate stylized facts about different types of relatedness, or a taxonomy.

Acknowledgments The Vietnamese Government sponsored this research in an overseas training program for Ph.D. candidates. We are indebted to Önder Nomaler and Cort MacLean Johns for their discussion and support. We acknowledge Higuchi Koichi for his technical support with the software KH Coder. We are thankful to have insights into the practical research of DNA Nanotechnology, presented and enlightened by experts at these conferences: DNA22, DNA meets Plasmonics, FDN2018. We are grateful to Nadrian Seeman for validating our results, and Jürgen Schmied and Sungi Kim for verifying our queries, Bas Rosier for sharing his insights on DNA Nanotechnology. We especially appreciate the constructive comments from discussants Virgilio Failla, Hans Christian Kongsted, the audience at the DRUID18 conference, from Piergiuseppe Morone at the ISS2018 conference, and two anonymous reviewers for this book chapter. We would also like to thank Nguyen Van Dan (Academy of Finance) for moral support.

Compliance with Ethical Standards

Funding This study was funded by a Vietnamese Government scholarship for conducting Ph.D. studies abroad, according to Decision No. 1908, 30 May 2013, by the Ministry of Education and Training. Mrs. Hanh Luong La was the recipient of this scholarship. She also received the travel grant from the Eindhoven University of Technology to present the earlier version of the chapter at the ISS2018 conference in Seoul.

Conflict of Interest The authors declare that they have no conflict of interest.

Annex. The Four Concepts Applied in the Concept Approach[31]

1. Description of the Four Concepts, as Well as the Exclusion Mechanisms Used

Concept A: Nanotechnology	"Nanotechnology is science, engineering, and technology conducted at the nanoscale, which is about 1 to 100 nanometers" (definition from the US National Nanotechnology Initiative, 2000). Thus, any science or technology that works below the scale of 100 nanometers is considered "nanotechnology." This definition is a broad one. We could therefore maximize our search by collecting synonyms referring to nanoscale or instruments used in nanotechnologies, such as specific types of microscopes (AFM, TEM, SEM)
Concept B: Design	The word "design" has two forms, the verb and the noun. As a noun, "design" refers to an object or an entity. As a verb, it refers to a process or series of activities. Design is the construction of an object or creation of an entity. An interesting feature of the DNA origami technique is that DNA strands are programmed, synthesized, and can self-assemble themselves afterward. We found all terms related to this process and listed them under the concept "design"
Concept C: Structure	Structure is defined by the Oxford Dictionary as "a particular arrangement of parts." We found several synonyms of "structure" based on publications and patents in DNA-Nano by top contributors in the field such as Nadrian Seeman, Paul Rothemund, and others. We also noted specific words related to DNA structures and included them in our search
Concept D: DNA	DNA is the abbreviation of "deoxyribonucleic acid," a type of nucleic acid, a chemical that carries genetic information in the cells of animals and plants (Oxford Dictionary), or any living organisms, and viruses (Wikipedia). It is interesting to note that the term DNA, as used in our research, refers to artificial DNA, not its natural form. However, its

(continued)

[31] It is worthwhile noting that some records where the concept "nanotechnology" is implicit, should be included in our datasets. Certain inventors choose not to mention nano-related terms explicitly or discuss only DNA or oligonucleotides. That might be the reason why a considerable number of patents belonging to DNA Nanotechnology is not classified under IPC-code B82 (Nanotechnology). From a conceptual point of view, DNA and nano are quite different. However, from a practical point of view, when discussing DNA or nucleotides, we should imply that the research is conducted at the nanoscale, since the dimension of a DNA strand is approximately 2.5 nm. Therefore, "DNA" and "*nucleotid*" are included in two concept areas (Nanotechnology and DNA) to avoid missing certain records that do not mention nano-related terms. Although DNA and Nanotechnology are closely related concepts, we have not grouped them because this leads to considerably more noise in the datasets selected. Thus, DNA-related terms must appear in the set under any conditions, while the presence of nano-related terms remains an option.

	synonyms and related terms are borrowed from molecular biology
Exclusion terms in Titles (E1)	At the first level of exclusion, we excluded specific terms relating to other closely linked fields (e.g., molecular biology, genetic engineering, forensics). However, these terms could still appear in abstracts or keywords
Exclusion terms in Titles, Abstracts, and Keywords (E2)	At the second level of exclusion, we excluded the terms that should not appear in titles, abstracts, and keywords. This strongest exclusion has improved the precision of our data

2. *Final Queries*

Query for Publications

(**Nanotechnology** AND **Design** AND **Structure** AND **DNA**) NOT (E1 OR E2)

.. where

Nanotechnology = NANO* OR 'ATOM* FORCE MICROSCOP*' OR AFM OR TEM OR 'TRANSMISSION ELECTRON MICROSCOP*' OR SEM OR 'SCANNING ELECTRON MICROSCOP*' OR 'FLUORESCENCE MICROSCOP*' OR 'CRYO-ELECTRON MICROSCOP*' OR 'CRYO-EM' OR MOLECUL* OR MULTIMER$ OR MONOMER$

Design = DESIGN* OR COMPUT* OR CONJUGAT* OR FORM* OR FOLD* OR JUXTAPOS* OR PROGRAM* OR BIND* OR BOUND OR ATTACH* OR LINK* OR CONNECT* OR CONSTRUCT* OR BRANCH* OR BOND* OR FABRICAT* OR 'SELF-ASSEMBL*' OR 'SELF-REPLICAT*' OR 'SELF-ORGANI*' OR 'DIRECTED-ASSEMBL*' OR SYNTHETIC OR ARTIFICIAL OR 'NON-NATURAL' OR UNNATURAL OR 'NON-GENETIC'

Structure = '*STRUCTURE$' OR DOMAIN$ OR SYSTEM* OR MOTOR* OR MACHIN* OR DEVICE$ OR ARRAY$ OR POLYHEDR* OR CONJUGATE $ OR LADDER$ OR '*ROBOT*' OR JUNCTION$ OR SCAFFOLD* OR TEMPLAT* OR TILE$ OR TILING$ OR LATTICE$ OR 'STICKY END*' OR 'COHESIVE END*' OR STAPL* OR 'LOGIC GATE*' OR CIRCUIT$ OR ORIGAMI

DNA = DNA* OR '*NUCLEIC ACID*' OR 'DOUBLE HELI*' OR HELICES OR '*STRAND*' OR '*NUCLEOTID*' OR FOLDAMER$ OR APTAMER$

E1 = RIBONUCLEIC OR CELL$ OR THERAP* OR INFLAMMAT* OR RIBOSOME$ OR BODY* OR SPECIES* OR BRAIN* OR 'MOLECULAR CLONING' OR EVOLUTION* OR IMMUN* OR DISORDER$ OR VIRUS* OR ORGANISM$ OR ORGAN$ OR BACTERI* OR ANTIBOD* OR HUMAN* OR MAMMAL$ OR TISSUE$ OR TRANSCRIPTION OR RAT$ OR MICE OR HSP* OR P53 OR STAT3 OR 'NON-NUCLEIC' OR 'DNA SEQUENCING' OR 'GENETIC ENGINEERING' OR GENETICS OR SYMPTOM$

E2 = METABOL* OR GEOGRAPH* OR NUTRI* OR YEAST$ OR TREE$ OR SOIL OR FISH* OR MARINE OR INJUR* OR WOUND* OR 'GENE EXPRESSION' OR 'GENETIC STRUCTURE' OR 'GENETICALLY MODIFIED' OR GMO OR 'GENETICALLY ENGINEERED' OR 'GENE REGULATION$' OR 'GENETIC ALGORITHM$' OR 'GENE DELIVERY' OR 'GENE INTERACTION$' OR 'GENO*' OR 'PHYLOGEN*' OR TRANSGENIC OR HORMON* OR ESTROGEN OR TESTOSTERONE OR PATIENT$ OR EMBRYO* OR POLYMERASE OR VACCIN* OR ANTIBIOTIC$ OR BLOOD OR FETAL OR FETUS OR OFFSPRING$ OR BLAST OR FUNG* OR MUTAT* OR CHROMOSOME OR 'PRO POLYPEPTIDE$' OR HELICASE OR INFECT* OR INSECT* OR PLANT$ OR ANIMAL$ OR FORENSIC$ OR NANOPLANKTON OR NANOFAUNA OR CAS9* OR NANO2 OR NANO3

Query for Patents

(**Nanotechnology** AND **Design** AND **Structure** AND **DNA**) NOT (E1 OR E2)

.. where

Nanotechnology = NANO* OR 'ATOM* FORCE MICROSCOP*' OR AFM OR TEM OR 'TRANSMISSION ELECTRON MICROSCOP*' OR SEM OR 'SCANNING ELECTRON MICROSCOP*' OR 'FLUORESCENCE MICROSCOP*' OR 'CRYO-ELECTRON MICROSCOP*' OR 'CRYO-EM' OR MOLECUL* OR MULTIMER$ OR MONOMER$ OR '*NUCLEOTID*' OR DNA

Design = CONJUGAT* OR FORM* OR FOLD* OR JUXTAPOS* OR PROGRAM* OR DESIGN* OR BIND* OR BOUND OR ATTACH* OR LINK* OR CONNECT* OR CONSTRUCT* OR BRANCH* OR BOND* OR FABRICAT* OR 'SELF-ASSEMBL*' OR 'SELF-REPLICAT*' OR 'SELF-ORGANI*' OR 'DIRECTED-ASSEMBL*' OR SYNTHETIC OR ARTIFICIAL OR 'NON-NATURAL' OR UNNATURAL OR 'NON-GENETIC' OR ORIGAMI

Structure = DOMAIN$ OR SYSTEM* OR MOTOR* OR MACHIN* OR DEVICE$ OR ARRAY$ OR POLYHEDR* OR CONJUGATE$ OR LADDER$ OR '*STRUCTURE$' OR '*ROBOT*' OR JUNCTION$ OR SCAFFOLD* OR TEMPLAT* OR TILE$ OR TILING$ OR LATTICE$ OR 'STICKY END*' OR 'COHESIVE END*' OR STAPL* OR 'LOGIC GATE*' OR CIRCUIT$

DNA[32] ='DNA ACTUAT*' OR 'DNA NANOTECHNOLOGY' OR 'FOLDING DNA' OR 'DNA STRUCTURE' OR 'DNA ORIGAMI' OR 'DNA COMPUT*' OR 'DNA HYBRIDIZ*' OR '*NUCLEIC ACID*' OR 'DOUBLE HELI*' OR HELICES OR '*STRAND*' OR '*NUCLEOTID*' OR FOLDAMER$ OR APTAMER$

E1 = RIBONUCLEIC OR '*RNA' OR RADIOTHERAPY OR SPECIES OR '*ORGANISM' OR ORGAN$ OR 'BIOLOGICAL AGENT$' OR BIOMARKER$ OR ENHANC* OR '*BASE' OR PAIR* OR '*NUCLEOTIDE SEQUENCE' OR

[32] It is harder practically to achieve precision in retrieving patents rather than retrieving publications. Therefore, we decided to adjust terminologies in this DNA concept group into more specific terms, which include DNA.

RECEPTOR$ OR '*WEAR' OR CLONING OR BIOSENSOR$ OR SYMPTOM$ OR AGGLOMERATION OR PURIF* OR INFLAMMAT* OR 'DNA SYNTHESIS' OR HEMOGLOBIN OR HIV OR BIOACTIVE OR 'DNA AMPLIFICATION' OR 'NUCLEIC ACID AMPLIFICATION' OR BLOOD OR VITAMIN$ OR IMMUN* OR ANTIBODY OR ANTIGEN$ OR REAGENT$ OR ENCOD* OR VIRUS* OR BACTERI* OR GENE$ OR 'GENE EXPRESSION' OR HUMAN$ OR PATIENT$ OR LIFE OR 'AMINO ACID$' OR TISSUE$ OR 'NON-NUCLEIC'

E2 = 'GENE INTERACTION' OR TRANSFECT* OR TRANSLOCAT* OR PHENOTYPE OR HYDROGEN OR ENHANCER$ OR EVOLUTION* OR EMBRYO* OR SEA OR FISH* OR 'SIDE EFFECT$' OR CULTURE OR FLOWER* OR CARBOHYDRATE$ OR INHIBITOR$ OR MOUSE OR MICE OR CO-EXPRESSION OR POLYMORPHISM OR NON-CODING OR COPY OR COPIES OR PARENT$ OR EXON*

References

Arora, S. K., Porter, A. L., Youtie, J., & Shapira, P. (2013). Capturing new developments in an emerging technology: An updated search strategy for identifying nanotechnology research outputs. *Scientometrics, 95*, 351–370.

Arthur, W. B. (2009). *The nature of technology: What it is and how it evolves*. Free Press.

Bekkers, R., & Martinelli, A. (2012). Knowledge positions in high-tech markets: Trajectories, standards, strategies and true innovators. *Technological Forecasting and Social Change, 79*, 1192–1216.

Benson, C. L., & Magee, C. L. (2013). A hybrid keyword and patent class methodology for selecting relevant sets of patents for a technological field. *Scientometrics, 96*, 69–82.

Benson, C. L., & Magee, C. L. (2015). Technology structural implications from the extension of a patent search method. *Scientometrics, 102*, 1965–1985.

Boschma, R., & Frenken, K. (2009). Technological relatedness and regional branching. Retrieved from http://econ.geo.uu.nl/peeg/peeg.html

Boschma, R., Heimeriks, G., & Balland, P. (2014). Scientific knowledge dynamics and relatedness in biotech cities. *Research Policy, 43*, 107–114.

Boyack, K. W., & Klavans, R. (2008). Measuring science–technology interaction using rare inventor–author names. *Journal of Informetrics, 2*, 173–182.

Breschi, S., & Catalini, C. (2010). Tracing the links between S&T: An exploratory analysis of scientists and inventors networks. *Research Policy, 39*, 14–26.

Chang, Y. W., Yang, H. W., & Huang, M. W. (2017). Interaction between S&T in the field of fuel cells based on patent paper analysis. *Electronic Library, 35*, 152–166.

Daim, T., Monalisa, M., Dash, P., & Brown, N. (2007). Time lag assessment between research funding and output in emerging technologies. *Foresight, 9*(4), 33–44.

Dosi, G. (1982). Technological paradigms and technological trajectories. *Research Policy, 22*, 102–103.

Douglas, K. (2016). *DNA nanoscience: From prebiotic origins to emerging nanotechnology*. CRC Press.

Drexler, K. E. (2013). *Radical abundance: How a revolution in nanotechnology will change civilization*. Public Affairs.

Dunn, K. E. (2020). The business of DNA nanotechnology: Commercialization of origami and other technologies. *Molecules, 25*, 377.

Evert, S. (2005). *The statistics of word cooccurrences word pairs and collocations*. Dissertation, Institut für maschinelle Sprachverarbeitung, Universität Stuttgart. Retrieved from http://elib.uni-stuttgart.de/bitstream/11682/2573/1/Evert2005phd.pdf

Finardi, U. (2011). Time relations between scientific production and patenting of knowledge: The case of nanotechnologies. *Scientometrics, 89*, 37–50.

Heinisch, D., Nomaler, Ö., Buenstorf, G., Frenken, K., & Lintsen, H. (2016). Same place, same knowledge–same people? The geography of non-patent citations in Dutch polymer patents. *Economics of Innovation and New Technology, 25*, 553–572.

Huang, Y., Schuehle, J., Porter, A. L., & Youtie, J. (2015). A systematic method to create search strategies for emerging technologies based on the Web of Science: Illustrated for 'Big Data'. *Scientometrics, 105*, 2005–2022.

Johns, C. M. (2020). *The industrial revolution-lost in antiquity-found in the renaissance*. Pumbo.nl.

Kilgarriff, A. (2001). Comparing corpora. *International Journal of Corpus Linguistics, 6*, 97–133.

Kuhn, T. S. (1970). *The structure of scientific revolutions* (2nd ed.). University of Chicago Press.

La, H. L., & Bekkers R. N. A. (2018, June 11–13). *The relation between scientific and technological knowledge in emerging fields: Evidence from DNA nanoscience and DNA nanotechnology*. Paper presented at DRUID18 conference, Copenhagen, Denmark.

Layton, E. T. (1974). Technology as knowledge. *Technology and Culture, 15*, 31–41.

Makri, M., Hitt, M. A., & Lane, P. J. (2010). Complementary technologies, knowledge relatedness, and invention outcomes in high technology mergers and acquisitions. *Strategic Management Journal, 31*, 602–628.

Meyer, M. (2000). Does science push technology? Patents citing scientific literature. *Research Policy, 29*, 409–434.

Mina, A., Ramlogan, R., Tampubolon, G., & Metcalfe, J. S. (2007). Mapping evolutionary trajectories: Applications to the growth and transformation of medical knowledge. *Research Policy, 36*, 789–806.

Murray, F. (2002). Innovation as co-evolution of scientific and technological networks: Exploring tissue engineering. *Research Policy, 31*, 1389–1403.

Nakagawa, H. (2000). Automatic term recognition based on statistics of compound nouns. *Terminology. International Journal of Theoretical and Applied Issues in Specialized Communication, 6*, 195–210.

Narin, F., Hamilton, K. S., & Olivastro, D. (1997). The increasing linkage between U.S. technology and public science. *Research Policy, 26*, 317–330.

Nature Research. (2018, January 1). DNA nanotechnology. Retrieved from https://www.nature.com/subjects/dna-nanotechnology

Nelson, R. R., & Winter, S. G. (1974). Neoclassical vs. evolutionary theories of economic growth: Critique and prospectus. *Economic Journal, 84*, 886–905.

Nomaler, O., & Verspagen, B. (2008). Knowledge flows, patent citations and the impact of science on technology. *Economic Systems Research, 20*(4), 339–366.

Nordmann, A. (2008). Philosophy of NanoTechnoScience. In G. Schmid, H. Krug, R. Waser, V. Vogel, H. Fuchs, M. Grätzel, K. Kalyanasundaram, & L. Chi (Eds.), *Nanotechnology, Vol. 1: Principles and fundamentals* (pp. 217–244). Wiley.

Patra, D. (2011). Nanotechnoscience, nanotechnology, or nanotechnoscience: Perceptions of Indian nanoresearchers. *Public Understanding of Science, 22*, 590–605.

Pavitt, K. (1987). The objectives of technology policy. *Science and Public Policy, 14*, 182–188.

Pinheiro, A. V., Han, D., Shih, W. M., & Yan, H. (2011). Challenges and opportunities for structural DNA nanotechnology. *Nature Nanotechnology, 6*, 763–772.

Porter, A. L., Youtie, J., Shapira, P., & Schoeneck, D. J. (2008). Refining search terms for nanotechnology. *Journal of Nanoparticle Research, 10*, 715–728.

Price, D. S. D. J. (1965). Is technology historically independent of science? A study in statistical historiography. *Technology and Culture, 6*, 553–568.

Rayson, P., & Garside, R. (2000). Comparing corpora using frequency profiling. In: *Proceedings of the workshop on comparing corpora* (vol. 9, pp. 1–6). Association for Computational Linguistics.
Rothemund, P. W. K. (2006). Folding DNA to create nanoscale shapes and patterns. *Nature, 440*, 297–302.
Suenaga, K. (2015). The emergence of technological paradigms: The evolutionary process of S&T in economic development. In A. Pyka & J. Foster (Eds.), *The evolution of economic and innovation systems. Economic complexity and evolution* (pp. 211–227). Springer.
Tripodi, G., Chiaromonte, F., & Lillo, F. (2020). Knowledge and social relatedness shape research portfolio diversification. *Scientific Reports, 10*(1) Nature.
US National Nanotechnology Initiative. (2000). What is nanotechnology? Retrieved from https://www.nano.gov/nanotech-101/what/definition
Verbeek, A., Debackere, K., Luwel, M., Andries, P., Zimmermann, E., & Deleus, F. (2002). Linking science to technology: Using bibliographic references in patents to build linkage schemes. *Scientometrics, 54*, 399–420.
Verspagen, B. (2007). Mapping technological trajectories as patent citation networks: A study on the history of fuel cell research. *Advances in Complex Systems, 10*(1), 93–115.
Wang, L., & Li, Z. (2018). Knowledge transfer from science to technology—the case of nano medical device technologies. *Frontiers in Research Metrics and Analytics, 3*, 11.
Zhao, Q., & Guan, J. (2013). Love dynamics between S&T: Some evidences in nanoscience and nanotechnology. *Scientometrics, 94*, 113–132.

Observable Factors of Innovation Strategy: Firm Activities and Industry Effects

Krzysztof Szczygielski, Wojciech Grabowski, and Richard Woodward

Abstract Responding to research questioning the significance of external factors such as industry and country in explaining the patterns of innovation-related activities, we examine the effects of factors both internal and external to the firm. Analyzing CIS data, we find that external factors are more helpful in explaining innovation strategies than internal factors. Our econometric model can quite adequately predict innovation strategies, implying that firm-specific factors might not dominate other factors as strongly as suggested by some prior studies.

Keywords Innovation · Innovation strategy · Sectoral analysis · National innovation systems · Sectoral innovation systems

JEL codes O31 · O32 · O33 · L21 · C31 · C38

1 Introduction

What factors do firms take into consideration when making choices about their approaches to technological innovation and the acquisition of knowledge needed in the innovation process, and how are they influenced by the characteristics of their environments? A number of innovation scholars have looked at what they have called variously "technology strategy" (see, e.g., Ford, 1988; Adler, 1989; Pavitt,

K. Szczygielski (✉)
Faculty of Economic Sciences, University of Warsaw, Warsaw, Poland
e-mail: kszczygielski@wne.uw.edu.pl

W. Grabowski
Faculty of Economics and Sociology, University of Łódź, Łódź, Poland

R. Woodward
CASE – The Center for Social and Economic Research, Warsaw, Poland

University of Edinburgh Business School, Edinburgh, UK
e-mail: Rick.Woodward@ed.ac.uk

A. Pyka, K. Lee (eds.), *Innovation, Catch-up and Sustainable Development*,
Economic Complexity and Evolution, https://doi.org/10.1007/978-3-030-84931-3_4

1990; Dodgson, 1991; Drejer, 1996), "innovation strategy" (Srholec & Verspagen, 2012; Clausen et al., 2011), "innovation orientation" (Prajogo et al., 2013; Yu & Lee, 2017), or "innovation mode" (Lundvall, 2007; Jensen et al., 2007). Some have suggested that industry (Zahra, 1996; Malerba, 2005) and/or the related technology (Lee, 2005; Hekkert et al., 2007) is important for the way firms innovate. Others have stressed the national dimension (Lundvall, 2007), whereas, for startups, a large literature studies the individual background and the knowledge base of the entrepreneurs (Hsu, 2008). More recently, however, Srholec and Verspagen (2012) have argued that factors such as industry and country account for a very small proportion of the variance among firms with respect to the patterns of their innovation-related activities, implying that the key explanatory factors for the relevant choices lie in the realm of (largely unobserved) properties of the firms themselves. In this context, this paper aims to answer the question to what extent firms' innovation strategies can be explained by observable factors, including those internal and external to the firm. This may have important implications for whether the national or sectoral innovation system frameworks provide valuable insights for innovation policy.

In our analysis, we investigate the variation in innovation strategies and examine to what extent it can be attributed to observable characteristics of firms and their environments. To do so, we use data from the 2014 edition of the Community Innovation Survey (CIS) of European manufacturing and services firms and apply factor analysis and regression analysis ('the Eurostat CD-Rom'). Our choice of methodology seeks to maintain as clear a boundary as possible between theory and empirics; in particular, we construct theory-guided measures of innovation strategy dimensions. Then we estimate a multivariate probit model of strategy indicators and assess its explanatory power by carefully analyzing a number of measures of fit.

The paper is organized as follows: In Sect. 2, we consider the relevant theoretical issues and develop our research questions. In Sect. 3, we present our data and methodology. In Sect. 4, we present our results. Section 5 concludes.

2 Background and Research Questions

2.1 What Is Innovation Strategy?

As with any strategy, innovation strategy concerns strategic choices and attempts to define innovation strategy vary widely in terms of which types of choices are studied. For Bhoovaraghavan et al. (1996) and Cheng et al. (2010), innovation strategy is about the choice between process and product innovation. For Turut and Ofek (2012) and Chen and Ergin Turut (2013), it is about the choice between radical and incremental innovation. For Prajogo et al. (2013), "innovation orientation" is about whether firms are oriented toward exploratory or exploitative innovation. And for Eesley et al. (2014) and Sharif and Huang (2012), innovation strategy simply refers to the choice of whether to innovate or not.

Instead of identifying strategy dimensions, some authors focus on the typical strategies firms might adopt. Lundvall (2007) and Jensen et al. (2007) distinguish between the "STI [science, technology, and innovation] mode of innovation," based on formal R&D activities in basic and applied scientific research and focused on the production of explicit, codified knowledge, and the "DUI [doing, using and interacting] mode of innovation," which is more experiential and focused on the sharing and reproduction of tacit knowledge and often involves organizational arrangements that stimulate incremental process innovation. Lundvall (2007) writes that the latter has been neglected by innovation research, which has tended to focus on the former, and argues—taking a cue from Mathews (2001)—that an appreciation of the role of DUI innovation is important for understanding learning processes in the economy. The distinction between these two fundamental types of approaches to innovation runs through much of the thinking about innovation strategy.

Does the STI-DUI dichotomy hold empirically? Prior research suggests that it does, at least in general terms. Srholec and Verspagen (2012), Clausen et al. (2011), and Szczygielski and Grabowski (2014) all distinguished clusters of firms, of which one or two can be interpreted as varieties of the STI mode of innovation, while others can be perceived as subcategories of the DUI type. In fact, the hierarchical factor analysis applied by Clausen et al. (2011) made it possible to formally confirm this interpretation, as the authors demonstrated that the number of clusters could be reduced by joining the clusters from previous rounds to arrive at two types of innovation strategies finally: "high profile" (STI-like) and "low profile" (DUI-like).

As will be seen in Sect. 4, we adopt elements of a number of these prior approaches to innovation strategies, as we examine such choices as radical vs. incremental innovation, process vs. product innovation, and the STI vs. DUI types of innovation.

2.2 The External Factors of Innovation Strategy

The firm's external environment, including customers, competitors, suppliers, government, technological conditions, etc., has often been invoked in the literature as an explanation for the decisions of firms and their success.

Authors in evolutionary economics have sought to classify industries and related firm strategies according to their technological characteristics. The classic Pavitt (1984) taxonomy rests on the criterion of the technology regime of the industry. This framework goes back to the concepts of technological paradigm and technological trajectory proposed by Dosi (1982): at each moment, some major technological advances (which may be more or less recent) have different effects on technological opportunities in different sectors. This, in turn, defines the technological trajectory—the direction of technological progress in the industry and the means of attaining it. It seems reasonable to expect that the technological trajectory or regime affects industries' innovation strategies. Taxonomical exercises are therefore a natural step in the analysis of those strategies (and in particular in examining the external factors of those strategies), especially in view of the related work on sectoral systems of innovation reviewed in Malerba (2005), situating the firm's choices about technological development and innovation in the context of the industry in which it is active.

In this paper, we largely follow Castellacci's (2008) extension of Pavitt's taxonomy since it encompasses both manufacturing and service industries.[1] In his version, two criteria are considered: the technological content and the place of the industry as a provider and/or recipient of advanced products, services and knowledge. The taxonomic groups are the following (note the abbreviations we use subsequently in the paper):

1. *Advanced knowledge providers* (further divided into *specialized supplier manufacturing* or *SSM*, and *knowledge-intensive business services* or *KIBS*).
2. *Mass production goods* (*science-based manufacturing*, *SBM*, and *scale-intensive manufacturing*, *SIM*).
3. *Supporting infrastructural services* (*network infrastructure services*, *NIS*, and *physical infrastructure services*, *PhIS*), and.
4. *Personal goods and services* (*supplier-dominated manufacturing goods*, *SDM*, and *supplier-dominated services*, *SDS*).

The two first groups are regarded as technologically sophisticated. Advanced knowledge providers consist of SSM industries that produce specialized machinery, equipment and precision instruments, mainly for mass production industries. Within the services sector, the KIBS group consists of the industries such as consulting, R&D, software or design, which can also be classified as providers of sophisticated technological content. Mass production goods industries generate advanced technology for their own use; however, the specific nature of innovation differs between the two subgroups of this category: while SBM relies on contacts with the science sector for knowledge utilized in the innovation process, SIM is more likely to work with providers of specialized machinery and equipment.

Firms from the third group provide "supporting infrastructure" for other businesses (even though they cater to individual clients too) and are characterized by a relatively low degree of own technological efforts. Castellacci draws a distinction between PhIS (logistics, wholesale trade) and NIS (finance and telecommunication), arguing that the latter represents a higher level of technological sophistication; however, both subgroups largely rely on other sectors for the provision of advanced technologies. This is particularly pronounced in the last group—personal goods and services—which is the least technologically advanced.

A number of external factors are related in one way or another to the country in which the firm operates. Benefiting from more qualified workforces, better knowledge infrastructure, and more demanding customers, companies in more developed countries stand better chances of introducing new products and production

[1] It is important to note that Castellacci's use of terms differs from ours; for example, he identifies taxonomic groups with innovation modes.

technology. This observation is conceptualized in the national innovation system framework (cf. Lundvall, 2007; Edquist, 2005), or more broadly in work on national technological capabilities (see the reviews in Fagerberg & Srholec, 2008; Fagerberg et al., 2010) and technology clubs (Castellacci & Archibugi, 2008). We, therefore, expect firms located in countries with better technological capabilities to be more likely to invest in R&D, pioneer technologies, introduce radical product innovations and engage in technological forecasting more often than firms from less advanced countries.

2.3 Internal Factors of Innovation Strategies

While the external environment obviously has an impact on firms' decisions and performance, one can also observe firms differing in these outcomes despite operating in seemingly similar conditions. Indeed, the need to explain the heterogeneity remarked upon by Marshall (cited in Laursen, 2012), and which tends to fly in the face of neo-classical assumptions that there is only one efficient way to do things and all inefficient ways are competed out of existence, was one of the most important motivations for the contribution of Nelson and Winter (1982) and the development of evolutionary economics. This heterogeneity is prominently displayed in the aforementioned finding of Srholec and Verspagen (2012) that industry and country are much less important than firm-specific factors in explaining the variance among firms with respect to the patterns of their innovation-related activities. On the other hand, they treat the unexplained heterogeneity as a black box and do not attempt to identify the factors behind it. This question is addressed by Szczygielski and Grabowski (2014), who analyze firm membership in clusters defined by the innovation activities of the firms. These clusters correspond, in fact, to innovation strategies. In their analysis, characteristics such as firm size and being a member of a group of firms are significant factors in membership in the clusters, and thereby in the firms' innovation strategies.

The resource-based school in strategic management argues that the firm is successful if it is able to create and sustain some unique capabilities—i.e., resources and competences—that the competitors find hard to imitate (cf. Penrose, 1959; Wernerfelt, 1984). These can lead to lower unit costs—e.g., due to superb internal logistics systems-—or to the firms' ability to develop unique and innovative products. More generally, the capabilities in question, rooted in the internal environment of a firm, and the way they are orchestrated by management and other internal actors will affect its position in the market together with the external factors considered in Sect. 2.1 (Henry, 2008: 126; Teece, 2019).

There is a large theoretical literature, most of it deriving from Schumpeter, on the relationship between technological innovation and firm size. According to the two main theories, either growth of the firm (hence they are becoming large) results from successful technological innovations, which allow it to acquire market share, or innovation is a very costly and capital-intensive process that larger firms are better able to afford. In either case, there should be a positive relationship between size and (successful) technological innovation. However, the empirical evidence for such a relationship between size (or the degree of industry concentration) on one hand and innovativeness or R&D intensity on the other is often contradictory or ambiguous (Degner, 2011; Dolfsma & van der Velde, 2014). More specifically, with regard to the subject of technology strategy and its relationship to internal factors such as size and resources of the firm, Pavitt (1990: 24) concluded that this strategy is "determined largely by the firm's size and the nature of its accumulated technological competences."

Sapprasert and Clausen (2012) find that firm age is an important explanatory factor for the frequency and success of organizational innovation (with older firms more likely to attempt such innovation, but younger ones more likely to benefit from it). We are unable to observe firm age in our data, but size may, to some extent, a proxy for age, since it is a common observation that young firms tend to either grow or exit the market (see, for example, Haltiwanger et al., 2010), making it unlikely that we could observe a considerable share of firms that are both small and old.

The governance or ownership structure of a firm is also of obvious relevance for all aspects of strategy, including innovation strategy. However, the influence of foreign ownership may be ambiguous. On the one hand, in low- and middle-income countries, foreign investors can be expected to be more liberally endowed with financial resources than the average domestically owned company and have a stronger technological base in general. However, we also know from the relevant literature that multinational companies tend to concentrate their R&D activity in their headquarters (see, e.g., Patel & Vega, 1999; Narula, 2002; Lee, 2005), meaning that the relative richness of available resources does not necessarily translate into their expenditure on R&D and other innovation-related activity within the subsidiary itself.

In light of the foregoing, one of the questions to be covered in our investigation in this paper of the role of internal factors in the firm's innovation strategy is whether resource-rich firms (in particular bigger firms and those that belong to groups of firms) are more likely to adopt more ambitious types of strategies than resource-poor firms: for this reason, we will also investigate whether such firms emphasize R&D and radical innovations. In particular, it will be verified whether foreign-owned firms tend to be more active innovators than domestically owned firms or vice versa and to adopt the pioneer posture more frequently and whether they do less R&D and monitor the science sector less intensively, preferring to rely for their technologies on their mother companies abroad. Finally, we will look at whether organizational innovations occur more frequently in firms that are group members and in bigger firms (because of their complexity).

Table 1 Composition of the sample by country groups

Group name	DE_NO	MED	V-3	BALT	NEW_EU
Countries in the group	Germany, Norway	Cyprus, Portugal, Spain	Czech Republic, Hungary, Slovakia	Estonia, Latvia, Lithuania	Bulgaria, Romania, Croatia
Share of the sample	0.12	0.41	0.15	0.06	0.26
Average score in the European Innovation Scoreboard in 2013	0.59	0.44	0.37	0.34	0.24

Note: V-3 stands for Visegrad group countries (Poland, the fourth Visegrad country, is missing from our dataset)
Source: Community Innovation Survey 2014 and European Commission (2015)

3 Data and Methodology

3.1 Data

Like Srholec and Verspagen (2012), we utilize the Community Innovation Survey data, which Eurostat makes available to certified research entities (i.e., we use the "Eurostat CD-Rom"); we look at the 2014 run of the CIS. Our dataset contains data for 14 countries, which, for the purpose of estimation, were aggregated into six categories (Table 1; for more information on the composition of the sample, see Table 14 in the appendix). As explained in the previous section, we expect the level of national technological capabilities to matter for innovation strategies, which is why for each group of countries, we include the average rank in the European Innovation Scoreboard in 2014.[2]

We analyze both manufacturing and services firms that are classified in 25 two-digit industries or industry groups: this is because in our dataset, some two-digit industries were merged. This is also the reason why we had to modify the Pavitt-Castellacci taxonomy and replace two of the groups in that taxonomy (specialized supplier manufacturing and science-based manufacturing) with other categories: "electrical and electronical equipment" (EEE and "chemicals and pharmaceutical manufacturing" (CPM). Finally, we add the category of miscellaneous repair and installation services (MRIS). The total of firms analyzed is 84,352; of these, 24,606 introduced product or process innovations, were in the process of introducing innovations or had attempted to introduce them (only such firms fill in the whole CIS questionnaire; this is not the case for firms that only introduced innovations in marketing or firm organization).

Table 2 presents the composition of the sample with respect to the taxonomy applied. About 30% of the sample is composed of the low-tech groups of industries

[2] Since the composition of the sample by country does not correspond to the actual composition (for example, the percentage of Spanish firms in the sample is too large), in the rest of the paper weighted estimations are conducted.

Table 2 Composition of the sample by industry categories

KIBS	NIS	PhIS	SIM	SDM	SDS	CPM	EEE	MRIS
0.15	0.03	0.26	0.16	0.23	0.04	0.03	0.08	0.02

Numbers in the table are fractions of the number of firms in the sample weighted by the inverse of the country shares. For the explanation of the abbreviations, see Sects. 2.2 and 3.1. The number of observations is 84,352
Source: Community Innovation Survey 2014

(supplier-dominated manufacturing and supplier-dominated services), and another 26% by physical-infrastructure services. At least 16% of firms operate in scale-intensive industries (the SIM category plus some firms from the CPM group). High-tech manufacturing is represented by CPM and EEE groups, which together constitute about 10% of the sample. Knowledge-intensive business services account for 15%, and network-intensive services (essentially, finance) for 3% of the sample.

The Community Innovation Survey was first implemented in 1993. It is a joint effort of national statistical offices in the European Economic Area, coordinated by Eurostat. The methodology follows the Oslo Manual (OECD and EC, 2005).[3] Most questions refer to the three-year period preceding the circulation of the questionnaire (2012–2014, in our case), while questions on turnover and outlays refer mainly to the year of issue. Although the CIS questionnaire has been developed over many editions, its structure remains relatively stable with well-known "chapters" such as "general information about the enterprise," "product (good or service) innovation," "process innovation," and "sources of information and co-operation for innovation activities."

The Community Innovation Survey includes only limited data about the participating firms, including their employment and sales as well as about whether the firm had any exporting activities or is a member of a group of firms (and if so, where the mother company is located). We use the latter information to define the dummy variables group_DOM and group_FDI, which equal 1 for firms that are members of groups and whose mother companies are located in the home country or abroad, respectively, as well as the dummy no_group for standalone firms. To exploit the information on the market the firms are exporting to, we employ dummy variables: market_LOC, market_DOM, market_EU, market_OTH, which equal 1 if and only if the firm's main market is the local, national, other-EU country, or other-non-EU country markets, respectively. Many studies have proved the exporting activities of firms to be correlated with higher productivity and innovation performance (e.g., Griffith et al., 2006; Hagemejer & Kolasa, 2008; Peters et al., 2018). Thus, although the choice of the market does not have to determine innovation strategy, it is likely to be correlated with (latent) firm characteristics that do have an impact on company decisions.

[3] Since 1992 CIS-like surveys have been implemented in a number of non-EEA countries, including the US (cf. Arora et al., 2016).

Table 3 Composition of the sample by firm size and industry categories

	KIBS	NIS	PhIS	SIM	SDM	SDS	CPM	EEE	MRIS	ALL
Below 250 workers	0.93	0.83	0.86	0.88	0.92	0.93	0.85	0.86	0.92	0.90
At least 250 workers	0.07	0.17	0.14	0.12	0.08	0.07	0.15	0.14	0.08	0.10

Numbers in the table are fractions of the number of firms in the sample weighted by the inverse of the country shares. For the explanation of the abbreviations, see Sects. 2.2 and 3.1. The number of observations is 84,352
Source: Community Innovation Survey 2014

Table 4 Composition of the sample by the membership in groups and industry categories

	KIBS	NIS	PhIS	SIM	SDM	SDS	CPM	EEE	MRIS	ALL
group_DOM	0.24	0.33	0.21	0.19	0.14	0.18	0.23	0.20	0.21	0.19
group_FDI	0.15	0.27	0.09	0.16	0.07	0.12	0.24	0.19	0.09	0.12
no_group	0.61	0.40	0.70	0.65	0.79	0.70	0.53	0.61	0.70	0.69

Source: Community Innovation Survey 2014

Table 5 Composition of the sample by firms' principal markets and industry categories

	KIBS	NIS	PhIS	SIM	SDM	SDS	CPM	EEE	MRIS	ALL
market_LOC	0.39	0.47	0.41	0.29	0.37	0.44	0.16	0.17	0.43	0.36
market_DOM	0.43	0.47	0.30	0.38	0.34	0.46	0.50	0.35	0.41	0.38
market_EU	0.12	0.04	0.23	0.29	0.26	0.07	0.23	0.35	0.12	0.21
market_OTH	0.06	0.02	0.06	0.04	0.03	0.03	0.10	0.13	0.04	0.05

Numbers in the table are fractions of the number of firms in the sample weighted by the inverse of the country shares. For the explanation of the abbreviations, see Sects. 2.2 and 3.1. The number of observations is 84,352
Source: Community Innovation Survey 2014

We also use the binary variable LARGE, which takes a value of 1 in the case of enterprises employing at least 250 workers and 0 otherwise. As one can see in Table 3, small and medium firms (LARGE = 0) constitute about 90% of our sample.

There is a much higher variability across industry groups when it comes to the extent of their internationalization and the membership in the groups of firms (cf. Table 4). About 30% of firms are members of either domestic or foreign groups, but this proportion is higher in the case of high-tech manufacturing (CPM and EEE), knowledge-intensive business services and infrastructure services, and lower for supplier-dominated manufacturing.

On average 22% of firms declare foreign markets to be their principal target (cf. Table 5), but this proportion is considerably higher for the scale-intensive and high-tech manufacturing industries (especially the CPM group). Interestingly, the KIBS firms are more domestically-oriented than services on average (however, presumably, the relatively high values for SDS are driven by tourism).

3.2 Methodology

Our work consists of three principal stages. First, we define the strategy variables. Second, we look at the factors of innovation strategies using the multivariate probit model. Thirdly, we see to what extent the differences in innovation strategies can be explained by observable firm characteristics.

The process of defining strategy variables is based on the analysis of CIS "chapters." In particular, we run factor analyses on two chapters—"Varieties of Innovation Activities" and "Co-operation for product and process innovation activities"—and based on their results, we propose indicators describing various aspects of the innovation strategies of companies. Note that this restricts our analysis only to firms that introduced product or process innovations, were in the process of introducing innovations or had attempted to introduce them, as only such firms answer the questions from these two CIS "chapters." The list of variables obtained in this way is supplemented by some additional indicators, according to the theory discussed above and prior studies of the problem. Suppose we extract K strategic variables and let $S^1, \ldots, S^K$ be the strategy variables identified in this part of the study.

In the second stage of the study, we estimate the parameters of the model explaining firms' propensity to apply a given innovation strategy. Since the values of strategy variables are observable only for a subset of firms, as explained in the previous paragraph, we apply a Heckman-type estimator to address the sample selection bias problem.

We start by estimating the parameters of the following probit model:

$$IN_i^* = \mathbf{x_i}\boldsymbol{\beta} + \mathbf{z_i}\boldsymbol{\gamma} + \varepsilon_i, \tag{1a}$$

$$IN_i = I\{IN_i^* > 0\}, \tag{1b}$$

where $i \in \{1, \ldots, I\}$ indexes all firms, $\varepsilon_i \sim N(0, 1)$, and

$$\mathbf{x_i} = (1, \text{group\_DOM}_i, \text{group\_FDI}_i, \text{FIRM\_SIZE}_i, \text{market\_LOC}_i, \ldots \quad \text{market\_OTH}_i, \text{KIBS}_i, .., \text{SDS}_i)$$

and, finally, z_i contains geographic control variables. Upon estimating the model (1a)-(1b), the inverse Mills ratio is calculated as follows:

$$\text{IMR}_i = IN_i * \frac{\varphi\left(\mathbf{x_i}\widehat{\boldsymbol{\beta}}\right)}{\Phi\left(\mathbf{x_i}\widehat{\boldsymbol{\beta}}\right)} - (1 - IN_i) * \frac{\varphi\left(\mathbf{x_i}\widehat{\boldsymbol{\beta}}\right)}{\left(1 - \Phi\left(\mathbf{x_i}\widehat{\boldsymbol{\beta}}\right)\right)} \tag{2}$$

Indicator IMR_i is then included as explanatory variables in the model of the strategy variables $S^1, \ldots, S^K$ so as to omit the sample selection bias problem (see: Heckman (1979)). More specifically, we estimate the following multivariate probit model:

$$S_n^{k,*} = \mathbf{x_n \beta_k} + \mathbf{z_n \gamma_k} + \lambda \mathrm{IMR}_n + \varepsilon_n^k, \quad (3a)$$

$$S_n^k = I\{S_n^{k,*} > 0\} \quad (3b)$$

where $n \in \{1, \ldots, N\}$ indexes all firms that introduced either product or process innovations or had ongoing or abandoned innovation activities, and it is assumed that $\left[\varepsilon_n^1 \ \varepsilon_n^2 \ \ldots \ \varepsilon_n^K\right]^T \sim N(\mathbf{0}, \mathbf{\Sigma})$.

Since all the dependent variables are binary variables, the parameters of the model (3a)-(3b) are estimated using GHK (Geweke-Hajivassiliou-Keane) smooth recursive conditioning simulator (cf. Geweke, 1992; Borsch-Supan & Hajivassiliou, 1993; Keane, 1994; Hajivassiliou & Ruud, 1994). Let us stress that vectors $\mathbf{x_i}$ and $\mathbf{z_i}$are just a starting point. The selection of variables in individual models is based on their statistical significance. We apply a strategy "from general to specific," following Davidson et al. (1978), who argued that, after starting from the most general model and subsequently imposing restrictions on it and verifying these restrictions, the appropriate specification of the model should be obtained. When this strategy is used, the most important problems associated with data mining are avoided (Lovell, 1983; Charemza & Deadman, 1997). In our case, this estimation strategy implies that we start with a model including all the variables listed above and all the geographic controls. We then verify significance and exclude those variables that are not significant at the 0.05 level of significance. Industry group dummies are exempted from this procedure; i.e., even if any of the variables KIBS through SDM prove insignificant in various estimations, we retain them. This is because we are particularly interested in the role the industry and market environment play in the formulation of innovation strategies.

One of our questions concerns the relative importance of internal and external factors. Using empirical techniques to assess the role different variables play in the model, we start by looking at the percentage of correct predictions. We regard the prediction of IN_i as correct if.

$$P\left(\mathbf{x_i}\widehat{\boldsymbol{\beta}} + \mathbf{z_i}\widehat{\boldsymbol{\gamma}} + \varepsilon_i > 0\right) > f_i \text{ and } IN_i = 1, \quad (4a)$$

or

$$P\left(\mathbf{x_i}\widehat{\boldsymbol{\beta}} + \mathbf{z_i}\widehat{\boldsymbol{\gamma}} + \varepsilon_i > 0\right) < f_i \text{ and } IN_i = 0, \quad (4b)$$

where f_k is the fraction of observations for which we have that $IN = 1$. In words, we require that the implied probability of a given result is at least as high as the observed probability. The percentages of correct predictions for variables $S^1, \ldots, S^K$ are calculated analogously (using formulae (3a)-(3b)), and the percentage of correct predictions of the entire multivariate model is defined as the average of the percentages of the correct predictions for all the variables. Moreover, we define.

FCP^{basic}: The percentage of correct predictions for the basic model.

FCP^{group}: The percentage of correct predictions for the model that omits variables GROUP_DOM and GROUP_FDI.

FCP^{large}: The percentage of correct predictions for the model that omits the variable LARGE.

FCP^{mkt}: The percentage of correct predictions for the model that omits variables market_LOC, market_DOM, market_EU, and market_OTH.

FCP^{ind}: The percentage of correct predictions for the model that omits industry group variables, and.

FCP^{ctr}: The percentage of correct predictions for the model that omits country dummies.

Next, for each of the above indicators, we calculate the relative decline in the explanatory power of the model resulting from the exclusion of the respective variables. More specifically

$$\mathrm{DROP}^{\nu} = \frac{\mathrm{FCP}^{\mathrm{basic}} - \mathrm{FCP}^{\nu}}{\mathrm{FCP}^{\mathrm{basic}}} \tag{5}$$

Where $\nu \in \{\text{group, size, mkt, ind, ctr}\}$. Finally, we look at the following ratios:

$$\mathrm{RI}^{\nu} = \frac{\mathrm{DROP}^{\nu}}{\mathrm{DROP}^{\mathrm{group}} + \mathrm{DROP}^{\mathrm{size}} + \mathrm{DROP}^{\mathrm{mkt}} + \mathrm{DROP}^{\mathrm{ind}} + \mathrm{DROP}^{\mathrm{ctr}}} \tag{6}$$

to assess the relative role of the (groups of) variables in the basic model.

In the last stage of our study, we examine to what extent the variation in innovation strategy can be explained by firm characteristics. This is done in two ways. First, we look at the measure of the fit of our model; i.e., we look at FCP^{basic} and at the more specific, conditional measures of fit (the percentage of correct predictions for a variable S^k).Second, we perform an analysis of variance of innovation dimensions, an extended version of the analysis proposed by Srholec and Verspagen (2012). We use a variance components model (see Goldstein, 2003), where a firm's strategy choice is explained by the country where the firm is located, its industry, size, membership in a group and principal market. However, since ANOVA models are not appropriate for discrete variables (cf. Kao & Green, 2008), we analyze the variance of factors obtained in the first stage of the analysis (denoted F^k) rather than the variance of strategic variables (S^k). A basic variance components model is given as follows:

$$F_n^k = \omega_n^k + \alpha_l^k + \kappa_m^k + \rho_o^k + \zeta_p^k + \eta_r^k \tag{7}$$

where k is the index of the strategic variable, n is the firm, l stands for the NACE industry, m differentiates firms according to group membership (we distinguish three categories: standalone firms, members of domestic groups, and members of foreign groups), o differentiates firms according to the variable LARGE (cf. Table 3),

Table 6 The results of the factor analysis of the varieties of innovation activities

Variable I	F^1	F^2	F^3
Internal R&D	0.4172	0.1087	0.3105
Acquisition of external R&D	0.7387	0.1156	0.1012
Acquisition of machinery, equipment and vehicles needed for innovation purposes	0.1498	0.4093	0.1039
Acquisition of software for innovation	0.2903	0.3207	0.1987
Training (internal or external) for innovative activities	0.2109	0.5109	0.3345
Marketing for product innovations (including market research and advertising)	0.2289	0.2189	0.6019
In-house or contracted out activities to design or alter the shape or appearance of goods or services	0.1754	0.1217	0.6194
Other preparatory activities for product or process innovations, such as feasibility studies, testing, software development)	0.2679	0.2356	0.4176

Note: Factors are listed in the heading of each column, and factor loadings are reported in the table. Extraction method: principal-components analysis. Rotation method: varimax. Number of observations: 24,606 (fsee text)
Source: Community Innovation Survey 2014

p differentiates firms according to their country and r differentiates firms according to the dominant market (cf. Table 5).

4 Results

4.1 Results of Factor Analysis and the Definition of Strategy Variables

We apply factor analysis to variables from two sets of questions ('chapters') in the CIS survey, namely "Varieties of Innovation Activities" and "Co-operation for product and process innovation activities." Then we use the results of the factor analysis to define the innovation strategy indicators. Our procedure is best explained by demonstrating how we apply it to the CIS chapter "Varieties of Innovation Activities." As shown in Table 6, for this chapter, three factors were extracted.[4] The variables *Internal R&D* and *Acquisition of external R&D* have the highest correlations with the first factor. On this basis, we have constructed the indicator *RD*, which takes on a value of 1 for companies that have carried out internal R&D or acquired external R&D.

[4] In order to determine the optimal number of factors, Kaiser's eigenvalue-greater-than-one rule was used (Kaiser, 1960). In order to check the robustness of this method, optimal numbers of clusters were determined using alternative methods (see Kanyongo, 2006, for a review). The results of the selection of the optimal number of factors turned out to be stable.

Turning to the correlations with the second factor, we define the variable "Capacity Building" (abbreviated *CapB*), which takes on a value of 1 for firms that indicated having engaged in at least two of the following three activities: *Acquisition of machinery, equipment and vehicles needed for innovation purposes, Acquisition of software for innovation, Training (internal or external) for innovative activities.*

As for the third factor, it correlates strongly with the "*the activities to design or alter the shape or appearance of goods or services*" and with "*marketing for product innovations*," and to a lesser extent with "*other preparatory activities for product and process innovations.*" Consequently, we define the variable DESIGN which equals one if and only if the firm claimed to be engaged in at least two of the three innovation activities.[5]

Next, to learn about the monitoring activities of firms, we analyze the question about collaborating during introducing innovations. Accordingly, we define two dummy variables.

Firstly, MARKETS, which equals 1 if and only if a firm cooperated with at least two of the following list of potential partners:

- Other enterprises within an enterprise group.
- Suppliers of equipment, materials, components or software.
- Clients or customers.
- Competitors or other enterprises within the sector.

Next, we define the variable SCIENCE, which takes the value of 1 if an enterprise cooperated with at least one partner from the following list:

- Consultants or commercial labs.
- Universities or other higher education institutes.
- Government, public or private research institutes.

We note that the RD vs. CapB and SCIENCE vs. MARKETS distinctions fit well with Lundvall's (2007) classification of innovation strategies into STI (science, technology, and innovation) and DUI (doing, using and interacting) types. The former is based on formal R&D activities in basic and applied scientific research and focused on the production of explicit, codified knowledge, while the latter is more experimental and focused on the sharing and reproduction of tacit knowledge and often involves organizational arrangements that stimulate incremental process innovation.

We note that the above results of the factor analysis are similar (though not identical) to the results of Srholec and Verspagen (2012). However, these authors did not define their own variables and instead used the factor values as strategic variables in their analysis, a choice we will discuss later when we address the fit of the model.

To complete the definition of strategy variables, we take some questions directly from the questionnaire. The dummy variable RADICAL equals 1 if and only if the

[5]Note that the three innovation strategy indicators roughly correspond with factors, and we utilize each CIS question in the construction of exactly one indicator, seeking the maximum correlation with the respective factor.

Table 7 The elements of innovation strategies employed by industry groups

	KIBS	NIS	PhIS	SIM	SDM	SDS	CPM	EEE	MRIS	ALL
RD	0.56	0.38	0.14	0.45	0.33	0.17	0.71	0.64	0.32	0.37
CapB	0.58	0.70	0.63	0.62	0.67	0.58	0.49	0.60	0.69	0.62
DESIGN	0.86	0.86	0.92	0.84	0.87	0.90	0.84	0.83	0.89	0.87
PRODUCT	0.34	0.26	0.09	0.25	0.20	0.11	0.46	0.44	0.15	0.22
PROCESS	0.27	0.27	0.14	0.27	0.20	0.14	0.39	0.33	0.15	0.22
ORGMARKT	0.40	0.42	0.22	0.30	0.27	0.26	0.49	0.40	0.24	0.30
RADICAL	0.23	0.12	0.05	0.15	0.11	0.07	0.27	0.27	0.09	0.13
SCIENCE	0.15	0.09	0.17	0.11	0.12	0.08	0.12	0.06	0.05	0.10
MARKETS	0.10	0.09	0.03	0.07	0.04	0.02	0.12	0.10	0.03	0.06

Numbers in the table are fractions of the number of firms in the sample for whom the dummy variable equals 1, weighted by the inverse of the country shares. For the explanation of the abbreviations, see Sects. 2.2, 3.1 and 4.1. The number of observations is 24,606 (see text).
Source: Community Innovation Survey 2014

firm has introduced innovations that were new not only to the firm but also to the market. Moreover, we define PRODUCT and PROCESS as dummy variables equal to 1 for firms that introduced product, and process innovations, respectively. By analogy, ORGMARKT is a dummy that equals 1 if the firm introduced innovations in organization or marketing.

Table 7 shows the distribution of strategic dummy variables by industry group. Quite predictably, in the high-tech sector (EEE, CPM and KIBS), the values of RD are considerably higher than the scores on CapB. Interestingly, however, the two indicators have comparable averages in other industry groups, although one would expect RD to lag behind CapB in low-tech sectors.

There seems to be a clear technology-related pattern when it comes to the question of the types of innovation engaged in. Product innovations are relatively more important for firms from the high-tech industries sectors than are process innovations. Organizational innovations show a quite interesting pattern. On the one hand, this type of innovation activity is relatively popular in services sectors, just as the literature on service innovation suggests (see, e.g., Miles, 2007). On the other hand, more technology-intensive manufacturing firms also include changes in the firm organization in their innovation strategies.

The introduction of radical product innovations is a relatively rare phenomenon (only 13% of innovating firms). What is more, it differs substantially across industries: 27–28% of high-tech manufacturing firms declared that they introduced products new to the markets where they operate, whereas the corresponding figure is 15% for SIM companies and only 5–6% of low-tech services.

Firms most frequently rely on information from customers and suppliers, and then on the information from the industry, with the science sector being least likely to serve as a source of inspiration: this percentage is particularly small for low-tech services (SDS) and exceptionally high for the chemicals and pharmaceutical manufacturing (CPM) and electrical and electronic equipment (EEE) groups. Note, however, that the EEE group scores the highest on *all* three "monitoring" variables.

4.2 Observable External and Internal Factors of Innovation Strategies

The results of the analysis of the factors of innovation strategies are presented in Tables 8 and 9, where we report the marginal effects (the estimation of the coefficients of the respective models (1a)-(1b) and (3a)-(3b) are presented in Tables 15 and 16 in Appendix). It is evident that large firms are more likely to innovate and to have higher values of our strategy variables: the effect is strongest for SCIENCE and PROCESS, and the only exception is DESIGN. Being a member of domestic groups increases the probability of R&D activities by almost 15%, while for foreign groups, this is only 5%, and the pattern is very similar to SCIENCE. The members of domestic and foreign groups of companies differ even more with respect to their focus on design and marketing innovations: the former are 10% more likely to implement them than the base group, while the latter are 9% less likely to do so. Finally, we note that the industry effects are considerable and have the expected signs, and the same can be said about the variables describing firms' markets. In particular, selling outside the EU marks the most innovative companies.

It should be stressed that the above exercise was about the *relative* importance of internal and external factors. However, we still would like to answer the question, to what extent the observable factors available in the CIS dataset can "explain" the innovation strategies as defined in this paper. We now turn to this problem.

Table 8 Marginal effects of the factors explaining whether firms engage in innovation activities: probit model (1)

	IN
LARGE	0.202
group_DOM	0.090
group_FDI	0.076
KIBS	0.054
CPM	0.225
EEE	0.119
MRIS	−0.034
NIS	−0.011
PhIS	−0.125
SDS	−0.090
SDM	−0.041
market_LOC	−0.053
market_EU	0.104
market_OTH	0.104
V-3	−0.163
NEW_EU	−0.301
MED	−0.193
BALT	−0.211

Note: the number of observations is 84,352. German or Norwegian SIM firms that are not members of a group and whose principal market is the national marker are the base category
Source: Community Innovation Survey 2014

Table 9 Marginal effects of the factors of innovation strategies: multivariate probit model (3a)-(3b)

	RD	CapB	DESIGN	SCIENCE	MARKETS	RADICAL	ORGMARKT	PRODUCT	PROCESS
LARGE	0.094	0.090	−0.009	0.143	0.095	0.086	0.129	0.120	0.159
group_DOM	0.149	0.068	0.100	0.102	0.091	0.017	–	0.027	0.169
group_FDI	0.051	0.055	−0.099	0.036	0.101	0.084	–	0.037	0.121
KIBS	0.173	0.007	0.075	0.079	0.018	0.116	0.028	0.043	−0.001
CPM	0.235	−0.014	0.135	0.096	0.014	0.032	0.048	0.115	0.104
EEE	0.179	0.058	0.082	0.053	0.018	0.102	−0.011	0.071	0.068
MRIS	−0.003	0.099	−0.065	0.005	−0.040	−0.011	−0.021	−0.042	−0.120
NIS	−0.088	0.123	−0.002	−0.049	0.082	−0.050	0.187	0.031	0.182
PhIS	−0.219	0.093	−0.078	−0.111	−0.025	−0.143	0.007	−0.093	−0.161
SDS	−0.215	−0.085	−0.103	−0.090	−0.054	−0.045	0.044	−0.061	−0.210
SDM	−0.135	−0.040	−0.065	−0.076	−0.058	−0.016	−0.018	−0.004	−0.032
market_LOC	−0.156	−0.058	−0.118	−0.088	−0.057	−0.109	–	−0.121	−0.021
market_EU	0.024	−0.012	−0.062	0.047	0.064	0.036	−0.040	0.052	0.047
market_OTH	0.208	0.127	0.159	0.114	0.035	0.098	0.067	0.073	0.049
V-3	−0.012	0.047	−0.354	–	0.080	0.061	−0.026	−0.021	–
NEW_EU	−0.327	−0.011	−0.485	−0.153	−0.061	−0.012	–	−0.077	−0.135
MED	−0.023	−0.362	0.332	0.025	−0.038	−0.043	–	−0.081	–
BALT	−0.085	0.018	−0.369	−0.009	0.083	0.086	−0.055	−0.073	0.039

Note: the number of observations is 24,606 (see text). German or Norwegian SIM firms that are not members of a group and whose principal market is the national marker are the base category

Source: Community Innovation Survey 2014 We now turn to the relative importance of the internal and external factors of innovation strategies. Table 10 refers to the model of the firm's decision to perform innovation activities or not (cf. Eqs. (4a)-(4b) and the accompanying definitions), while Table 11 presents the same analysis for the multivariate probit models. The variables describing firms' principal markets and group membership are the most helpful in explaining whether the firm engages in innovation activities, while external factors (industry and country) are most important in explaining the kind of innovation strategy adopted

Table 10 The role of explanatory variables: the probit selection model

Model	FCP	Drop in explanatory power ($DROP^{\nu}$)	Relative importance (RI^{ν})
Basic model	0.69	–	–
GROUP_DOM and GROUP_FDI omitted	0.57	0.17	0.26
SIZE omitted	0.68	0.01	0.02
market_LOC, market_DOM, market_EU, and market_OTH omited	0.51	0.26	0.38
Industry group dummies omitted	0.64	0.07	0.11
Country dummies omitted	0.58	0.16	0.23

Note: For the definition of indicators see Sect. 3.2 and formulae (4a)-(4b)
Source: Community Innovation Survey 2014

Table 11 The role of explanatory variables: the multivariate probit model of innovation strategy

Model	FCP	Drop in explanatory power ($DROP^{\nu}$)	Relative importance (RI^{ν})
Basic model	0.78	–	–
GROUP_DOM and GROUP_FDI omitted	0.72	0.08	0.12
LARGE omitted	0.72	0.08	0.12
market_LOC, market_DOM, market_EU, and market_OTH omited	0.70	0.10	0.16
Industry group dummies omitted	0.64	0.18	0.28
Country dummies omitted	0.62	0.20	0.32

Note: For the definition of indicators see Sect. 3.2
Source: Community Innovation Survey 2014

4.3 Can Observable Factors "Explain" Innovation Strategies?

Table 12 shows three measures of the percentage of correct predictions for both models (i.e. (1a)-(1b) and (3a)-(3b)). The overall percentage of correct predictions is between 69% and 85%, which indicates a high degree of predictive power. Importantly, the model tends to predict correctly both "ones" (the Sensitivity column) and "zeros" (the Specificity column): the variables that consistently tend to be the best-predicted ones are SCIENCE, MARKETS and RADICAL. Thus, judging from the criterion of correct predictions, it seems that although the fit of the model is far from perfect, we are able to "explain" innovation strategies to a considerable extent.

Can this optimism be sustained if we perform an analysis of variance similar to that carried out by Srholec and Verspagen? In fact, our results for the bulk of the variance in the factors extracted in the first step of our study, while the observable factors play a minor role (Table 13).

Table 12 The percentages of correct predictions for the model (1)–(4)

	Percentage of correctly predicted units (%)	Sensitivity (%)	Specificity (%)
IN	69	75	65
RD	72	86	56
CapB	83	88	63
DESIGN	71	53	87
SCIENCE	84	70	86
MARKETS	80	73	81
RADICAL	76	72	78
ORGMARKT	74	55	79
PRODUCT	70	67	72
PROCESS	71	68	73

Note: "Sensitivity" is the probability that the prediction equals 1 conditioned on the variable being equal to 1. "Specificity" is the probability that the prediction equals 0 conditioned on the variable being equal to 0. The prediction is regarded as correct if the probability of a given result is at least as high as the observed probability

Source: Community Innovation Survey 2014

Table 13 Analysis of variance

	Country	Industry	Size	Group	Market	Firm
F^1	11.25%	7.23%	3.78%	1.35%	2.34%	74.05%
F^2	10.79%	3.45%	0.23%	0.98%	0.75%	83.80%
F^3	5.68%	4.50%	0.26%	1.05%	0.93%	87.58%

Source: Community Innovation Survey 2014

So, why does the ANOVA suggest that observable factors account for a small portion of the variance in firms' innovation strategies, while our model can predict innovation strategies quite well using precisely these factors? We believe there are at least four reasons behind this discrepancy, and which make our model more fit for purpose in assessing the weight of observable factors in explaining innovation strategy.

First, in our approach, we directly address the sample selection bias by employing the Heckman procedure (in fact, an alternative probit model that did not control for sample selection proved to be a much worse predictor than models (1a)-(3b)[6]). Second, our econometric framework makes it possible to differentiate between factors that affect innovation strategies more strongly and those whose effects are less important. Thirdly, by estimating the multivariate probit model, we account for the possible correlation among the error terms, which contributes to more accurate predictions. Finally, note that our econometric model and the analysis of variance (7) differ with regard to dependent variables: while the former uses relatively simple,

[6]Results of this alternative estimation are available on request.

CIS-based indicators, the latter applies the factor values. It might be the case that, since the factor values depend on *all* the questions from the respective CIS "chapters" (cf. Tables 5 and 6), these variables show more variation that is hard to explain by observable factors. (We illustrate the latter point by an example. Suppose there are two companies that both engage in internal R&D activities but differ with respect to some other "varieties of innovation activities," say, marketing for product innovations (cf. Table 6). Their values of the RD variable are obviously the same, while their respective values of the factor F^1 are different.)

5 Conclusions

With this paper, we hope to have contributed to research on the role that factors external and internal to the firm play in its innovation strategy. We applied a number of statistical techniques to the firm-level data from the 2014 edition of the Community Innovation Survey. While we build on previous work in the field, our empirical approach is novel in that we address the selection problem in the analysis of strategies, and we use the measures of fit to assess the relative role of various factors in formulating the innovation strategies.

We found that the external factors, such as the country and the industry in which the company operates, play a smaller role than internal factors in the decision whether to innovate or not, but they are more important in the choice of the specific strategy (e.g., based on R&D or capacity building).

In general, we have demonstrated that, if innovation strategies are measured in a relatively simple way, then the observable factors are able to explain innovation strategies quite satisfactorily. While we certainly would not wish to dismiss the heterogeneity in firms' R&D behavior, we do believe our results imply that it is important for innovation policy debates to continue to be informed by the body of work on national and sectoral innovation systems.

If this is so, we believe the future research agenda on national and sectoral systems of innovation should move from the descriptive approach that has tended to characterize much work in this area to a more analytical and comparative one. What has been seen as a framework should become a method. To accomplish this, it will be necessary to build tools for capturing the characteristics of systems in ways that facilitate comparison. We agree with the call by Srholec and Verspagen (2012) for more work on disentangling sectoral and national effects from heterogeneous behavior within sectors and countries, for example, by employing data aggregated at lower levels of NACE classification. Recent work by Radosevic and Yoruk (2013, 2018) provides examples of how quantitative techniques can be developed that allow for comparisons across countries (and, by extension, sectors).

Appendix

Table 14 Composition of the sample by NACE industries and the attribution to taxonomy groups

NACE groups	Frequency	taxonomy group
10–12	0.08	Supplier-dominated manufacturing (SDM)
13–15	0.06	Supplier-dominated manufacturing (SDM)
16–17	0.04	Supplier-dominated manufacturing (SDM)
18	0.02	Supplier-dominated manufacturing (SDM)
19–21	0.03	Chemicals and pharmaceutical manufacturing (CPM)
22–23	0.06	Scale-intensive manufacturing (SIM)
24–25	0.07	Scale-intensive manufacturing (SIM)
26–28	0.08	Electrical and electronic equipment (EEE)
29–30	0.03	Scale-intensive manufacturing (SIM)
31–32	0.04	Supplier-dominated manufacturing (SDM)
33	0.02	Miscellaneous repair and installation services (MRIS)
45–47	0.16	Supplier-dominated services (SDS)
49–51	0.06	Physical infrastructure services (PhIS)
52–53	0.03	Physical infrastructure services (PhIS)
55–56	0.02	Supplier-dominated services (SDS)
58–63	0.08	Knowledge-intensive business services (KIBS)
64–66	0.03	Network-intensive services (NIS)
68	0.00	Physical infrastructure services (PhIS)
69–75	0.07	Knowledge-intensive business services (KIBS)
77–82	0.02	Physical infrastructure services (PhIS)

Source: Community Innovation Survey 2014

Table 15 Estimates of the parameters of the model explaining whether firms engage in innovation activities: probit model (1)

Explanatory variable	IN
LARGE	0.695***
group_DOM	0.310***
group_FDI	0.260***
KIBS	0.184***
CPM	0.776***
EEE	0.409***
MRIS	−0.118***
NIS	−0.079***
PhIS	−0.432***
SDS	−0.311***
SDM	−0.022**
market_LOC	−0.183***
market_EU	0.359***
market_OTH	0.359***
V-3	−0.559***
NEW_EU	−1.034***
MED	0.162***
BALT	−0.727***

Source: Community Innovation Survey 2014

Table 16 Estimates of the parameters of the factors of innovation strategies: multivariate probit model (3a)-(3b)

	RD	CapB	DESIGN	SCIENCE	MARKETS	RADICAL	ORGMARKT	PRODUCT	PROCESS
IMR	–	2.096***	2.381***	0.456***	0.211*	0.741***	−0.405***	0.798***	1.479***
LARGE	0.373***	0.479***	−0.058**	0.642***	0.664***	0.282***	0.351***	0.321***	0.439***
group_DOM	0.077**	0.184***	0.423***	0.383***	0.605***	0.250***	–	0.178***	0.493***
group_FDI	−0.075*	0.250***	0.281***	0.294***	0.741***	0.378***	–	0.284***	0.349***
KIBS	0.297***	0.035	0.632***	0.229***	0.081***	0.254***	−0.019	0.344***	−0.001
CPM	0.630***	0.713***	1.674***	0.493***	0.101**	0.398***	−0.189***	0.609***	0.302***
EEE	0.369***	0.447***	1.099***	0.117***	−0.185***	0.400***	−0.231***	0.574***	0.188***
MRIS	−0.135***	−0.184***	−0.198***	−0.061*	−0.091**	−0.352***	−0.243***	−0.134***	−0.326***
NIS	−0.071	0.395***	0.769***	0.024	0.011	0.159***	0.223***	0.180***	0.495***
PhIS	−0.394***	−0.707***	−0.619***	−0.522***	−0.466***	−0.594***	0.054*	−0.505***	−0.439***
SDS	−0.562***	−0.833***	−0.579***	−0.837***	−0.605***	−0.557***	0.405***	−0.273***	−0.569***
SDM	−0.160***	−0.191***	0.063***	−0.322***	−0.292***	−0.110***	−0.020*	−0.019	−0.089***
market_LOC	−0.279***	−0.557***	−0.281***	0.213***	0.201***	−0.107***	–	−0.720***	−0.070***
market_EU	0.203***	0.576***	0.639***	0.242***	0.169***	0.334***	−0.043**	0.399***	0.338***
market_OTH	0.342***	0.692***	0.782***	0.400***	0.168***	0.571***	0.075***	0.458***	0.348***
V-3	−1.593***	−2.568***	−2.656***	–	0.436***	0.096***	−0.096***	−0.111***	–
NEW_EU	−1.991***	−3.406***	−3.841***	−0.526***	0.140*	−0.470***	–	−0.538***	−0.544***
MED	−0.186***	−3.176***	−1.802***	−0.147***	0.193***	−0.282***	–	−0.590***	–
BALT	−2.057***	−3.223***	−3.197***	−0.415***	0.236***	−0.371***	−0.167***	−0.548***	0.153***

Source: Community Innovation Survey 2014

References

Arora, A., Cohen, W. M., & Walsh, J. P. (2016). The acquisition and commercialization of invention in American manufacturing: Incidence and impact. *Research Policy, 45*(6), 1113–1128.

Adler, P. (1989). 'Technology strategy: A guide to the literatures', in R.S. Rosenbloom and R.A. Burgelman (eds.). *Research in Technological Innovation, Management and Policy, 4*, 25–151.

Bhoovaraghavan, S., Vasudevan, A., & Chandran, R. (1996). Resolving the process vs. product innovation dilemma: A consumer choice theoretic approach. *Management Science, 42*(2), 232–246.

Borsch-Supan, A., & Hajivassiliou, V. (1993). Smooth unbiased multivariate probability simulators for maximum likelihood estimation. *Journal of Econometrics, 58*(3), 347–368.

Castellacci, F. (2008). Technological paradigms, regimes and trajectories: Manufacturing and service industries in a new taxonomy of sectoral patterns of innovation. *Research Policy, 37* (6–7), 978–994.

Castellacci, F., & Archibugi, D. (2008). The technology clubs: The distribution of knowledge across nations. *Research Policy, 37*, 1659–1673.

Charemza, W. W., & Deadman, D. F. (1997). *New directions in econometric practice. General to specific modelling, cointegration and vector autoregression*. Edward Elgar.

Chen, Y., & Ergin Turut, Ö. (2013). Context-dependent preferences and innovation strategy. *Management Science, 59*(12), 2747–2765.

Cheng, C. F., Lai, M. K., & Wu, W. Y. (2010). Exploring the impact of innovation strategy on R&D employees' job satisfaction: A mathematical model and empirical research. *Technovation, 30* (7–8), 459–447.

Clausen, T., Pohjola, M., Sapprasert, K., & Verspagen, B. (2011). Innovation strategies as a source of persistent innovation. *Industrial and Corporate Change, 21*(3), 553–585.

Davidson, J. H., Hendry, D. H., Srba, F., & Yeo, S. (1978). Econometric modelling of the aggregate time-series relationship between consumers' expenditure and income in the United Kingdom. *Economic Journal, 88*, 661–692.

Degner, H. (2011). Do technological booms matter? New evidence on the relationship between firm size and innovativeness. *Cliometrica, 5*(2), 121–144.

Dolfsma, W., & van der Velde, G. (2014). Industry innovativeness, firm size, and entrepreneurship: Schumpeter Mark III? *Journal of Evolutionary Economics, 24*(4), 713–736.

Dodgson, M. (1991), 'The management of corporate technology strategy', *International Journal of Technology Management* (Special edition on the *Role of Technology in Corporate Policy*), 95–102.

Dosi, G. (1982). Technological paradigms and technological trajectories: A suggested interpretation of the determinants and directions of technical change. *Research Policy, 11*(3), 147–162.

Drejer, A. (1996). Frameworks for the management of technology: Towards a contingent approach. *Technology Analysis and Strategic Management, 8*(1), 9–2.

Edquist, C. (2005). Systems of innovation: Perspectives and challenges. In J. Fagerberg, D. C. Mowery, & R. R. Nelson (Eds.), *The Oxford handbook of innovation*. Oxford University Press.

Eesley, C. E., Hsu, D. H., & Roberts, E. B. (2014). The contingent effects of top management teams on venture performance: Aligning founding team composition with innovation strategy and commercialization environment. *Strategic Management Journal, 35*(12), 1798–1817.

European Commission. (2015). *Innovation union scoreboard 2015*. Brussels.

Fagerberg, J., & Srholec, M. (2008). National innovation systems, capabilities and economic development. *Research Policy, 37*(9), 1417–1435.

Fagerberg, J., Srholec, M., & Verspagen, B. (2010). Innovation and economic development. In B. H. Hall & N. Rosenberg (Eds.), *Handbook of the economics of innovation* (Vol. 2). Amsterdam.

Ford, D. (1988). Develop your technology strategy. *Long Range Planning, 21*(5), 85–95.

Geweke, J. (1992). Evaluating the accuracy of sampling-based approaches to the calculation of posterior moments. In J. M. Bernardo, J. O. Berger, A. P. Dawid, & A. F. M. Smith (Eds.), *Bayesian statistics*. Oxford University Press.

Goldstein, H. (2003). *Multilevel statistical models*. Arnold.

Griffith, R., Huergo, E., Mairesse, J., & Peters, B. (2006). Innovation and productivity across four european countries. *Oxford Review of Economic Policy, 22*(4), 483–498.

Hagemejer, J., & Kolasa, M. (2008). *Internationalization and economic performance of enterprises: Evidence from firm-level data*. National Bank of Poland Working Paper, 51.

Hajivassiliou, V., & Ruud, P. A. (1994). Classical estimation methods for LDV models using simulation. *Handbook of Econometrics, 4*, 2383–2441.

Haltiwanger, J., Jarmin, R., & Miranda, J. (2010). Who creates jobs? Small vs. Large vs. Young. In *Working Paper 16300*. NBER.

Heckman, J. J. (1979). Sample selection bias as a specification error. *Econometrica, 47*(1), 153–161.

Hekkert, M. P., Suurs, R. A., Negro, S. O., Kuhlmann, S., & Smits, R. E. (2007). Functions of innovation systems: A new approach for analysing technological change. *Technological Forecasting and Social Change, 74*(4), 413–432.

Henry, A. (2008). *Understanding strategic management*. Oxford University Press.

Hsu, D. H. (2008). Technology-based entrepreneurship. In S. Shane (Ed.), *Handbook of technology and innovation management*. Wiley-Blackwell.

Jensen, M. B., Johnson, B., Lorenz, E., & Lundvall, B.-Å. (2007). Forms of knowledge and modes of innovation. *Research Policy, 36*(5), 680–693.

Kaiser, H. F. (1960). The application of electronic computers to factor analysis. *Educational and Psychological Measurement, 20*, 141–151.

Kao, L. S., & Green, C. E. (2008). Analysis of variance: Is there a difference in means and what does it mean? *Journal of Surgical Research, 144*(1), 158–170.

Keane, M. (1994). A computationally practical simulation estimator for panel data. *Econometrica, 62*(1), 95–116.

Laursen, K. (2012). Keep searching and you'll find: What do we know about variety creation through firms' search activities for innovation? *Industrial and Corporate Change, 21*(5), 1181–1122.

Lee, K. (2005). Making a technological catch-up: Barriers and opportunities. *Asian Journal of Technology Innovation, 13*(2), 97–131.

Lovell, M. C. (1983). Data mining. *Review of Economics and Statistics, 65*, 1–12.

Lundvall, B.-Å. (2007). National innovation systems — Analytical concept and development tool. *Industry and Innovation, 14*(1), 95–119.

Malerba, F. (2005). Sectoral systems: How and why innovation differs across sectors. In J. Fagerberg, D. C. Mowery, & R. R. Nelson (Eds.), *The Oxford handbook of innovation*. Oxford University Press.

Mathews, J. A. (2001). National systems of economic learning: The case of technology diffusion management in East Asia. *International Journal of Technology Management, 22*(5/6), 455–479.

Miles, I. (2007). Research and development (R&D) beyond manufacturing: The strange case of services R&D. *R&D Management, 37*(3), 249–268.

Narula, R. (2002). Innovation systems and 'inertia'in R&D location: Norwegian firms and the role of systemic lock-in. *Research Policy, 31*(5), 795–816.

Nelson, R. R., & Winter, S. G. (1982). *An evolutionary theory of economic change*. Harvard University Press.

OECD. (2005). *Oslo manual: Guidelines for collecting and interpreting innovation data*. OECD.

Patel, P., & Vega, M. (1999). Patterns of internationalisation of corporate technology: Location vs. home country advantages. *Research Policy, 28*(2–3), 145–155.

Pavitt, K. (1984). Sectoral patterns of technical change: Towards a taxonomy and a theory. *Research Policy, 13*(6), 343–373.

Pavitt, K. (1990). What we know about the strategic management of technology. *California Management Review, 32*(3), 17–26.
Penrose, E. (1959). *The theory of the growth of the firm*. John Wiley and Sons.
Peters, B., Riley, R., Siedschlag, I., Vahter, P., & McQuinn, J. (2018). Internationalisation, innovation and productivity in services: Evidence from Germany, Ireland and the United Kingdom. *Review of World Economics, 154*(3), 1–31.
Prajogo, D. I., McDermott, C. M., & McDermott, M. A. (2013). Innovation orientations and their effects on business performance: Contrasting small- and medium-sized service firms. *R&D Management, 43*(5), 486–450.
Radosevic, S., & Yoruk, E. (2013). Entrepreneurial propensity of innovation systems: Theory, methodology and evidence. *Research Policy, 42*(5), 1015–1038.
Radosevic, S., & Yoruk, E. (2018). Technology upgrading of middle income economies: A new approach and results. *Technological Forecasting and Social Change, 129*, 56–75.
Sapprasert, K., & Clausen, T. (2012). Organizational innovation and its effects. *Industrial and Corporate Change, 21*(5), 1283–1305.
Sharif, N., & Huang, C. (2012). Innovation strategy, firm survival and relocation: The case of Hong Kong-owned manufacturing in Guangdong province, China. *Research Policy, 41*(1), 69–78.
Srholec, M., & Verspagen, B. (2012). The voyage of the Beagle into innovation: Explorations on heterogeneity, selection, and sectors. *Industrial and Corporate Change, 21*(5), 1221–1253.
Szczygielski, K., & Grabowski, W. (2014). Innovation strategies and productivity in the Polish services sector. *Post-Communist Economies, 26*(1), 17–38.
Teece, D. J. (2019). A capability theory of the firm: An economics and (Strategic) management perspective. *New Zealand Economic Papers, 53*, 1–43.
Turut, Ö., & Ofek, E. (2012). Innovation strategy and entry deterrence. *Journal of Economics & Management Strategy, 21*(3), 583–631.
Wernerfelt, B. (1984). A resource-based view of the firm. *Strategic Management Journal, 5*, 171–180.
Yu, G. J., & Lee, J. (2017). When should a firm collaborate with research organizations for innovation performance? The moderating role of innovation orientation, size, and age. *The Journal of Technology Transfer, 42*(6), 1451–1465.
Zahra, S. A. (1996). Technology strategy and financial performance: Examining the moderating role of the firm's competitive environment. *Journal of Business Venturing, 11*(3), 189–219.

The Value of Industry Studies: Impact of Luigi Orsenigo's Legacy on the Field of Innovation and Industry Evolution

Junguo Shi and Bert M. Sadowski

Abstract New solutions in artificial intelligence and machine learning require researchers to study, in greater depth, the nature, and dynamics of emerging industries like biotechnology or pharmaceuticals. With his pioneering work, Luigi Orsenigo has demonstrated, in great detail, how new technologies create technological opportunities, change appropriability conditions, and cumulativeness in these emerging industries. Rooted in the evolutionary economics tradition, this approach is better suited in explaining the patterns of innovation, technological change, and the growth in very dynamic industries. In this context, our article reviews the evidence of Luigi Orsenigo's contribution to the economics of innovation, to the tradition of history-friendly models, and to the discussion on the sectoral system of innovation. It concludes by pointing at some unresolved questions in these traditions and new fruitful alleys for future researchers.

Keywords Innovation · Industrial dynamics · Neo-Schumpeterian · History-friendly model · Sectoral system of innovation

1 Introduction

With the emergence of artificial intelligence (AI) and machine learning (ML), a renewed interest has surfaced in studying the nature and the dynamics of growth of firms in the biotechnology and pharmaceutical industry (Buvailo, 2018). This

---

J. Shi (✉)
School of Finance & Economics, Jiangsu University, Zhenjiang, China

Institute of China Studies, Seoul National University, Seoul, South Korea
e-mail: junguoshi@outlook.comm

B. M. Sadowski
School of Innovation Sciences, Eindhoven University of Technology, Eindhoven, the Netherlands
e-mail: B.M.Sadowski@tue.nl

A. Pyka, K. Lee (eds.), *Innovation, Catch-up and Sustainable Development*, Economic Complexity and Evolution, https://doi.org/10.1007/978-3-030-84931-3_5

interest in the role of AI- and ML-driven solutions in early-stage drug discovery has not only been vital for understanding the market entry of small firms but also the growth patterns of large conglomerates in the industry. This explains the onset of a renaissance of ideas originally developed by Luigi Orsenigo 20 years earlier. His pioneering research on the pharmaceutical and biotechnology industry has shed some new light on the field of economics of innovation and technological change by linking emerging technological opportunities to industrial dynamics while examining the effects of science and technology policy, industry–university relations as well as firm collaborations on these processes. In contrast to the neoclassical economic literature, his research was focused on studying the nature of emerging technologies, the role of market structure, the degree of industry concentration, and the function of government intervention in explaining the growth of industries. This renewed interest has also been echoed by newly established research centers in Asia, where researchers utilized these ideas to create a better understanding of these dynamic industries.

During his scientific career, Luigi Orsenigo has undertaken a number of in-depth empirical industry studies that were outstanding in terms of originality and variety of themes ranging from analyzing the nature of biotechnology in order to develop micro-foundations of the emerging industry, from linking the role of intellectual property rights to the concepts of national and sectoral systems of innovation (Dosi & Malerba, 2018). He developed an in-depth understanding of the technology, which allowed him to provide a sound empirical basis for new theoretical insights. In the following, we examine quantitively how this research has diffused throughout the international academic community and attracted, in particular, in Asia increasing attention. The ideas and concepts were vital in stimulating new insights in the economics of innovation and technological change by developing new frameworks to (a) study industrial dynamics, in particular, in the biotechnology and pharmaceutical industry; (b) model industrial change in a history friendly manner; and (c) study processes of innovation and technological change on a sectoral level.[1]

2 The contribution of Luigi Orsenigo's research

2.1 General statistics

In this paper, we mainly use the original 40 papers published by Luigi Orsenigo in renowned journals as our research sample. We find 2024 papers citing Luigi Orsenigo's publications in both Scopus and WOS systems, which are distributed across 560 journals (with self-citation excluded). Figure 1 presents a sharp increase

[1] In Luigi Orsenigo's lifelong academic research, he developed theory and methodologies with his co-authors. We use the term *legacy* to discuss his contribution to the academy through the joint works.

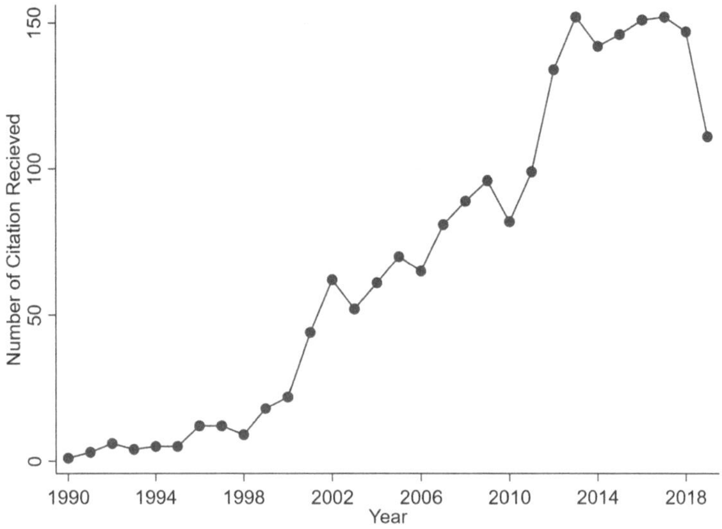

Fig. 1 Growth of papers citing Luigi Orsenigo's publication

in citation during the past two decades. Using indicators like a total number of papers, total citations, g-index, and h-index, we found 30 journals which are intensely citing Luigi Orsenigo's publications and received high citations (see Table 1).

We cluster these 30 journals into the following categories: (1) The most influenced area is (Neo-)Schumpeterian related research journals, namely *Research Policy, Industrial and Corporate Change, Journal of Evolutionary Economics, Economics of Innovation and New Technology, Small Business Economics,* and *Structural Change and Economic Dynamics*. These journals mainly publish papers related to innovation studies that intensely explore Schumpeterian ideas. This is consistent with Luigi Orsenigo's research contribution in the Neo-Schumpeterian tradition. In addition, *Cambridge Journal of Economics* is a journal that welcomes contributions from heterodox economics. (2) The second cluster shows journals related to broadly innovation studies, namely *Technovation, Technological Forecasting and Social Change, International Journal of Technology Management, Science and Public Policy, Technology Analysis and Strategic Management, R&D Management,* and *Journal of Technology Transfer*. These journals deal with issues related to innovation studies. Different from cluster (1), it is not necessary to develop a theory falling in Schumpeterian economics tradition. They focus more on management issues related to innovation. (3) Geography-based fields, like *Regional Studies, Entrepreneurship and Regional Development,* and *Journal of Economic Geography*. Papers published in these journals are mainly fall into the so-called Evolutionary Economic Geography which can be regarded as one branch of Neo-Schumpeterian tradition. (4) Environmental related journals, namely *Ecological Economics, Journal of Cleaner Production, Environmental Innovation* and

Table 1 Influenced journals citing Luigi Orsenigo's publication

Journal name	Total papers	Total citations	g-index	h-index
Research Policy	178	13,053	112	60
Industrial and Corporate Change	126	5539	72	39
Journal of Evolutionary Economics	92	2166	44	26
Technovation	47	1892	43	23
Economics of Innovation and New Technology	66	1316	35	20
Technological Forecasting and Social Change	78	1352	34	21
Small Business Economics	43	1149	33	19
Industry and Innovation	44	832	28	14
Regional Studies	27	971	27	11
Cambridge Journal of Economics	25	1253	25	16
International Journal of Technology Management	26	569	23	8
Strategic Management Journal	19	3980	19	14
Structural Change and Economic Dynamics	31	406	19	11
Science and Public Policy	22	342	18	11
Technology Analysis and Strategic Management	34	370	18	10
European Planning Studies	26	363	18	9
R and D Management	20	315	17	9
Organization Science	15	1832	15	12
Scientometrics	17	234	15	9
Journal of Technology Transfer	14	169	13	5
Ecological Economics	12	419	12	10
Entrepreneurship and Regional Development	11	142	11	7
Journal of Cleaner Production	11	145	11	6
International Journal of Industrial Organization	10	586	10	8
Journal of Economic Geography	9	1289	9	7
Journal of Economic Behavior and Organization	9	124	9	6
Environmental Innovation and Societal Transitions	9	157	9	5
Applied Economics	9	95	9	3
Organization Studies	8	400	8	7
Review of Industrial Organization	8	117	8	6

Societal Transitions. This is an emerging field in Neo-Schumpeterian studies in recent years. This means our society needs more and more innovation to address the current environmental challenges. With the development of manufacturing in Asian economies, environmental problems like acid rain, air pollution, urban sprawl, waste disposal, water pollution, and climate change are received wide concern. It needs to be addressed by the new advanced technologies, like green ICTs, AI, and MI. (5) Industrial organization clusters, like *International Journal of Industrial Organization, Journal of Economic Behavior and Organization, Review of Industrial Organization,* and other related journals like *Applied Economics, Organization Science,* and *Organization Studies*. This reflects the application of the theory of Sector Innovation Systems (one of the contribution by Luigi Orsenigo) into mainstream economics journals.

We also calculate the author distribution in each region citing Luigi Orsenigo's publications. We map this result in Table 2. In general, the authors are mainly from European and north American areas. In Europe, Italy, the United Kingdom, Netherlands, Germany, France, Spain, Sweden, and Demark, count for almost 60% of the papers. Several well-known research institutes like SPRU, UNU-MERIT, LEM, ECIS, IKE, are in these areas, and united cooperated by some projects like ISS, GLOBELICS, DRUID, EUSPRI, or DIME. Asia, Latin America, and Australia are emerging regions for Luigi Orsenigo's research, particularly in China and Korea.

In the following, we will discuss Luigi Orsenigo's main contributions and raise some prospects in each aspect.

2.2 Economics of Innovation and Technological Change in the Biotechnology and Pharmaceutical Industry

In order to explain the dynamics of industrial innovation in the pharmaceutical and biotechnology sector, Luigi Orsenigo examined the institutions and market structure by studying in great detail the network of emerging small firms and their interaction with large companies in the industry (Orsenigo, 1989a). In his thesis, he further developed the economics of innovation and technology change by using concepts like technological opportunities, regimes, learning, market selection, institutions to explain the industrial dynamics in the industry. By using the development of biotechnology as a benchmark, he demonstrated that the nature of biotechnology and the patterns of industrial innovative activities in this emerging industry are interrelated. He showed, in addition, why the role of technological regimes, scientific advances, industry–university relationships, government and public policies have to be considered in order to explain industrial dynamics in the biotechnology sector. These key variables he used later to develop the concept of sectoral systems of innovation. His in-depth understanding of the technology and the industry enabled him to provide ample evidence for his propositions. This empirical basis generated a solid foundation for his follow-up research on the biotechnology industry and allowed him to develop new insights into the economics of innovation and technological change. By leaning on his extensive network of colleagues, he received valuable suggestions to further improve his ideas and encouragement for a wider popularization of his insights.

Table 2 Geography distribution of authors citing Luigi Orsenigo's Publication

Europe (Total number 1931)	Italy	UK	Netherlands	Germany	France	Spain	Sweden	Denmark	Finland	
	383	361	213	194	157	149	107	51	49	
	Norway	Portugal	Austria	Belgium	Switzerland	Greece	Poland	Russia	Czech Republic	
	47	41	36	34	34	21	14	14	7	
	Hungary	Luxembourg	Estonia	Cyprus	Serbia	Iceland	Macedonia	Romania	Croatia	
	5	5	2	2	1	1	1	1	1	
Americas (Total number 451)	United States	Canada	Brazil	Argentina	Colombia	Chile	Uruguay	Mexico	Peru	Dominican
	319	58	32	15	10	7	4	3	2	1
Asia (Total number 261)	China	Korea	Taiwan	Malaya	India	Singapore	Iran	Turkey	Israel	
	68	61	43	14	12	12	10	9	7	
	Macau	Hong Kong	United Arab Emirates	Pakistan	Indonesia	Thailand	Iraq	Bahrain		
	7	6	3	2	2	2	2	1		
Africa (Total number 20)	South Africa	Cameroon	Nigeria	Tunisia	Ghana					
	10	4	3	2	1					
Austilia (Total number 73)	Australia	New Zealand								
	62	11								

In his follow-up research, Luigi Orsenigo devoted his energy in developing a better understanding of the nature of biotechnology and of processes of convergence between the biotechnology and pharmaceutical industry by examining, in particular, the dynamics of firm collaboration (Barbanti et al., 1999; Orsenigo et al., 1998, 2001), differential processes of innovation and industry evolution (Malerba & Orsenigo, 2002), the role of technological regimes (Garavaglia et al., 2012) and innovation policies (Rosiello & Orsenigo, 2008). As a result, several books and book chapters edited by Luigi Orsenigo appeared focusing on economics of innovation and technological change in the biotechnology and pharmaceutical industry such as *The Economics of Biotechnology* (McKelvey & Orsenigo, 2006), and *The Emergence of Biotechnology. Institutions and Markets in Industrial Innovation* (Orsenigo, 1989b). Due to his original way of thinking in this field, he was invited as editor of special issues in academic journals like the *International Journal of Biotechnology*.

As the development of biotechnology increasingly generates technological opportunities for a variety of sectors as well as provides already a significant contribution to economic output (OECD, 2009), topics addressed by Luigi Orsenigo like technological regimes, university–industry linkage, IPR, innovation policy are still fundamental in understanding the dynamics in the industry. In addition, there are new themes like catching up for emerging country firms or convergence among different technological areas in biotechnology which research still needs to address. His techno-economic understanding of the evolution of biotechnology and the pharmaceutical industry has been central to his way to study innovation and industrial evolution in greater detail not only in terms of methodology but also in the way it spurred theory development. In the following, we discuss his contribution to methodology, in particular to the development of history-friendly models (HFMs), and the concept of Sectoral System of Innovation (SSI).

2.3 *Impact on History Friendly Model Development*

With Luigi Orsenigo, research in the evolutionary theory tradition has taken agent-based simulation models (ABMs) to a new level by including history-based details into account in formal complex modelling exercises. As complexity has been at the heart of modern adaptive and dynamic economic systems (Tesfatsion, 2001), simulations provided researchers with tools to translate complex economic relationships of agents and their interactions into economic models. In order to explore the complexity of industrial dynamics, ABMs have been a suitable option available to economists to undertake such complex analysis (Garavaglia, 2010). As ABMs have been considered as a convenient way of exploring evolution in economics, these models have been criticized as limited in their explanatory power (see Yoon and Lee (2009) for a detailed review). As a result, a search process for more elaborated methodologies for ABMs started driven by two different, but complementary theoretical traditions. One tradition, e.g., Silverberg et al. (1988), Bottazzi et al. (2001),

Winter et al. (2000), Fagiolo and Dosi (2003) and Dosi et al. (2006), focused on more general models to explore fundamental principles of evolutionary economics, explaining as many observed phenomena as possible with as few assumptions as possible. In this tradition, more general models were developed that had the potential to cover areas of neoclassical economics like the business cycle or economic growth theories, in more realistic ways. These models were aimed at providing more fundamental results to evolutionary economics (Orsenigo, 2007). A second theoretical tradition, in contrast, was aimed at studying the evolution of industries in greater detail. In this tradition, Luigi Orsenigo and his colleagues developed a family of the HFMs focusing on the evolution of industries and on "stylized" facts that have been identified and examined by historical analyses and case studies in order to add history-based details to the formal representation (Malerba et al., 1999).

The "stylized" facts in HFMs that are included in ABM are derived from qualitative theories about mechanisms and factors affecting innovation and industry evolution. These mechanisms and factors are generated based on empirical research in industrial organization, business strategy and organization, and by analyzing histories of industries. The objective in using these "stylized" facts is to link empirical evidence to stand-alone simulation models in order to generate new insights into formal theory. In this respect, HFMs are aimed at exploring whether particular mechanisms and forces built into the model can generate (explain) the patterns predicted. The model building in the HFMs tradition is guided by verbal explanations and appreciative theorizing.

As a variety of models have been developed for different industries in a history-friendly fashion, the challenge for Luigi Orsenigo was to generate some more general determinants of industry development. Comparisons between different models became a way forward to generate new and more general hypotheses about the factors shaping the interactions between technological change and industrial evolution. Almost two decades have passed between the first HFM (Malerba et al., 1999) and later HFMs focusing on a greater variety of industries. Luigi Orsenigo and his colleagues developed different history-friendly models focusing on the evolution of three industries: computers, semiconductors, and pharmaceuticals (Malerba et al., 2016). As a result of their analysis, they were able to generate a new HFM style of analysis that combined the investigation of technological progress and its relationships with competition and the evolution of industry structures. Based on their joint effort to develop this methodology, they won the prestigious Schumpeter Prize from the International Joseph A. Schumpeterian Society in 2012.

In comparing these three industries, Luigi Orsenigo and his colleagues were able to use several topics and factors to explain industrial dynamics, like the role of segmented demand, user–producer interaction, public policy, entry and the dynamics of concentration, IPR, technological regimes, vertical structure of production, and market selection. Table 3 lists the main HFMs publications written by Luigi Orsenigo with his colleagues.

Luigi Orsenigo's work has been influential for the analysis of other industries like the synthetic dye industry (Brenner & Murmann, 2003) or the DRAM industry (Kim & Lee, 2003) and to explore new topics, e.g., product portfolio (Mäkinen & Vilkko,

Table 3 The main HFMs publications by Orsenigo

Author(s)	Title	Journal	industry	year
Malerba, F., Nelson, R., Orsenigo, L. and Winter, S.	'History-friendly' models of industry evolution: the computer industry	Industrial and Corporate Change	Computer	1999
Malerba, F., Nelson, R., Orsenigo, L. and Winter, S.	Competition and industrial policies in a 'history friendly' model of the evolution of the computer industry	International Journal of Industrial Organization	Computer	2001
Malerba, F., Nelson, R., Orsenigo, L. and Winter, S	Product Diversification in a "History-Friendly Model of the Evolution of the Computer Industry	in E. Larsen and A. Lomi (eds.), "Simulating organizational societies.", Cambridge (Ma.), MIT Press	Computer	2001
Malerba, F. and Orsenigo, L.	Innovation and market structure in the dynamics of the pharmaceutical industry and biotechnology: towards a history-friendly model.	Industrial and Corporate Change	Pharmaceutical & Biotechnology	2002
Malerba, F., Nelson, R., Orsenigo, L. and Winter, S. G.	Firm Capabilities, Competition and Industrial Policies in a History-Friendly Model of the Computer Industry	in C. Helfat (ed.) "The SMS Blackwell Handbook of Organizational Capabilities. Emergence, Development and Change", Blackwell, Oxford	Computer Industry	2003
Garavaglia, C., Malerba, F., Orsenigo, L. and Pezzoni, M.	Entry, Market Structure and Innovation in a History-Friendly Model of the Evolution of the Pharmaceutical Industry	in G. Dosi and M. Mazzuccato (eds.), Knowledge Accumulation and Industry Evolution. The Case of Pharma-Biotech", Cambridge University Press	Pharmaceutical Industry	2006
Malerba, F., Nelson, R., Orsenigo, L. and Winter, S.	Demand, Innovation and the Dynamics of Market Structure: the Role of Experimental Users and Diverse Preferences	Journal of Evolutionary Economics	Computer Industry	2007
Malerba, F., Nelson, R., Orsenigo, L. and Winter, S.	Public policies and changing boundaries of firms in a "history-friendly" model of the co-evolution of the computer and semiconductor industries	Journal of Economic Behavior & Organization	Computer & semiconductor	2008
Malerba, F., Nelson, R.,	Vertical integration and disintegration of	Industrial and Corporate Change	Computer & semiconductor	2008

(continued)

Table 3 (continued)

Author(s)	Title	Journal	industry	year
Orsenigo, L. and Winter, S.	computer firms: a history-friendly model of the coevolution of the computer and semiconductor industries			
Garavaglia, C., Malerba, F., Orsenigo, L. and Pezzoni, M.	Technological regimes and demand structure in the evolution of the pharmaceutical industry	Journal of Evolutionary Economics	Pharmaceutical industry	2012
Garavaglia, C., Malerba, F., Orsenigo, L. and Pezzoni, M.	Innovation and Market Structure in Pharmaceuticals: An Econometric Analysis on Simulated Data	Jahrbücher für Nationalökonomie und Statistik	Pharmaceutical industry	2014

2014), the dynamics and evolution of technologies (Fontana et al., 2008), successive changes in industrial leadership (Fontana & Zirulia, 2015; Landini et al., 2017; Yu et al., 2020) and the evolution of National Innovation Systems (Yoon, 2009). In addition to analysis on the micro and meso levels, HFMs have recently been used to analyze at macro level, e.g., to study catch-up of a latecomer with an incumbent country (Landini & Malerba, 2017). There still is some work to be done in this area to follow Luigi Orsenigo's style of HFM modelling (Malerba, 2011; Garavaglia, 2010; Yoon & Lee, 2009). First of all, more industries should be considered that are quite different compared to the already examined one's (such as business service industries or agro-food environmental friendly industries) in order to model the specificities and dynamics of these industries. Secondly, a stronger focus should be on deriving factors affecting technological change, the dynamics of market structure, industrial leadership, the vertical and horizontal structure of production, and the division of innovative labor in industries. In this context, the work on selection and on the role of institutions will become more important. These more "general models" can be considered as the second generation of ABMs adopting HFM frameworks. Finally, it would be interesting to study "future counterfactuals," in which the researcher investigates potential future conditions that could lead to different outcomes. This prospect is highly ambitious but it may contribute to stimulating a debate about the normative role of simulation models in economics (Garavaglia, 2010).

2.4 Sectoral Systems of Innovation

The development of the concept of sectoral systems of innovation provided in evolutionary economics a new framework for examining factors that affect innovation in sectors that are based on three building blocks: knowledge and technologies, actors and networks, and institutions (Malerba, 2005). Luigi Orsenigo explored these factors further in greater detail during his academic career. The idea that knowledge is of crucial importance for the performance and growth of firms, regions, and countries became in recent years widely acknowledged in the literature (Nelson, 1982). As a result, research has increasingly focused on the question of how knowledge can be characterized and what is the impact of knowledge on the economy. This led to a number of studies focusing on a better conceptualization of knowledge, its relevant dimensions and economic consequences as well as the mechanisms through which knowledge leads to greater economic welfare (Malerba & Orsenigo, 2000). An important area of research has been on tacit and codified knowledge (Nelson & Winter, 1982). By using a distinction between tacit and codified knowledge, the literature has been increasingly recognized that the concept of knowledge is more complex and multifaceted. Thus, the types and forms of knowledge are likely to exert in quite different ways effects on the organization of economic activities, productivity, and the overall rates of the technological and economic process. Malerba and Orsenigo (2000) argued that the distinction between tacit and codified knowledge constitutes only a part of the categorization of the dimensions of knowledge relevant to an understanding of innovative activities of firms and the evolution of industries. They further identified other main dimensions of knowledge that are relevant for an understanding of a firms' innovation processes and the evolution of industries. The authors emphasized, in addition, the relevance of competencies and some further properties of knowledge, like technological regimes, different domains of knowledge (in terms of technology, demand, and applications), and knowledge complementarities (and the related issues of coordination and the integration of these complementarities).

Luigi Orsenigo proposed that there are persistence and heterogeneity of innovative activities at the firm level determining patterns of technological change in different industries as well as countries. In their paper, Malerba et al. (1997) computed indicators of persistence and heterogeneity using the OTAF-SPRU patent database at the firm level for five European countries over the period 1969–1986 for 33 technological classes to answer the following questions, i.e., are persistence and heterogeneity associated with higher degrees of concentration in innovative activities, stability in the ranking of innovators, and lower degrees of entry and exit in the population of innovators? Or, do the patterns of innovation depend on other variables like firm size and industrial concentration? Moreover, they focused on the question of what are the relationships between the patterns of innovative activities, their determinants, and the technological specialization of countries. The results of their analysis show that persistence and asymmetries are important (and strongly related) phenomena that affect the patterns of innovative activities across countries and sectors, while the role of market structure variables is less clear. Furthermore, international technological specialization is associated with the competitive core of persistent innovation. In Cefis and Orsenigo (2001), the authors further examine the persistence of innovative activities at the firm level from a comparative perspective by using a new data set composed of panel data for France, Germany, Italy, the UK,

Japan, and the USA. Using a transition probability matrix approach, they found empirical evidence for the existence of persistence in innovative activities. However, the significance of these results was not very high at the aggregate level and there were signs that persistence was declining over time. However, both innovators and non-innovators had a high probability to remain at their positions and persistent innovators were responsible for a disproportionately high share of innovative activities. In this context, the authors showed that persistence in innovative activities is rather strong. The observed trends could be found in all countries in the sample, even there were also some country-specific properties of these processes. In addition, the authors found that there was heterogeneity across industries and with respect to firm size. Furthermore, intersectoral differences were invariant across countries, suggesting that persistence is (at least partly) a technology-specific variable. Persistence tends to increase with firm size, but the relationship between firms' size and persistence is strongly country specific.

By using empirical data, Malerba and Orsenigo (1995) demonstrated that Schumpeterian patterns of innovation are technology-specific and are related to specific technological regimes. Their empirical analysis based on patent data from four countries found that patterns of innovation activities differ systematically across technological classes, while remarkable similarities emerge across countries for each technological class. These results strongly suggested that "technological imperatives" and technology-specific factors (which are closely linked to technological regimes) play a major role in determining the patterns of innovative activities across countries. In a later study, Malerba and Orsenigo (1996) investigated—based on patent data of 49 technological classes from six countries—these patterns of innovation activities at technological and country levels in greater detail. In this paper, two groups of technological classes were identified: "*Schumpeter Mark I*" and "*Schumpeter Mark II.*" These innovative activities in these two groups were structured and organized in a different way. The first group was characterized by a *widening pattern* in which the concentration of innovative activities was low, innovators were small, the stability in the ranking of innovators was low and the entry of new innovators was high. The second group represented a *deepening pattern* in which concentration of innovative activities was higher than in the first group, innovators were larger in terms of size, there was more stability in the ranking of innovators, and the rate of entry was lower. The first group composed of mechanical technologies and traditional sectors, while the latter group included chemicals and electronics. These results suggested that technology-related factors (such as technological regimes, defined in terms of conditions of technological opportunity, appropriability, cumulativeness, and properties of the knowledge base) play a major role in determining the specific patterns of innovative activities of a technological class across countries. Within these constraints, country-specific factors introduce variances across countries in the pattern of innovative activities for a specific technological class. In addition, the authors also examined the relationships between specific features of the patterns of innovative activities and international technological specialization. Technological advantages appear in general to be linked to higher degrees of asymmetries among innovators, higher stability of the ranking of innovators, smaller economic size of the innovating firms, and lower entry rates of new innovators. These relationships, however, are across the two groups of technological classes. In the Schumpeter Mark I (widening) technological classes, international technological specialization was associated with relatively higher degrees of asymmetries among innovators and entry of new innovators (as well as smaller firm size) while in the Schumpeter II (deepening) technological classes, international technological specialization was linked to the existence of a stable but competitive core of persistent innovators. To further confirm these conclusions, Luigi Orsenigo conducted additional studies using other databases to further characterize technological regimes and Schumpeterian patterns of innovation (Breschi et al., 2000; Malerba & Orsenigo, 1996, 1997). In focusing on the relationship between technological regimes and patterns of innovative activities, he studied, in addition, how technological regimes influence industrial evolution (Dosi et al., 1994, 1995, 1997; Malerba & Orsenigo, 1999). Earlier studies had already revealed the effects of more specific determinants of technological regimes on firm behavior (Malerba & Orsenigo, 1993).

In their 2013 article, Luigi Orsenigo and his co-authors examined the moderating role of demand and technological regimes in shaping the relationship between consumers switching costs and first-mover advantage (Capone et al., 2013). Their research results showed that the extent to which switching costs can be an effective mechanism in generating first-mover advantage depends on demand regimes, i.e., whether demand is homogeneous or fragmented. The dimensions of technological regimes do not matter when demand is homogenous. However, in the case of fragmented demand, these regimes can be key determinants of the existence of advantages for early movers.

Luigi Orsenigo found some exceptional cases that did not follow the general role of technological regimes and industrial dynamics. The pharmaceutical industry—one of Luigi Orsenigo's favorite study subjects—represented such an exception. The pharmaceutical industry has been described as a sector characterized by high R&D and marketing expenditure. These characteristics would suggest that—as a first approximation—the industry should be characterized by a high degree of concentration. However, the concentration has been consistently lower over the whole history of the growth of the industry. Furthermore, competition in the industry does not occur among many small (relative to the market) firms of approximately similar size. Rather, the industry is largely dominated by a core of innovative firms which have remained quite small and stable for a prolonged period of time. To understand the structure and dynamics in the industry, Luigi Orsenigo had to delve deeper into the analysis of the determinants by developing a modified version of his previous "history-friendly" model of the evolution of the pharmaceutical industry (Malerba & Orsenigo, 2002; Garavaglia et al., 2012). The simulation results presented in the paper in 2012 (Garavaglia et al., 2012) demonstrated that technological regimes remain the fundamental determinants of the patterns of innovation. Furthermore, the authors showed that the demand structure played a crucial role in preventing the emergence of concentration through a partially endogenous process of discovery of new submarkets. In addition, they indicated that it is not simply market fragmentation as such that produces these results, but rather the entity of the "prize" that innovators can gain relative to the overall size of the market. Finally, the paper provided some evidence on the proposition that emerging industry leaders start-up as innovative early entrants in large submarkets.

By looking at the networks of actors in the transformation of industries, Malerba and Orsenigo (2008) explored the notion of how user–producer interaction affects innovation and the dynamics of market structure in industry evolution. In Malerba and Orsenigo (2010), they extended this analysis by examining how the benefits of user–producer interactions influence the rates of innovation and the evolution of market structure in two related industries under alternative contractual arrangements, namely the length and the exclusivity of the contracts. In the 2010 paper, they showed that (a) there is a trade-off between the exploitation of past experience and the exploration of new suppliers; (b) even if externalities are existing, advantages arising from interactions do not spill over to other firms; (c) imperfect information and agents heterogeneity are crucial factors in determining the consequences of alternative contractual arrangements on industry dynamics; and (d) vertical interdependencies influence the effects of specific firms' decisions across industries and over time, so that the resulting dynamics can be characterized as an interacting path-dependent process.

In an earlier academic report, Luigi Orsenigo and his co-author focused on university–industry collaboration in Sweden and provided an analytical overview of the trends in the governance of public R&D in Sweden during the period 1990–2005 (Jacob & Orsenigo, 2007). In addition, the report examined three of the most, to date, influential perspectives on policy namely the concepts of systems of innovation, Mode 2, and Triple Helix.[2]

In one of his earlier studies, Luigi Orsenigo analyzed the evolution of partnership agreements among firms in biotechnology industry (Barbanti et al., 1999). The study showed that there is a strong complementarity between internal and external research. In addition, as there are co-existing processes of specialization and consolidation of competencies, there is not necessarily a contradiction between increasing degrees of vertical integration and increasing collaboration. This trend toward collaboration is reinforced by the fact that the experience accumulated in managing collaborative relations improves their attractiveness. The analysis supports the idea of the emergence of a very structured and hierarchical network, made by the expansion of constellations of firms, linked together by a relatively small number of key agents. In Bruno and Orsenigo (2003), Luigi Orsenigo further analyzes the links between industry and academia by using data on the performance of university departments and institutes involved in attracting funding from industrial sources. It shows that conventional political strategies to support industry–academia links by building up intermediary organizations might fail as industry is mainly interested in excellent academic quality.

[2]System of innovation is oriented toward the macro level, and the Mode 2 argument is concerned almost exclusively with the conditions for the organization and production of knowledge.

Luigi Orsenigo expanded his research and focused on the dynamics of the network of collaborative agreements in R&D in the pharmaceutical and biotechnology industry after the "molecular biology revolution" (Orsenigo et al., 1998, 2001). In Orsenigo et al. (1998), he and his co-authors found that the topological properties of network structure remained relatively unchanged while the size of the network was increasing over time due to net entry. Moreover, the evolution of the network occurred without relevant deformations in the core-periphery profile. With regards to the age-dependent propensity to collaborate, the extent of inter-generational collaboration was much more significant compared to intra-generational collaboration. In addition, the propensity of firms of a given generation to enter into collaboration with firms of a different generation increased with the distance between the two, while the total number of intra-generational collaborations decreasing over time and tending to decrease for most recent generations. The paper then moves a step forward in the direction of establishing a connection between the structure and evolution of knowledge bases and the structure and evolution of organizational forms in innovative activities in a science-intensive industry. In Orsenigo et al. (2001), this research is taken a step further by investigating how the underlying relevant technological conditions induce distinguishable patterns of change in the structure and the evolution of an industry. The graph-theoretic techniques introduced in the paper were mapping the major technological discontinuities on changes observed at the level of dominant organization forms. The paper concludes that there might be more applications in other domains, whenever the identification of structural breaks and homological relationships between technological and industrial spaces are considered important issues.

In summary, Luigi Orsenigo touched on almost all aspects and elements of the concept of sectoral systems of innovation, provided original insights into the further development of the concept by using new methodologies. His studies provided new directions for theory development. Future studies must examine other industries and check whether existing within this tradition is sufficient to explain their development. There are a variety of emerging research questions related to industrial evolution which can be analyzed within this framework.

3 Innovation, Industrial Change, and Economics Evolution

Professor Luigi Orsenigo was a remarkably talented and influential scholar, well known for his contributions in developing conceptual frameworks to analyze innovation and study industrial dynamics as well as providing empirical evidence on evolutionary processes especially in focusing on the evolution of the biotechnology industry. Luigi Orsenigo's lifelong work was focused on studying innovation and industrial dynamics from an evolutionary economics perspective leading to valuable contributions within the Neo-Schumpeterian tradition. This article has attempted to capture three important elements in his pioneering research in the areas of the economics of innovation by focusing, in particular, on biotechnology and the pharmaceutical industry, in the area of history-friendly models, and in the area of the sectoral system of innovation. His studies in these three areas have highlighted hitherto unknown mechanisms of sectoral development that caused industries to evolve and transform over time. Luigi Orsenigo was without any doubt a leading authority in these areas of research. With his contribution to theory development, he was pushing the frontiers in modelling technological change and innovation forward. Based on analytical rigor, he combined both empirical and theoretical works.

His work provided for the plethora of innovation studies a strong and coherent intellectual framework aimed at a more general understanding of the relationship between innovation and industrial evolution. Luigi Orsenigo developed history-friendly models that combined advanced agent-based simulation techniques with "stylized" facts of a specific industrial history. By using a variety of methodologies, he made a series of path-breaking contributions leading to a better understanding of the mechanisms of industry evolution. Interestingly, recent research has applied in greater detail agent-based simulation techniques to the catch-up growth of Asian companies (Li et al., 2019; Yu et al., 2020).

Based on his contributions, some research avenues for future scholarly work can be identified. First, HFMs can be used to develop and analyze more general assumptions about the determinants of the evolution of market structures. As HFMs are developed in order to provide original insights and suggestions for the study of the evolution of industrial structures, particularly their dynamic properties, there is a need to examine in greater detail the sources of increasing returns in markets. There surely is ample scope for constructing new models of different industries with their respective histories and generate new theoretical questions. HFMs might, therefore, provide better tools for progress to a more general and a more empirically as well as historically founded theory of industry evolution and economic change. The fundamental contributions in this area have been discussed in Sect. 2. Publications based on HFMs have increased the understanding of factors affecting the relationship between innovation and market structure in an evolutionary and (Neo-)Schumpeterian tradition. Luigi Orsenigo and his colleagues developed their research in the hope that HFMs might be a tool to foster dialogue and cross-fertilization between different traditions in the literature by identifying not only differences but also similarities in the different frameworks. A promising area of future work has therefore been to compare results generating by HFMs with the empirical evidence and the prediction of other models.

Second, Luigi Orsenigo has developed his theory based on the nuanced investigation of the biotechnology industry. Within an emerging bioeconomy, biotechnology already significantly contributes to economic output but the growth of biotechnology remains an interesting field of investigation. With the introduction of information and communication technologies, some traditional topics that Luigi Orsenigo has discussed like technological regimes, university–industry linkage, IPR, innovation policy, and some new themes like catching up from emerging countries, technological convergence among different areas, are still worthy of research. As a science-based industry, the technological regimes within biotechnology and the pharmaceutical industry are characterized by high R&D input, high marketing investment, and high uncertainty about the potential of the technology, however, more factors that facilitate the development of the industry need to be further explored. For example, many different agents are involved in the process of exploitation of new opportunities in the industry, scientists, large incumbent companies as well as new emerging firms, government regulators, universities, and research institutes. The agents have established a variety of complex relationships, encompassing cooperation and competition, contractual and hierarchical forms of interaction. Open questions in this tradition are related to the role of knowledge flows and spillovers among different agents, the function of different channels of technological spillovers influencing the dynamics of industry. Luigi Orsenigo has investigated how technological conditions and the knowledge base can induce distinguishable patterns of change in network dynamics (Orsenigo et al., 1998, 2001). Later this has been taken up by Malerba (2007) in order to point at some possible research opportunities about collaborations in innovation and R&D network. Research found also that there is a rich-club phenomenon in the evolution of cooperation networks among different agents owing to its technological regimes. Further research must address factors like collaborative capability, cohesive effect, even some geographic proximity factors, that are contributing to his kind of network dynamics. The recent weighted social network technique provides as a good tool to investigate these questions related to the structural change of cooperation network in biotechnology and the pharmaceutical industry. In addition to the cooperation network, identifying the technological trajectories or core knowledge of this industry has been fundamental to explore research questions related to knowledge flows and industrial dynamics. In this tradition, main path analysis, which is based on evolutionary theorizing of the growth of technological paradigms and technological trajectories (Dosi, 1982), and the exploration of different technological contexts based on patent data (e.g., Verspagen, 2007) and paper information (Hung et al., 2014) are useful tools for further research in this tradition.

Thirdly, Luigi Orsenigo has contributed to the concept of sectoral systems of innovation. Several steps need to take to further enrich this concept. First, the current structure should be replenished and adjusted to suit different contexts. For example, Lee and Lim (2001) extended the original sectorial systems of innovation framework to the context of catch-up in developing or latecomer countries. Some modifications or adaptations are necessary to make these models "friendlier" to different contexts. In contrast to the original framework, it will increasingly become important to categorize technological regimes in terms of uncertainty and fluidity of the technological trajectory, the frequency of innovation, and the need to access external knowledge bases. In this respect, the role of scientists, the relationship between science and technology, as well as market structure in upstream or downstream industries, different knowledge base and competence, and some other elements should also be considered in the framework of sectoral systems of innovation. Second, the framework should be used to analyze more industries not only technological intensity industries but also in some low technological industries, not just in manufacturing sectors but also in service sectors (one notable exception has been Castellacci (2008)). Third, as the elements in the sectoral system of innovation are co-evolving, the analysis of these elements still remains a necessity. For example, Luigi Orsenigo discussed in some of his papers that the role of technological regimes is exogenously determined and related parameters are not able to change the whole industry history. Some progress in this area has been made (e.g., Malerba & Mani, 2009). Future extensions should be encouraged like considering the coevolution of technological regimes and industry dynamics in simulation models. Finally, public policy proposals may be developed on how to affect the transformation of sectoral systems, the innovation and diffusion processes, and the competitiveness of firms, regions, and countries. In this context, Luigi Orsenigo has started to analyze the failure or side effects of public policy (Malerba et al., 2008). A sectoral system perspective may help to identify mismatches and blocks that parts of the system exert on the rest and it may help overcome vicious cycles that block systems in their growth, development, and transformation. In the evolutionary (and innovation system) tradition, this work should go hand in hand, and be continuously confronted with in-depth empirical work.

In contrast to the neoclassical paradigm on technological change and market structure, Orsenigo's contribution to the importance of innovation and the dynamics of industrial change are increasingly vital in understanding the structure and the growth of indigenous companies in Asia. In order to develop a better understanding of the growth of companies in China (Guo et al., 2019), South Korea (Giachetti & Marchi, 2017; Lee & Lim, 2001) or Japan (Lee, 1996), a focus on the determinants of technological change and market structure at the sectoral level has shown surprising results. As a number of studies have developed new insights on the firm-internal dynamics of these companies (Lee & Malerba, 2017), a few papers have been able to show in a rigorous empirical manner that the interaction between firms across different sectors has been vital to their growth (Lee, 1996).

Surely there is much more to Luigi Orsenigo's work than his emphasis on cross-disciplinarily. He influenced with his synthesis of existing knowledge about innovation and industrial dynamics with new insights theoretical development. In studying the legacy of Luigi Orsenigo, it seems that much of what is on the research agenda today actually consists of relatively modest elaborations on the themes he has taken up there much earlier. We hope that future scholarly work will benefit from developing new answers to the currently unresolved research questions and will utilize the new insights which Luigi Orsenigo identified during his career.

References

Barbanti, P., Gambardella, A., & Orsenigo, L. (1999). The evolution of collaborative relationships among firms in biotechnology. *International Journal of Biotechnology, 1*(1), 10–29.

Bottazzi, G., Dosi, G., & Rocchetti, G. (2001). Modes of knowledge accumulation, entry regimes and patterns of industrial evolution. *Industrial and Corporate Change, 10*(3), 609–638.

Brenner, T., & Murmann, J. P. (2003). The use of simulations in developing robust knowledge about causal processes: Methodological considerations and an application to industrial evolution. In *Computing in economics and Finance*. Society for Computational Economics.

Breschi, S., Malerba, F., & Orsenigo, L. (2000). Technological regimes and Schumpeterian patterns of innovation. *The Economic Journal, 110*(463), 388–410.

Bruno, G. S., & Orsenigo, L. (2003). Variables influencing industrial funding of academic research in Italy: An empirical analysis. *International Journal of Technology Management, 26*(2–4), 277–302.

Buvailo, A. (2018). *How big pharma adopts AI to boost drug discovery*. BiopharmaTrend.com 8 October 2018.

Capone, G., Malerba, F., & Orsenigo, L. (2013). Are switching costs always effective in creating first-mover advantage? The moderating role of demand and technological regimes. *Long Range Planning, 46*(4–5), 348–368.

Castellacci, F. (2008). Technological paradigms, regimes and trajectories: Manufacturing and service industries in a new taxonomy of sectoral patterns of innovation. *Research Policy, 37* (6–7), 978–994.

Cefis, E., & Orsenigo, L. (2001). The persistence of innovative activities: A cross-countries and cross-sectors comparative analysis. *Research Policy, 30*(7), 1139–1158.

Dosi, G. (1982). Technological paradigms and technological trajectories: A suggested interpretation of the determinants and directions of technical change. *Research Policy, 11*(3), 147–162.

Dosi, G., Fagiolo, G., & Roventini, A. (2006). An evolutionary model of endogenous business cycles. *Computational Economics, 27*(1), 3–34.

Dosi, G., & Malerba, F. (2018). In memory of a friend and distinguished scholar: Luigi Orsenigo (1954–2018). *Economia e Politica Industriale, 45*(2), 109–109.

Dosi, G., Malerba, F., Marsili, O., & Orsenigo, L. (1997). Industrial structures and dynamics: Evidence, interpretations and puzzles. *Industrial and Corporate Change, 6*(1), 3–24.

Dosi, G., Malerba, F., & Orsenigo, L. (1994). Evolutionary regimes and industrial dynamics. In *Evolutionary and neo-Schumpeterian approaches to economics* (pp. 203–229). Springer.

Dosi, G., Marsili, O., Orsenigo, L., & Salvatore, R. (1995). Learning, market selection and the evolution of industrial structures. *Small Business Economics, 7*(6), 411–436.

Fagiolo, G., & Dosi, G. (2003). Exploitation, exploration and innovation in a model of endogenous growth with locally interacting agents. *Structural Change and Economic Dynamics, 14*(3), 237–273.

Fontana, R., Guerzoni, M., & Nuvolari, A. (2008). Habakkuk revisited: A history friendly model of American and British technology in the nineteenth century (No. 2008, 064). Jena economic research papers.

Fontana, R., & Zirulia, L. (2015). "... then came Cisco, and the rest is history": A 'history friendly' model of the Local Area Networking industry. *Journal of Evolutionary Economics, 25*(5), 875–899.

Garavaglia, C. (2010). Modelling industrial dynamics with "history-friendly" simulations. *Structural Change & Economic Dynamics, 21*(4), 258–275.

Garavaglia, C., Malerba, F., Orsenigo, L., & Pezzoni, M. (2012). Technological regimes and demand structure in the evolution of the pharmaceutical industry. *Journal of Evolutionary Economics, 22*(4), 677–709.

Giachetti, C., & Marchi, G. (2017). Successive changes in leadership in the worldwide mobile phone industry: The role of windows of opportunity and firms' competitive action. *Research Policy, 46*(2), 352–364.

Guo, L., Zhang, M. Y., Dodson, M., & Gann, D. (2019). Huawei's catch-up in the global telecommunication industry: Innovation capability and transition to leadership. *Technology Analysis & Strategic Management, 31*(12), 1395–1411.

Hung, S. C., Liu, J. S., Lu, L. Y., & Tseng, Y. C. (2014). Technological change in lithium iron phosphate battery: The key-route main path analysis. *Scientometrics, 100*(1), 97–120.

Jacob, M., & Orsenigo, L. (2007). Leveraging Science for innovation: Swedish policy for university-industry collaboration 1990–2005, SNS Förlag Report.

Kim, C. W., & Lee, K. (2003). Innovation, technological regimes and organizational selection in industry evolution: A 'history friendly model' of the DRAM industry. *Industrial and Corporate Change, 12*(6), 1195–1221.
Landini, F., Lee, K., & Malerba, F. (2017). A history-friendly model of the successive changes in industrial leadership and the catch-up by latecomers. *Research Policy, 46*(2), 431–446.
Landini, F., & Malerba, F. (2017). Public policy and catching up by developing countries in global industries: A simulation model. *Cambridge Journal of Economics, 41*(3), 927–960.
Lee, K. R. (1996). The role of user firms in the innovation of machine tools: The Japanese case. *Research Policy, 25*, 491–507.
Lee, K., & Lim, C. (2001). Technological regimes, catching-up and leapfrogging: Findings from the Korean industries. *Research Policy, 30*(3), 459–483.
Lee, K., & Malerba, F. (2017). Catch-up cycles and changes in industrial leadership: Windows of opportunity and responses of firms and countries in the evolution of sectoral systems. *Research Policy, 46*(2), 338–351.
Li, D., Capone, G., & Malerba, F. (2019). The long march to catch-up: A history-friendly model of China's mobile communications industry. *Research Policy, 48*(3), 649–664.
Mäkinen, S. J., & Vilkko, M. K. (2014). Product portfolio decision-making and absorptive capacity: A simulation study. *Journal of Engineering and Technology Management, 32*, 60–75.
Malerba, F. (2005). Sectoral systems of innovation: A framework for linking innovation to the knowledge base, structure and dynamics of sectors. *Economics of Innovation and New Technology, 14*(1–2), 63–82.
Malerba, F. (2007). Innovation and the dynamics and evolution of industries: Progress and challenges. *International Journal of Industrial Organization, 25*(4), 675–699.
Malerba, F. (2011). *Modelling innovation and the evolution of industries: History-friendly models*. Presentation in GLOBELICS ACADEMY.
Malerba, F., & Mani, S. (2009). *Sectoral systems of innovation and production in developing countries: Actors, structure and evolution*. Edward Elgar Publishing.
Malerba, F., Nelson, R., Orsenigo, L., & Winter, S. (1999). 'History-friendly' models of industry evolution: The computer industry. *Industrial and Corporate Change, 8*(1), 3–40.
Malerba, F., Nelson, R., Orsenigo, L., & Winter, S. (2008). Public policies and changing boundaries of firms in a "history-friendly" model of the co-evolution of the computer and semiconductor industries. *Journal of Economic Behavior & Organization, 67*(2), 355–380.
Malerba, F., Nelson, R., Orsenigo, L., & Winter, S. (2016). *Innovation and the evolution of industries-history-friendly models*. Cambridge University Press.
Malerba, F., & Orsenigo, L. (1993). Technological regime and firm behaviour. *Industrial and Corporate Change, 2*, 45–71.
Malerba, F., & Orsenigo, L. (1995). Schumpeterian patterns of innovation. *Cambridge Journal of Economics, 19*(1), 47–65.
Malerba, F., & Orsenigo, L. (1996). Schumpeterian patterns of innovation are technology-specific. *Research Policy, 25*(3), 451–478.
Malerba, F., & Orsenigo, L. (1997). Technological regimes and sectoral patterns of innovative activities. *Industrial and Corporate Change, 6*(1), 83–118.
Malerba, F., & Orsenigo, L. (1999). Technological entry, exit and survival: An empirical analysis of patent data. *Research Policy, 28*(6), 643–660.
Malerba, F., & Orsenigo, L. (2000). Knowledge, innovative activities and industrial evolution. *Industrial and Corporate Change, 9*(2), 289–314.
Malerba, F., & Orsenigo, L. (2002). Innovation and market structure in the dynamics of the pharmaceutical industry and biotechnology: Towards a history-friendly model. *Industrial and Corporate Change, 11*(4), 667–703.
Malerba, F., & Orsenigo, L. (2008). User-producer relationships, innovation and the evolution of two related industries, paper presented at the DIME Conference on Innovation and Industrial Dynamics, Bocconi University, Milan, 2008.

Malerba, F., & Orsenigo, L. (2010). User–producer relations, innovation and the evolution of market structures under alternative contractual regimes. *Structural Change and Economic Dynamics, 21*(1), 26–40.
Malerba, F., Orsenigo, L., & Peretto, P. (1997). Persistence of innovative activities, sectoral patterns of innovation and international technological specialization. *International Journal of Industrial Organization, 15*(6), 801–826.
McKelvey, M., & Orsenigo, L. (2006). *The economics of biotechnology* (Vol. 198). Edward Elgar.
Nelson, R. R. (1982). The role of knowledge in R&D efficiency. *Quarterly Journal of Economics, 93*, 453–470.
Nelson, R. R., & Winter, S. (1982). *An evolutionary theory of economic change*. Harvard University Press.
OECD Publishing. (2009). *The bioeconomy to 2030: Designing a policy agenda*. Organisation for Economic Co-operation and Development.
Orsenigo, L. (1989a). *Institutions and markets in the dynamics of industrial innovation: The theory and the case of biotechnology*. Thesis, .
Orsenigo, L. (1989b). *The emergence of biotechnology: Institutions and markets in industrial innovation*. Pinter Publishers Ltd..
Orsenigo, L. (2007). History-friendly models of industrial evolution. In H. Hanusch & A. Pyka (Eds.), *Elgar companion to neo-schumpeterian economics*. Edward Elgar Publishing Limited.
Orsenigo, L., Pammolli, F., & Riccaboni, M. (2001). Technological change and network dynamics: Lessons from the pharmaceutical industry. *Research Policy, 30*(3), 485–508.
Orsenigo, L., Pammolli, F., Riccaboni, M., Bonaccorsi, A., & Turchetti, G. (1998). The evolution of knowledge and the dynamics of an industry network. *Journal of Management & Governance, 1* (2), 147–175.
Rosiello, A., & Orsenigo, L. (2008). A critical assessment of regional innovation policy in pharmaceutical biotechnology. *European Planning Studies, 16*(3), 337–357.
Silverberg, G., Dosi, G., & Orsenigo, L. (1988). Innovation, diversity and diffusion: A self-organisation model. *The Economic Journal, 98*(393), 1032–1054.
Tesfatsion, L. (2001). Introduction to the special issue on agent-based computational economics. *Journal of Economic Dynamics and Control, 25*(3–4), 281–293.
Verspagen, B. (2007). Mapping technological trajectories as patent citation networks: A study on the history of fuel cell research. *Advances in Complex Systems, 10*(01), 93–115.
Winter, S. G., Kaniovski, Y. M., & Dosi, G. (2000). Modeling industrial dynamics with innovative entrants. *Structural Change and Economic Dynamics, 11*(3), 255–293.
Yoon, M. (2009). A History-friendly model on the relationship between NISs and performances in frontier industries of Korea and Taiwan. In: *2009 Convention of the Korean Association of Technology Economics and Management*.
Yoon, M., & Lee, K. (2009). Agent-based and "history-friendly" models for explaining industrial evolution. *Evolutionary and Institutional Economics Review, 6*(1), 45–70.
Yu, P., Shi, J., Sadowsk, B., & Nomaler, Ö. (2020). Catching up in the face of technological discontinuity: Exploring the role of demand structure and technological regimes in the transition from 2G to 3G in China. *Journal of Evolutionary Economics*. https://doi.org/10.1007/s00191-020-00673-9

Part II
Catching-up

National innovation systems, economic complexity, and economic growth: country panel analysis using the US patent data

Keun Lee and Jongho Lee

Abstract This study examines the impacts of national innovation systems (NIS) and economic complexity index (ECI) on economic growth. A composite index of NIS is developed by using US patent data as a weighted sum of three, four or five variables among the following: concentration of assignees, localization, originality, diversification, and cycle time of technologies. Growth regressions confirm the significant and robust impacts of NIS3a, NIS4a, and NIS5 indices on economic growth. The common feature of these NIS indices is that they have the same component variables as their ingredients, and these are originality, cycle time, and technological diversification. NIS3a is the most parsimonious and powerful among all indices. The robustness of ECI is questionable because ECI loses significance after adding government expenditure and terms of trade variables into the regression model. Results confirm the overall importance of NIS in economic growth and justify policy efforts to improve NIS. This research is one of the first to generate a robust NIS index by using patent data only without many data requirements and free from the problem of cross-country comparability of underlying variables.

This paper draws partly from the presidential address given by the corresponding author at the 2018 International Schumpeter Society Conference held in Seoul, and was also presented at the Korea's Allied Economic Associations Annual Meeting held in Seoul, February 2019 . The authors would like to thank the editor of this journal (Uwe Cantner), Justin Lin, Sangsoo Park, and other participants of the two conferences for useful feedbacks and comments. . This work was supported by the Laboratory Program for Korean Studies through the Ministry of Education of Republic of Korea and Korean Studies Promotion Service of the Academy of Korean Studies (AKS-2018-LAB-1250001).

K. Lee (✉)
Department of Economics, Seoul National University, Seoul, South Korea
e-mail: kenneth@snu.ac.kr

J. Lee
Barun ICT Research Center, Yonsei University, Seoul, South Korea
e-mail: jongholee@yonsei.ac.kr

A. Pyka, K. Lee (eds.), *Innovation, Catch-up and Sustainable Development*,
Economic Complexity and Evolution, https://doi.org/10.1007/978-3-030-84931-3_6

Keywords National innovation systems · Economic complexity · Economic growth · Patents · Index

JEL classification B52 · C43 · C81 · O31 · O34 · O38

1 Introduction

Early literature focused on the differences in the amount of accumulated capital per worker to explain differences in economic growth across countries (Solow 1956). Other research streams have concentrated on differences in other dimensions or various capabilities, especially among advanced and latecomer economies (Gerschenkron 1962; Abramovitz 1986). Related concepts include social capability (Ohkawa and Rosovsky 1973; Abramovitz 1986), absorptive capacity (Cohen and Levintal 1990), and innovative capacity (Furman et al. 2002). Following the intellectual legacy of Schumpeter (Schumpeter 1934), Schumpeterian literature on economic growth has explored technological capabilities (Fagerberg 1987, 1988; Dosi et al. 1990; Verspagen 1991; Furman et al. 2002). In Schumpeterian economics, strong economic growth is considered to prevail in countries with an effective "innovation system" (Freeman et al. 1982; Lundvall 1992; Nelson 1993; Edquist 1997). The focus on innovation as the driving force of economic growth was subsequently absorbed by the so-called new growth theory in the neo-classical school (Lucas 1988; Romer 1990; Aghion and Howitt 1992).

Innovation systems have been established as the core concept of Schumpeterian economics and discussed in various dimensions, such as national, sectoral, and firm levels, and in latecomer economies or catching-up contexts (Malerba 2005; Fagerberg and Godinho 2004; Lee 2013). Lundvall (1992) defined national innovation systems (NIS) as "elements and relationships which interact in the production, diffusion and use of new and economically useful knowledge." Therefore, NIS is about efficiency in production, diffusion, and use of knowledge. Empirical studies on the relationship between innovation systems and economic growth have been flourishing since the 2000s. These studies have considered and measured various factors and dimensions of NIS, including techno-economic or socio-institutional dimensions and ICT-related infrastructures (Desai et al. 2002; Fagerberg and Verspagen 2002; Archibugi and Coco 2004; Fagerberg and Srholec 2008; Castellacci 2008, 2011; Lee and Kim 2009; Filippetti and Peyrache 2011; Lee 2013; Castellacci and Natera 2015). They also focused on different factors of NIS to quantify them.

Which approach works best is debatable because the selection depends on the key research questions in each study. Given that one source of challenge in measuring and comparing NIS across countries is the comparability of variables across countries, using a homogenous set of data, such as patent data, provides certain advantages. Lee (2013) attempted to measure innovation systems by using US patent data at country, sector, and firm levels. He used five variables, namely, localization of knowledge creation and diffusion, originality, concentration at the assignee level, cycle time of technologies, and technological diversification, to express diverse aspects of NIS. The NIS of high-income economies shows a dispersed distribution of assignees, high localization of knowledge creation and diffusion, and high technological diversification. The knowledge base of NIS also has high originality and long cycle time of technologies. Then, Lee (2013) further explored the sources of catching-up growth by east Asian economies and showed that these economies specialize in short-cycle technology-based sectors, such as information technology (IT), which makes sense because these sectors are where frontier technologies frequently change and soon become outdated. Therefore, low entry barriers are faced by latecomers from Asia who are approaching the technological frontier.

The growth analysis of Lee (2013) was conducted with regard to each of the five NIS variables. By contrast, free from the problem of correlations among the five variables, the current study proposes one composite NIS index based on the five variables and relates it to general economic growth in the world. This study also compares the impacts of the NIS index on growth to those of the economic complexity index (ECI) developed by Hidalgo in his joint work, specifically, Hausmann et al. (2011). ECI attempts to measure the amount of productive knowledge that each country holds from trade data. ECI has a positive effect on economic growth. Moreover, both indices (NIS and ECI) can explain economic growth, but their robustness varies in certain contexts.

The rest of this paper is organized in the following manner. Section 2 discusses related literature that measured NIS and ECI and the strengths and weaknesses of diverse approaches. Section 3 discusses and compares various methods to construct an NIS index using the three, four or five NIS variables and shows the development of the NIS indices. Section 4 presents the results of a country panel analysis relating the NIS indices to economic growth. Section 5 concludes by summarizing the main results and discussing their implications.

2 Literature: NIS, economic complexity, and economic growth

2.1 Importance of innovation in achieving economic growth

Fagerberg and Verspagen (2002) confirmed the increasing importance of innovation to economic growth. They measured innovation by the growth rate of the number of patents and discovered that the link between innovation and growth is significant in the period of 1966–1995; however, the study covered 26 countries only. Castellacci (2008) considered patents and scientific articles and found that both are related to economic growth in long- and short-term Schumpeterian growth models. Castellacci used dynamic panel model estimation in this research. A similar approach that adopts patents and articles was employed by Castellacci (2011) for 131 countries for the period 1985–2004.

Lee and Kim (2009) investigated the idea that different factors are crucial for different country groups divided by income levels. They found that innovation, measured by the number of patents per million and R&D/GDP ratio, is significant in upper middle- and high-income countries only, whereas basic human capital and political institutions are significant in low-income countries. Similarly, other studies uncovered the different roles of innovation in different groups of countries. Lee and Kim (2015) focused on the different natures of NIS in East Asia and Latin America. Both groups are different not only in terms of the quantity of innovation measured in patent counts or scientific articles but also in the sequence of emphasis between technological knowledge (patents) and scientific knowledge (articles). Their key finding is that unless NIS is mature or sufficiently developed, scientific knowledge does not translate into technological knowledge and is thus not significant in growth regressions, as in the case of Latin America. By contrast, East Asia emphasizes technological knowledge first and promotes scientific knowledge only at a later stage of development.

In a similar vein, Castellacci and Natera (2015) explored within-group differences among 18 countries in Latin America from 1970 to 2010 by using the Johansen co-integration approach. They found that Latin American countries exhibit different growth trajectories depending on the combination of policies (openness, industrial transformation, and/or innovation policy). In addition, countries that have managed to combine imitation and innovation policies experienced higher growth rates than economies that have only exerted efforts to improve their imitation capability.

In view of the purpose of the current research, one implication of these studies is that innovation matters differently and is even not evident in certain groups of countries. Moreover, one composite index can be used to reflect various aspects of innovation systems. We discuss the literature that attempted to develop indices of innovations and innovation systems for countries in which innovation matters to economic growth.

2.2 *Composite index of innovation for economic growth*

Desai et al. (2002) proposed the technology achievement index (TAI) and measured it for 72 countries. Its objective is to measure technological achievements in four dimensions: creating new technology (e.g., patents per person), diffusing recent innovations (e.g., share of high-technology exports), diffusing existing technologies that are still basic inputs to the industry and network age (e.g., telephones per person), and building a human skill base for technological creation and adoption (e.g., educational attainment). The research of Desai et al. focused on how well a country creates and uses technologies. TAI is derived by assigning equal weights to the components.

Archibugi and Coco (2004) generated a new index of technological capabilities that aims to explain developed and developing countries for two periods, 1987–1990 and 1997–2000. Three main factor, namely, technological infrastructures, technology creations, and human skill development, were contemplated. Eight subcategories were included, and these were (1) patents, (2) scientific articles, (3) Internet penetration, (4) telephone penetration, (5) electricity consumption, (6) tertiary science and engineering enrollment, (7) mean years of schooling, and (8) literacy rate.

Fagerberg and Srholec (2008) also measured the level of national capabilities. They identified capabilities through a factor analysis between 1992 and 2004. They discovered three dimensions: innovation systems, governance and political systems, and openness. They argued that innovation systems and quality of governance have a positive and significant relationship with economic development. In their research, innovation systems have factors based on the following 10 variables: United States Patent Trademark Office (USPTO) patents (per capita), science and engineering articles (per capita), ISO 9000 certifications (per capita), fixed line and mobile phone subscribers (per capita), Internet users (per capita), personal computers (per capita), primary school teacher–pupil ratio, secondary school enrollment (% gross), and tertiary school enrollment (% gross).

Filippetti and Peyrache (2011) investigated the patterns of technological capabilities of 42 countries from 1995 to 2007. This study used seven component variables, such as patent counts, business R&D, scientific articles, and number of PCs and telephones. These variables were transformed into a composite index. The World Intellectual Property Organization (WIPO) recently developed its own index, the global innovation index (GII). GII considers institutions, human capital and research, infrastructures, market sophistication, and business sophistication as innovation inputs and sub-indices (Cornell University et al. 2018). Knowledge, technology, and creative outputs are considered innovation output indices. Similarly, the European innovation scoreboard (EIS) measures 27 components in several sections, such as framework conditions, investments, innovation activities, and impacts EC (2018). A composite index in EIS uses the equal-weighting method.

Determining which index is the best among all the above-mentioned ones is impossible because they have different purposes and attributes. An index that covers diverse aspects is good but demanding in terms of collection effort. Another problem is that data qualities and their measurement vary across countries. Thus, the present research proposes an index using homogenous data, namely, US patents, which enables us to express the key dimensions of NIS. Existing indices reflect diverse variables (e.g., education and IT infrastructures) that are directly and indirectly related to innovation processes and outcomes. However, they do not contribute much in terms of reflecting the detailed aspects of creation, diffusion, and nature of knowledge. By contrast, this study aims to develop an index that directly and thoroughly considers such dimensions by focusing on the following aspects.

The first aspect is the degree of local creation and diffusion of knowledge, which is equivalent to country-level self-citation. This aspect is also a dimension of whether a country relies on domestic or foreign knowledge when it creates new knowledge. Lee (2013: ch.3) found that this measure of knowledge localization is high in high-income countries. The second aspect is who creates new knowledge, such as whether knowledge is created by a few or a large number of inventors. Thus, this aspect is a dimension of concentration versus decentralization. The third aspect focuses on technological diversification or width dimension (narrow versus wide dimension), that is, whether a country has a knowledge portfolio in narrow or wide fields. The fourth dimension (how) is about the sourcing of knowledge, that is, whether it relies on knowledge from diverse or narrow fields when a country creates new knowledge. The fifth dimension involves the longevity of a country's knowledge, that is, whether a country has knowledge in short- or long-cycle technologies.

Lee (2013: ch.3) showed that high-income countries show a high degree in all of the five aspects. Thus, these five variables can be considered relevant components of an effective NIS. We also think that these five dimensions are sufficiently comprehensive because they cover diverse dimensions of nationality (domestic vs. foreign), concentration, diversification (width), sourcing, and longevity. For example, we do not use the direct measure of university–industry interaction, but the variable is indirectly reflected in knowledge localization and concentration and even in diversification. In other words, if a country has an active university–industry collaboration, then the country may have high local creation and diffusion of knowledge, low concentration, and/or high diversification. University–industry linkages affect several of the five variables. Therefore, having one composite index is encouraged. Similarly, if a country has a strong science basis, then it will have long-lasting knowledge, which means long-cycle technologies, and will generate knowledge relying on other diverse fields, thereby suggesting high originality.

However, no proof exists that an index combining these five components is comprehensive enough to cover all of the important dimensions of NIS. In addition, one may not have to use all five; a few of them may be enough to reflect the NIS of a country. Thus, we use several different combinations of these five variables to construct different indices and to examine their explanatory power to check their comprehensiveness and robustness in predicting economic growth.

We also compare the NIS index we constructed with ECI in the growth regression context to determine how successful and robust the indices are in predicting economic growth. ECI attempts to measure the amount of productive knowledge of each country. Hausmann et al. (2011) defined economic complexity as "the composition of a country's productive output, which reflects the structures that hold and combine knowledge." Hausmann et al. (2011) also showed that ECI has a positive effect on future economic growth. However, ECI does not directly use data, such as patents, which reflect knowledge or innovation directly. Instead, ECI uses trade data. Therefore, it may underestimate the economic complexity of nations with a highly developed domestic (e.g. Tulip production using high-tech as in the Netherlands) or non-tradable sector (Inoua 2016).

Another limitation is that ECI does not reflect the global supply chain. ECI assumes that production factors are constrained within national borders and that goods are produced entirely within a given economy (Schölkopf et al. 1997; Colombage 2016; Coe et al. 2004; Hanson et al. 2005; Orefice and Rocha 2014). This condition means that the productive capabilities of countries specializing in intermediate goods in the global value chain are not directly considered or reflected in the user countries' complexity (Hausmann et al. 2014). Furthermore, the endogenous path-dependent nature of economic growth assumed as countries move through the product space to complex export baskets does not consider asymmetric or idiosyncratic shocks (Fidrmuc 2004; Toya and Skidmore 2007). However, events, such as natural and man-made disasters or technological breakthroughs, may result in a sudden change in a nation's trajectory from a high-growth to a low-growth path or vice-versa (Palmer and Richards 1999). Despite these limitations, ECI is regarded as a useful index that can predict future economic growth.

3 Five NIS variables and the composite NIS index

3.1 Five NIS variables and US patent data

We use the patent data registered at USPTO (1976-2017). Information on newly granted patents is released weekly in the amount of approximately 4000 patents per week. USPTO uploads full-text files of granted patents on its website (https://bulkdata.uspto.gov/). The format of these files are ASCII text for patents for the period 1976–2001 and standard generalized markup language for the period 2001–present. The text files of patents include diverse information, such as patent identification number, granted date, inventor information, assignee names, classification codes, citation information, and Patent Cooperation Treaty information. Through a text mining process using the statistical software SAS, we construct a dataset of registered US patents and their citations that covers five million patents and 80 million citations. In this process, the nationalities of patents are classified based on the first assignee's country of origin. Then, the five variables quantifying the NIS of each country are calculated.

The five NIS variables are those that were identified and used in the country-panel analysis of Lee (2013), and several of them have been previously introduced in early studies, such as those of Jaffe et al. (1993), Trajtenberg et al. (1997), and Hall et al. (2001). These variables are localization of knowledge creation and diffusion, degree of concentration among assignees, technological diversification, originality, and the average cycle time of technologies. The following text explains each variable on the basis of Lee's study (2013).

Localization of knowledge creation and diffusion is defined and calculated by adopting the idea of Jaffe et al. (1993). To compare the geographic localization of the citations made by the patents of different countries, Jaffe et al. (1993) suggested an approach to compare the probability of a patent matching the original patent by geographic area, conditional on its citing of the original patent, with the probability of a match not conditioned on the existence of a citation link. Thus, this study measures the degree of localization of knowledge creation and diffusion in a country by considering the difference between the probability of one country's patents citing its own patents and the probability of the rest of the world's patents citing that country's patents. Therefore, we obtain the following formula.

$$Localization_{xt} = \frac{n_{xx}}{n_{xt}} - \frac{n_{cxt}}{n_{ct}},$$

where $\frac{n_{xx}}{n_{xt}}$ is the probability of x country's patent citing its own patent, n_{xxt} is the number of citations made to country x's patents by its own patents granted in year t, n_{xt} is the number of all citations made by country x's patents granted in year t, n_{cxt} is the number of citations made to country x's patents by all patents except for its patents filed in year t, and n_{ct} is the number of all citations made by all patents granted in year t except for country x's patents.

Patenting concentration across assignees is a variable that measures the degree of inventor concentration, particularly the degree of patent concentration across assignees (excluding unassigned patents). It is measured by HHI. The HHI of country x in year t is calculated as follows:

$$HHI_{xt} = \sum\nolimits_{i \in I_x} \left(\frac{N_{it}}{N^*_{xt}} \right)^2,$$

where I_x is the set of assignees, N_{it} is the number of patents granted by assignee i in year t, and N^*_{xt} is the total number of patents granted by country x in year t excluding unassigned patents. We use 1–HHI to express the decentralization or inverse of concentration.

Originality measures the degree to which a patent makes (backward) citations to patents from a wide range of technological classes instead of from a narrow field of technologies. The originality of the knowledge base of a country can be calculated based on the definition of originality in Hall et al. (2001) and Trajtenberg et al. (1997). Conceptually, the originality of a patent is defined as follows for each patent i of country x in year t.

$$Originality_{xt} = \left(1 - \sum\nolimits_{k=1}^{N_i} \left(\frac{Ncited_{ik}}{Ncited_i} \right)^2 \right)_{xt},$$

where k is the technological sector (especially US patent classification), $Ncited_{ik}$ is the number of citations made by patent i to patents that belong to patent class k, and $Ncited_i$ is the total number of citations made by patent i.

Technological diversification measures how many diverse fields of technologies a country files patents on. Following Lee (2013), we define this variable as the ratio in percentage of the number (N in the following formula) of technological classes, i, in which a country x has registered patents to a number in year t, 438, which is the number of three-digit classes in the US patent classification system until 2016.

$$Diversification_{xt} = \left(\frac{N_i}{438}\right)_{xt}$$

Cycle time of technologies measures the time lags between the application (or granted) years of citing and cited patents or the time span between predecessors and successors (Jaffe and Trajtenberg 2002). A long cycle time indicates a high significance of old knowledge and a great need to study it from the point of view of latecomers. In a country-level analysis, this variable is the average of technological cycles shown in citations made by patents assigned to a corresponding country. This study uses grant years in calculating mean backward citation lags. After calculating the average backward lags, they are transformed to a relative cycle time, which is defined as (cycle time of patent A granted in year *t*)/(average cycle time of all patents belonging to the same class granted in year *t*).

The five variables are calculated for countries with a certain number of US patents that is large enough to generate reliable estimates. No absolute criterion is adopted, and we include countries with 10 or more registered patents each year since 2000. Thus, the number of countries in the sample is 45, including Chile, Indonesia, and the Philippines. These three countries have failed to register 10 or more patents for some years but are included in terms of their country size and importance. The US and Japan are among the 45 but are excluded in the regression analysis because both can be outliers with much more registered patents than the other countries. Another reason the US is excluded is the possible home bias in calculating certain variables, such as localization of citations.

Table 1 shows the average values of the five NIS variables for the 45 countries in the period 2010–2015. We have estimates of these variables for each year in the period 1984–2015. In the growth regressions in the next section, we use the data for the period 1990–2015, which is divided into five sub-periods.

3.2 Generating an NIS composite index: Statistical methods versus simple summation

The key issue in generating a composite index of NIS is how to combine the five sub-indicators measured in different scales into one index in a meaningful manner. This issue implies that weighting for each indicator is required (Nardo et al. 2005). Different weights may be assigned to sub-indicators to reflect various circumstances, such as economic importance, statistical adequacy, cyclical conformity, and speed of available data (Nardo et al. 2005). Weighting schemes have an important impact on the meaning of the composite index and the resulting ranking among countries. However, no definite methodology has been established to weigh individual indicators. Several researchers may apply a large weight to components that they consider important. Others may pay attention to the correlations among factors or weights derived from related statistical analyses. In many composite indices, all variables are

Table 1 Five NIS variables of 45 countries and their ranking during 2011–2015

Country	Localization	Diversification	Originality	Relative cycle time	1-HHI	NIS5	Rank of NIS5
Japan	0.407	0.866	0.354	0.942	0.980	3.566	1
United States	0.246	0.937	0.503	1.005	0.994	3.495	2
Germany	0.140	0.844	0.455	1.106	0.984	3.147	3
France	0.111	0.735	0.402	1.083	0.975	2.873	4
United Kingdom	0.070	0.687	0.450	1.157	0.993	2.855	5
Italy	0.090	0.611	0.408	1.163	0.981	2.763	6
Australia	0.134	0.469	0.466	1.176	0.923	2.742	7
Switzerland	0.042	0.657	0.434	1.159	0.984	2.730	8
Canada	0.065	0.671	0.486	1.014	0.935	2.709	9
Taiwan	0.129	0.674	0.331	0.828	0.971	2.575	10
Netherlands	0.075	0.582	0.434	1.041	0.903	2.564	11
Israel	0.066	0.431	0.498	1.044	0.990	2.551	12
South Korea	0.137	0.705	0.339	0.846	0.854	2.533	13
Denmark	0.081	0.374	0.429	1.169	0.971	2.516	14
Norway	0.080	0.268	0.482	1.200	0.985	2.503	15
Austria	0.076	0.405	0.422	1.133	0.967	2.496	16
Sweden	0.098	0.568	0.390	0.992	0.824	2.435	17
Belgium	0.065	0.378	0.418	1.130	0.955	2.421	18
China	0.048	0.643	0.332	0.854	0.944	2.343	19
New Zealand	0.043	0.172	0.481	1.251	0.976	2.341	20
Spain	0.044	0.324	0.400	1.107	0.986	2.308	21
Finland	0.095	0.418	0.426	0.976	0.770	2.249	22
South Africa	0.072	0.116	0.424	1.231	0.959	2.249	23
Brazil	0.022	0.158	0.390	1.237	0.957	2.134	24
Mexico	0.014	0.096	0.485	1.216	0.933	2.129	25
Hong Kong	0.037	0.289	0.388	0.978	0.965	2.126	26

Ireland	0.023	0.241	0.465	0.993	0.929	2.109	27
Singapore	0.037	0.323	0.437	0.889	0.915	2.106	28
India	0.028	0.243	0.371	1.057	0.969	2.097	29
Luxembourg	0.007	0.221	0.472	1.032	0.928	2.088	30
Poland	0.069	0.074	0.369	1.156	0.952	2.072	31
Saudi Arabia	0.020	0.191	0.467	1.130	0.774	1.999	32
Malaysia	0.035	0.084	0.399	1.129	0.917	1.982	33
Chile	0.014	0.042	0.426	1.175	0.939	1.976	34
Portugal	0.032	0.045	0.418	1.106	0.932	1.956	35
Hungary	0.033	0.049	0.384	1.116	0.939	1.934	36
Argentina	0.041	0.028	0.392	1.135	0.909	1.926	37
Russia	0.039	0.102	0.423	0.934	0.889	1.871	38
Czech Republic	0.018	0.056	0.332	1.110	0.945	1.845	39
Thailand	0.009	0.031	0.467	1.107	0.824	1.837	40
Slovenia	0.014	0.038	0.335	1.272	0.831	1.822	41
Greece	0.016	0.031	0.327	1.179	0.870	1.781	42
Iceland	0.039	0.038	0.420	1.300	0.563	1.735	43
Indonesia	0.000	0.006	0.445	1.361	0.442	1.562	44
Philippines	0.002	0.011	0.465	1.121	0.547	1.528	45

Source: the authors

given the same weight when no statistical or theoretical reasons exist for selecting a different plan. For example, the Environmental Sustainability Index of Columbia University and the EIS of the European Commission were constructed by assigning an equal weight to each component. By contrast, the GII of WIPO uses statistical methods, such as data envelopment analysis (DEA) and principal component analysis (PCA), which allow different weights.

Therefore, a basic decision is either to use the simple summation of the five components with equal weights or to assign different weights to each component by following certain statistical methods.

We now compare several statistical methods of building a composite index. These methods include PCA, DEA, and the benefit of the doubt (BOD) method. They are compared before selecting a simple equal-weighting method. The issue is determining which method is the most appropriate in predicting economic growth.

Pearson (1901) invented PCA, although Hotelling (1933) also developed it in the 1930s. PCA uses orthogonal transformation to convert a set of observations of correlated variables into a set of values of linearly uncorrelated variables. The DEA method, which was initially developed by Charnes et al. (1978), is a linear programming technique for evaluating the performance of a set of peer entities (countries in this research) that uses inputs to produce outputs. In the current research, the inputs are the five NIS variables, and the output is the growth rate of per capita GDP or the level of per capita income. The BOD method is a variation of the DEA method proposed by Melyn and Moesen (1991) to evaluate macroeconomic performance.

Figure 1 shows the distribution of NIS indices estimated by PCA, DEA, and BOD methods over the space of their scores of countries and their per capita GDP. Simple regression lines show the relationship between each index and the income level of countries. The regression result indicates that the NIS indices produced by PCA and BOD methods show a positive correlation to the logged values of GDP per capita, whereas the DEA index shows a negative correlation to GDP per capita. The DEA index cannot thus be used. The method is difficult to use in analyzing the changes in NIS level over time because DEA measures efficiency. The first factor scores of PCA are skewed to the left, whereas the BOD index is skewed to the right, implying that both are not that appropriate. BOD is a method of imposing a different (high) weight to the specific component most favorable to each country. Thus, the values for most countries are distributed to the high ends (or between 0.8 and 1.0), implying the possibility of overestimating the level of innovation systems of all countries.

We then discuss the simple summation method, that is, simply aggregating the five variables without any weight difference. However, given the differences in the range and scale of the values of these variables, we must standardize the values before taking their summation. Thus, each NIS component variable (called K) is standardized over its value during the entire sample period (1990 to 2015 in our case) by using the following formula:

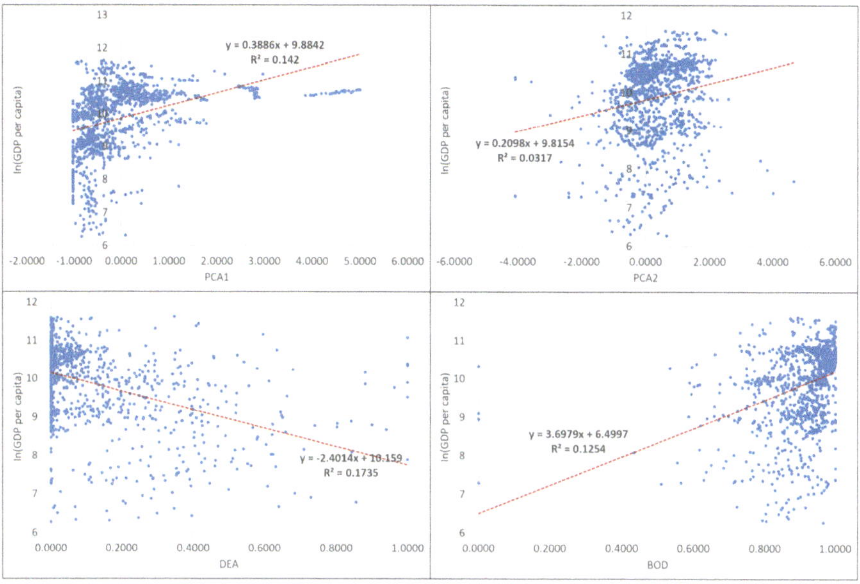

Fig. 1 Distribution of NIS indices generated by the statistical approach. Notes: NIS indices constructed by PCA1, PCA2, DEC, and BOD methods, respectively, from the top-left to top-right, bottom left, and bottom-right. Source: the authors

$$\text{Standardized value of K variable} = (\text{actual value of K} - \text{minimum value of K}) / (\text{maximum value of K} - \text{minimum value of K})$$

Another issue is whether we should use all five variables or only several of them to predict economic growth effectively. Without a priori theory, we examine several combinations of the five variables. Thus, six different combinations are used in making an NIS composite index as follows ("S" means the standardized values of NIS sub-components):

1)
$$\text{NIS3a} = \text{S\_Originality} + \text{S\_Relative cycle time} + \text{S\_Diversification}$$

2)
$$\text{NIS3b} = \text{S\_Originality} + \text{S\_Relative cycle time} + \text{S\_1} - \text{HHI}$$

3)
$$\text{NIS3c} = \text{S\_Relative cycle time} + \text{S\_1} - \text{HHI} + \text{S\_Localization}$$

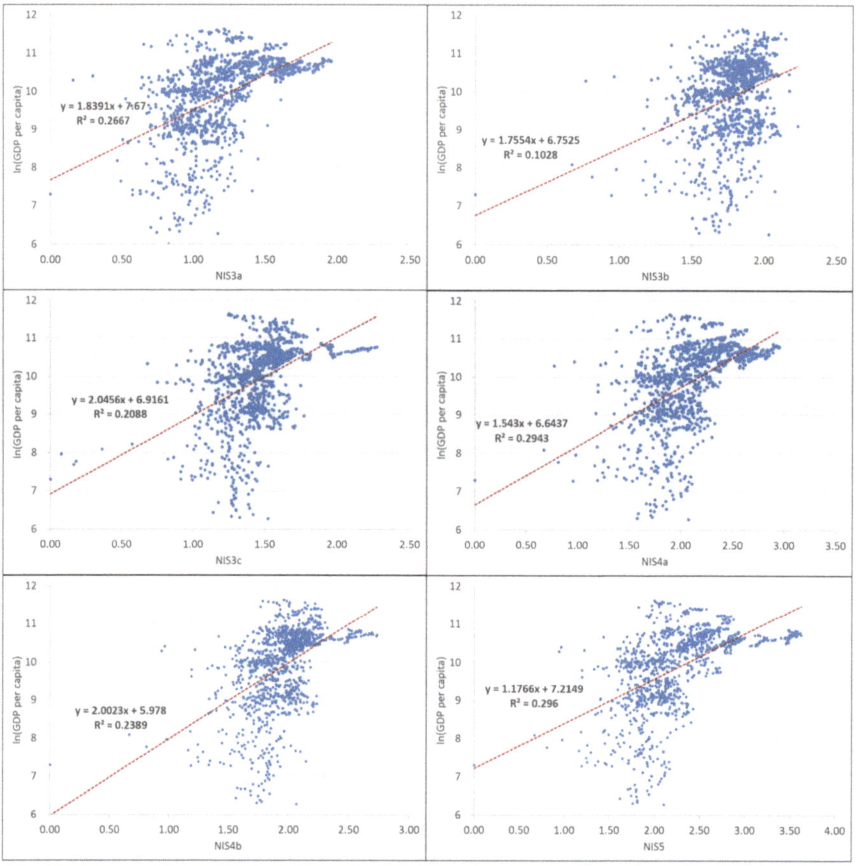

Fig. 2 Distribution of Six different NIS indices generated by the equal-weighting method. Notes: NIS indices, such as NIS3a, NIS3b, NIS3c, NIS4a, NIS4b, NIS5, from the top-left to bottom-right. Source: the authors

4)
$$\text{NIS4a} = \text{S\_Originality} + \text{S\_Relative cycle time} + \text{S\_1} - \text{HHI} + \text{S\_Diversification}$$

5)
$$\text{NIS4b} = \text{S\_Originality} + \text{S\_Relative cycle time} + \text{S\_1} - \text{HHI} + \text{S\_Localization}$$

6)
$$\text{NIS5} = \text{S\_Originality} + \text{S\_Relative cycle time} + \text{S\_1} - \text{HHI} + \text{S\_Diversification} + \text{Localization}$$

NIS3 is constructed to take values from 0 to 3, whereas NIS5 has values from 0 to 5. Figure 2 depicts the results of the equal-weighting method applied to different

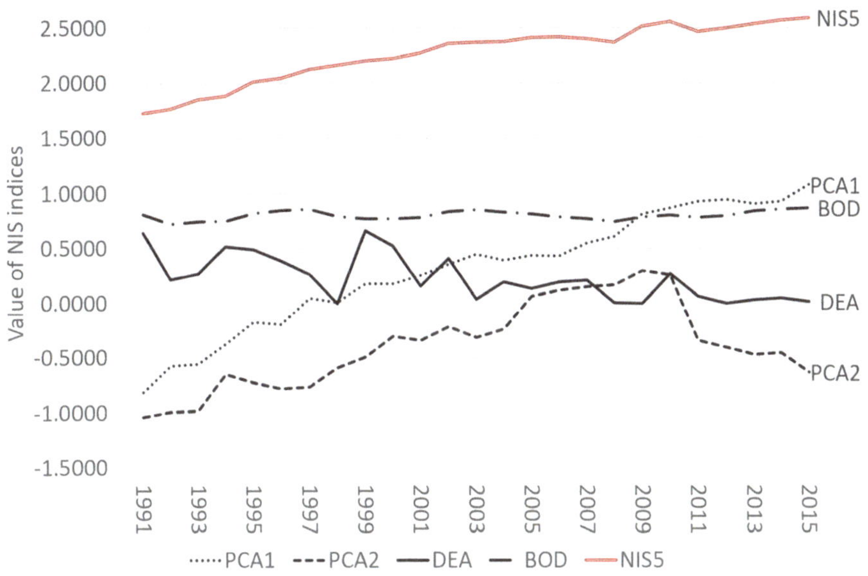

Fig. 3 Distribution of NIS indices in South Korea. Source: the authors

definitions of NIS from NIS3abc and NIS4ab to NIS5, which aggregate the standardized values of three, four, or five different variables with equal weights. Compared with the discussed statistical approaches (PCA, DEA, and BOD), the distribution appears relatively good without much skewing to either end regardless of the differences across NIS3, NIS4, and NIS5. Although the range of the values in each index has a certain difference, the values in general range from 0% to 70% of the maximum value. Therefore, further increasing the NIS level in the future is possible.

The overall R^2 values are relatively high. The overall R^2 values of NIS3a, NIS4a, and NIS5 are close to 0.18 and much higher than those of PCA and DEA (below 0.10) or that of BOD (i.e., 0.15). Figure 3 shows the NIS trends of one country, South Korea, by using the different methods. The second factor score from the PCA method shows an even declining period, which does not make sense for Korea. The trends from DEA and BOD are flat and do not make sense either. Thus, the above discussion appears to support the use of the equal-weighting method. Uniformly determining which factors are important in the process of economic growth is difficult. Moreover, identifying which specific mechanisms differ across countries in different stages of development and initial conditions is challenging.

Figure 4 provides another example of countries in terms of their dynamic changes in the NIS5 index and per capita income space. Panel A in Fig. 4 demonstrates the case of economies with successful growth experiences, such as South Korea, China, and Taiwan. Such countries mostly show upward sloping lines over time. By contrast, panel B presents somewhat different patterns in the case of economies

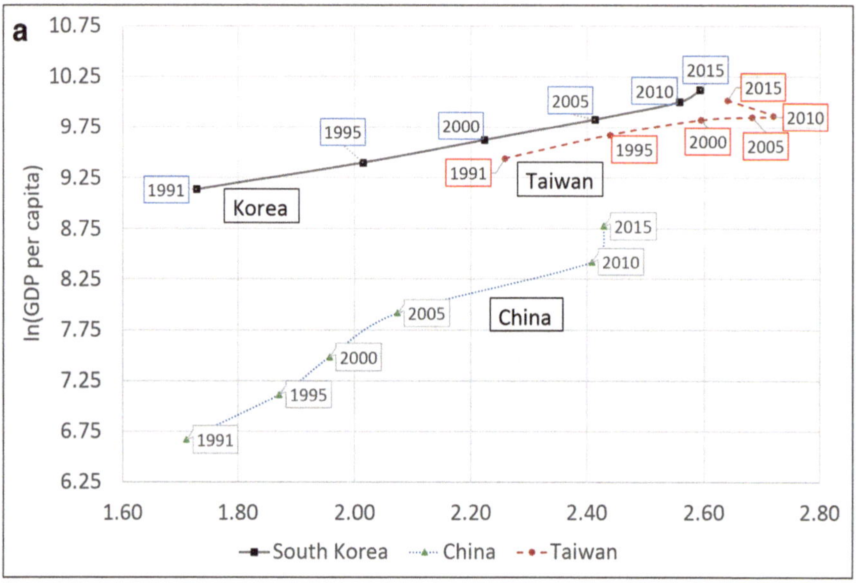

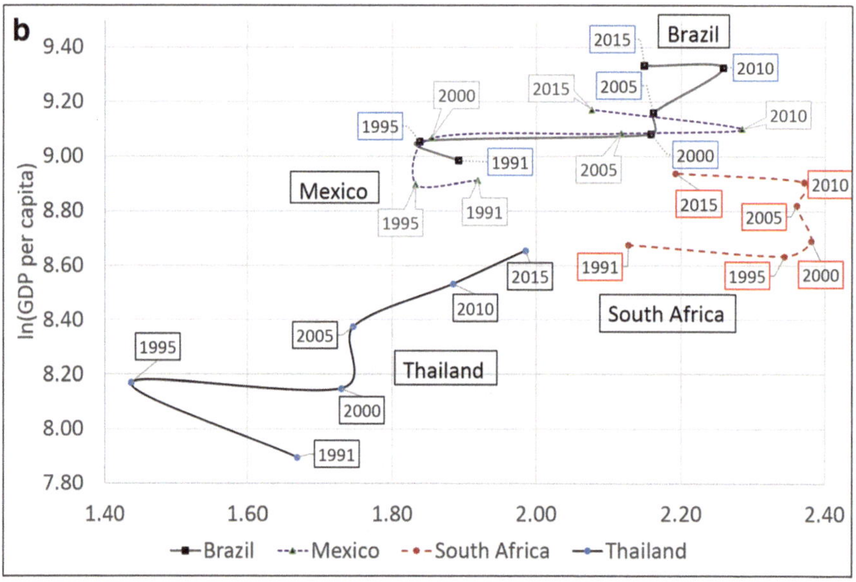

Fig. 4 **a** Trends of NIS5 in China, Korea, and Taiwan. Source: the authors. **b** Trends of NIS5 in Brazil, Mexico, Thailand, and South Africa. Source: the authors

with less successful growth experiences, such as Brazil, Mexico, Thailand, and South Africa. The value of the NIS5 index does not increase much in certain periods or even declines.

4 Econometric model and results

4.1 Models and key variables

The baseline model specification for estimating the effects of NIS level on the growth rate of real GDP per capita follows a conventional growth equation (Mankiw et al. 1992; Sala-i-Martin 1997), namely,

$$\mathrm{GR}_{i,t} = \alpha_i + \beta \log \mathrm{GDP}_{i,t} + \gamma \mathrm{X}_{i,t} + \delta \mathrm{Z}_{i,t} + \mu_{i,t} + \varepsilon_{i,t}, \quad (1)$$

where i is the country and t is the time period. $\mathrm{GR}_{i,\ t}$ is the growth rate of GDP per capita; $\log\mathrm{GDP}_{i,\ t}$ is the logarithm of initial GDP per capita in each period; $\mathrm{X}_{i,\ t}$ is a set of conventional control variables, such as population growth rate, ratio of fixed investment to GDP, and enrollment rates of secondary education; $\mathrm{Z}_{i,\ t}$ is the variable of interest (NIS index); $\mu_{i,\ t}$ is the unobserved time-invariant individual effect; and $\varepsilon_{i,\ t}$ is the error term. Another variable of interest is ECI by Hausmann et al. (2011), which has been discussed in Section 2.

The estimation method generally used to analyze the growth equation is the panel fixed effect (FE) or panel random effect (RE) model. By conducting the Hausmann test, we select the suitable model between these two models, that is, FE estimation. To exclude the yearly or cyclical variance of data values and focus on long-term economic growth, we use reconstructed five-year average data for the 1990–2015 period divided into five sub-periods. To confirm robustness in consideration of the possible endogeneity of explanatory variables, we also apply the first-difference generalized method of moments (GMM) econometric model introduced by Arellano and Bover (1995), with the following equation:

$$\begin{aligned} GR_{i,t} - GR_{i,t-1} = \alpha L.(GR_{i,t} - GR_{i,t-1}) + \beta(GDP_{i,t} - GDP_{i,t-1}) \\ + \gamma(X_{i,t} - X_{i,t-1}) + \delta(\mathrm{Z}_{i,t} - \mathrm{Z}_{i,t-1}) + \varepsilon_{i,t} - \varepsilon_{i,t-1} \end{aligned} \quad (2)$$

where $GR_{i,\ t}$ is the growth rate of real per capita GDP; $L.\ (GR_{i,\ t} - GR_{i,\ t-1})$ is the lagged value of the dependent variable; $GDP_{i,\ t}$ is the initial level of per capita income; $\mathrm{X}_{i,\ t}$ is a set of conventional control variables, such as population growth rate, fixed investment per GDP, and enrollment rate of secondary education; $\mathrm{Z}_{i,\ t}$ refers to NIS and ECI indices; and $\varepsilon_{i,\ t}$ is the error term.

Most variable data are from the World Development Indicators (World Bank 2017). The dependent variable, GDP per capita growth rate, is calculated by the average annual growth rate during each period (1990–1995, 1995–2000, 200–2005, 2005–2010, and 2010–2015). Independent variables are measured as follows: the log of GDP per capita is measured using constant 2010 US dollars for the initial year of each period, population growth rates are in percentage per annum, gross fixed capital formation is in % of GDP, and secondary school enrollment rates are in % gross. We also consider two additional control variables in certain models to show robustness. Institution variables and democracy are from the POLITY™ IV

PROJECT of Marshall, Gurr, and Jaggers (2017). The openness variable and the export of goods and services as % of GDP are also from the World Bank (2017). This dataset is an unbalanced panel because certain variables are missing.

Appendix Table 9 presents the descriptive statistics of the key variables, and Appendix Table 10 shows the correlations among NIS components, NIS indices, and ECI. ECI has a high correlation with certain components of NIS, such as technological diversification, localization, and decentralization, with the values of 0.60, 0.62, and 0.49, respectively. These three NIS component variables are correlated, which can be a justification not to use all of them together in the regressions but to develop a composite index as several combinations. ECI has almost no correlations with the other component, such as originality (0.05), and an intermediate level of correlations with the variable of cycle time of technologies (−0.31). The correlations between ECI and NIS indices vary mostly within the range of 0.4 to 0.6; the highest correlation is with the NIS5 index (0.58), except for a very low correlation with NIS3b (0.16). It is interesting to note that ECI reflecting trade-based diversification and NIS reflecting technological (patent-based) diversification are related to each other. The high correlations between ECI and NIS indices may be a warning against using both in the same regressions in consideration of possible collinearity. Thus, econometric analyses must be performed with this point in mind.

4.2 *Results: From NIS and ECI to economic growth*

Table 2 presents the baseline results of regressing the growth of per capita GDP on the conventional control variables and our NIS indices following Eq. (1). The chi-square values of the Hausmann test are significant at the 1% level, thereby justifying the use of FE estimation instead of RE models. All NIS indices are positive and significant in the FE estimations. However, the GMM results reported in Table 3 reveal that NIS3b, NIS3c, and NIS4 are not significant at the 5% level. The robustness of the remaining indices of NIS3a, NIS4a, and NIS5 5 becomes noticeable when the overall R^2 values of the different models in Table 2 are compared. This robustness pattern and the explanatory power of the three indices are repeated in the following regressions with additional variables. The first column of Table 2 presents the results without the NIS indices for a comparison with the results with various NIS indices. A 4% increase in overall R^2 is observed in the results with NIS3a, which also shows a larger coefficient than NIS4a or NIS5.

With regard to the other control variables, the results are consistent with those in previous studies, such as that of Lee and Kim (2009) who discovered the weak robustness of certain variables, such as secondary enrollment and political democracy, in upper-middle and high-income countries as in the current study. For example, the coefficients of democracy in Table 2 are positive but insignificant in all models. Lee and Kim (2009) found this result unsurprising because most sample countries show high democracy, with seven as the average democracy index. The coefficient of the enrollment rate of secondary education is also insignificant in all

Table 2 NIS and economic growth: fixed effect results

	1990/2015						
	(1)Base	(2)NIS3a	(3)NIS3b	(4)NIS3c	(5)NIS4a	(6)NIS4b	(7)NIS5
ln (Initial GDP)	−0.047***	−0.059***	−0.051***	−0.048***	−0.058***	−0.053***	−0.059***
	(−6.33)	(−7.42)	(−6.49)	(−6.40)	(−7.03)	(−6.45)	(−6.50)
POP growth Rate	−1.90***	−1.81***	−1.97***	−1.87***	−1.85***	−1.90***	−1.79***
	(−3.40)	(−3.31)	(−3.66)	(−3.50)	(−3.45)	(−3.61)	(−3.39)
Fixed Investment Rate	0.30***	0.29***	0.32***	0.32***	0.31***	0.33***	0.32***
	(4.77)	(4.80)	(5.14)	(5.09)	(5.26)	(5.36)	(5.47)
Secondary School Enrollment	0.0095	0.017	0.0072	0.0071	0.0069	0.011	0.011
	(0.64)	(1.10)	(0.48)	(0.47)	(0.45)	(0.70)	(0.74)
Democracy	0.00025	0.000028	−0.0000070	0.00016	−0.000039	0.000050	0.000045
	(0.11)	(0.013)	(−0.0031)	(0.070)	(−0.018)	(0.022)	(0.020)
Openness	0.037**	0.025	0.032**	0.042***	0.027*	0.038**	0.036**
	(2.56)	(1.60)	(2.14)	(2.80)	(1.74)	(2.66)	(2.42)
NIS3a		0.048***					
		(3.08)					
NIS3b			0.030**				
			(2.34)				
NIS3c				0.023**			
				(2.05)			
NIS4a					0.039***		
					(2.72)		
NIS4b						0.028**	
						(2.02)	
NIS5							0.034**
							(2.14)

(continued)

Table 2 (continued)

	1990/2015						
	(1)Base	(2)NIS3a	(3)NIS3b	(4)NIS3c	(5)NIS4a	(6)NIS4b	(7)NIS5
Constant	0.40***	0.47***	0.39***	0.37***	0.44***	0.40***	0.44***
	(6.31)	(7.30)	(5.93)	(5.82)	(6.91)	(6.11)	(6.96)
adj. R-sq	0.25	0.29	0.27	0.26	0.29	0.27	0.28
N	209	209	209	209	209	209	209
Hausmann	29.89***	37.49***	34.72***	30.35***	37.16***	33.58***	36.04***

1) ***, **, and * in the cells indicate 1%, 5%, and 10% levels of significance, respectively
2) The t-values are in parentheses
3) The dependent variable is the annual growth rate of real per capita GDP in each period

Table 3 NIS and economic growth: GMM results

	1990/2015						
	(1)Base	(2)NIS3a	(3)NIS3b	(4)NIS3c	(5)NIS4a	(6)NIS4b	(7)NIS5
L.GDP per Capita Growth	−0.11	−0.10	−0.11	−0.11	−0.10	−0.11	−0.10
	(−0.87)	(−0.81)	(−0.87)	(−0.85)	(−0.83)	(−0.87)	(−0.83)
ln(Initial GDP)	−0.061***	−0.072***	−0.065***	−0.061***	−0.070***	−0.066***	−0.071***
	(−4.44)	(−5.60)	(−4.80)	(−4.49)	(−5.43)	(−4.82)	(−5.36)
POP growth Rate	−1.82*	−1.68*	−1.83*	−1.77*	−1.73*	−1.80*	−1.69*
	(−1.88)	(−1.87)	(−2.01)	(−2.01)	(−1.93)	(−1.99)	(−1.91)
Fixed Investment Rate	0.27***	0.26***	0.28***	0.29***	0.27***	0.28***	0.27***
	(2.79)	(2.81)	(2.88)	(2.94)	(2.85)	(2.93)	(2.92)
Secondary School Enrollment	0.0046	0.018	0.011	0.0046	0.013	0.013	0.014
	(0.31)	(1.11)	(0.69)	(0.32)	(0.83)	(0.77)	(0.89)
Democracy	0.0037	0.0029	0.0034	0.0034	0.0032	0.0034	0.0031
	(1.23)	(1.04)	(1.17)	(1.23)	(1.13)	(1.20)	(1.17)
Openness	0.050*	0.041	0.047*	0.054**	0.043	0.050*	0.046*
	(1.92)	(1.61)	(1.81)	(2.05)	(1.62)	(1.93)	(1.79)
NIS3a		0.044**					
		(2.57)					
NIS3b			0.023				
			(1.40)				
NIS3c				0.033*			
				(1.71)			
NIS4a					0.032**		
					(2.09)		
NIS4b						0.023	
						(1.56)	

(continued)

Table 3 (continued)

	1990/2015						
	(1)Base	(2)NIS3a	(3)NIS3b	(4)NIS3c	(5)NIS4a	(6)NIS4b	(7)NIS5
NIS5							0.031**
							(2.19)
AR(2) z-statistics (*p* value)	−1.62	−0.82	−1.34	−1..16	−0.63	−1.18	−0.51
	(0.105)	(0.410)	(0.180)	(0.247)	(0.528)	(0.238)	(0.607)
Hansen χ^2 statistics (p value)	9.80	9.28	9.48	9.27	8.77	9.30	8.52
	0.081	(0.098)	(0.091)	(0.099)	(0.118)	(0.098)	(0.130)
N	126	126	126	126	126	126	126

1) ***, **, and * in the cells indicate 1%, 5%, and 10% levels of significance, respectively
2) The t-values are in parentheses

Table 4 NIS, economic complexity, and economic growth: fixed effect results

	1990/2015						
	(1) Base	(2) NIS3a	(3) NIS3b	(4) NIS3c	(5) NIS4a	(6) NIS4b	(7) NIS5
ln(Initial GDP)	−0.046***	−0.057***	−0.049***	−0.046***	−0.056***	−0.051***	−0.057***
	(−6.48)	(−7.83)	(−7.22)	(−6.47)	(−7.25)	(−6.93)	(−6.60)
POP growth Rate	−1.66***	−1.57***	−1.71***	−1.66***	−1.61***	−1.68***	−1.58***
	(−2.81)	(−2.76)	(−2.99)	(−2.87)	(−2.83)	(−2.98)	(−2.82)
Fixed Investment Rate	0.30***	0.29***	0.32***	0.31***	0.31***	0.32***	0.32***
	(5.52)	(5.61)	(6.09)	(5.66)	(6.12)	(6.16)	(6.15)
Enrollment Rate Secondary	−0.0034	0.0047	−0.0048	−0.0051	−0.0045	−0.0024	−0.0014
	(−0.23)	(0.31)	(−0.32)	(−0.34)	(−0.30)	(−0.15)	(−0.095)
Democracy	0.0018	0.0016	0.0015	0.0018	0.0015	0.0016	0.0016
	(0.95)	(0.85)	(0.81)	(0.92)	(0.84)	(0.89)	(0.93)
Openness	0.045**	0.035**	0.040**	0.047***	0.036**	0.044**	0.043**
	(2.71)	(2.09)	(2.35)	(2.81)	(2.13)	(2.60)	(2.44)
ECI	0.017**	0.017**	0.018**	0.017**	0.017**	0.017**	0.015**
	(2.32)	(2.54)	(2.54)	(2.21)	(2.52)	(2.43)	(2.32)
NIS3a		0.045***					
		(3.23)					
NIS3b			0.027**				
			(2.06)				
NIS3c				0.016			
				(1.35)			
NIS4a					0.036**		
					(2.66)		
NIS4a						0.026*	
						(1.84)	

(continued)

Table 4 (continued)

	1990/2015						
	(1) Base	(2) NIS3a	(3) NIS3b	(4) NIS3c	(5) NIS4a	(6) NIS4b	(7) NIS5
NIS5							0.033**
							(2.15)
Constant	0.36***	0.43***	0.35***	0.34***	0.40***	0.36***	0.40***
	(6.49)	(7.69)	(6.15)	(5.81)	(7.17)	(6.32)	(7.04)
adj. R-sq	0.29	0.32	0.30	0.29	0.32	0.30	0.32
N	194	194	194	194	194	194	194
Hausmann	34.31***	40.55***	36.94***	34.50***	40.01***	37.11***	39.79***

1) ***, **, and * in the cells indicate 1%, 5%, and 10% levels of significance, respectively
2) The t-values are in parentheses
3) The dependent variable is the annual growth rate of real per capita GDP in each period

models. This result is consistent with that of Lee and Kim (2009) and not surprising because most of the sample countries have high secondary enrollment. Openness has a positive effect on economic growth and is significant at the 5% level in all models. The coefficient of logarithm of initial GDP per capita, as well as population growth, has a negative effect on economic growth. Moreover, the coefficient of fixed capital investment per GDP is positive and significant at the 1% level in all models.

Table 4 shows the results with the variable of ECI added. ECI is positive and significant in all specifications with different NIS indices.[1] As shown in the first column with ECI but without NIS, overall R^2 also increases by 3% to 4% on the average to 0.29, compared with 0.25 in the first column of Table 2. The increase is in a similar magnitude as the case of NIS in Table 2 (comparing the first and second columns). Several NIS indices, such as NIS3c and NIS4a, are insignificant, again at the 5% level. The overall R^2 values are high in the models with NIS3a, NIS4a, and NIS5. However, the ECI coefficient loses significance in the results presented in Table 5 with additional controls for the terms of trade and government expenditure, which are added following Barro (2003). ECI losing significance is related to the fact that ECI is a variable generated by trade data and thus correlated with the variable of terms of trade. The power and robustness of NIS3a, NIS4a, and NIS5 are observed again in Table 5.

Table 6 presents the results without ECI, given the somewhat high correlation between ECI and NIS indices. The three NIS indices remain significant at the 5% level, in which one index is significant at 10%, with NIS3b and NIS4b being insignificant. The high explanatory power (overall R^2) of the three indices is unchanged, with the coefficient of NIS3a being larger than that of NIS4a or NIS5. The significance of other variables is unchanged, except for the openness variable that is affected by the terms of trade variable.

Table 7 and 8 shows the results with different model specifications, particularly a different dependent variable of per capita income rather than its growth rate, as in Acemoglu et al. (2001).[2] In these specifications, we only use the three NIS indices (NIS3a, NIS4a, and NIS5) that are robust and powerful. They are also significant with and without ECI in the FE and GMM results. The ECI variable remains insignificant, similar to the preceding Table 5. In general, the overall R^2 values increase further compared with those in the preceding tables. The explanatory power of the NIS indices is noticeable from the jump of overall R^2 from 0.48 in Model 1 without NIS to 0.57 in the second column with NIS3a. The estimated coefficient of NIS3a is larger than that with NIS4a or NIS5.

---

[1]The results of GMM estimations for the models in Tables 4, 5, and 6 are mostly consistent with the FE results and are available upon request.

[2]We follow Acemoglu et al. (2001) in not adding the variable of initial per capita income in the regression models. However, the results do not change with and without this variable.

Table 5 NIS, economic complexity, and economic growth with government and TOT: fixed effects results

	1990/2015					
	(1) NIS3a	(2) NIS3b	(3) NIS3c	(4) NIS4a	(5) NIS4b	(6) NIS5
ln(Initial GDP)	−0.050***	−0.045***	−0.044***	−0.049***	−0.046***	−0.050***
	(−6.34)	(−6.61)	(−6.27)	(−6.41)	(−6.76)	(−6.47)
POP growth Rate	−1.71**	−1.81**	−1.75**	−1.73**	−1.77**	−1.70**
	(−2.42)	(−2.56)	(−2.46)	(−2.44)	(−2.48)	(−2.37)
Fixed Investment Rate	0.25***	0.28***	0.28***	0.27***	0.28***	0.27***
	(5.11)	(5.49)	(5.28)	(5.46)	(5.42)	(5.42)
Enrollment Rate Secondary	0.016	0.011	0.0074	0.010	0.012	0.012
	(1.06)	(0.79)	(0.58)	(0.76)	(0.88)	(0.87)
Democracy	−0.00041	−0.00037	−0.00026	−0.00034	−0.00027	−0.00025
	(−0.44)	(−0.37)	(−0.28)	(−0.33)	(−0.28)	(−0.25)
Openness	0.014	0.017	0.024	0.016	0.020	0.019
	(0.94)	(1.18)	(1.56)	(1.03)	(1.38)	(1.28)
Government Expenditure	−0.29**	−0.30**	−0.27**	−0.28**	−0.29**	−0.27**
	(−2.46)	(−2.48)	(−2.38)	(−2.45)	(−2.39)	(−2.35)
Terms of Trade	0.0014	−0.0036	−0.00092	−0.0013	−0.0025	−0.00051
	(0.23)	(−0.62)	(−0.16)	(−0.23)	(−0.43)	(−0.088)
ECI	0.010	0.012	0.012	0.011	0.012	0.011
	(1.45)	(1.65)	(1.58)	(1.52)	(1.65)	(1.53)
NIS3a	0.037**					
	(2.27)					
NIS3b		0.023*				
		(1.76)				
NIS3c			0.026**			
			(2.13)			
NIS4a				0.025**		

				(2.23)		
NIS4a					0.019	
					(1.67)	
NIS5						0.020**
						(2.06)
Constant	0.45***	0.40***	0.38***	0.43***	0.41***	0.43***
	(7.04)	(6.37)	(5.98)	(6.86)	(6.65)	(7.03)
adj. R-sq	0.47	0.46	0.45	0.46	0.45	0.46
N	170	170	170	170	170	170
Hausmann	47.24***	44.98***	44.84***	46.25***	44.58***	45.45***

1) ***, **, and * in the cells indicate 1%, 5%, and 10% levels of significance, respectively
2) The t-values are in parentheses
3) The GMM results are available upon request

Table 6 NIS and economic growth with government and TOT: fixed effects results

	1990/2015					
	(1) NIS3a	(2) NIS3b	(3) NIS3c	(4) NIS4a	(5) NIS4b	(6) NIS5
ln(Initial GDP)	−0.049***	−0.044***	−0.042***	−0.048***	−0.045***	−0.048***
	(−6.58)	(−6.79)	(−6.35)	(−6.73)	(−6.89)	(−6.71)
POP growth Rate	−1.82***	−1.92***	−1.86***	−1.86***	−1.88***	−1.82***
	(−2.83)	(−3.03)	(−2.92)	(−2.90)	(−2.94)	(−2.81)
Fixed Investment Rate	0.24***	0.26***	0.27***	0.25***	0.26***	0.26***
	(4.72)	(4.92)	(4.83)	(4.93)	(4.90)	(4.95)
Enrollment Rate Secondary	0.023	0.018	0.015	0.017	0.020	0.019
	(1.53)	(1.40)	(1.22)	(1.33)	(1.46)	(1.44)
Democracy	−0.00038	−0.00030	−0.00021	−0.00031	−0.00022	−0.00022
	(−0.35)	(−0.26)	(−0.19)	(−0.26)	(−0.19)	(−0.19)
Openness	0.011	0.015	0.022	0.012	0.018	0.016
	(0.84)	(1.15)	(1.64)	(0.92)	(1.42)	(1.25)
Government Expenditure	−0.35***	−0.36***	−0.34***	−0.35***	−0.35***	−0.34***
	(−3.30)	(−3.28)	(−3.30)	(−3.30)	(−3.25)	(−3.22)
Terms of Trade	−0.0044	−0.0096**	−0.0074	−0.0069	−0.0088*	−0.0064
	(−1.01)	(−2.09)	(−1.64)	(−1.59)	(−1.98)	(−1.42)
NIS3a	0.034**					
	(2.03)					
NIS3b		0.020				
		(1.51)				
NIS3c			0.026**			
			(2.06)			
NIS4a				0.024**		
				(2.09)		
NIS4b					0.017	

					(1.50)	
NIS5						0.020*
						(2.02)
Constant	0.46***	0.42***	0.40***	0.45***	0.43***	0.45***
	(7.86)	(7.17)	(6.69)	(7.74)	(7.46)	(7.92)
adj. R-sq	0.46	0.45	0.45	0.46	0.45	0.46
N	178	178	178	178	178	178
Hausmann	50.58***	48.45***	47.54***	49.71***	48.12***	49.16***

1) ***, **, and * in the cells indicate 1%, 5%, and 10% levels of significance, respectively
2) The t-values are in parentheses
3) G MM results are available upon request

Table 7 NIS, complexity, and per capita income: fixed-effect results

	1990/2015						
Dep: ln(per capita *GDP)*	(1) Base	(2) NIS3a	(3) NIS4a	(4) NIS5	(5) ECI & NIS3a	(6) ECI & NIS4a	(7) ECI & NIS5
POP growth Rate	−9.01*	−6.15	−7.10*	−5.47	−4.31	−4.71	−3.58
	(−1.80)	(−1.41)	(−1.74)	(−1.47)	(−1.07)	(−1.32)	(−1.04)
Fixed Investment Rate	2.67**	2.01*	2.44**	2.49**	2.12**	2.57**	2.60**
	(2.06)	(1.94)	(2.28)	(2.45)	(2.04)	(2.43)	(2.56)
Enrollment Rate Secondary	0.70*	0.72**	0.60**	0.62**	0.66**	0.55**	0.58**
	(2.00)	(2.51)	(2.14)	(2.33)	(2.45)	(2.14)	(2.35)
Democracy	0.025	0.014	0.016	0.016	0.016	0.017	0.017
	(1.65)	(0.93)	(1.05)	(1.13)	(1.01)	(1.11)	(1.18)
Openness	0.75***	0.47**	0.51**	0.55***	0.56**	0.60**	0.62***
	(3.52)	(2.33)	(2.66)	(3.06)	(2.33)	(2.66)	(2.82)
Government Expenditure	3.19**	2.10	2.19	2.18*	2.64*	2.67**	2.60**
	(2.44)	(1.51)	(1.64)	(1.74)	(1.96)	(2.13)	(2.19)
Terms of Trade	−0.24*	−0.12	−0.18	−0.15	−0.085	−0.14	−0.11
	(−1.71)	(−0.99)	(−1.44)	(−1.30)	(−0.68)	(−1.15)	(−1.04)
ECI					0.086	0.093	0.080
					(1.01)	(1.06)	(0.91)
NIS3a		0.75***			0.72***		
		(3.76)			(3.55)		
NIS4a			0.55***			0.54***	
			(3.42)			(3.32)	
NIS5				0.57***			0.55***
				(3.77)			(3.63)
Constant	7.68***	7.20***	6.99***	6.77***	6.95***	6.71***	6.56***
	(17.3)	(16.7)	(14.4)	(13.3)	(15.0)	(13.1)	(12.5)
adj. R-sq	0.48	0.57	0.56	0.59	0.58	0.57	0.59

N	178	178	178	178	170	170	170
Hausmann	35.45***	46.89***	47.23***	42.73***	41.41***	43.67***	40.06***

1) ***, **, and * in the cells indicate 1%, 5%, and 10% levels of significance, respectively
2) The t-values are in parentheses
3) Dependent variables are the levels of per capita GDP

Table 8 NIS, complexity, and per capita income: GMM results

	1990/2015					
*Dep: ln(*per capita *GDP)*	(1) NIS3a	(2) NIS4a	(3) NIS5	(4) ECI & NIS3a	(5) ECI & NIS4a	(6) ECI & NIS5
L.*ln(*per capita *GDP)*	0.78***	0.80***	0.79***	0.80***	0.81***	0.82***
	(12.8)	(14.0)	(13.6)	(11.9)	(12.5)	(12.7)
POP growth Rate	−3.61*	−3.92*	−3.60*	−2.78	−3.00	−2.69
	(−1.75)	(−1.90)	(−1.83)	(−1.47)	(−1.57)	(−1.35)
Fixed Investment Rate	1.59***	1.67***	1.71***	1.48***	1.60***	1.60***
	(4.07)	(4.25)	(4.43)	(4.27)	(4.53)	(4.47)
Enrollment Rate Secondary	−0.037	−0.066	−0.066	−0.036	−0.068	−0.086
	(−0.40)	(−0.72)	(−0.75)	(−0.36)	(−0.72)	(−0.93)
Democracy	−0.0014	−0.00062	−0.00035	−0.0036	−0.0017	−0.0016
	(−0.13)	(−0.063)	(−0.037)	(−0.35)	(−0.18)	(−0.17)
Openness	0.076	0.079	0.11	0.074	0.085	0.11
	(0.95)	(0.96)	(1.42)	(0.95)	(1.08)	(1.41)
Government Expenditure	−0.85	−0.85	−0.68	−0.87	−0.85	−0.70
	(−1.37)	(−1.64)	(−1.41)	(−1.29)	(−1.53)	(−1.31)
Terms of Trade	0.011	−0.0089	−0.0030	0.037	0.018	0.033
	(0.25)	(−0.21)	(−0.069)	(0.68)	(0.36)	(0.69)
ECI				0.049	0.056	0.069*
				(1.31)	(1.44)	(1.75)
NIS3a	0.30***			0.32***		
	(4.20)			(3.82)		
NIS4a		0.24***			0.24***	
		(4.47)			(3.21)	
NIS5			0.22***			0.20***
			(4.06)			(3.07)
AR(2) z-statistics (p value)	−2.12	−2.25	−1.90	−1.64	−1.94	−2.11
	(0.034)	(0.024)	(0.057)	(0.100)	(0.053)	(0.035)
Hansen x^2 statistics (*p* value)	6.22	5.56	6.18	4.50	4.60	4.97
	(0.286)	(0.351)	(0.290)	(0.480)	(0.466)	(0.419)
N	124	124	124	118	118	118

1) ***, **, and * in the cells indicate 1%, 5%, and 10% levels of significance, respectively
2) The t-values are in parentheses

5 Concluding remarks

This study examined the impacts of NIS on economic growth by using a composite NIS index in the context of growth regression with static (FE) and dynamic (first-difference) GMM estimation models. To develop the index, this research used US patent data to generate the five NIS variables for expressing the diverse dimensions of NIS (i.e., concentration of assignees, localization, originality, diversification, and cycle time of technologies). To generate a composite NIS index, this study compared several weighting methods, such as PCA, DEA, and BOD, which is a variation of the DEA method. We opted for a simple equal-weighting method and tested the robustness of the constructed NIS indices as diverse combinations of the five NIS variables.

The growth regressions in general confirmed the significant and robust impacts of NIS3a, NIS4a, and NIS5 indices on economic growth. The importance of NIS in economic growth was confirmed by an increase in R^2 after adding the NIS indices to the growth equations, apart from the typical control variables. The three NIS indices are similar in terms of explanatory power (or additional R2), which implies that adding one or more component variables to make NIS6 or NIS7 does not make any difference. The common feature of the three NIS indices is that they have the three component variables as their ingredients, namely, originality, cycle time, and technological diversification. These results are reasonable in view of the high correlations of technological diversification with localization and decentralization, implying that adding these two components does not bring additional explanatory power. In other words, economies with high technological diversification have high localization and decentralization.

Thus, NIS3 may be a parsimonious and powerful NIS index because NIS3 combines only three NIS variables of technological diversification, originality, and cycle time of technologies, and it has the largest coefficient among others in all the regression results. The R^2 values of the growth equations with NIS3 are consistently higher than, or similar to, those with other NIS indices in the benchmark results (Table 2), results with ECI (Table 4), and results with government and terms of trade (Tables 5 and 7). Although NIS4a and NIS5 have smaller coefficients than NIS3a, their sub-components, such as knowledge localization and concentration, are still useful variables on their own, especially in terms of showing the diverse aspects of the NIS of countries. Having more sub-components, the values of NIS5 may be more stable over time and thus be better when the objective is to show ranking of countries and their change over time.

By contrast, ECI robustness is somewhat questionable because it loses significance after adding government expenditure and terms of trade variables into the regression models. We also found that ECI and our NIS indices are correlated at varying degrees. NIS3a has the lowest correlation degree (0.46) with ECI among the NIS indices, such as NIS4a (0.54) and NIS5 (0.59). This result may be another reason to claim that NIS3a may be a good or distinctive index for having the lowest correlation with ECI and the largest coefficient among NIS indices. The component variables of NIS3a have a low correlation with ECI, such as originality (0.05) and cycle time of technologies (−0.31). By contrast, NIS3b has the least correlation with ECI (0.16) but is not a robust predictor of economic growth.

The results confirmed the overall importance of NIS in economic growth and justify the policy effort to improve NIS. The findings suggest that the simple NIS index constructed using US patent data is as powerful as other indices in reflecting diverse, complicated, or nuanced aspects of NIS. While this statement does not mean to depreciate the value of other indices, it means that predicting economic growth by using a simple NIS index (NIS3a) constructed in a parsimonious manner is technically possible as long as the intention is to explain and predict the economic growth of countries (mostly upper-middle or high-income ones) at certain stages of development. According to the estimated coefficient (0.034) of NIS3a (Table 6), the increase in the NIS index by the amount of one standard deviation (0.262) (e.g., from its average value of 1.174 to 1.436) increases the growth rates of per capita income by 0.17% (e.g., from the current sample average of 2.25% to 2.42%).

However, to the extent that NIS is more than what can be captured by patent data, this study has its limitations. Nevertheless, this research is one of the first to generate a robust NIS index by using patent data only without many data requirements and free from the problem of cross-country comparability of underlying variables. This statement does not mean to depreciate the value of the research that examines different importance (weights) of other NIS variables in certain stages of development or certain groups of countries.

Publisher's note Springer Nature remains neutral with regard to jurisdictional claims in published maps and institutional affiliations.

Appendix

Table 9 Basic statistics

Variable	Observations	Mean	Std. Dev.	Min	Max
GDP per Capita Growth	214	0.0225	0.0241	−0.0900	0.1305
ln(Initial GDP)	214	9.8014	1.0880	6.2746	11.5642
POP growth Rate	215	0.0091	0.0077	−0.0055	0.0348
Fixed Investment Rate	215	0.2316	0.0486	0.1264	0.4489
Enrollment Rate Secondary	210	0.9836	0.2025	0.3835	1.5506
Government Expenditure	210	0.1761	0.0492	0.0665	0.2812
Openness	215	0.4827	0.3885	0.0768	2.1360
Democracy	215	8.1699	2.8832	0.0000	10.0000
Net Barter Terms of Trade	187	1.0006	0.2181	0.4886	2.7047
1-HHI	215	0.8850	0.1173	0.4417	0.9945
Originality	215	0.4084	0.0653	0.1989	0.5684
Localization	215	0.0573	0.0414	0.0000	0.1906
Diversification	215	0.2746	0.2516	0.0064	0.8598
Relative cycle time	215	1.1131	0.1268	0.7891	1.4748
ECI	200	0.8822	0.7172	−0.6944	2.2867
NIS3a	215	1.1740	0.2628	0.5277	1.8633
NIS3b	215	1.7790	0.1615	1.0234	2.0936
NIS3c	215	1.4192	0.1747	0.8599	1.8110
NIS4a	215	2.0637	0.3353	1.0306	2.8543
NIS4b	215	1.9172	0.1971	1.1024	2.3496
NIS5	215	2.2019	0.4053	1.1096	3.2250
PCA1	215	−0.1908	0.5998	−1.0209	1.7374
PCA2	215	0.2825	0.6968	−1.9529	1.9898
DEA	215	0.0545	0.0836	0.0000	0.4362
BOD	215	0.9201	0.0807	0.4783	0.9998

1) S_´variable name` equals the standardization of variables
2) NIS3a = S_Originality + S_Relative cycle time + S_Diversification
3) NIS3b = S_Originality + S_Relative cycle time + S_1-HHI
4) NIS3c = S_Relative cycle time + S_1-HHI + S_ Localization
5) NIS4a = S_Originality + S_Relative cycle time + S_1-HHI + S_Diversification
6) NIS4b = S_Originality + S_Relative cycle time + S_1-HHI + S_Localization
7) NIS5 = S_Originality + S_Relative cycle time + S_1-HHI + S_Diversification + S_Localization
Sources: Author's calculation

Table 10 Correlations during the sample periods

	Originality	1-HHI	Localization	Diversification	Relative cycle time	NIS3a	NIS3b	NIS3c	NIS4a	NIS4b	NIS5	ECI
Originality	1.0000											
1-HHI	0.1157	1.0000										
Localization	−0.0161	0.4281	1.0000									
Diversification	0.1016	0.5253	0.7709	1.0000								
Relative cycle time	0.0428	−0.2693	−0.1923	−0.3336	1.0000							
NIS3a	0.4043	0.4577	0.6851	0.8964	0.0184	1.0000						
NIS3b	0.6051	0.6485	0.2017	0.2523	0.3862	0.5509	1.0000					
NIS3c	0.0891	0.7555	0.7252	0.5949	0.2202	0.6807	0.7303	1.0000				
NIS4a	0.3607	0.7093	0.6915	0.8927	−0.0787	0.9514	0.6614	0.8014	1.0000			
NIS4b	0.4685	0.7152	0.6370	0.5673	0.2120	0.7612	0.8835	0.9217	0.8513	1.0000		
NIS5	0.2935	0.6846	0.8034	0.9157	−0.1097	0.9441	0.5923	0.8298	0.9857	0.8504	1.0000	
ECI	−0.0538	0.4884	0.6189	0.5959	−0.3133	0.4628	0.1593	0.4988	0.5361	0.4214	0.5863	1.0000

Sources: Author's calculation

References

Abramovitz M (1986) Catching up, forging ahead, and falling behind. J Econ Hist 46:385–406

Acemoglu D, Johnson S, Robinson JA (2001) The colonial origins of comparative development: an empirical investigation. AER 91:1369–1401

Aghion P, Howitt P (1992) A model of growth through creative destruction. ECTA 60:323–351

Archibugi D, Coco A (2004) A new indicator of technological capabilities for developed and developing countries (ArCo). WD 32:629–654

Arellano M, Bover O (1995) Another look at the instrumental variable estimation of error-components models. J Econ 68:29–51

Barro RJ (2003) Determinants of economic growth in a panel of countries. Ann Econ Financ 4:231–274

Castellacci F (2008) Technological paradigms, regimes and trajectories: manufacturing and service industries in a new taxonomy of sectoral patterns of innovation. Res Policy 37:978–994

Castellacci F (2011) Closing the technology gap? Rev Dev Econ 15:180–197

Castellacci F, Natera JM (2015) The convergence paradox: the global evolution of national innovation systems. In: Archibugi D, Filippetti A (eds) The handbook of global science, technology, and innovation. Wiley Blackwell, Chichester

Charnes A, Cooper WW, Rhodes E (1978) Measuring the efficiency of decision making units. Eur J Oper Res 2:429–444

Coe NM, Hess M, HWc Y, Dicken P, Henderson J (2004) 'Globalizing' regional development: a global production networks perspective. T I Brit Geogr 29:468–484

Cohen WM, Levinthal DA (1990) Absorptive capacity: a new perspective on learning and innovation. Adm Sci Q 35:128–152

Colombage, S (2016) A grounded demolition of Richard Hausmann's economic thinking for Lanka. Thuppahi's Blog. https://thuppahi.wordpress.com/2016/01/27/a-grounded-demolition-of-richard-hausmanns-economic-thinking-for-lanka/. Access 27 November 2016

Cornell University, INSEAD, WIPO (2018) The global innovation index 2018: energizing the world with innovation. Ithaca, Fontainebleau, and Geneva

Desai M, Fukuda-Parr S, Johansson C, Sagasti F (2002) Measuring the technology achievement of nations and the capacity to participate in the network age. J Hum Dev Capabil 3:95-122

Dosi, G, Pavitt K, Soete L (1990) The economics of technical change and international trade. LEM Book Series

Dosi M, Fukuda-Parr S, Johansson C, Sagasti F (2002) Measuring the technology achievement of nations and the capacity to participate in the network age. J Hum Dev 3:95–122

Edquist C (1997) Systems of innovation approaches: their emergence and characteristics. In: Edquist C (ed) Systems of Innovation: technologies, institutions and organizations. Pinter/Cassell, London

European Commission (2018) European innovation scoreboard. Publications Office of the European Union, Luxembourg

Fagerberg J (1987) A technology gap approach to why growth rates differ. Res Policy 16:87–99

Fagerberg J (1988) International competitiveness. EJ 98:355–374

Fagerberg J, Godinho M (2004) Innovation and catching-up. In: Fagerberg J, Mowery D (eds) The Oxford handbook of innovation. Oxford University Press, Oxford

Fagerberg J, Srholec M (2008) National innovation systems, capabilities and economic development. Res Policy 37:1417–1435

Fagerberg J, Verspagen B (2002) Technology-gaps, innovation-diffusion and transformation: an evolutionary interpretation. Res Policy 31:1291–1304

Fidrmuc J (2004) Migration and regional adjustment to asymmetric shocks in transition economies. J Comp Econ 32:230–247

Filippetti A, Peyrache A (2011) The patterns of technological capabilities of countries: a dual approach using composite indicators and data envelopment analysis. WD 39:1108–1121

Freeman C, Clark J, Soete L (1982) Unemployment and technical innovation. Frances Pinter, London
Furman JL, Porter ME, Stern S (2002) The determinants of national innovative capacity. Res Policy 31:899–933
Gerschenkron A (1962) Economic backwardness in historical perspective: a book of essays. Harvard University Press, Cambridge
Hall, BH, Jaffe AB, Trajtenberg M (2001) The NBER patent citation data file: lessons, insights and methodological tools. NBER discussion paper series, 3094
Hanson GH, Mataloni RJ Jr, Slaughter MJ (2005) Vertical production networks in multinational firms. REStat 87:664–678
Hausmann R, Hidalgo CA, Bustos S, Coscia M, Chung S, Jimenez H, Simoes A, Yildirim MA (2011) The atlas of economic complexity: mapping paths to prosperity. MIT Press, Cambridge
Hausmann R, Hidalgo CA, Bustos S, Coscia M, Simoes A, Yildirim MA (2014) The atlas of economic complexity: mapping paths to prosperity. MIT Press, Cambridge
Hotelling H (1933) Analysis of a complex of statistical variables into principal components. J Educ Psychol 24:417
Inoua, S (2016) A simple measure of economic complexity. arXiv preprint arXiv:1601.05012
Jaffe AB, Trajtenberg M (2002) Patents, citations, and innovations: A window on the knowledge economy. MIT press, Cambridge
Jaffe AB, Trajtenberg M, Henderson R (1993) Geographic localization of knowledge spillovers as evidenced by patent citations. QJE 108:577–598
Kim YK, Lee K (2015) Different Impacts of Scientific & Technological Knowledge on Economic Growth: Contrasting S&T Policy in East Asia and Latin America. Asian Econ Policy R 10:43-66
Lee K (2013) Schumpeterian analysis of economic catch-up: knowledge, path-creation, and the middle-income trap. Cambridge University Press, Cambridge
Lee K, Kim B-Y (2009) Both institutions and policies matter but differently for different income groups of countries: determinants of long-run economic growth revisited. WD 37:533–549
Lucas RE Jr (1988) On the mechanics of economic development. J Monet Econ 22:3–42
Lundvall B-Å (1992) National systems of innovation: toward a theory of innovation and interactive learning. Anthem Press, London
Malerba F (2005) Sectoral systems of innovation: a framework for linking innovation to the knowledge base, structure and dynamics of sectors. Econ Innovat New Tech 14:63-82
Mankiw NG, Romer D, Weil DN (1992) A contribution to the empirics of economic growth. QJE 107:407–437
Marshall MG, Gurr TR, Jaggers K (2017) Polity IV project: Political regime characteristics and transitions, 1800-2016. Center for Systemic Peace
Melyn, W, Moesen W (1991) Towards a synthetic indicator of macroeconomic performance: unequal weighting when limited information is available. K.U. Leuven Public Economics Research Papers 17
Nardo, M, Saisana M, Saltelli A, Tarantola S, Hoffman A, Giovannini E (2005) Handbook on constructing composite indicators. OECD Statistics Working Papers 03
Nelson RR (1993) National Innovation Systems: a comparative analysis. Oxford University Press, Oxford
Ohkawa K, Rosovsky H (1973) Japanese economic growth: trend acceleration in the twentieth century. Stanford University Press, Stanford
Orefice G, Rocha N (2014) Deep integration and production networks: an empirical analysis. World Econ 37:106–136
Palmer J, Richards I (1999) Get knetted: network behaviour in the new economy. J Knowl Manag 3:191–202
Pearson K (1901) LIII. On lines and planes of closest fit to systems of points in space. Lond.Edinb. Dubl.Phil.Mag. 2:559–572
Romer PM (1990) Endogenous technological change. J Polit Econ 98:S71–S102

Sala-i-Martin XX (1997) I just ran four million regressions. AER 87:178-183
Schölkopf B, Smola A, Müller KR (1997) Kernel principal component analysis. In International Conference on Artificial Neural Networks. Springer, Berlin Heidelberg, pp.583-588
Schumpeter JA (1934) The theory of economic development. Harvard University press, Cambridge
Solow RM (1956) A contribution to the theory of economic growth. Q J Econ 70:65-94
Toya H, Skidmore M (2007) Economic development and the impacts of natural disasters. Econ Lett 94:20–25
Trajtenberg M, Henderson R, Jaffe A (1997) University versus corporate patents: a window on the basicness of invention. Econ Innov New Technol 5:19–50
USPTO (1976-2017) Patent Grant Red Book (Full Text)
Verspagen B (1991) A new empirical approach to catching up or falling behind. Struct Chang Econ Dyn 2
World Bank (2017) World development indicators. The World Bank

Regulation and product innovation: the intermediate role of resource reallocation

Fang Wang and Xiaoyong Dai

Abstract Regulation has been identified as an important determinant of the innovation activities of companies, industries, and entire economies. As such, this paper investigates the potential effects of regulation on the innovative performance of firms in China. We identify an inverted U-shaped relationship between regulation and product innovation performance. That is, in China, regulation plays a positive role in promoting innovation: the more actively firms deal with regulations within certain threshold levels, the better their product innovation performance is. However, after reaching the threshold, the relationship reverses. Further, actively coping with regulations facilitates firms' access to financial resources, which in turn promotes product innovation. Meanwhile, output distortion significantly impedes product innovation performance. However, regulation does not show a measurable impact on output distortion.

Keywords Regulation · Product innovation · Resource reallocation · China

JEL F14 · D22 · P31 · O31 · L51

1 Introduction

The term regulation generally refers to the implementation of rules by government institutions to influence market activity and the behavior of private actors in the economy. While it has been identified as an important determinant of the innovation activities of companies, industries, and entire economies, the effects of regulation on

---

F. Wang (✉)
Institutes of Science and Development, Chinese Academy of Sciences, 15 Zhongguancun Beiyitiao, Beijing 100190, People's Republic of China
e-mail: fwang@casisd.cn

X. Dai
School of Economics and Finance, Xi'an Jiaotong University, Xi'an, China
e-mail: daixy87@gmail.com

A. Pyka, K. Lee (eds.), *Innovation, Catch-up and Sustainable Development*, Economic Complexity and Evolution, https://doi.org/10.1007/978-3-030-84931-3_7

innovative performance have been a topic of debate for several decades. The Regulatory Capture view (Stigler 1971) and the Public Interest perspective pioneered by Pigou (1938) hold opposite views on the role of regulation for industry development. The former addresses the manipulation of regulations by specific industries for their own benefit, while the latter advocates the positive impact of regulation in correcting market failure. The degree to which regulation promotes or inhibits competition can affect innovative performance by influencing the cost of innovative projects or by changing industry structure. A major issue for the government is thus achieving a balance between over- and under-regulation, to the benefit of the society (Amable et al. 2016). Due to the lack of a coherent theoretical framework to analyze the impacts of regulation on innovation performance (Blind 2012), the causal relationship between the degree or scope of regulation and innovation performance still remains unclear. Meanwhile, the emergence of new technologies and of the sharing economics brings new challenges for regulations such as car sharing platforms, Fintech, or green energy.

The extent to which governments have used regulation to drive technological change varies across countries and sectors. Firms in developing and transitioning economies often face different problems in regard to setting regulations to stimulate innovation compared with their counterparts in developed countries. The successful catching-up experience of East Asian economies highlights the importance of regulation (Wade 1990). For example, regulations on intellectual property rights (IPR) in Korea shifted from a loose form of control toward a higher level of protection in the late 1980s to provide more incentives for increasing innovation efforts (Lee 2016). It is acknowledged that the regulations for the entry and operation of firms helped the technological leapfrogging of the automotive industries in Japan and Korea, although the regulations differed by country. As regulation shapes the potential paths to technological development, it is important to understand their influence and functionality to increase innovation performance.

From the viewpoint of empirical analysis, China provides a particularly interesting context, given its highly centralized governance structure and massive efforts for promoting innovation- oriented growth (Li 2018). On the one hand, in China, the government controls the allocation of resources to a large degree, which leaves rooms for high-level bureaucracy and strong regulations in certain areas, such as market entry and financial control. This may cause rent-seeking and distortions in resource allocation, and, therefore, result in poor innovation performance. On the other hand, China has witnessed continuous regulatory reforms in different sectors, such as the financial market, new energy, and IPR during its marketization over the past three decades. However, due to the path dependency in innovative behaviors, industrial foundation, and capital constraints, the response to regulation in terms of innovation varies substantially across firms.

Consequently, this paper intends to answer the following two questions: (1) what are the potential effects of regulation on the innovative performance of firms in China; and (2) how does the regulation affect their innovative performance?

While regulation has been widely identified as the main cause of resource misallocation in the literature (Restuccia and Rogerson 2017), the impacts of resource misallocation on the causal relationship between regulation and product innovation are still under-explored. Therefore, following Hsieh and Klenow (2009), we construct a measure for firm-level distortions and use financial resource accessibility to reflect across-firm resource reallocation. Further, a simultaneous equation model is proposed to investigate the relationship between regulation, resource reallocation, and product innovation performance.

Analyzing the causal relationship between regulation and firm performance in terms of innovation presents two challenges. First, it is difficult to define and measure the regulation level quantitatively. Second, regulations normally interweave and generate both positive and negative effects on firms. The main implication of this phenomenon is that any analysis on the relationship between regulations and firm performance should identify and distinguish between these two aspects.

This paper contributes to the studies on the determinants of innovation in two ways. First, it builds a conceptual framework for analyzing the potential relationship between regulation and innovation performance at the firm level by using resource allocation as a mediating factor, thus providing evidence on the impact of regulation on the innovative behaviors of firms in China. Specifically, it establishes a mechanism by which government intervention establishes its role on innovation performance via resource allocation across and within firms. Second, it proposed an identification strategy to identify the potential negative and positive effects of regulation, which helps us better understand micro-level performance in response to macro-level regulations in a transitional environment.

The remainder of this article is organized as follows. Section 2 reviews the literature on the relationship between regulation and innovation, and proposes a conceptual framework to analyze this relationship. Section 3 constructs the econometric model for analyzing the effects of regulation on the tendency and intensity of product innovation, as well as the mediating effects of resource allocation, and presents the data and measurements used for the empirical analysis. Section 4 shows the empirical results. Section 5 concludes the article and discusses the research findings.

2 Literature review and conceptual framework

The occurrence of regulations is typically traced back to the presence of market failure. Market and government intervention are identified as two main channels for distributing resources. Although a free market provides information and incentives for agents, market failure arises in the presence of monopoly, externalities, and asymmetric information. While some studies consider regulation and government intervention interchangeable, conventional economic studies view regulation as one type of government intervention, often in the form of information requirements, proscriptions (things firms may not do), or mandates (things firms must do) (Stiglitz 2012). According to Trebing (1969), "the salient feature of government regulation is that it involves an attempt to impose social judgments and goals upon existing market judgments and goals insofar as the actions of persons, firms and industries are concerned".

In this paper, we follow the conventional treatment in distinguishing regulation from a host of other forms of "market-based" government intervention, such as fiscal and monetary policies. By "regulation", we refer to direct legislation and administrative regulation of economic behavior on the market. These regulations can be divided into three categories: economic regulations designed to avoid market failure, such as market entry, competition policy, and price regulation; social regulations designed to prevent negative externalities, such as environmental and consumer safety regulations; and more generic institutional regulations based on liability law, such as IPR (Blind 2012; OECD 2016).

Innovation performance heavily relies on advances in science and technology, a feature of public goods. Ordinary markets fail to incentivize firms to produce them in as much quantity as optimally required (Schot and Steinmueller 2018), and, therefore, regulations addressing market failure and externalities can particularly influence innovation performance, for example, by creating such incentives or removing barriers. Firms are typically subject to all these types of regulations, making it difficult to analyze the effects of only one type in isolation from others. We thus focus our discussion on the effects of the general regulatory environment. This enables us to restrict our study to an extensive but well-defined literature subset.

2.1 Review of the regulatory framework in China

With China's rapid transformation from an agricultural to an industrialized economy, its regulatory framework has also undergone changes. Since its introduction in the late 1970s, regulatory reform has been an integral part of economic reforms in China. Its main goal is to reduce the governments intervention in the economy and create a unified market system with orderly competition by expanding the role of the market in resource allocation. In the process of transforming from a highly centralized regulatory state to a market economy, a strategy of incremental reform has been adopted, in contrast to the "shock therapy" approach pursued by the former Soviet Union and Eastern European countries (Zhou 2018).

The regulatory reforms of the 1990s and early 2000s enabled an expanded role of the market in major decisions on price, production, investment, market structure, and more (Yeo and Pearson 2008). The Corporate Law, enforced in 1994, paved the way for the foundation of a market environment where enterprises under different types of ownership can compete with state-owned enterprises. The government has launched a series of science and technology initiatives to match the strategic directions of enterprises. The decentralization process delegates more decision-making powers in investment approval, firm entry, revenue mobilization, and expenditure responsibilities to the lower levels of the government and grants more autonomy to state-owned enterprises in production and marketing (Lin et al. 2006).

Since China's accession to the World Trade Organization in 2001, the Chinese government has made further efforts to standardize its regulatory framework across the country, carrying out a series of regulatory reforms to strengthen competition and openness (OECD 2009). These include additional reduction in the scope of state ownership, reform of regulations among central and local governments, firmer establishment of the rule of law, and strengthening of regulatory institutions and processes. These efforts have resulted in simpler and more transparent regulation, less burdensome compliance, and more effective enforcement of laws on intellectual property rights and other areas. The incremental regulatory reforms in China can be considered successful when judged based on various indicators of economic development and living standards (Garnaut et al. 2018). Nevertheless, the strict control of the financial system, stringent market entry regulation for foreign investors, and the close ties between government authorities and state-owned enterprises continue to exist. Therefore, measures formulated by regulatory bodies at all levels need to be continuously reviewed and revised with experience and with further development of the economy.

2.2 *Regulation and innovation: A review*

Previous studies have analyzed the impacts of government regulations on innovation performance from three perspectives. First, regulation influences the direction and rate of innovation by creating markets and reshaping the competitional landscape (Crafts 2006; Blind 2012). Specifically, strict market entry regulations may hinder the introduction and diffusion of product or process innovation by reducing competitive pressure, increasing the costs of introduction and diffusion, or delaying the entry of new high-tech firms. Entrepreneurs are particularly affected by administrative regulations that create entry barriers. Countries with a quicker market entry process have seen more entries in industries that experience expansionary global demand and technology shifts (Nicoletti and Scarpetta 2003; Kaplan et al. 2011). Further, regulations on prices and competition change the pattern of the expected returns to innovation. As such, shifting from price to non-price competition could increase the incentives for the rapid adoption of product innovations (Joskow and Rose 1989). Haley and Haley (2012) argue that the patent law changes in India's pharmaceutical industry hindered the domestic efforts for innovation because uncertain property rights reduced the appropriability of returns to innovation.

Regulation may help create an overall favorable climate for certain technological trajectories to innovation by reducing the risks associated with innovation, for example the establishment of standardization or the new energy regulations. Regulation may also drive out firms that show no compliance with existing products and processes, thus spurring either compliance or circumventive innovation (Nakamura and Kajikawa 2018). Yoon et al. (2018), by analyzing cross-country panel data on 47 countries from 2002 to 2012, document that more regulations on credit, labor, and business increase the transformation of scientific knowledge into innovative, nascent entrepreneurship. Further, Blind et al. (2017) find that the impacts of regulation on innovation efficiency of firms vary with market uncertainty. Regulations have a positive impact on firms innovation efficiency in markets with low uncertainty as they create transparent and non-discriminating rules and are less susceptible to regulatory capture. The incompatibility between regulations and the underlying technologies is much lower in such markets than in highly uncertain markets, where regulations have a negative impact on firm innovation efficiency because of the greater efforts required to comply with the emerging regulatory framework.

Second, the red tape arising from strong regulations creates a compliance burden for would-be innovators (Ciccone and Papaioannou 2007; Ciriaci et al. 2019). This research stream generally considers regulation compliance costs or a "time tax" imposed on firms (De Rosa et al. 2010). Such costs, including resources and the time used for filling out paperwork, for obtaining permits from different offices, among others, reflect different opportunity costs, which are typically increasing with individual ability. More efficient agents are thus able or willing to accept more red tape.

The Schumpeterian creative destruction process is favored by a dynamic business environment (Aghion et al. 2009). High administrative entry costs, stringent product market regulation, and excessive employment protection legislation increases transaction costs and leads to less efficient reallocation of resources, damaging the most innovative and productive firms and sectors. Hence, lower levels of market and product regulation is more attractive to R&D-intensive multinationals seeking dynamic innovation ecosystems and regulatory framework that supports returns on innovative investments (Ciriaci et al. 2019). While Krammer (2009) finds a significantly negative relationship between the cost of starting up a new business and the number of granted patents, according to Amici et al. (2016), the effects of entry regulation on firms can be divided into two aspects: the time costs associated with getting permits and authorizations to start a new business (red tape costs), and the fees and duties that must be paid for this purpose (monetary costs). While lowering time costs increase the average survival rate and time of new firms, reducing monetary costs may lower it for Italian firms.

Finally, the public choice approach links regulatory intervention with resource misallocation, rent-seeking, preferentialism, and corruption, which ultimately leads to the distortion of resource allocation among firms and lowers the incentives for innovation (Duvanova 2014; Stigler 1971). Regulatory capture occurs when the interests of firms or political groups are prioritized over the interests of the public, leading to a net loss to the society as a whole; an example is lobbying a standard, which in turn influences the technological infrastructure of a particular market (Blind and Mangelsdorf 2016). Efficiency might decrease by increasing the cost of government goods and services, distortion, and creating additional competition efficiency costs (Olken and Pande 2012). Such distortion distracts entrepreneurial talent from improving productivity and directs it toward rent extraction, which lowers the product innovation level (Acemoglu and Verdier 1998; Waldemar 2012).

Overall, it is not surprising that the effects of regulation on innovation performance are mixed, implying regulation can both promote and suppress innovation. Stewart (2012) proposes that regulation affects innovation by three dimensional

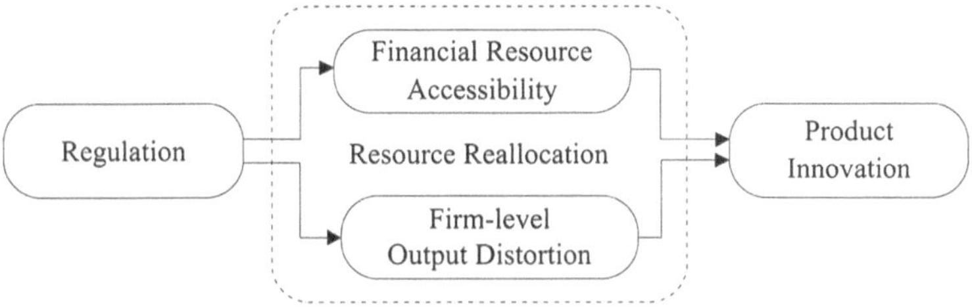

Fig. 1 Conceptual framework for the impacts of regulations on product innovation

factors, that is, flexibility, information, and stringency. Greater flexibility and more complete information generally aid innovation, while there is a trade-off between stringent compliance and the desired innovation. Studies in this field tend to adopt case studies approaches to analyze certain industries, with specific regulations (Faulkner 2009).

One important indication is that the impact of government regulations on firm performance varies in response to other factors such as political organization of structure, prevailing economic conditions, financial market, or stages of technological development. Guan and Yam (2015) argue that a centrally planned system is ineffective for the innovative performance of manufacturing firms in China. The focus of government regulations should thus shift from high centralization to a high level of freedom when approaching the technological frontier (Mahmood and Rufin 2005). Amable et al. (2016) find that the effect of product market regulation on patenting intensity increases with proximity to the technological frontier, measured by multifactor productivity, for OECD industries. While some studies investigate the impact of regulation on innovation performance for certain industries in China such as energy, telecommunications, automobiles, and pharmaceuticals, such studies still do not provide a clear picture of the overall regulation level and its interaction with innovation performance in China.

2.3 *Conceptual framework*

The above three research streams show that allocation of resources is an important mediator in relating regulations to innovation performance. Hence, we propose the analytical framework shown in Fig. 1 to identify the causality between regulations and innovation. The fundamental assumption is that regulations determine the allocation of resources that are required for product innovation across firms. Further, the regulations that create heterogeneity in the prices faced by individual producers can lead to sizeable differences in product innovation.

This idea corresponds to the two channels by which regulations influence the performance of product innovation, namely, incentive impacts and compliance costs or burdens. Essentially, this idea is in line with the theory of Carlin and Soskice

(2006), which demonstrates that, under the Schumpeter relation, with regulation increasing capital intensity, more resources are available for R&D investments. This consequently fosters innovation, while the compliance cost of regulations reduces resources for innovation in a manner similar to taxes. On the one hand, regulations influence the distribution of financial resources across incumbent firms, thereby affecting their innovative performance. Easier access to financial resources can generally foster product innovation (Barbosa and Faria 2011). From the viewpoint of public-private partnerships, Mazzucato (2013) argues that radical innovation, such as the Internet or nanotechnology, did not occur because the private sector could not find the resources to invest in it. All the government has to do is to "nudge" the private sector in the right direction.

On the other hand, regulations may cause resource misallocation in production, or output distortion, which in turn hinders product innovation. Output distortion could be high for firms that face size restrictions or high transaction costs, and low for firms that benefit from favorable regulations. Restuccia and Rogerson (2008) demonstrate that resource misallocation across firms caused by poorly designed policies can lead to aggregate productivity loss, for example, by subsidizing unproductive firms and taxing productive firms. Following this idea, Hsieh and Klenow (2009) identify a potential 30 to 50% increase in the aggregate productivity in China as a result of more efficient resource allocation. Cicala (2015) identifies asymmetric information, capital bias, and regulatory capture as important sources of regulatory distortion, and demonstrates that deregulation led to a shift toward more productive coal mines in the U.S.

By this analytical framework, we assume over-regulation causes an increase in resource misallocation, which in turn has a negative effect on product innovation. On the other hand, firms that actively respond to government regulations may gain easier access to certain financial resources, which in turn has a positive impact on product innovation. As discussed in Guan and Yam (2015), firms in China that actively comply with regulations gain more financial resources and regulatory provisions. Financial constraints have been found to be a major reason that prevents firms from investing in R&D activities (Antunes and Cavalcanti 2007), while more efficient allocation of financial resources can promote capital-intensive innovations (Blind 2012). Hence the overall impact of regulations on product innovation depends on the trade-off between the two. Generally, whichever one is stronger will largely determine whether the regulation stifles or stimulates innovation. As Wang (2018) demonstrates, too much government interference could lead to the concentration of resources among a small number of players, while too little government support would result in missing development opportunities, such as in the cases of Singapore and Hong Kong.

3 Methodology

3.1 Econometric models

According to the conceptual framework in Fig. 1, we propose three econometric models to estimate empirically the impacts of regulations on product innovation. First, we estimate the impact of regulations on the tendencies of firms to conduct product innovation using the probit specification in Eqs. 1 and 2.

$$Prob(BPI_i = 1|X) = c + ß_1 REG_i + ß_2 REGsq_i + ß\mathbf{Z_i} + e_i \quad (1)$$

$$\widehat{REG_i} = c_0 + \gamma_1 ILR_i + \gamma \mathbf{Z_i} + \varepsilon_i \quad (2)$$

where BPI_i denotes the tendency of firm i to conduct product innovation; REG_i denotes the regulation level; $REGsq_i$ is the square term of regulation level REG_i. According to Blind et al. (2017), many other factors can influence product innovation performance. For example, innovation activities are driven by the competition level. As such, Aghion et al. (2005) demonstrate an inverted U-shaped relationship between competition and innovation. Leff (1964) points out that new firms usually turn to the government for the protection of their investments and future returns. The existing economic interests depend on their longstanding associations with bureaucratic and political supporters for protection, and, therefore, firm age is relevant for their responses to regulations and innovative performance. Wang (2014) identifies the importance of R&D investment and trade choices, such as exports and imports, in improving innovative performance. Hence, the control variable set $\mathbf{Z_i}$ includes the process innovation PRC_i, the decision to conduct R&D RND_i, skill level of employees SKL_i, training TRA_i, size SIZ_i, years since established AGE_i, export ratio EXP_i, import ratio IMP_i, competition COM_i, ownership dummy, region dummy, and industry dummy.

The endogeneity problem arises because firms with better performance might also put more effort into managing their relationships with government officials. The regulation level might thus be determined by the performance of product innovation. This results in a bidirectional causality between product innovation and regulation. Rothwell (1980) demonstrates that bureaucrats have discretionary power, given a certain regulation of firms, according to their innovative performance. We address the endogeneity issue by the specification of a two-stage probit regression. Inspired by Fisman and Svensson's (2007) approach in addressing the endogeneity between corruption and growth, we use the industry-average IRA_i and location-average of regulation LRA_i (at city level) as measures for the regulation level. It is arguable that the industry and location averages are closely related to firms' practical responses to regulation but not with their product innovation performance.

In practice, we first estimate the regulation determination regression with the instruments and other explanatory variables as in Eq. 2; we then substitute the predicted regulation values into the probit estimation in the innovation tendency regression in Eq. 1.

Second, we estimate the intensity of product innovation using the ordinary least squares (OLS) and two-stage least squares (2SLS) regressions in Eqs. 3 and 4.

$$PDI_i = c + ß_1 REG_i + ß_2 REGsq_i + ß\mathbf{Z_i} + e_i \tag{3}$$

$$\widehat{REG}_i = c_0 + \gamma_1 ILR_i + \gamma\mathbf{Z_i} + \varepsilon_i \tag{4}$$

where PDI_i denotes the intensity of product innovation for firm i. The control variable set $\mathbf{Z}_i$ includes the same variables as Eq. 1. As before, we use the industry and location averages of regulation, IRA_i and LRA_i, respectively, as instruments for the regulation level in the 2SLS estimation to address the endogeneity problem.

Finally, to understand how regulation affects firm performance in terms of product innovation, we propose a simultaneous equation model (SEM) that incorporates a measure of firm-level distortions DIS_i and the accessibility of financial resources (FIN_i), as shown in Eq. 5,

$$\begin{aligned} PDI_i &= c + ß_1 REG_i + ß_2 REGsq_i + ß_3 FIN_i + ß_4 DIS_i + ß\mathbf{Z_i} + e_i \\ REG_i &= c_0 + \gamma_1 ILR_i + \gamma\mathbf{Z_i} + \varepsilon_i \\ DIS_i &= c_1 + \eta_1 REG_i + \eta_2 INV_i + \eta_3 OWN_i + \xi_i \\ FIN_i &= c_2 + \eta_4 REG_i + \eta_5 LAN_i + \eta_6 OWN_i + \upsilon_i \end{aligned} \tag{5}$$

where DIS_i represents the measure of firm-level distortions and FIN_i financial resource accessibility. The two indicators are designed to capture across-firm resource allocations, which enables us to investigate the role of resource reallocation in the observable relationship between regulation and product innovation. The distortion of resource allocation, DIS_i, is specified as a function of regulation REG_i, investment in fixed assets INV_i, and ownership dummy OWN_i. Financial resource accessibility FIN_i is specified as a function of regulation REG_i, land ownership LAN_i, and ownership dummy OWN_i. The control variable set $\mathbf{Z}_i$ includes the same variables as Eq. 1.

This specification addresses two potential impacts of regulation on innovation: the efficiency of resource allocation within and across firms, that is, the accessibility to financial resources, and production resource distortion. The prevalence of regulation distortion may increase the returns for rent-seeking compared to those of productive activities (Baumol 1990). Restuccia and Rogerson (2008) demonstrate that differences in resource allocation across establishments that differ in productivity may be an important factor accounting for cross- country differences in output per capita.

3.2 Data and measurement

The data are taken from Business Environment Enterprise Performance Survey (BEEP), conducted by the World Bank in 2012. This survey was designed to assess the impacts of government policies and practices on business activities worldwide. The sample in China was selected using stratified random sampling in 25 cities. The data provide detailed information about innovation performance and business environment, such as firm characteristics, financial performance, as well as business-government relationships, among other aspects. Table 1 summarizes the measurements of the main variables and the descriptive statistics.

Following theoretical studies on regulations, we consider regulation as a manner of time tax imposed on firms, measured by the time of senior managers in dealing

Table 1 Variables, measurements, and their descriptive statistics

Variables	Measurements	Obs.	Mean	SD	Min	Max
Product innovation	Ratio of new product to sales	2719	11.04	18.1	0	100
Innovation tendency	Binary variable indicating whether firms have new product sales	2719	.44	0.50	0	1
Regulation	Percentage of time spent by senior manager dealing with regulations	2595	1.34	3.86	0	100
Process Innovation	Percentage of establishment's annual production volume associated with new or improved processes introduced over the last three years	2719	8.93	15.61	0	100
Skill	Average education years of employees	1657	10.18	1.89	1	18
R&D	Binary variable indicating whether firms conduct R&D	2719	0.98	0.86	0	1
Size	Number of full-time employees in logarithm	2699	4.15	1.37	1.39	10.30
License	The use of foreign licenses	2719	−2.37	5.24	−9	2
Competition	Number of competitors divided by 100	2719	5.54	1.59	0	6.01
Age	Years established	2627	16.72	7.91	4	129
Export	Ratio of export to sales	2698	10.87	24.63	0	100
Import	Ratio of imported intermediate input to in puts	1690	3.78	13.38	0	100
Capital distortion	Calculated based on eq. 6	980	1.13	1.79	−4.13	12.26
Output distortion	Calculated based on eq. 7	1558	0.36	0.47	−4.29	1.9
Finance accessibility	Percentage of the firm's working capital that was borrowed from banks	2639	6.90	14.86	0	100

Notes: Missing values under Product innovation, Process innovation, R&D, and Competition are replaced with zeros, while missing values are coded as −9 for the License variable with regulations.[1] Stiglitz (2012) argues that regulations (whether restrictions or mandates) can be viewed as hidden tax/expenditure programs. Similarly, De Rosa et al. (2010) account the enforcers of regulatory requirements to a "time tax" imposed on firms. The measures adopted in this study do not directly measure the regulation magnitude imposed on firms but the heterogeneous reactions of firms in response to regulations. The rationale behind this is that the longer senior managers take to deal with regulations, the more stringent the regulatory environment is and higher the compliance costs.

We use the location and industry averages of the time needed to deal with regulations as instrumental variables to control for industry- and region-specific regulatory circumstances. Whereas regulatory environmental circumstances are beyond the choice set of individual firms, firms (managers) still have some degree of autonomy in deciding their time (as one types of resources) allocation in response to regulations, which affects firm level innovation. In China and other developing economies, this indicator incorporates the active efforts of firms in seeking better government relationships, apart from red tape, in order to obtain technical resources, government fundings, and market entry permits. As in developing markets, government behavior is one of the main potential risks (Acemoglu and Verdier 2000), policy uncertainty occurs when a firm or industry anticipates the enactment of a regulation at some time in the future. The responses of firms to regulations by firms acts as a way to hedge and safeguard against losses due to poorly designed regulations. This measurement reflects both the constraints of government regulations and the comprehensive responses of Chinese firms to regulations.

Innovation performance is measured by both the tendency to conduct product innovation and the ratio of new products to sales. Missing values under product innovation are considered to appear in the absence of new products in sales and are thus replaced by zeros. This applies to process innovation as well.

Following the pioneer work by Hsieh and Klenow (2009), we construct the distortion variables as follows:

$$\tau_{K_{si}} = \frac{\alpha_s}{1 - \alpha_s} \frac{\omega L_i}{RK_i} - 1 \tag{6}$$

where τ_{Ksi} captures capital distortion, K_i is the capital input of firm i, L_i is the labor input of firm i, ω denotes wage, α_s is the share of capital in industry s, and R is the interest rate, assumed as 10%. τ_{Ksi} is larger when a firm has more difficulties in accessing financial credit.

Output distortion reflects the additional operational cost or impediment to production caused by regulations that are not tied to capital,

[1] The survey question asked "In a typical week, over the last year, what percentage of the total senior management's time was spent on dealing with requirements imposed by government regulations?" Some examples of government regulations are taxes, customs, labor regulations, licensing and registration, including dealings with officials and completing forms.

$$\tau_{Y_{si}} = 1 - \frac{\alpha_s}{1-\alpha_s}\frac{\sigma}{\sigma-1}\frac{\omega L_i}{\mathrm{PY}_i} \tag{7}$$

where τ_{Ysi} is the output distortion, and σ is the elasticity of substitution between different firms' goods, which is assumed to be 3, following Hsieh and Klenow (2009).

The measure of distortions reflects the consequences of government regulations on firm production. $\tau_{Ksi} > 0$ or $\tau_{Ysi} > 0$ implies firms face capital or output burdens, which may take the form of taxes, in terms of either finance or time. These firms thus produce less than their counterfactual optimal levels. If $\tau_{Ksi} < 0$, $\tau_{Ysi} < 0$, firms are experiencing preferential regulations, for example, R&D subsidies on certain technologies, and are expected to produce more than their counterfactual optimal level, that is, regulation may distort firms' production behaviors and lead to resource misallocation across firms.

As seen from the correlation coefficients in Table 2, the time spent dealing with government regulations (*REG*) presents a significantly positive relationship with the intensity of product innovation (*PRD*) and the accessibility of financial resources (*FIN*), but does not significantly correlate with output distortion (*DIS*). The time spent dealing with government regulations (*REG*) significantly correlates with process innovation (*PRC*), skill level of employees (*SKL*), R&D investment (*RND*), size (*SIZ*), export (*EXP*), and import (*IMP*), while it does not show a significant correlation with training (*TRA*), competition(*COM*), and time established (*AGE*).

To review comprehensively the relationships among regulation, resource allocation, and product innovation, we present a scatter plot with the three variables at the firm and industrial levels in Fig. 2. Figure 2 (a) indicates an inverted U-shaped relationship between the time spent dealing with regulations and the intensity of product innovation. We then calculate the average capital distortion, product innovation, and time spent dealing with regulations for each industry. Figure 2 (b) shows that the more time is spent dealing with government regulations, the higher the level of product innovation at the industrial level and the higher the level of capital distortion. This preliminary evidence is consistent with the hypothesis of econometric model 5.

4 Results

We conduct empirical analyses to identify the causality between government regulations, resource allocation, and product innovation by applying the econometric models in section 3.1 to the survey data.

Table 2 Cross-correlation table

	PRD	REG	PRC	SKL	RND	TRA	SIZ	LIC	COM	AGE	EXP	IMP	DIS
REG	0.12***												
PRC	0.29***	0.05*											
SKL	0.06*	0.09***	0.09***										
RND	0.40***	0.13***	0.29***	0.12***									
TRA	0.08***	0.03	0.10***	0.04	0.13***	1.00							
SIZ	0.07***	0.04*	0.21***	0.06*	0.24***	0.19***							
LIC	−0.10***	−0.06**	0.35***	−0.13***	−0.18***	0.01	0.19***						
COM	−0.06**	−0.01	0.20***	−0.11***	−0.13***	- 0.00	0.12***	0.62***					
AGE	−0.01	−0.00	0.01	0.05*	0.02	0.02	0.25***	0.04*	0.06**				
EXP	0.03	0.10***	0.12***	0.01	0.08**	0.03	0.15***	0.10***	−0.11***	0.00			
IMP	0.07**	0.08**	0.06*	0.08***	0.07**	0.02	0.10***	−0.15***	−0.14***	−0.02	0.32***		
DIS	−0.02	0.00	−0.00	0.08**	0.07**	0.10***	−0.02	−0.01	0.04	0.04	−0.10***	−0.02	
FIN	0.11***	0.11***	0.10***	0.14***	0.15***	0.01	0.18***	0.01	−0.05**	0.02	0.07***	0.04	0.02

Notes: Significance levels: * $p < 0.05$, ** $p < 0.01$, *** $p < 0.001$

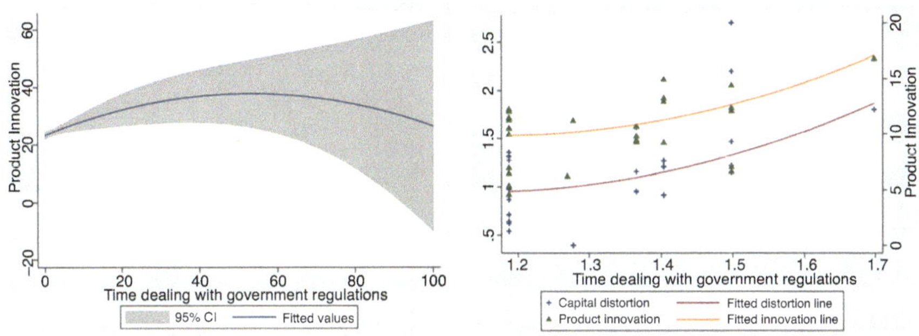

Fig. 2 Regulation and product innovation

4.1 Impact of regulation on the decision of product innovation

First, the impact of regulations on the tendency to conduct product innovation is estimated using probit and instrument variable probit (IV-probit) specifications. The dependent variable is a binary variable indicating whether firms have new product revenues. Robust standard errors are used to address heteroskedasticity. Table 3 presents the estimation results generated by both the probit regression in columns (1) and (2) and IV-probit regression in columns (3) and (4). In both cases, the squared regulation $REGsq_i$ is incorporated into the estimation separately. The coefficients of the instrument variables industry-average and location-average are significant in the IV-probit regression. The Wald test rejects the null hypothesis of no endogeneity and, therefore, the estimation of the IV-probit regression is valid.

As per Table 3, the coefficient of the squared regulation (*Regulationsq*) is significant in both the probit regression (column (2)) and the IV-probit one (column (4)). This indicates that the time spent dealing with government regulations has a concave effect on firms' tendency to conduct product innovation, that is, firms that spend more time in dealing with government regulations, within a rational level, are more likely to conduct product innovation. However, after this time reaches a threshold point, it has negative effects on innovation decisions. Based on the estimation results, the IV-probit regression incorporating the squared term of regulation in column (4) is the most appropriate estimation. Process innovation and R&D investment show significantly positive effects on firms' tendency to conduct product innovation. Further, state- owned firms are less likely to conduct product innovation compared to private firms (−0.513). However, training, time since established, skill level of workers, competition, and trade variables do not show significant effects on the decision of firms to conduct product innovation.

It is not appropriate to interpret the coefficients in the probit and the IV-probit regressions directly, and, therefore, their marginal effects are computed at the sample means and presented in Table 4. Based on the two-stage probit estimation in column (4), there is an inverted U- shaped relationship between regulation and product

Table 3 Impact of regulation on product innovation decision

	(1)	(2)	(3)	(4)
	Probit	Probit	IV-probit	IV-probit
Regulation	0.042*	0.121***	0.110***	0.175**
	(1.90)	(4.20)	(2.68)	(2.25)
Regulationsq		−0.004***		−0.006**
		(−3.93)		(−2.07)
Process innovation	0.012***	0.012***	0.012***	0.012***
	(4.92)	(4.92)	(5.03)	(4.87)
R&D	1.180***	1.192***	1.141***	1.184***
	(14.98)	(15.04)	(12.92)	(14.66)
Skill	0.005	0.005	0.008	0.002
	(0.21)	(0.21)	(0.34)	(0.10)
Training	0.162	0.154	0.152	0.147
	(1.50)	(1.42)	(1.44)	(1.36)
Size	0.027	0.023	0.060*	0.020
	(0.82)	(0.70)	(1.93)	(0.62)
Age	−0.003	−0.003	−0.003	−0.003
	(−0.55)	(−0.61)	(−0.71)	(−0.64)
Export	−0.002	−0.002	−0.001	−0.002
	(−1.06)	(−1.15)	(−0.84)	(−1.24)
Import	0.002	0.002	0.002	0.001
	(0.68)	(0.56)	(0.66)	(0.48)
Competition	0.011	0.012	0.007	0.012
	(0.75)	(0.85)	(0.77)	(0.82)
Foreign license	0.307	0.115		0.092
	(0.52)	(0.21)		(0.17)
State-owned	−0.531***	−0.534***	−0.504***	−0.513***
	(−2.95)	(−2.96)	(−3.06)	(−2.89)
Region	Yes	Yes	Yes	Yes
Industry	Yes	Yes	Yes	Yes
Constant	−2.180***	−2.076***	−1.963***	−2.050***
	(−3.37)	(−3.36)	(−5.33)	(−3.29)
Industry-average			0.927***	0.504***
			(7.76)	(9.15)
Location-average			0.631***	0.240**
			(2.86)	(2.15)
N	1549	1549	1549	1549
AIC	1606.576	1597.572	9030.589	6797.607
BIC	1740.210	1736.551	9292.511	7091.602
athrho2			−0.200*	−0.077
			(−1.81)	(−0.74)
lnsigma2			0.950***	0.241***
			(10.30)	(4.99)

Notes: Robust standard errors. *t* statistics in parentheses. Significance levels: * $p < 0.10$, ** $p < 0.05$, *** $p < 0.01$

Table 4 Marginal effects of regulation on product innovation decisions

	(1)	(2)	(3)	(4)
	Probit	Probit	IV-probit	IV-probit
Regulation	0.017*	0.048**	0.013	0.045*
	(1.90)	(4.19)	(0.82)	(1.48)
Regulationsq		−0.002***		−0.002*
		(−3.92)		(−1.32)
Process innovation	0.005***	0.005***	0.005***	0.005***
	(4.90)	(4.90)	(5.13)	(4.84)
R&D (d)	0.443***	0.448***	0.449***	0.448***
	(16.72)	(16.82)	(15.01)	(16.50)
Skill	0.002	0.002	0.008	0.002
	(0.21)	(0.21)	(0.86)	(0.23)
Training(d)	0.063	0.060	0.064	0.061
	(1.52)	(1.44)	(1.58)	(1.47)
Size	0.010	0.009	0.025**	0.010
	(0.82)	(0.70)	(2.01)	(0.74)
Age	−0.001 (−0.55)	−0.001 (−0.61)	−0.001 (−0.71)	−0.001 (−0.64)
Export	−0.001	−0.001	-0.000	−0.001
	(−1.06)	(−1.15)	(−0.64)	(−1.14)
Import	0.001	0.001	0.001	0.001
	(0.68)	(0.56)	(0.83)	(0.56)
Competition	0.004	0.005	0.006	0.012
	(0.75)	(0.85)	(1.09)	(0.87)
Foreign licenses (d)	0.341	0.269		0.265
	(1.63)	(1.30)		(1.27)
State-owned (d)	−0.192***	-0.193***	−0.195***	-0.192***
	(−3.34)	(−3.36)	(−3.52)	(−3.32)
N	1549	1549	1549	1549
AIC	1606.576	1597.572	9030.589	6797.607
BIC	1740.210	1736.551	9292.511	7091.602

Notes: Robust standard errors. t statistics in parentheses. Marginal effects are estimated at the sample means. (d) stands for discrete change of dummy variable from 0 to 1. Significance levels: $^{*}p < 0.10$, $^{**}p < 0.05$, $^{***}p < 0.01$

innovation decisions. The turning point is 11.25, that is, when senior managers spend more than 11.25% of their time in dealing with regulations, firms' tendency to sell new products decreases, a situation faced by approximately 1.8% of the sample firms (46). R&D investment significantly improves firms' tendency to sell new products by 0.45, while process innovation improves this tendency by 0.005.

Again, compared to private firms, state-owned firms are less likely to conduct product innovation (− 0.192). As before, training, time established, skill level of workers, competition, and trade variables do not show significant effects on the decision of firms to conduct product innovation. The inverted U-shaped relationship suggests that actively dealing with regulations is associated with a higher innovation probability when the time spent on regulations is within a rational level. However, an environment characterized by over-regulation can hinder firm innovation, and firms that spend too much time in dealing with regulations experience decreases in their tendency to product innovation.

4.2 Impacts of regulation on product innovation intensity

We estimate the effects of regulation on product innovation intensity based on Eqs. 3 and 4 and show the results in Table 5. The control variables are gradually incorporated into the OLS estimation in order to justify the validation of those variables. Robust standard errors are used to address the heteroskedasticity problem. The adjusted R^2 increases from 0.071 to 0.346 in the OLS estimation, suggesting that adding more variables increases the goodness-of-fit and explanatory power of the model. Hence, we adopt the entire variable set to conduct instrument 2SLS estimation in the last two columns. Instrument variables, that is, the industry-average and location-average level of regulation, show significantly positive effects on the regulation variable. The Wald test rejects the null hypothesis of no endogeneity on regulation, and a weak instrument test rejects the null hypothesis of weak instruments. Hence, the instrument 2SLS estimation including the squared item of regulation is preferred.

As shown in Table 5, regulation has positive effects on product innovation intensity for all regressions in question. The squared term of regulation shows significantly negative signs in both the OLS and 2SLS estimations, indicating an inverted U-shaped relationship between the time spent dealing with regulations and product innovation performance. The trend is similar to that in the previous probit regression. The turning point for regulations in the 2SLS estimation is 14.4, slightly higher than the 11.25 estimated by the IV-probit regression. Senior managers in 42 firms (1.6%) in the sample spend more than 14.4% of their time on government regulations. The result is in line with the study by D'Este et al. (2012), which distinguishes between deterring and revealing effects of different barriers of regulations on the innovative performance of firms, and suggests that deterring effects are more prominent for firms that are heavily engaged in innovation. They reveal a non-linear relationship between market barriers and innovative performance of firms: which effect—learning or deterring—is stronger depends on the specific phase in the innovation trajectory.

As before, both process innovation and R&D investment significantly improve product innovation performance (0.312 and 8.397, respectively). The ratio of exports to sales shows a negative effect on product innovation intensity. This result is consistent with Wang (2014), who argues that exports show negative effects on learning and productivity improvement in labor-intensive sectors in China. Training, firm age, skill level of employees, competition, imports, license, and ownership variables do not show significant effects on product innovation intensity.

Table 5 Impacts of regulation on product innovation intensity

	(1)	(2)	(3)	(4)	(5)	(6)	(7)
	OLS	OLS	OLS	OLS	OLS	2SLS	2SLS
Regulation	0.570**	0.460***	0.603***	0.562***	0.976***	1.890***	3.312***
	(4.15)	(3.85)	(3.18)	(3.17)	(3.39)	(4.57)	(4.32)
Regulationsq					−0.022*		−0.115**
					(−1.68)		(−3.69)
Process innovation		0.409**	0.339**	0.318***	0.318***	0.306***	0.312***
		(11.16)	(8.42)	(8.02)	(8.02)	(13.52)	(14.01)
R&D			9.192***	8.624***	8.638***	7.952***	8.397***
			(9.61)	(9.22)	(9.23)	(9.36)	(10.21)
Skill			0.184	−0.005	−0.013	−0.224	−0.144
			(0.76)	(−0.02)	(−0.05)	(−1.00)	(−0.66)
Size			0.107 (0.34)	−0.256 (−0.81)	−0.283 (−0.90)	−0.203 (−0.63)	−0.374 (−1.16)
Age			−0.055	−0.053	−0.054	−0.062	−0.064
			(−1.34)	(−1.31)	(−1.34)	(−1.28)	(−1.34)
Export			−0.029*	−0.038**	−0.039**	−0.045***	−0.048***
			(−1.76)	(−2.25)	(−2.32)	(−2.74)	(−2.89)
Import			0.009	0.004	0.003	−0.004	−0.008
			(0.29)	(0.13)	(0.09)	(−0.14)	(−0.25)
Training			0.238	0.287	0.212	0.157	−0.163
			(0.22)	(0.28)	(0.20)	(0.14)	(−0.14)
Competition			−0.056	−0.109	−0.104	−0.200	−0.122
			(−0.38)	(−0.75)	(−0.71)	(−1.33)	(−0.84)
Foreign license				11.207***	10.255***	17.085***	8.838*
				(2.90)	(2.87)	(3.36)	(1.84)

(continued)

Table 5 (continued)

	(1)	(2)	(3)	(4)	(5)	(6)	(7)
	OLS	OLS	OLS	OLS	OLS	2SLS	2SLS
State-owned	−5.492**	−2.597*	−0.289	−0.048	0.055	0.387	0.681
	(−3.79)	(−1.87)	(−0.25)	(−0.04)	(0.05)	(−0.03)	(0.03)
Industry	Yes	Yes	Yes	Yes	Yes	Yes	Yes
Region	Yes	Yes	Yes	Yes	Yes	Yes	Yes
Constant	5.225**	0.363	−2.451	−3.868	−3.127	−8.423	−2.011
	(3.17)	(0.21)	(−0.69)	(−0.79)	(−0.66)	(−1.42)	(−0.35)
N	2594	2594	1549	1549	1549	1549	1549
R^2	0.071	0.171	0.319	0.344	0.346	0.302	0.313

Notes: Robust standard errors. *t* statistics in parentheses. Significance levels: $^{*}p < 0.10$, $^{**}p < 0.05$, $^{***}p < 0.01$

4.3 *Impact of regulation on product innovation via resources allocation*

As previously discussed, regulation may create rent for bureaucrats, induce resource misallocation, and increase the size of the bureaucracy. Therefore, we investigate the potential impacts of regulation on product innovation via resource allocation using simultaneous equation model shown in Eq. 5. The estimation results are described in Table 6 and the path diagram in SEM (2) is illustrated in Fig. 3.

As shown in Table 6, column (2), the squared term of regulation does not show a significant effect on product innovation. A possible explanation is that resource

Table 6 Regulation effects on product innovation through resources allocation

	SEM (1)		SEM (2)	
- > Product innovation				
Regulation	0.640^{***}	(4.37)	0.747^{***}	(2.58)
Regulationsq			−0.006	(−0.43)
Finance	0.055^{*}	(1.86)	0.054^{*}	(1.84)
Distortion	-1.573^{*}	(−1.88)	-1.576^{*}	(−1.88)
Process innovation	0.322^{***}	(14.31)	0.323^{***}	(14.31)
R&D	8.363^{***}	(9.98)	8.367^{***}	(9.99)
Training	0.949	(0.84)	0.921	(0.82)
Size	-0.573^{*}	(−1.74)	-0.581^{*}	(−1.76)
Age	−0.057	(−1.20)	−0.057	(−1.20)
Export	-0.034^{**}	(−2.08)	-0.034^{**}	(−2.09)
Import	0.007	(0.24)	0.007	(0.23)
Foreign-owned	11.700^{**}	(2.42)	11.369^{**}	(2.32)
Skill	−0.231	(−1.07)	−0.233	(−1.08)
Competition	−0.048	(−0.32)	−0.047	(−0.32)
Constant	−2.125	(−0.36)	−1.864	(−0.31)
Regulation - > Finance accessibility	0.381^{***}	(2.83)	0.381^{***}	(2.83)
Foreign-owned - > Finance accessibility	-4.807^{***}	(−2.62)	-4.807^{***}	(−2.62)
Land ownership - > Finance accessibility	0.001	(0.07)	0.001	(0.07)
Regulation - > Distortion	0.002	(0.41)	0.002	(0.41)
State-owned - > Distortion	0.282^{***}	(4.53)	0.282^{***}	(4.53)
Investment in fixed assets - > Distortion	0.149	(0.86)	0.149	(0.86)
Industry-average - > Regulation	0.944^{***}	(14.90)	0.944^{***}	(14.90)
Location-average - > Regulation	0.750^{***}	(3.66)	0.750^{***}	(3.66)
var(e.PRD)	192.469^{***}	(26.57)	192.444^{***}	(26.57)
var(e.REG)	6.084^{***}	(26.57)	6.084^{***}	(26.57)
var(e.FIN)	181.164^{***}	(26.57)	181.164^{***}	(26.57)
var(e.DIS)	0.206^{***}	(26.57)	0.206^{***}	(26.57)
N	1412		1412	

Notes: Robust standard errors. *z* statistics in parentheses. Significance levels: $^{*}p < 0.10$, $^{**}p < 0.05$, $^{***}p < 0.01$

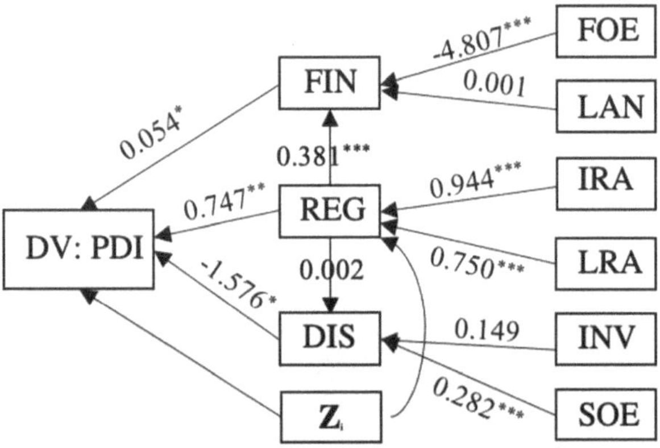

Fig. 3 Path diagram of simultaneous equation model

allocation variables mitigate the negative impacts of regulation to a certain degree. As such, regulation shows a significantly positive effect on product innovation (0.774). Firms that actively deal with government regulations, identified as spending more time in dealing with regulations, have easier access to financial resources (0.381), which in turn increases product innovation intensity (0.054).

Output distortion has a significantly negative effect on product innovation (−1.576), while regulation does not show a significant effect on output distortion. The latter case is inconsistent with the hypothesis, implying regulation does not cause significant out distortion. However, previous studies present inconsistent results on the impact of regulation on distortion. The insignificant effect of regulation on distortion is assumed to be related to the measurement of regulation in our analysis. The measure of regulation captures both the stringency of government regulations and the efforts of firms in dealing with regulations, and these two aspects have completely opposite impacts on resource distortion. More stringent regulation can act as a form of tax and lead to resource misallocation, suggesting that the regulation variable is assumed to cause higher level distortions for firms. However, firms actively dealing with regulations are more likely to build better political connections and obtain more insider information and, consequently, are able to obtain more resources and re-direct them toward compliance innovation. As a result, more time spent dealing with regulations can negatively correlate with firm-level distortion. Therefore, the two opposite driving forces can result in an overall insignificant relationship between regulation and distortion.

Meanwhile, different firm ownership types exhibit various performance levels in resource allocation as follows. Foreign-owned firms are less likely to obtain financial resources in China (−4.874), while state-owned firms experience a higher level of output distortion (0.282). R&D investment presents a significantly positive effect on product innovation intensity. Firm size and export level have significantly negative effects on product innovation intensity. Training, time established, skill level of employees, competition, import, license, and ownership variables do not show significant effects on product innovation intensity. Consequently, our study confirms that resource reallocation is an important channel through which regulation can affect product innovation.

4.4 *Robustness check*

We conduct a robustness check by including the distortion variables, accessibility to financial resources, and their interaction items with regulations into a 2SLS estimation. The results are shown in Table 7. The first column shows the 2SLS estimation with output distortion and its interaction term with regulation, and the second column presents the 2SLS estimation with financial resource accessibility and its interaction term with regulation.

As per Table 7, column (3), the 2SLS estimation confirms the results of the SEMs, with significantly negative coefficients for the squared term of regulation. The turning point for regulation is 17.9, higher than those in the previous IV-probit and 2SLS analyses without resource allocation variables. While easier access to financial resources significantly improves the performance of product innovation, its interaction term with regulation does not show a significant effect.

The interaction term between output distortion and regulation presents a significantly negative effect on product innovation intensity, implying that, given a certain regulation level, output distortion will impede product innovation. Similar to the above analyses, process innovation and R&D investment have significantly positive effects (0.319 and 8.229, respectively), while export and size have significantly negative effects (0.039 and 0.737, respectively). Training, time established, skill level of employees, competition, import, license, and ownership variables do not show significant effects on product innovation intensity.

Additionally, the estimation results for the tendency to conduct product innovation using the IV-probit regression are similar to those of the 2SLS regression on product innovation intensity. This indicates the robustness of the estimation.

5 Conclusions and discussion

5.1 *Conclusion*

The aim of this study is to understand how Chinese firms respond to government regulation in terms of product innovation. Unlike the majority of studies that investigate the impact of certain regulations on innovation performance using anecdotal evidence, this paper investigates the regulation level in China and analyzes its impacts on resource allocation, which plays an important role in firm performance in terms of product innovation. Utilizing Business Environment Performance data collected by the World Bank in 2012, we obtain the following research findings

Table 7 Impact of regulation on product innovation via resource allocation

	(1) 2SLS	(2) 2SLS	(3) 2SLS
Regulation	3.894***	3.366***	3.793***
	(4.04)	(3.74)	(3.65)
Regulationsq	−0.115***	−0.108***	−0.106***
	(−3.31)	(−3.42)	(−2.98)
Distortion	0.174		−0.038
	(0.16)		(−0.04)
Distortion*Regulation	−1.652***		−1.484***
	(−2.76)		(−2.67)
Finance		0.047	0.068*
		(1.36)	(1.92)
Finance*Regulation		−0.021	−0.017
		(−1.44)	(−1.20)
Process innovation	0.313***	0.324***	0.319***
	(13.52)	(14.11)	(13.57)
Training	−0.227	0.590	0.542
	(−0.19)	(0.51)	(0.46)
R&D	8.374***	8.404***	8.229***
	(9.66)	(10.05)	(9.44)
Size	−0.579*	−0.494	−0.737**
	(−1.69)	(−1.50)	(−2.12)
Competition	−0.099	−0.150	−0.101
	(−0.64)	(−1.01)	(−0.65)
Age	−0.073	−0.056	−0.065
	(−1.46)	(−1.15)	(−1.30)
Export	−0.038**	−0.051***	−0.039**
	(−2.21)	(−3.01)	(−2.28)
Import	−0.009	−0.003	−0.003
	(−0.28)	(−0.11)	(−0.09)
Foreign license	10.086**	10.075**	11.022**
	(2.06)	(1.99)	(2.15)
Skill	−0.270	−0.209	−0.352
	(−1.19)	(−0.95)	(−1.55)
State-owned	2.021	1.007	2.477
	(0.97)	(0.51)	(1.17)
Region	Yes	Yes	Yes
Industry	Yes	Yes	Yes
Constant	−2.169	−2.892	−2.398
	(−0.36)	(−0.48)	(−0.39)
N	1434	1522	1412
R^2	0.304	0.318	0.312

Notes: t statistics in parentheses. Significance levels: $^{*}p < 0.10$, $^{**}p < 0.05$, $^{***}p < 0.01$

regarding the impact of regulation on product innovation performance by using instrumental variable regression and simultaneous equation modeling.

First, we identify an inverted U-shaped relationship between regulation and product innovation in China, that is, regulation plays a positive role in promoting innovation within a threshold, and the more actively firms respond to regulation, which we express as more time spent dealing with regulation by senior managers, the better the product innovation performance experienced by firms. However, after a threshold, the situation reverses. The turning point of the regulation variable is approximately 14.4, which implies that 1.7% of the sample firms experience side effects due to regulation. During the period covered by the survey, most firms spent time on government regulations within the threshold, implying that, in China, regulation plays an overall positive role in influencing firms innovative behaviors. These findings are in line with studies addressing the managerial ties–innovation link (Gao et al. 2017). In other words, the institutional void in China force managers to rely on personal ties and connections to substitute for formal institutional support. Social network theory suggests that managerial ties play a "conduit" role by providing opportunities to approach external resources. Nevertheless, over- regulation or too much time spent dealing with government regulations may have a negative effect. For example, Wang and Chung (2013) argue that political ties hinder the relationship between inter-functional coordination and innovation in China.

Second, regulation influences firm innovation performance via the allocation of financial resources among firms. Consistent with the posited hypothesis, actively coping with regulation, measured as spending more time in dealing with regulations, facilitates firms' access to financial resources in China, which accordingly promotes product innovation. This finding confirms the arguments by De Massis et al. (2018) and Ayyagari et al. (2011), who state that externally financed investment is positively related to firm innovation. Meanwhile, this result implies that private firms in China have less access to the formal banking system, possibly due to the insufficient enforcement of enterprise law and to information asymmetry (Mayer 2010). Further, financial friction distorts entry and technology adoption decisions, generating dispersion in the returns to capital across existing producers (Midrigan and Xu 2014).

Finally, output distortion significantly impedes product innovation performance, but regulation has no measurable effect on output distortion. The latter finding occurs because the measurement of regulation in this study captures both the stringency of government regulations and the heterogeneous efforts of firms in dealing with these regulations. More stringent regulation is fundamentally associated with more severe output distortion. For example, Ranasinghe (2014) and Fisman and Allende (2010) confirm the various effects of regulation on output distortion for industry structure and inter-sectoral allocations. However, firms actively dealing with regulations are more likely to establish closer political connections and obtain more insider information, which in turn leads to easier access to certain resources. The ultimate impact of regulation on output distortion is shown as a net effect of both positive and negative influences. Nevertheless, our results confirm that regulations result in resource reallocations across firms and, accordingly, affect the innovative performance of firms.

5.2 Discussion

Our findings imply that actively dealing with regulations is associated with higher innovation probability and intensity when it is within a rational level. However, an over-regulating environment potentially increases resource misallocation, which hinders firm innovation. When firms spend an appropriate amount of time or resources in dealing with regulations, the incentive impact of regulation, that is, easier access to financial resources, dominates the ultimate effects of regulation on product innovation. Firms spending too much time in dealing with regulations may direct talent and resources towards rent extraction, and returns to resources are maximized by appropriating wealth rather than by product innovation. Under these circumstances, resource misallocation and output distortion overtake the incentive impact of regulation. Hence, the impact of regulation on product innovation ultimate depends on the trade-off between these two aspects.

Theoretically, we can associate this inverted U-shaped relationship with a balanced relationship between transaction costs and risks. One of the standard arguments for regulation is that it economizes on transactions costs (Stiglitz 2012). Regulation thus stimulates product innovation by reducing transaction costs in the vertical transactions between the state and firms, such as influencing input choices, for example, capital.

An important feature for firms to conduct innovation is "risk". Mazzucato (2013) argue that the main task for the government to stimulate innovation is to regulate the risk-reward nexus, achieving a balance between risk socialization and reward privatization. Many government regulations are designed to absorb risk and reduce the risk exposure of firms and consumers. The time and resources spent by firms in complying with such regulations are essentially translated as dealing with the risk associated with innovation and, therefore, this may spur either compliance or circumventive innovation.

However, when firms spend too much time or resources in dealing with regulations, either caused by poor-quality regulation or by their own efforts at rent-seeking or building political connections, regulation increases compliance costs and leads to unnecessary complexity and the associated uncertainty of regulatory obligations. In this case, regulation increases transaction costs, which can cause firms to divert resources from innovative activities to compliance.

Our results must be viewed in light of the study's limitations. First, regulation is measured as the time spent dealing with regulations. We assume this indicator includes the efforts to deal with red tape and build government relationships, as well as managerial ties. However, these different activities are not separately analyzed. Second, the research is based on cross-sectional data. As with all cross-sectional analyses, our results suffer from endogeneity bias by arguing the causal relationship between product innovation and regulation. Although we apply instrument 2SLS and a simultaneous equation model to address endogeneity, a longitudinal structure would reveal the dynamic changes in regulations and their impacts over time. Finally, regulation affects the incentives to innovate in various ways and interacts with all phases of the innovation cycle. As we limit our research scope to product innovation, the impacts of regulation on process innovation and its interaction with product innovation would be a future research agenda.

Publisher's note Springer Nature remains neutral with regard to jurisdictional claims in published maps and institutional affiliations.

Acknowledgments The authors are grateful for discussion with the attendants in the International Conference on "Innovation, Institutions, and Governance" 2017 in Tallinn and the 17th International Schumpeter Society Conference on "Innovation, Catch-up, and Sustainable Development" 2018 in Seoul. The usual disclaimer applies.

Funding information This study was funded by the National Natural Science Foundation of China (grant number 71503247 and 71804140), the Beijing Social Science Foundation (grant number 15JDJGA040), and Institutes of Science and Development, Chinese Academy of Sciences (grant number Y9X3581H).

Compliance with ethical standards

Conflict of interests The authors declare that they have no conflict of interest.

References

Acemoglu D, Verdier T (1998) Property rights, corruption and the allocation of talent: a general equilibrium approach. Econ. J. 108(450):1381–1403

Acemoglu D, Verdier T (2000) The choice between market failures and corruption. Am Econ Rev 90(1):194–211

Aghion P, Bloom N, Blundell R, Griffith R, Howitt P (2005) Competition and innovation: an inverted-U relationship. Q J Econ 120(2):701–728

Aghion P, Blundell R, Griffith R, Howitt P, Prantl S (2009) The effects of entry on incumbent innovation and productivity. Rev Econ Stat 91(1):20–32

Amable B, Ledezma I, Robin S (2016) Product market regulation, innovation, and productivity. Res Policy 45(10):2087–2104

Amici M, Giacomelli S, Manaresi F, Tonello M (2016) Red tape reduction and firm entry: new evidence from an Italian reform. Econ Lett 146(C):24–27

Antunes A, Cavalcanti T (2007) Start up costs, limited enforcement, and the hidden economy. Eur Econ Rev 51(1):203–224

Ayyagari M, Demirgüç-Kunt A, Maksimovic V (2011) Firm innovation in emerging markets: the role of finance, governance, and competition. J Financ Quant Anal 46(6):1545–1580

Barbosa N, Faria AP (2011) Innovation across Europe: how important are institutional differences? Res Policy 40(9):1157–1169

Baumol W (1990) Entrepreneurship: productive, unproductive, and destructive. J Polit Econ 98 (5):893–921

Blind K (2012) The influence of regulations on innovation: a quantitative assessment for OECD countries. Res Policy 41(2):391–400

Blind, K & Mangelsdorf, A (2016). Motives to standardize: empirical evidence from Germany, *Technovation* **48–49**(Supplement C): 13–24

Blind K, Petersen SS, Riillo CA (2017) The impact of standards and regulation on innovation in uncertain markets. Res Policy 46(1):249–264

Carlin W, Soskice DW (2006) Macroeconomics: imperfections, institutions and policies. Oxford University Press, Oxford

Cicala S (2015) When does regulation distort costs? Lessons from fuel procurement in US electricity generation. Am Econ Rev 105(1):411–444

Ciccone A, Papaioannou E (2007) Red tape and delayed entry. J Eur Econ Assoc 5(2–3):444–458

Ciriaci D, Grassano N, Vezzani A (2019) Regulations and location choices of top R&D investors worldwide. Struct Chang Econ Dyn 49:29–42

Crafts N (2006) Regulation and productivity performance. Oxf Rev Econ Policy 22(2):186–202

D'Este P, Iammarino S, Savona M, von Tunzelmann N (2012) What hampers innovation? Revealed barriers versus deterring barriers. Res Policy 41(2):482–488

De Massis A, Audretsch D, Uhlaner L, Kammerlander N (2018) Innovation with limited resources: management lessons from the German mittelstand. J Prod Innov Manag 35(1):125–146

De Rosa, D., Gooroochurn, N. & Gorg, H. (2010). Corruption and productivity: firm-level evidence from the BEEPS survey, *Policy Research working paper WPS 5348*, World Bank

Duvanova D (2014) Economic regulations, red tape, and bureaucratic corruption in post-communist economies. World Dev 59:298–312

Faulkner A (2009) Regulatory policy as innovation: constructing rules of engagement for a technological zone of tissue engineering in the European Union. Res Policy 38(4):637–646

Fisman R, Allende VS (2010) Regulation of entry and the distortion of industrial organization. J Appl Econ 13:91–111

Fisman R, Svensson J (2007) Are corruption and taxation really harmful to growth? Firm level evidence. J Dev Econ 83(1):63–75

Gao Y, Shu C, Jiang X, Gao S, Page AL (2017) Managerial ties and product innovation: the moderating roles of macro- and micro-institutional environments. Long Range Plan 50 (2):168–183

Garnaut R, Song L, Fang C (eds) (2018) *China's 40 Years of Reform and Development: 1978–2018*. ANU Press, Canberra

Guan J, Yam RC (2015) Effects of government financial incentives on firms' innovation performance in China: evidences from Beijing in the 1990s. Res Policy 44(1):273–282

Haley GT, Haley UCV (2012) The effects of patent-law changes on innovation: the case of India's pharmaceutical industry. Technol Forecast Soc Chang 79(4):607–619

Hsieh C-T, Klenow PJ (2009) Misallocation and manufacturing TFP in China and India. Q J Econ 124(4):1403–1448

Joskow PL, Rose NL (1989) The effects of economic regulation, in Vol. 2 of *Handbook of Industrial Organization*. Elsevier, pp 1449–1506

Kaplan DS, Piedra E, Seira E (2011) Entry regulation and business start-ups: evidence from Mexico. J Public Econ 95(11):1501–1515

Krammer SM (2009) Drivers of national innovation in transition: evidence from a panel of eastern European countries. Res Policy 38(5):845–860

Lee, K (2016). Economic catch-up and technological leapfrogging, Books, Edward Elgar Publishing

Leff NH (1964) Economic development through bureaucratic corruption. Am Behav Sci 8(3):8–14

Li L (2018) China's manufacturing locus in 2025: with a comparison of "made-in-China 2025" and "industry 4.0". Technol Forecast Soc Chang 135:66–74

Lin J, Tao R, Liu M (2006) Decentralization and local governance in China's economic transition. In: *Decentralization and Local Governance in Developing Countries: A Comparative Perspective*. The MIT Press, pp 305–327

Mahmood IP, Rufin C (2005) Government's dilemma: the role of government in imitation and innovation. Acad Manag Rev 30(2):338–360

Mayer J (2010) The finance of innovative investment in emerging economies. Palgrave Macmillan UK, London, pp 147–169

Mazzucato, M. (2013). The entrepreneurial state: debunking public Vs. *Private Sector Myths*, anthem frontiers of global political economy, Anthem Press
Midrigan V, Xu DY (2014) Finance and misallocation: evidence from plant-level data. Am Econ Rev 104(2):422–458
Nakamura H, Kajikawa Y (2018) Regulation and innovation: how should small unmanned aerial vehicles be regulated? Technol Forecast Soc Chang 128:262–274
Nicoletti G, Scarpetta S (2003) Regulation, productivity and growth: OECD evidence. Econ Policy 18(36):9–72
OECD (2009) OECD reviews of regulatory reform: China 2009. OECD Publishing, Paris
OECD (2016). Regulatory reform and innovation, Technical report, OECD
Olken BA, Pande R (2012) Corruption in developing countries. Annual Review of Economics 4 (1):479–509
Pigou, A (1938). The economics of welfare, Macmillan and Co., Ltd
Ranasinghe A (2014) Impact of policy distortions on firm-level innovation, productivity dynamics and TFP. *Journal of Economic Dynamics and Control* **46**(Supplement C):114–129
Restuccia D, Rogerson R (2008) Policy distortions and aggregate productivity with heterogeneous plants. Rev Econ Dyn 11(4):707–720
Restuccia D, Rogerson R (2017) The causes and costs of misallocation. J Econ Perspect 31 (3):151–174
Rothwell R (1980) The impact of regulation on innovation: some U.S. data. Technol Forecast Soc Chang 17(1):7–34
Schot J, Steinmueller WE (2018) Three frames for innovation policy: R&D, systems of innovation and transformative change. Res Policy 47(9):1554–1567
Stewart, L. A. (2012). The impact of regulation on innovation in the United States: a cross-industry literature review, in *Health IT and Patient Safety: Building Safer Systems for Better Care*, number ISBN 978–0–309-22112-2, The National Academies Press
Stigler G (1971) The theory of economic regulation. Bell J Econ 2(1):3–21
Stiglitz JE (2012) Government failure vs. market failure: principles of regulation. In: *Government and Markets: Toward a New Theory of Regulation*. Cambridge University press, pp 13–51
Trebing HM (1969) Government regulation and modern capitalism. Journal of Economic Issues 3 (1):87–109
Wade R (1990) Governing the market: economic theory and the role of government in east Asian industrialization. Princeton University Press
Waldemar FSD (2012) New products and corruption: evidence from Indian firms. Dev Econ 50 (3):268–284
Wang F (2014) Complementarities between R&D investment and exporting–evidence from China. China Econ Rev 31:217–227
Wang J (2018) Innovation and government intervention: a comparison of Singapore and Hong Kong. Res Policy 47(2):399–412
Wang CL, Chung HF (2013) The moderating role of managerial ties in market orientation and innovation: an Asian perspective. J Bus Res 66(12):2431–2437
Yeo Y, Pearson M (2008) Regulating decentralized state industries: China's auto industry. China Rev 8(2):231–259
Yoon HD, Kim N, Buisson B, Phillips F (2018) A cross-national study of knowledge, government intervention, and innovative nascent entrepreneurship. J Bus Res 84:243–252
Zhou Z (2018) China's regulatory reform: experiences, challenges, and prospects. University of Pennsylvania Asian Law Review 13(1):1–23

Catch-Up and *Reverse Catch-Up* Processes in the Market for Lithium-Ion Batteries

Alexander Gerybadze and Helen Mengis

Abstract The diffusion of electric vehicles (EV) represents a cornerstone of climate control and innovation policy in Europe, North America and Asia. Greater penetration of EV crucially depends on sourcing strategies for advanced batteries and their continuous price decreases. Lithium-ion batteries (LIB) are the most critical technology and attract increasing R&D funds. Our paper describes the evolution of LIB technology over time and the changing patterns of technological capabilities in this field. Asian countries and multinational firms from Japan and South Korea were successful in absorbing LIB technology originally invented in the USA and in Europe. At present, Asian manufacturers are dominating the world market for LIB cells and are presently leading in terms of technology and manufacturing capacity for LIB cells, specifically for automotive applications. International innovation, however, is a dynamic process and technological leadership changes over time. The novelty of our paper involves *reciprocal* processes of learning and technology transfer between Europe and Asia. International technology transfer is not a one-way road. Emerging countries can follow successful catch-up strategies. But this does not necessarily imply that former lead countries will lose international competitiveness forever. Winning back and reciprocal catch-up may be possible under specific conditions. Based on the present transformation of the European EV market, there are some chances for reversing the flow of technology from Asia to Europe and for regaining international competitiveness in battery technology.

Keywords Catch-up · Global innovation · Electric Vehicles (EV) · Lithium-ion batteries (LIB) · *Reverse catch-up*

JEL Codes O19 · O31 · O33 · O52 · O53

A. Gerybadze · H. Mengis (✉)
Center for International Management and Innovation, University of Hohenheim, Stuttgart, Germany
e-mail: gerybadze@uni-hohenheim.de; helen.mengis@uni-hohenheim.de

A. Pyka, K. Lee (eds.), *Innovation, Catch-up and Sustainable Development*, Economic Complexity and Evolution, https://doi.org/10.1007/978-3-030-84931-3_8

1 Introduction

Studies on international technology transfer and on catch-up processes typically focus on uni-directional transfer processes between leaders and former laggard countries. In many cases, emerging countries have effectively absorbed technologies originally developed in advanced countries. Early catch-up theories describe uni-directional technology transfer of former developing countries that were able to close the gap between leaders and laggards (Gerschenkron, 1962; Abramovitz, 1986; Amsden, 1989; Lall, 1992). More recent studies of innovation-based catch-up processes analyze the dynamic relation between innovation and diffusion. Firms and industries in emerging countries are often able to outperform their rivals in the former advanced countries (Lee, 2005, 2013; Lee & Malerba, 2017). Still, these studies also emphasize uni-directional processes from the perspective of the emerging nation.

Our paper analyzes more recent developments in the global market for lithium-ion batteries (LIB). While Western countries were dominating the invention and early development of the LIB, selected Asian countries were more successful in commercializing this promising new technology. At present, Asian manufacturers are dominating the world market for LIB cells, and South Korean and Japanese firms are presently leading in terms of technology and manufacturing capacity (EU, 2017). Early applications of LIBs that were driving the innovation process were primarily consumer electronic (CE) products. More recently, the automotive industry has become the driving application area for battery technology. Battery technology has become a core competence for most automobile firms and their suppliers: the LIB cell constitutes approximately 30%–40% of value added in an EV and substitutes the key technology of automotive OEM manufacturers, the combustion engine. Car manufacturers, as well as automotive suppliers, have become dependent on battery cell technology, for which Japan and South Korea are more advanced.

The novelty of our paper involves *reciprocal* processes of learning and technology transfer between Europe and Asia. While earlier studies concentrate on catch-up processes of emerging countries and analyze under which conditions follower nations may be successful in the long run (Malerba & Nelson, 2011; Lee, 2013), we are interested in the dynamic relationship between former leaders and new catch-up nations. *Reverse catch-up* processes describe situations where a former lead country has temporarily lost out in international competitiveness but attempts to overcome this deficiency. The key issue of *reverse catch-up* then addresses the conditions for success.

Through an in-depth industry study, we try to explain the major reasons for changes in the geography of innovation during the period 1980 to 2018. We will illustrate the transfer of LIB capabilities from North America and Europe to Japan and South Korea, and more recently to China. We will then examine the dynamic relationship between countries that are the leader in battery technology and those countries which attempt to gain a stronger position in the production and sales of the driving application of LIBs, EVs. Is it necessary to combine both strengths, or is it feasible to attain international specialization between upstream activities (e.g. battery technology) and downstream R&D and production activities for the next generation of automobiles? South Korea and Japan as the present leader in battery cell technology and Western countries like Germany that continue to play a strong role in premium car manufacturing are thus involved in an interesting competitive relationship.

Today, car manufacturers and automotive suppliers are dependent on battery cell technology, for which South Korea is more advanced. The theoretical framework of our study is presented in Sect. 2. Section 3 explains the applied methodology. We study the evolution of the battery technology and successive catch-up cycles in Sect. 4. Here we distinguish between different types of catch-up processes. We introduce the concept of *reverse catch-up* in Sect. 5 and conclude our findings in Sect. 6.

2 Theoretical Background

So far, most studies on catch-up processes of economic and industrial development have concentrated on formerly less-developed nations that were adopting technologies already used in other, more advanced countries. The classical product life cycle theory based on Vernon (1966) has assumed a three-stage flow from (1) advanced industrial countries to (2) other industrialized countries, followed in later phases (3) by the transfer of technology and production capabilities to less-developed nations. We label this type as "classical catch-up."

The revived interest in Asian development processes since 1997 (World Bank, 1998; Nelson & Pack, 1999) has led to empirical studies on catch-up processes in Japan, South Korea, Singapore and Taiwan, but has also followed a more or less uni-directional view of technology transfer from the USA or Europe to these Asian nations. More recent studies of Schumpeterian analysis of economic catch-up have emphasized more differentiated views of diffusion and innovation. As Lee (2013) and Lee and Malerba (2017) show, persistent innovation and the build-up of complementary assets often lead to situations where the former catch-up country is able to attain a world leadership position during later phases. Especially the successful catch-up stories of South Korean firms in several industries have been studied in detail (Lee, 2013; Wade, 2004). We will use the term *innovation-enhanced catch-up* to describe the development of South Korean firms, which is outlined in Sect. 4.2. Existing case studies on *innovation-enhanced catch-up* processes in electronics, IT and automobiles provide rich insight for analyzing the ongoing changes in the market for LIBs.

On the firm level, most explanations for catch-up success are based on the theory of absorptive capacity (Cohen & Levinthal, 1990). According to the absorptive capacity theory, latecomer firms have to undergo a learning process and build up their own technological capabilities to sustain in the long run. Lower dependence on established routines and entrepreneurial behaviors enable new firms from emerging countries to better absorb technological and managerial knowledge from their external environment and to make the best use of it internally. Most of the examined success stories illustrate how catching-up firms initially start by imitating technologies available through licensing or JV agreements and later innovate during follow-on generations of these technologies on their own (Lee & Malerba, 2017; Malerba & Nelson, 2011). Since all of these studied catch-up examples refer to emerging country firms where no prior R&D or production-wise knowledge was available in these countries, the assumption does not hold for our suggested *reverse catch-up* hypothesis where frontier technological knowledge is available in the catch-up nations.

We will use a widely used and accepted concept amongst catch-up researchers: the windows of opportunity approach suggested by Perez and Soete (1988) and extended by Lee and Malerba (2017). They suggest three windows of opportunity for a potential market entry by latecomer firms: (1) technology or knowledge-related changes, (2) demand changes and (3) institutional or policy changes. We will examine how South Korean and Chinese firms have strategically responded to changing windows of opportunity. Potentially, all three windows of opportunity are relevant to explain the current situation for *reverse catch-up* within the battery and EV industry: (1) The next generation of battery technology is already examined in advanced research projects, (2) the shift on the demand side from consumer electronics as key customers to the automotive industry as driving application area. In addition, (3) institutional and policy changes can be important in the EV field and offer opportunities for battery manufacturers. Worldwide policy regulations on the reduction of combustion engines' emissions and promotion of electrification of automobiles will strongly influence further developments in battery technology and will open up windows of opportunity for new rivals.

The study of changes in the market for new EVs and LIBs, however, requires a new perspective. The former catch-up nations have turned into leaders, while corporations in Europe and North America have lost their former strengths. While we know much about technology transfer from Western to Asian countries, we need to understand better how effective technology transfer can be reversed, i.e., moving from East to West. We define a situation where a firm from a developed country, e.g., Germany or the USA, is catching up to the leading position of firms from former emerging countries as South Korea or China as *reverse catch-up*. In such a situation, firms from emerging countries are operating at the technology frontier, whereas firms from developed countries lag behind. *Reverse catch-up* assumes that firms from developed countries highly depend on that key technology for sustaining their competitive position in other technological markets. Thus, the necessity arises to learn from emerging markets' firms and to trigger a reverse knowledge transfer from East to West.

The automotive LIB cell is nowadays mainly delivered by Japanese and South Korean producers. The EV market, due to its projected high growth within the next 5–10 years and its accompanying substantial need for high-performance batteries, is expected to change the market structure for LIBs radically. The role of Asian, especially South Korean firms, as the supplier of a key component for the automotive industry, may thus also affect these existing dependency patterns. Especially demand changes and regulatory changes in the European EV market may offer new windows of opportunity for European firms to regain international competitiveness in the LIB field. The conditions for such a reversal in LIB competence from Asia to Europe will be discussed in Sect. 5.

Although we support the argument that incumbent firms' advantages as, e.g., in terms of know-how and mass production competence, favors their competitiveness in the future, we will further address the potential incumbent trap of Asian producers (Lee & Ki, 2017), offering further opportunities for latecomer firms. Building on the previous results on the explanations of catch-up, we have not been able to find an approach in theory that describes the current situation. *Reverse catching-up* firms in our case study on the LIB market are threatened by radical technological changes in their industry, resulting in a high dependency on foreign firms in a key technology. In our example, this dependency is intensified by oligopolistic supplier market structures and conflicting aims of suppliers and customers. Both parties aim to dominate the automotive supply chain in the long run and thus become the system integrator. The aim of our article is to first-off outline these reverse dependency patterns and to contribute to the understanding of catching up from the perspective of a developed country catch-up firm.

3 Methodology

With regard to the fact that we are the first to examine *reverse catch-up* situations, we have employed an explorative case study approach (Stebbins, 2001) in studying the global LIB and EV market as a case example. Our findings are based on insights from semi-structured expert interviews, a patent as well as an industry analysis. We have based our industry analysis on firm-specific information that has been retrieved from the databases such as Orbis (Bureau van Dijk, 2018) as well as publicly available industry reports as, e.g., from the International Energy Agency (IEA, 2017) or the Joint Research Centre of the European Union (EU, 2016, 2017).

We have identified our primal sample of experts through an initial patent analysis within the IPC for LIB cells (H01M10/0525) at the European Patent Office (EPO).[1] Starting with R&D experts in the field, we have further identified industry experts by following the recommendations of our interviewees. In total, we have conducted 32 interviews with 25 experts in China, Germany and South Korea from March 2017 to January 2019. With respect to the novelty of our topic and currently fast-changing developments, several experts have been repeatedly interviewed. Table 1 gives an overview of the interviewed experts.

On average, the interviews lasted between 45 and 60 min and have been recorded, if in consent with the respective interviewee. Based on an interview guideline, interviewees, with regards to their expertise, have been asked about (1) the

[1] Patent data was retrieved from the OECD Regpat database (version February 2018).

Table 1 Interviewees' expertise

Expertise	Context	#
LIB	Research	6
LIB	Industry	6
Asian markets	Industry	5
Asian markets	Research	4
Automotive	Industry	4
		25

contributors and development of the early evolution of the battery technology, (2) the (catch-up) strategies of selected Asian firms and (3) a critical assessment of Western, especially automotive, firms ability for a *reverse catch-up*. The interview transcripts and memos have been qualitatively analyzed with the use of the document analysis software MAXQDA (Bryman & Bell, 2015; Mayring, 2000).

4 Classical Catch-Up Processes in the Market for Lithium-Ion Batteries

4.1 The Early Evolution of the LIB Technology and Japanese Commercialization

Lithium-ion Batteries represent the second generation of rechargeable batteries and have experienced strong research and investment activities during the last 30 years. Due to their superior performance characteristics, they have substituted earlier battery types as lead-acid batteries in an increasing number of applications (Yoshino, 2014). During the first two decades, CE and IT products were accounting for the largest share of LIB applications. During the last 10 years, the focus of innovation in battery technology has shifted towards new EVs and other high-power applications, such as energy storage systems. As can be seen from the development of driving LIB applications, newer applications compared to CE applications are increasing at a higher rate and are expected to continue to grow even more. Especially the Chinese market until 2030 is expected to account for the largest growth share (EU, 2017; IEA, 2017).

Technological progress for new generations of lithium-based batteries is expected to continue for the next decade, which has led to increased funding for R&D in many countries. The third generation of rechargeable batteries, the so-called solid-state batteries, is still examined in several research projects worldwide, even though it is not expected to be commercialized within the next decade (VDMA, 2018; Fraunhofer, 2016).

Basic research and early discovery processes for the LIB were concentrated in North America and Europe. Most research is conducted on the components' materials used and on the design of the cell. These two aspects crucially determine the overall performance of the cell. Every component of the LIB cell requires know-how related to the material and design, but also regarding the complexity and sensitivity of its production process. Several researchers from North America and Europe contributed to the early discovery processes of LIB technology during the early 1980s. The most significant scientific discoveries are attributed to John B. Goodenough and his research team at the University of Texas, as well as to researchers at Argonne National Laboratory.[2] The early breakthrough discovery was Goodenough's invention related to the composition of the cathode materials $LiCoO_2$, for which he filed two US patents in 1979 and 1980. This invention paved the ground for follow-on material research and contributed to several classes of commercial LIB cells, which are still used today. Other early inventors were involved in significant research in Canada, Germany and France, primarily in the field of electrochemistry and material science. However, this remained a basic research activity, with just limited efforts for commercial applications and manufacturing. In Germany, Jürgen O. Besenhard pursued advanced research during the 1970s and 1980s at the University of Munich and later at the University of Graz in Austria. He is seen as one of the early pioneers of the so-called rocking chair principle resp.—the intercalation of lithium.

Even though leading research was carried out in Europe and North America, researchers were missing driving application projects and the support of local industrial investors. Early lead markets for LIB during the early 1990s were primarily in CE and IT applications. As these user industries in Europe and North America have been lost out to Asian manufacturers, Western researchers did not get enough support from the industry. One repeatedly mentioned example during the interviews was the German automotive industry. Although product development plans for an electrified car already existed during the 1990s in Germany, mainly based on the lead-acid technology, the German automotive industry cohesively decided against a radical technological change, the battery technology and electrification of cars, and instead favored to further improve and rely on the already established Diesel technology. In our interviews, the rather reluctant (investment) behavior of German automotive firms was, in particular, explained in two streams: (1) the not-invented-here-syndrome and (2) risk-averse firm strategies. The Diesel technology was invented by German automotive engineers, whereas the battery technology was invented by electrochemists and at that time mainly applied in CE products. Jin (2019) offers an explanation for this by empirically testing and finding that researchers from incumbent countries tend to more likely engage in sustaining technologies (hybrid EVs) and are more likely to neglect disruptive technologies (battery EVs). As a consequence, entering the battery market was entailed with higher risks, especially with regards to the at that time already prevalent efforts in the battery technology of Japanese firms. The selected risk-averse firm strategy was further explained by several failure events causing the automotive industry negative

[2]For a detailed description of the early evolution of LIB technology in the USA see Levine (2016) and Crabtree et al. (2015).

public attention as, e.g., the failed Daimler and Chrysler fusion or some technical issues with the first generation of the Mercedes A-Class. In accordance with and as a consequence of industrial policy, government funding for R&D projects was not available, and public electrochemical research institutes have been gradually reduced. Thus, and with regards to the high expenses of battery R&D projects, European research institutions have been appreciative of international collaboration partners, especially funding partners. This was when Japanese industry came into play. Japanese firms were interested in advanced battery technology, and European researchers were in need of funding and potential applications of their research findings. One of the interviewees confirmed that the abovementioned German battery researcher Jürgen O. Besenhardt was involved in several collaboration projects with Japanese firms, too. Interviewees of leading German LIB research institutions have described the collaboration projects as win-win situations where knowledge was transferred in exchange for the financing of expensive R&D projects. Many of the graduate and post-graduate electrochemical students came from Asia. Even today, after a revived national interest and available national funding for LIB R&D projects since 2009, a large share of their funds still comes from foreign, especially from Asia.

Furthermore, early Western commercial applications were sometimes plagued by safety issues. As an example, the Molicel was the first rechargeable LIB introduced to market by the Canadian Moli Energy Ltd. but was soon withdrawn from the market for safety reasons (Julien et al., 2016). These activities have later been acquired by a Japanese firm. Another Western firm involved in the early commercialization of the LIB was the German battery firm Varta. Varta was formerly owned by the family Quandt, one of the largest shareholders of the German automotive company BMW, and was separated by the family Quandt into several independent business units and sold to differing investors in 2002. The automotive lead acid-based division was sold to Johnson Controls, whereas the lithium-based battery production stayed within the Varta Microbattery Group and focused on micro application markets as hearing devices where they constitute the world market leader today. There exist several more European battery firms from Switzerland or France from these early commercialization phases which have specialized on Niche markets, e.g., in Switzerland on watches, in smaller quantities. Recently, these battery producers have received more attention with regards to their potential to contribute to European automotive cell production.

While Western firms either did not or failed to commercialize the LIB on larger scales, more and more Japanese corporations became interested in this promising technology and stepped up their R&D investment in the field. Japanese researchers were sent to the USA and Germany for acquiring technology and skills, and they implemented fruitful innovation projects after their return to Japan. These returnees contributed to the successful commercialization of Japanese firms as Sony and Panasonic.

The landmark event of LIB commercialization was Sony's first introduction of this type of rechargeable battery for CE products in 1991, soon followed by a wave of adoption of LIB cells for several IT applications by Japanese companies including

Matsushita, Sharp and Toshiba. It is noticeable that one Japanese researcher, A. Yoshino, repeatedly appears in the international patent filing. Yoshino (2014) claims that his US patent filed in 1985 explains the basic principle of LIB cells that is still in use today. As can be seen in Fig. 2 in the next section, inventors from Japan have strongly increased the number of patent filings since the early 1990s.

During the 1990s, the locus of innovation for LIB technology shifted from Western public research laboratories to industrial R&D laboratories in Japan. Major channels of technology transfer from West to East included co-publications and cooperation projects between European, North American and Japanese researchers. In our interviews, German researchers from leading LIB research institutions have mentioned that collaboration with Japanese corporations was a vehicle to get projects going as a reaction to reduced support at home. This was partly due to the lack of interest of German corporations in their research and was also seen as a consequence of a gradual reduction of public research institutions for electrochemistry. Until the turn of the century, Japanese firms have been dominating the world market with monopolistic market shares of above 90% (see Fig. 1). Within the last 10 years, Japanese incumbent firms have been challenged in sustaining their competitive position by the demand-induced window of opportunity for latecomer firms in the automotive application. Especially the intense competition from China has caused significantly decreasing market shares. One of the Japanese incumbent firms, Panasonic, managed to enter the automotive application successfully. Mainly based on its collaboration with one leading US EV producer, Tesla, Panasonic managed to sustain its leading position in the LIB market and to develop into a leading automotive cell producer. The first company marketing the LIB cell, Sony, however, failed to enter the automotive application and finally sold its battery business to Murata in 2018. South Korean CE firms as Samsung and LG in the 1990s aimed at reducing the dependency on their few Japanese suppliers. Thus, they started their LIB activities in the mid-1990s and managed to obtain significant market shares approximately 10 years later. The catch-up process of South Korean and later Chinese firms is described in the next section.

4.2 *Catch-Up of South Korean and Chinese Firms*

Japanese firms were pioneers in the application of these new types of batteries for electronic products (video recorders, audio and video equipment etc.). Korean firms started a few years later but improved upon LIB technology and became more competitive in developing LIB cells for secondary applications (automobiles, energy storage, power tools etc.). They have gradually built up R&D and technological capabilities and have successively penetrated new growth markets that demand high-power batteries. While the center of gravity of LIB research and innovation shifted from Europe and North America to Japan during the 1980s to '90s, similar patterns of international technology transfer can be observed between Japan and South Korea almost 10 years later.

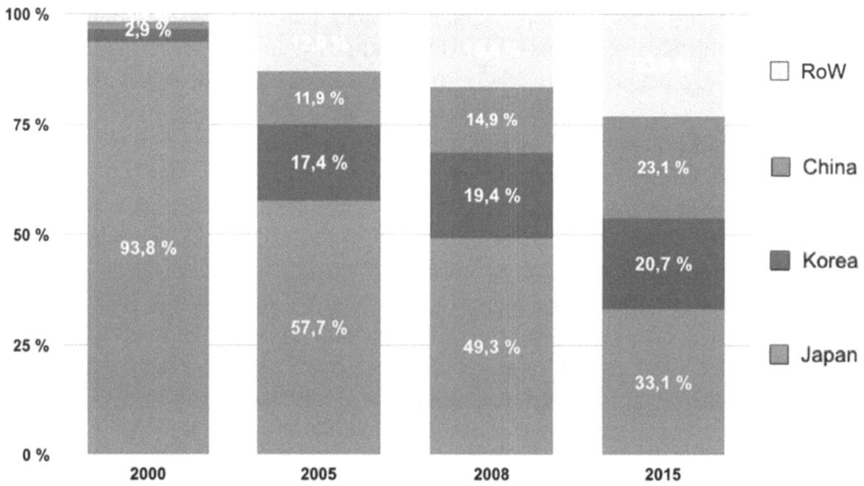

Fig. 1 Market Shares in Sales Values for High-Power LIB (in %). Source: own illustration based on Kawamoto (2010); EU (2016)

Based on their increased technological strengths, South Korean firms have increasingly penetrated major application markets for high-power batteries. This is illustrated in Fig. 1, where we compare market shares of major suppliers primarily from three Asian countries. At the turn of the new century, Japanese firms still dominated LIB world markets with a share of 94%. South Korean firms became more successful since 2005, and their market shares have reached 19% in 2008 and 21% in 2015.[3] More recently, Chinese firms are increasingly active in this market and have attained a share of 23% (mainly obtained on their large home market).[4] Figure 1 thus illustrates the consecutive catch-up processes of first-off South Korean and later Chinese LIB firms by increasing market shares of these and vice versa for Japanese incumbents.[5]

4.2.1 The South Korean Successful Catch-Up

Application markets, as well as investment efforts of major corporations, were driving the innovation process and the locus of LIB research. South Korean firms started their first attempts in the LIB market with a time lag, but have since then implemented a successful catch-up strategy. Japanese and South Korean corporations have emphasized the strong complementarity between LIB technology and

[3]Market shares of South Korean firms are primarily related to the two leaders LG Chem and Samung SDI.

[4]However, a major share of this is attained in the captive Chinese market, while Chinese battery firms are still less active than Japanese and South Korean firms in markets outside Asia.

[5]The sales of SK Innovation are not included in this survey.

their strategy to attain a strong position in the electronics market. The leading supplier firms of CE have also become the leading suppliers of LIB cells applied in other secondary markets. South Korean and Japanese firms today, after almost 30 years of LIB experience, represent the dominant player in the worldwide LIB market. One repeatedly acknowledged factor in their catch-up process was South Koreans' organizational structure of conglomerates, as the huge initial costs have been cross-subsidized by more profitable business units. The majority of interviewed experts have even voiced their doubts about today's profitability of the battery business of these leading firms. This was on the one side reasoned by high R&D and production costs and the need to extend production capacities while at the same time applying price-cutting strategies to attain a competitive position. Samsung SDI and LG Chem have been attributed with a pro-aggressive strategy in cutting the price to half when competing with Japanese Panasonic "until their competitor has left their territory" (*interviewed manager, September 2018*).

After a decade of CE cell experience, mainly based on their large internal market, South Korean firms have started their first attempts in entering the automotive application. The main Korean automobile producer electrifying its cars is the Hyundai Group, especially its daughter firm, Kia Motors. To our experts' knowledge, the Hyundai Group has very early contracted LG Chem as a cell supplier. LG Chem further supplies Indian group Mahindra and Japanese Mitsubishi by exporting. South Korean firms have internationalized their businesses with production sites in China,[6] the USA,[7] and Europe. Samsung's production in Changchun has been a result of its acquisition of the battery division of the Austrian-Canadian battery firm Magna Steyr Battery. Changchun has proven to be an attractive location for automotive firms, too. Chinese FAW, as well as German VW and BMW, are located there, too. Samsung SDI has managed to enter BMW's supplier network mainly due to its failed JV with German first-tier automotive supplier Bosch, SB LiMotive. The same has happened in the JV between German first-tier supplier Continental and South Korean cell producer SK Innovation. Although the two parties in both cases seemed to meet ideal prerequisites in terms of complementary assets (automotive vs. battery cell know-how), the collaborations have not been continued.

Their market success is based on high R&D and patenting activities. Samsung SDI showed a drastically increased R&D intensity from 1.5% in 2013 to 10.9% in 2016, whereas LG Chem's R&D intensity within the same years grew even more, but at lower rates from 0.1% to 3.6% (EU R&D Scoreboard, 2014, 2017). Figure 2 illustrates the development of patent applications over time and shows the predominance of Japanese applicants and an increased patenting of Korean firms in Europe

[6] Samsung SDI 2 GWh in Xian, 1.4 GWh (5.6 GWh announced for 2020) in Changchun and planned in Tianjin; LG Chem 3 GWh in Nanjing; SK Innovation canceled plans on a Chinese production plant in Beijing in 2017. The respective production capacities in Korea are for Samsung SDI 2.8 GWh in Cheonan and 3.3. GWh for LG Chem in Cheongju-si 3.3 GWh.

[7] Samsung SDI 1.2 GWh in Michigan for supply of Ford, GM and Tesla; LG Chem 3 GWh in Michigan, too, for the supply of Chevrolet and Chrysler.

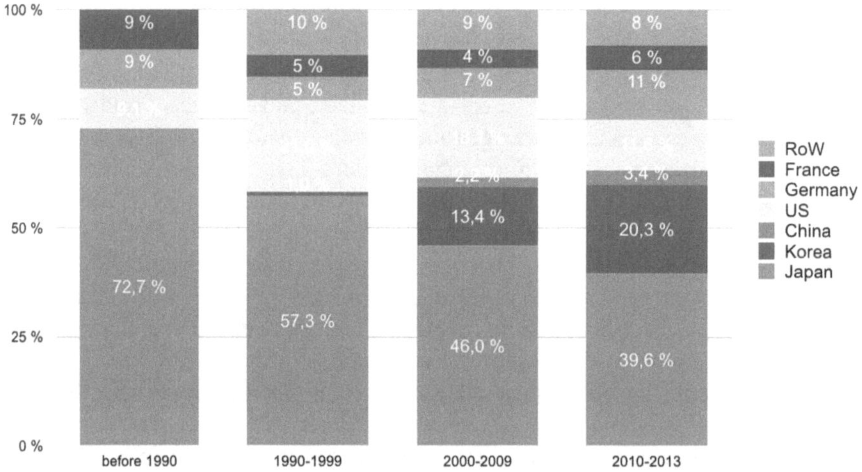

Fig. 2 EPO Patent Applications by the origin of applicant (IPC H01M10/0525). Source: Own illustration based on OECD (2018)

since 2003. Japanese applicants with 1612 applications at the EPO rank first and account for the largest share of total patent applications (44%), followed by Koreans (16%), USA (15%), German (9%), and French (5%) applications. Samsung SDI[8] applied for its first patent at the EPO in 1999, LG Chem in 2001 and SK Innovation in 2007. The applications of the two leading South Korean firms, Samsung SDI and LG Chem, account for 93% of all South Korean patents applied in Europe. Patent applications of these two firms in Europe have stepped up strongly since 2010. More than 70% of applications have been filed since then. The increasing activity in Europe suggests a technological protection strategy in markets for EVs. This can be explained on the one side by the location of their target customers, the automotive industry, and on the other side by the aim to reduce the freedom to operate of potential future competitors coming from the automotive (supplier) industry. Corporations from South Korea have developed into a leading power of battery technology and this is increasingly transformed into export and sales activities.

The market for automotive applications is divided between batteries for hybrid cars and for battery EVs. The second segment was still in its infancy until 2015, but is growing much faster than the hybrid car market. South Korean battery firms have been particularly successful in the early growth phase of battery-powered EVs worldwide. This is shown in Table 2, where the two major firms have reached an annual sales volume of 403 Mio. USD (Samsung SDI) and 365 Mio. USD (LG Chem), just closely behind the main Japanese rival (Panasonic).

[8]Patent applications of the former JV between Samsung SDI and Robert Bosch GmbH, SB LiMotive, have been included within Samsung's patents as a result of their termination agreements.

Table 2 Revenues from LIB cells for battery EVs (in Mio. USD)

Company	Country	2014	2015	2016
Panasonic/Sanyo	JP	43	94	135
Panasonic Corp	JP	417	413	449
Lithium Energy Japan	JP	74	73	76
AESC	JP	394	384	373
Toshiba	JP	33	24	23
Japanese Firms		961	988	1,056
LG Chem	KR	220	244	365
Samsung SDI	KR	197	250	403
South Korean Firms		417	494	768
BYD	CN	30	32	35
A123 Systems LLC	CN	62	72	86
Tianjin Lishen Battery	CN	44	48	52
Chinese Firms	CN	136	152	173

Source: Andermann (2016); Sauer (2018)

As can be seen in Table 2, South Korean firms are now among the top three worldwide suppliers of LIB cells for automotive applications. In total, Japanese firms are still leading, but on a firm-level Samsung SDI and LG Chem have accomplished to supply target customers in equal magnitudes as their presently leading Japanese rival Panasonic. South Korean production capacities have developed on a constant level until 2015 and increased by over 55% in 2016. This increase is equivalent to the growth of EV car production worldwide.

Table 3 in the next section shows the expected production capacities for LIB cell production plants for the periods 2016, 2020 and 2025. Manufacturers from South Korea, Japan and China have published announcements for new production plants in different regions of the world. This table shows that overall planned capacities will increase by 150% within 4 years from 2016 to 2020. Still, in 2014, one-third of worldwide LIB cell capacity of 27.2 Gwh/a was produced by three South Korean firms: LG Chem (4,9), Samsung SDI (3,4) and SK Innovations (0,8) (NPE, 2016). South Korean firms are expected to increase their production capacities, particularly through foreign manufacturing plants close to major automobile clients. Major investment projects of South Korean firms are presently built in China, Europe and the USA. As soon as these plants will be operating, South Koreans will become major vendors of LIB automotive cells and will thus strengthen their position as key suppliers for the automotive industry. The next section will deal with the subsequent South Korean's and ongoing catch-up process of Chinese firms.

4.2.2 The Chinese Ongoing Catch-Up

The Chinese EV market constitutes the largest and fastest-growing application of LIB cells worldwide. Since 2012 average yearly market growth lied above 100% and has reached a market volume of approximately 5 Billion USD in 2016. In 2017

Table 3 Production capacities and locations for LIB cells worldwide in GWh

Supplier	Location	2018	2020	2025	2030
Chinese	Asia	239	550	615	615
Chinese	Europe	0	0	14	14
Chinese	**Total**	**239**	**550**	**629**	**629**
Korean	Asia	30	87	87	87
Korean	Europe	8	47	47	47
Korean	US	3	3	3	8
Korean	**Total**	**41**	**137**	**137**	**142**
Japanese	Asia	16	23	63	63
Japanese	Europe	2	2	37	37
Japanese	US	29	39	109	109
Japanese	**Total**	**47**	**64**	**209**	**209**
US	Asia	14	41	51	51
US	Australia	0	3	15	15
US	US	3	6	18	18
US	**Total**	**17**	**50**	**84**	**84**
European	Europe	2	14	56	70
European	**Total**	**2**	**14**	**56**	**70**
Row		**15**	**18**	**71**	**96**

Based on calculated expected maximum values
Source: VDMA Batterieproduktion (2018)

770,000 EVs have been registered in China (IEA, 2017). On the one side, this has attracted foreign firms to set up or extend existing production plants in China, while at the same time, many local LIB cell start-ups are aroused on the market. To our experts' knowledge, in 2018, there have been more than 200 Chinese cell producers that are expected to be consolidated to below five major producers by 2020. The decisive factors are mass production competence, an ensured (inter)national value chain and the ability to receive automotive supplier contracts. The companies BYD and CATL are considered to count to these few successful catching-up firms since they have already attained significant market shares and moreover managed to enter the driving automotive application. Their success stories vary widely and are outlined in the following section.

Figure 3 illustrates market shares for the automotive LIB cell market in China in 2015. One example of how volatile the Chinese cell market is the company Optimum Nano. As can be seen, the firm ranked third in 2015, but had to close its production in the first quarter of 2018. Moreover, Fig. 3 shows that incumbent foreign firms do not play a significant role in the Chinese market. The highly dynamic environment on the Chinese market has challenged incumbent firms from Japan and South Korea, too. This was mainly induced by policy regulations. In order to set up production in (restricted) regions in China,[9] foreigner LIB firms had to

[9]These are Fujian, Guangdong, Shanghai and Tianjin.

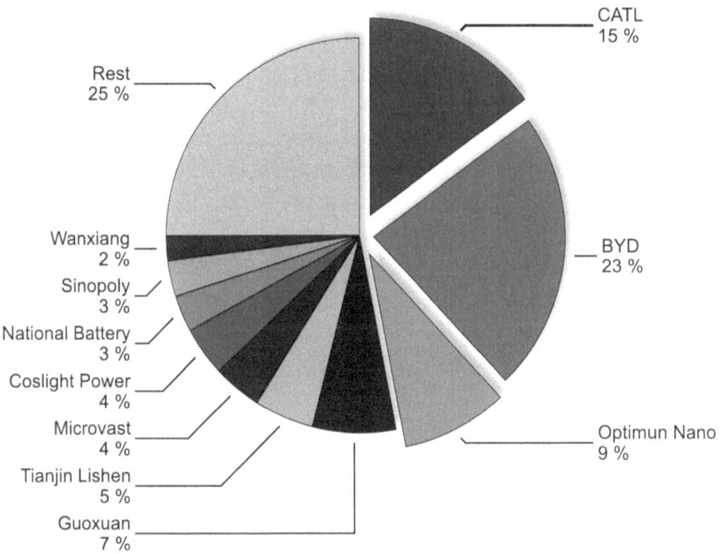

Fig. 3 Market Shares EV LIB cells in China, 2015. Source: Park et al. (2016)

register Chinese subsidiary companies with a local Chinese partner. The Chinese partner is especially important with regard to local governmental know-how and the identification of available subsidies.

The Chinese government has offered subsidy programs for battery cell production in China with either production volume thresholds (>8 GWh) or specific technical requirements regarding the density of the cell and the materials used. The cells of incumbent foreign suppliers from Japan and South Korea did not meet these requirements. Thus, these firms faced major issues regarding their competitiveness in the Chinese market. These subsidy programs were employed upstream to encourage R&D and production of these types of cells as well as downstream in terms of a sales promotion of EVs that contain these cells. This is why B2B, as well as B2C customers, favored Chinese cells enabling subsidy payments. After 2016 however, these subsidies have been decreased and, as a consequence, enhanced the ongoing consolidation process.

As with South Korean, the Chinese catch-up must be differentiated by the two major applications, CE and automobiles. While Chinese firms have caught up in the CE industry, especially in mobile communication technology, several years after South Korean firms, likewise a delay can be observed in the LIB market. The major application of LIB cells in China in early phases has also been portable CE products.

With regards to best environmental effects, the Chinese government started the electrification offense with the electrification of public transport, resp. busses. This is how the Chinese company BYD, as a supplier of these busses as well as cells in these, was able to grow rapidly. BYD was founded in 1995 in Shenzhen (Guangdong province) as a privately owned company. Until the start of automotive production in

2003, BYD was a cell manufacturer for CE products. Today, the businesses of BYD cover automotive production, conventional combustion engines and EVs, battery cell production as well as photovoltaic. The automotive know-how has been especially absorbed from its 2011 founded JV with German premium car manufacturer Daimler. The failure of this JV, Denza, can be explained by the conflicting interest of both parties to become a leading EV supplier. The LIB cells produced by BYD are, until today, exclusively applied in its own products. The large internal market constitutes a major competitive advantage with regards to the challenging supplier requirements of the worldwide automotive manufacturers. Besides its Chinese cell production, BYD produces the LIB cells applied for its busses on the Brazilian market in Sao Paulo, too. Furthermore, BYD, as well as CATL, have, amongst others, set up production in the Chinese city Xining, Qinghai province, where lithium deposits are high.

Just as BYD, CATL has started its cell business in the CE industry. CATL was founded as a privately-owned firm by its CEO, Zeng Yuqun, in Ningde, Fujian province, in 2011 and has managed a successful initial public offering at the Shenzhen stock exchange by 2018. Besides its battery pack and energy storage system activity, CATL mainly focuses on the development and production on LIB cells. The CEO, Zeng Yuqun, was the founder of the 1999 spin-offed Chinese-Japanese company of the Japanese cell producer TDK, named ATL, too and accounts for the human-embodied knowledge transfer in the build-up of technological capabilities in the early years. Until 2015, ATL held 15% of the shares of CATL. These shares have been especially sold due to the fact that the Japanese participation prevented the firm from higher governmental subsidies.

The human-embodied knowledge transfer within CATL is further based on its ability to attract foreign experts (e.g., from Korea). On their site in Ningde, CATL has even introduced a separate canteen for their numerous foreign employees, especially from Japan and South Korea.

In 2015, production capacities of CATL were 3 GWh, whereas these have been drastically increased to 17 GWh by 2017 and are expected to reach 88 GWh by 2020. The increased production capacities of CATL and the ability to attract customers of the rapidly growing Chinese EV industry go in line with the standstill of foreign LIB producers in China as Samsung SDI and LG Chem. Having premium electronic product manufacturer Apple as a reference customer, CATL has attracted numerous R&D and production collaboration projects with the automotive industry. Amongst others, two JVs with SAIC (for battery pack and cell) and an R&D collaboration with BMW. The increased interest of foreign automotive firms can be on the one side explained by the missing alternatives on the Chinese market and simultaneously by the objective to reduce the dependency on the existing few leading suppliers from South Korea and Japan and to encourage a set out of the oligopolistic market structure. Although Chinese firms until today do not satisfy the high quality of Japanese and South Korean firms, most of the Western automotive manufacturers voice an optimistic attitude, especially in view of the ongoing intense R&D and production collaborations. BMW, for example, had reduced its dependency on Samsung SDI by additionally collaborating with CATL. As a consequence, and in addition to its already established R&D site in Germany, CATL in 2018 has announced to set up production in Erfurt, Germany, to supply its automotive customers, e.g., BMW, locally. Even though the CATL's German production plant will be a replication of one of its Chinese plants, the company is challenged to replicate its supply chain in Europe with the constraints of higher production costs (labor, energy, resources, as well as equipment manufacturers). As a start, CATL has acquired 22% of the shares of the Finnish automotive supplier, Valmet, of customers as Daimler, Porsche as well as VW.

Whereas innovation of Chinese cell manufacturers within the CE application was mainly based on licensing or JV agreements, these are nowadays more induced by own internal R&D activities. Though increasing, the quantity of Chinese patent applications in Europe compared to those of incumbent firms from Japan and South Korea are negligible low (see Fig. 2). Interestingly, BYD as well as CATL as latecomers in the battery industry, make use of already expired patents of their competitors as Panasonic, Samsung SDI and LG Chem. For BYD 17 and for CATL 16 of the 30 most cited patents have been already expired. This suggests a special IPR strategy of a free-of-charge knowledge transfer. On the other hand, the increased innovation capabilities can be seen in the forward citations of these two firms. BYD patents, on average, are more frequently cited, especially by leading incumbent firms (Samsung SDI 56, LG Chem 35, Panasonic 22), confirming a successful knowledge catch-up by BYD.

The learning curve of the CE application and attained mass production competence, especially on the large Chinese market, offers competitive advantages for BYD and CATL. Moreover, they can benefit from shorter product life cycles of the CE industry compared to the automotive one. According to our interviewed experts, cells developed for the automotive application are first-off tested in CE products due to faster market response and consequently faster response possibilities. Table 3 finally illustrates the development of worldwide LIB cell production capacities and illustrates the Chinese catch-up process.

In this section, we have analyzed development strategies and the competence level of major countries, with a focus on catch-up strategies of South Korea and China. Based on strengths for strategic materials and technologies, corporations from both countries were able to control world markets for a wide range of electronic products and information technology markets. This linkage effect between downstream product and systems markets on one side, and strategic LIB components on the other, is replicated in the uprising market for new EVs. Control of advanced LIB cells is translated into capturing the LIB systems market and, as a next step, serves to attain a stronger presence in the market for automotive products and services. In the long run, this strength in the LIB market may allow Asian firms to capture value within the European and North American automotive market.

During the last 10 years, Korean LIB producers have managed to outpace even the former leading Japanese LIB firms, and Chinese companies have rapidly increased their production capacities. Control in the market for LIB cells does not only constitute the majority of value added of new EVs, but also has a crucial influence on the functionality and performance of automobiles. There are scenarios that the leading providers of battery cells and electronic systems may in the future become providers of advanced mobility.

Today, the worldwide LIB market is experiencing a major transformation. New EVs represent the driving application area of the next decade. The EV market is expected to increase the LIB cell demand by a multiple during the period 2018 to 2025 (Fraunhofer, 2016). The supplier structure will thus not only depend on the previous LIB knowledge but also on the ability of LIB firms to respond to the demand of the world automotive industry, especially in regions where the EV development is most advanced. The automotive application thus also constitutes a challenge for Japanese and South Korean LIB producers.

5 *Reverse Catch-Up* for Europe and the USA?

The preceding part of our article has documented the present dominance of Asian manufacturers in the market for advanced LIB cells. Will success breed success or will new entrants create a more open and dynamic competitive environment? Will the large incumbent corporations from Japan, South Korea and China continue to dominate the market for LIB cells in the period 2020 to 2040? Will they even be able to move downstream and control the market for battery systems and eventually also the market for EVs worldwide? Or will the existing system providers in the world automobile industry be able to successfully integrate backwards, and thus reduce their dependence on the Asian LIB oligopoly? This last scenario would require a strong move of regaining competitiveness among large systems integrators primarily from Europe and North America. This scenario builds on successful activities of *reverse catch-up*, on the locus of innovation again shifting towards Western countries. In the following, we will analyze under which conditions it may be possible for Western corporations to regain international competitiveness.

Reverse catch-up in the field of LIB cells is feasible under three conditions.[10] (1) There occur favorable technology or knowledge-related changes that support new entrants, (2) demand patterns change and open up a window of opportunity or (3) institutional and policy changes in Europe and North America could create specific favorable conditions for a *reverse catch-up*. As a result of our empirical analysis, we found support for the demand- and technology-induced opportunities specifically applicable and in favor of Western firms, but not for policy-related opportunities. The majority of experts regarded Western policymakers rather as a risk than an opportunity as industrial policy regulations are mainly induced by locally leading industry representatives. This usually leads to regulation protecting more mature, established industries whereas not sufficiently promoting uprising

[10] Here we use the three arguments on windows of opportunity for successful catch-up put forth by Lee and Malerba (2017). We analyze the reciprocal process: what are the windows of opportunity and the conditions under which *reverse catch-up* can happen?

markets. As opposed to the Chinese government's long-term strategy in attaining a competitive position in future technologies, Western policymakers in preserve mature industries might miss opportunities in key future technologies as it was the case for the LIB in Germany in the 1990s. Furthermore, our experts explained that most policy promotion in Western countries, especially in Europe, is related to R&D activities and does not promote the commercialization of these technologies. Thus, European firms lack experience in commercializing disruptive technologies. In the following, we will analyze two potential windows of opportunities for *reverse catch-up*: demand and technology related. The counterargument would emphasize conditions under which the present dominant position of Asian LIB cell manufacturers is sustained and further strengthened, which in turn would mean that a *reverse catch-up* is not feasible.

5.1 Technology Induced Window of Opportunity

As described in the previous sections, inventors from the USA, but also from France, Germany and Canada, were most influential during the basic research and discovery phase of LIB, particularly during the period 1977 to 1990. The locus of innovation shifted to Asia when product development and advanced manufacturing were becoming critical activities. Japan became stronger during the 1990s, following the first commercial application in CE. South Korea and China succeeded in exploiting new business opportunities in information technology as well as for automotive applications. The expected future evolution in technology may offer new windows of opportunity. Technology experts are anticipating several waves of major changes in battery technology in the years after 2030. These imply incremental improvements of the today used lithium-based technology as well as the next expected generation of rechargeable batteries, the so-called solid-state batteries.[11] While Asian manufacturers will most probably benefit from an incumbent's advantage for lithium-based cell technologies of the current generations, new cell designs and material technologies accompanied with the next generations' technologies will open opportunities for new firms. This is especially the case in view of the argument of the so-called incumbent trap (Lee & Ki, 2017) that incumbent firms tend to behave resistant to radical innovations as next generations' technologies due to a stickiness with their current businesses. Due to the rapidly increasing worldwide demand for LIB cells, incumbent firms are currently heavily investing in an extension of their current generations' production sites and even setting up new productions in high-cost, developed countries in Europe and the USA. These activities in unfamiliar territory—country and industry wise—bear risks and thus even higher

[11]This technological roadmap is based on expert assessments published by the working group on batteries within the German Platform on Electric Vehicles (See NPE, 2016, Chap. 3). Similar technological forecasts were developed by other institutions (e.g. IEA, 2017).

costs, especially in the absence of governmental support. This is why our interviewed experts have assigned this technology-related window of opportunity to offer market entry possibilities, specifically for Western countries.

Furthermore, leading battery research institutions in Europe and the USA are assessed to be equally competent related to R&D achievements as leading researchers of the leading countries from Japan and South Korea. Next generations' technology is still examined in research laboratories, and no commercially viable prototype is available yet. A prerequisite for successful *reverse catch-up* would afford a holistic approach. Such a strategy implies an intense collaboration between research and industry and a direct transfer of current research findings into the education of future practitioners. This will lead to an optimal absorbing of frontier technology and simultaneous industrial education and application. The sheer size of R&D spending both in industrial firms and in public laboratories, the ability to combine material research with cell design and advanced manufacturing can work in favor of innovation in Europe and the USA again. Leapfrogging strategies and their success are also influenced by standard-setting strategies for new battery cell generations and their integration in larger systems. The dynamics between standards and the appropriation of patents and complementary assets may open up opportunities in Europe and North America.

An integral approach would moreover imply use of and collaboration with locally available production know-how. Future cell producers should start co-developing the future cell production plan together with leading research institutions and machinery firms. For example, Chinese firm CATL has announced to look for collaboration projects in Germany with locally available production excellence as the Fraunhofer Institute for Production Technology as well as robotic firms as the Kuka Group. It is further crucial to build on previous experiences and technological capabilities of the leading firms from Asia. Besides the learning effects from ongoing collaborations between Asian cell producers and Western automotive firms, the ability to attract experts from these countries will be decisive for absorbing tacit knowledge. The newly founded Swedish LIB firm, Northvolt, serves as an example for technology transfer from Asia to Europe as most of their battery engineers come from Asia.

5.2 Demand Induced Window of Opportunity

Different countries have different demand patterns. Knowledge about preferences and these demand patterns in end-user markets provides business opportunities for companies close to final customers. The argument of customer proximity as a decisive factor in the catch-up success of Chinese firm Haier has been illustrated in Wu et al. (2014). Asian companies had specific advantages in CE and IT in the past, and these have in turn favored innovation in the LIB field. For the next years, a growing percentage of batteries will be required for automobile applications, for storage systems and for special-purpose equipment, for which specific know-how of user preferences is more critical. The dominance of CE as the driver of change in LIB technology will certainly become reduced during the next years. Applications in the field of EVs are expected to grow at a higher rate, and when considering worldwide announced EV registration targets, even higher shares can be expected by 2030 (Fraunhofer, 2016; IEA, 2017).

Until recently, so far, produced LIB cells have been mainly applied in CE devices. The EV applications require adapted technological specifications, e.g., compared to CE products, higher power is needed. Furthermore, the market itself bears challenges for battery suppliers. LIB manufacturers have detected these needs early and have thus started cooperating with automotive companies as outlined in the previous sections. Western automotive firms are leading in automobile production, especially in premium car manufacturing. The key issue remains: will the stronger presence of Western automobile firms and suppliers lead to strong backward integration into battery cells? Will Western companies be able to manage the *reverse catch-up* process in advanced batteries? At present, the Achilles heel of the European EV market lies in the supply and production capacities for LIB cells. R&D capacities and patenting by German institutions have been stepped up, but this does not solve the immediate challenge of large-scale manufacturing. As has been shown in the preceding sections, this element of the EV value-chain is dominated by Asian manufacturers from Japan, South Korea and China. *Reverse catch-up* in Germany, as well as in several European countries, will thus crucially depend on the mastering of an integrated value chain for the electric drivetrain, with the battery-cell as its most strategic component. According to our experts' assessment the integration process and the manufacturing of the so-called battery pack and battery management systems will be controlled by the automotive OEM. The European supply and production architecture for battery cells, however, is still debated. The following options may be considered: (1) existing large Asian battery firms are opening production plants in Europe, (2) first-tier or second-tier automotive suppliers from Germany are starting battery cell manufacturing; and (3) new entrants that will start battery production in Europe as, e.g., in the case of the Swedish firm Northvolt. The first option is the most likely one, and there are ongoing investment projects. If it is not complemented by one of the other two options, however, *reverse catch-up* in Europe will not be sustainable.

Furthermore, high-power special-purpose applications of LIBs, as, e.g., power tools, for which strong user industries are still present in Europe may shift the focus of R&D activities and manufacturing investments away from the presently predominant Asian manufacturing locations. While German car manufacturers have been more hesitant so far in shifting to battery technology, other manufacturers of special-purpose equipment, including power tools, garden equipment or industrial handling equipment, have been much faster during the last years. This has led to a strong innovation move and to vertical integration at least into battery systems integration. The formation of BMZ, a subcontracting unit for special-purpose battery packs for different users in Europe, is an interesting case. Eventually, this will also lead to the formation of battery cell production plants. The project on joint European cell production, TerraE,[12] may be a viable move in this direction. In many cases, it is difficult for a former leader to gain back industries that have once been lost out to more successful catch-up nations. First of all, disinvestment of capital and human skills over longer periods will lead to high investment requirements once a country or a region may decide to reinvest. The level of innovation, entrepreneurship and continuous improvement in the catch-up nation may have led to such a level of superiority that the former incumbent can no longer respond. Ignorance on the side of the business community in the country that has encountered a downturn may lead to a failure in understanding key performance factors and new rules of the game now defined by challengers from earlier catch-up nations.

6 Concluding Remarks

As has been shown in the preceding, Europe and the USA have lost out in key technologies for advanced LIB cell production between 1995 and 2015. Strong market inducements from electronic consumer products, strong investments and complementary investments in the product, as well as process technology, have shifted the locus of innovation to Japan, South Korea and China. Western countries have lost out in application capabilities and in advanced manufacturing during the first two generations of rechargeable batteries. Even though innovation in cell technology and manufacturing for CE and EV has not been followed, some remaining European LIB manufacturers have specialized in niche markets, such as Varta, Johnson Controls, Saft and Leclanché. When analyzing the catch-up possibilities of Europe, it is necessary also to address the competencies within Europe. In the field of fundamental research and material science, there are still strong capabilities and a large enough talent pool. Europe has leading R&D institutions in battery cell technology.

There is a long tradition in electrochemistry and research that can be re-activated, particularly for the third and fourth generation of battery technology. Public support programs at the federal as well as state level have strengthened these capabilities during the last years and are complemented by European research funds. There is a vivid and stable scientific community. Since the early days of advanced battery research, German inventors, for example, were quite active in publishing and patenting. Robert Bosch GmbH was among the first firms to file international LIB patents (both in the USA and in Europe in 1983). However, German commercialization then and even after a revived approach within the last years has not been followed due to a risk-averse strategy in view of the challenging competition with experienced incumbent firms.

[12]TerraE is a consortium of the following companies: Manz AG, Electrovaya Litarion, BMZ Group, Thyssen-Krupp AG and M + W GmbH.

The German passenger car manufacturers were comparatively slow in adapting to EVs until now. One of the main reasons was the strong reliance on Diesel technology as well as the strong resistance among engineers with a preference for sophisticated internal combustion engines. The challenge by the US automotive start-up Tesla, as well as the "Dieselgate" scandal since 2015 led to behavioral changes among automobile companies, consumers as well as regulators. So far, typical "teething problems" were upholding stronger growth, including high purchase prices and the limited supply of attractive new EV models. Furthermore, the limited number of EV charging stations in Germany provided another bottleneck. The most recent update of the report of the national German platform on E-mobility (NPE, 2018) shows that European automobile firms are able to attain high market shares also in other European EV markets, which offer the best opportunities for a demand-induced catch-up strategy.

We have examined past and recent developments on the market for lithium-ion batteries. We found support for catch-up successes of Korean and Chinese firms with a similar route to previously studied catch-up processes of these countries in other industries as consumer electronics or semiconductors. The novelty of our analysis includes recent reverse dependency patterns where firms from developed countries as Germany and the USA are dependent on frontier technology dominated by firms from the Far East. With our findings, we have outlined a framework for *reverse catch-up* and its conditions and have thereby contributed to the understanding of catching up from a developed country's perspective. Our findings, however, are based on an in-depth case study analysis of one industry, LIBs, and can thus not be generalized. Owed to the novelty of this topic, very little is known about the conditions for a reverse knowledge transfer from East to West. More research is needed on this new phenomenon and on the role of emerging markets' firms as incumbents. Therefore, we suggest further investigations on the role of catching-up firms from developed countries, (2) the role of incumbent firms from emerging markets and the conditions for successful knowledge transfer from East to West.

Acknowledgments We would like to thank two anonymous referees for their helpful comments and recommendations on an earlier version of this article. Furthermore, we thank the Unibund of the University of Hohenheim for the received travel funding for a presentation of this article at the 17th International Schumpeter Society Conference, held in Seoul in 2018. The authors further declare that they do not have any conflict of interest.

References

Abramovitz, M. (1986). Catching up, forging ahead, and falling behind. *The Journal of Economic History, 46*(2), 385–406. https://doi.org/10.1017/S0022050700046209

Amsden, A. (1989). *Asia's next giant: South Korea and late industrialization.* Oxford University Press.

Andermann. (2016). *The xEV industry insider report, 2016.* Total Battery Consulting.

Bryman, A., & Bell, E. (2015). *Business research methods* (4th ed.). Oxford University Press.

Cohen, W. M., & Levinthal, D. A. (1990). Absorptive capacity: A new perspective on learning and innovation. *Administrative Science Quarterly, 35*(1), 128–152. https://doi.org/10.2307/2393553
Crabtree, G., Kocs, E., & Trahey, L. (2015). The energy-storage frontier: Lithium-ion batteries and beyond. *MRS Bulletin, 40*(12), 1067–1076. https://doi.org/10.1557/mrs.2015.259
EU. (2016). *Lithium-ion battery value chain and related opportunities for Europe*. EU JRC Science for Policy Report.
EU. (2017). *EU competitiveness in advanced Li-ion batteries for e-mobility and stationary storage applications – Opportunities and actions*. EU JRC Science for Policy Report, Netherlands.
EU R&D Scoreboard. (2014). *The 2014 EU industrial R&D investment scoreboard*. EU JRC Science for Policy Report.
EU R&D Scoreboard. (2017). *The 2017 EU industrial R&D investment scoreboard*. EU JRC Science for Policy Report, Luxembourg.
Fraunhofer. (2016). *Gesamt-Roadmap Lithium-Ionen-Batterien 2030*. Fraunhofer Institut für System- und Innovationsforschung (FHG-ISI), Karlsruhe.
Gerschenkron, A. (1962). *Economic backwardness in historical perspective*. Harvard University Press.
IEA. (2017). *Global EV outlook 2017. Two million and counting*. International Energy Agency, OECD/IEA.
Jin, B. (2019). Country-level technological disparities, market feedback, and scientists' choice of technologies. *Research Policy, 48*(1), 385–400. https://doi.org/10.1016/.j.respol.2018.09.007
Julien, C., Mauger, A., Vijh, A., & Zaghib, K. (2016). Lithium batteries. In *In lithium batteries, science and technology, 29-67*. Springer.
Kawamoto, H. (2010). Trends of R&D on materials for high-power and large-capacity lithium-ion batteries for vehicles application. *Quarterly Review, 36*, 34–54.
Lall, S. (1992). Technological capabilities and industrialization. *World Development, 20*(2), 165–186. https://doi.org/10.1016/0305-750X(92)90097-F
Lee, K. (2005). Making a technological catch-up: Barriers and opportunities. *Asian Journal of Technology Innovation, 13*(2), 97–131. https://doi.org/10.1080/19761597.2005.9668610
Lee, K. (2013). Schumpeterian analysis of economic catch-up. In *Knowledge, path-creation, and the middle-income trap*. Cambridge University Press.
Lee, K., & Ki, J. (2017). Rise of latecomers and catch-up cycles in the world steel industry. *Research Policy, 46*(2), 365–375. https://doi.org/10.1016/j.respol.2016.09.010
Lee, K., & Malerba, F. (2017). Catch-up cycles and changes in industrial leadership: Windows of opportunity and responses of firms and countries in the evolution of sectoral systems. *Research Policy, 46*(2), 338–351. https://doi.org/10.1016/j.respol.2016.09.006
Levine, S. (2016). *The powerhouse*. Penguin Books.
Malerba, F., & Nelson, R. (2011). Learning and catching up in different sectoral systems: Evidence from six industries. *Industrial and Corporate Change, 20*(6), 1645–1675. https://doi.org/10.1093/icc/dtr062
Mayring, P. (2000). Qualitative content analysis. *Forum Qualitative Social Research, 1*(2), 20. Retrieved from http://nbn-resolving.de/urn:nbn:de:0114-fqs0002204
Nelson, R. R., & Pack, H. (1999). The Asian miracle and modern growth theory. *The Economic Journal, 109*(457), 416–436. https://doi.org/10.1111/1468-0297.00455
NPE. (2016). *Roadmap integrierte Zell- und Batterieproduktion Deutschland*. AG 2 – Batterietechnologie, Gemeinsame Geschäftsstelle Elektromobilität der Bundesregierung (GGEMO), Berlin & Munich.
NPE. (2018). *Fortschrittsbericht 2018 – Markthochlaufphase*. Nationale Plattform Elektromobilität (NPE).
OECD. (2018, February). *Regpat database*.
Park, S., Taguchi, H., Kan, J., Han, S. H., Dunwoodie, M., Kim, C., & Ha, V. (2016). *F.I.t.t* (For investors – Charging the car of tomorrow). Deutsche Bank Markets Research.

Perez, C., & Soete, L. (1988). Catching-up in technology: Entry barriers and windows of opportunity. In G. Dosi, C. Freeman, R. Nelson, G. Silverberg, & L. Soete (Eds.), *Technical change and economic theory* (pp. 458–479). Pinter Publishers.

Sauer, A. (2018). *Funktionale Dynamik von Technologischen Innovationssystemen im Bereich der Erneuerbaren Energietechnologien: Das Beispiel der weltweiten Durchsetzung von batteriebetriebenen Fahrzeugen und Plug-in-Hybridfahrzeugen.* Dissertationsschrift Universität Hohenheim. http://opus.unihohenheim.de/volltexte/2018/1547/pdf/Dissertation_Andreas_Sauer_November_2018.pdf

Stebbins, R. A. (2001). Exploratory research in the social sciences. In *Qualitative research methods series* (Vol. 48). Sage.

van Dijk, B. (2018). *Orbis database. As of May 2018.*

VDMA Batterieproduktion. (2018). *Roadmap Batterie-Produktionsmittel 2030 – Update 2018.* VDMA Verlag GmbH.

Vernon, R. (1966). International investment and international trade in the product cycle. *The Quarterly Journal of Economics, 80*(2), 190–207. https://doi.org/10.2307/1880689

Wade, R. H. (2004). Is globalization reducing poverty and inequality? *World Development, 32*(4), 567–589. https://doi.org/10.1016/j.worlddev.2003.10.007

World Bank. (1998). *The east Asian miracle, economic growth and public policy.* Oxford University Press.

Wu, X., Dou, W., Gao, Y., & Huang, F. (2014). How to implement secondary product innovations for the domestic market: A case from Haier washing machines. *International Journal of Technology Management, 64*(2/3/4), 232–254. https://doi.org/10.1504/IJTM.2014.059930

Yoshino, A. (2014). Development of the lithium-ion battery and recent technological trends. In *Lithium-ion batteries. Advances and applications* (pp. 1–20). Elsevier. https://doi.org/10.1016/C2011-0-09658-8

Is Drug Patent Protection a Determinant of the Location of Pharmaceutical FDI? China's Experience

Nejla Yacoub and Hajer Souei

Abstract The economic literature reveals that the relationship between patents and Foreign Direct Investments (FDI) depends on industries and countries' features. Our research considers the pharmaceutical industry in China. This choice stems from a contradictory observation: China is known for its important imitation capacities, but at the same time, it is becoming one of the most attractive destinations to technology intensive FDI, for instance, pharmaceutical FDI. To explore whether patent protection plays a role in attracting pharmaceutical FDI in China we conduct a documentary analysis over the 1980–2015 period. Data is compiled from specialized press and international and national economic institutions (*such as the World Trade Organization-WTO* and *the Chinese Intellectual Property Office—SIPO*). Using these statistics, we construct a composite index measuring the pharmaceutical patent protection in China (PPP index) to analyze its correlation with inward pharmaceutical FDI. For a better reliability of the results, the study considers only the forms of FDI that are—according to economic literature—the most sensitive to patent protection, i.e., drugs producing and/or research and development (R&D) FDI. Our analysis suggests that enhancing drug patent protection could have had a positive impact on inward pharmaceutical FDI in China, especially R&D subsidiaries. However, this impact is conditioned by the existence of other advantages for FDI location such as the development of technology parks and the knowledge-based human capital policy. Hence, drug patent protection would be a determinant for attracting pharmaceutical FDI provided that it is a part of a strong innovation system and active innovation policies.

Keywords Attractiveness · China · FDI · Patent protection · Patent index, Pharmaceuticals

N. Yacoub (✉) · H. Souei
Faculté des Sciences Economiques et de Gestion de Mahdia (FSEG Mahdia), Université de Monastir, Mahdia, Tunisia

A. Pyka, K. Lee (eds.), *Innovation, Catch-up and Sustainable Development*, Economic Complexity and Evolution, https://doi.org/10.1007/978-3-030-84931-3_9

JEL L65 · O34 · O53 · F21 · F23

1 Introduction

Most developing countries strive to ameliorate their attractiveness to foreign direct investment (FDI). They invest to build an economic and institutional framework favorable for foreign investors. Until the late 1990s developing countries have usually focused on their comparative advantages (*market size, geographic location, etc.*) and short run constructed advantages (*especially tax incentives*). This policy has been effective in attracting low technology-intensive FDI. But in the era of information society, it is high-tech investments that are targeted by the host economies, especially developing ones. Attractiveness to these investments requires implementing structural advantages, for instance, a sound logistic and communication infrastructure, active innovation policies, a stable political and legal framework.

The economic literature stresses the importance of intellectual property rights (IPR)—especially patents—as a determinant of the location of technology-intensive FDI (Pratomo & Hastiadi, 2017; Shapiro and Mathur, 2014; Lippoldt & Park, 2003; Combe and Pfister, 2001). In fact, firms operating in the high-tech industries are found to be attracted by fairly strict patent protection (Smarzynska, 2002). In addition to the industry's characteristics, those related to the host country also influence the significance and the nature of the impact of patents on inward FDI. For some economists, these characteristics include the economic development (Yacoub & Yacoub, 2011; Lippoldt & Park, 2003) and governance (Aho, 2013). Yet, for other economists, the imitation capacities of host countries are the main feature that influences the relationship between patents and inward FDI (Smith, 2001). In this line, patent protection is found to be significantly attractive to FDI in countries that present a strong threat of new technologies imitation.

Globally, the economic literature reveals divergent conclusions about the "patent-FDI" relationship since it depends on countries, industries, and even firms. Therefore to reveal precise results, it is more efficient to target one industry of a specific country. In this perspective, our research considers the pharmaceutical industry in China. Undoubtedly, this is not a random choice; it is argued by a curious observation: China is known for its high imitation capacities, but at the same time, it is becoming one of the most attractive destinations toward technology-intensive FDI; for instance, pharmaceutical ones.

On the basis of elements provided, our research aims to explore whether to and to which extent has drugs patentability played a role in attracting pharmaceutical FDI to China.

Answering this question requires a methodology combining a theoretical and an empirical approach. Our chapter will be then divided into four main parts. In the first one, we make a literature review on the relationship between patent protection and attractiveness to FDI. In the second part, we analyze the main features and transformations of the Chinese economy and pharmaceutical sector since 1980. In the third part, we proceed with a documentary analysis based on data compiled basically from the specialized press and reports of economic institutions both national (*such as the Chinese Intellectual Property Office—SIPO*) and international (*such as the World Trade Organization—WTO*). Using these statistics we measure a composite index assessing the pharmaceutical patent protection (PPP) in China. Then, we analyze the correlation of our PPP index with inward pharmaceutical FDI. For a better reliability of the results, the study considers only the forms of FDI that are—according to the economic literature—the most sensitive to patentability, i.e., producing Greenfield investments and research and development (R&D) subsidiaries. In the fourth and last sections, we discuss our study's main concluding remarks.

2 Patent Protection and FDI: A Literature Review

The economic literature reveals that due to many factors (2.2) the relationship between patent protection and FDI is divergent (2.1).

2.1 The Divergent Relationship Between Patent Protection and FDI

According to some studies, patent protection has a positive impact on inward FDI while for other studies the impact is negative for some of them or even insignificant for some others.

2.1.1 Insignificant Impact of Patent Protection on FDI

Ferrantino (1993) and Primo-Braga and Fink (1998) conclude that there is no statistically significant influence of patent protection on the US multinationals' location decisions. The research conducted by Maskus and Eby-Konan (1994) about the pharmaceutical industry in four countries (Argentina, Brazil, India, and Mexico) shows that the impact depends mainly on whether patents can transform the market structure from competition into monopoly. Also, patent protection seems to play a marginal role in attracting FDI when foreign firms are able to centralize their sophisticated technologies and thus decrease the likelihood of being imitated by local firms (Pfister, 2003).

2.1.2 A Positive Impact of Patent Protection on Inward FDI

Several scientific works result in a positive impact of patent protection on inward FDI (Kirkilis & Koboti, 2015; Yacoub, 2007, 2012; Combe and Pfister, 2001; Lesser, 2000; Saggi, 2000; Maskus, 1998; Lee & Mansfield, 1996; Seyoum, 1996). In a survey on US chemical multinationals Maskus (1998) shows that 80% of them would not locate their subsidiaries in countries where patent protection is weak. These results are confirmed by Lesser (2000) who shows that an increase by 10% of the patent's coefficient in a sample of host countries generates an increase by 200 million $ of their inward FDI from the USA, Germany, and Japan. A similar conclusion has been revealed by Yacoub and Yacoub (2011) for 30% of the drug-producing foreign subsidiaries they have surveyed in Tunisia which confirm that patent protection is a guarantee allowing them protecting their technologies.

In this same framework Hassan et al. (2010) refer to the Dunning's OLI paradigm[1] to argue that strong patent protection in host countries offers foreign investors an ownership advantage (by preserving their technological monopoly) and a location advantage (by reducing the risk of imitation). However, the study results in an insignificant impact of patents on the internalization advantage since they rather encourage externalization via licenses.

2.1.3 A Negative Impact of Patent Protection on Inward FDI

The negative impact of patent protection on inward FDI is shown mostly in studies on developing countries (Glass & Saggi, 2002; Kumar, 2000). This is mainly explained by failures in patent *enforcement* in these countries (Yacoub, 2007). Moreover, in some cases when the patent protection is weak or inexistent, foreign firms can decide to locate abroad in order to prevent being imitated by local firms. In this case, strengthening patent protection would decrease the imitation risk in the host country and encourage the foreign firm to dislocate from that country. In this same line, the US multinationals studied by Ferrantino (1993) are shown to prefer locating their subsidiaries in countries where patent protection is not quite strong. Combe and Pfister (2001) present similar findings showing that the weak patent protection in Brazil in the 1990s did not hinder US multinationals to prefer entering the Brazilian market by FDI (700 million $) rather than by exports (50 million $).

[1] Ownership, Location, Internalization.

2.2 *Factors Explaining the Divergent Relationship "Patent Protection—FDI"*

We can divide factors explaining the divergent relationship between patent protection and FDI into three main groups: firm-related factors, industry-related factors, and factors related to the host countries.

2.2.1 Factors Related to the Firm's Intrinsic Characteristics

These factors trace back to the reasons behind the firm's very decision of investing abroad. This leads to understanding the firm's intrinsic characteristics as regards its risk aversion, the phases of its products' life cycle, the degree of sophistication of its technology, and many other specific features (Yacoub & Yacoub, 2011). For example, a firm that locates abroad in order to valorize its monopolistic advantage would be positively influenced by patent protection in the host country. However, firms offering standardized products (i.e., products with low levels of innovation and technology) generally choose to locate abroad in order to reduce production and/or transaction costs. In this case, the role of patent protection would be trivial. The research of Yacoub and Yacoub (2011) surveying all the foreign pharmaceutical firms in Tunisia shows that patent protection is important as a location determinant for only 30% of them while the other 70% chose the Tunisian location basically to benefit from the local human capital advantage combining competencies and qualifications on the one hand and relatively low costs on the other hand.

The type of the FDI is also an important factor that determines the existence and the sign of the relationship between patent protection and FDI. Maskus (1998) shows that strengthening patent protection influences vertical FDI more than horizontal FDI since technology externalities and imitation risk are higher with vertical FDIs. The influence is even more important in joint-ventures and licenses: "*foreign firms are less willing to invest in joint-ventures with local companies, if they risk losing their proprietary assets*" (Primo-Braga & Fink, 1998, p. 173). Indeed the weaker the foreign firm's control on its technologies abroad is, the more positively significant the impact of patent protection would be.

2.2.2 Factors Related to the Industry

The relationship between patent protection and FDI varies significantly depending on the different industries. The impact is likely to be positive on technology-intensive FDI (Kirkilis & Koboti, 2015; Park and Lippoldt, 2005; Smarzynska Javorcik, 2004; Maskus, 1998). Thus, countries with a strong patent system are shown to be more attractive to pharmaceutical FDI (Yacoub & Yacoub, 2011; Coriat & Orsi, 2004; Saggi, 2000), while according to Maskus (1998) multinationals operating in labor-intensive sectors, for instance, the textile industry, are attracted rather by production costs advantages. Indeed in this survey on a sample of US multinationals operating in six different industries and located in 16 host countries Maskus (1998) confirms that even though all the production subsidiaries are sensitive to the potential of patent protection in the host countries, the impact is specifically more important in the chemical industry. Similar findings are revealed for the German (Maskus, 2004; Fink, 1997) and the Japanese (Lesser, 2000) multinationals.

2.2.3 Factors Related to the Host Countries

Several studies assert that the relationship between patent protection and inward FDI depends on the host country's characteristics, especially as regards the level of economic development. This thesis is confirmed particularly by studies considering samples combining developed and developing countries. For example, Seyoum (1996) estimates the impact on inward FDI in a sample of 27 developed, developing, and least developed countries on the period going from 1975 to 1990. The impact of patent protection is revealed to be positive and strong on FDI in developed countries, while it is moderate in developing ones (explaining 43% of their FDI inflows) and marginal in the least developed ones (explaining only 13% of their inward FDI).

In the same line, Pfister and Mayer (2001) use a microeconomic approach to assess the impact of patent protection on the choice of FDI location of 755 French multinationals within 37 countries of different development levels. Unlike Seyoum (1996) their empirical analysis covering 20 years (1980s–1990s) reveals that the strongest positive correlation between patent protection and the inward FDI is for developing countries.

This unexpected result can be explained by the role of the host country's imitation capacities. This variable has been highlighted in the economic literature as a crucial determinant of the relationship between patent protection and FDI (Yacoub, 2017, 2012; Kirkilis & Koboti, 2015; Yacoub & Yacoub, 2011; Pfister, 2003; Smith, 2001, 1999; Nair-Reichert, 2000). The imitation capacities depend on the local country's absorption capacities of new and sophisticated technologies (Smith, 1999). Hence, strengthening patent protection would be an attractive factor towards inward FDI in developing countries with high imitation capacities, such as China, India and Brazil. Indeed countries with higher imitation capacities are obviously riskier for foreign investors but also they are more likely to be a source of innovativeness. The elasticity of their attractiveness toward FDI is high. Therefore, when these countries enhance their patent protection systems their FDI inflows would increase significantly. Delving further into this point, Smith (1999) suggests considering the question rather in terms of the "*threat-of-imitation*" which can be defined as the combination resulting of the degree of "imitation abilities" and the level of "patent protection." Then the impact of patent protection strengthening on FDI will depend on the degree of the "threat-of-imitation." As shown in Fig. 1, this combination results in three degrees of threat-of-imitation: weak, moderate, and high.

According to the Fig. 1, when the threat-of-imitation is weak (case 1), patent protection strengthening generates a negative impact on inward FDI; an impact

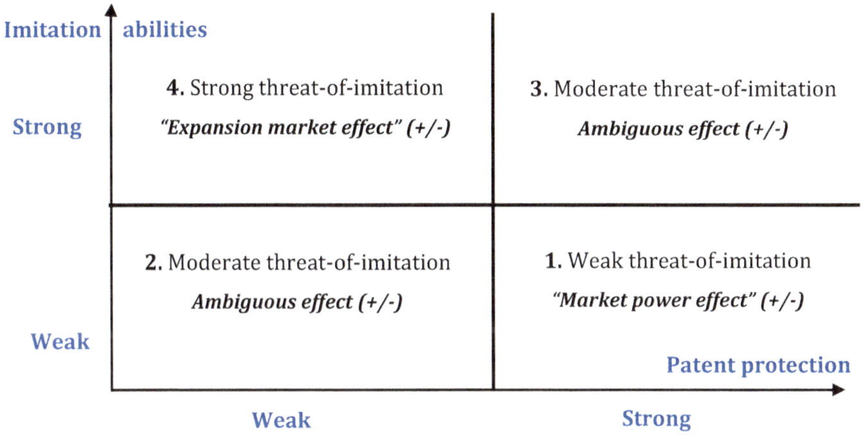

Fig. 1 The impact of patent protection strengthening on FDI, according to the host country's threat-of-imitation. Source: Authors' version, based on Smith (1999), p. 155

called "market power effect" and explained by an abusive monopoly power. It is the case of countries that combine weak imitation capacities and strong patent protection. *Per contra*, strong imitation abilities combined with weak patent protection result in a strong threat-of-imitation (case 4). So strengthening patent protection generates a positive impact on inward FDI called an "expansion market effect."

In the two remaining situations the threat-of-imitation is moderate (cases 2 and 3), either resulting from the combination of both strong patent protection and strong imitation abilities or of both, weak patent protection, and weak imitation abilities. In these both situations, the impact of patent protection strengthening on FDI is ambiguous. It can be either negative or positive depending on industry-related factors, firm-related factors, and other factors related to the host country's features and policies.

These findings are confirmed by Smith (2001) where the US multinationals are shown to be attracted by the strengthening of patent protection (measured by the signature of TRIPS agreements) in countries with high threat-of-imitation; illustrating then the advent of an *expansion market effect*. However, the study of the Tunisian pharmaceutical industry confirms the advent of a *market power effect* due to a moderate threat-of-imitation (resulting from relatively moderate imitation capacities and strong patent protection) (Yacoub & Yacoub, 2011).

According to our literature review, it is obvious that the relationship between patent protection and FDI is ambiguous since it depends on several factors that overlap with each other. Therefore, we restate that clarifying this issue requires analyzing it on an empirical scale all by considering a specific country and a specific sector. In order to clarify this ambiguity the remaining of our study targets the case of the pharmaceutical industry in China.

3 Pharmaceutical Patent Laws and FDI Trends in China: Inventory of Fixtures

Since the end of the 1970s, China has witnessed important economic and institutional changes. The State's economic openness policy is the main axis of these changes and it has considerably influenced the local pharmaceutical industry.

3.1 A Preview of the Pharmaceutical Industry in China

In 1978, China implemented an economic development plan aiming to become the *world's manufactory* by facilitating business to foreign investors, mobilizing its important human resources and benefitting from globalization.

3.1.1 The Trends of Pharmaceutical FDI in China

Until the end of the 1980s, China has been an attracting destination mainly for labor-intensive foreign investments, especially in the textile and leather industries (Lasserre, 2007). Yet since the 1990s, it has become an interesting location for technology-intensive multinationals, such as in electronics and pharmaceuticals. As shown in the following graph, pharmaceutical FDIs have recorded a notable growth. This growth has known four main slowdowns, though. The first and the second ones are recorded in 1998 and 2000 and could be explained by the Asian crisis. The third slowdown has occurred from 2004 till 2006 and the fourth one occurred in 2012 (Fig. 2).

Since the 2000s China has transformed from the world's manufactory into the world's pool for R&D and technology-intensive FDI. In fact, by the year 2004 there

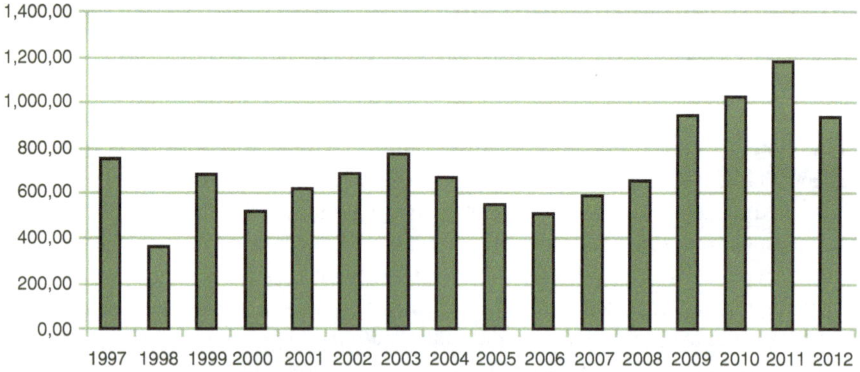

Fig. 2 Inward pharmaceutical FDI trends in China *(millions $)*. Source: Spigarelli and Wei (2014) and CEIC (2017)

have been about 700 R&D foreign centers. Likewise, by 2015 we notice that most of the pharmaceutical leaders have set R&D subsidiaries in China (IHEST, 2015).

3.1.2 The Location Advantages for Pharmaceutical FDI in China

China's location determinants for pharmaceutical FDI are mainly related to comparative advantages such as the market size (ranked as the second in the world in 2018 with a share of 8.2%) and the competitive production costs, especially those of labor, energy, and lands (LEEM, 2019). On a different scale, China is an attractive location for FDI as regards clinical trials. Indeed, on the one hand, clinical trials costs in China represent only 40% of those in the USA (Samedan Ltd, 2011). On the other hand, the Chinese regulation as regards those trials is much more flexible than in Western countries (Noury, 2017).

Even though comparative advantages play an important role they remain insufficient to attract pharmaceutical FDI. Attractiveness to technology-intensive FDI requires the implementation of structural advantages, for instance, logistic and communication infrastructures, active innovation policies, regulation, and institutional advantages. In this framework, China has invested in restructuring and strengthening its intellectual property rights (IPR) system in order to meet the foreign investors' requirements in terms of protection of their new and sophisticated technologies.

3.2 The Patent System in China: Special Features and Trends

Patent protection reforms in China have resulted from both internal and external factors. Internal factors are related to the innovation policy requirements. External factors stem from pressures by the WTO to lead China complying with the TRIPS agreements' standards.

However, before even the creation of the WTO, China has also been pressured by some developed countries in order to protect pharmaceutical patents. Bosworth and Yang (2000) explain these pressures by the important losses undergone by occidental multinationals in the Chinese market. Hence, since 1979 China has signed several international IPR agreements such as the World Intellectual Property Organization (WIPO) membership agreement in 1980 and the Paris convention on Industrial Property in 1985. Yet, China signing the TRIPS agreements in 1994 and joining the WTO in 2001 after 15 years of negotiations (Yang, 2003), remain the most outstanding facts in the country's IPR history. Thenceforth the Chinese State has started implementing technical and administrative institutions specialized in dealing with IPR applications, for instance, the Sino Intellectual Property Rights Office (*SIPO*).

Through these reforms, China's IPR system has started transforming into a relatively conform and up-to-date one. This resulted in a notable increase of patent

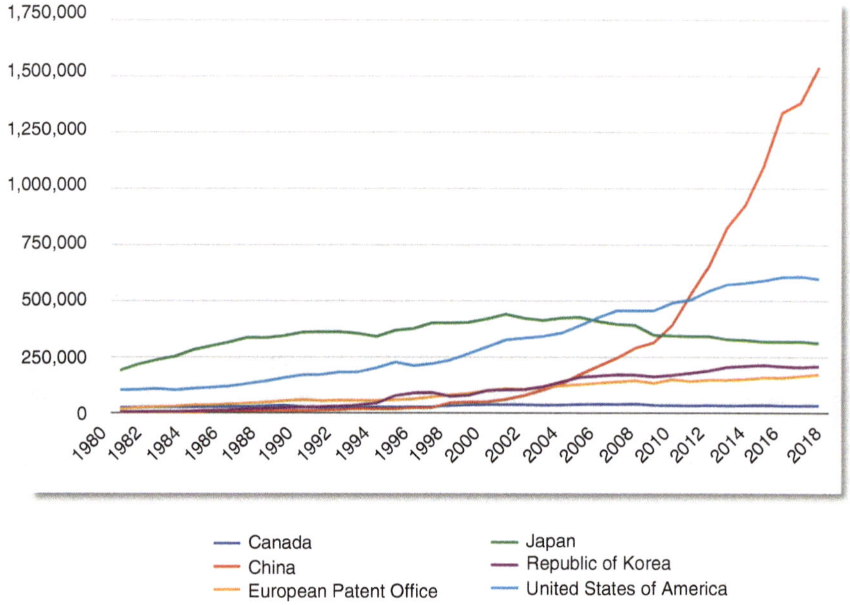

Fig. 3 Patent applications trends in the world's top 6 patent offices. Source: WIPO (2020)

applications in China growing with a steady annual rate of 15% since the first patent law was promulgated in 1984 and of 23% since this law's reform in 2001 (Fig. 3).

Since 2012 China is top ranked in terms of patent applications worldwide before the USA (second rank) and Japan (third rank). In 2018, China has recorded more than 1.542 million patent applications that is a growth rate of 11.6% comparing with 2017 (WIPO, 2020).

Pharmaceutical investors are among the most active sectors in terms of patent applications in China with a share of 5.37%. Most of the applications are made by leader pharmaceutical foreign investors such as *Novartis* (Switzerland), *MSD* (USA), *Takeda* (Japan), and *Bayer* (Germany) (Drug Patent Watch, 2017), which confirms the interest shown by pharmaceutical multinationals in patent protection in China.

4 The Impact of Patent Protection on Pharmaceutical FDI in China: A Documentary Analysis

At this stage, we intend to analyze empirically whether patent protection has played a significant role in attracting pharmaceutical FDI in China.

4.1 Methods

Previous empirical studies of the relationship between patents and FDI estimate econometric models such as gravity models, panels, and times series (Tanaka & Iwaisako, 2014; Kirkilis & Koboti, 2015; Lippoldt & Park, 2003; Glass & Saggi, 2002; Smith, 2001) or conduct firm-level surveys on multinationals (Yacoub & Yacoub, 2011; Pfister, 2003; Maskus, 1998; Seyoum, 1996; Ferrantino, 1993). We use a different method that is a documentary analysis based on data from international and national institutions such as the WTO and the SIPO, and from specialized press in the global pharmaceutical industry. Our choice is argued by two main arguments. The first one is that our research considers one country which makes panel and gravity models unusable. The second argument is that required data to explore the patent-FDI question in the pharmaceutical industry needs to be limited to the FDI that would be influenced by patent protection. These include firms producing drugs and active ingredients, R&D centers, clinical trials subsidiaries, joint ventures, and other similar investment forms where technology externalities are high.

Our analysis refers mainly to Smith (1999) as regards the threat-of-imitation of the pharmaceutical industry in China in order to analyze the impact of patent protection on the country's inward FDI.

4.2 Assessing the Pharmaceutical Threat-of-Imitation in China

We restate that according to Smith (1999) the impact of patent protection is expected to be positive (i.e., expansion market effect) on FDI inflows in countries with a high threat-of-imitation. Then assessing China's pharmaceutical threat-of-imitation requires first measuring both its imitation capacities and its patent protection potential.

4.2.1 The Pharmaceutical Imitation Capacities in China

The following map illustrates the origins, routes, and destinations of drugs. The logos' size indicates the extent of the counterfeit activity (production, transit, imports). A bigger drug tablet logo refers to an active zone in counterfeit drugs production (IRACM, 2017) (Fig. 4).

The map shows that Asia (China and India) is obviously the most active region in the production and the trade of counterfeit drugs. South America (especially Brazil) comes in the second rank followed by Russia, South Africa, and Turkey. Sub-Saharan Africa is shown to be the most dynamic market of counterfeit drugs followed by Russia and South America and then developed countries such as

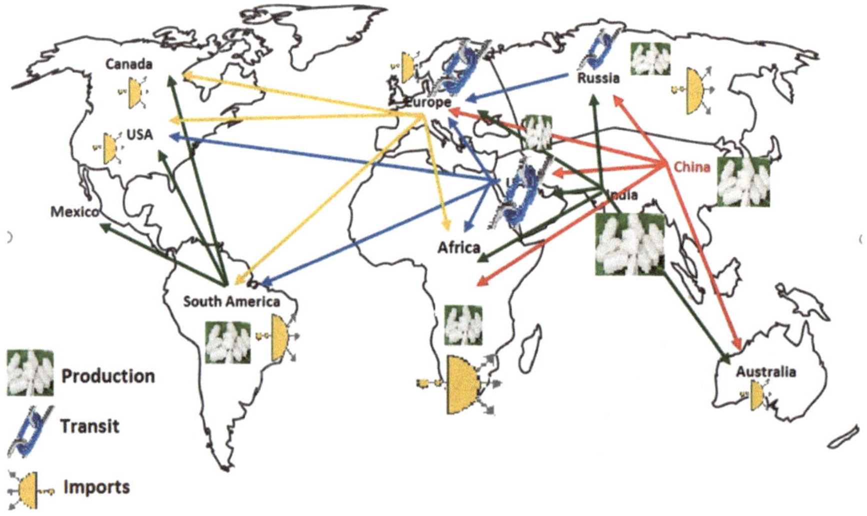

Fig. 4 Cartography of counterfeit drugs (2012). Source: Authors' version, based on Robert (2013)

Northern Europe, the USA, Canada, and Australia. The Gulf and Middle-East regions are the core route of counterfeit drugs.

Since the early 2000s, China has been ranked second over the 25 greatest imitator countries worldwide (Wang, 2013). It has reached the first rank since 2015 (Mackey et al., 2015), allowing to call it "*the counterfeiting empire*" (Robert, 2013).

4.2.2 The Pharmaceutical Patent Protection in China

One common problem encountered in patent studies is the measurement of the patent protection. To overcome this problem several authors have—since the 1990s—developed different patent indexes (Rapp & Rozek, 1990; Ginarte and Park, 1997; Pugatch, 2006; Yacoub, 2007; Lesser, 2011; La Croix & Liu, 2014, Pratomo & Hastiadi, 2017).

Our research refers to four main studies to construct an up-to-date and adequate pharmaceutical patent index. Our index is adapted from the two general indexes of Ginarte and Park (1997) and Yacoub (2007) and at the same time from the two pharmaceutical indexes of Pugatch (2006) and La Croix and Liu (2014). We called it the "*Pharmaceutical Patent Protection index*" (PPP index). Required data to construct our index is collected from official documents of national and international institutions and from interviews with intellectual property professionals. Our composite PPP index is aggregated from five sub-indexes.

The pharmaceutical patent international agreements index

The pharmaceutical patent international agreements (PPIA) index considers three major international agreements that recognize patent protection: (i) the Paris convention on the industrial property (1883) and its revisions; (ii) the Patent Cooperation Treaty (PCT, 1979), and (iii) the TRIPS agreements (1994). For each one of these agreements, the mark is "1/3" starting from the date China has signed it and "0" otherwise. Thus the value of the PPIA index ranges between "0" and "1."

The pharmaceutical patent coverage index

The pharmaceutical patent coverage (PPC) index indicates whether the following drugs-related domains are patentable in China: (i) new molecular entities, (ii) new medical indications, (iii) incremental drug innovations, and (iv) pharmaceutical processes. For each one of these components, the mark is "¼" starting from the date China has signed it and "0" otherwise. Thus, the PPC index ranges between "0" and "1."

The pharmaceutical patent enforcement index

The pharmaceutical patent enforcement (PPE) includes 4 components related to patent strengthening and enforcement: (i) the burden of proof reversal, (ii) provisions for pre-trial injunctions, (iii) contributory infringements, and (iv) supplementary protection certificates (SPC). Each of these components takes "¼" if it is protected by the patent law in China and "0" otherwise. Same as the PPIA and the PPC indexes, the PPE index ranges between "0" and "1."

The pharmaceutical patent restrictions index

The pharmaceutical patent restrictions (PPR) index measures the restrictions on pharmaceutical patent protection that are: (i) working requirements, (ii) compulsory licensing, and (iii) revocation of patents. Each one of these components takes "1/3" if the patent law in China *does not* recognize it and "0" otherwise. The PPR index also ranges between "0" and "1."

The pharmaceutical patent length index

The pharmaceutical patent length (PPL) index measures the legal duration of pharmaceutical patents in China. According to the TRIPS agreements, this duration is of 20 years starting from the date of the application submission. Then "PPL = n/20." The value of PPL is "1" if the legal patent duration is full and "<1" otherwise. It is considered equal to "0" during the years where pharmaceuticals were not patentable in China.

The pharmaceutical patent protection index

The global composite pharmaceutical patent protection index ranges between "0" (no protection) and "5" (strongest full protection). Computing our Chinese pharmaceutical patent protection (PPP) index over the period between 1980 and 2019 reveals an important increase in the degree of the pharmaceutical patent protection. As shown in Fig. 5, the PPP index increased from 1.05 in 1980 to 3.6 in 2019, that is, a growth of 242.85%.

The PPP index recorded three major rises. The first important one traces back to 1993 and results from the 1992 patent law reform. The second rise (slight) is noticed in 1996 which is explained by the signature of the TRIPS agreements in 1994 and their entry into effect in 1995. We notice a second important rise in 2001 to a value of 3.6 against 2.4 in 2000 and it results from both the 2000 patent law reform and China's entry to the WTO Since 2001 the PPP index has stabilized at a value of 3.6.

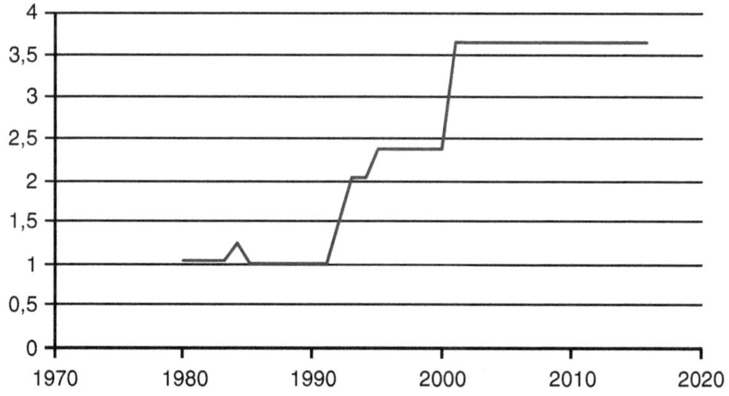

Fig. 5 Trends in the pharmaceutical patent protection index in China (1980–2019)

The trends in the PPP index confirm that since the 1980s China has made notable investments toward strengthening its patent regulation. However, its efficiency remains questioned, especially as regards failures in laws enforcement, the lack of genuine mechanisms to fight counterfeit, and the overcrowded patent examination system (Liu, 2016; Spigarelli & Wei, 2014; Yacoub, 2007; Fai, 2005).

4.2.3 The Pharmaceutical Threat-of-Imitation in China

On the one hand, China is a country with strong imitation capacities. On the other hand, the PPP index value (3.6 over a 5-point full value) allows ranking China as a country with strong pharmaceutical patent protection. Theoretically, both variables are high resulting in a moderate threat-of-imitation (case 3). The impact of further patent strengthening is then ambiguous.

Until the 1980s, the pharmaceutical patent protection was weak in China, the threat-of-imitation was at very high levels since the local imitation capacities are also at a very high level; China was obviously ranked at the case 4 of the table (a country with a strong threat-of-imitation). The strengthening of patent protection would first generate an expansion market effect on FDI inflows. However, as the Chinese government continues to strengthen its patent system, the local threat-of-imitation is supposed to turn from strong into moderate (case 3) generating an ambiguous impact on the FDI inflows. In this situation, two possible—but opposite—scenarios would occur.

(i) The first one is that the patent protection potential could be so high that it counteracts the high imitation capacities, which would weaken the threat-of-imitation and then generate a market power effect (case 1 of Table 1).
(ii) The second one is that the imitation capacities could be so high that they counteract the high patent protection, which makes the threat-of-imitation remain strong and generate thus an expansion market effect on inward FDI.

Table 1 Threat-of-imitation in China and expected impacts on pharmaceutical FDI

	Weak patent protection	Strong patent protection
Strong imitation capacities	**4.** Strong threat-of-imitation *« Expansion market effect » (+)*	**3.** Moderate threat-of-imitation *Ambiguous effect (+/-)*

Source: Authors' version, based on Smith (1999)

Table 2 The real threat-of-imitation in China and expected impacts on pharmaceutical FDI

	Weak patent protection	Strong patent protection
Strong imitation capacities	**4.** Strong threat-of-imitation *« Expansion market effect » (+)*	**3.** Moderate threat-of-imitation *Ambiguous effect (+/-)*

Source: Authors' version, based on Smith (1999)

Beyond these theoretical scenarios, real observation shows that patent protection in China still suffers from genuine technical and enforcement failures. This means that the local threat-of-imitation is still relatively high in China (case 4) (Table 2).

In these conditions, strengthening the patent system, especially as regards enforcement would generate a further expansion market effect on inward pharmaceutical FDI.

4.3 *Research Assumptions, Data Analysis, and Results*

Our research assumption is that "*strengthening pharmaceutical patent protection enhances China's attractiveness towards FDI.*" To examine whether this assumption is valid we analyze the correlation between the PPP index and the pharmaceutical FDI inflows. These are reduced to the drugs producing and R&D Greenfield investments as they are the most responsive FDI to patent protection.

4.3.1 Exploring the Pharmaceutical FDI Activities in China

Until the 1980s, China was viewed by foreign firms as an attractive giant market. Thenceforth, it has become the world's manufactory thanks to its large labor resources and production low costs. Since the early 2000s, the Chinese economy has prevailed as an attractive location to production seeking FDI but also to R&D

Table 3 Main pharmaceutical leader having R&D subsidiaries in China

Firm	Country of origin	R&D fields in China	Date of establishment
Astra-Zeneca	Sweden/GB	Biological drugs, active ingredients	2001
Bayer	Germany	Chemical pharmacy	2003
Chiral Quest	USA	Pharmaceutical biotechnologies	2009
Eli Lilly	USA	Diabetes	1999
GSK	Great Britain	Neurological troubles, breathing diseases	2006
Johnson & Johnson	USA	New therapeutic approaches, traditional Chinese medicine	2009
Lonza	Switzerland	Active ingredients, organic chemistry	2003/2004
Novo Nordisk	Denmark	Diabetes, traditional Chinese medicine	2002
Pfizer	USA	Pharmaceutical biotechnologies	2005
Roche	Switzerland	Chemical pharmacy, traditional Chinese medicine	2004
Sanofi-Aventis	France	Diabetes, cancer, traditional Chinese medicine	2008/2010/2014

Source: Authors' version, based on the firms' different reports

seeking FDI. As illustrated in Table 3, all the top 20 big pharmaceutical firms have already set up R&D subsidiaries in China.

We notice that the main world's pharmaceutical leaders have settled their R&D units in China after 1999 (Spigarelli & Wei, 2014). China's increasing attractiveness to pharmaceutical innovation seeking FDI is mainly consequent to the economic policy aiming to build structural and innovation-driven location advantages. This policy is concretized by the strengthening of the patent system, the notable improvement of the human capital's academic formation and competencies and the multiplication of technology clusters all over the country. Technology clusters encourage R&D and innovation thanks to the territorial (Uzunidis, 2010) and the technological proximity effect and contribute to building a strong innovation system.

Pharmaceutical foreign R&D centers are concentrated mainly in the regions of *Shanghai* and Beijing which have become two of the most dynamic pharmaceutical research poles in the world (Spigarelli & Wei, 2014). In fact, the *Zhangjiang Park in* Shanghai and the *Zhongguancun Park* in *Beijing* have transformed into a genuine pharmaceutical FDI *magnet* worldwide. China has also become an attractive location for pharmaceutical FDI thanks to its competitiveness in the field of active ingredients production and innovation.

In this pharmaceutical branch, the Chinese industry combines high quality, low costs, and innovativeness benefitting from the famous and renowned traditional Chinese medicine (Yacoub, 2012). In this context, the leader Astra-Zeneca (Sweden-Great Britain) has located its active ingredients production chain in China since 2009 in order to benefit from the "ideal" value for money competencies in this field (2017).

All these factors explain the fact that a large number of pharmaceutical multinationals settled in China's parks are specialized in R&D activities and employing

Chinese human resources. In these conditions, it is obvious that the risk of imitating new technologies is very high confirming the theoretical interesting role played by patent protection in China.

4.3.2 Correlation Between the PPP Index and the Pharmaceutical FDI Inflows in China

Observing that the world pharmaceutical industry leaders are located in China would confirm the theoretical literature as regards the positive role of patent protection. On the one hand, the pharmaceutical industry is technology intensive and easily imitable (Yacoub, 2012). On the other hand, China is a country with strong imitation capacities in pharmaceuticals. Thus, the questionable patent protection results in a high threat-of-imitation which is a dissuasive factor for foreign investors; especially those operating in R&D. Consequently strengthening the patent protection generates an expansion market effect on inward FDI whose elasticity toward China's legal changes is high.

The increase in the pharmaceutical FDI inflows in China during the 1990s and in the R&D foreign investments since the early 2000s would be partially explained by the patent system strengthening during the 1980s and 1990s. China's entry to the WTO in 2001 has announced a new era for the Chinese patent law history. This advent concretizes a formal and irretrievable commitment to respect patent protection, which is a guarantee for foreign investors.

Figure 6 shows simultaneously the trends in the PPP index (graph on the left) and in the number of drugs foreign subsidiaries in China (graph on the right) over the period between 2000 and 2016.

The graphs above confirm that the number of drugs producing FDI has notably increased since the early 2000s going from 560 foreign subsidiaries to 1190 in 2009, and then 1500 in 2012, 1800 in 2014 to reach its highest level in 2016 with about

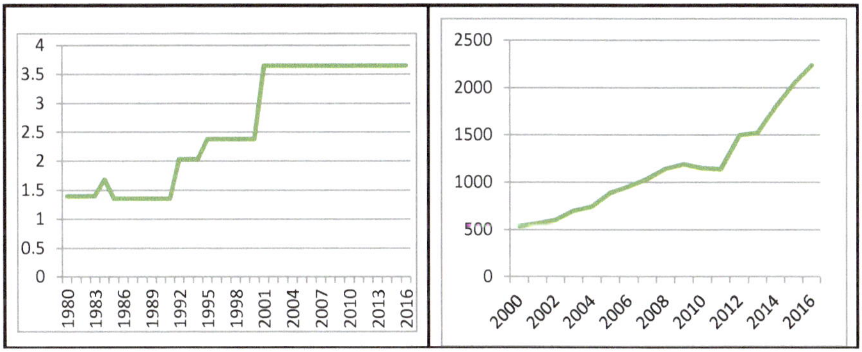

Fig. 6 Trends in the PPP index (1980–2016) and the number of foreign pharmaceutical subsidiaries in China (2000–2016). Source: Authors' version, based on Spigarelli & Wei (2014) and different reports

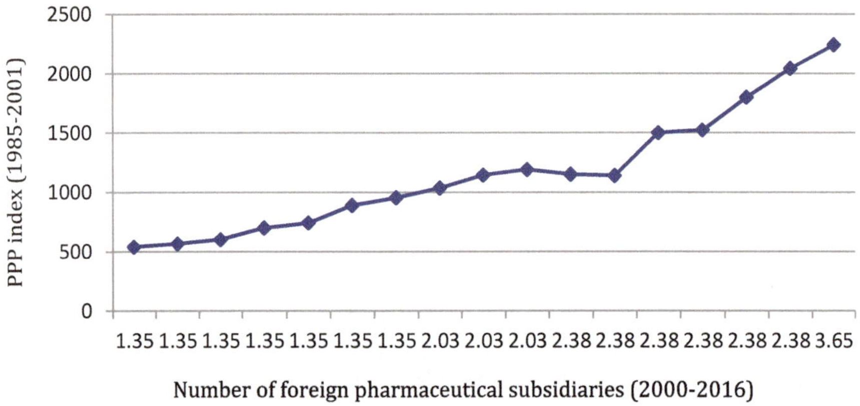

Fig. 7 Time-delayed correlation between the PPP index and the number of foreign pharmaceutical subsidiaries in China. Source: Authors' version

2042 firms. Pharmaceutical foreign investors in China are mainly from Asia (especially Japan), the USA and Western Europe (France, the UK, Switzerland, Germany, etc.).

At this stage of the research, we attempt to further explore our findings by estimating the correlation between the PPP index and the number of drugs producing FDI in China over the period going from 2000 to 2016. Our result reveals a moderate correlation coefficient of "0.442." This result is not statistically significant though, since from 2001 to 2016 the PPP index is at a constant value of 3.6.

In order to overcome this problem, we have estimated a time-delayed correlation between our two variables. We consider a 16-year period for both variables: (1985–2001) for the PPP index and (2000–2016) for the FDI. This statistical manipulation has resulted in a correlation coefficient of "0.89." We can suggest a positive high correlation between patent protection and the pharmaceutical FDI in China (Fig. 7).

Beyond the statistical concerns, using a time-delayed correlation between the PPP index and the FDI inflows is economically founded. Indeed patent protection stems from structural location advantages and generates impacts in the *long term*. Hence, apart from other factors, the important increase of inward pharmaceutical FDI in China since the 2000s could be the consequence of the patent protection strengthening during the 1980s and 1990s.

5 Concluding Discussion

Since the first patent law of 1984 China has enhanced its patent system in order to comply with the international institutions' requirements. Thus, in addition to the major reforms made in 1992 and 2000 China has implemented an important revision of its patent law in 2010 in order to comply further with the European standards. This last reform has not affected our PPP index since it refers to a statutory aspect that is not considered in our study. Hence our PPP index has stabilized since 2001.

Nevertheless, the pharmaceutical inward FDI in China continues to increase, which confirms that the multinationals are still attracted by the Chinese location. Also, the continuous increase of pharmaceutical patent applications by nonresident investors (WIPO, 2020) upholds the fact that patent protection is a determinant of FDI in China. The fact that the PPP index has stabilized means that the Chinese patent system regulation has—only legally or theoretically—reached the maturity phase. It is exactly at this stage that its positive impacts on FDI are likely to be more important.

Beyond the patent protection issue, the impressive attractiveness of China to pharmaceutical FDI—especially those of R&D—is explained by other joint factors mainly related to the innovation policy aiming to build a strong national sectoral innovation system (NSIS). In this context, patent protection is a necessary element of the NSIS but insufficient to attract FDI. Multiplying technological clusters, improving the human capital competencies (at both the academic and professional levels), facilitating procedures for doing business, strengthening the logistic and communication infrastructures, and other innovation and industrial policy mechanisms implemented since the 1980s have been the main key success factors of making from China one of the most attractive destinations of pharmaceutical FDI.

References

Aho, E. (2013). Les déterminants des investissements directs étrangers dans la Communauté des Etats de l'Afrique de l'Ouest (CEDEAO), Revue d'Economie Théorique et Appliquée, Volume 3 – Numéro 2.

Bosworth, D., & Yang, D. (2000). Intellectual Property law, technology flow and licensing opportunities in China. *International Business Review, 9*(4), 453–477.

CEIC. (2017). *China foreign direct investment*. CEIC Institutional Investor Company. https://www.ceicdata.com/en/indicator/china/foreign-direct-investment

Combe, E., & Pfister, E. (2001). Le Renforcement International des Droits de Propriété Intellectuelle, Economie Internationale, La Revue du CEPII, N°85, Premier Trimestre 2001, pp 63–81.

Coriat, B., & Orsi, F. (2004). Les Enjeux de L'Innovation. Droits de Propriété Intellectuelle et Innovation. *Cahiers Français*, N°323, pp. 90–95.

Drug Patent Watch. (2017). *Profile for patents*. https://www.drugpatentwatch.com/

Fai, F. M. (2005). Using intellectual property data to analyze china's growing technological capabilities. *World Patent Information, 27*, 49–61.

Ferrantino, M. J. (1993). The effect of intellectual property rights on international trade and investment. *Weltwirtschaftliches Archiv, 129*, 300–331.

Fink, C. (1997). Intellectual property rights and US and German international transactions in manufacturing industries. *Duke Journal of Comparative and International Law, 9*, 163.

Ginarte, J. C., & Park, W. G. (1997). Determinants of patent rights: A cross-national study. *Research Policy, 26*(3), 283–301.

Glass, A. J., & Saggi, K. (2002). Intellectual property rights and foreign direct investment. *Journal of International Economics, 56*, 387–410.

Hassan, E., Yaqub, O., & Diepeveen, S. (2010). *Intellectual property and developing countries: A review of literature*. RAND Corporation prepared for the UK Intellectual Property Office and the UK Department for International Development.

IHEST. (2015). *« L'industrie pharmaceutique, l'innovation et la Chine »*. Institut des Hautes Études pour la Sciences et la Technologie, Septembre 2015. http://www.ihest.fr/IMG/pdf/l_industrie_pharmaceutique_en_chine_maj_2015_final.pdf

IRACM. (2017). *Définition de la falsification de médicaments*. Institut International de Recherche Anti-contrefaçon des médicaments. http://www.iracm.com/falsification/definition/

Kirkilis, D., & Koboti, S. (2015). Intellectual property rights as determinant of foreign direct investment entry mode: The case of Greece. *Procedia Economics and Finance, 19*, 3–16.

Kumar, N. (2000). Explaining the geography and depth of international production: The case of US and Japanese multinational enterprises. *Weltwirtschaftliches Archiv, 136*(3), 442–476.

La Croix, S. J., & Liu, M. (2014). A cross-country index of intellectual property rights in pharmaceutical inventions. *Research Policy, 44*, 206–216.

Lasserre, M. (2007) *« Les différentes formes de délocalisations »*. https://www.mlasserre.com/educpop/dossierdelocs/lesdifferentesformesdedelocalisations.htm

Lee, J.-Y., & Mansfield, E. (1996). Intellectual property protection and U.S. foreign direct investment. *Review of Economics and Statistics, 78*(2), 181–186.

LEEM. (2019). *Les entreprise du médicament*. https://www.leem.org/marche-mondial

Lesser, W. (2000) *The effects of TRIPS mandated intellectual property rights on economic activities in developing countries*. Cornell University/WIPO. http://www.wipo.org/about-ip/en/index.html?wipo_content_frame=/aboutip/en/studies/index.html

Lesser, W. (2011). Measuring intellectual property 'strength' and effects: An assessment of patent scoring systems and causality. *The Journal of Business, Entrepreneurship and the Law, 4*(2), 345–382.

Lippoldt, D., & Park, W. G. (2003). The impact of trade-related intellectual property rights on trade and foreign direct investment in developing countries. *OECD working papers: Special Issue on trade policy, 4*(11), 294.

Liu, W. H. (2016). Intellectual property rights, FDI, R&D and economic growth: a cross-country empirical analysis. *The World Economy, 39*(7), 983–1004.

Mackey, T. K., Lian, B. A., York, P., & Kubic, T. A. (2015). Counterfeit drug penetration into global legitimate medicine supply chains: A global assessment. *The American Journal of Tropical Medicine and Hygiene, 92*, 59–67.

Maskus, K. E. (1998). The role of intellectual property rights in encouraging foreign direct investment and technology transfer. *Duke Journal of Comparative and International Law, 9* (1), 109–161.

Maskus, K. E. (2004). Encouraging International Technology Transfer, UNCTAD-ICTSD Project on IPRs and Sustainable Development, Issue Paper No 7.

Maskus, K. E., & Eby-Konan, D. (1994). Trade-related intellectual property rights: Issues and exploratory results. In A. V. Deardorff & R. M. Stern (Eds.), *Analytical and negotiation issues in the global trading system*. University of Michigan Press.

Nair-Reichert, U. (2000). *Patent regimes and the internationalization of economic activities: Some empirical evidence from US multinationals*. Georgia Institute of Technology.

Noury, M. (2017). Après les paradis fiscaux, les « paradis » des essais cliniques ? *The Conversation*. https://theconversation.com/apres-les-paradis-fiscaux-les-paradis-des-essais-cliniques-86375

Park, W. G., & Lippoldt, D. C. (2005). International licensing and the strengthening of intellectual property rights in developing countries during the 1990s. *OECD Economic Studies, 2005*(1), 7–48.

Pfister, E. (2003). Propriété Intellectuelle et Choix de Localisation. Une Modélisation Théorique. *Revue Économique, 54*(3), 697–706.

Pfister, E., & Mayer, T. (2001). Investissements Directs et Droits de Propriété Intellectuelles dans les Pays En Voie de Développement. Une Étude Empirique des Choix de Localisation des Multinationales Françaises. *Revue Région et Développement, 13*, 99–123.

Pratomo, M., & Hastiadi, F. F. (2017). Patent Rights protection system and foreign direct investment (FDI) in developing countries. *Advances in Social Science, Education and Humanities Research, 126*, 37–42.

Primo-Braga, C. A., & Fink, C. (1998). The relationship between intellectual property rights and foreign direct investment. *Duke Journal of Comparative and International Law, 9*, 163–188.

Pugatch, N. P. (2006). Measuring the strength of national pharmaceutical intellectual property regimes: Creating a new pharmaceutical IP index. *The Journal of World Intellectual Property, 16*(4), 373–391.

Rapp, R. T. & Rozek, R. P. (1990). Benefits and costs of intellectual property protection in developing countries. National Economic Research Associations, Inc., Working Paper No. 3.

Robert, J. (2013). « *La contrefaçon des produits de santé dans le monde: moyens de lutte et implication du pharmacien d'officine* », Thèse de Doctorat Es science pharmaceutiques et ingénierie de la santé, soutenue publiquement le 26 Avril 2013, Universités Angers, France.

Saggi, K. (2000). Trade, Foreign direct investment, and international technology transfer: A survey. *World Trade Organization, WT/WGTI/W/88*, 19 September 2000.

Samedan Ltd. (2011). *International clinical trials*. Samedan Pharmaceutical Publisher. http://www.samedanltd.com/magazine/13/issue/162/article/3073

Seyoum, B. (1996). The impact of intellectual property rights on foreign direct investment. *Columbia Journal of World Business, 31*(1), 50–59.

Smarzynska, B. (2002). *Composition of foreign direct investment and protection of intellectual property rights: Evidence from transition economies*. World Bank working papers, WP No. 2786, February, 2002.

Smarzynska Javorcik, B. (2004). Does foreign direct investment increase the productivity of domestic firms? In search of spillovers through backward linkages. *American Economic Review, 94*(3), 605–627.

Smith, P. J. (1999). Are weak patent rights a barrier to U.S. exports? *Journal of International Economics, 48*, 151–177.

Smith, P. J. (2001). How do foreign patent rights affect U.S. exports, affiliate sales, and licenses? *Journal of International Economics, 55*, 411–439.

Spigarelli, F., & Wei, H. (2014). The Chinese pharmaceutical market: Driving forces and emerging trends. *L'Industria, Rivista di Economia e Politica Industrial, 35*(3), 505–530.

Tanaka, H., & Iwaisako, T. (2014). Intellectual property rights and foreign direct investment: A welfare analysis. *European Economic Review, 67*, 107–124.

Uzunidis, D. (2010). Innovation et Proximité: Entreprises, Entrepreneurs et Milieux Innovateurs. *La Revue des Sciences de Gestion, 241*, 13–22.

Wang, L. (2013). Intellectual property protection in China. *International Information & Library Review, 36*(3), 253–261.

WIPO. (2020). *Statistiques de propriété intellectuelle dans le monde, différents rapports*. http://www.wipo.int/ipstats/fr/

Yacoub, L., & Yacoub, N. (2011) « Quelles politiques d'attractivité ? Les Déterminants de la localisation des investissements directs étrangers pharmaceutiques en Tunisie. ». In Uzunidis D, Laperche B, Boutillier S (Eds) « *L'Entreprise dans la Mondialisation. Contexte et Dynamiques d'Investissement et de Développement* », 536p, Éditions LeManuscrit, Paris, pp. 405–445.

Yacoub, N. (2007). « Renforcement de la Protection des Brevets, Impact sur les Flux Mondiaux de Commerce et d'Investissements Directs Étrangers. Étude Théorique et Validation Empirique pour L'économie Chinoise », Mémoire de Master de Recherche en Économie, soutenu publiquement le 23 Janvier 2007, Institut Supérieur de Gestion de Sousse.

Yacoub, N. (2012). « Brevetabilité des Médicaments et Innovation Pharmaceutique. Étude Théorique et Validation Empirique pour le cas de la Tunisie », Thèse de Doctorat en Économie de l'innovation, soutenue publiquement le 27 Janvier 2012, Université de Lille Nord de France & Université de Tunis el Manar.

Yacoub, N. (2017). The role of public policies in building up a national pharmaceutical innovation system in Tunisia: Challenges after the Jasmine Revolution. In A. Tsvetkova et al. (Eds.), *Innovation in developing and transition countries* (pp. 68–85). Edward Elgar Publishing.

Yang, D. (2003). The development of intellectual property in China. *World Patent Information, 25*, 131–142.

Total factor productivity, catch-up and technological congruence in Italy, 1861–2010

Cristiano Antonelli and Christophe Feder

Abstract In the catch-up literature, more attention has been paid to the rate rather than the direction of technological change. This paper presents and implements a novel methodology to identify and measure the effects of the direction of technological change in terms of technological congruence and its effects on total factor productivity (*TFP*). Evolution of the match between technology direction and the idiosyncrasies of its endowments and factor markets is a key factor in country growth. We elaborate its implications for the theory of induced technological change, and apply it to an empirical analysis of Italy's economic history from 1861 to 2010. The results confirm the important role of the introduction of biased technological change in the assessment of the levels of technological congruence and *TFP*, and for supporting the long-run convergence of an early-late-comer. N13 N14 O33

This paper contributes to the PRIN 20177J2LS9 research project which provided funding and support in combination with Università di Torino and the Collegio Carlo Alberto research funding. The authors acknowledge useful suggestions and contributions from the editors and the referees, and detailed and constructive comments from Federico Barbiellini Amidei, Claudio Bermont, and Emanuele Felice. We benefited also from comments and criticisms on previous versions of the paper presented at "La società Italiana e le grandi crisi economiche 1929–2016" conference organized for the 90th anniversary of the foundation of ISTAT, and the 2018 International Schumpeter Society Conference. The authors are responsible for any shortcomings in the paper.

C. Antonelli
Dipartimento di Economia e Statistica, Università di Torino and BRICK, Collegio Carlo Alberto, Turin, Italy

C. Feder (✉)
CT-TEM, Università della Valle d'Aosta, Aosta, Italy
e-mail: c.feder1@univda.it

A. Pyka, K. Lee (eds.), *Innovation, Catch-up and Sustainable Development*, Economic Complexity and Evolution, https://doi.org/10.1007/978-3-030-84931-3_10

Keywords Total factor productivity · Biased/induced technological change · Output elasticity of input · Italian growth · Congruence/convergence · Catching-up

JEL classification N13 · N14 · O33

1 Introduction

The historical evidence confirms that growth is a long and complex process characterized by systematic variance in the performance of participating countries: some are able to forge ahead, others fall behind, a few manage to catch-up (Abramovitz 1986; Jung and Lee 2010). Long-term analysis is useful in particular to analyze the causes and consequences of national catch-up processes (Gerschenkron 1955, 1962). The literature on innovation tends to focus on understanding the determinants and consequences of the rate of technological change. Much less attention has been paid to understanding these determinants and the effects of the direction of technological change, i.e., on which factors innovation has a positive effect. Some scholars claim that the catch-up process is characterized by country specificities, especially countries' indigenous capabilities (Amsden 1989; Kim 1997; Porcile and Spinola 2018) and knowledge relatedness (Boschma 2017; Boschma et al. 2017).

The comparative evidence confirms that convergence cannot be assumed: many late-comers fail to converge and implement sustained catch-up. Baumol (1986) and Baumol et al. (1994) suggest rather that convergence and catch-up are sustainable and successful in the long-run only if: i) the follower is able to command the direction of technological change so as to improve its congruence, and ii) the structure of the follower's endowments is not too different from that of the leaders.

Knowledge externalities and technological congruence play a major role in the process. There is a large literature showing that knowledge externalities support catching-up because the followers benefit from the opportunities provided by spillovers of technological knowledge generated at high cost by the leaders (Metcalfe 1994; Malerba and Nelson 2011). Spillovers enable access and exploitation of technological knowledge at much lower cost than those required for its generation. Spillovers provide followers with opportunities to imitate innovators' products, and in turn generate new knowledge. However, the literature has paid insufficient attention to the idiosyncratic aspects of the knowledge spilling across countries (Le Bas and Sierra 2002).

Knowledge spillovers from directed technologies are likely to exhibit high levels of technological congruence with their origin countries but much lower levels of congruence with the factor markets of recipient countries. Exploitation of knowledge externalities may reduce the technological congruence of the would-be catching-up countries. Thus, directing the generation of technological knowledge appropriate to the local structure of endowments and relative factor costs is a major condition for successful catch-up.

The notion of technological congruence and hypotheses about induced technological change provide a powerful analytical tool that enables investigation of the role of technological change in Italian economic growth, and identifies an important yet neglected component. At the same time, the case of long-run Italian economic growth provides an excellent opportunity to test the restated induced technological change hypothesis and the validity of the notion of technological congruence.

In the first part of the nineteenth century, the club of early industrial countries was relatively small and was led by the UK and the US. Landes (1969) documents how, in the 1830s, the industrialization gap was rendering France, Germany and Belgium late-comers while England was entering a more mature stage. Italy's catching-up was part of a second catch-up wave, and was achieved in two steps. The first step in the second part of the nineteenth century was limited to the north-western regions; the second, which occurred after WWII, included the eastern and central regions. The catch-up in the second part of the nineteenth century can be regarded as one of the earliest of such cases in contemporary economy history. Some nations, such as Hungary and Ireland, saw Italy as an example to be emulated and went so far as to adopt the Italian tricolor as their flag (de Cecco 2013). The case of Italy's catch-up provides relevant insights into the growth of more recent emerging countries the catch-up process in which paid special attention to the dynamics of directed knowledge externalities and technological congruence (Lee and Kim 2016; Lee 2013).

Italy is a classic and one of the earliest examples of catch-up (Zamagni 1993, 2009; Rossi and Toniolo 1992; Malanima and Zamagni 2010; Felice and Carreras 2012). The case of Italy provides strong evidence about a two-step catch-up process. Until 1875, Italian economic growth was fairly stationary. After 1875 there was a lengthy process of increasing convergence with the richer countries, which culminated in the start a second stationary phase in the 1970s. In the course of 150 years, the Italian economy experienced a radical and rapid evolution from being a developing country with low levels of productivity and low wages, and the inability to master technological change or command its direction, to achieving the conditions to qualify it as an advanced country, namely, high levels of productivity, wages, and technological capability. Technological change has played a major role in the continuous increase in total factor productivity (*TFP*) (Antonelli and Barbiellini Amidei 2007; Antonelli and Barbiellini 2011). This paper extends and complements the results of previous analyses assessing the impact of the direction of technological change alongside its neutral effects, and allows identification of the role of technological congruence in the case of an early-late-comer.

The long-term evidence shows that income shares were far from the "magic constant" advocated by Solow (1958). The increasing levels of congruence experienced in almost a century between 1874 and 1964 can be regarded as both the cause and the consequence of sustained convergence towards the productivity levels of more advanced economies. However, after 1964, the Italian economy was unable fully to realize this growth potential enabled by increased levels of technological congruence. The literature suggests that Italy's limited achievements post-1966 were due to the limited accumulation of technological knowledge and a weak national innovation system. The new evidence provided by the analysis in this paper supports the two phases of the Italian catching-up (Patel and Pavitt 1994).

The notion of catch-up includes some qualifications that are examined in this paper. First, the initial catching-up process appears to be exogenous, and therefore cannot be explained. Second, the dynamics of the whole process and its interruption are not explained. Third, the role of technological congruence in supporting catch-up is poorly understood. Finally, the catch-up literature tends to ignore the contingency and potentiality related to catching-up. Although late-comers have the chance to reduce the gap with the first movers, the outcomes of their efforts are far from automatic. Achieving catch-up requires radical changes to the structure of the economy, its industry composition, and the working of its labor markets. Successful catch-up as occurred in Italy requires the capability not only to adopt foreign technologies but also to adapt them to the local endowments (Nelson 1981, 2005; Nelson and Pack 1999).

The present paper integrates the theory of economic growth with an analysis of the direction of technological change, and proposes a measure of technological congruence that improves the measurement of *TFP* and contributes to the debate on induced technological change and catching-up (Lee and Malerba 2017; Miao et al. 2018).

The results of the analysis shed some light on the role of directed knowledge externalities and technological congruence in supporting the convergence of late-comers to the productivity levels of advanced economies. We provide an analysis of conditional convergence in an early-late-comer, and show that technological congruence matters for shaping the outcome of the catching-up even within the convergence club.

This methodology allows us to hypothesize that successful search for technological congruence has contributed to Italian economic growth. The consistent and systematic introduction of biased technological change allowed reductions to the excess levels of output elasticity of capital by means of systematic increases in the levels of output elasticity of labor, which augmented the overall level of technological congruence (Antonelli et al. 2017).

The paper is organized as follows. Section 2 introduces the main economic tools used to capture the notion of technological congruence. Section 3 applies the methodology to study the evolution of the direction of technological change in Italian economic growth, and the role of technological congruence in Italy's catch-up. Section 4 concludes the paper.

1.1 Technological congruence

The introduction of biased technological change exerts direct effects on the general levels of *TFP* according to the matching between the output elasticity of the inputs and their relative cost. Using the notion of biased technological change, it is possible to improve measurement of the actual level of *TFP* (Feder 2018a). The standard measure of *TFP* during the overall period $[0, t]$ in logarithmic terms, $ln(NFP_t)$, captures the effect of neutral technological change on *TFP* and is written as:

$$ln\left(NFP_t\right) = ln\left(Y_t\right) - ln\left(K_t^{\alpha_t} L_t^{1-\alpha_t}\right) \tag{1}$$

and, from the Euler Theorem:

$$K_t = \frac{\alpha_t Y_t}{r_t} \tag{2}$$

$$L_t = \frac{(1-\alpha_t) Y_t}{w_t} \tag{3}$$

where r and w are the unit costs of capital and labor, respectively.

Equation (Abramovitz 1986) compares, on the one hand the observable output with the current technological level, and, on the other hand, the theoretical output that would occur if the level of neutral technology did not move from time 0. In other words, (Abramovitz 1986) measures only the effect of neutral technological change on *TFP*, *NFP*, because it is able to exclude the effect of biased technological change on *TFP*, *BFP*, determined by the variation in the output elasticity that qualifies the introduction of directed technological change.

Biased technological change alters the output elasticity, and, therefore, not only the production function but also the firm's decisions about the optimal amount of factors $\widehat{K}$ and $\widehat{L}$. From (Abramovitz and David 1996) and (Acemoglu 2015), we can determine the theoretical amount of the factors present at time t if the technology remains available at time 0:

$$\underset{t}{K} = \frac{\alpha_0 Y_t}{r_t} \tag{4}$$

$$\underset{t}{L} = \frac{(1-\alpha_0) Y_t}{w_t} \tag{5}$$

Using the same method as in (Abramovitz 1986), we can measure the bias of technological change by comparing the production function without the neutral technological change, $K_t^{\alpha_t} L_t^{1-\alpha_t}$, to the production function without neutral and biased technological change, $\underset{t}{K}\,\alpha_0 \underset{t}{L}\,1 - \alpha_0$.

This implies that the logarithmic effect of biased technological change on *TFP* in t, $ln(BFP_t)$, is given by the (logarithmic) difference between the two *TFP* measures (Feder 2018b)[1]:

[1] The non-neutral assumption of technological change could introduce an index number problem on all the proposed measures (Fisher 1922; Törnqvist 1936). However, this problem is resolved by finding the correct scaling parameters of capital and labor (Zuleta 2012; Feder 2018a, 2019).

$$ln\,(BFP_t) = ln\,(K_t^{\alpha_t} L_t^{1-\alpha_t}) - ln\left(K_t\,\alpha_0 L_t\,1 - \alpha_0\right) \quad (6)$$

A new measure of *TFP* must consider both neutral and biased technological change. Therefore, the *TFP* is[2]:

$$ln\,(TFP_t) = ln\,(Y_t) - ln\left(K_t\,\alpha_0 L_t\,1 - \alpha_0\right) \quad (7)$$

Exactly similar to the standard measure of *TFP* described in (Abramovitz 1986), the *TFP* described in (Antonelli 2006) compares the observable output to the current technological level and the theoretical output. However, now the theoretical production function must also fix the level of biased technological change at time 0, i.e. α_0.

A technology is congruent with the factor markets if, for given levels of total costs, it allows larger levels of output and hence higher levels of *TFP*, given the factor costs (David 1975; Abramovitz and David 1996). Remembering that a change in the biased component of the technology means a variation in the output elasticity of inputs, $d\alpha$, we can formalize the notion of technological congruence starting from:

$$\frac{dY_t}{d\alpha_t} = \ln\left(\frac{\alpha_t}{1-\alpha_t}\frac{w_t}{r_t}\right)Y_t \quad (8)$$

Equation (Antonelli and Barbiellini Amidei 2007) measures how the variation in output elasticity affects gross domestic product (GDP). Therefore, by definition, the rate of technological congruence can be written formally as:

$$\frac{dY_t}{Y_t} = \ln\left(\frac{\alpha_t}{1-\alpha_t}\frac{w_t}{r_t}\right)d\alpha_t. \quad (9)$$

Equation (Antonelli and Barbiellini 2011) shows that if the logarithmic argument is greater than 1, $\alpha_t w_t > (1-\alpha_t) r_t$, then only a technological change in favor of capital productivity will increase the level of technological congruence, $d\alpha_t > 0$. Conversely, if the logarithmic argument is less than 1, then only a technological change in favor of labor will increase the level of technological congruence, $d\alpha_t < 0$.

The rate of technological congruence is measured as a percentage, and is determined by three factors in combination: i) the relative output elasticity of the

[2]Non-parametric measures such as data envelopment and stochastic frontier analyses are other methodologies that can be used to measure the biased technological change (Färe et al. 1997; Tsekouras et al. 2004, 2016; Hampf and Krüger 2017). In particular, the Malmquist productivity index has some relevant similarities to our proposed measure (Feder 2018a). However, to the best of our knowledge, no measures of technological congruence can be employed for the non-parametric approach. For an extended comparison of (Abramovitz 1986) and (Antonelli 2006), and for a comparison of this method with others such as data envelopment analysis or stochastic frontier analysis, see Feder (2018a).

production factors, $\alpha/(1-\alpha)$; ii) the relative cost of factors, w/r; iii) the direction of technological change, $d\alpha \lesseqgtr 0$. From (i) and (ii) we can identify a threshold level of α, called $\overline{\alpha}$, such that, for a given slope of isocost, w/r, the improvement in the biased component has a positive effect on the Y:

$$\overline{\alpha}_t = \frac{r_t}{w_t + r_t} \tag{10}$$

The level of technological congruence for the overall period $[0, T]$, TC_T, is the sum of all of the rates of technological congruence from the base year 0 to the year T. In other words, technological congruence is defined as:

$$TC_T = \int_0^T \frac{dY_t}{Y_t} dt = \int_0^T \ln\left(\frac{\alpha_t}{1-\alpha_t}\frac{w_t}{r_t}\right) d\alpha_t dt \tag{11}$$

The evolution of technological congruence can affect the country's pattern of growth and long-term economic changes but not its economic cycle. However, the economic cycle has relevant effects on the short-term variability in technological congruence. Indeed, during crises the least productive and least efficient firms fail. This creative destruction effect (Schumpeter 1942) increases the level of technological congruence in the economic system because it increases the share of highly congruent firms. Symmetrically, in periods of economic boom, technological congruence decreases due to the growth of firms that are less technologically congruent, and thus less efficient and productive.

The counter-cyclicity of biased technological change corrects the pro-cyclicity of *TFP* (Inklaar et al. 2011, 2016; Watanabe 2016): the opposing effects of *BFP* and *NFP* lead, in fact, to a smoother than standard trend.

The proposed measure of technological congruence is a percentage that allows comparison to include years in the remote past. In addition, (Antonelli et al. 2014) clarifies the variables influencing technological congruence.

1.2 The Italian evidence 1861–2010

For the empirical implementation, we use the Italian National Accounts, available from the Bank of Italy for the whole economy for the years 1861 to 2010 (Baffigi 2013; Broadberry et al. 2013; Giordano and Zollino 2016; Giordano and Zollino 2017). This database includes the standard variables Y_t, K_t, L_t, and w_t for each year. The proposed methodological extension to measure *TFP* and split it to reveal the effects of *NFP* and *BFP* clearly relies on the traditional growth accounting approach.

According to Euler's theorem, under constant returns to scale, it is possible to estimate the output elasticity of capital at each time t:

$$\alpha_t = 1 - \frac{w_t L_t}{Y_t} \tag{12}$$

In particular, it allows us to estimate the output elasticity of inputs at time 0, and thus to calculate the effect of NFP_t, using (Abramovitz 1986) and normalizing TFP_0 at 1 (Feder 2018a). So far, the implementation is in line with Solow's (1957) methodology. Hence, we need to estimate K_t and L_t as defined by (Amatori and Bigatti 2003) and (Amsden 1989). First, again applying Euler's theorem, we can calculate the unit cost of capital:

$$r_t = \frac{\alpha_t Y_t}{K_t} \tag{13}$$

NFP, *BFP*, and *TFP* are measured in (Abramovitz 1986), (Antonelli 1995) and (Antonelli 2006), respectively. Finally, (Antonelli and Feder 2019) and (Baffigi 2013) allows us to measure technological congruence, as described in (Antonelli et al. 2014).

The data do not allow empirical estimation of the specific roles of other important factors such as human capital, intermediate goods, and land (Prados de la Escosura and Rosés 2009; Schivardi and Torrini 2010; Moro 2012; Felice and Vasta 2015). Statistical reporting of R&D expenditure dates are collected only from the Frascati Manual (OECD 1962); there have been no attempts - at least for Italy - to collate historical data for the years starting in 1861. These limitations do not allow us to explore the role of technological knowledge. The empirical evidence available for 150 years, does not include the data required to explore the central role of structural change in the transformation of the agricultural economy initially to a highly industrialized manufacturing system and then into a service economy.

The standard assumption is that the levels and dynamics of wages capture the levels of labor and the changes to labor skills and capabilities. According to the induced technological change approach, an increase in the availability of technological knowledge and human capital, and the consequent reductions in their costs, should be reflected by the respective increases in capital and labor productivity, and their respective output elasticities.

GDP is the sum of the final goods and services produced in a period of time. However, the value of the final goods and services could be interpreted as the sum of all intermediate goods and services plus the value added in the final step in the value chain.

Finally, although land is an important factor in Italy's pre-industrialization history, its productivity is mostly constant over time with no clear directionality emerging until the start of the catching-up process when its factor share in GDP becomes irrelevant. However, the inclusion of its value in the amount of capital, *K*, helps to reduce potential bias in the measures. This methodology allows us to assess the effect of the direction of technological change in the evolution of Italian *TFP*.

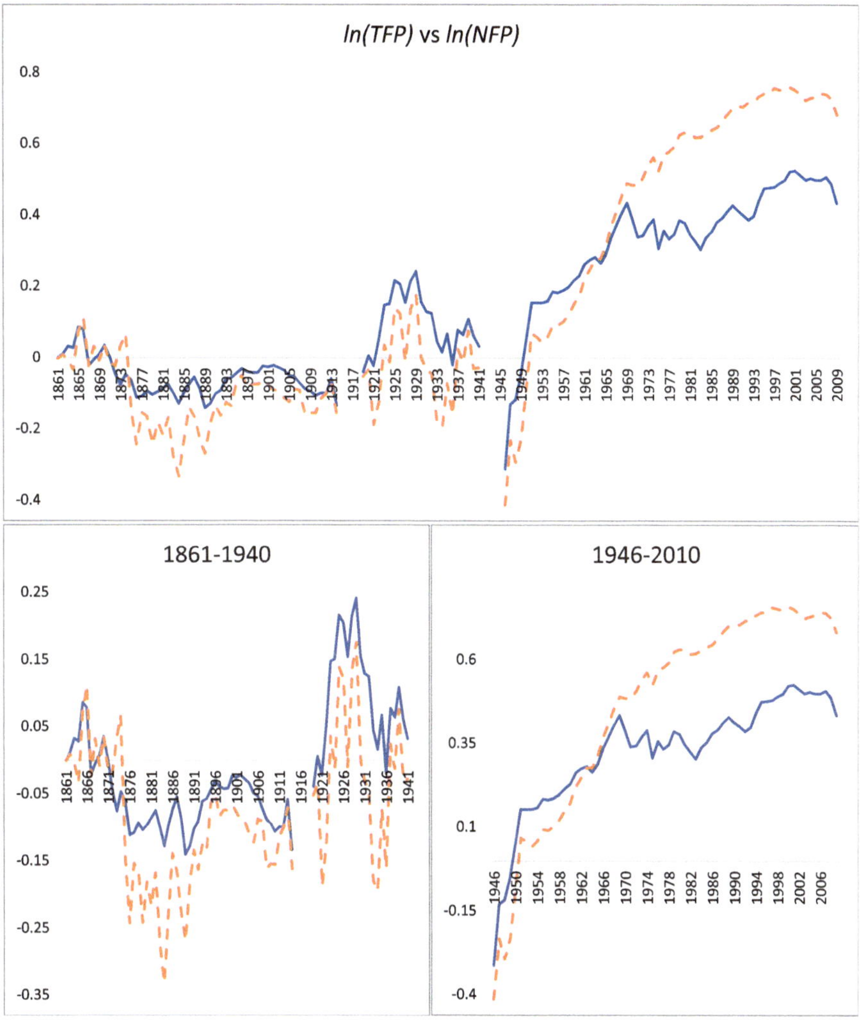

Fig. 1 Comparison of Italian *NFP* (dashed line) and *TFP* (solid line) from 1861 to 2010 and the two sub-periods 1861–1940 and 1946–2010. Source: Elaboration of Broadberry et al. (2013)

1.3 The dynamics of total factor productivity

The solid lines in Fig. 1 show the new logarithmic measure of *TFP*, which takes account of both the neutral and the biased effects of technological change; the dashed lines are the standard measure of *TFP* and considers only the neutral effects of technological change (as measured by Broadberry et al. 2013). The distance between the two lines in each of the graphs is a measure of the effects of the introduction of biased technological change.

NFP exhibits negligible negative and positive values until 1874, then mostly negative values up to WWI with the (absolute) minimum of −0.33 in 1884. In the period between the two world wars, there were wide variations in *NFP*: from a low point in 1921 (−0.19) to the 1929 peak (0.18), which was followed by negative growth until 1936. From 1951 to 2000 the economy grew, pushing *NFP* from 0.10 to 0.76. Growth was especially rapid up to until 1969 after which it slowed and was mostly stable in the last 10 years. The evidence described by the dashed lines representing *NFP*, which is able to assess only the shift effects from the introduction of technological innovations, confirms the evidence in the rich literature on Italian economic growth including the long period of stagnation (Toniolo 2013; Rossi and Toniolo 1996; Giannetti 1998, 1999; Barca 1997).

TFP, represented by the solid lines provides interesting information that challenges established interpretations about the slow rate of technological change and the long stagnation of Italian productivity, and highlights the important role of the effects of the increased levels of technological congruence in both the second post-war period and especially in the years after WWI (Toniolo 2013; Barca 1997; Giannetti 1998, 1999). Note that this does not say that the former *TFP* is incorrect, but only incomplete.

The *TFP* measure shows also that the effects on productivity of the 1873 and 1929 crises were less negative than previously estimated, and highlights the relevance of the effect of biased technological change during these periods. In line with recent contributions on technology shocks and the great depression, we observe that, in Italy also, technology was not the driving force in these two crises (Cafagna 1989; Luzzato 1963; Inklaar et al. 2011, 2016; Watanabe 2016).

Figure 1 allows reconsideration of the evolution of *TFP*. *TFP* is positive but not significant in most of the first ten years (except 1867–1868) of Italy's economic history. In the succeeding years, the rate of *TFP* shows negative values up to WWI but less negative than suggested by the *NFP*. In the interwar years, *TFP* grew from −0.04 to 0.03. However, up to 1929 there was significant growth in *TFP* value and then a fall from 1930 to 1941. Hence, these results support Eichengreen's (2007) thesis of extensive growth in post-war Europe after both WWI and WWII.

Figure 1 shows also that, during the economic miracle, *TFP* levels were underestimated until 1964, after which they were overestimated. This allows a re-assessment of our understanding of the second part of the twentieth century, which stresses the slow rate of *TFP* increase, well below previous estimates. These results suggest that the origins of Italy's low-growth in the twenty-first century emerged almost 40 years earlier.

The use of this new measure shows that *TFP* played a significant role not only during the years of the economic miracle but also in the preceding 90 years of Italy's history. In particular, it sheds light on the limitations in the traditional literature in relation to the supposed irrelevance of technological change and low levels of *TFP* for Italy's economic history (Toniolo 2013). Rather, it calls attention to the important role of productivity growth, which stemmed from the introduction of biased technological change alongside its –light- shift effects.

It is relevant to note that, after 1874, the bias effect augmented the –poor- shift effects in Italy, at least until 1964. During the period 1875–1963, Italy was unable to rely much on 'shift technologies' but took advantage of the direction of 'biased technologies' quite effectively. The new growth accounting procedure implemented in this essay confirms that technological change played an important role in Italian economic growth because its direction enabled increasing levels of congruence throughout the period analyzed and especially in the years following the end of WWI. The evidence seems to suggest that, since the beginning of the twentieth century, the Italian economy was able to improve its control over the direction of technological change. The buildup of its technological competence allowed the adoption of capital-intensive technologies generated abroad and their adaptation to local factor markets, and created a stock of knowledge that allowed the rapid introduction of new, radical technologies in the "Golden Age" (Antonelli 1995; Antonelli 2006).

The distance between the two lines in Fig. 1 shows the effects of the direction of technological change in Italy from 1861 to 2010. In the years 1865–1873, the direction of technological change was capital-intensive, despite Italy's typical abundance of labor rather than capital. The consequent decline in technological congruence seems to have been determined by the wide scale adoption of imported capital-intensive production techniques, as modeled by Basu and Weil (1998).

With the exception of these years, technological congruence in *TFP* continually and significantly increased until the outbreak of WWI. The extent on *TFP* of the positive effect of biased technological change gradually began to disappear from 1973 onwards. The economic miracle was not motivated purely by the neutral component of technological change; the biased component played a fundamental role during the boom in terms of adaptation (as opposed to passive adoption) of foreign technologies, making them more efficient and more congruent to local endowments (Antonelli and Barbiellini 2011; Antonelli et al. 2017).

Toniolo (2013) suggests that the Italian case provides strong evidence of a two-tailed catch-up process. Following an initial stationary phase –the first tail, from 1875– there was a long process of increasing congruence and convergence with the richer countries. A modern stationary phase –the second tail– began to exert its effects from the 1970s (Antonelli and Feder 2019).

Note that the new measure of *TFP*, which includes the effects of biased technological change, provides solid cliometric evidence that modifies the descriptive evidence identified by economic historians: technological change played a continuous important and positive role between the 1920s and the 1990s in terms of both a shift in and congruence of its direction. Nevertheless, it is clear that, since the 1960s, the country has missed important opportunities to improve its technological congruence further, and to support the rate of neutral technological change.

From this perspective, these results have implications for the notion of "conditional convergence": convergence takes place only if congruence increases. Convergence is not an automatic outcome of the flows of international knowledge spillovers from advanced to developing countries and their import for innovations embodied in capital and intermediary goods. Late-comer catch-up is sustainable in the long-run only if the late-comer country is able to adapt the foreign technologies to its specific endowments structure, and to introduce localized technological change (Baumol 1986; Bernstein 1996; Keller 2004; Cameron et al. 2005). The Italian case confirms these hypotheses and provides an interesting case of an early-late-comer that was able to use congruence as a tool for effective convergence.

To summarize, this process suggests that: i) the passive adoption of foreign technologies designed to cope with other and different factor markets may have positive shift effects but also includes some drawbacks in terms of biased technological change; ii) the implementation of a national innovation system is necessary to generate localized technological change and to adapt foreign technologies to local factor conditions; iii) when a country approaches the international technological frontier, it can no longer rely only on the adoption and adaptation of foreign technologies; iv) top down research and development activities combined with active valorization of bottom-up learning processes are required to build the stock of localized technological knowledge necessary for the introduction of technological innovations with appropriate bias to increase levels of technological congruence and valorize the local endowments structure (Antonelli 2006).

1.4 Technological congruence and its determinants

This section highlights the central role of the direction of technological change in the Italian catch-up. We have argued that the catching-up process depends inherently on the country's level of technological congruence. Figure 1 shows that an initial negative technological change bias impedes the catch-up process, and a period of introduction of the new technologies is needed to exert a congruent bias after which catch-up begins and consolidates. The weakening in this effect led to the weakened economic growth in the final years of the twentieth century.

The implications of our results are important. They show the crucial need not only to invest more resources in research and development, but to combine these activities with the valorization of bottom-up learning processes to direct the localized technological stock toward the introduction of biased technological innovations congruent with the relative abundance of production factors and the state of the existing technology.

Table 1 provides a decomposition of the average rate of output growth in average rate of growth of labor, capital, and productivity. It also summarizes the average rate of growth of the neutral and biased effects of technological change on *TFP*.

The new *TFP* measure provides better evidence for Italian growth and helps to shed light on the divergence between the national accounts and economic history. The rate of output growth is positive but small up to 1940. This position is reversed during the economic boom, with *TFP* growth becoming positive and significant and

Table 1 Decomposition of output growth - each variable is described at the average growth rate

Years	*Y*	*L*	*K*	*NFP*	*BFP*	*TFP*
1861–1895	1.20%	0.50%	1.91%	−0.18%	0.06%	−0.12%
1896–1914	1.72%	0.96%	3.13%	−0.59%	0.05%	−0.54%
1919–1940	2.26%	0.70%	2.64%	0.10%	0.35%	0.46%
1946–1973	6.47%	0.96%	5.80%	3.46%	−0.97%	2.46%
1974–1992	2.44%	0.82%	3.56%	0.82%	−0.82%	−0.01%
1993–2010	0.91%	0.37%	1.63%	−0.20%	0.40%	0.20%

Elaboration of Broadberry et al. (2013)

increasing.[3] After the oil crisis, growth rates returned to pre-boom trends. Observe also that the accumulation of capital is a key variable explaining output growth.

Also Table 1 shows the rate of growth of the two components of productivity growth. It is interesting that, throughout the whole period, these two components seem to substitute for each other, i.e., if one component increases the other decreases. In particular, during the nineteenth century and in the first post-war period, the effects of biased technological change gain momentum, while neutral technological change is weak. However, during the economic boom, we observe an increased effect of neutral technological change and weaker effects of biased technological change. Both trends become positive only between the two wars.

To apply the notion of technological congruence to analyze Italian history provides an understanding of the direction of technological change and allows assessment of whether it was consistent with the Italian economic structure and its evolution, in turn allowing identification of its effects in terms of *TFP*.

The evolution of technological congruence reveals the changing levels of firms' abilities to match their technological choices to their factor markets. As such, technological congruence is expected to exert significant effects on the patterns of long-term rather than short-term growth. In contrast, the economic cycle is likely to affect the level of technological congruence: downturns spur the exclusion of firms less able to select the appropriate technologies, while upturns favor the survival of less congruent firms. As a consequence, we would expect an increase in the level of technological congruence among the former group, and a relative decline among the latter group.

Our understanding of the role of biased technological change would be improved and become clearer through an analysis of the rate of technological change and its effect on Italian economic growth. In fact, the direction of technological change in Italy has been far from neutral (Federico 2003). In the Italian experience, the trend toward technological change was clearly labor-intensive for more than 80 years, with strong directionality that has exerted relevant and positive economic effects. This bias itself and its positive effects have declined in the most recent decades.

[3] From 1946 to 1973, accounting for Italian growth is probably underestimated by the emergence and diffusion of the Fordist mode of production organization (Boyer 2000).

The evidence confirms that, for nearly a hundred years from 1874 to 1964, the Italian economy has been characterized by a sharp increase in the level of technological congruence. At the beginning of the period analyzed in this paper, the level of technological congruence was extremely low and was in fact negative between 1865 and 1873; the Italian economic system was characterized by excessively high levels of technology capital-intensity and low levels of wages, which were systematically lower than capital user costs. Since then, the Italian economy has experienced a consistent capital-intensive technological change. In the most recent decades since 1993, the increasing abundance of capital and the strong increase in wages have resulted in technological congruence, favoring adoption of capital-intensive technologies. The strong increase in technological congruence between 1874 and 1964 can be considered the result of increased technological knowledge that has enabled control over the direction of technological change towards higher levels of congruence with the national endowments structure. However, between 1966 and 1993, the Italian economy was less able to improve its technological congruence through the introduction of labor-intensive technologies. Also, after 1993, when the slope of the isocost was greater than 1 and the state of the technology was tilted in favor of a capital-intensive bias, the economy was unable to steer technological change towards the introduction of more capital-intensive technologies.[4]

Section 2 provides some background to explain why and how levels of technological congruence increased as the result of the reduction in of the output elasticity of capital while wages experienced a rapid increase. The traditional formulation of induced technological change hypothesis would suggest that countries have an incentive to cope with increased wages by increasing the output elasticity of capital. However, the notion of technological congruence in the context of the Italian evidence shows that, especially if starting levels of output elasticity of capital are too high, it is more convenient and appropriate for countries where $w < r$, to cope with these increased wages by introducing more labor-intensive technologies.

Figure 2 describes the evolution of the relative output elasticity of factors, $\alpha/(1-\alpha)$. The line is always below 1, and throughout the whole period the productivity of capital, α, is larger than the productivity of labor, $1-\alpha$. Moreover, we observe that the initial period and the final period values are similar. The shape of the graph line in Fig. 2 is characterized by a long flat period between 1900 and the 1970s.[5] This trend is notable since it contrasts with the global trend among the industry leaders toward technological change characterized by a steady increase in the relative output elasticity of the production factors. However, in Italy, the evolution was two-tailed with a maximum of 0.82 in 1873–1874, and a minimum of 0.22 in 1949. More precisely, from a decade after Unification up to 1889, the

[4]Note that, in 1966, the slope of the isocost was greater than 1 (see: Figure 5). Yet, because of the complementary role of the state of the technology ($\overline{\alpha}$) in assessing the effects of technological congruence, the bias in favor of capital-intensity did not exert a positive effect until after 1993.

[5]The dotted line in figure 2 is based on the econometric interpolation of the following equation:

$$y = -1 \cdot 10^{-12}x^6 + 6 \cdot 10^{-10}x^5 - 8 \cdot 10^{-8}x^4 + 4 \cdot 10^{-6}x^3 - 6 \cdot 10^{-5}x^2 - 0.0095x + 0.685.$$

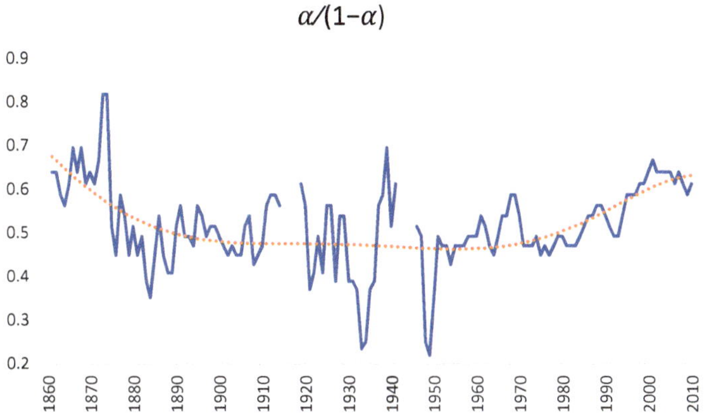

Fig. 2 Italian evolution of the relative output of elasticity of factors from 1861 to 2010. Note: The dotted line is the econometric interpolation of $\alpha/(1-\alpha)$. Source: Elaboration of Broadberry et al. (2013)

relative output elasticity decreased, then until WWI was around 0.5, although with a fair amount of variance. At the end of WWI, the value of $\alpha/(1-\alpha)$ fell, reaching its lowest point (0.23) in 1933 before rising sharply to its relative maximum (0.69) in 1939. In the second post-war period, the relative output elasticity of factors continued to increase, although at a declining rate. In particular, there was a strong increase in the years 1945–1955 while the decade between 1970 and 1980 seems to be characterized by lateral changes: 1980 values are close to 1970s' values. The increase in relative output elasticity, exhibits clear signs of steady growth only after the 1980s. The years 1950–1980 are characterized by high levels of variance around low mean values. This variance could be interpreted as the outcome of the interaction among three forces: i) the state-owned enterprise-led growth of corporations driven by the introduction of technological change and high levels of capital output elasticity; ii) the emergence and diffusion of the Fordist mode of production (Boyer 2000); and iii) the bottom-up industrialization of the peripheral regions characterized by labor-intensive technological change (Antonelli et al. 2014).

Figure 2 also shows that the variance is influenced by some regularities: i) in the first years of the three global crises (1873, 1929, 2007) the value of the relative output of elasticity of capital decreased sharply; ii) the rearmament rush before each world war $\alpha/(1-\alpha)$ caused a significant increase (Bardini 1998; Giordano and Giugliano 2015); iii) in the years following these conflicts, the reconstruction and the dismantling of the war economy significantly reduced the value of the relative output elasticity of capital.

However, to assess whether the technology is congruent with the economic endowment such that it was able to exert a positive effect on *TFP*, we need to analyze this evolution jointly with the endowments structure and the relative factor costs.

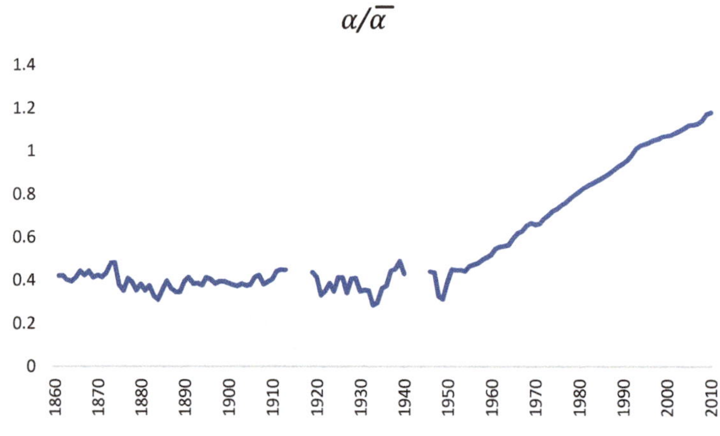

Fig. 3 The size of the Italian output elasticity of capital compared to its minimum from 1861 to 2010. Source: Elaboration of Broadberry et al. (2013)

Thus, the relative output elasticity of capital and the relative factor costs need to be considered together to understand their effect on technological congruence. From (Antonelli et al. 2017) and (Antonelli and Feder 2019), if their value is greater than 1, $\alpha > \overline{\alpha}$, then only technological change in favor of capital productivity will increase levels of technological congruence. Conversely, if the total value is less than 1, $\alpha < \overline{\alpha}$, then only a technological change in favor of labor will increase the levels of technological congruence.

Figure 3 compares the actual values of capital productivity, α, to the levels that inhibit technological congruence, $\overline{\alpha}$, in order to analyze the extent of technological congruence. Since the graph line means that, if $\ln(\alpha w/(r - \alpha r))$ tends to zero, the ratio $\alpha/\overline{\alpha}$ tends to 1, and a less efficient (or inefficient) direction of technological change affects the levels of technological congruence. The path of $\alpha/\overline{\alpha}$ increases at a slow pace until 1954, with a minimum point in 1933 (0.28) and a maximum point in 1939 (0.49), then grows at a faster rate to 1.18 in 2010.

Figure 3 shows the working of technological congruence: the relative output elasticity and the relative cost of the factors shaping the effects of technological change have played a major role for almost a century. In the most recent decades, the increased congruence eventually declines, with its effects becoming smaller and smaller. Figure 3 allows us to conclude that, although the ratio w/r continued to increase, the changes in $\alpha/(1 - \alpha)$ did not match the rate of adjustment of the slope of the isocosts efficiently.

Figure 3 also shows that, up to 1993, the search for more labor-intensive technologies had positive effects in terms of increased technological congruence $(\alpha < \overline{\alpha})$. In contrast, after 1993, the direction of technological change should have been capital-intensive $(\alpha > \overline{\alpha})$.

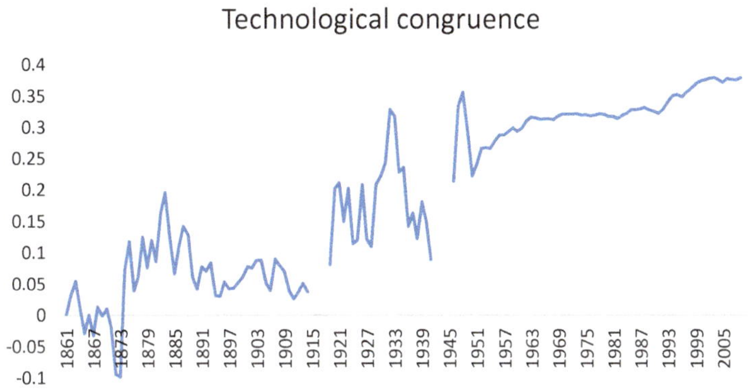

Fig. 4 Technological congruence in Italy from 1861 to 2010. Source: Elaboration of Broadberry et al. (2013)

Figure 4 depicts the technological congruence suggested by (Antonelli et al. 2014), and summarizes all the previous figures.[6] Specifically, it describes the yearly levels of technological change congruence, or a measure of the extent to which the technology in place at each year affects the level of congruence. For example, in 2009, the congruence of technology with the structure of endowments was positive and equal to 37.93%. Comparing Figures 4 and 1 shows that, certainly up to 1964, and to a lesser extent up to 1980, the introduction of labor-intensive technologies increased *TFP* because they were congruent with the country's economic endowments. Indeed, the only period of negative technological congruence (1865–1873) was characterized by the introduction of capital-intensive technology associated with the broad range of activities related to the railways. From 1980 to 1993, the direction of technological change was again capital- rather than labor-intensive, with the result that levels of technological congruence stopped increasing. After 1993, although congruent, the capital-intensity of the direction of technological change was not sufficient to cope with the increasing abundance of capital. Note that both these effects are negligible due to the small changes to α shown in Fig. 2.

The historical analysis of the technological congruence levels provided in Fig. 4 suggests that, at the beginning of the period, the Italian economy was characterized by levels of α far larger than the ratio w/r would suggest. The sharp decline in the output elasticity of capital increased the overall levels of technological congruence with positive effects on *TFP*.

Figure 5 compares relative output elasticity to relative cost of factors during the 150 years analyzed, and provides a partial explanation for the evolution of technological congruence. The dashed and solid lines represent $\alpha/(1-\alpha)$ and w/r,

[6] Since we have only discrete not continuous time data, it was not possible to use the integers but only the sum of all of the rates of technological congruence described in (Antonelli and Barbiellini 2011). Also, the measure of technological congruence directly follows (Antonelli et al. 2014) and thus is not in logarithmic terms.

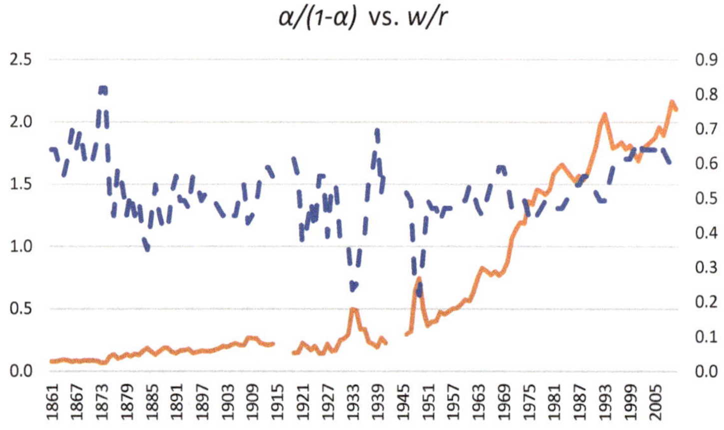

Fig. 5 Comparison of relative output elasticity, $\alpha/(1-\alpha)$, (dashed line and right axis) and relative factor costs, w/r, (solid line and left axis) in Italy: 1861 to 2010. Source: Elaboration of Broadberry et al. (2013)

respectively. At the beginning of the period, the Italian economy was characterized by very low wages, far lower than the capital rental costs, but high levels of capital output elasticity. In other words, the Italian economy was characterized by very low levels of technological congruence with a clear contradiction between a highly capital-intensive technology and a labor abundant structure of endowments where capital was scarce.

The relative decline in the -low- levels of technological congruence in the first years following Unification seems to confirm the role of knowledge externalities from imported technologies associated with both imports and important flows of foreign direct investments attracted by the significant spending on the railways, and transportation more generally, which took place at that time. This evidence is important to understand the contradiction between the neutral effects and the biased effects of new technologies: because of the bias related to technological spillovers from the advanced countries, catching-up countries often are "obliged" to rely on inappropriate foreign technologies if the positive (neutral) shift effects far exceed the negative bias effects (Basu and Weil 1998; Colli and Rinaldi 2015).

The characteristics of the Italian economy in the first ten years of the growth process can be considered typical of a newcomer with a weak national system of innovation that is unable to command the direction of technological change and must rely passively on the technological externalities from foreign direct investments and goods imported from more advanced countries characterized by relative capital abundance. The shift from 1874 onward to positive values of technological congruence signals the increasing capability of the Italian economic system to direct technological change towards labor-intensive technologies more consistent with its structure of endowments and local factor markets. This, in turn, can be considered the cause and the consequence of the gradual consolidation of the role in the Italian economy, of an emerging indigenous manufacturing industry.

Since Unification, the evolution of the Italian economy has been characterized by the following processes: i) a constant rise in the slope of the isocost; ii) before 1950 – and to a lesser extent until 1980- the introduction of biased technological changes directed consistently towards an increase in the output elasticity of labor; iii) fast rates of increase in the *TFP* component stemming from the introduction of biased technological change; iv) fast rates of economic growth. Our basic contention is that there is a strong and effective causal and sequential relationship between these processes.

The long-run history of the Italian economy provides clear evidence about the case of a country where: i) historically wages have been much lower than capital user costs for many decades; ii) wages have been increasing at a steady and fast rate[7]; iii) for almost a century, especially up to 1964 –and then slightly less in the following 16 years- the labor-intensive direction of technological change has been able to increase the levels of technological congruence; iv) the labor-intensive direction of Italian technological change is particularly remarkable when compared to the strong bias in favor of increased capital output elasticity among the technology leaders; v) consistent with restatement of the induced technological change hypothesis enabled by the notion of technological congruence, the introduction of biased technological change has contributed to an increase in *TFP* and economic growth that was significant up to 1964, and slightly lower to 1980; vi) after 1964, the direction of technological change was increasingly less able to cope with the changing characteristics of factor markets, and consequently was less able to contribute to *TFP* growth.

This process can be interpreted as the outcome of four distinct but complementary forces: progressive reduction of technological dependence; emergence of a national system of innovation able to support the introduction of localized technological changes; a bottom-up light industrialization process; low levels of accumulation of technological stock. Let us consider these in more detail.

It seems plausible to argue that, in the year of the Unification, the excess levels of capital output elasticity and the consequent low levels of technological congruence were determined by lack of domestic technological capabilities. Technological change at Unification and the following 10 years was driven mainly by passive adoption of foreign technologies that reflected the endowment structures in the countries of origin, and the active role of foreign investors whose technologies were applied to their Italian factories (Barbiellini Amidei et al. 2013; Colli 2014).

The adoption of foreign technology enabled an increase in *TFP* determined by its neutral effects but at the cost of reduced level of technological congruence. The foreign technology was superior to the domestic technology but was less efficient in Italy than in its origin countries where it was technologically congruent. Eventually, domestic command of technological knowledge became stronger and the increasing levels of technological capability enabled the Italian economy to implement the

[7] See the debate on wage levels (Zamagni 1989, 1991, 2002; Malanima 2007, 2013a, 2013b).

biased technological changes in a labor-intensive direction, which was a better fit with the local factor markets.

The analysis of the composition of the Italian economy identifies some important elements that contribute to these dynamics. Early industrialization of the Italian economy was based on affiliates of multinational corporations and a small oligopolistic core of large firms heavily subsidized by the State and specializing in capital-intensive activities (Zamagni 2009; Malanima and Zamagni 2010).[8] High levels of labor unionization favored an increase in the wages of the workers in those firms - the slope of the isocost of the oligopolistic core was very different from the aggregate averages. The rest of the country continued to specialize in agricultural and craft activities.

In the succeeding decades, Italian economic growth was characterized by a strong bottom-up industrialization process that allowed entry to the market of an array of small firms specialized in labor-intensive activities consistent with the marked labor abundance of peripheral labor markets. The reduced output elasticity of capital revealed by the aggregate statistical evidence reflects the bottom-up industrialization process in traditional labor-intensive sectors and labor abundant regions that eventually complemented the oligopolistic core of large capital-intensive industries (Amatori and Bigatti 2003; Antonelli and Barbiellini Amidei 2007).

These dynamics enabled the country to rely on technological congruence with clear benefits for output and *TFP* growth rates. Italian long-run economic growth confirms that, in a labor abundant country, it is convenient to introduce biased technological change that makes more intensive use of the factor at each point in time that is cheaper irrespective of its increases.

2 Conclusions

The analysis of Italian long-term growth provides rich evidence on the dynamics of catch-up. The Italian experience can be regarded as one of the earliest cases of catch-up, with the north-western regions of the country able in the second half of the nineteenth century to absorb the relevant knowledge externalities spilling over from the small club of early industrialized countries. The Italian evidence shows that international spillovers can be a two-edged sword: on the one hand, they foster growth in countries able to absorb the foreign technology, with relevant shift effects, while on the other hand, foreign technologies may not match local factor market conditions. International knowledge externalities are directed, and their adoption has negative bias effects.

[8] As Acemoglu (2015) notes, the composition of the economic system exerts relevant effects. The Italian evidence suggests that some larger firms faced different factor prices to the rest of the economy, which may have affected their technological choices and favored their specialization in capital-intensive activities. Here a clear composition effect may account for the bifurcation in the technological path.

The Italian evidence suggests the need to consider the role of doing, using and interacting learning processes in the accumulation of stocks of technological knowledge, which help to direct technological change towards a labor-intensive bias that reflects the receiving country's endowment structure. This learning can modify the direction of global technological change mastered by the technology leaders through the implementation of top-down science, technology and innovation activities (Jensen et al. 2007).

The increasing effect of the grassroots process of industrialization was the simultaneous cause and consequence of the increasing levels of technological congruence. The industrialization of Italy's peripheral regions and the growth of industrial districts specializing in light industry were driven by the accumulation of tacit knowledge based on bottom-up learning processes that increased command of labor-intensive technologies (David et al. 1998; Saviotti and Pyka 2004; Antonelli and Barbiellini 2011).

The evidence from the Italian case confirms various hypotheses; it confirms that the notion of technological congruence enables a redefinition of the induced technological change hypothesis and sheds new light on the role of the direction of technological change for determining its outcomes. Exploration of the evolution of Italian technological congruence, and the effects of the introduction of biased technological change on *TFP*, identified five periods: i) up to 1873, the technological congruence trend decreased but with high variability; ii) from 1874 to 1948, technological congruence was significant and positive supporting an increase in the general efficiency of economic activity; iii) throughout the early period of the economic miracle (1949–1963), technological congruence had a positive sign and exerted a significant effect; iv) from 1964 to 1992, technological congruence had a negligible impact; v) after 1993, technological congruence again increased, although the neutral effect declined.

To sum up, at the time of Unification, Italy encompassed all the characteristics of an underdeveloped country. To improve its situation, it tried to organize a classical catching-up process by implementing an export led strategy based upon labor-intensive products. This was enabled initially by access to knowledge externalities from the advanced countries but at the cost of low levels of technological congruence. In the second stage, it was characterized by increasing command of technological knowledge built mainly on the valorization of bottom-up learning processes that enabled the country to support catch-up and the convergence to the productivity levels of more advanced countries accompanied by a systematic -and systemic-increase in technological congruence. The process of industrialization in Italy has been particularly congruent with its economic structure for almost a century. Our understanding of the direction of technological change towards increased output elasticity of labor and its positive effects contribute to the debate on long-term Italian economic growth. The stagnation of traditional *TFP* growth in the period 1874–1964 has been very much emphasized to support the hypothesis of the "weakness" of the contribution of technological change to Italy's economic growth. However, this new evidence related to biased technological change suggests that, during that period, Italy was able to improve its control over the type of technological knowledge it received, allowing the related technological changes to be more technologically congruent. The acquisition of greater control over technological congruence was the foundation for the introduction of radical technological changes during the period 1964–1993.

Technological change inherently is directed and exhibits high levels of technological congruence with the country of adoption. Knowledge spillovers are not neutral: they reflect the direction of technological change in the origin country. Access to international knowledge spillovers enables followers to exploit relevant knowledge externalities but imposes constraints in the form of bias. Late-comers that try to catch-up with the leaders initially may experience the introduction of new foreign technologies with low levels of technological congruence. Accumulation of a local stock of technological knowledge is necessary to adapt knowledge spilling from abroad to the local factor endowment conditions and factor markets, and enable adoption of a new technological path (Lee and Lim 2001; Lee et al. 2005).

This essay proposes a novel methodology to understand the effects of the introduction of biased technological change according to its level of technological congruence with local factor market characteristics. This analysis of the direction and congruence of technological change in Italy's economic history during the period 1861 to 2010 provides another relevant result. It offers interesting evidence on a successful case of catch-up by an early-late-comer based on systematic increase to its technological congruence enabled by an appropriate direction of technological change toward the introduction of labor-intensive technologies. The Italian evidence supports the notion of increased technological congruence and the bias component of *TFP* as important factors in economic growth.

The long-term cliometric evidence for the Italian case confirms the strong complementarity between convergence and congruence, and its interpretation provides some hints for the current economy: i) to return to growth, Italy must increase the size of its stock of national technological knowledge and the strength of its national innovation system to better exploit the opportunities provided by increased technological congruence through the introduction of biased technological change able to valorize the use of relatively cheaper inputs; ii) the Italian catching-up experience provides important insights into both the benefits and the constraints of knowledge externalities from the leading countries, and the need for followers to combine the adoption of foreign technology with its adaptation to the actual endowment structure in order to increase levels of technological congruence; (iii) the combination of top-down research activities and bottom-up learning processes can provide late-comers with more control over the global direction of technological change led by the science-based countries, and introduce technological change with higher levels of technological congruence to the knowledge coming from abroad.

Based on the literature, it cannot be argued that the slow rates of accumulation of a localized stock of technological knowledge slowed the search for higher levels of congruence and productivity growth. Rather, the evidence seems to suggest that, from the early 1960s, Italy missed the opportunity to continue the positive trend experienced since 1875. To exploit this opportunity would have required Italy to strengthen its knowledge base (Felice and Vasta 2015).

The finding in this paper call for more studies to implement the proposed methodology using richer data that account for changes in the sectoral mix and the specific roles of human capital and skills. In the case of Italy, it would be interesting to extend both the technological congruence and the new *TFP* measures to include skilled and unskilled labor and the stock of technological knowledge, and to incorporate land. It would be interesting also to measure how much biased technological change is due to the adoption of new technologies or to sectoral shifts. Although the availability and quality of Italian historical data is considerable (Felice and Vasta 2015; Giordano and Zollino 2016, 2017), we need additional data to allow better measurement of the effects of the direction of technological change on technological congruence and *TFP* at the disaggregated level.

Publisher's note Springer Nature remains neutral with regard to jurisdictional claims in published maps and institutional affiliations.

Compliance with ethical standards

Conflict of interest The authors declare that they have no conflict of interest.

References

Abramovitz M (1986) Catching up, forging ahead, and falling behind. J Econ Hist 46(2):385–406

Abramovitz M, David PA (1996) Convergence and delayed catch-up: productivity leadership and the waning of American Exceptionalism. In: Landau R, Taylor T, Wright G (eds) The mosaic of economic growth. Stanford University Press, Stanford, pp 21–62

Acemoglu D (2015) Localized and biased technologies: Atkinson and Stiglitz's new view, induced innovations, and directed technological change. Economic Journal 125(3):443–463

Amatori F, Bigatti G (2003) Business history in Italy at the turn of the century. In: Amatori F, Geoffry J (eds) Business history around the world. Cambridge University Press, Cambridge, pp 215–232

Amsden A (1989) Asia's new Giant: South Korea and late industrialization. Oxford University Press, New York

Antonelli, C. (1995). Il cambiamento tecnologico: Innovazione e modernizzazione (1945-1990), in Barbagallo, F. (ed.), *Storia dell'Italia Repubblicana. La trasformazione dell'Italia: Sviluppi e squilibri*, Torino: Einaudi, 477-526

Antonelli C (2006) Diffusion as a process of creative adoption. J Technol Transfer 31(2):211–226

Antonelli C, Barbiellini AF (2011) The dynamics of knowledge externalities: localized technological change in Italy. Edward Elgar, Cheltenham

Antonelli C, Barbiellini Amidei F (2007) Innovazione tecnologica e mutamento strutturale nell'industria italiana nel secondo dopoguerra. In: Antonelli C, Barbiellini Amidei F, Giannetti R, Gomellini M, Pastorelli S, Pianta M (eds) *Innovazione Tecnologica e Sviluppo Industriale nel Secondo Dopoguerra,* Collana Storica della Banca d'Italia. Roma, Laterza, pp 3–358

Antonelli C, Feder C (2019) A long-term comparative analysis of the direction and congruence of technological change. Soc Econ Rev. https://doi.org/10.1093/ser/mwy048

Antonelli C, Barbiellini Amidei F, Fassio C (2014) The mechanisms of knowledge governance: state owned corporations and Italian economic growth, 1950-1994. Struct Chang Econ Dyn 31:43–63
Antonelli C, Barbiellini Amidei F, Feder C (2017) Directed technological change and productivity growth. The Italian evidence 1861–2010, *International Journal of Computational Economics and Econometrics, Special Issue in Honor of Mario Amendola: "Innovation, economic change and policies: An out-of-equilibrium perspective"* 7(3):238–255
Baffigi A (2013) National accounts. In: Toniolo G (ed) The Oxford handbook of the Italian economy since unification. Oxford University Press, Oxford, pp 157–186
Barbiellini Amidei F, Cantwell J, Spadavecchia A (2013) Innovation and foreign technology. In: Toniolo G (ed) The Oxford handbook of the Italian economy since unification. Oxford University Press, Oxford, pp 378–416
Barca F (1997) Storia del Capitalismo Italiano dal Dopoguerra ad Oggi. Donzelli, Roma
Bardini C (1998) Dictatorship and catching-up. The use of benchmark productivity comparisons to evaluate the impact of fascism on Italian industrial convergence. In: Núnez CE (ed) Proceedings of the twelfth international economic history congress. Fundación Fomento de la Historia Económica, Madrid, pp 93–106
Basu S, Weil DN (1998) Technology and growth. Q J Econ 113(4):1025–1054
Baumol WJ (1986) Productivity growth, convergence, and welfare: what the long-run data show. Am Econ Rev 76(5):1072–1085
Baumol WJ, Nelson RR, Wolff EN (1994) Convergence of productivity cross-national studies and historical evidence. Oxford University Press, Oxford
Bernstein JI (1996) International R&D spillovers between industries in Canada and the United States. Can J Econ 29(Special issue):463–467
Boschma R (2017) Relatedness as driver behind regional diversification: a research agenda. Reg Stud 51(3):351–364
Boschma R, Coenen L, Frenken K, Truffer B (2017) Towards a theory of regional diversification: combining insights from evolutionary economic geography and transition studies. Reg Stud 51 (1):31–45
Boyer R (2000) Is a finance led growth regime a viable alternative to Fordism? A preliminary analysis. Econ Soc 29(1):111–114
Broadberry S, Giordano C, Zollino F (2013) Productivity. In: Toniolo G (ed) The Oxford handbook of the Italian economy since unification. Oxford University Press, Oxford, pp 187–227
Cafagna L (1989) Dualismo e Sviluppo nella Storia d'Italia. Marsilio, Venezia
Cameron G, Proudman J, Redding S (2005) Technological convergence. R&D, trade and productivity growth, *European Economic Review* 49:775–807
de Cecco M (2013) The Italian economy seen from abroad. In: Toniolo G (ed) The Oxford handbook of the Italian economy since unification. Oxford University Press, Oxford, pp 134–154
Colli A (2014) Multinational and economic development in Italy during the twentieth century. Business History Review 88(2):302–327
Colli A, Rinaldi A (2015) Institutions, politics, and the corporate economy. Enterp Soc 16 (2):249–269
David PA (1975) Technological choice, innovation and economic growth. Cambridge University Press, Cambridge
David PA, Foray D, Dalle JM (1998) Marshallian externalities and the emergence and spatial stability of technological enclaves. Econ Innov New Technol 6(2–3):147–182
Eichengreen B (2007) The European economy since 1945: coordinated capitalism and beyond. Princeton University Press, Princeton
Färe R, Grifell-Tatje E, Grosskopf S, Lovell CAK (1997) Biased technical change and the Malmquist productivity index. Scand J Econ 99(1):119–127
Feder C (2018a) A measure of total factor productivity with biased technological change. Econ Innov New Technol 27(3):243–253

Feder C (2018b) The effects of disruptive innovations on productivity. Technological Forecasting & Social Change 126(C):186–193
Feder C (2019) Biased and neutral technological change: empirical evidence from a sample of OECD countries. Appl Econ Lett 26(11):943–947
Federico G (2003) A capital intensive innovation in a capital-scarce world: steam-threshing in nineteenth century Italy. Adv Agric Econ Hist 2:75–114
Felice E, Carreras A (2012) When did modernization begin? Italy's industrial growth reconsidered in light of new value-added series, 1911-1951. Explor Econ Hist 49(4):443–460
Felice E, Vasta M (2015) Passive modernization? The new human development index and its components in Italy's regions (1871-2007). Eur Rev Econ Hist 19(1):44–66
Fisher I (1922) The making of index numbers. Houghton-Mifflin, Boston, MA
Gerschenkron A (1955) Notes on the rate of industrial growth in Italy, 1881-1913. J Econ Hist 15 (4):360–375
Gerschenkron A (1962) Economic backwardness in historical perspective, a book of essays. Belknap Press of Harvard University Press, Cambridge, MA
Giannetti R (1998) Tecnologia e Sviluppo Economici Italiano 1870–1990. Il Mulino, Bologna
Giannetti R (1999) Il progresso tecnologico. In: Amatori F, Bigazzi D, Giannetti R, Segreto L (eds) Storia d'Italia, Annali 15, L'industria. Einaudi, Torino
Giordano C, Giugliano F (2015) A tale of two fascisms: labour productivity growth and competition policy in Italy, 1911-1951. Explor Econ Hist 55:25–38
Giordano C, Zollino F (2016) A historical reconstruction of capital and labour in Italy, 1861–2013. Quaderni di Storia Economica, Economic History Working Papers
Giordano C, Zollino F (2017) Macroeconomic estimates of Italy's mark-ups in the long-run, 1861–2012. Quaderni di Storia Economica, Economic History Working Papers
Hampf B, Krüger JJ (2017) Estimating the bias in technical change: a nonparametric approach. Econ Lett 157:88–91
Inklaar R, de Jong H, Gouma R (2011) Did technology shocks drive the great depression? Explaining cyclical productivity movements in U.S. manufacturing, 1919-1939. J Econ Hist 71(4):827–858
Inklaar R, de Jong H, Gouma R (2016) A note on technology shocks and the great depression. J Econ Hist 76(4):934–936
Jensen M, Johnson B, Lorenz E, Lundvall BA (2007) Forms of knowledge and modes of innovation. Res Policy 36:680–693
Jung M, Lee K (2010) Sectoral systems of innovation and productivity catch-up: determinants of the productivity gap between Korean and Japanese firms. Ind Corp Chang 19(4):1037–1069
Keller W (2004) International technology diffusion. J Econ Lit 42:752–782
Kim L (1997) Imitation to innovation: the dynamics of Korea's technological learning. Harvard Business School Press, Cambridge
Landes DS (1969) The unbound Prometheus. Cambridge University Press, Cambridge
Le Bas C, Sierra C (2002) Location versus home country advantages in R&D activities: some further results on multinationals' locational strategies. Res Policy 31(4):589–609
Lee K (2013) Schumpeterian analysis of economic catch up: knowledge, path-creation, and the middle-income trap. Cambridge University Press, Cambridge
Lee K, Kim YK (2016) Intellectual property rights and technological catch-up in Korea, chapter 4. In: Lee K (ed) Economic catch-up and technological leapfrogging. Edward Elgar, Cheltenham, pp 56 85
Lee K, Lim C (2001) Technological regimes, catching-up and leapfrogging: findings from the Korean industries. Res Policy 30(3):459–483
Lee K, Malerba F (2017) Catch-up cycles and changes in industrial leadership: windows of opportunity and responses of firms and countries in the evolution of sectoral systems. Res Policy 46(2):338–351

Lee K, Lim C, Song W (2005) Emerging digital technology as a window of opportunity and technological leapfrogging: catch-up in digital TV by the Korean firms. Int J Technol Manag 29 (1–2):40–63

Luzzato G (1963) L'Economia Italiana dal 1861 al 1914. Banca Commerciale Italiana, Milano

Malanima P (2007) Wages, productivity and working time in Italy, 1270-1913. The Journal of European Economic History 36:127–174

Malanima P (2013a) When did England overtake Italy? Medieval and early modern divergence in prices and wages, *European Review of Economic History* 17:45–70

Malanima, P. (2013b). Prezzi e salari 1734-1860, in P. Malanima and N. Ostuni (eds.), Il Mezzogiorno Prima dell'Unità. *Fonti, Dati, Storiografia*, Soveria Mannelli: Rubbettino, 339–394

Malanima P, Zamagni V (2010) 150 years of the Italian economy, 1861-2010. J Mod Ital Stud 15 (1):1–20

Malerba F, Nelson R (2011) Learning and catching up in different sectoral systems: evidence from six industries. Ind Corp Chang 20(6):1645–1675

Metcalfe JS (1994) Evolutionary economics and technology policy. Economic Journal 104 (425):931–944

Miao Y, Song J, Lee K, Jin C (2018) Technological catch-up by east Asian firms: trends, issues, and future research agenda. Asia Pac J Manag 35(3):639–669

Moro A (2012) Biased technical change, intermediate goods and total factor productivity. Macroecon Dyn 16(2):184–203

Nelson RR (1981) Research on productivity growth and productivity differences: dead ends and new departures. J Econ Lit 19(3):1029–1064

Nelson RR (2005) Technology, institutions and economic growth. Harvard University Press, Cambridge, MA

Nelson RR, Pack H (1999) The Asian miracle and modern growth theory. Economic Journal 109 (457):416–436

OECD (1962). The measurement of scientific and technical activities: proposed standard practice for surveys of research and experimental development, DAS/PD/62.47

Patel P, Pavitt K (1994) National innovation systems: why they are important, and how they might be measured and compared. Econ Innov New Technol 3(1):77–95

Porcile, G., Spinola, D.S. (2018). Natural, effective and BOP-constrained rates of growth: adjustment mechanisms and closure equations, *PSL Quarterly Review* S.I 71(285), 139-160

Prados de la Escosura L, Rosés JR (2009) The sources of long-run growth in Spain, 1850-2000. J Econ Hist 69(4):1063–1091

Rossi N, Toniolo G (1992) Catching up or falling behind? Italy's economic growth, 1895-1947. Economic History Review 45(3):537–563

Rossi, N., Toniolo, G. (1996). Italy, in N. crafts, Toniolo, G. (eds.), *Economic Growth in Europe since 1945*, Cambridge: Cambridge University press, 427-454

Saviotti P, Pyka A (2004) Economic development by the creation of new sectors. J Evol Econ 14 (1):1–35

Schivardi F, Torrini R (2010) Structural change and human capital in the Italian productive system. Giornale degli Economisti e Annali di Economia 69(3):119–167

Schumpeter, J.A. (1942). Capitalism, *Socialism and Democracy*, New York: First Harper Colophon edition Harper & Row

Solow RM (1957) Technical change and the aggregate production function. Rev Econ Stat 39 (3):312–320

Solow RM (1958) A skeptical note on the constancy of relative shares. Am Econ Rev 48 (4):618–631

Toniolo G (2013) An overview of Italy's economic growth. In: Toniolo G (ed) The Oxford handbook of the Italian economy since unification. Oxford University Press, Oxford, pp 3–37

Törnqvist L (1936) The bank of Finlands consumption price index. Bank of Finland Monthly Bulletin 10:1–8

Tsekouras KD, Pantzios CJ, Karagiannis G (2004) Malmquist productivity index estimation with zero-value variables: the case of Greek prefectural training councils. Int J Prod Econ 89 (1):95–106

Tsekouras KD, Chatzistamoulou N, Kounetas KE, Broadstock DC (2016) Spillovers, path dependence and the productive performance of European transportation sectors in the presence of technology heterogeneity. Technol Forecast Soc Chang 102:261–274

Watanabe S (2016) Technology shocks and the great depression. J Econ Hist 76(3):909–933

Zamagni, V. (1989). An international comparison of real industrial wages 1890-1913: methodological issues and results, in P. Scholliers (ed.), Real wages in 19th and 20th century Europe. *Historical and Comparative Perspectives*, Oxford: Berg, 107–139

Zamagni V (1991) Industrial wages and workers' protest in Italy during the "Biennio Rosso" (1919-1920). The Journal of European Economic History 1:137–153

Zamagni V (1993) The economic history of Italy 1860–1990. Clarendon Press, Oxford

Zamagni V (2002) Salari e profitti nell'industria italiana tra decollo industriale e anni '30. In: Zaninelli S, Taccolini M (eds) Il Lavoro come Fattore Produttivo e come Risorsa nella Storia Economica Italiana. Milano, Vita e Pensiero, pp 243–254

Zamagni V (2009) Governing the Italian economy: a comparative perspective. J Mod Ital Stud 14 (1):46–51

Zuleta H (2012) Variable factor shares, measurement and growth accounting. Econ Lett 114 (1):91–93

Acting as an innovation niche seeder:how can the reverse salient of southeast Asian economies be overcome?

Hsien-Chen Lo, Ching-Yan Wu, and Mei-Chih Hu

Abstract Taking Southeast Asian emerging economies as an empirical case, this study explores how the reverse salients that have emerged during the transitional process may be overcome efficiently and effectively. In particular, three action-oriented case studies derived from a heuristic research approach are presented to show how Taiwan is empowering its universities and public research institutes to act as innovation niche seeders for Southeast Asian economies, thereby compensating for the weakness of their socio-technical systems (i.e. the reverse salients). Presently, the government-led policies of Southeast Asian countries are largely oriented towards incentivizing foreign multinational corporations to lead the development of domestic production networks. This strategy allows these countries to acquire the necessary resources for an economic transition in the era of digitalization, although at the expense of developing their own innovation niches. This study presents the urgency of a need for a new approach, and a new avenue for emerging countries to develop an effective and efficient governance model. The proposed model would allow external institutional mechanisms, such as universities and public research institutes, to act as critical intermediaries providing an alternative solution for the dilemmas faced by small and medium-sized enterprise-centric emerging countries. Policy implications for building sustainable socio-technical regimes in Southeast Asia's transitional emerging countries are also discussed.

Keywords Southeast Asia · Reverse salient · Socio-technical regime · Innovation niche · Taiwan

JEL codes O33 · O14 · I23 · O25 · L52 · F23

H.-C. Lo · C.-Y. Wu (✉) · M.-C. Hu
Institute of Technology Management, National Tsing Hua University, NO.101, Sec. 2, Guangfu Rd., 30013 Hsinchu, Taiwan
e-mail: lohsienchen.eric@gmail.com; wuchingyan@mx.nthu.edu.tw; mchu@mx.nthu.edu.tw

A. Pyka, K. Lee (eds.), *Innovation, Catch-up and Sustainable Development*,
Economic Complexity and Evolution, https://doi.org/10.1007/978-3-030-84931-3_11

1 Introduction

With an ambition to secure the techno-economic opportunities brought on by the era of digitalization, many emerging economies are experiencing profound socio-technical transitions toward more productive and competitive structures. As latecomers in technology development, emerging economies such as those in Southeast Asia (SEA) treat the sector of Internet of Things (IoT) as a critical leverage point to accelerate their transition (e.g. MIMOS Berhad 2015). Taking advantage of domestic markets as a test bed, local firms in SEA countries are increasingly prosperous while at the same time largely incentivized by state-led intervention. Inspired by the East Asian model, such state-led intervention is aimed at acquiring and securing necessary capital, advanced technologies and manpower for their transition, catching-up, and competition in the global market. While the model of incentivizing local firms is expected to generate knowledge diffusion and the learning effect, it is increasingly acknowledged that SEA economies generally lack the necessary innovation infrastructure and capabilities to absorb IoT-based applications and innovations. This has hampered efforts to build indigenous innovations critical for driving transition, not to mention securing a dominant position in either domestic or global markets. In the face of this weakness of national/sectoral systems, for SEA emerging economies to foster their indigenous innovative capabilities, leveraging external sources in association with institutional governance and mechanisms is needed (Hu and Mathews 2005; Lee and Lim 2001).

Governing a successful catch-up transition has been a major challenge for latecomer countries. It is widely agreed that the transitions in latecomer countries suffer from critical reverse salients[1] due to resource disadvantage (Hughes 1987; Mathews 2006). To overcome the reverse salient embedded in the transitional process, most latecomer countries have traditionally focused their catch-up efforts on encouraging foreign direct investment (FDI) and promoting knowledge transfer via multinational corporations (MNCs). It is thought that this method will open up opportunities for economies to link and leverage the required resources and capacities for building indigenous innovations and drive the system's transition as a whole. However, reaping the benefits of knowledge transfer requires economies to have an underpinning absorptive capacity and a flourishing of entrepreneurial activities to sustain the indigenous sectoral system as the external environment is rapidly evolving and changing. If the indigenous sectoral system (including both resources and institutional support) is not sufficient to deal with the absorption and internalization of foreign technology, there is significant risk of being crowded-out

[1]It was Hughes (1987) who first proposed the concept of a 'reverse salient.' In his book explaining the evolution of a large technological system, he refers to a 'reverse salient' as *components in the system that have fallen behind, or out of phase with, the others.* He further explains that a reverse salient impedes the evolution or hampers the achievement toward the final goal of the collective system. In this study, we follow Hughes's metaphor for describing a reverse salient as a significant difficulty faced during system transition.

by foreign companies or MNCs. Such scenarios are being witnessed in SEA emerging latecomer economies, especially in technology-driven sectors such as the automobile, electronics, and biotechnology industries, where the domestic markets have come to be dominated by foreign MNCs. The crowded-out effect has dragged some SEA economies into the middle-income trap (Asian Development Bank 2017). Transitions among SEA emerging latecomers are proceeding at an unprecedented rate, yet MNCs overwhelmingly dominate their domestic production networks. To move forward, an external source of institutional mechanisms aimed at infusing innovative and entrepreneurial resources into the economy is critical to help increase mobilization and amplification capacities toward building indigenous learning and innovative activities. Based on the literature of latecomer strategies, external public actors such as universities and public research institutes (PRIs) from more industrialized countries that possess active innovative and entrepreneurial resources may play a significant role in helping transitional emerging economies overcome the reverse salients that have emerged (Mathews and Hu 2007).

Our research interest in this study is to explore that possibility by examining an approach aimed at helping emerging latecomer countries to overcome their reverse salient during the process of transition. In particular, the transition management literature views socio-technical transition as a multi-level structure evolving from an existing regime toward a new regime. In this process, both the state-led policy landscape and aggregated firm-driven innovation niches essentially re-configure, re-shape, and re-combine to create the new regime. However, the literature has little to say about how a reverse salient that emerges in the transitional process is to be overcome effectively and efficiently so that a sustainable new regime is formulated. Drawing from this perspective, this paper wishes to explore how Taiwan, as an industrialized latecomer country, is empowering its universities and PRIs to act as seeders of indigenous innovation niches, further enabling SEA countries to overcome reverse salients in the process of transitions as they develop new socio-technical regimes. While the state-led policy landscape is helpful to leverage external resources to build a transitional socio-technical regime (particularly with foreign government-led FDIs), its weakness is the lack of a highly developed sectoral system that can initiate endogenous learning activities and sustain self-propagating co-evolutionary dynamics (Viotti 2002). This study identifies the absence of indignenous innovation niches as the pertinent reverse salient of emerging economies, especially for those adopting the FDI-leveraging model for catch-up transitions, such as the SEA latecomers. Where these state-led approaches have been widely adopted by SEA emerging economies, we have also seen many government-led FDIs, such as investments from China, Singapore, Japan, and Korea, gain their footholds in emerging economies (ASEAN Secretariat and UNCTAD 2016). Accordingly, this study aims to use three cases generated from the action research method to demonstrate how SME-centric Taiwan is adopting a different approach by laying the foundation for an aggregated firm-level niche so as to help SEA emerging economies overcome their reverse salients and co-evolve with the transitional socio-technical regime.

The remainder of this paper is structured as follows: Section 2 presents the theoretical background of transitional management in the context of Asian latecomer emerging economies as well as the framework addressing the reverse salient of SEA latecomers in their catch-up transition. The methodology of this study is described in Section 3. Section 4 provides a brief introduction to FDI flows into SEA emerging markets, while Section 5 elaborates the three action-oriented cases. The last section presents our conclusion.

2 Theoretical background

Transition is widely acknowledged as the evolutionary process of shifting an existing undesirable socio-technical system toward a more sustainable, productive and competitive structure in which new technologies and institutions are legitimized while new forms of interactions among innovation actors are developed (e.g. Geels 2002; Wong et al. 2015; Weber and Rohracher 2012). The topic has generated substantial interests in recent years as the existing systems of many modern economies are increasingly either locked in a path-dependent trap or need to be restructured for further growth. This is especially a concern for sustainable energy and digitalization systems. To understand better *why* and *how* evolutionary dynamics are driving transitions, studies have widely adopted a multi-level perspective of transition management in their analytical framework.

In fact, the development of a transition management framework is, to some extent, derived from the innovation system literature (Geels 2005). In mainstream innovation studies, the innovation system literature has been focused on exploring how institutional settings and network compositions shape a system's innovation dynamics (Castellacci 2009; Nelson 1993; Teubal 2002). This literature has shown how, at the sectoral level, the characteristics of an innovation system—including its knowledge base, learning mechanisms, public-private linkages and relationships between firms—significantly influence the innovation performance and competitiveness of firms within the system context (Hu and Hung 2014; Kim and Lee 2008; Malerba 2004). As such, innovation system literature is able to provide a full understanding of the *structural features* leading to an 'innovative' system in terms of sectoral and national perspectives. Nevertheless, we have also seen that the interactive relationships between elements within the system can inadvertently become locked-in, leading the structure to turn rigid due to institutional inertia and path-dependence. Despite this, the innovation system approach has not given attention to issues of momentum within the existing sectoral system toward socio-technical transition (see, for example, Weber and Rohracher 2012). It is here that the transition management framework provides a conceptual foundation explaining how system transition occurs, and this framework has increasingly come to dominate theoretical discussions and policy debates in recent years. Accordingly, we draw upon the framework of transition management to lead the discussion of the reverse salients faced by emerging economies in the process of transition.

2.1 *Reverse salients in the multi-level transitional process*

The transition of a sectoral system is complex and widely assumed to evolve in a multi-level context as it deals with struggles between public policies, market environments, industrial structures and firm capabilities. Studies of transition management are therefore focused on linking dynamics at different macro, meso and micro levels to articulate how the transitional process responds to new economic development and competitiveness in a more systematic and holistic way. For example, Geels (2002) suggested that the socio-technical transition of a sectoral system is the outcome of the dynamic interplay between a meso-regime, a macro policy landscape and micro-level innovation niches. The meso-regime accounts for the deep structure of the socio-technical system and refers to a semi-coherent set of rules and institutions that guide and coordinate the activities of various incumbent industrial stakeholders. The macro policy landscape is critical to break the evolutionary equilibrium of the regime, whereas the key to alter the regime structure itself is the aggregation of firm-driven innovation niches at the micro-level which bring 'novelty' into the regime and ultimately lead to its re-configuration (Geels 2002, 2004).

This multi-level approach is now serving as a major foundation for managing the direction and rate of transition, as well as for coordinating the socio-technical innovation process that involves multiple actors such as governments, universities, research institutes and private firms. In particular, this research stream has provided a coherent view of how socio-institutional settings and policy landscapes can promote changes in a socio-technical regime, while at the same time providing protected spaces and scale-up mechanisms for firm-driven innovation niches through various supporting institutions until these niches are able to compete with the dominant structure of the incumbent regime. For example, Kern (2012) conducted an analysis of the UK's transition to sustainable industrial structures, and showed how well-designed policy initiatives were able to unlock the network configuration dominated by several powerful groups in the local socio-technical regime. Focused on the Dutch energy industry, Verbong et al. (2008) attributed the failure of Dutch industries to deploy sustainable technological niches to the failure of policies to guarantee sufficient protection mechanisms for innovators. Much of the literature suggests important implications for the role of governance in the transitional process, but these discussions have been confined to industrialized countries (Grillitsch et al. 2019; Nykvist and Whitmarsh 2008). Researchers have yet to devote much effort to address issues for the development of sustainable socio-technical regimes in emerging latecomer countries, especially in the Asian context.

It was argued in Bai et al. (2009) that recent research on technological and industrial transitions in industrialized countries may not provide appropriate developmental guidelines for Asian emerging latecomer countries now experiencing technological upgrading and industrialization. A basic premise behind this argument is that, compared to industrialized countries that have large endowments of innovative and entrepreneurial resources, the indigenous sectoral systems and embedded socio-institutional settings of Asian latecomer countries are not capable of managing, affecting, and organizing the emergence and formation of self-sustained innovation niches. This inability remains a fundamental reverse salient in the transitional process of these latecomer economies. This reverse salient has forced Asian emerging countries to develop socio-political landscapes dedicated to the promotion of high levels of international linkages in terms of technology, knowledge flows and especially large amounts of financial capital via multinational corporations into the local socio-technical regime in order to nurture indigenous firm-level innovative capabilities (Berkhout et al. 2009; Wong et al. 2015; Lee and Lim 2001).

The transitions of Asian emerging economies have been largely influenced by how effectively they can interact with such international linkages and secure the benefits of technology transfer and knowledge spillover. A call to identify the appropriate way to overcome this reverse salient in Asian emerging economies has emerged with the increasing recognition of their importance in the global economy. Despite an increasing body of literature investigating the distinct transitional trajectories of emerging Asian economies (e.g. Berkhout et al. 2009; Rock et al. 2009), the question of how to overcome the reverse salient that arises during transition has not been well addressed. The aim of this paper is therefore to fill this gap by examining the approach used by Taiwan, an industrialized latecomer country, to help SEA economies resolve their reverse salients while building their sustainable socio-technical regimes. In particular, the traditional approach of Asian latecomer countries for addressing reverse salients during transitions has been an overwhelming reliance on the acquisition of FDI through MNCs. This tactic has put their learning processes and catch-up efforts at risk. While the spillovers of technology and know-how from FDI are expected to upgrade the manufacturing capacities of local firms through technology adoption, it is historically evidenced that, due to the inability of indigenous sectoral systems to deliver learning effects to local firms, the strong presence of MNCs in these economies will lead to the dominance of MNC technological activities in the domestic market at the expense of indigenous firms.

2.2 The pros and cons of the FDI-leveraging catch-up model

Due to the limits of critical resources and socio-institutional settings to support the development of innovation activities, international technology transfer through FDI has been one of the major vehicles for promoting industrial transition and catch-up in latecomer countries. As a bundle of technological and management knowledge as well as financial capital, previous studies have shown that FDI contributes to the technological upgrading of latecomer economies in significant ways (Dunning 1994; Lall 1992). The introduction of FDI into a country's socio-technical regime helps latecomer countries join in the operations and production of foreign MNCs in both local and global markets. Spillover from MNCs enables latecomer countries to upgrade manufacturing process capacities for new and advanced products with the hope that, during the catching-up process, the local firms connected to MNCs can leverage and obtain the required resources and capacities for building their own technological capabilities.

The FDI-leveraging model that aimed at promoting technology transfer via MNCs was adopted by a number of latecomer countries for managing their catching-up transition, including Singapore, China, Brazil and India. More recently, this strategy has been utilized by SEA emerging economies. But recent studies have observed that reliance on FDI spillover for indigenous innovations may not achieve the expected and desired effects (see, for example, Fu and Gong 2011; Lee et al. 2017 and Wong and Goh 2015). In order to benefit from the spillover effects of FDI and MNCs, the economy's sectoral system needs to have a strong absorptive capacity and a flourishing of entrepreneurial activities so that indigenous firm-level innovation niches are able to develop. If the absorptive capacity and entrepreneurial activities in latecomer countries are not capable of capturing the values of FDI spillovers, MNCs can only make limited contributions to the proliferation of indigenous innovations niches despite their intensive presence in local socio-technical regime. Under these circumstances, MNCs not only enjoy the benefits of access to local resources (in terms of cheap labor and inputs for production), but they are also in a position to appropriate indigenous knowledge and technological outcomes for their own economic and innovational gain. This crowding-out effect has been evidenced by many African and Central and South American latecomers, and is currently being witnessed in SEA emerging economies.

Electronics, for example, has been the most prominent industry supporting the rapid growth and export-led industrialization of SEA latecomers over the past decades. The development of this prosperous industry can be largely attributed to the government policies that encourage MNCs to bring manufacturing activities and capitals flows into the SEA economies. The main motivation for MNCs investing in SEA latecomers has been the potential to utilize their relatively cheaper labor forces and natural resources. Taking advantage of the offered access to local labor forces, this has facilitated the formation of domestic production networks across various sectors and also led to those networks becoming dominated by MNC operations. Knowledge flow has been largely dependent on MNCs articulation of proprietary networks. The local firms in SEA latecomers are marginalized, acting only as lower level value-added 'assemblers' (Felker 2003; Hobday 2001; Steinberg 2010). Due to the lack of knowledge and absorptive capabilities, indigenous innovation and entrepreneurial activities remain underdeveloped, seriously harming the considerable efforts made by SEA countries to accelerate their socio-technical transitions.

As suggested by Fu et al. (2011), the benefits of technology transfer and knowledge diffusion can only be reaped and realized in the presence of indigenous innovative and entrepreneurial activities. Their presence plays a dual role in self-sustaining and enhancing indigenous capacities for learning and creating new knowledge. Otherwise, foreign technology remains 'exogenous' to the latecomer innovation systems and will never turn into real indigenous innovation niches (Fu et al. 2011). In line with this point, Pietrobelli and Rabellotti (2011) futher indicate that building innovation capacity is not just about advancing functions along the value chain (e.g. from manufacturing to marketing), but also about accumulating the specific capabilities to explore and exploit new technological opportunities through spillovers (e.g. recombination of knowledge for innovation). It appears that the central problem facing the latecomer countries in building their transitional socio-technical regimes is often an overemphasis on attracting MNCs to set up operations within the regime, combined with lack of attention to the active promotion of innovation and entrepreneurial resources. These resources are critical to sustaining an evolving indigenous sectoral system because they establish channels of knowledge diffusion and learning feedback between the regime and niches, fostering locally-generated innovative activities. The consequence of the under-development of such resources is the weakened innovative capability of firm-level niches through self-propagation and co-evolution along with knowledge-driven MNCs.

2.3 Lessons from Taiwan's SMEs: from a mass producer to a niche innovator

The importance of proliferating indigenous innovation niches among Asian latecomers has been evidenced in the experience of Taiwan (Mathews et al. 2011). As an industrialized latecomer, Taiwan has achieved a successful catch-up transition from labor-intensive to a high value-added and knowledge-based system structure (Hu and Mathews 2005). On one hand, the inflow of FDI and technology transfer via MNCs were encouraged by Taiwan's government to accelerate the transition. On the other hand, the state-intervention focused heavily on assisting local firms to internalize knowledge spillovers and rapidly diffuse knowledge into both national and sectoral innovation systems. For example, public research institutes built with the goal of diffusing technologies and related knowledge to local firms as quickly as possible acted as critical agents to assimilate foreign advanced technologies. Simultaneously, universities were encouraged to engage in industrial solutions and made responsible for supplying and training the needed local techno-entrepreneurs. In this respect, industrial policies such as the development of industrial parks, venture capital support, and talent-centric education systems have demonstrated their prominent effect. This allowed local firms to secure the benefits of knowledge diffusion and rapidly develop their own technological capabilities, making them able to co-evolve with the advanced knowledge and technological demands made by MNCs. In turn, this attracted further MNCs investments in Taiwan's local firms. Since the 2000s, MNC investments in Taiwan have been shifted from production-oriented to innovation-focused (Zheng and Hu 2008).

Strategically, MNCs were treated by Taiwan as a proxy for the acquisition of external resources. Facilitated by the advanced technologies of MNCs in combination with state-intervention, a substantial population of techno-entrepreneurs has emerged over time to re-structure the existing regime and impact the endogenous system of industrial development. As a result, Taiwanese firms have been able to develop niche innovations complementary to MNCs, enabling them to function as critical partners for MNCs in the global market. The implications of this situation are two-fold. First, while the acquisition of FDI and foreign technology is an indispensable catalyst to enable and facilitate the building of a transitional socio-technical regime, the fueling of endogenous innovative capabilities and entrepreneurial activities act as antenna to identify precisely the *fit* model during the process of transitions. Notable examples such as Go-Jek in Indonesia and Grab in many SEA economies demonstrate the importance of localized innovation niches that allow latecomers to define the emerging structure of the regime so as to secure a unique niche advantage over the MNCs (such as Uber) in the local market. Second, niched techno-entrepreneurs who are capable of exploring and exploiting knowledge spillovers from the MNCs by engaging in interactive learning are crucial for latecomers. The identified niche opportunity is complementary and compatible with the core competence of MNCs, driving them together with MNCs toward the technology frontier in the global market. Based on these lessons, we now turn to discuss the reverse salients in SEA latecomers in transition.

2.4 The reverse salient of SEA latecomers

Although SEA latecomers have made considerable efforts in transforming themselves toward a more competitive structure, they have achieved only limited progress in building indigenous innovations (Wong 2011; Asian Development Bank 2017). The innovation systems of SEA latecomers have remained under-developed due to their highly fragmented structures. We identify this as a reverse salient in SEA transitional economies caused by ineffective interactions between the policy landscape, the socio-technical regime, and innovation niches.

On the state-led policy landscape, the national intent was to develop a socio-technical regime where MNCs act as a central hub in the industrial structure, leading to interactions between the actors embedded in the manufacturing networks. This was initially aimed to help build absorptive capability as well as indigenous innovative capability through knowledge spillovers from the MNCs by following the experience of Asian Tiger latecomers. Nevertheless, the ill-planned institutional arrangements failed to support the emergence of techno-entrepreneurs at the niche-level due to the lack of learning-by-doing engagement and interaction with MNCs.

In addition, within the socio-cultural bureaucratic context, corruption in SEA countries disabled effective industrial policies and prevented supporting mechanisms from promoting collective niches (Gomez 2009; Govindaraju and Wong 2011). Consequently, industrial policies were designed to favor a few large firms with strong political connections interested in establishing a monopoly over resource exploitation in traditional industries rather than seeking learning opportunities in technology-advanced sectors (Wong 2011). Under such scenario, the policy landscape is not able to help build indigenous capabilities; neither can it facilitate knowledge spillovers from the socio-technical regime to techno-entrepreneurs at the niche level. Based on the lessons learned from Taiwan's SMEs, the collective effect created by niched-level techno-entrepreneurs is the indispensable and underpinning driver in the process of transitions. Moreover, the enhancement of niche-level innovation dynamics in SEA economies would heavily rely on a broad base of small and medium-sized enterprises (SMEs), which have been characterized as more flexible and thus more able to innovate than established giants (Hung and Whittington 2011). This study thus argues that the reverse salient of SEA economies in transitions can be identified as the lack of techno-entrepreneurs at the collective and niche levels.[2]

As shown in Fig. 1, we have developed a conceptual framework to address this reverse salient of SEA economies. In particular, this study emphasizes the role of external public actors, i.e. universities and PRIs from more industrialized economies, which act as important agents to help address the transitional reverse salient encountered by SEA latecomers. They do this by facilitating demand-driven knowledge diffusion and entrepreneurial resources through specialized institutional capabilities and well-articulated innovation networks. Taking Taiwan's approach as a demonstrative case, this study will show how Taiwan's universities and public research institutes are helping SEA economies to overcome their reverse salients by focusing on building collective firm-level niches in SEA countries.

3 Methodology

Given that there is a lack of structured understanding of an effective approach for addressing reverse salients in the transitional process, especially in the context of emerging countries, this study adopts a qualitative heuristic method. Specifically, the method employed in this paper is heuristic action research, a method that has been regarded as a useful approach for enhancing the impact of development and change-oriented research (e.g. German and Stroud 2007). In contrast with other social research methods that consider specific social actors as objects of a study, heuristic action research emphasizes taking actions for practical problem solving while simultaneously building up a body of knowledge. Reason and Bradbury (2001, p.1) argued that action research is *a participatory, democratic process concerned with developing practical knowing in the pursuit of worthwhile human purpose*. In this sense, one can recognize that the major purpose of applying action research is not only to gain an understanding of a specific social arrangement, but also to apply the needed action-solutions to practical problems by including in the research project itself the co-operation of researchers and relevant social members who experience

[2]While there are some successful startups that are being developed in SEA economies, for example Wongnai in Thailand (an app startup providing restaurant search service) and Go-Jek in Indonesia, it is important to note that these startups are imitating business models generated from advanced Western countries then adapting them into the local context.

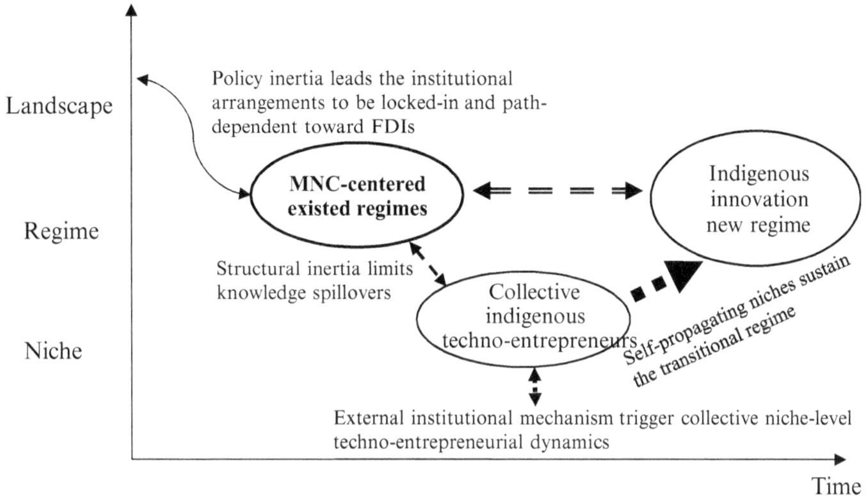

Fig. 1 Conceptual framework. Source: Adapted from Geels (2002)

the chosen research issues (Bradbury-Huang 2010; Brydon-Miller et al. 2003). Implementing action research therefore requires researchers to evaluate iteratively practices, actions and theories in order to generate desired solutions to the immediate problems being addressed while also making a contribution to scientific knowledge (Coughlan and Coghlan 2002).

All the authors are currently involved in project teams that have been organized to help SEA emerging economies to engage in building new socio-technical regimes by allowing them finally to achieve a sustainable catch-up transition. This involvement allowed the authors to conduct heuristic action research for an in-depth exploration of how to overcome the reverse salients in the transitions of SEA emerging economies through reflecting on practices and taking the necessary action solutions. For the purpose of this study, we first surveyed and reviewed the recent efforts made by SEA emerging economies related to industrial upgrading and catch-up strategies in order to understand the context of the transitional processes in which comprehensive data were to be collected. The authors relied on this background information for on-site interviews and all discussions in project meetings across SEA economies from March 2016 to April 2019. The participants in the meetings were practitioners engaged in facilitating transitions in SEA economies, including representatives of private firms, government agencies, research institutes and universities from Taiwan and SEA emerging countries. Numerous questions were raised for discussion regarding the major difficulties SEA emerging economies face in transforming their industrial structures toward a more competitive position, and for articulating the process of collaborative inquiry and collective actions among researchers and various agencies to address transitional reverse salients. Our involvement in the project teams also enabled us to make deep and detailed observations of how each participating entity designed and implemented institutional mechanisms geared toward addressing the transitional reverse salients they face. Additionally, we conducted a series of semi-structured interviews with professionals who have been operating their businesses or conducting research in SEA economies. This was intended to clarify our understandings of the transitional trajectories of SEA emerging economies, and provided us with positive views of the action principles that can assist them in implementing the systematic development of their own sectoral systems.

The details of a selective list of main interviewees are shown in Table 1. The results were achieved and evaluated through an iterative process of meeting discussions and interviews until the research team members reached a consensus. This iterative process enabled us to generate interactively and test emerging ideas through every interview and meeting discussion. In fact, our exploration was not originally based on transition management studies, but rather on a grounded principle emphasizing implementation research without a presumed framework. However, as the research progressed, we found the transition management framework to be a useful analytical lens to explore the factors hindering the catching-up and transitions of the SEA economies.

To illustrate clearly the approach for closing the transitional reverse salient, we provide three action-oriented case studies in which Taiwanese universities and PRIs play significant roles in assisting innovation niche actors to pursue transformational change in response to the transitional ambition of SEA countries. The action emphasis was to coordinate the flow of various innovative and entrepreneurial resources into SEA countries, with the aim of enhancing their institutional capacity so that they may build a sustainable socio-technical regime in transition. Before presenting the three case studies, we first demonstrate the current transition efforts of SEA economies and describe the strong presence of foreign MNCs in these economies as made present through FDI flows.

3.1 Locking-in the FDI and internet-of-thing as an opportunity for transitions

SEA emerging economies are proving to be the leaders in terms of IoT adoptions around the world. As shown in Table 2, according to a recent study of the International Data Corporation, IoT installed units in the Asia Pacific region is expected to grow from 3.6 billion in 2014 to 10.1 billion by 2020, bringing its IoT market opportunity to USD 2602.6 billion (International Data Corporation 2014). In view of their state-directed change and current economic development, the astonishing growth in IoT adoption and revenue is widely acknowledged as the major contribution of SEA emerging markets, China and India. Following the previous catch-up model used in the electronics industry, SEA emerging economies are again aggressively encouraging local firms to attract foreign investments and set up joint ventures

Table 1 List of interviewees (selected), 2016–2019

No.	Interviewee	Affiliation	Position	Date	Time
1	Mr. F	Industry Technology Research Institute (Taiwan)	Associate researcher	Jul 12, 2016 Dec 21, 2017 April 3, 2018	3 h 2 h 2 h
2	Dr. L	Foundation for Commerce and Culture Interchange (Taiwan)	CEO	Sep 29, 2016	2.5 h
3	Dr. C	Institute for Information Technology (Taiwan)	Researcher	May 3, 2016 Nov 12, 2016	2 h 2 h
4	Mr. C	Private firm (Taiwan-based)	CEO	Nov 1, 2016	3 h
5	Ms. H	Private firm (Taiwan-based)	CEO	Sep 18, 2016	2 h
6	Mr. C	Private firm (Taiwan-based)	Manager	Aug 31, 2016	1.5 h
7	Ms. G	Private firm (Taiwan-based)	Market coordinator	Aug 31, 2016	1.5 h
8	Mr. L	Fu Jen Catholic University (Taiwan)	Doctoral student	Oct 22, 2016	3 h
9	Ms. F	National Chiao Tung University (Taiwan)	Master student	Dec 12, 2016	1.5 h
10	Dr H	Ministry of Science and Technology (Taiwan)	General Director	Aug 24, 2016 Oct 5, 2016	2 h 1 h
11	Mr. H	Private firm (Indonesia-based)	General manager	Aug 20, 2016	1 h
12	Mr. T	Private firm (Indonesia-based)	Manager	Aug 22, 2016	1.5 h
13	Mr. L	Investment Department, West Kalimantan Government (Indonesia)	Coordinator	Aug 24, 2016	2 h
14	Dr. S	University of Atma Jaya (Indonesia)	Associate professor	Jun 8, 2016 Aug 23, 2016	2 h 3 h
15	Ms. L	Startup firm (Thailand-based)	CEO	Aug 21, 2017 Apr 18, 2018 Apr 15, 2019	3 h 2 h 1 h
16	Ms. C	Private firm (Thailand-based)	COO	Aug 22, 2017 Apr 18, 2018 Apr 13, 2019	1 h 1.5 h 2 h
17	Mr. R	Private Bank (Thailand-based)	Vice general president	Apr 15, 2018 Dec 20, 2018 Jan 14, 2019	1 h 2 h 2 h
18	Mrs. J	Private accelerator(Thailand-based)	Manager	Jan 15, 2019	1.5 h
19	Dr J	Chulalongkorn University (Thailand)	Associate Professor	Dec 21, 2018	1 h
20	Dr K	King Mongkut's University of Technology Thonburi (Thailand)	Professor	Dec 22, 2018	2 h
21	Mr. N	Private firm (Thailand-based)	CEO	Dec 20, 2018 Jan 15, 2019	2.5 h 1 h
22	Mr. L	Startup firm (Vietnam-based)	CTO	Sept 16, 2018	3 h
23	Dr. R	Tôn Đức Thắng University (Vietnam)	Professor/ Dean	Sept 17, 2018	2 h
24	Mr. C	Private firm (Vietnam-based)	COO	Sept 16, 2018	2 h
25	Dr. F	Private firm (Vietnam-based)	CEO	Sept 15, 2018	3 h

(continued)

Table 1 (continued)

No.	Interviewee	Affiliation	Position	Date	Time
26	Dr. W	University of Malaya (Malaysia)	Lecturer	Mar 15, 2017 Jun 20, 2018 Jan 22, 2019	1 h 1.5 h 1 h
27	Mr. F	Private firm (Malaysia-based)	Manager	Jun 20, 2018	1.5 h
28	Dr. W	National University of Singapore (Singapore)	Professor	Jul 18, 2017 Sept 4, 2018	2 h 2 h
29	Mr. C	Private firm (Cambodia-based)	Manager	Oct 11, 2018	1 h
30	Mr. L	Private bank(Cambodia-based)	Manager	Oct 11, 2018	1.5 h

Table 2 Worldwide IoT installed base by region, 2013–2020 Unit: billion

	2013	2014	2015	2016	2017	2018	2019	2020	2013–2020 CAGR(%)
Total	9.1	11.4	13.7	16.3	19.2	22.2	25.2	28.1	17.5
Asia/Pacific	2.8	3.6	4.4	5.4	6.4	7.6	8.9	10.1	20.1
Central and Eastern Europe	0.3	0.3	0.4	0.5	0.6	0.7	0.8	0.8	15.0
Latin America	0.2	0.2	0.3	0.2	0.4	0.4	0.5	0.6	17.0
Middle East/ Africa	0.3	0.4	0.4	0.5	0.5	0.7	0.7	0.8	15.0
North America	3.1	3.8	4.5	5.2	5.9	6.5	7.0	7.5	13.5
Western Europe	2.4	3.1	3.7	4.5	5.4	6.3	7.3	8.3	17.5

Source: International Data Corporation (2014)

with MNCs that have advanced IoT-abilities in order to accelerate their technological upgrading and catch-up transition. To that end, most SEA emerging economies have claimed to embrace the proliferation of use and industrialization of IoT as a critical part of their national policy landscapes for transformation. Thailand, for example, has launched the 'Smart Thailand 2020' strategy and combined it with the 'Industrial 4.0 Program,' to facilitate the abilities of local firms to increase competitiveness by leveraging the benefits of IoT. As a leading country in the digital transformation of the SEA region, Malaysia unveiled the 'National IoT Strategic Roadmap' as its plan to transform the traditional sectors of agriculture and manufacturing toward digitalization, and enable private sectors to move up the global value chain (Chulavachana 2014; MIMOS Berhad 2015). In addition, Vietnam, the Philippines and Indonesia have different scales of national masterplans for upgrading their traditional industries by introducing IoT, regardless of what stage of economic development and phase of transition they currently occupy (e.g. Talavera 2017; Van 2016). By taking advantage of their domestic markets, a basic principle of such national policies is that they are favorable to FDI-inflow and to MNC activities in their local economies.

Under such favorable policy landscapes, SEA emerging economies have been the main investment targets of MNCs among developing countries for last couple of

Table 3 Top 10 investors in SEA emerging economies, 2015 and 2016 Unit: Millions of dollars

Rank	Country/region	2015	Rank	Country/region	2016
1	Intra-ASEAN	22,149	1	Intra-ASEAN	25,800
2	Japan	17,395	2	United States	18,800
3	United States	12,191	3	Japan	14,100
4	China	8155	4	China	11,300
5	Netherlands	7907	5	Luxembourg	9600
6	United Kingdom	6698	6	Ireland	9000
7	South Korea	5680	7	United Kingdom	8700
8	Australia	5193	8	Hong Kong(China)	8600
9	Denmark	2693	9	Korea, Republic of	6500
10	New Zealand	2241	10	Netherlands	4800
Total		90,303	Total		117,300
% of Top 10 FDI in ASEAN		75%	% of Top 10 FDI in ASEAN		95.5%

Source: ASEAN Secretariat and UNCTAD (2017)

years, accounting for around 19% of global FDI-flows in 2016. Table 3 indicates the top 10 investors in SEA economies in both 2015 and 2016, and provides evidence that foreign MNCs have made a strong footprint in these emerging economies, especially the USA, Japan, China, Europe and South Korea. One notable point is that intra-regional investment was the largest source of FDI flows. While this is in part due to the regional investment of increasingly prosperous local firms, supported by the acquisition of foreign assets, the strong and aggressive expansion by MNCs is also a major factor. More and more foreign MNCs chose to set up headquarters or subsidiaries in SEA economies. These headquarters and subsidiaries in turn invest in other countries across the SEA region on behalf of their parent companies (ASEAN Secretariat and UNCTAD 2017).

The major investors in SEA countries focus their investment interests in different industries. In general, FDI flows into SEA economies have been largely focused in three industries: finance (33%), manufacturing (24%) and wholesale and retail (9%). For example, the investments of Korean and Japanese MNCs were highly concentrated in manufacturing activities. In fact, approximately 50% of FDI from these two countries flowed into manufacturing industries across SEA economies and that percentage continues to rise significantly (ASEAN Secretariat and UNCTAD 2017). The demand derived from digitalization has induced further investment opportunities from MNCs whereby IoT-enabled manufacturing products have become a driving agenda for economic growth in the SEA economies.

From the perspective of transition management, the policy landscape of SEA emerging economies has been implemented to incentivize MNCs to act as the agent, leading the formation of production networks in the IoT sector. This is designed to build indigenous firm-driven innovation niches through knowledge spillover from MNCs. However, SEA economies are not successfully detached from the MNC-centric dependent path. To the contrary, we have seen that MNCs put indigenous innovation activities at risk, mostly because the policy landscape and socio-institutional setting has become locked-in and relies too heavily on MNCs (Wong and Goh 2015). This is particularly evidenced in the electronics industry of SEA economies, which is also the main concern raised by many practitioners and professionals when they were interviewed for this study.

This concern thus calls for SEA emerging economies to create a set of socio-institutional settings where foreign technology, indigenous niched innovation capability, and entrepreneurial activities are coordinated in parallel. Therefore, taking Taiwan's approach as an example, this study seeks to offer evidence of an accessible method that may be able effectively to help SEA emerging economies overcome their reverse salients by building collective niched-based techno-entrepreneurship.

3.2 *Taiwan's innovation niche seeder approach and three action-oriented cases*

As discussed earlier, Taiwan is an industrialized latecomer country and has proven to be remarkably successful in sustaining its transitional socio-technical regime through self-propagating and firm-driven innovation niches. As Taiwan's sectoral system is mainly composed of SMEs that suffer from resource constraints, the policy landscape has put much emphasis on the promotion of techno-entrepreneurial activities and the creation of innovation clusters (e.g. science parks) to grow indigenous high-tech industries. In such approach, the roles of universities and PRIs are largely enhanced to underpin the evolving sectoral system for promoting knowledge diffusion and learning effects through intensive interactions with local firms.

In seeking to achieve the current mission of enhancing regional competitiveness and entrepreneurship in Asia, Taiwan is creating new approaches for enabling exchange and interaction among innovative and entrepreneurial resources across the region. The ambition that lies at the core of this mission is to enable Taiwan to become one of the global/Asian hubs in terms of innovation and entrepreneurship in the forthcoming digital socio-technical regime that is largely driven by IoT technologies and applications. While state-led policy is currently trying to reduce economic dependence on the Chinese market, numerous flagship projects initiated by the Taiwanese government, such as the New Southbound Policy, have been launched to aggregate institutional capacities embedded in Taiwan's sectoral system. These projects aim at providing multifaceted platforms and solutions to help SEA emerging economies overcome the reverse salients they face. In particular, three platforms, namely the Business Models Innovation Research Center (BMIRC) operated by National Tsing Hua University, the Taiwan Rapid Innovation Prototyping League for Entrepreneurs (TRIPLE) and the Taiwan Innovation & Technology Arena (TITAN) operated by the Industry Technology Research Institute (ITRI), are increasingly demonstrating their contribution through the infusion of techno-entrepreneurial capacities into SEA emerging countries.

3.3 Business models innovation research center (BMIRC)

BMIRC was created by National Tsing Hua University (one of the elite universities in Taiwan, located in Hsinchu Science Park) with the aim of implementing Taiwan's 'New Southbound Policy.' Recognizing the reverse salient in the SEA economies, BMIRC realized that Taiwan needed to establish close linkages with SEA emerging economies and help them foster collective niched-level indigenous techno-entrepreneurship. To relieve the reverse salient faced by SEA latecomers, the major activities implemented by BMIRC focus on facilitating knowledge flows and manpower exchanges between Taiwan and SEA economies.

Considering the weaknesses of the indigenous socio-institutional setting, Taiwanese firms based in SEA economies are acting as intermediaries to bridge technology/knowledge gaps between SEA small firms and MNCs, as shown in Fig. 2. Many Taiwanese firms based in SEA economies operate in traditional industries but actively engage in the upgrade and transformation of their local businesses through IoT-enabled solutions. BMIRC thus leverages these Taiwanese firms as agents to diffuse IoT-enabled solutions into the innovation systems of SEA latecomers, triggering technological connections and learning opportunities for local niche techno-entrepreneurs. In addition, BMIRC aims to gather SEA alumni who have graduated from Taiwanese universities to act as catalysts for the promotion of indigenous techno-entrepreneurship. (On average, there are more than 30 thousand students from SEA countries studying in Taiwan's universities annually, a high percentage of whom are from Malaysia and Vietnam). These SEA students/alumni are encouraged to take advantage of the entrepreneurial resources available from Taiwan to create new ventures that link the societal and industrial needs of SEA economies with technological solutions from Taiwan. The goal is establishing a bridging mechanism between SEA countries and Taiwan in terms of innovation and entrepreneurship, toward a vision of building a mutual beneficiary techno-entrepreneurial system for fueling indigenous innovation niches.

3.4 Taiwan rapid innovation prototyping league for entrepreneurs (TRIPLE)

The TRIPLE platform implemented by ITRI takes a novel approach to help foster not only niche-level techno-entrepreneurs in SEA economies, but also those from the rest of the world. One of the critical problems faced by niche-level innovators is the lack of capabilities and resources to scale up niche development. This includes realizing an idea into a product prototype or service model (i.e. from zero to one) and scaling up from the prototype to mass production (i.e. from one to thousands). TRIPLE is designed as a platform to assist techno-entrepreneurs in acquiring critical resources and capacities for their early-stage development by leveraging institutional capacities accumulated in Taiwan's sectoral systems. (Please see Fig. 3 for a graphic

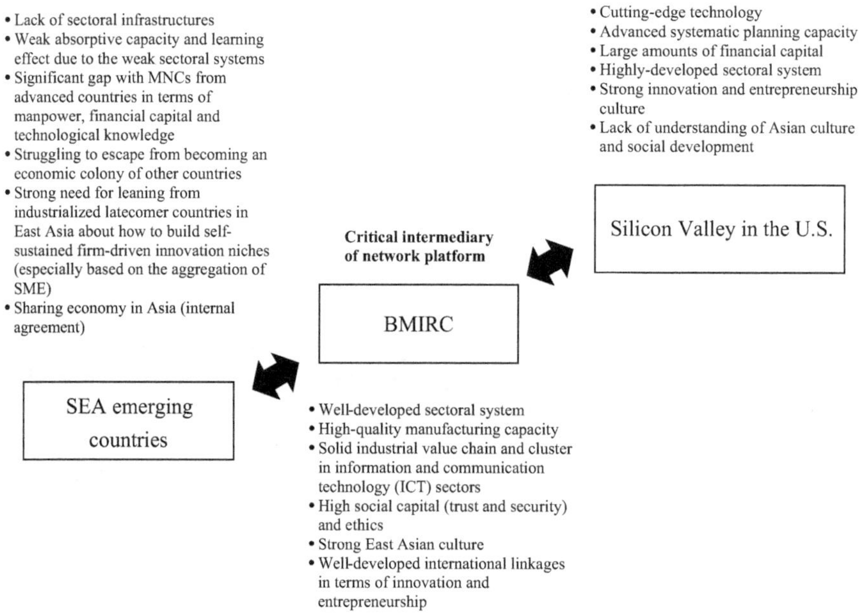

Fig. 2 A graphical representation of the mission of BMIRC. Source: derived from this study

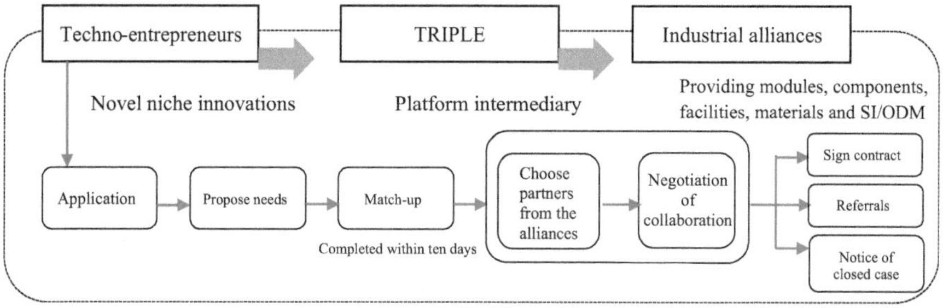

Fig. 3 TRIPLE's Two-week working flow. Source: Information retrieved from www.triplelinkage.com

of TRIPLE's approach.) As a whole, TRIPLE has formed diverse portfolio-wide industrial networks based on different types of modules, components, facilities, and materials, while it also offers total-solution system integration (SI) and Original Design Manufacturing (ODM) to early-stage developers. In addition, TRIPLE provides various institutional mechanisms, which have been developed and accumulated through ITRI for fostering Taiwan's innovation niches, to enhance the capability of techno-entrepreneurs in terms of intellectual property rights and financial arrangement, reinvestment and other value-added services.

Niche innovators from SEA latecomers that connect with TRIPLE are able to economically and efficiently secure advanced solutions and develop self-enhancing cycles. There are already some successful cases to report from the SEA economies, such as Sybo Tech (which developed a 'smart ball device' enabling pet owners to monitor and interact with their pets anytime and anywhere) and eVida (which created a pressure sensor to monitor fall-prone patients and alert nurses for early assistance). More cases provide evidence that TRPLE is acting as an effective mechanism to help foster techno-entrepreneurs in the niche-level.

3.5 . Taiwan Innovation & Technology Arena (TITAN)

TITAN is a platform implemented by ITRI to stimulate techno-entrepreneurial dynamics in Asia. Functioning to fulfill needs sequential to TRIPLE, TITAN is developed to support and fund overseas entrepreneurs to come to Taiwan to leverage Taiwan's innovative and entrepreneurial resources. One of the examples is the 'soft-landing' program, which provides funds for startups or small companies seeking to address their technologies, capital, manpower, or market needs to come to Taiwan for a period of one to a few months. In this way, the entrepreneurs participating in the TITAN platform are able to relocate temporarily to Taiwan and engage intensively and interact with Taiwan's sectoral actors. TITAN thus functions as an intermediary in the process to articulate the needs of techno-entrepreneurs, and connect them with solution providers in Taiwan. To date, many start-ups from SEA emerging countries, such as Vietnam and Malaysia, have taken advantage of TITAN as early engagers with potential Taiwanese corporate partners and clients.

3.6 Overcoming the reverse salient of SEA economies in transition

The three flagship projects, namely, BMIRC, TRIPLE, and TITAN, launched in Taiwan are presented as action-oriented cases in this study. They are novel socio-institutional mechanisms working to provide institutional support, build innovation capacities and establish international linkages by linking indigenous techno-entrepreneurs across Taiwan and SEA countries. In particular, we aggregate the three policy-driven platforms as an innovation niche seeder approach to help SEA emerging economies overcome the reverse salients that have emerged during their catch-up transition by means of promoting their niche-level techno-entrepreneurial capabilities. We expect to see this innovation niche-driven approach enable the formulation of new socio-technical regimes, where inclusive growth and indigenous collective techno-entrepreneurial activities are able to play significant roles (see Fig. 4).

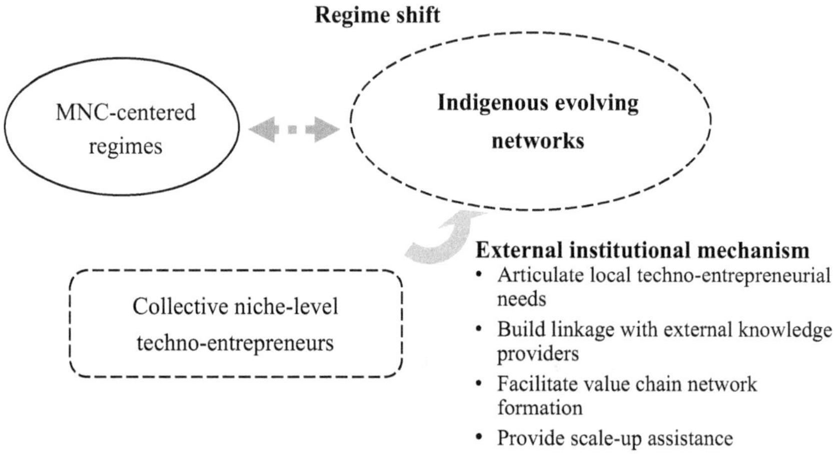

Fig. 4 Overcoming the reverse salient to build a new sustainable socio-technical regime through the assistance of external institutional mechanisms

Instead of the supply-driven dissemination induced by FDI, it is observed that universities and PRIs from Taiwan are leading a demand-focused diffusion process. To help foster indigenous niches in SEA latecomer economies, the three Taiwanese organizations examined here aim to assist SEA techno-entrepreneurs link with external knowledge/solution providers. The effectiveness of such innovation-niche driven approach is preliminarily highlighted by the two successful cases of niche innovators mentioned in this study, i.e. Sybo Tech and eVida. Both techno-entrepreneurial startups encountered difficulties in their early stage of development, but successfully addressed them by leveraging institutional and resource support from Taiwan's sectoral system. Coordinated by TRIPLE, Sybo Tech was able to solve its technological bottleneck through innovation collaboration with Taiwan's module suppliers, and to develop its value chain networks, and eVida successfully leveraged the TRIPLE platform to identify its strategic partners.

4 Discussion and conclusion

This study has implications for both theoretical and practical management. For its theoretical contribution, we demonstrate that institutional theory and resource-based views are mutually reinforced and reflected in their rational contexts. They are not necessarily intented to stand alone or against each other as shown in prior literature. Our empirical study shows that (external) institutions are able to act as a catalyst, rather than a constraint, to induce (internal) resources by triggering collective niche-level techno-entrepreneurial dynamics. In the transitional process, we explored *why* and *how* the industrial dynamics of emerging economies, such as those of SEA countries, have difficultly evolving because their socio-institutional settings mostly favor FDIs. Such socio-institutional difficulty has commonly and widely caused current global protests, especially in the emerging economies such as Chile, Ecuador, Lebanon, Iraq, Haiti, Hong Kong, etc. where further development of 'inclusive growth' is urgently needed. For its practical contribution, we identified the reverse salient of SEA economies in transitions to be the lack of indigenous collective niche-level and firm-driven techno-entrepreneurial capabilities. We also provided an accessible solution for policy makers by demonstrating how such reverse salients can be overcome by means of leveraging external institutional mechanisms such as the three Taiwanese university and PRI institutes examined here.

Given that the sectoral system and the embedded socio-institutional settings are insufficient to support indigenous techno-entrepreneurs, the building of sustainable socio-technical regimes in transitions has become more complicated as regimes suffer from critical system barriers (Bai et al. 2009). This indicates the need for substantial state-intervention to address the reverse salient in the transitional process. In this respect, we have witnessed SEA emerging economies implementing various macro-level policies to attract FDIs and MNCs to support their domestic industrial clusters. This top-down approach is intended to secure resources for the rapid development of industrial infrastructures as well as induce learning effects that will allow for the upgrade of the manufacturing capacity of local firms with the hope of achieving a successful industrial upgrade as a whole. However, the effectiveness of the FDI-leveraging approach is increasingly questionable (Lee et al. 2017; Wong and Goh 2015). As argued in this study, when the existing indigenous sectoral system is incapable of providing sufficient resources and institutional support to local firms for internalizing their absorptive capabilities, the knowledge diffusion and learning effect derived from the FDI will not occur. For emerging latecomer countries to avoid such a dilemma, the innovation niches seeder approach demonstrated by Taiwan's universities and public research institutes may represent a novel avenue to address a reverse salient and locate solutions, especially for SMEs in the Asian context.

The limitation of this study, by means of action research, is that the ultimate effectiveness of the proposed approach in addressing the reverse salients of SEA emerging economies takes time to accumulate and verify. It will be dependent on future policy designs and the development of means for SEA economies to explore and utilize the external sources of institutional mechanisms so as to reinforce indigenous niche capabilities. It will also depend on how such mechanisms are able effectively to mobilize aggregated firm-level niches to shape the structure into a new endogenous regime.

The persistently widening gap between the North and the South has called for an inclusive globalization model, which allows newly-industrializing economies to co-create and co-share growth opportunities and economic gains with advanced economies. In this respect, governments from more advanced economies may have significant impacts by promoting inclusive growth in which their universities and PRIs can act as coordinators to help solve the reverse salients faced by emerging economies. Accordingly, the policy implication derived from this study is that emerging economies are urged to develop an effective and efficient governance model that includes not only attracting FDI and MNCs to facilitate knowledge diffusion but also exploring and utilizing the external sources of institutional mechanisms able to reinforce indigenous niche capabilities that are critical for building a self-sustaining sectoral system.

Highlights • The article elaborates the urgent need for emerging economies to focus catch-up efforts on building indigenous innovation niches.

• The study identifies and demonstrates how reverse salients can be overcome effectively and efficiently in emerging latecomer countries.

• The authors argue that universities and public research institutes from industrialized latecomer countries, such as Taiwan, are able to help compensate for the weaknesses of the socio-technical systems in emerging economies.

• The article proposes a novel governance model for building sustainable socio-technical regimes in transitional Southeast Asian economies.

Compliance with ethical standards The authors would like to acknowledge that this study was funded by the Ministry of Science and Technology, Taiwan (grant number: 106–2420-H-007-008-). The authors declare that they have no conflict of interest.

References

ASEAN Secretariat and UNCTAD (2016) ASEAN investment report 2016: foreign direct investment and MSME linkages. http://asean.org/storage/2016/09/ASEAN-Investment-Report-2016.pdf. Accessed 29 April 2018

ASEAN Secretariat and UNCTAD (2017) ASEAN investment report 2017: foreign direct investment and economic zones in ASEAN. http://asean.org/storage/2017/11/ASEAN-Investment-Report-2017.pdf. Accessed 9 April 2018

Asian Development Bank (2017) ADB annual report 2016. https://www.adb.org/sites/default/files/institutional-document/414776/adb-annual-report-2016.pdf. Accessed 28 May 2019

Bai X, Wieczorek AJ, Kaneko S, Lisson S, Contreras A (2009) Enabling sustainability transitions in Asia: the importance of vertical and horizontal linkages. Technol Forecast Soc Change 76:255–266

Berkhout F, Angel D, Wieczorek AJ (2009) Asian development pathways and sustainable socio-technical regimes. Technol Forecast Soc Change 76:218–228

Bradbury-Huang H (2010) What is good action research? Why the resurgent interest? Action Res 8:93–109

Brydon-Miller M, Greenwood D, Maguire P (2003) Why action research? Action Res 1:9–28

Castellacci F (2009) The interactions between national systems and sectoral patterns of innovation. J Evol Econ 19(3):321–347

Chulavachana TJ (2014) Thai government targets "smart Thailand 2020" combined "national ICT" & "National Broadband" policies. Thai Intel Economics News. https://entrepreneurthai.wordpress.com/2014/03/10/thailands-government-combined-national-ict-policy-national-broadband-policy-for-smart-thailand-2020/. Accessed 9 April 2018

Coughlan P, Coghlan D (2002) Action research for operations management. Int J Oper Prod Manag 22:220–240

Dunning JH (1994) Multinational enterprises and the globalization of innovatory capacity. Res Policy 23:67–88
Felker GB (2003) Southeast Asian industrialisation and the changing global production system. Third World Q 24(2):255–282
Fu X, Gong Y (2011) Indigenous and foreign innovation efforts and drivers of technological upgrading: evidence from China. World Dev 39(7):1213–1225
Fu X, Pietrobelli C, Soete L (2011) The role of foreign technology and indigenous innovation in the emerging economies: technological change and catching-up. World Dev 39(7):1204–1212
Geels FW (2002) Technological transitions as evolutionary reconfiguration processes: a multi-level perspective and a case-study. Res Policy 31(8–9):1257–1274
Geels FW (2004) From sectoral systems of innovation to socio-technical systems: insights about dynamics and change from sociology and institutional theory. Res Policy 33:897–920
Geels FW (2005) Processes and patterns in transitions and system innovations: refining the co-evolutionary multi-level perspective. Technol Forecast Soc Change 72(6):681–696
German L, Stroud A (2007) A framework for the integration of diverse learning approaches: operationalizing agricultural research and development (R&D) linkages in eastern Africa. World Dev 35(5):792–814
Gomez ET (2009) The rise and fall of capital: corporate Malaysia in historical perspective. J Contemp Asia 39(3):345–381
Govindaraju VC, Wong C-Y (2011) Patenting activities by developing countries: the case of Malaysia. World Pat Inf 33(1):51–57
Grillitsch M, Hansen T, Coenen L, Miörner J, Moodysson J (2019) Innovation policy for system-wide transformation: the case of strategic innovation programmes (SIPs) in Sweden. Res Policy 48(4):1048–1061
Hobday M (2001) The electronics industries of the Asia–pacific: exploiting international production networks for economic development. Asian-Pac Econ Lit 15(1):13–29
Hu M-C, Hung S-C (2014) Taiwan's pharmaceuticals: a failure of the sectoral system of innovation? Technol Forecast Soc Change 88:162–176
Hu M-C, Mathews JA (2005) National innovative capacity in East Asia. Res Policy 34 (9):1322–1349
Hughes TP (1987) The evolution of large technological systems. In: Bijker WE, Hughes TP, Pinch TJ (eds) The social construction of technological systems. The MIT Press, Cambridge, pp 51–82
Hung S-C, Whittington R (2011) Agency in national innovation systems: institutional entrepreneurship and the professionalization of Taiwanese IT. Res Policy 40(4):526–538
International Data Corporation (2014) Worldwide and regional Internet of Things (IoT) 2014–2020 Forecast: a virtuous circle of proven value and demand. http://branden.biz/wp-content/uploads/2017/06/IoT-worldwide_regional_2014-2020-forecast.pdf. Accessed 27 Jan 2017
Kern F (2012) Using the multi-level perspective on socio-technical transitions to assess innovation policy. Technol Forecast Soc Change 79(2):298–310
Kim Y-Z, Lee K (2008) Sectoral innovation system and a technological catch-up: the case of the capital goods industry in Korea. Glob Econ Rev 37(2):135–155
Lall S (1992) Technological capabilities and industrialization. World Dev 20(2):165–186
Lee K, Lim C (2001) Technological regimes, catching-up and leapfrogging: findings from the Korean industries. Res Policy 30(3):459–483
Lee K, Szapiro M, Mao Z (2017) From global value chains (GVC) to innovation systems for local value chains and knowledge creation. Eur J Dev Res 30(3):424–441
Malerba F (2004) Sectoral systems of innovation: concepts, issues and analyses of six major sectors in Europe. Cambridge University Press, London
Mathews JA (2006) Dragon multinationals: new players in 21 st century globalization. Asia Pac J Manag 23(1):5–27
Mathews JA, Hu M-C (2007) Enhancing the role of universities in building national innovative capacity in Asia: the case of Taiwan. World Dev 35(6):1005–1020

Mathews JA, Hu M-C, Wu C-Y (2011) Fast-follower industrial dynamics: the case of Taiwan's emergent solar photovoltaic industry. Ind Innov 18(2):177–202

MIMOS Berhad (2015) National Internet of things (IoT) strategic roadmap: a summary. http://www.mimos.my/iot/National_IoT_Strategic_Roadmap_Summary.pdf. Accessed 15 Jan 2018

Nelson RR (ed) (1993) National innovation systems: a comparative analysis. Oxford University Press, New York

Nykvist B, Whitmarsh L (2008) A multi-level analysis of sustainable mobility transitions: niche development in the UK and Sweden. Technol Forecast Soc Change 75(9):1373–1387

Pietrobelli C, Rabellotti R (2011) Global value chains meet innovation systems: are there learning opportunities for developing countries? World Dev 39(7):1261–1269

Reason P, Bradbury H (eds) (2001) Handbook of action research: participative inquiry and practice. Sage Publications, London

Rock M, Murphy JT, Rasiah R, van Seters P, Managi S (2009) A hard slog, not a leap frog: globalization and sustainability transitions in developing Asia. Technol Forecast Soc Change 76 (2):241–254

Steinberg DI (ed) (2010) Korea's changing roles in Southeast Asia: expanding influence and relations. Institute of Southeast Asian Studies, Singapore

Talavera C (2017) World's biggest 'smart city' to rise in Philippines. The Philippine Star. https://www.philstar.com/business/real-estate/2017/07/06/1717043/worlds-biggest-smart-city-rise-philippines. Accessed 15 Jan 2018

Teubal M (2002) What is the systems perspective to innovation and technology policy (ITP) and how can we apply it to developing and newly industrialized economies? J Evol Econ 12 (1–2):233–257

Van H (2016) IoT has major potential in Vietnam. Vietnam Economic Times. http://vneconomictimes.com/article/vietnam-today/iot-has-major-potential-in-vietnam. Accessed 8 Jan 2018

Verbong G, Geels FW, Raven R (2008) Multi-niche analysis of dynamics and policies in Dutch renewable energy innovation journeys (1970–2006): hype-cycles, closed networks and technology-focused learning. Technol Anal Strateg Manag 20(5):555–573

Viotti EB (2002) National learning systems: a new approach on technological change in late industrializing economies and evidences from the cases of Brazil and South Korea. Technol Forecast Soc Change 69(7):653–680

Weber KM, Rohracher H (2012) Legitimizing research, technology and innovation policies for transformative change: combining insights from innovation systems and multi-level perspective in a comprehensive 'failures' framework. Res Policy 41(6):1037–1047

Wong C-Y (2011) Rent-seeking, industrial policies and national innovation systems in southeast Asian economies. Technol Soc 33(3–4):231–243

Wong C-Y, Goh K-L (2015) Catch-up models of science and technology: a theorization of the Asian experience from bi-logistic growth trajectories. Technol Forecast Soc Change 95:312–327

Wong C-Y, Hu M-C, Shiu J-W (2015) Governing the economic transition: how Taiwan transformed its industrial system to attain virtuous cycle development. Rev Policy Res 32 (3):365–387

Zheng C, Hu M-C (2008) Challenge to ICT manpower planning under the economic restructuring: empirical evidence from MNCs in Singapore and Taiwan. Technol Forecast Soc Change 75 (6):834–853

Embeddedness and local patterns of innovation: evidence from Chinese prefectural cities

Giorgio Prodi, Francesco Nicolli, and Federico Frattini

Abstract The diffusion of innovative activities has been very fast in China since the mid-1990s. The literature nonetheless suggests that internationally-relevant innovation may have delayed gaining embeddedness in some places, depending on the strategy it was "seeded". This paper posits that different degrees of embeddedness are linked with different local patterns of innovation and investigates these linkages across Chinese prefectural cities. Four research hypotheses are stated, one for each indicator identified in the literature to investigate technological catching up. The empirical exercise is set as an ordered logistic regression of data rearranged from the OECD Patent Databases for the period 1981–2009. The results show that embeddedness is positively linked with innovation that increasingly relies on its own local past and negatively linked with innovative activities more concentrated across patent owners. The evidence of a nexus with originality and technology cycle time is less clear and requires appropriate investigation in future research. At the state of the art, the main hint is that embeddedness is gained where the knowledge paths increase in complexity.

Keywords China · Embeddedness · Innovation · Patent · Technological catching up

JEL Classification O33 · O53 · R19

G. Prodi · F. Frattini (✉)
University of Ferrara, 44121 Ferrara, Italy
e-mail: giorgio.prodi@unife.it; federico.frattini@unife.it

F. Nicolli
University of Ferrara, 44121 Ferrara, Italy

European University Institute, 50133 Fiesole, Florence, Italy
e-mail: francesco.nicolli@unife.it

A. Pyka, K. Lee (eds.), *Innovation, Catch-up and Sustainable Development*,
Economic Complexity and Evolution, https://doi.org/10.1007/978-3-030-84931-3_12

1 Introduction

Technological catching up is essential to the economic rise in middle-income countries (Lee 2013). Laggards are actually required to accumulate technologically less-vintaged capital to close the gap with the more industrialized economies representing the global technology frontier (Abramovitz 1986). On this frontier, up-to-date capital accumulation is mostly an endogenous process, while indigenous capital accumulation in emerging economies can critically benefit from being complemented by capabilities imported from abroad (Lall 1992).

Despite a debate in the literature (De Marchi et al. 2018; Fagerberg et al. 2018; Lee et al. 2018), several channels are reckoned to favor a local absorption of foreign capital and technologies in middle-income countries, such as the import of goods, capital, brains and the involvement in global value chains (GVC). This very absorption is essential for indigenous-innovation patterns to grow less-and-less dependent upon exogenous sources and to"seed" local innovation systems (Chung and Lee 2015; Lee et al. 2018).

The interaction between endogenous and exogenous capabilities may nonetheless produce side effects in the medium–long term, such as foreign activities displacing some of those indigenous (Fu and Gong 2011; Lin and Kwan 2016). For this reason, the strategy by which technological catching up is "seeded" is critical for innovative activities to embed at a local level (Prodi et al. 2018). Embeddedness is referred to here as the depth that innovation takes roots into a local environment, focusing on where innovative activities are performed. This idea of local roots and anchors is related to the theory in economic sociology that individual economic actions depend on collective or social structures (Granovetter 1985), that is, on the configuration of networks of nodes and ties (Moran 2005). Accordingly, structural embeddedness is mostly associated with the stability and potential of relations emerging as a sort of impersonal features of networks not in the domain of single nodes to change (Feld 1997; Nahapiet and Ghoshal 1998).

Network structures and embeddedness are relevant in innovation and management studies as they help capture non-individual elements in collaborations that can foster the potential of learning and value creation and so improve firms' performance (among others: Ahuja 2000; Kogut 2000; Dhanaraj and Parkhe 2006). Among these elements, economic geography has focused on identifying those more place-specific that, agglomerating, "develop into more or less specialised industrial milieux [where] knowledge tends to become embedded, not only in individual skills and in the routines and procedures of organisations, but indeed in the milieux as such" (Maskell 1999, 180). Hence, embeddedness is considered a key property of Regional Innovation Systems (RIS) (Doloreux 2002), so that technology creation, absorption and exploitation in "mature" systems are expected to be substantially anchored and governed at a local level (Cooke et al. 1998).[1]

[1]The literature also identifies types of RIS based on the characteristics of nodes and ties (among others: Cooke 2004; Asheim and Coenen 2005; Zukauskaite 2018). Their discussion is beyond the

Unfortunately, a precise quantification of the embeddedness of innovative activities is impossible to obtain, as both embeddedness and innovation are not directly measurable. On the one hand, structural embeddedness refers to the overall composition of the linkages and is proxied by measuring the frequency that ties occur to be shared by nodes (Feld 1997). On the other hand, possible approximations of innovation rely on observing the input of innovative activities such as the amount of the R&D expenditure or personnel, its output such as patent applications or grants, or the effects that innovative activities may have produced, such as the changes in total factor productivity (Keller 2004). A choice among these alternatives often depends on the aims of the empirical investigation.

Prodi et al. (2018) suggest that the embeddedness of innovative activities in small regions can be proxied comparing the prevalence of patent inventors and applicants (or assignees). The higher the presence of indigenous applicants in the local pool, the more innovative activities are said to be embedded in their local environment. The idea behind this is quite simple: innovation is anchored more tightly to where it is promoted, funded, managed and exploited than where it just happens. Take for instance the theories about multinational corporations (MNC) and global value chains (GVC). Value creation is more diffused in the network "peripheries" as competences and resources are more dispersed across and actually governed by subsidiaries and suppliers (Ghoshal and Bartlett 1990; Gereffi et al. 2005). The same holds for innovative activities on which value creation extensively depends: they need more than being just performed in a place to embed.

Network structures are usually investigated in the literature with Social Network Analysis (SNA) (Scott 1991). Prodi et al. (2018) present an alternative approach, making use of data in the same dyadic form and comparing the frequency that two types of nodes (local patent applicants and inventors) are linked with one another. Nonetheless, this method takes advantage of an oversimplification of the overall relational set to investigate a large number of very small networks simultaneously.

The literature offers a wide set of patent statistics to investigate the features of innovative activities (Squicciarini et al. 2013). Breschi et al. (2000) first took some of these indicators to qualify different patterns of innovation in separate technological regimes. Park and Lee (2006) later enriched and tuned that selection to investigate specifically the role of technological regimes for technological catching up in emerging economies. Lee (2013) finally identified the localization, originality, concentration, and technology cycle time of innovations as the most critical indicators in cross-country comparison. These indicators are built upon patent information, each one capturing a specific driver of technological catching up.

More in detail, technological catching up is positively related to more original inventions and to an increasing localization of the knowledge sources in the same place where innovation is carried out, while it tends to slow down where the concentration of innovative activities across applicants and the technology cycle

scope of this paper, however. What concerns us here is the extent, not the modes, that innovative activities can be said to be anchored into a place.

time increase (Lee 2013). The main assumption here is that, at a local level, all these patterns but technology cycle time are related to the embeddedness of innovative activities in the same way they are to technological catching up in middle-income countries. Embeddedness is expected indeed to grow along with technological catching up and its highest levels are to be found in mature innovative environments. For this reason, a higher embeddedness can be also expected to support more complex paths of knowledge creation than those required to boost filling technological gaps in capital accumulation. These hypotheses are tested in an ordered logistic regression where the dependent variable is represented by ranked levels of embeddedness in Chinese prefectural cities and the four indicators of the local patterns of innovation are included as continuous explanatory variables.

The empirical exercise is based on the set of patent applications from China filed at the European Patent Office (EPO) in the period 1981–2009 that Prodi et al. (2018) rearranged at a prefectural level from the OECD REGPAT Database (January 2014). The REGPAT database is rich in systematized details about the location of patent inventors and applicants that can be used to build a measure of embeddedness. In addition, patent records in REGPAT are linkable with those in the OECD Citations Database and the OECD Patent Quality Indicators Database, from which the indicators for the local patterns of innovation can be derived.

For what concerns the selected case, China is paradigmatic for the purpose of this paper as one of the most successful catching up economies, experiencing unprecedented economic growth and a specific developmental model since the early 1980s (Brandt and Thun 2010). Success led the country to the role of "world factory" (Thun 2014), so that China is today a provider of manufacturing activities to many GVCs (Sun and Grimes 2018) and also capable of international technological collaborations and world leadership in some industries (Ma et al. 2009; Zhang and Zhou 2015). Several gaps are then filled, at least in some cities. China's developmental attainments follow in fact from an articulated and unbalanced strategy of technological catching up, mixing indigenous and foreign seeds diversely over time (Fu et al. 2016). As a result, innovative activities are strongly concentrated in some regions (Crescenzi et al. 2012) and variously embedded as well (Prodi et al. 2018).

This paper offers a threefold contribution to the innovation studies applied to economic development. First, it reinforces the bridge between two streams of research, one focusing on the political economy of developmental upgrading in China (among others: Naughton 2007; Brandt et al. 2008; Jin et al. 2008; Brandt and Thun 2010; Chen and Naughton 2016; Brandt and Thun 2016) and the other on the relevance of technological catching up to that change (among others: Lee and Lim 2001; Park and Lee 2006; Lee 2013, 2017). Second, the empirical exercise somehow validates the methodology to approximate embeddedness proposed in Prodi et al. (2018), as it offers evidence of theoretically consistent linkages between embeddedness and previous findings in the literature. Third, the findings here provide additional support to the idea that technology cycle time works differently for technological catching up, on the one hand, and for pushing on the technological frontier, on the other hand (Lee 2013). In doing this, the remainder of the paper is outlined as follows.

Section 2 illustrates the diffusion and dispersion of innovative activities in China, showing how they are variously embedded across Chinese prefectural cities. Section 3 describes the indicators capturing the local patterns of innovation that are relevant to the analysis here and reports summary statistics at the prefectural level. Section 4 is devoted to introducing the empirical test of the linkages between embeddedness and the local patterns of innovation and, then, to reporting and discussing the results also with the support of robustness tests. Section 5 makes room for conclusive remarks highlighting the main findings, their limitations and implications.

2 Embeddedness of innovative activities in China

Innovative activities have grown very fast in China since the mid-1990s. Domestic patent applications to the State Intellectual Property Office of the People's Republic of China (SIPO) rose on average 24.6% a year, from 7.7 to 207 per million inhabitants between 1995 to 2010.[2] Despite much smaller count, the growth pace is even steeper where applications to international patent offices are considered. As an example, the number of patent applications from China to the EPO rose on average 34.5% a year, from 0.03 to 2.5 per million inhabitants during the same period.[3] Several factors are mentioned in the literature as fostering that upsurge of patents, such as the amendments to the national law on intellectual property rights (Hu and Jefferson 2009), a competition between local authorities (Li 2012) and, of course, a substantial reinforcement of technological capabilities (Hu and Mathews 2008; Lee et al. 2017).

The rise of innovative activities is tightly intertwined with economic development and strongly concentrated where it cumulated first (Crescenzi et al. 2012). In 1995, around 55% of patent applications from China to the EPO were actually located in Beijing, the capital city, and they amounted up to 71% including those from Shanghai and the provinces of Guangdong, Jiangsu and Zhejiang. Concentration further increased afterwards, with the EPO applications from these regions reaching

[2] Compound Annual Growth Rate. The counts here consider domestic applications for creations and inventions from China's National Bureau of Statistics, China Statistical Yearbooks. Editions referred for data collection are 1996, 1998 to 2003 and 2005 to 2011, available at the National Bureau of Statistics of China, Annual Data: http://www.stats.gov.cn/english/Statisticaldata/AnnualData. Population data are from the United Nations, Department of Economic and Social Affairs, Population Division, World Population Prospect 2017: https://esa.un.org/unpd/wpp. Hong Kong, Macao and Taiwan are not included for statistical consistency. Data extracted on May 21, 2018.

[3] Compound Annual Growth Rate. Patent counts refer to the priority date and applicant location based on fractional counts from the OECD.Stat: http://stats.oecd.org. Population data are from the United Nations, Department of Economic and Social Affairs, Population Division, World Population Prospect 2017: https://esa.un.org/unpd/wpp. Hong Kong, Macao and Taiwan are not included for statistical consistency. Data extracted on May 21, 2018.

86% in 2010. Nonetheless, the distribution has substantially changed over years, with Beijing as counting for about 10% of the total national patent applications, Guangdong 62% and Shenzhen in Guangdong almost 57%.[4] Evidence is mitigated but not confuted by referring to the domestic applications to the SIPO: 31% of innovative activities in China were located in the same regions as above in 1995, then grown to 60% in 2010.[5]

These figures are the product of a specific, multilayered and evolving set of science, technology and innovation (STI) policies at a national level, as well as of more local drivers of development (Fu et al. 2016; Zhang et al. 2010). For instance, major cities such as Beijing and Shanghai were better endowed with local R&D capacity to attract seeds of local innovation (Zhang et al. 2010). Other cities such as Shenzhen took advantage of dramatically rescaling alongside the country's development since the early 1980s (Zeng 2010). It was in the post-Mao strategy of transition and industrialization that foreign direct investments (FDI) and new imported capabilities started agglomerating in a limited number of places, such as special economic zones (SEZ), to experiment with the market economy (Heilmann 2008). Then, a number of STI initiatives, such as the Torch Programme launched in 1988 to create new industry and technology parks, worked as a connection between separate governmental layers (Heilmann et al. 2013) and as an additional boost for local economic growth (Hu 2007).

Concentration is the most immediate but not the only side effect of unbalanced growth. Structural differences may also emerge over time as much for income as for innovative activities. Especially where the seeds vary across regions, innovative activities can grow to feature place-specific institutional and structural traits, which include embeddedness (Prodi et al. 2017; Prodi et al. 2018). To gain an insight into this aspect of the diffusion of innovative activities in China, the discussion now focuses on the patent applications from China to the EPO. Patentability is usually more binding and patenting costs higher than to national patent offices, so that referring to one or more international patent offices is advantageous as it introduces an implicit quality threshold to the analysis (Dernis and Khan 2004). Some very recent literature also suggests that the quality issue should be carefully considered in the case of China, where international patents are shown to be far more reliable than domestic patents to measure the quality and relevance of the innovative output (Prud'homme and Zhang 2017; Long and Wang 2019).

[4] Shares are computed on fractional counts of patent applications to the EPO by priority date and applicant location. Data are collected from the OECD.Stat: http://stats.oecd.org. Hong Kong, Macao and Taiwan are not included for statistical consistency. Data extracted on May 21, 2018.

[5] Shares are computed on domestic applications for creations and inventions from China's National Bureau of Statistics, China Statistical Yearbooks available at the National Bureau of Statistics of China, Annual Data: http://www.stats.gov.cn/english/Statisticaldata/AnnualData. Hong Kong, Macao and Taiwan are not included for statistical consistency. Data extracted on May 21, 2018.

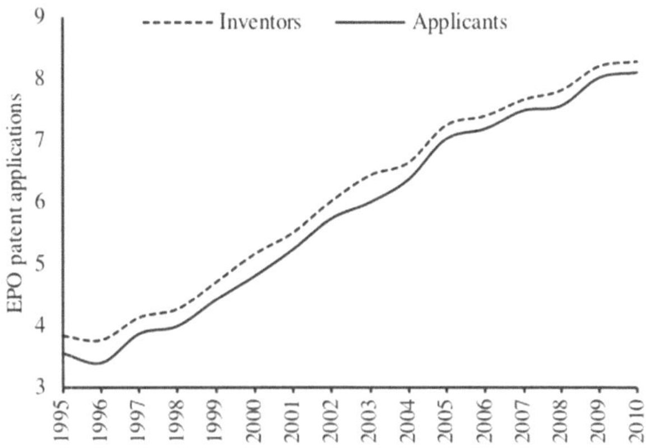

Fig. 1 Diffusion of innovative activities in China by inventor and applicant location, 1995-2010, fractional counts, log scale. Source: authors' arrangement from the OECD.Stat

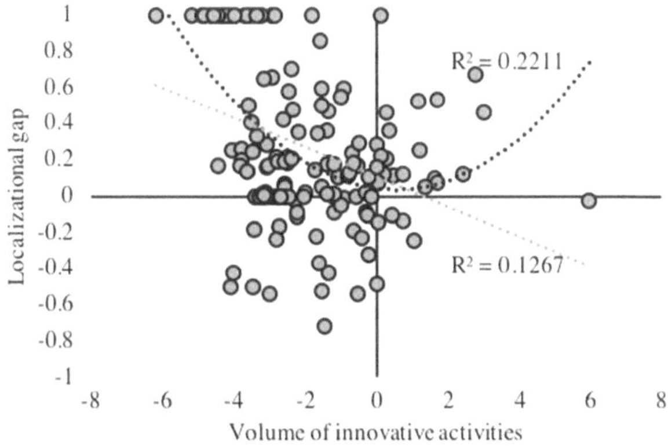

Fig. 2 Gaps between applicant- and inventor-located EPO patent applications (rescaled counts) and total number of EPO patent applications considered in Chinese prefectural cities (patent per million inhabitants, log scale), 2002-2009, period-pooled counts. Source: authors' arrangement from the OECD REGPAT Database, January 2014 and China Data On Line

Figure 1 starts from reporting the overall trends of the EPO patent applications from China between 1995 to 2010.[6] The black solid line counts the patents located in China by applicant (a) and the black dashed line those located by inventor (b). The pair of lines exhibit a fast growth but the gap between (g) highlights that the count by applicant location is 15 to 25% smaller. In this sense, internationally relevant innovation appears frequently to be performed locally but appropriated abroad or in other Chinese prefectural cities. The question is now whether this evidence is homogeneously distributed over the local innovative centers in China.

Data on the EPO patent applications between 1981 to 2009 from the OECD REGPAT Database (January 2014) rearranged at a prefectural level by Prodi et al. (2018) can help to get an answer. Based on these data, it is possible to quantify the gap ($g_i = b_i - a_i$) between the counts of EPO patent applications by applicant (a_i) and inventor (b_i) in Chinese prefectural cities i. Figure 2 focuses on the period

[6]Data are collected from the OECD.Stat: http://stats.oecd.org. Hong Kong, Macao and Taiwan are not included for statistical consistency. Data extracted on May 21, 2018.

between 2002 to 2009, that is, the latest period considered in Prodi et al. (2018), where the number of cities hosting at least one EPO-patent inventor or applicant is the largest (187 over 345 total). As innovative activities have been said strongly concentrated in some of these cities, the gap measure is rescaled on the overall number of the EPO patent applications considered for each city (f_i), that is, the combination of the applicant- and inventor-based counts: $f_i = a_i + b_i - c_i$, where c_i are patent documents which report applicants and inventors located in the very same city i. Put into a different perspective, the overall number of patent applications (f_i) is the union of two sets: $f_i = a_i \cup b_i$, that is, the usual count of total patent applications by applicant location a_i and the usual count of total patent applications by inventor location b_i, which intersect in the subset $c_i = a_i \cap b_i$.[7] The rescaled gaps (g_i/f_i) are scattered against the total number of EPO patent applications per million inhabitants (f_i/pop_i) in Fig. 2.[8]

The feedback from Fig. 2 is straightforward: the gaps (g_i/f_i) weight differently across cities and they appear weakly related to the volume of innovative activities performed in cities. Prodi et al. (2018) interpreted this picture as evidence that innovative activities are variously embedded across cities and, going a step further, as a sort of trace of the mix seeding technological catching up locally. In this sense, more (less) embedded innovative activities are expected to come from more endogenous (exogenous) seeds. Innovative activities were found indeed to have increased faster, although they have delayed gaining embeddedness in places such as the SEZ, where imported capabilities mainly agglomerated in the origin. Nonetheless, there is no solution to trigger innovative activities in developing countries to be necessarily preferred *ex ante*. What concerns us here is that different mixes can lead to different structures at a local level.

The key to this piece of evidence was to get a measure of embeddedness. The method proposed in Prodi et al. (2018) is to perform a grouping of cities into clusters based on the values of the three rescaled indicators. Put in the terms of network theory, these indicators represent the frequency that two types of nodes are linked. In more details, an observed city is treated as an *ego* within a very simple *ego*-network where all the other locations are treated as an *alter*. Hence, there are just two relevant linkages: *ego-ego* and *ego-alter*. The frequency of the first linkage corresponds to the count c_i above, i.e., the fractions of patents that are located in a city i by both applicant and inventor. Differently, the nature of the second linkage changes depending on the focal point. When patent applicants (inventors) are considered, the frequency broadly corresponds to the count a_i (b_i).

The aim of clustering is to separate observations into groups according to some measure of association in order to summarize their multidimensional variability (Hair et al. 2009). Records are separated here considering three locational sets:

[7] By definition, f_i is never less than a_i or b_i ($f_i \geq a_i, b_i \forall i$) and the rescaled gaps (g_i/f_i) are consequently ranging between –1 and +1 ($-1 \leq g_i/f_i \leq +1$).

[8] Data on population in prefectural cities (*pop*) are from China Data On Line, City statistics, http://chinadataonline.org/member/city/. Data extracted on February 18, 2016.

Table 1 Classes of embeddedness by prevailing patent indicator and period, Chinese prefectural cities, 1981–2009

Class	Description	# of prefectural cities		
		1981–1992	1993–2001	2002–2009
4	Prevalence of *c*/*f* and *d*/*f*	0	0	5
3	Prevalence of *c*/*f*	8	12	14
2	Prevalence of *c*/*f* and *e*/*f*	3	7	38
1	Prevalence of *e*/*f*	29	68	130
Total grouped		40	87	187
Total excluded for no activity recorded at the EPO		305	258	158

c = number of EPO patent applications with local inventor and applicant
d = number of EPO patent applications with local applicant only
e = number of EPO patent applications with local inventor only
$f = c + d + e$ = total number of EPO patent applications counted
Source: authors' arrangement from Prodi et al. (2018), Table 5 (partial), p. 91

applications where the applicants only are from a city i ($d_i = a_i - c_i$); those where the inventors only are from a city i ($e_i = b_i - c_i$); those where both the applicants and inventors are from the same city i (c_i). Counts are then rescaled on the total number of the EPO patent documents considered ($f_i = c_i + d_i + e_i = a_i + b_i - c_i$) and their period-average values.

The resulting groups are classes of observations, and they can be ordered according to motivated criteria. In this specific case, the motivation is inherently related to how innovative activities are supposed to evolve as they gain embeddedness, that is, those patents located by applicant come to weight more, while those located by inventor do less. Table 1 reports the results as obtained by Prodi et al. (2018) for the EPO patent applications from China for three separate periods in the country's developmental experience between 1981 to 2009 (letters amended as above). The total number of prefectural cities grouped, i.e., those reporting at least one application record at the EPO, has increased over time as well as "higher" classes of embeddedness has grown. In the latest period (2002–2009), 130 cites grouped into class 1 among 187 total are those where embeddedness is assumed to be the lowest because innovative activities are mostly or even exclusively associated with these cities by inventor (e/f), while the applicants are located elsewhere in China or abroad. Embeddedness is then expected to increase, climbing up the classes, and the 38 cities grouped into class 2 are those shown to host also innovative activities where both the inventors and applicants are local (c/f). This last set of innovative activities is the most relevant alone among the 14 cities in class 3, while it emerges together with innovative activities located only by applicant (d/f) in the five cities grouped into class 4. This evidence suggests that, despite a growing diffusion over time, internationally relevant innovative activities are far from reaching high levels of embeddedness in a large majority of the Chinese prefectural cities where they are performed. About 70% of the cities with a record at the EPO between 2002 to 2009 predominantly host inventors only (class 1) and fewer than 3% record a sizeable presence of local applicants (class 4). For the remainder 27% of cities, the local pool of innovative activities is in between (classes 2-3).[9]

3 Local patterns of innovation across Chinese prefectural cities

Embeddedness is just one of the qualities of local innovative activities that can be detected by patent statistics. As mentioned above, the literature offers several patent quality indicators aimed to reveal manifold characteristics of innovation (Squicciarini et al. 2013). Some of these indicators have been adopted to investigate the patterns of innovation featured by separate technological regimes (Breschi et al. 2000) and to estimate how technological catching up appears to foster economic growth, including the originality of innovation, the localization of its knowledge base, the concentration of activities across innovators, and the cycle time of technologies (Lee 2013).

First, an originality index (O_p) focuses on "the breath of the technology fields on which a patent relies" (Squicciarini et al. 2013, 49). Based on the seminal contribution by Trajtenberg et al. (1997), it is defined as follows:

$$O_p = 1 - \sum_{k \in K_p} s_{pk}^2 \tag{1}$$

where p is a patent document, k a eight-digit class of technologies in the International Patent Classification (IPC) and s the share of citations to a technological class k among those reported in the documents cited by the patent p (K_p). A higher variety of the referred technological fields then corresponds to more originality. But, as the analysis here is put into a regional perspective, patent indicators p are taken their average value within the sets of patents P_i relating to each city i:

$$O_i = \frac{1}{|P_i|} \sum_{p \in P_i} O_p \tag{2}$$

Values can range between 0 and 1, corresponding to the lowest and the highest level of originality, respectively ($0 \leq O_i \leq 1$).

Second, the localization of knowledge creation and diffusion (L_i) is based on the idea "to compare the probability of a patent matching the originating patent by geographic area, conditional on it citing the originating patent, with the probability

[9] An additional rank 5, that is, a prevalence of *d*/*f* alone, may result in theory from grouping. It is hard (not impossible), however, to find out that innovators largely agglomerate in a place while their activities are mostly performed elsewhere. The results presented in Prodi et al. (2018) actually report this hypothetical rank 5 as an empty group.

of a match not conditioned on the existence of a citation link" (Jaffe et al. 1993, 581). Following from this idea, Lee and Yoon (2010) proposed to measure localization as the difference between the propensity to regional self-citation and the citations from other regions. Lee (2013) then amended the indicator as follows:

$$L_i = \frac{c_{ii}}{c_i} - -\frac{\sum_{j \in J} c_{ij}}{\sum_{j \in J} c_j} \tag{3}$$

where: c_{ii} is the number of citations to patents in a region i by patents from the same region; c_{ij} is the number of citations to patents in the region i from another region $j \neq i$; c_i is the total number of citations by patents from the region i; c_j is the total number of citations by patents from the region $j \neq i$. The set $J = \{j \neq i\}$ is restricted here to Chinese prefectural cities so that the value of L_i is the percentage points that a city i is exceeding or failing the other cities j to reference its knowledge base. In other words, L_i increases as innovative activities tend to build more and more on their own local past. The indicator can take both positive and negative values, theoretically ranging between -1 and $+1$ inclusive ($-1 \leq L_i \leq +1$).

Third, "high technological opportunities allow for the entry of new innovative firms, thereby reducing concentration" (Breschi et al. 2000, 393). Accordingly, the concentration of innovative activities (H_i) is negatively related to technological catching up (Lee 2013). As the same as market concentration, it can be approximated by a Herfindahl-Hirschman index:

$$H_i = \sum_{a:i} \left(\frac{\pi_{a:i}}{\pi_i}\right)^2 \tag{4}$$

where π_i is the count of patent applications located in a region i by inventor and $\pi_{a:i}$ the subset of these patent applications that are attributable to the same applicant a. Values can range between 0 and 1, corresponding to the lowest and the highest level of concentration, respectively (**$0<Hi\leq 1$**).

The fourth indicator considered is technology cycle time (T_i). It was introduced to measure how knowledge differs "in its obsolescence over time" (Park and Lee 2006, 726) based on citation lags, that is, the approximation of the time span between the appearance of a predecessor and a successor technology (Jaffe and Trajtenberg 2002). The indicator is amended here to investigate the differences not across technological classes k but regions i, so that:

$$T_i = \frac{1}{|P_i|} \sum_{p \in P_i} \tau_{pc} \tag{5}$$

where p are citing patent documents (those collected), c cited patent documents, τ the citation lag in years, and P_i the set of citing patent applications in a city i. By definition, the indicator can take only non-negative values ranging between 0 and the longest citation lag ($0 \leq T_i \leq \max\tau_{pc} : p \in P_i$).

Table 2 Indicators of local patterns of innovation, Chinese prefectural cities, 1981–2009, summary statistics

	Obs	Mean	sd	$z(W)$	Min	25%	50%	75%	Max
O_i	262	0.702	0.154	6.926***	0.000	0.638	0.730	0.791	0.947
L_i	262	0.003	0.014	10.932***	– 0.002	0.000	0.000	0.000	0.143
H_i	262	0.461	0.349	6.422***	0.011	0.165	0.366	0.762	1.000
T_i	262	13.333	9.077	8.931***	1.800	8.000	11.809	15.986	89.000

p-value: * < 0.1;** < 0.05;*** < 0.01
Source: authors' arrangement from the OECD REGPAT Database, January 2014, the OECD Citations Database, March 2018, and the OECD Patent Quality Indicators, March 2018

All the indicators here are produced looking at the inventor side, as it is recommended to use the inventors' location to "compile patent statistics aimed at reflecting inventive activities" (OECD 2009, 63). The index of concentration H_i is built on the same data set rearranged from the OECD REGPAT Database, Janaury 2014, by Prodi et al. (2018). The citations from the EPO applications in the data set to patents worldwide (not depending on the granting authority) are extracted from the OECD Citations Database, March 2018, and merged with the information about the inventor location to build a measure of the localization of knowledge creation and diffusion L_i. Technology cycle time T_i is computed on the citation lags reported in the OECD Citations Database, March 2018, while the index of originality O_i is taken from the OECD Patent Quality Indicators, March 2018. Records are linked across databases and releases by application number. The data set is a collection of period-average values for 262 complete observations overall, that is, 35 prefectural cities in the first period (1981–1992), 67 in the second period (1993–2001), and 160 in the third (2002–2009).

Table 2 reports the summary statistics for each indicator. It is worth noting that their distribution is mostly not well-behaved. As an example, the distribution is negatively skewed for originality O_i and positively for the other indicators, as well as there are many zeros in the case of localization L_i. The Shapiro-Wilk test $z(W)$ confirms that the (null) hypothesis of normal distribution should be rejected for all the indicators. As a consequence, quantile thresholds are to be preferred to mean values as meaningfully representative of regressors in the empirical exercise presented in the next section (Field et al. 2012).

4 Linking embeddedness with local patterns of innovation

The core of this paper is to test whether innovative activities exhibit local patterns that are linked with their degree of embeddedness. The idea is that separate levels of embeddedness gained by local innovative activities correspond to different patterns. The research hypotheses are specified as follows: (H1) embeddedness is positively correlated with the originality of local innovation; (H2) embeddedness is positively correlated with the more local knowledge sources referenced by local innovation; (H3) embeddedness is negatively correlated with the concentration of local innovative activities; (H4) embeddedness is not negatively correlated with the technological cycle time of local innovation. No assumption is posited on the nature of these linkages, and no causal relation is implied.

As the measure of embeddedness reported in Section 2 is in the form of ranked classes into which Chinese prefectural cities are grouped, the most appropriate model to test the hypotheses above is an ordered logistic regression. This technique belongs to a set of models based on Maximum Likelihood Estimators (MLE), that is, non-linear functions of the dependent variable. In the empirical exercise presented here, non-linearity arises from the categorical nature of the dependent variable and regression parameters are to be interpreted as the effects of regressors on a latent continuous variable y^* entailed by the classes of the dependent one (Cameron and Trivedi 2005). The model specification is as follows:

$$y^*_{it} = \beta X_{it} + u_{it} \tag{6}$$

where y^*_{it} is a one-dimensional array of 262 observations for the response variable that "crosses a series of increasing unknown thresholds [moving] up the ordering of alternatives" (Cameron and Trivedi 2005, 519). X_{it} is then a two-dimensional array of 262 observations for each one of the four regressors and u_{it} the usual one-dimensional array of error terms that are assumed to be logistic distributed. Finally, t henceforth identifies the period observed: 1981–1992 for $t = 1$, 1993–2001 for $t = 2$, 2002–2009 for $t = 3$.

4.1 Main estimates

Table 3 reports the distribution of observations by class of the dependent variable. The most of them fall into the class $Y_{it} = 1$ (about 67%) and frequency decreases fast, with very few observations grouped into the class $Y_{it} = 4$ (2%). Table 3 also gives an insight into the behavior of regressors reporting their representative values by class of the dependent variable. Regardless as to whether these values are means or

Table 3 Distribution of observations and representative values of regressors by class of the dependent variable, pooled 1981–2009

			Mean				Median			
Y_{it}	obs	% obs	O_{it}	L_{it}	H_{it}	T_{it}	O_{it}	L_{it}	H_{it}	T_{it}
1	175	66.79	0.707	0.002	0.600	13.304	0.744	0.000	0.510	11.142
2	48	18.32	0.713	0.004	0.165	13.950	0.721	0.000	0.115	12.182
3	34	12.98	0.656	0.008	0.202	12.544	0.685	0.000	0.183	12.691
4	5	1.91	0.774	0.000	0.195	13.772	0.744	0.000	0.158	14.416
All	262	100.00	0.702	0.003	0.461	13.333	0.730	0.000	0.366	11.809

Table 4 Regression output (scores for unit and percentage for standard-deviation increase of regressors)

		M1		M2		M3	
	sd	Scores	%	Scores	%	Scores	%
O_{it}	0.154	−1.470	−20.3	−5.580**	−57.7	−5.867**	−59.5
		(1.227)		(2.439)		(2.465)	
L_{it}	0.014	9.055	13.0	9.518	13.8		
		(11.02)		(11.14)			
H_{it}	0.349	−5.735***	−86.5	−5.692***	−86.2	−5.791***	−86.7
		(0.820)		(0.825)		(0.818)	
T_{it}	9.077	0.002	2.0	−0.154**	−75.4	−0.162**	−77.0
		(0.022)		(0.095)		(0.097)	
$O_{it} \times T_{it}$	5.283			0.261**	297.8	0.272**	320.4
				(0.148)		(0.150)	
L_{i1}	0.002					7.585	1.4
						(52.95)	
L_{i2}	0.006					−49.01	−23.8
						(41.71)	
L_{i3}	0.012					20.35*	28.6
						(10.94)	
θ_1		−2.182**		−4.752***		−4.997***	
		(1.052)		(1.692)		(1.707)	
θ_2		−0.782		−3.333**		−3.543**	
		(1.043)		(1.678)		(1.691)	
θ_3		1.553		−0.991		−1.158	
		(1.114)		(1.719)		(1.731)	
# obs		262		262		262	
$LR\chi^2(4)$		105.34***		109.75***		114.98***	
Pseudo R^2		0.218		0.227		0.238	
Log Likelihood		−188.638		−186.430		−183.817	

p-value: $^{*} < 0.1$;$^{**} < 0.05$;$^{***} < 0.01$
standard errors in brackets

medians, regressors tend to behave homogeneously (increase or decrease) across classes, but class $Y_{it} = 4$.

The output of regressing the classes of embeddedness against the four pattern indicators in Chinese prefectural cities is reported in Table 4, both in the form of scores and percentages. Scores quantify the effect that one unit increase in regressors x_{it} produces on the response variable y^*_{it}. More precisely, this effect is an increase in the log odds that the response variable moves from values below to values above a threshold θ_y. The scores estimated for the specification in M1 suggest that the odds are affected by regressors as follows: (H1) negatively and non-significantly by an increase of the originality of innovative activities O_{it}; (H2) positively and non-significantly by an increase in the localization of knowledge creation and diffusion L_{it}; (H3) negatively and significantly by an increase of the concentration of innovative activities across applicants H_{it}; (H4) positively and non-significantly by an increase of technology cycle time T_{it}.

The baseline specification in M1 can be improved to capture a more consistent relationship between the four regressors and the classes of embeddedness. It is worth recalling, indeed, that originality O_{it} focuses on "the breath of the technology fields on which a patent relies" (Squicciarini et al. 2013, 49), which can therefore be interpreted as positively related to more complex knowledge paths. In turn, T_{it} is an inverse proxy of the speed of obsolescence of technologies (Park and Lee 2006) and it is also expected to increase with complexity. It is then reasonable to argue that, despite the fact that the two variables do not exert a significant effect individually, their interaction can reveal some room of significance. This is exactly the result obtained with the specification in M2, where the coefficient associated with the interacted term $O_{it} \times T_{it}$ is positive and statistically significant, providing evidence of some degree of complementarity between the two variables, so that the linkage between the embeddedness and originality of innovative activities O_{it} is positively coupled with, or mediated by, technology cycle time T_{it}.

The specification in M3 finally digs more deeply into the nature of knowledge localization L_{it}, interacting this indicator with three period dummies $t = \{1, 2, 3\}$. The estimated coefficients are positive and statistically significant for L_{i3} only, i.e., the period 2002–2009. The intuition behind M3 is straightforward. Given that L_{it} compares the probability of self-citation against the probability to be cited (Jaffe et al. 1993), it is reasonable to expect meaningful values of the indicator only some "technological time" after a consistent number of a local predecessor technologies have been published. In the case of China, a middle-income country having experienced a tremendous surge of patent applications since the mid-1990s, it could be accordingly guessed that an appreciable evidence about localization L_{it} is possible, but just limited to the latest period. Before that, the indigenous materials that can be cited are so sparse that the probability to have been cited is almost null.

The quantification of all these linkages is nonetheless easier where the scores are transformed. The transformations reported in Table 4 are the percentage changes in the odds that the response variable crosses a threshold θ_y due to one standard-deviation increase of regressors. The discussion is now limited to the specification in M3, which exhibits the most statistically significant results. Accordingly, the odds of moving up classes of embeddedness are: (H1) decreasing by 59.5% where the value of originality O_{it} increases by one standard deviation (0.154); (H2) increasing by 28.6% with one standard-deviation increase of localization in the third period L_{i3} (0.012); (H3) decreasing by 86.7% with one standard-deviation increase of concentration H_{it} (0.349); (H4) decreasing by 77.0% where technology cycle time T_{it} increases by one standard deviation (9.077). Furthermore, the odds increase by 320% with one standard-deviation increase of the interaction term $O_{it} \times T_{it}$ (5.283). Despite two single coefficients failing to meet the assumptions of a consistent linkage specification (L_{i1} and L_{i2}), test statistics suggest that the assumption of correct specification is met overall. First, the estimates actually converge to a log likelihood (–183.8) and, second, the log likelihood ratio test between the constrained and unconstrained model (*LR*) is statistically significant.

4.2 Predicted probabilities

The regression output has returned a quantification of the changes in the odds that the latent variable y^*_{it} crosses the thresholds θ_y.[10] Nothing has been said, however, about the actual odds that the dependent variable y_{it} falls into alternative classes of Y_{it} as predicted by regressors x_{it}. These probabilities can be obtained computing the marginal effects at given values of regressors for each one of the possible dependent outcomes or classes of Y_{it} ($\omega_y = 1, 2, 3, 4$). Those reported in Table 5 are then the odds that a Chinese prefectural city *i* is grouped into a given class of embeddedness ($Y_{it} = \omega_y$) conditionally on the four local patterns of innovation (x_{it}), more formally, $\partial Pr(y_{it} = \omega_y)/\partial x_{it}$ at some representative values of x_{it}.

Let us start from the indicator of concentration H_{it} for which a very robust prediction has been produced across specifications. The odds that an observation falls into the class $Y_{it} = 1$ are 35% if the 25th-percentile value of H_{it} is taken, and they increase up to 96% at the 75th-percentile value of H_{it}. By contrasts, the odds of falling into the class $Y_{it} = 2$ decrease from 34% to 3% moving from the 25th-percentile to the 75th-percentile of H_{it}, and the same happens for the classes $Y_{it} = 3$ (from 21% to 1%) and $Y_{it} = 4$ (from 3% to 0%). The array of estimated odds is obviously bound to the original distribution of observations in the sample, so that observations here are more likely to fall into the class $Y_{it} = 1$ unconditionally as well as conditionally on regressors. Nonetheless, substantial changes in the odds are produced by taking alternative points within the distribution of H_{it} (and supposing that the other regressors are held at their mean values).

In sum, an increase in the concentration of innovative activities across applicants H_{it} is associated with an increase in the odds that a city is grouped into the class $Y_{it} = 1$ and a decrease in those that the same city is grouped into another class $Y_{it} > 1$. Although less evident, the same happens with the originality of inventions O_{it}. By

[10]The ordered logistic regression is based on the assumption of proportional odds or parallel regressions. More precisely, the changes in regressors x_{it} are assumed to produce the very same increase in the odds that the response variable crosses any threshold θ_y (Agresti 2013). Given that the dependent variable takes four possible outcomes $\omega_y = 1, 2, 3, 4$, there are three implied thresholds to be considered ($\theta_y = \omega_y - 1$). As an example, one standard-deviation increase in the concentration indicator H_{it} is expected to reduce about 87% the probability that the response variable y^*_{it} moves, let's say, from the lowest class ($Y_{it} = 1$) to the three-class block above ($Y_{it} > 1$) as much as from the lowest two-class block ($Y_{it} = 1, 2$) to the highest two-class block ($Y_{it} = 3, 4$). A Brant test based on $\chi^2(2)$ statistics (p-values between brackets) confirms that the assumption is met by each individual regressor in M3: O_{it} 0.79 (0.674); L_{it} 2.43 (0.296); H_{it} 8.40 (0.103); T_{it} 1.18 (0.554); $O_{it} \times T_{it}$ 1.08 (0.582). Accordingly, the null hypothesis of proportional odds cannot be rejected.

Table 5 Predicted probabilities at the most representative values of regressors in M3

			Outcomes of the dependent variable			
Regressor	Value		$Y_{it} = 1$	$Y_{it} = 2$	$Y_{it} = 3$	$Y_{it} = 4$
O_{it}	p25	0.638	0.779***	0.159***	0.056***	0.006**
			(0.042)	(0.031)	(0.016)	(0.003)
	p50	0.730	0.812***	0.136***	0.046***	0.005**
			(0.038)	(0.028)	(0.014)	(0.003)
	p75	0.791	0.832***	0.123***	0.041***	0.004**
			(0.040)	(0.029)	(0.013)	(0.002)
L_{i3}	p50	0.000	0.816***	0.157***	0.021**	0.005
			(0.050)	(0.042)	(0.010)	(0.003)
	mean	0.004	0.803***	0.169***	0.023**	0.006*
			(0.052)	(0.044)	(0.010)	(0.003)
H_{it}	p25	0.165	0.345***	0.336***	0.214***	0.029**
			(0.057)	(0.041)	(0.034)	(0.013)
	p50	0.366	0.691***	0.208***	0.081***	0.009**
			(0.055)	(0.032)	(0.019)	(0.004)
	p75	0.762	0.959***	0.031**	0.009**	0.000
			(0.021)	(0.014)	(0.005)	(0.001)
T_{it}	p25	8.000	0.826***	0.127***	0.042***	0.005*
			(0.040)	(0.030)	(0.014)	(0.002)
	p50	11.809	0.810***	0.138***	0.047***	0.005**
			(0.038)	(0.028)	(0.014)	(0.003)
	p75	15.986	0.790***	0.151***	0.053***	0.006**
			(0.042)	(0.031)	(0.015)	(0.003)

p-value: * < 0.1;** < 0.05;*** < 0.01
standard errors in brackets

contrasts, the odds that a city is grouped into the class $Y_{it} = 1$ decrease and those that a city is grouped into the class $Y_{it} > 1$ increase with an increase in the localization of knowledge creation and diffusion L_{i3}, as well as with an increase of technology cycle time T_{it}.

Based on the overall evidence reported, it can therefore be said that the original hypothesis of a positive relation between the gains in embeddedness and the originality of local innovative activities O_i (H1) is partially verified, limited to a complementarity with a longer technology cycle time T_i, and this is not sufficient for the odds of falling into higher classes of embeddedness to increase. Also a non-negative relation between embeddedness and technology cycle time T_i (H4) is verified only for the same complementarity, but the odds are affected as expected in this case. On the other hand, the hypothesis that embeddedness is positively linked with the localization of its knowledge base L_i (H2) is verified, limited to the period between 2002 to 2009 ($t = 3$), while the hypothesis of a negative linkage with the concentration of innovative activities H_i (H3) is fully verified.

Table 6 Robustness tests (scores for unit increase of regressors)

	M4	M5	M6
		$t = 3$	$t = 3$
O_{it}	–5.694**	1.023	1.932
	(2.547)	(2.194)	(4.994)
H_{it}	–5.899***	– 6.624***	– 6.660***
	(0.857)	(1.500)	(1.511)
T_{it}	–0.162	0.056	0.095
	(0.101)	(0.036)	(0.193)
$O_{it} \times T_{it}$	0.291*		–0.057
	(0.158)		(0.281)
L_{i1}	–26.964		
	(55.969)		
L_{i2}	–63.205		
	(50.876)		
L_{i3}	21.672**	23.573**	23.490**
	(10.961)	(11.193)	(11.226)
gdp_{i3}		–0.633	–0.649
		(0.583)	(0.588)
pop_{i3}		0.241	0.256
		(0.608)	(0.613)
fdi_{i3}		0.459	0.459
		(0.298)	(0.299)
ind_{i3}		0.603	0.626
		(0.482)	(0.496)
θ_1	–5.618**	–5.483	–4.931
	(1.906)	(3.530)	(4.459)
θ_2	–4.121**	–3.229	–2.676
	(1.888)	(3.513)	(4.448)
θ_3	–1.713	–1.563	–1.009
	(1.921)	(3.512)	(4.449)
Regional dummies	Yes	Yes	Yes
Time trend	Yes	No	No
# obs	262	153	153
$LR\chi^2(4)$	121.07***	90.58***	90.62***
Pseudo R^2	0.251	0.306	0.306
Log Likelihood	–180.772	–102.965	–102.945

p-value: * < 0.1;** < 0.05;*** < 0.01
standard errors in brackets

4.3 Tests of Robustness

Before moving to conclusions, Table 6 presents three additional specifications to test the robustness of the evidence provided by M3. The model M4 is augmented with

Table 7 Indicators of local patterns of innovation and control variables, Chinese prefectural cities, 2002–2009, summary statistics

	obs	Mean	sd	$z(W)$	Min	25%	50%	75%	Max
O_{i3}	160	0.716	0.132	5.55***	0.000	0.669	0.732	0.789	0.932
L_{i3}	160	0.004	0.016	9.77***	– 0.001	0.000	0.000	0.000	0.142
H_{i3}	160	0.442	0.351	5.23***	0.012	0.130	0.341	0.701	1.000
T_{i3}	160	13.333	9.744	7.90***	2.000	8.173	11.674	16.333	89.000
gdp_{i3}	153	1168.0	1342.3	8.54***	122.0	411.2	726.0	1310.3	10242.3
pop_{i3}	153	4026.7	2681.4	7.62***	582.7	2430.1	3646.0	5294.4	25524.1
fdi_{i3}	153	–4.066	1.159	3.46***	– 7.922	–4.661	–4.071	–3.121	–2.244
ind_{i3}	153	3.202	0.771	1.23	– 5.234	–3.704	–3.173	–2.641	–0.784

Source: indicators are an authors' arrangement from the OECD REGPAT Database, January 2014, the OECD Citations Database, March 2018, and the OECD Patent Quality Indicators, March 2018; control variables are from China Data On Line, City statistics

four regional dummies (Midland, East, West, Northeast)[11] and a time trend t to capture possible sources of unobserved heterogeneity related to structural differences and a different economic climate in the long term. The results here broadly confirm those in M3 and suggest that augmenting the specification with geographical and temporal fixed effects does not substantially affect the estimates, at least qualitatively.

The two specifications in M5 and M6 are then augmented taking the period average of a set of socio-economic variables to control for additional sources of unexplained heterogeneity. These variables are summarized in Table 7, where *gdp* is the log of GDP per capita at constant prices (2009 Yuan); *pop* is the log of population (10 thousand inhabitants); *fdi* is the log of foreign capital actually utilized per inhabitant (Yuan); *ind* is the log of the employment share in the secondary industry as a proxy of the economic structure.[12] Unfortunately, information at a prefectural level is collected since 1996 and include several missing values for the starting years, so that they can be tested to the period $t = 3$ only. The distribution of the 160 observations in this period by class of the dependent variable is nonetheless quite similar to that in the full sample: 103 (64.38%) for $Y_{i3} = 1$, 38 (23.75%) for $Y_{i3} = 2$, 14 (8.75%) for $Y_{i3} = 3$, and 5 (3.13%) for $Y_{i3} = 4$.

The coefficient associated to L_{i3} in M5 is positive, statistically significant, and similar in size to those obtained in M3 and M4. This evidence supports the empirical strategy to augment the model specification with an interaction of the localization of

[11] Regional dummies are based on the three initiatives of coordinated development launched by China's national government since the late-1990s to support reducing economic gaps across regions (Li and Wu 2012).

[12] Data for control variables are from China Data On Line, City statistics, http://chinadataonline.org/member/city/. Data extracted on February 18, 2016.

knowledge creation and diffusion L_{it} and the period dummies t to obtain consistent results. By contrasts, the interaction between the originality of inventions O_{i3} and technology cycle time T_{i3} is no longer significant in M6, suggesting that the complementarity estimated in the long term (M2, M3 and M4) is harder to appear in a much shorter time span (M6). In the subsample for the period 2002–2009 (t = 3), the average technology cycle time T_{i3} (13.33) is in fact higher than the number of years observed (8).

5 Conclusions

Innovative activities have grown very fast in China since the mid-1990s, intertwining with the geography of national economic development. Along this process, the structural traits of innovative activities have emerged as varying over time and, for what concerns us most here, over cities. Those traits include embeddedness, that is, the depth innovative activities are anchored to their local environment and expected to gain in mature innovation systems (Cooke et al. 1998; Doloreux 2002). Previous research relying upon patent statistics shows internationally relevant activities to be far from reaching high levels of embeddedness in several Chinese prefectural cities where they are performed (Prodi et al. 2018). In the present paper, the accomplishments on this front have been supposed to be associated with corresponding local patterns of innovation, especially those identified for cross-country comparison of the role of technological catching up in economic development (Lee 2013).

Accordingly, the core of the paper has been to present an empirical exercise based on data rearranged from the OECD Patent Databases to investigate the correlation between the measure of embeddedness proposed in Prodi et al. (2018) and the indicators of the originality of innovation, the localization of its knowledge base, the concentration of innovation across innovators, and the cycle time of technologies selected in Lee (2013). Four research hypotheses were posited, two of which are fully verified: embeddedness increases with an increase in the localization of knowledge creation and diffusion (H2), and it decreases with an increase of the concentration of local innovative activities across patent applicants (H3). Differently, the positive linkage of embeddedness with the originality of innovative activities (H1) and the non-negative linkage supposed with technology cycle time (H4) have been shown to appear limited only to the long period and a room of complementarity between these two innovation patterns.

These results clearly suggest that the empirical settings suffer some limitations. First, there is a sort of misalignment potentially contributing to a weakening of the evidence. The methodology proposed in Prodi et al. (2018) is indeed purposely penalizing those cities with a poor patenting history at the EPO, taking the period average of values after and not before computing the locational indicators on which embeddedness is measured. This strategy is possible because null values are simply summed as zeros in counting patents, but the case is unfortunately different for the innovation-pattern indicators that are built on more sophisticated algorithms. Since period-pooled data have to be preferred, explanatory variables here are probably overestimating some aspects of the local innovative activities compared to the dependent variable that, by contrasts, features to relatively underestimate another one.

Second, the innovation-pattern indicators could be not very precise for the long-term analysis presented in this paper. In particular, the originality index in the OECD Patent Quality Database is computed on a set of eight-digit technological classes (Squicciarini et al. 2013), and this set have been extended over time to better describe an evolving technological landscape (OECD 2009). If a precise comparison can be obtained limited to patent documents in the same cohort, the treatment of the originality index in the analysis presented here can be supposed to entail a positive trend in the background due to a larger number of classes that can be combined over time. Accordingly, it cannot be excluded that the evidence of a negative linkage between the embeddedness and originality of local innovative activities is in part triggered or, at least, emphasized by this hidden trend.

Third, also the overall strategy to build the analysis on patent applications to the EPO is not flawless. As described in the introductory section, the OECD Patent Databases are important sources of systematized data, but there are international technology "markets", such as Japan and the US, which are closer to China than Europe, and where it is possible to find a stronger record of innovative activities from China than at the EPO. Relying on patent applications rather than patent grants reduces in part the problem of potentially poor records but at the cost of bringing some noise into the analysis.

Fourth, the analysis is limited to Chinese prefectural cities. Though China is a paradigmatic case for the aims of this paper, it does not allow a full-scale investigation of the linkages between the embeddedness and local patterns of innovation as the highest among the classes of embeddedness considered remains very small in size. As a consequence, $Y_i = 4$ represents a weak alternative in the ordering of the dependent variable and this fact can be fairly supposed to affect the evidence obtained.

Despite these limitations, the analysis has been able to unveil some important traits of the evolution of innovative activities in China, contributing to the literature with new insights into the linkages between the embeddedness and the local patterns of innovation. First, the diffusion of innovative activities along economic development is shown to exhibit place-specific features that appear related to the cumulation as well as to the nature of the local development paths. The embeddedness of innovative activities can therefore contribute to a better understanding of the political economy of industrial upgrading and technological catching up, especially in China's developmental model. Second, despite the limitations of the empirical exercise, the findings here suggest that the methodology recently proposed in Prodi et al. (2018) to measure the embeddedness of innovative activities is quite robust to a number of theoretically consistent assumptions, so that it is worth further development, potentially leading to an enrichment of the state of the art of patent statistics. Third, among the patterns considered, a shorter technology cycle time is confirmed to characterize technological catching up even where higher grades of embeddedness are achieved. Nonetheless, where the maturity of local innovation systems is appreciable, innovative activities may also develop into more complex knowledge paths. Again, this step does not exclusively depend on cumulative dynamics, but also on bridging complementary patterns.

Further investigation is required to emphasize better this last point. As a matter of fact, the analysis presented here is in a pure descriptive fashion and relies on an extreme stylization. In particular, the channels through which technological capabilities can be transferred from external to indigenous innovators, such as FDI, import of capital goods, import and re-export of intermediate goods within the GVC, licensing and imitation, human-capital mobility (De Marchi et al. 2018; Fagerberg et al. 2018; Lee et al. 2018), are not considered. The empirical exercise has been purposefully modeled as the simplest possible in order to offer some straightforward insights. The findings are deemed robust enough to support delivering that local innovation systems, i.e., relevant agglomerations of indigenous innovative activities, in emerging economies can grow and strengthen featuring both shared and distinctive characteristics. Those shared are (1.1) an increase in the number of local companies and entities that are capable of engaging in internationally-relevant innovation, so that innovative activities become less concentrated, and (1.2) an increase in the capability of setting local knowledge paths and technological trajectories as developmental change cumulates over time. The pair of these characteristics can be considered as first-level conditions for local innovation systems to develop in emerging economies. Distinctive or second-level characteristics are instead (2.1) the capability to enter more or less complex paths of knowledge creation and (2.2) a focus on more or less radical changes, the pair of which appear to be more tightly related to local opportunities or strategies.

Publisher's note Springer Nature remains neutral with regard to jurisdictional claims in published maps and institutional affiliations.

Acknowledgements The authors are truly thankful to the editors and the two anonymous reviewers whose comments have helped pave a path towards more consistent evidence and results.

Compliance with Ethical Standards

Conflict of interests The authors declare that they have no conflict of interest.

References

Abramovitz M (1986) Catching up, forging ahead, and falling behind. J Econ Hist 46:385–406. https://doi.org/10.1017/S0022050700046209

Agresti A (2013) Categorical data analysis, 3rd edn. Wiley, Hoboken

Ahuja G (2000) Collaboration networks, structural holes, and innovation: a longitudinal study. Adm Sci Q 45:425. https://doi.org/10.2307/2667105

Asheim BT, Coenen L (2005) Knowledge bases and regional innovation systems: comparing Nordic clusters. Res Policy 34:1173–1190. https://doi.org/10.1016/j.respol.2005.03.013
Brandt L, Thun E (2010) The fight for the middle: upgrading, competition, and industrial development in China. World Dev 38:1555–1574. https://doi.org/10.1016/j.worlddev.2010.05.003
Brandt L, Thun E (2016) Constructing a Ladder for growth: policy, markets, and industrial upgrading in China. World Dev 80:78–95. https://doi.org/10.1016/j.worlddev.2015.11.001
Brandt L, Rawski TG, Sutton J (2008) China's industrial development. In: Brandt L, Rawski T G (eds) China's great economic transformation: economic development and growth. Cambridge University Press, Cambridge, pp 1–26
Breschi S, Malerba F, Orsenigo L (2000) Technological regimes and schumpeterian patterns of innovation. Econ J 110:388–410. https://doi.org/10.1111/1468-0297.00530
Cameron AC, Trivedi PK (2005) Microeconometrics: methods and applications. Cambridge University Press, Cambridge
Chen L, Naughton B (2016) An institutionalized policy-making mechanism: China's return to techno-industrial policy. Res Policy 45:2138–2152. https://doi.org/10.1016/j.respol.2016.09.014
Chung MY, Lee K (2015) How absorptive capacity is formed in a latecomer economy: different roles of foreign patent and know-how licensing in Korea. World Dev 66:678–694. https://doi.org/10.1016/j.worlddev.2014.09.010
Cooke P (2004) Regional innovation systems - an evolutionary approach. In: Cooke P, Heidenreich M, Braczyk H-J (eds) Regional innovation systems: the role of governance in a globalized world, Routledge, pp 1–18
Cooke P, Uranga MG, Etxebarria G (1998) Regional systems of innovation: an evolutionary perspective. Environ Plan A 30:1563–1584. https://doi.org/10.1068/a301563
Crescenzi R, Rodriguez-Pose A, Storper M (2012) The territorial dynamics of innovation in China and India. J Econ Geogr 12:1055–1085. https://doi.org/10.1093/jeg/lbs020
De Marchi V, Giuliani E, Rabellotti R (2018) Do global value chains offer developing countries learning and innovation opportunities? Eur J Dev Res 30:389–407. https://doi.org/10.1057/s41287-017-0126-z
Dernis H, Khan M (2004) Triadic patent families methodology. OECD Science, Technology and Industry Working Papers 2014/02. OECD Publishing, Paris
Dhanaraj C, Parkhe A (2006) Orchestrating innovation networks. Acad Manag Rev 31:659–669. https://doi.org/10.5465/amr.2006.21318923
Doloreux D (2002) What we should know about regional systems of innovation. Technol Soc 24:243–263. https://doi.org/10.1016/S0160-791X(02)00007-6
Fagerberg J, Lundvall B-Å, Srholec M (2018) Global value chains, national innovation systems and economic development. Eur J Dev Res 30:533–556. https://doi.org/10.1057/s41287-018-0147-2
Feld SL (1997) Structural embeddedness and stability of interpersonal relations. Soc Networks 19:91–95. https://doi.org/10.1016/S0378-8733(96)00293-6
Field A, Miles J, Field Z (2012) Discovering statistics using R. SAGE Publications, London
Fu X, Gong Y (2011) Indigenous and foreign innovation efforts and drivers of technological upgrading: evidence from China. World Dev 39:1213–1225. https://doi.org/10.1016/j.worlddev.2010.05.010
Fu X, Woo WT, Hou J (2016) Technological innovation policy in China: the lessons, and the necessary changes ahead. Econ Chang Restruct 49:139–157. https://doi.org/10.1007/s10644-016-9186-x
Gereffi G, Humphrey J, Sturgeon T (2005) The governance of global value chains. Rev Int Polit Econ 12:78–104. https://doi.org/10.1080/09692290500049805
Ghoshal S, Bartlett CA (1990) The multinational corporation as an interorganizational network. Acad Manag Rev 15:603–626. https://doi.org/10.5465/AMR.1990.4310825
Granovetter M (1985) Economic action and social structure: the problem of embeddedness. Am J Sociol 91:481–510. https://doi.org/10.1086/228311

Hair JFJ, Black WC, Babin BJ, Anderson RE (2009) Multivariate data analysis seventh. Prentice Hall, Upper Saddle

Heilmann S (2008) Policy experimentation in China's economic rise. Stud Comp Int Dev 43:1–26. https://doi.org/10.1007/s12116-007-9014-4

Heilmann S, Shih L, Hofem A (2013) National planning and local technology zones: experimental governance in China's torch programme. China Q 216:896–919. https://doi.org/10.1017/S0305741013001057

Hu AG (2007) Technology parks and regional economic growth in China. Res Policy 36:76–87. https://doi.org/10.1016/j.respol.2006.08.003

Hu AG, Jefferson GH (2009) A great wall of patents: what is behind China's recent patent explosion? J Dev Econ 90:57–68. https://doi.org/10.1016/j.jdeveco.2008.11.004

Hu M-C, Mathews JA (2008) China's national innovative capacity. Res Policy 37:1465–1479. https://doi.org/10.1016/j.respol.2008.07.003

Jaffe AB, Trajtenberg M (2002) Patents, citations and innovations: a window on the knowledge economy. MIT Press, Cambridge

Jaffe AB, Trajtenberg M, Henderson R (1993) Geographic localization of knowledge spillovers as evidenced by patent citations. Q J Econ 108:577–598. https://doi.org/10.2307/2118401

Jin F, Lee K, Kim YK (2008) Changing engines of growth in China: From exports, FDI and marketization to innovation and exports. China World Econ 16:31–49. https://doi.org/10.1111/j.1749-124X.2008.00105.x

Keller W (2004) International technology diffusion. J Econ Lit 42:752–782. https://doi.org/10.1257/0022051042177685

Kogut B (2000) The network as knowledge: generative rules and the emergence of structure. Strateg Manag J 21:405–425. https://doi.org/10.1002/(SICI)1097-0266(200003)21:3<405::AID-SMJ103>3.0.CO;2-5

Lall S (1992) Tcchnological capabilities and industrialization. World Dev 20:165–186. https://doi.org/10.1016/0305-750X(92)90097-F

Lee K (2013) Schumpeterian analysis of economic catch-up knowledge path creation and middle income trap. Cambridge University Press, Cambridge

Lee K, Lim C (2001) Technological regimes, catching-up and leapfrogging: findings from the Korean industries. Res Policy 30:459–483. https://doi.org/10.1016/S0048-7333(00)00088-3

Lee K, Yoon M (2010) International, intra-national and inter-firm knowledge diffusion and technological catch-up: the USA, Japan, Korea and Taiwan in the memory chip industry. Technol Anal Strateg Manag 22:553–570. https://doi.org/10.1080/09537325.2010.488059

Lee K, Gao X, Li X (2017) Industrial catch-up in China: a sectoral systems of innovation perspective. Cambridge J Reg Econ Soc 10:59–76. https://doi.org/10.1093/cjres/rsw037

Lee K, Szapiro M, Mao Z (2018) From global value chains (GVC) to innovation systems for local value chains and knowledge creation. Eur J Dev Res 30:424–441. https://doi.org/10.1057/s41287-017-0111-6

Li X (2012) Behind the recent surge of Chinese patenting: an institutional view. Res Policy 41:236–249. https://doi.org/10.1016/j.respol.2011.07.003

Li Y, Wu F (2012) The transformation of regional governance in China: the rescaling of statehood. Prog Plann 78:55–99. https://doi.org/10.1016/j.progress.2012.03.001

Lin M, Kwan YK (2016) FDI technology spillovers, geography, and spatial diffusion. Int Rev Econ Financ 43:257–274. https://doi.org/10.1016/j.iref.2016.02.014

Long CX, Wang J (2019) China's patent promotion policies and its quality implications. Sci Public Policy 46:91–104. https://doi.org/10.1093/scipol/scy040

Ma Z, Lee Y, Chen C-FP (2009) Booming or emerging? China's technological capability and international collaboration in patent activities. Technol Forecast Soc Change 76:787–796. https://doi.org/10.1016/j.techfore.2008.11.003

Maskell P (1999) Localised learning and industrial competitiveness. Cambridge J Econ 23:167–185. https://doi.org/10.1093/cje/23.2.167

Moran P (2005) Structural vs. relational embeddedness: social capital and managerial performance. Strateg Manag J 26:1129–1151. https://doi.org/10.1002/smj.486
Nahapiet J, Ghoshal S (1998) Social capital, intellectual capital, and the organizational advantage. Acad Manag Rev 23:242–266. https://doi.org/10.5465/amr.1998.533225
Naughton B (2007) The Chinese economy: transitions and growth. MIT Press, Cambridge MA
OECD (2009) OECD patent statistics manual. OECD Publishing, Paris
Park K-H, Lee K (2006) Linking the technological regime to the technological catch-up: analyzing Korea and Taiwan using the US patent data. Ind Corp Chang 15:715–753. https://doi.org/10.1093/icc/dtl016
Prodi G, Nicolli F, Frattini F (2017) State restructuring and subnational innovation spaces across Chinese prefectures. Environ Plan C Polit Sp 35:94–112. https://doi.org/10.1177/0263774X16664519
Prodi G, Frattini F, Nicolli F (2018) The diffusion and embeddedness of innovative activities in China. Econ Polit 35:71–106. https://doi.org/10.1007/s40888-017-0088-9
Prud'homme D, Zhang T (2017) Evaluation of China's intellectual property regime for innovation: summary report for the World Bank, Washington DC. https://ssrn.com/abstract=3118079
Scott J (1991) Social network analysis. SAGE Publications, London
Squicciarini M, Dernis H, Criscuolo C (2013) Measuring patent quality: indicators of technological and economic value. OECD Science, Technology and Industry Working Papers 2013/03. OECD Publishing, Paris
Sun Y, Grimes S (2018) China and global value chains. Routledge
Thun E (2014) the globalization of production. In: Ravenhill J (ed) Global political economy. 4th edn. Oxford University, Oxford, pp 283–304
Trajtenberg M, Henderson R, Jaffe AB (1997) University versus corporate patents: a window on the basicness of invention. Econ Innov New Technol 5:19–50. https://doi.org/10.1080/10438599700000006
Zeng DZ (2010) How do special economic zones and industrial clusters drive China's rapid growth? In: Zeng D Z (ed) Building engines for growth and competitiveness in china: experience with special economic zones and industrial clusters. The World Bank, Washington DC, pp 1–54
Zhang Y, Zhou Y (2015) The source of innovation in China. Palgrave, Macmillan
Zhang F, Wu F, Cooke P (2010) China's changing national and regional innovation systems and regional distribution of R&D. Geogr Compass 4:532–544. https://doi.org/10.1111/j.1749-8198.2010.00323.x
Zukauskaite E (2018) Variety of regional innovation systems and their institutional characteristics. In: Isaksen A, Martin R, Trippl M (eds) New avenues for regional innovation systems - theoretical advances, empirical cases and policy lessons. Springer, Cham, pp 41–60

Patent, Utility Model, and Economic Growth

Gokay Canberk Bulus and Ibrahim Bakirtas

Abstract The main purpose of this study is to examine the impact of patent rights and utility model on both economic growth and firm performance. The research hypothesis is tested using the Generalized Method of Moments (GMM) technique. Empirical findings imply that the impact of intellectual property rights protection on economic growth depends upon the level of development. While patent protection positively effect on economic growth for developed countries, utility model protection positively effect on economic growth for developing countries. Using Turkish firm-level data as a case study, analysis results show that patent protection and utility model do not contribute to firm performance in Turkey.

Keywords Patent · Utility model · Intellectual property rights · Economic growth

JEL Classification O31 · O34 · O47 · O57

1 Introduction

Competition affects the economic performance of countries in macro terms and firms in micro terms. Although the factor that compels countries to compete is to maximize economic welfare, the factor for companies is to maximize profit. Under the conditions of imperfect competition, the most important stage during which competition was associated with prosperity and profits was the Industrial Revolution; during this stage, technology began to be integrated into every aspect of life. However, the integration of technology is a matter of curiosity as to whether the accumulation of knowledge is a natural consequence or a consequence of knowledge being seen as a source of profitability and prosperity. Whichever consideration is adopted, the high externality of information and the difficulty in pricing can affect the production of

G. C. Bulus (✉) · I. Bakirtas
Department of Economics, Aksaray University, Aksaray, Turkey
e-mail: gcbulus@aksaray.edu.tr; ibakirtas@aksaray.edu.tr

A. Pyka, K. Lee (eds.), *Innovation, Catch-up and Sustainable Development*,
Economic Complexity and Evolution, https://doi.org/10.1007/978-3-030-84931-3_13

knowledge in a negative direction. These two problems reduce the speed of knowledge and the internalization of technology whenever the production of information is not protected by law. However, if the information is protected by law, the transformation of information into technology will accelerate. This showed itself during the production process, with property rights beginning to be protected in Europe after the Glorious Revolution in England (North, 1990). For instance, the long-term average growth rate in Europe during the two centuries between 1500 and 1700 was only 0.13%, which rose to 0.16% after the Glorious Revolution. Because knowledge is regarded as a factor of production and its protection has gained momentum with the Paris Convention (1883) and the Bern Convention (1886) in the second half of the nineteenth century. This regulation is also the first example of contemporary property law. The securing of intellectual property rights and knowledge as a factor of production created a macro and micro prosperity effect. Until the outbreak of World War I, Europe's long-term average annual growth rate rose by only 1.2%. Except for the public war-focused technological developments, both World War I and World War II threatened the legal security of traditional production factors and knowledge and caused the market economy and national prosperity to decline. For example, from 1913 to 1923, Europe's long-term average annual growth rate declined to –0.49%. The effect of the expanded production function of national refinement and creative destruction on firm profitability assumed its present-day form with arrangements signed such as the Universal Copyright Convention (1952), the Geneva Convention (1971), and the Trade-Related Aspects of Intellectual Property Rights Agreement (TRIPS 1994) during the second half of the twentieth century (Drahos, 1998; Lee, 2016; Maskus, 2000; Reichman & Samuelson, 1997). These arrangements ensure the continuity of Schumpeterian invention as the driving engine of growth in the theory of creative destruction.

Intellectual property rights in practice are classified as patents, utility models, trademarks, or industrial designs. These classifications are made according to the invention's stage, inventive step, shape, duration, and cost. The intellectual property rights of patents and utility models are directly related to the manufacturing industry production process. The patent is an intellectual property right that requires high R&D expenditures, so the length of protection of the rights is long and the information regarding the production process is added as an innovative invention. The utility model is an intellectual property right that does not require high R&D expenditures; an invention that is not an inventive step but is, at least, valuable as an invention; and generated from the technology with an addition to the production process. While patent rights provide a high monopoly power, they lead to prosperity-reducing effects for competitors. However, this effect is not the same for all sectors (Javorcik, 2004) and is not the same in all countries (Hudson & Minea, 2013). It has been stated that the high level of patent rights of developed economies and the tight assurance of intellectual property rights through TRIPS Agreement would negatively affect the growth of developing economies (Albert & Ping, 2013; Falvey et al., 2006; Grossman & Lai, 2002). A similar situation applies to firms: Patent rights give big firms more advantages than they do smaller firms in imperfect markets, especially in sectors where product differentiation affects profitability (Cho et al., 2015; Lanjouw

& Schankerman, 2004). In the face of these allegations, Maskus and McDaniel (1998) and Kim et al. (2012) argued that these disruptive effects on emerging economies and firms can translate positively in the long run with utility model applications. Considering these allegations, few studies are available in the current literature that examine the economic growth of developing countries and the impact to firms on output. The outcome of the research in which patent rights and utility models are examined together is very important in terms of developing economic policies for firms and firms' strategies. This is the most important motivation behind this work. Based on this motivation, the purpose of this study is to examine the effect of patent rights and utility models on economic growth and sales of firms, taking into account the level of development of each country. To this end, Sect. 2 provides a review of the literature, Sect. 3 contains the theoretical framework, Sect. 4 defines the data and the model, and Sect. 5 offers analysis and results. Conclusions are discussed in Sect. 6.

2 Literature

Intellectual property rights affect national economies and the revenue of companies. A body of literature constituting empirical research on the level of this effect, especially at the national level, began to accumulate after 1990. The reason for this timing is that the TRIPS Agreement, which was signed in 1994 and was the most comprehensive intellectual property rights agreement in international standards, came into force. Following the TRIPS Agreement, rights have been reported more systematically, and thus the increase in the quantity of data and the number of case studies has allowed researchers to make analyses.

There are two basic theoretical views on the effect of intellectual property rights on economic growth. One of these views is that strong intellectual property rights encourage innovation and technical production, ensure the protection of the resulting economic rent, and increase economic growth; therefore, intellectual property rights positively affect the production function. The other view is that strong intellectual property rights constitute a barrier to market economies and their economic growth, which means that such rights negatively affect the production function. This dilemma is also evident in the empirical literature. Table 1 provides a detailed literature summary of empirical studies as a reflection of these developments.

The empirical literature in Table 1 exhibits three important characteristics. The first is that research results vary on a common point in the relationship between intellectual property rights and economic growth. For example, according to Park (2005), intellectual property rights positively affect economic growth, whereas Hu et al. (2014) maintained that the strong protection of intellectual property rights negatively affects economic growth. Gould and Gruben (1996) stated that intellectual property rights positively affect economic growth in both developed and developing countries. However, Hu and Png (2013) emphasized that intellectual property rights increase economic growth in developed countries but have a negative

Table 1 Intellectual property rights and economic growth

Study	Methodology	Period	Country	Research findings
Eaton and Kortum (1996)	Panel OLS	1988	19 developed countries	Patent rights affect economic growth positively in developed countries
Gould and Gruben (1996)	Panel regression analysis	1960–1988	76 countries	Intellectual property rights have positive impact on economic growth in both developed and developing countries
Seyeum (1996)	Panel regression analysis	1975–1990	27 countries	Strong protection of intellectual property rights increases economic growth in both developed and developing countries
Schneider (2005)	Panel OLS	1970–1990	47 countries	Intellectual property rights increase economic growth in developed countries, while decreasing economic growth in developing countries
Park (2005)	Panel regression analysis	1980–1995	41 countries	Intellectual property rights affect economic growth positively
Falvey et al. (2006)	Threshold regression analysis	1975–1994	80 countries	Intellectual property right is positively and significantly related to growth for low- and high-income countries, but not for middle-income countries
Adams (2008)	Panel regression analysis	1985–2001	62 countries	Intellectual property rights have a significant positive impact on growth
Hu and Png (2013)	Panel regression analysis	1981–2000	72 countries	While strengthening intellectual property rights increases economic growth in high-income countries, prevent economic growth in low-income countries
Hu et al. (2014)	Seemingly unrelated regression model (SUR)	2000–2007	46 countries	Strengthening intellectual property rights reduces economic growth
Sudsawasd and Chaisrisawatsuk (2014)	Panel regression analysis	1995–2010	57 countries	While strong intellectual property rights positively affects economic growth in developed countries, this effect is not valid in developing countries
Liu (2016)	Panel GMM analysis	1970–2007	72 countries	Strong intellectual property rights protection positively affects economic growth in both high-income and low-income countries.

(continued)

Table 1 (continued)

Study	Methodology	Period	Country	Research findings
				However, no statistically significant relationship was found in middle-income countries
Chan and Tang (2017)	Panel cointegration analysis	1980–2014	35 countries	There is a long-term relationship between intellectual property rights and economic growth in high-income countries. However, this relationship is not valid for middle- and low-income countries
Sesay et al. (2018)	Panel GMM analysis	2000–2013	BRICS countries	Strict protection of intellectual property rights supports economic growth in BRICS countries
Evan et al. (2018)	Panel GMM analysis	2005–2014	146 countries	Intellectual property rights have not significant effect on economic growth
Gold et al. (2019)	Panel regression analysis	1995–2011	124 developing countries	Strong intellectual property protection increases economic growth in developing countries

effect on economic growth in developing countries. Though, according to Mohtadi and Ruediger (2008), strong intellectual property rights affect economic growth in economies with human capital above only a certain threshold, according to Evan et al. (2018), intellectual property rights have no effect on the economic growth of countries. Second, despite the controversy surrounding research and theoretical views on the relationship between intellectual property rights and growth, a wealth of literature has involved investigation at the macro level with country panels. In fact, a relationship is found between intellectual property rights and variables such as foreign capital investments (Adams, 2010; Lee et al., 2018), R&D expenditures (Branstetter et al., 2006; Cho et al., 2015), innovation (Hudson & Minea, 2013), export quality (Zhang & Yang, 2016), export amount (Raizada & Dhillon, 2017), and technology transfer (Gentile, 2017). Thus, the indirect effects of intellectual property rights on growth seem to attract researchers' attention Third, despite the abundance of research at the macro level, research at the firm level is extremely limited. The reason for the dearth of firm-level studies is the unwillingness of companies to share information and the difficulty of converting the reports published by companies into a specific systematic data. Therefore, it was not possible to carry out the analyses in terms of macroeconomics on a firm basis.

The literature has expanded over time to include patents, utility models, and trademarks, which are subcomponents of intellectual property rights. However, patent research has the largest share among them because the term "patents" is frequently used synonymously with "intellectual property rights." Moreover the effects of each of these components on the economic performance of developed or developing countries and also firms should differ from each other. The literature review shows that only a few researchers have examined the relationship between the utility model and growth. Possible reasons for the paucity of studies on this relationship are as follows: (1) the TRIPS Agreement came into force at a very late date compared to other agreements related to intellectual property rights; (2) many countries did not protect the utility model by law before the TRIPS Agreement; (3) lack of observation can be seen in the data related to the utility model; (4) developed economies, such as the USA, UK, and Canada, do not protect the utility model under a specific law; and (5) because intellectual property rights and patent rights are considered to be almost the same, and sufficient attention is not paid to the utility model in the literature.

Only two important studies have concerned the effects of the utility model on economies. According to Maskus and McDaniel (1998), the utility model increased technological diffusion and positively affected economic growth in Japan in the period after World War II. In a more recent study, Kim et al. (2012) stated that growth and innovation can be explained by patent rights for high-income countries but cannot be explained by the utility model. In addition, patent protection positively affects economic growth in developed countries, whereas the utility model supports and promotes innovation and economic growth in developing countries. Kim et al.'s (2012) finding is the main starting point of this research. We used the growth model they had developed as a reference and expanded it with trade openness in this research. Through this framework, the effect of utility model applications on economic growth in developed and developing countries as well as on firm performance in Turkey was analyzed.

3 Theoretical Framework

Kim et al. (2012) expanded the Solow growth model by adding knowledge capital. According to Kim et al. (2012), the experience gained through the utility model leads to the use of new utility models through knowledge dissemination and the use of patents through knowledge accumulation. Knowledge capital is defined on the basis of this process. Kim et al. (2012) showed the knowledge capital function as in the following equation:

$$Z = Z(P, U|D) \tag{1}$$

where Z is knowledge capital, P is patentable innovation, and U is utility model innovation. Z is a function of both P and U. The bar "|" denotes the conditional operator and D an indicator of technological development, where $D = 1$ demonstrates a high level and $D = 0$ indicates low level. This model is based on the following assumptions: (1) utility model innovation and patent innovation are not exactly substitutes for each other. (2) the marginal technical substitution rate of utility model innovation and patent innovation in developed countries is lower than in developing countries. (3) if $D = 1$, technological development is at the highest level. (4) if $D = 0$, there is no technological development. Based on this information, Eqs. (2) and (3) are functions defined for each sub-intellectual property right:

$$P = P(\mathrm{IPR}, U, \ldots | D), \quad P_U > 0 \tag{2}$$

$$U = U(\mathrm{UML}, \ldots | D), \quad U_{\mathrm{UML}} > 0 \tag{3}$$

where IPR represents the level of patent rights and UML represents utility model law in the economy. The condition in Eq. (2) indicates that the knowledge production obtained with the utility model positively affects the patent capacity provided that the firm or economy adheres to the technology level. The condition in Eq. (3) states that the production of utility model innovations is a positive function of the existence of laws protecting utility model. This condition also reflects the general belief that protecting firms or small inventors by law encourages creative activity. The underlying reason is that firms and small inventors have a greater incentive to engage in minor inventive activity if the rewards to it are available through legal protection. For this reason, the entrepreneurial spirit of small inventors reflects more on the market in economies that provide legal protection for utility models. These arrangements would increase the number of utility model applications that may be useful commercially. Kim et al. (2012) also point out that existing patent innovations are a function of utility model innovations in the past in the knowledge accumulation process. In other words, patents are the result of learning by doing through some small inventions and utility models.

Kim et al. (2012) extended their models based on the work of Mankiw et al. (1992), Caselli et al. (1996), and Bond (2002) by incorporating knowledge capital into the growth equations. The steady-state production function in efficiency units postulates the following:

$$y^* = k^{\alpha_1} z^{\alpha_2} \tag{4}$$

where $y^* = Y^*/\mathrm{AL}$ is output per efficiency worker, $k = K/\mathrm{AL}$ physical capital per efficiency worker, and $z = Z/\mathrm{AL}$ knowledge capital per efficiency worker. Assuming that the economy is growing, on the one hand, with physical capital and, on the other hand, with knowledge capital, the mathematical representation of the two capital accumulation can be as in Eqs. (5) and (6)[1]:

$$\dot{k} = s_K y - nk \tag{5}$$

$$\dot{z} = s_Z y - nz \tag{6}$$

[1]To avoid cluttering up the derivation of the growth equation, Kim et al. (2012) suppress depreciation rates of capital (δ) and technological knowledge (A) in the equations.

where s_K is physical capital, s_Z knowledge capital, and n is labor force growth rate. Taking the natural log of Eq. (1), time differentiating the result and substituting the accumulation equations into it, and then further linearizing the result around steady state demonstrates that the instantaneous growth rate of output per efficiency worker is inversely related to the positive deviation of the natural log of y above its steady-state level:

$$\frac{\partial \ln y}{\partial t} = -\lambda(\ln y - \ln y^*) \tag{7}$$

where $\lambda = n(1 - \alpha_1 - \alpha_2)$ is speed of adjustment. Solving (2) from $t - 1$ to t yields the following equation for estimation [where Kim et al. (2012) used subscript t to index time and i to index the unit country or firm]:

$$\Delta \ln y_{it} = \gamma_0 + \gamma_1 \ln y_{it-1} + \gamma_2 \ln s_{Z_{it}} + \gamma_3 \ln s_{K_{it}} + \gamma_4 \ln n_{it} + \gamma_{\mathrm{i}} + \gamma_{\mathrm{t}} + \varepsilon_{it} \tag{8}$$

where $\gamma_1 = -(1 - e^{-\lambda})$, t is index of time, i is index of the unit firm or country. In addition, γ_{i} is individual fixed effects, γ_{t} is time effects, and ε_{it} is spherical error term. According to Kim et al. (2012) the physical capital investment rate (s_K) is a function of both per capita human capital (η) and per capita physical capital (k). In this case, the capital investment rate is as in Eq. (9):

$$s_{K_{it}} = k_{it}\eta_{it} \tag{9}$$

When all data are available on intellectual property types, the knowledge capital investment rate is $s_Z = s_Z(p, u)$, where p and u are patenting and utility model intensities, respectively ($p = P / L$ and $u = U / L$). In addition, the utility model innovation is assumed to be a function of utility model laws. The utility model is defined as delayed (u_{it-j}) due to the assumption that utility model law affects economic growth with delays. Thus, Kim et al. (2012) utilize firm-level and country level data to assess the effects of utility model innovations on growth based on the following equation:

$$s_{Z_{it}} = p_{it}^{\Phi_1} u_{it-j}^{\Phi_2} \tag{10}$$

Kim et al.'s (2012) basic prediction of the growth model expanded with knowledge capital; the efficiency of information production is that it will be influenced not only by patent rights but also by utility model law that protects small inventions. Developing countries and firms with low-technology utilization make significantly small inventions. The technology-learning capacities and technology-usage skills of these countries and companies start with the small-invention process. The number of these small inventions increases over time, and, in the future, small inventions may be replaced by patentable inventions. Given this interaction process, Kim et al. (2012) stated that the implementation of the utility model as a policy that protects small inventions is extremely important, especially for developing countries. When designing these policies, it is important for the success of the policy to define sufficient time for the adoption of the utility model in the economy, taking into account the delay length of the utility model that protects small innovation activities. Although successful policies increase the number of small technological activities, they positively affect the use of more advanced technology and the number of patentable inventions in the long run.

4 Data and Methodology

Definitions of the variables used in the analysis of research questions developed in the light of theoretical and empirical literature and the method of the research are included in this section.

4.1 Data

Macro and micro data were used in the analysis. Macro data in the country panel were compiled from the World Bank Statistics Database. The country panel was limited to 122 countries included in the patent rights index. In addition, low-income countries were excluded from the panel because they could not fully answer the research question. Therefore, lower middle income and upper middle income countries were included in the analysis as developing countries. As a result, macro analysis included 88 countries, 34 developed and 54 developing countries.[2] These 88 countries constituted the N dimension of the analysis. The t dimension of the analysis covered the period from 1996 to 2010. The TRIPS Agreement, which was used as a reference in the period selection, was put into practice in 1995, and the last date that the patent rights index data were compiled was 2010. The dependent variable was the growth rate of real GDP per capita in macro models.[3] The independent variables were initial real GDP per capita, gross fixed capital formation, population growth rate, human capital, patent rights index, openness and utility model law Kim et al. (2012) was used as a reference in the macroeconometric estimation model of this study. Trade openness was added to this model, based on Gould and Gruben's (1996) claims that, as the openness increases, the positive effect of intellectual property rights on growth will also increase. The variables, symbols, sources, and definitions used in the macro model are shown in Table 2.

We compiled a detailed database of firm-level patent and utility model applications and matched the data to the firms' financial data in the study. The micro part of

[2]The country list is given in Appendix.

[3]GDP and related data are in constant 2010 international purchasing power parity dollars.

Table 2 Data used in macroeconometric analysis

Variable	Symbol used	Sources	Definition
Economic growth	Δy	World Bank, World Development Indicator	GDP per capita growth rate in purchasing power parity constant 2010 international dollars
Utility model law	uml	World Intellectual Property Organization Official Website	Depending on whether countries have utility model law or not, they are included in the model to take the values of 1 and 0. It is defined as uml = 1 for countries have utility model law, and uml = 0 for countries have not
Initial GDP per capita	y_0	World Bank, World Development Indicator	Initial GDP per capita for each country
Investment	k	World Bank, World Development Indicator	Gross capital formation as a % of GDP
Population growth	n	World Bank, World Development Indicator	Percentage increase in the total population over the years
Human capital	h	Penn World Table (version 9.0)	Human capital index, based on years of schooling and returns to education
Patent index	pr	Park index data[a]	The index provides a score that reflects a given country's overall level of patent rights and restrictions at a given point in time. Data for this variable takes values in the range of 1–5. As the numerical value increases, patent protection increases. pr data is published at 5-year intervals. Therefore, interpolation method was used to derive annual data
Trade openness	op	World Bank, World Development Indicator	The ratio of import and export total to GDP

[a]The current version of the patent rights index has not been published. We used it in analyses with the written permission of Professor Park

the analysis, which involved examining the effects of the utility model on the growth of the firm, included 80 firms that were traded on the Istanbul Stock Exchange for the period from 2003 to 2015. The selection criterion was that a firm had applied for at least one utility model or patent during that time. The reference for the selection of this period was that the sales, investment, and export data of the firms had been published after 2003 and that the number of patents and utility models were as of the last publication date in 2016. The variables used in the micro analysis were the firm's annual growth rate of sales, initial sales, capital stock, age, number of employees, and number of patents and utility models registered, which Kim et al. (2012) had used in their study. In addition to these variables, exports, which were expressed as an openness indicator by Hahn (2004) and Buch et al. (2009), were included in the model. The variables, symbols, sources, and definitions used in the micro model are shown in Table 3.

Table 3 Data used in microeconometric analysis

Variable	Symbol used	Sources	Definition
Firm sales growth rate	Δr	The statistical extension of the official website of Borsa Istanbul and the official website of the Public Disclosure Platform	Annual growth rate of firm real sales (firm sales divided by consumer price index for realization process 2003 = 100)
Utility model number	umn	Turkish Patent and Trademark Office	Utility model applications
Initial sales	r_0	The statistical extension of the official website of Borsa Istanbul	Initial firm sales for each firm
Investment	fk	The statistical extension of the official website of Borsa Istanbul and the official website of the Public Disclosure Platform	Change in fixed assets as a percentage of total assets
Employment	l	Ministry of Labor Data Archive Directorate Reports	Number of firm employees
Firm age	a	Official website of the Public Disclosure Platform	How many years companies have been operating in the market
Patent number	pn	Turkish Patent and Trademark Office	Patent applications
Export	ex	The statistical extension of the official website of Borsa Istanbul and the official website of the Public Disclosure Platform	The ratio of the export made by the companies in the total revenue is considered as openness.
Research and development expenditures	rd	The statistical extension of the official website of Borsa Istanbul and the official website of the Public Disclosure Platform	Share of R&D expenditures in total expenditures made by companies
Firm value	fv	The statistical extension of the official website of Borsa Istanbul and the official website of the Public Disclosure Platform	The value of a firm is found by multiplying the stock price of that firm by the total number of stock

In Turkey, as in many other developing countries, a legal right to recognition of the utility model began in 1995. Figure 1 shows the number of patents and utility models that have been registered in Turkey since 1995.

The application paths of both the utility model and patent show a positive trend in Turkey. Though the number of utility model applications has increased over the years, this trend is lower than that of patent applications in Turkey. The point that should be emphasized in Fig. 1 is that, though the numbers of patents and utility models in countries leading in technological progress, such as South Korea, Germany, and Japan, are expressed in tens of thousands, these numbers go only to the thousands in Turkey. Figure 2 shows utility model and patent applications of the top five Turkish utility model applicant firms.

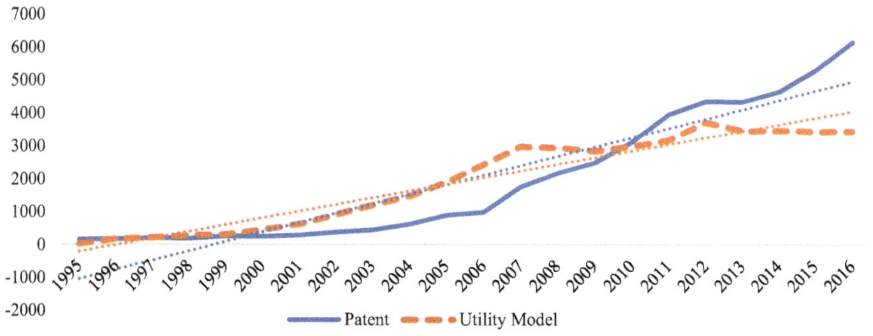

Fig. 1 Utility model and patent applications in Turkey. Source: Turkish Patent and Trademark Office (website: https://www.turkpatent.gov.tr/TURKPATENT/?lang=en)

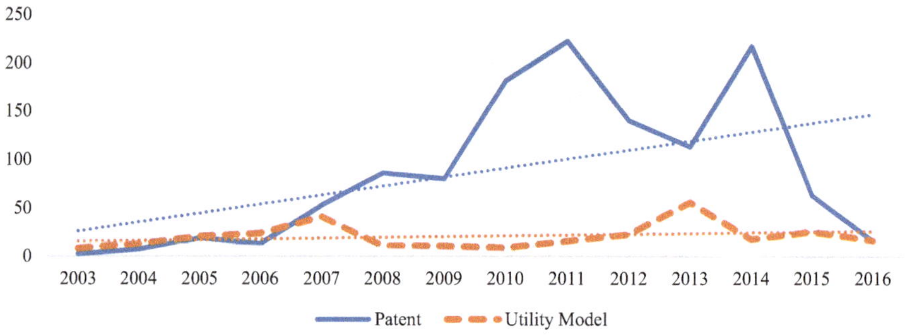

Fig. 2 Utility model and patent applications of the top five Turkish utility model applicant firms. Source: Turkish Patent and Trademark Office (website: https://www.turkpatent.gov.tr/TURKPATENT/?lang=en)

According to the trend curve of Fig. 2, the tendency is toward competition, even though the utility model in companies with the highest number of utility models is too low in Turkey. As a result, the value of the intellectual property rights component in Turkey does not appear to be as steady patterns.

4.2 *Methodology*

The model was estimated by system generalized method of moments (GMM), as well as by pooled ordinary least squares (POLS) and fixed effect (FE) estimations. A traditional dynamic panel data equation containing both time and unit size is as follows.

$$y_{it} = \alpha y_{it-1} + \beta X_{it} + u_{it} \quad i = 1, \ldots, N; t = 1, \ldots, T \tag{11}$$

The lagged value of the dependent variable (y_{it-1}) is the explanatory variable in the model. Dynamic panel data estimates can be made by various estimation methods. Dynamic panel data analysis can be made by various estimation methods. The POLS method is also known as the traditional regression method. The correlation between the lagged value of the dependent variable (y_{it-1}) and error term (u_{it}) leads to inconsistent estimation results in the POLS method. In addition, the existence of unit and time effects is ignored in the FE method. Therefore, the dependent variable has a correlation between the lagged value and the error, and the estimation results are inconsistent in this method (Baltagi, 2005). The system GMM method is used in the research in order to eliminate the biased results due to autocorrelation and heteroskedasticity problems arising in the researches using traditional regression methods (POLS, FE). Also, according to Arellano and Bond (1991) and Arellano and Bover (1995), particular framework is well suited for datasets with small T and larger N. Additional benefits of the GMM approach are that is also well suited for dealing with the bidirectional causality between variables; the possible endogeneity of explanatory variables, as well as omitted variable biases. In addition, Bond (2002) suggests that the GMM estimator is reliable; the predicted value of β_1 parameter should be OLS> GMM> FE. For this reason, POLS and FE analyses will be estimated to test the reliability of the System GMM estimator.

To test the robustness of system GMM estimates, AR(2) and Sargan tests were used, on the basis of which the null hypothesis of no serial correlation and instrument validity cannot be rejected, respectively. More specifically, results support the validity of the overidentifying restrictions and the absence of second-order serial correlation in all regressions, thus providing support to the reliability of the estimates.

5 Empirical Results

This section contains the test results of the research hypotheses. Preceding the results of the econometric analysis, basic descriptive statistics and correlation matrices of the data are presented. Subsequent to these analyses, the findings of POLS, FE, and GMM analysis of the research hypotheses for the country panel and firm panel are presented. Table 4 presents a summary of descriptive statistics of the variables included in the macro and micro models.

Table 4 reports the mean, median, minimum, maximum, and standard deviation of the series used in the analysis for both the developed/developing and firm panels. Mean values of the patent rights index and utility model law for the country panel are higher in developed countries than in developing countries. Descriptive statistics for the number of patents and utility models in the number of firms operating in Turkey are highly interesting as well as strange. Although utility model applications do not

Table 4 Descriptive statistics

	Mean	Median	Max	Min	Std. dev.	Observation	Number of country/ firm
Developed Countries Panel							
GDP per capita annual growth rate	0.02	0.03	0.11	–0.09	0.03	480	34
Utility model law (dummy)	0.61	1.00	1.00	0.00	0.48	480	34
Patent right index	4.20	4.33	4.87	1.83	0.49	480	34
Trade openness (%)	96.71	74.50	432.93	18.75	66.03	480	34
Population growth (%)	0.67	0.53	4.43	–1.04	0.64	480	34
Investment to GDP (%)	23.44	22.92	36.01	13.59	3.79	480	34
GDP per capita (PPP, constant 2000 international dollars)	37,863.9	37,529.1	11,0001.1	6949.1	19,243.2	480	34
Human capital (index)	3.15	3.19	3.70	2.10	0.34	480	34
Developing Countries Panel							
GDP per capita annual growth rate	0.03	0.02	0.40	–0.43	0.04	756	54
Utility model law (dummy)	0.40	0.00	1.00	0.00	0.49	756	54
Patent right index	2.94	2.97	4.67	0.99	0.67	756	54
Trade openness (%)	78.31	69.91	220.40	16.43	37.23	756	54
Population growth (%)	1.42	1.47	4.25	–2.09	0.99	756	54
Investment to GDP (%)	23.41	22.28	61.46	5.46	7.18	756	54
GDP per capita (PPP, constant 2000 international dollars)	4473	3663.75	14,687.98	695.39	3108.64	756	54
Human capital (index)	2.25	2.27	3.30	1.25	0.47	756	54
Firms Panel							
Sales (million USD)	988.92	204.36	26,238.90	0.37	2382.47	1014	80
Sales growth	0.04	0.04	1.51	–4.11	0.27	1014	80
Utility model	0.45	0	26	0	1.88	1014	80
Patent	3.85	4	272	0	18.81	1014	80
R&D expenditure (million USD)	3.57	0.15	127.18	0	10.67	1014	80
Employees	2950.59	1008.50	31898	8	4883.33	1014	80

Investment (%)	2.42	5.67	76.22	−64	8.55	1014	80
Firm age	37.95	39	81	5	12.79	1014	80
Export (%)	26.13	19.81	97.48	0	22.91	1014	80

Note: This table summarizes the statistics for all observations for the macro model from 1996 to 2010, for the micro model from 2003 to 2016. Descriptive statistical values were calculated with EViews-9 package program. In addition, Sales and R&D expenditures were in constant 2003 Turkish Lira and converted to U.S. dollars require an inventive step and high R&D expenditures, the expectation is that utility model applications should be higher than the number of patents. However, this is not the case in Turkey. Though the highest number of patents registered is 272, this value is only 26 for the utility model in the firm panel. Though the average patent registration value of firms is 3.85, utility model registration values are only 0.45.

The correlation matrix is one of the tools commonly used to identify the problem of multicollinearity. Table 5 shows correlations for the developed/developing- and firm-level data. The correlation coefficients among the variables used in analyses are less than 0.80. Therefore, there is no multicollinearity between variables (Kennedy, 2008).

As a next step, the research hypotheses were tested with FE, OLS, and the two-step system GMM. Because of the robust and reliable results of GMM, the findings were based on the results of the GMM analysis.

5.1 Country Panel Results

The regression equation of the model created to examine the effects of the utility model on economic growth is as follows:

$$\Delta \ln y_{it} = \beta_0 + \beta_1 \ln (y_0)_{it-1} + \beta_2 \ln k_{it} + \beta_3 \ln n_{it} + \beta_4 \ln h_{it} + \beta_5 \ln \mathrm{pr}_{it} + \beta_6 \mathrm{uml}_{it-1} + \beta_7 \mathrm{op}_{it} + \varepsilon_{it}$$

The utility model law (uml), which is the main explanatory variable in the regression equation, is expected to positively affect economic growth($\Delta \ln y$), especially in developing countries. The main rationale behind this expectation is that the utility model does not require especially high R&D expenditures and provides added value to the economies by making additions to existing inventions. In addition, the utility model variable is included in the regression with a lag because utility model innovations or adoption of utility model laws will affect economic growth with lag. Table 6 shows the POLS, FE, and GMM estimation results of the regression equation established for the macro model.

Before interpreting the panel regression results in Table 6, the consistency of the GMM predictors was tested. The suitability of the estimation method applied was tested with two tests, Sargan and AR(2), proposed by Arellano and Bond (1991). According to the analysis results of the model, the probability value of the Sargan test was greater than 0.05 for both developed countries and developing countries. According to this result, the instrument variables used in the model were valid. Also, AR(2) test results indicated no second-order autocorrelation. Wald chi^2 test results showed that the model was significant at 1% level as a whole. According to Bond (2002) GMM results, if valid, should produce a coefficient estimate of lagged GDP per capita lying between the OLS and FE estimates (OLS > GMM > FE). Analysis findings indicate the coefficient values of y_{t-1} parameter are (–0.201) > (–

Table 5 Sample correlation

	GDP per capita annual growth rate	Utility model	Patent right	Trade openness	Population growth	Investment	Human capital
Developed Countries Panel							
GDP per capita annual growth rate	1.00	–0.08	0.19	0.17	0.15	0.31	0.10
Utility model law	–0.08	1.00	0.38	0.15	–0.42	0.28	–0.09
Patent right	0.19	0.38	1.00	0.27	–0.04	–0.17	0.32
Trade openness	0.17	0.15	0.27	1.00	0.11	–0.04	–0.18
Population growth	–0.15	–0.42	–0.14	0.11	1.00	0.04	–0.09
Investment	0.31	0.28	0.37	–0.04	0.04	1.00	–0.03
Human capital	0.10	–0.09	0.32	–0.18	–0.09	–0.03	1.00
Developing Countries Panel							
GDP per capita annual growth rate	1.00	0.04	0.10	0.01	–0.15	0.21	0.09
Utility model law	0.04	1.00	0.28	–0.15	–0.14	0.14	0.32
Patent right	0.10	0.28	1.00	0.09	0.02	0.10	0.63
Trade openness	0.01	–0.15	0.09	1.00	0.19	0.19	0.13
Population growth	–0.15	–0.11	–0.48	0.01	1.00	–0.02	–0.64
Investment	0.21	–0.14	0.02	0.14	–0.02	1.00	0.02
Human capital	0.09	0.32	0.63	0.13	–0.64	0.02	1.00

Firms Panel

	Sales growth	Utility model	Patent	Employees	Investment	Firm age	R&D expenditure	Export
Sales growth	1.00	0.02	0.24	0.51	0.03	–0.07	0.34	0.06
Utility model	0.05	1.00	0.07	0.04	0.01	–0.02	0.24	0.10
Patent	–0.01	0.07	1.00	0.41	0.02	0.15	0.56	0.26
Employees	0.04	0.04	0.41	1.00	0.04	0.02	0.45	0.14
Investment	0.03	0.01	0.02	0.04	1.00	0.02	0.02	0.01
Firm age	–0.08	–0.02	0.15	0.01	0.02	1.00	0.18	0.14
R&D expenditure	0.01	0.24	0.56	0.45	0.02	0.18	1.00	0,34
Export	0.06	0.10	0.26	0.14	0.01	0.14	0.34	1.00

Table 6 Estimates of macro model

Dependent variable: GDP per capita growth rate (Δy)	Developed Country Panel			Developing Country Panel		
	POLS	FE	GMM	POLS	FE	GMM
(Log of GDP per capita)$_{t-1}$	–0.201 (0.039) ***	–0.203 (0.391) ***	–0.202 (0.015) ***	–0.010 (0.003) ***	–0.051 (0.002) ***	–0.046 (0.027)*
(Utility model law dummy)$_{t-1}$	–1.406 (0.135) ***	–1.345 (0.134) ***	–1.348 (0.078)	0.006 (0.004) *	0.0206 (0.003) **	0.035 (0.016)**
(Log of patent intensity)$_t$	0.514 (0.631)	1.297 (0.651) ***	1.296 (0.245) ***	0.003 (0.009)	–0.010 (0.009)	0.013 (0.042)
(Log of population growth)$_t$	–0.673 (0.149) ***	0.723 (0.148) ***	–0.724 (0.062) ***	–0.008 (0.003) ***	–0.008 (0.002) ***	–0.022 (0.010)**
(Log of human capital)$_t$	1.092 (0.548) **	1.633 (0.552) ***	1.634 (0.143) ***	0.003 (0.006) *	0.006 (0.005)	0.016 (0.035)
(Log of investment)$_t$	1.276 (0.151) ***	1.300 (0.149) ***	1.301 (0.056)**	0.042 (0.001) ***	0.041 (0.001) ***	0.042 (0.001)*
(Trade openness)$_t$	0.006 (0.001) ***	0.006 (0.000) ***	0.006 (0.001) ***	0.615 (0.003) *	0.590 (0.020) *	0.002 (0.0001) **
Constant	–18.244 (1.470) ***	–20.394 (1.512) ***	–20.401 (0.420) ***	0.064 (0.025) **	0.309 (0.166) *	–0.344 (0.215)
R^2	0.659	0.677		0.476	0.258	
Wald Chi^2			187.46***			63.30***
Sargan			0.20			0.61
AR(2)			0.15			0.38
Observations	480	480	480	756	756	756
Number of countries	34	34	34	54	54	54

Note: Panel data tests were performed using the Stata 14 software program. The results of the Sargan test and the AR2 test indicate p values expressing the validity of the instrumental variables and second-order autocorrelation, respectively. *, **, and *** represent significance at the 10%, 5%, and 1% levels, respectively

0.202) > (–0.203) in developed countries and (–0.010) > (–0.046) > (–0.051) in developing countries.

According to the GMM estimation results applied for the macro model, patent rights in developed countries positively affect economic growth, whereas patent rights in developing countries do not have a statistically significant effect on economic growth. Besides, the type of intellectual property rights that positively affects economic growth is the utility model in developing countries. Evidence on the impact of utility models and patent rights on growth implies that different types of intellectual property protections are appropriate for different country groups.

GMM analysis results also provide clues to conditional convergence for both developed and developing countries. The coefficient of the lagged dependent variable is negative and statistically significant in both panel groups, indicating conditional convergence in growth rates across countries. As for the control variable, while human capital has a mixed significance level, investment and trade openness have a consistently significant positive impact, and population growth has a negative impact on economic growth. These results are consistent with previous empirical studies (Islam, 1995; Kim et al., 2012; Schneider, 2005).

5.2 Firm Panel Results

The effect of the utility model on firm sales growth is defined by the regression equation:

$$\begin{aligned}\Delta \ln r_{it} = \beta_0 + \beta_1 \ln (r)_{it-1} + \beta_2 \ln \text{fk}_{it-1} + \beta_3 \ln l_{it-1} + \beta_4 \ln \text{umn}_{it-1} + \beta_5 \ln \text{pn}_{it-1} \\ + \beta_6 \ln a_{it} + \beta_7 \text{ex}_{it} + \varepsilon_{it}\end{aligned}$$

The main explanatory variable in the regression equation is the utility model. The utility model is expected to have a positive impact on firm sales growth. Table 7 shows the POLS, FE, and GMM estimation results of the regression equation established for the micro model.

The Sargan test was performed to check whether the instrumental variables employed in the model were valid. AR(2) test showed no second-order autocorrelation. Wald chi^2 test results indicated that the model was significant as a whole. Also, the coefficient values of the log of sales parameter were (–0.256) > (–0.476) > (–0.715). These results indicate that the GMM estimator also gives reliable and robust results for the micro model.

According to the regression results of the micro model, utility model and patent applications do not have a statistically significant effect on firm sales growth in Turkey. However, investment, openness, and number of employees have a positive and statistically significant effect on firm sales growth in Turkish firms. In contrast, the effect of firm age on sales growth is negative. According to the results of the analysis, the coefficient of the lagged dependent variable is negative and statistically significant in firms operating in Turkey, indicating conditional convergence in sales growth across firms.

Technological progress emerges as an innovation as a result of R&D activities carried out by the firms. Therefore, technological progress and innovation increase the economic growth at the macro level and the revenues of the firms at the micro level. Ginarte and Park (1997) determined that the main factor affecting the level of patent protection is the R&D activities associated with the development level of the country. In addition, according to Helpman (1993), R&D investments have a positive effect on total factor productivity. Because R&D activities are an input of

Table 7 Estimates of micro model

Dependent variable: Annual sales growth rate (r)	POLS	FE	GMM
(Log of sales)$_{t-1}$	–0.256 (0.133)*	–0.715 (0.163)**	–0.476 (0.088)***
(Log of utility model)$_{t-1}$	0.086 (0.047)*	–0.059 (0.067)	–0.060 (0.073)
(Log of patent)$_{t-1}$	–0.004 (0.032)	–0.052 (0.042)	–0.074 (0.055)
(Log of investment)$_{t-1}$	0.344 (0.794)	3.287 (3.898)	7.546 (3.597)**
(Log of export)$_t$	0.267 (0.065)***	0.277 (0.072)***	0.206 (0.113)*
(Log of firm age)$_t$	0.019 (0.069)	–1.048 (0.652)	–1.806 (0.745)**
(Log of employees)$_{t-1}$	–0.004 (0.050)	0.507 (0.398)*	0.783 (0.445)*
Constant	1.039 (2.121)	–10.331 (10.135)	–22.806 (9.795)**
R^2	0.31	0.43	
Wald Chi^2			592.22
Sargan			0.09
AR(2)			0.15
Observations	823	823	823
Number of firms	80	80	80

Note: Panel data tests were performed using the Stata 14 software program. The results of the Sargan test and the AR2 test indicate p values expressing the validity of the instrumental variables and second-order autocorrelation, respectively. *, **, and *** represent significance at the 10%, 5%, and 1% levels, respectively

innovation, many authors even use R&D expenditures as a substitute for intellectual property rights or generations of input for intellectual property rights (Bosworth & Rogers, 2001; Eom & Lee, 2010; Lee, 2009; Park, 2001; Rogers, 2002; Zhao, 2006). Therefore, to determine whether R&D spending has any impact on the performance of firms operating in Turkey, the following regression equation was estimated:

$$\begin{aligned}\Delta \ln r_{it} = \beta_0 + \beta_1 \ln (r)_{it-1} + \beta_2 \ln \text{fk}_{it-1} + \beta_3 \ln l_{it-1} + \beta_4 \ln \text{umn}_{it-1} + \beta_5 \ln \text{pn}_{it-1} \\ + \beta_6 \ln a_{it} + \beta_7 \text{ex}_{it} + \beta_8 \text{rd}_{it-1} + \varepsilon_{it}\end{aligned}$$

POLS, FE, and GMM estimation results of the extended regression equation with R&D expenditures on the basic model are shown in Table 8.

According to the regression results of the model, R&D expenditures, utility model applications, and patent applications do not have a statistically significant effect on firm performance in Turkey. As a robustness check of the micro analysis results, we conducted the same test using firm values instead of sales growth. The effect of utility models on firm values is defined by the regression equation:

Table 8 Estimates of micro model with R&D expenditures

Dependent variable: Annual sales growth rate (*r*)	POLS	FE	GMM
$(\text{Log of sales})_{t-1}$	–0.027 (0.004)*	–0.073 (0.079)	–0.030 (0.015)**
$(\text{Log of utility model})_{t-1}$	0.025 (0.013)*	0.019 (0.018)	0.010 (0.035)
$(\text{Log of patent})_{t-1}$	0.023 (0.007)	–0.017 (0.012)	–0.005 (0.055)
$(\text{Log of research and development})_{t-1}$	0.002 (0.004)	0.001 (0.010)	0.002 (0.013)
$(\text{Log of investment})_{t-1}$	0.319 (0.130)	2.801 (0.523)***	12.640 (2.444)***
$(\text{Log of export})_{t}$	0.209 (0.018)***	0.195 (0.018)***	0.127 (0.037)***
$(\text{Log of firm age})_{t}$	0.007 (0.021)*	–0.339 (0.095)***	-1.921 (0.635)***
$(\text{Log of employees})_{t-1}$	0.198 (0.035)***	0.175 (0.037)***	0.159 (0.074)**
Constant	–0.036 (0.357)	-7.114 (1.351)***	-30.922 (5.411)***
R^2	0.25	0.28	
Wald Chi^2			336.42
Sargan			0.95
AR(2)			0.84
Observations	916	916	916
Number of firms	80	80	80

Note: Panel data tests were performed using the Stata 14 software program. The results of the Sargan test and the AR2 test indicate *p* values expressing the validity of the instrumental variables and second-order autocorrelation, respectively. *, **, and *** represent significance at the 10%, 5%, and 1% levels, respectively

$$\Delta \ln \text{fv}_{it} = \beta_0 + \beta_1 \ln (r)_{it-1} + \beta_2 \ln \text{fk}_{it-1} + \beta_3 \ln l_{it-1} + \beta_4 \ln \text{umn}_{it-1} + \beta_5 \ln \text{pn}_{it-1} + \beta_6 \ln a_{it} + \beta_7 \text{ex}_{it} + \varepsilon_{it}$$

In the case the dependent variable has firm value, the effects of utility model and patent on firm value are shown in Table 9.

According to the regression results, utility models and patents do not have a statistically significant effect on firm value in Turkey.

Table 9 Estimates of micro model with firm values

Dependent variable: Log of firm value (fv)	POLS	FE	GMM
(Log of firm value)$_{t-1}$	0.884 (0.014)***	0.551 (0.0269)***	0.481 (0.060)***
(Log of utility model)$_{t-1}$	0.028 (0.034)	0.044 (0.041)	0.101 (0.103)
(Log of patent)$_{t-1}$	–0.002 (0.018)	0.071 (0.027)**	0.078 (0.055)
(Log of investment)$_{t-1}$	1.946 (0.324)***	1.516 (0.831)**	5.181 (2.276)**
(Log of export)$_t$	0.078 (0.038)*	0.092 (0.036)**	0.132 (0.081)
(Log of firm age)$_t$	–0.027 (0.040)	0.013 (0.149)	–0.312 (0.169)*
(Log of employees)$_{t-1}$	0.152 (0.073)**	0.207 (0.069)***	0.345 (0.172)**
Constant	–3.731 (0.813)	3.157 (2.143)	–5.599 (5.877)
R^2	0.49	0.44	
Wald Chi^2			386.08
Sargan			0.77
AR(2)			0.07
Observations	937	937	937
Number of firms	80	80	80

Note: Panel data tests were performed using the Stata 14 software program. The results of the Sargan test and the AR2 test indicate *p* values expressing the validity of the instrumental variables and second-order autocorrelation, respectively. *, **, and *** represent significance at the 10%, 5%, and 1% levels, respectively

6 Conclusions

The components of intellectual property rights have different effects on different levels of development. The abundance of data on patents combined with more systematic observations and reporting has led to the creation of extensive literature on patent rights. However, this does not validate the utility model. In this study, the effects of utility models on economic growth and firm performance were investigated through the country and firm panels. Thus, the subject was combined in a single text at both macro and micro levels.

According to the macro analysis findings, the intellectual property rights component that positively affects economic growth in developed economies is patents and in developing economies utility models. This finding also guides policy makers as to which appropriate intellectual property right is beneficial for economic growth according to their country's level of economic development. One of the important findings of this study is that the utility model, which provides cheaper and faster protection compared to patent rights, should be preferred, especially by developing countries in the field of industry. Policy makers can support growth by increasing the efficiency and number of inventions that can be applied to the industry through the utility model. For this purpose, policy makers can increase and sustain the economic growth rate by encouraging the application of the utility model in developing countries. Therefore, in addition to pursuing international standards, the production, use, and dissemination of information can be accelerated, and economic growth can be supported in this way through changes made under a national intellectual property law or existing law.

According to the micro analysis findings, utility model and patent applications do not have a statistically significant effect on sales growth in Turkish firms. However, in countries that are pioneers in high-tech goods manufacturing, such as South Korea, Japan, and Germany, patent and utility model practices have a positive impact on both performance and market values of firms. However, these two intellectual property rights applications do not have a significant effect on firm performance and value in Turkey. These findings mean that firms have non-innovation-based growth in Turkey. The managers of large companies in Turkey are mostly trained by the Anglo-Saxon education system, in which the patent is emphasized among intellectual property rights. For this reason, the utility model lags far behind the patent in terms of implementation in Turkey. In addition, the sectoral distribution of firms confirms that Turkey has mostly non-innovative firms. Only 19 of the 507 firms in the stock exchange operate in the technology sector. In fact, only 3 of those 19 companies registered patents and utility models during the period examined. Considering the sectoral distribution of firms operating in Turkey, out of a total of 507 firms, 127 are financial institutions; 46 are investment companies; 33 are real estate investment companies; and 27 appear to be in the food, beverage, and tobacco sector. Therefore, it can be stated that the number of innovative firms investing in R&D expenditures, patents, and utility models is insufficient in Turkey. If Turkey wants to become a developed country and catch up with technologically leading countries, it should adopt utility model applications and other intellectual property rights as national policies; moreover, firms should learn how to use these rights. For this purpose, it is necessary to carry out informative advertising campaigns regarding the utility model, provide training to the relevant institutions, and organize policies to promote the utility model. The fact that R&D spending does not have a significant impact on sales growth supports these statements in Turkish companies. Overall, the companies operating in Turkey that make the non-innovation-based growth and production are stunning results of this study. Thus, Turkish firms cannot shake off the traditional company structure. The findings of this research regarding brings to mind the question of whether imitation can be source of growth for Turkey's economy. Thus, future researchers could explore other types of economic activity such as imitation. In addition, studies conducted using single-country samples generally feature investigations of firms operating in all sectors of a country. However, analyzing the firms operating in different sectors within the same sample group imposes problems in terms of reaching a common conclusion for overall sectors. Studies whose authors examine both intellectual property rights and the types of these rights will lead the literature and provide a basis for more accurate policy recommendations on a sectoral basis.

Acknowledgements An earlier version of the paper was presented at the 17th Conference of International Schumpeter Society, Seoul, South Korea from July 2 to 4, 2018. In addition, we would like to thank the seminar participants for their feedback at Center for Economic Catch-up, Seoul. We would also like to thank Prof. Keun Lee for sharing his ideas and helpful suggestions for our work. This research was supported by Scientific and Technological Research Council of Turkey (TUBITAK), 2214-A International Doctoral Research Fellowship Programme.

Appendix. List of Countries

Developed Country Panel			Developing Country Panel		
Australia	Greece	Malta	Algeria	Ghana	Pakistan
Austria	Hong Kong	Netherlands	Angola	Guatemala	Panama
Belgium	Hungary	New Zealand	Argentina	Honduras	Paraguay
Canada	Iceland	Norway	Bolivia	Iran	Peru
Cyprus	Ireland	Poland	Botswana	Iraq	Romania
Chile	Israel	Portugal	Brazil	India	Russia
Czechia	Italy	Slovakia	Bulgaria	Indonesia	Senegal
Denmark	Japan	Spain	Cameroon	Jamaica	South Africa
Finland	Korea	Sweden	Chile	Jordan	Sri Lanka
France	Lithuania	Switzerland	China	Lithuania	Sudan
Germany	Luxembourg	UK	Colombia	Malaysia	Swaziland
		USA	Costa Rica	Mauritania	Thailand
			Dominican Republic	Mauritius	Tunisia
			Egypt	Mexican	Turkey
			El Salvador	Morocco	Ukraine
			Equator	Nigeria	Uruguay
			Fiji	Nicaragua	Venezuela
			Gabon	Philippines	Vietnam

References

Adams, S. (2008). Globalization and income inequality: Implications for intellectual property rights. *Journal of Policy Modeling, 30*(5), 725–735.

Adams, S. (2010). Intellectual property rights, investment climate and FDI in developing countries. *International Business Research, 3*(3), 201–209.

Albert, H., & Ping, I. (2013). Patent rights and economic growth: Evidence from cross-country panels of manufacturing industries. *Oxford Economic Papers, 65*(3), 675–698.

Arellano, M., & Bond, S. (1991). Some tests of specification for panel data: Monte Carlo evidence and an application to employment equations. *The Review of Economic Studies, 58*(2), 277–297.

Arellano, M., & Bover, O. (1995). Another look at the instrumental variable estimation of error-components models. *Journal of Econometrics, 68*(1), 29–51.

Baltagi, B. H. (2005). *Econometric analysis of panel data*. Wiley.

Bond, R. S. (2002). Dynamic panel data models: A guide to micro data methods and practice. *Portuguese Economic Journal, 1*(2), 141–162.

Bosworth, R., & Rogers, M. (2001). Market value, R&D and intellectual property: An empirical analysis of large Australian firms. *Economic Record, 77*(239), 323–337.

Branstetter, G. L., Fisman, R., & Foley, F. C. (2006). Do stronger intellectual property rights increase international technology transfer? Empirical evidence from U.S. firm-level data. *The Quarterly Journal of Economics, 121*(1), 321–349.

Buch, M. C., Döpke, J., & Strotmann, H. (2009). Does export openness increase firm-level output volatility? *The World Economy, 32*(4), 531–551.

Caselli, F., Esquivel, G., & Lefort, F. (1996). Reopening the convergence debate: A new look at cross-country growth empirics. *Journal of Economic Growth, 1*, 363–389.

Chan, M. S., & Tang, C. T. (2017). Foreign direct investment inflows and intellectual property rights: Empirical evidence from different income groups. *Global Economic Review, 46*(4), 1–30.

Cho, K., Kim, C., & Shin, J. (2015). Differential Effects of intellectual property rights on innovation and economic performance: A cross-industry investigation. *Science and Public Policy, 42*(6), 827–840.

Drahos, P. (1998). The universality of intellectual property rights: Origins and development. *Intellectual Property and Human Rights*, 1–36.

Eaton, J., & Kortum, S. (1996). Trade in ideas patenting and productivity in the OECD. *Journal of International Economics, 40*(3-4), 251–278.

Eom, B. Y., & Lee, K. (2010). Determinants of industry–academy linkages and, their impact on firm performance: The case of Korea as a latecomer in knowledge industrialization. *Research Policy, 39*(5), 625–639.

Evan, T., Vazarova, P., & Bolotov, I. (2018). Some effects of intellectual property protection on national economies: Theoretical and econometric study. *Prague Economic Papers, 27*(1), 73–91.

Falvey, R., Foster, N., & Greenaway, D. (2006). Intellectual property rights and economic growth. *Review of Development Economics, 10*(4), 700–719.

Gentile, E. (2017). *Intellectual property rights and foreign technology licensing in developing countries: An empirical investigation Asian* (Development Bank Economics Working Paper No. 515). Retrieved from https://papers.ssrn.com/sol3/papers.cfm?abstract_id=3187778.

Ginarte, J. C., & Park, W. G. (1997). Determinants of patent rights: A cross-national study. *Research Policy, 26*, 283–301.

Gold, E. R., Shadeed, E., & Morin, J. (2019). Does intellectual property lead to economic growth? Insights from a novel IP dataset. *Regulation & Governance, 13*, 107–124.

Gould, M. D., & Gruben, C. W. (1996). The role of intellectual property rights in economic growth. *Journal of Development Economics, 48*(2), 323–350.

Grossman, M. G., & Lai, E. C. (2002). *International protection of intellectual property* (NBER Working Paper No.8704). Retrieved from https://www.nber.org/papers/w8704.

Hahn, H. C. (2004). *Exporting and performance of plants: Evidence from Korean manufacturing* (NBER Working Paper No. 10208). Retrieved from https://www.nber.org/papers/w10208.

Helpman, E. (1993). Innovation, imitation, and intellectual property rights. *Econometrica, 61*(6), 1247–1280.

Hu, A., & Png, I. (2013). Patent rights and economic growth: Evidence from cross-country panels of manufacturing industries. *Oxford Economic Papers, 65*(3), 675–698.

Hu, J., Chen, H., & Tsai, F. (2014). Exploring the endogenous relationship between intellectual property rights protection and economic growth. *Journal of Information and Optimization Sciences, 35*(3), 255–274.

Hudson, J., & Minea, A. (2013). Innovation, intellectual property rights, and economic development: A unified empirical investigation. *World Development, 46*, 66–78.
Islam, N. (1995). Growth empirics: A panel data approach. *The Quarterly Journal of Economics, 110*(4), 1127–1170.
Javorcik, S. B. (2004). The composition of foreign direct investment and protection of intellectual property rights: Evidence from transition economies. *European Economic Review, 48*(1), 39–62.
Kennedy, P. (2008). *A guide to econometrics*. MIT Press.
Kim, K. Y., Lee, K., Park, W. G., & Choo, K. (2012). Appropriate intellectual property protection and economic growth in countries at different levels of development. *Research Policy, 41*(2), 359–375.
Lanjouw, J. O., & Schankerman, M. (2004). Protecting intellectual property rights: Are small firms handicapped? *The Journal of Law & Economics, 47*(1), 45–74.
Lee, K. (2009). *How can Korea be a role model for catch-up development? A 'capability-based view'* (WIDER Research Paper, No. 2009/34). Retrieved from https://www.econstor.eu/bitstream/10419/45072/1/601792939.pdf.
Lee, K. (2016). *Economic catch-up and technological leapfrogging: Path to development and macroeconomic stability in Korea*. Edward Elgar.
Lee, M., Alba, D. J., & Park, D. (2018). Intellectual property rights, informal economy, and FDI into developing countries. *Journal of Policy Modeling, 40*, 1067–1081.
Liu, W. (2016). Intellectual property rights, FDI, R&D and economic growth: A cross-country empirical analysis. *The World Economy, 39*(7), 983–1004.
Mankiw, G. N., Romer, D., & Weil, N. D. (1992). A contribution to the empirics of economic growth. *The Quarterly Journal of Economics, 107*(2), 407–437.
Maskus, E. K. (2000). *Intellectual property rights in the global economy*. Institute for International Economics.
Maskus, E. K., & McDaniel, C. (1998). Impacts of the Japanese patent system on productivity growth. *Japan and the World Economy, 11*(4), 557–574.
Mohtadi, H., & Ruediger, S. (2008). Intellectual property rights and growth: Is there a threshold effect? *International Economic Journal, 28*(1), 1–42.
North, D. C. (1990). *Institutions, institutional change and economic performance*. Cambridge University Press.
Park, W. (2005). Do intellectual property rights stimulate R&D and productivity growth? Evidence from cross-national and manufacturing industries data. In J. Putnam (Ed.), *Intellectual property rights and innovation in the knowledge-based economy* (pp. 1–51). University of Calgary Press.
Park, W. G. (2001). R&D, spillovers, and intellectual property rights. In *Annual World Bank conference on development economics, Washington, DC*. Retrieved from https://observer.american.edu/cas/faculty/wgpark/upload/rd-spillovers-iprs.pdf.
Raizada, G., & Dhillon, S. S. (2017). Impact of intellectual property rights on international trade: Evidence from India. *Journal of Intellectual Property Rights, 22*(4), 200–210.
Reichman, H. J., & Samuelson, P. (1997). Intellectual property rights in data. *Hein Online*, 52–166.
Rogers, M. (2002). *Firm performance and investment in R&D and intellectual property* (Melbourne Institute Working Paper No. 15/02). Retrieved from https://minerva-access.unimelb.edu.au/bitstream/handle/11343/33681/65813_00000135_01_wp2002n15.pdf?sequence=1.
Schneider, H. P. (2005). International trade, economic growth and intellectual property rights: A panel data study of developed and developing countries. *Journal of Development Economics, 78*(2), 529–547.
Sesay, B., Yulin, Z., & Wang, F. (2018). Does the national innovation system spur economic growth in Brazil, Russia, India, China and South Africa economies? Evidence from panel data. *South African Journal of Economic and Management Sciences, 21*(1), 1–12.

Seyeum, B. (1996). The impact of intellectual property rights on foreign direct investment. *The Columbia Journal of World Business, 31*(1), 50–59.

Sudsawasd, S., & Chaisrisawatsuk, S. (2014). Foreign direct investment, intellectual property rights, and productivity growth. *Journal of International Commerce, Economics and Policy, 5* (3), 1–19.

Zhang, H., & Yang, X. (2016). Intellectual property rights protection and export quality. *International Journal of Development Issues, 15*(2), 1–12.

Zhao, M. (2006). Conducting R&D in countries with weak intellectual property rights protection. *Management Science, 52*(8), 1185–1189.

Part III
Sustainability

Schumpeterian economic dynamics of greening: propagation of green eco-platforms

John A. Mathews

Abstract The greening of business is now widely recognized as firms take the lead from reluctant governments in making sustainable operations profitable. The greening of business may be contrasted with the "business of greening" – in the sense that greening may be associated with the emergence of smart green platforms that propagate and expand as they creatively destroy industries that are rooted in a fossil fuelled past. Such considerations bring into focus the evolutionary economic dynamics of greening, involving business concepts like emergence of platforms and networks, the capture of increasing returns, the role of manufacturing, mass production and learning curves, which help to account for green innovation and green growth as drivers of the global green shift. This is a perspective that is distinguished from "zero growth" and "natural capitalism" approaches to greening; and it is one that is as applicable as much to China and emerging industrial powers as to advanced industrial countries. Fundamentally, greening is characterized as the emergence of green business platforms which create new possibilities for green growth as they propagate, driven by supply-side dynamics as much as by demand-side dynamics involving changed consumer behavior, as in the rise of the sharing economy. Fundamentally it is cost reduction (via learning curves) and capture of increasing returns that open up opportunities for new business strategies that creatively destroy the old business models associated with fossil fuels and resource wastage.

Keywords Smart green platforms · Green growth · Green economy · Renewable energy · Circular economy · China

JEL classifications O14 · O25 · O33 · P18 · Q50

J. A. Mathews (✉)
Faculty of Business and Economics, Macquarie University, Sydney, NSW 2109, Australia
e-mail: john.mathews@mgsm.edu.au

A. Pyka, K. Lee (eds.), *Innovation, Catch-up and Sustainable Development*,
Economic Complexity and Evolution, https://doi.org/10.1007/978-3-030-84931-3_14

1 Introduction

Concern over the sustainability of current business models is widespread; it has been a theme of discussion and enquiry at least since Hart and Milstein raised the issues in pointed fashion over two decades ago (1999). It is widely believed that business is greening in response to environmental/ecological threats, with global warming as the headline danger, posing a great moral challenge. But if responding to this challenge were what is really driving greening strategies, then there would be little hope for the planet – for as many companies that wished to do the right thing, there would certainly be as many companies looking to make profits by doing the wrong thing. For every company like Tesla looking to clean transport systems with Electric Vehicles (EVs), there would be a VW looking to cut corners with vehicle emission standards. For every oil company like Statoil looking to diversify from its offshore drilling operations towards offshore wind power generation, there would be an ExxonMobil that remains rooted to its fossil fuel past. Neither would there be much hope for a greener planet if it were left solely to governments and regulatory controls like carbon taxes or vehicle emissions standards to drive the transition; these are demonstrably too weak to achieve the desired result unless they work to complement the economic dynamics that are the real drivers of change.

In this paper, the argument is developed that the greening of business is really a *business phenomenon*, driven by business fundamentals. It can be described in terms of the emergence of multiple green business platforms, each of which is already profitable and promises to become much more profitable as the platforms link with each other and propagate across the economy in aggregate fashion. There are platforms in transport, involving electric vehicles where – notwithstanding the idolization of Tesla and Elon Musk – the initial profits are being made in fleets of EV buses, taxis and commercial vehicles, creating linked value chains in vehicles, motors, and charging infrastructure. There are platforms in energy generation and storage and with increasing focus on home systems like rooftop solar. There are platforms that link energy generation to previously expensive operations like water desalination and recycling, thus bringing clean water in reach of all. There are platforms in previously carbon-intensive heavy industry – as in green steel making, and in generation of solar fuels. There are platforms now transforming urban/indoor production of food, enhancing yield and ensuring clean and green operations. These business model innovations are true platforms in that they provide a base for multiple businesses; they involve scope for IT (as in smart grids and smart cities) as well as generation and analysis of big data. They are scalable in that they can operate at local-level or city-wide level – as in the emergence of new eco-cities. They can be facilitated by government policies and regulations but are fundamentally driven by diminishing costs and technoeconomic drivers.

Just over a century ago the Austrian economist Joseph Schumpeter tackled economic fluctuations and dynamics and revealed their fundamental economic drivers, characterizing the process of change as one involving creative destruction – the destruction of the old and its replacement by the creation of something new. He insisted that what fundamentally characterized capitalism is its ceaseless creativity – the creation of new modes of production, new markets, new forms of organization – and now, to bring the story into the twenty-first century, new business platforms. He described how creative destruction was given an economic rationale in the ability of the capitalist financial system to advance credit to entrepreneurs bringing in the new to allow them to operate on a level playing field with the incumbents. Now we are witnessing in the twenty-first century a new "great transformation" that involves multiple sectors and multiple countries in a global process of renewal.

These new green business platforms are emerging not just where they might be expected, in the advanced economies. Surprisingly, they are emerging also in China – where green business platforms that generate cleaner air, water and soil, and generate energy and resource security, are proving to be a top priority for the communist government. And as the platforms mature in China, driven by diminishing costs, so they get taken up in India – and from there they can be expected to diffuse to the rest of the industrializing world. This is how the world of business is greening, creating a new green paradigm of profit generation and entrepreneurial opportunities.

It is the emergence of the IT-enhanced platform economy and the rise of new green industries that together create the new eco-platform economy, which promises to become one of the dominant business trends of the next several decades. It promises to create a trend that all extant businesses will have to respond to, either by creating their own new eco-platform business models or reacting to those developed by others. The green economy is not conceived as an end-product but as an evolving entity, where new eco-business models can be expected to create new platforms which in turn would generate new business opportunities and stimulate the emergence of new business models. This is a very different conception from one that sees green developments as high-cost initiatives that can be sustained only by the wealthy, through subsidies or through moral/ethical commitments. It is different from a view that sees such developments as essentially political in nature (e.g. the politics of sustainable development) rather than as driven by industrial and business dynamics. Likewise this is an approach that is quite different from that advanced by "zero-growth" advocates like Daly and Cobb, or by "natural capital" proponents like Hawken.[1] On the other hand this is an approach that is consistent with and compatible with the sociotechnical transition (STT) perspective (or multi-level perspective) that views innovation processes like the green shift that is under way as complex

[1]The notion of "zero growth" derives from a consideration of what is possible for an economy that is growing within the limits of a finite world e.g. Daly and Cobb 1989). Because it ignores the possibilities of enhanced resource and energy productivity associated with green growth, it has little to offer emerging industrial powers like China, and indeed its strict pursuit today would condemn China et al. to perpetual poverty. The idea of "natural capital" as underpinning the operations of capitalism, is advanced by authors such as Hawken (1993), who characterize natural capital as intrinsically measurable and capable of carrying a price that reflects its scarcity. No such hypotheses are called for in the green platforms approach.

processes that involve technologies and the institutional settings within which they evolve.[2]

The argument of this paper is that greening is a business matter—a pre-eminent business matter. There is the *greening of business*, making it less energy- and resource-intensive. But there is also the *business of greening* – viewing the phenomenon of the greening of business through the lens of business and entrepreneurial calculation and the propagation of green platforms. Such a perspective is very different from that which views greening as a moral challenge and as an extension of the firm's corporate social responsibilities, i.e. as fundamentally a matter of moral choice. The trouble with such an argument is that it poses the issue as a choice to be made by individual firms. There is an important element here of subjectivity; one firm decides to move in one direction, which may be viewed as a response to the moral crisis of confronting global warming, but others find ample ways to justify to themselves (and their shareholders) the adopting of a different choice, upholding business as usual. This is why most of the literature on "greening of business" consists of cases of "good" firms like Tesla or SolarCity, advancing an argument that if more firms behaved like this, then the system as a whole would be expected to shift to a more sustainable trajectory. Firms' best interests would drive them in the desired direction. The problem is that there is precious little evidence to indicate that business is really changing due to firms' taking their CSRs seriously.

At the same time there is the issue that the traditional "Western" model of industrialization, based as it is on fossil fuels and resources throughput (rather than circularity) is simply not scalable to the degree demanded by China and other emerging industrial powers. It comes as a shock to many that it is actually the newly industrializing giants like China (and to some extent India) that are driving the competitive dynamics of the process of greening. This is because they are less prone to the effects of "carbon lock-in" and can benefit from strong state intervention in driving a new energy and resource trajectory (Unruh 2002). As China makes choices that favor solar PV and wind power (and associated energy storage) over fossil fuel alternatives, so it helps to drive down the trends of falling costs for solar PV (and for other renewable sources such as wind power) by expanding the market. The diffusion of industrialization as an evolutionary economic process now encompasses the world. Industrialization was concentrated last century in Europe and East Asia and is now diffusing globally to encompass the emerging giants China, India and Brazil, to be followed by the other major countries of the presently developing world such as in Africa.[3]

The OECD has captured this fundamental phenomenon in what it calls "shifting wealth" – as depicted clearly in Fig. 1. Here the top line indicates the falling proportion of world manufacturing value-added by the OECD countries, and the

[2]The most widely cited study in the sociotechnical transition (STT) tradition is that of the transition from sailing ships to steam-powered vessels in the nineteenth century, as developed by Geels (2002).

[3]For an argument along these lines, see for example Mathews and Tan (2014).

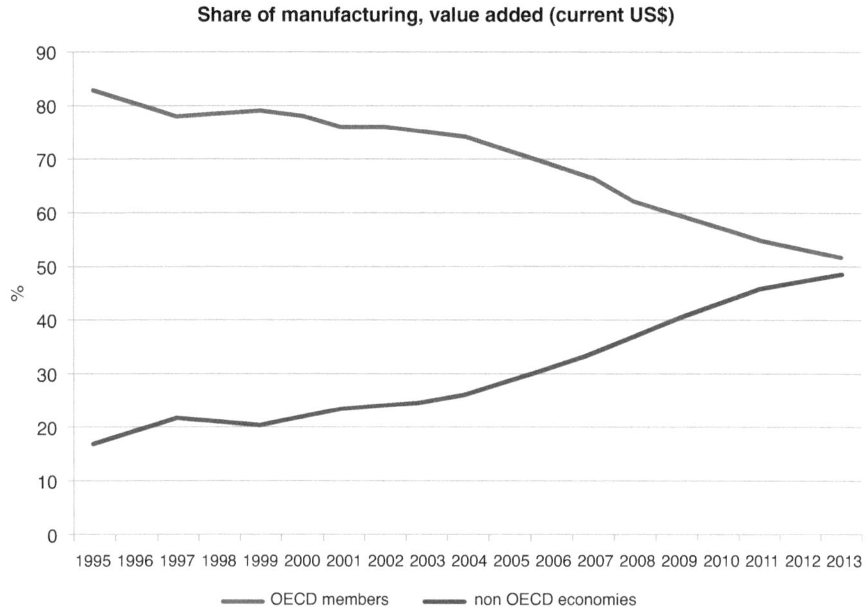

Fig. 1 Shift eastwards of manufacturing value-added. Source: OECD Development Centre, as carried at: https://bluenotes.anz.com/posts/2017/10/LONGREAD-Chinas-green-shift-and-how-Australia-should-respond

rising lower line the manufacturing value-added of the non-OECD countries – for which, read China, India and Brazil. The two lines can be expected to cross over by the year 2020 if not sooner.

All would be well if this phenomenon of shifting wealth could extend "business as usual" indefinitely -- but this is not possible. Even if the planet allowed such expansion in fossil fuel usage and resource spoliation to continue indefinitely, the geopolitical pressures arising from tightening pressure on peaking oil, coal and gas supplies, and on peaking commodity supplies more generally, would rule out continued Business as Usual (BAU) expansion. The fact is that the Western model of industrialization cannot scale to accommodate the rising industrial powers of the twenty-first century.[4] This is a profoundly inconvenient truth.

Let us then elaborate on the perspective that sees greening in terms of emergence of smart green business platforms, and as applicable to emerging industrial powers like China as much as to advanced industrial countries, in that this is a perspective that views greening as the propagation of platforms that are (in principle) scalable and replicable without hitting geopolitical limits.

[4] See Michael Spence, "Asia's new growth model," *Project Syndicate* (1 June 2011), available at: http://www.project-syndicate.org/commentary/spence23/English, for an argument that the Asian powers are moving towards a new development model; while a much more explicit argument is provided by Hu Angang (2006).

2 Greening of business: Emergence of eco-platforms

By the "greening of business" I mean the emergence of smart green business platforms, or "eco-platforms" at multiple levels, from that of a group of firms, to industries, to groups of complementary industries, to cities (as in "eco-cities"). These are business developments because they are products of business model innovation; they generate new sources of profits; and they create new business opportunities as they are scaled up through interlinkage and propagation. They are products of Schumpeterian creative destruction.

Smart green platforms are extending their operations in classic formations or configurations that link one firm's prosperity with another's. Take electric vehicles. As the case for EVs becomes more pressing, due to technological improvements such as battery innovations that reduce their size, weight and cost, and renewable energy contributions to the grid make EVs less and less dependent on carbon flows, so the economic drivers of the shift away from internal combustion engine (ICE) vehicles become stronger. Of course, government regulations can help to shape these drivers – as when governments intervene with demanding fuel standards that make ICE vehicles less and less attractive. These regulations to be truly effective need to work with the technological and business drivers, not at odds with them. Is it moral/ethical imperatives that drive them, or are firms responding to new business opportunities generated by the global green shift that is already underway?

The point is that we are living through the beginnings of a green transition and yet it is difficult to see it clearly because our language disguises the reality. Take the comparable case of networks or clusters. For over a century, business scholars were more or less blind to the realities of platforms, networks, clusters and other suprafirm phenomena, while their language emphasized the primacy of individual firms and their business calculations. Economists' language failed to acknowledge or recognize the ways in which firms strategized around interfirm linkages or complementarities. Now the situation is different and platform firms like Facebook, Google and Alibaba all emphasize their contributions towards the development of platforms as part of the evolution of their business models. Likewise, we need some expressions and forms of words that capture the reality of the green transition that is working through business processes and not just through assumed drivers in the form of moral and ethical considerations (weak at the best of times) and government regulatory drivers such as carbon taxes (even weaker when considered over the past 20 or 25 years). We need language that reflects and captures the industrial dynamics and scale of the transition involved.

It is not so much a question of describing what should be done or ought to be done but what *is* being done – if only we had the language to capture it. I am suggesting that the greening of business is already a reality that is building on what is already happening with smart platform initiatives and their building of criss-crossing chains of complementary value creation; the greening is an amplification or intensification of trends that already exist. *Intensification* is the preferred word – because it conjures up intensification of economic growth (or creation of green growth via intensification) with an emphasis on improvements in resource efficiency (and resource security) via creation or closure of circular industrial loops. This perspective will allow for an appreciation of the scale of the transition and which roots it to the industrial dynamics of capitalism – as insisted on by Schumpeter.

3 Green platforms

Consider three such smart green platforms (eco-platforms) to capture their main effects and characteristics as they propagate through the economy.

3.1 Green steel platform

Consider first the green steel platform and its propagation as an exemplar of the industrial dynamics of the greening economy within the existing carbon-intensive economy. "Green steel" as described by one such entrepreneur promoting the concept, Sanjeev Gupta, with his Liberty House group in the UK, consists of three major innovations in a mature industry, steel. The first is increasing reliance on recirculated steel (scrap steel) which can be accommodated using mini steel mills with electric arc technology; in the Liberty House business model, this reliance on recirculated steel is increased – thereby reducing dependence on virgin iron ore mined from the earth, and thereby reducing the planetary impact of the industry. Secondly the green steel platform increasingly generates its own electric power from renewable sources, integrating wind and solar power facilities into the operations of the steel mills. The innovative platform thus has the potential to reduce costs and (more significantly) reduce cost uncertainty, because electric arc mills use electricity which, in principle, can be generated from renewable sources rather than from coal (fossil fuels) as in traditional open-hearth furnaces. Third, the green steel platform offers possibilities of being extended into associated activities, such as the use of the green steel produced and the power generated from renewable sources in an activity like electric vehicle (EV) production and operation. In this way, the Green Steel platform demonstrates the potential to extend its activities across multiple industrial sectors, linking value chains in steel production, power production and vehicle production.[5] It is striking that "green steel" is now expressed through hydrogen being used as reductant in place of coal, so that steel production can become

[5] The green steel entrepreneur, Sanjeev Gupta, has proposed a link with EV production, utilizing the abandoned production facilities for the Holden car company in Adelaide – just as Elon Musk was able to utilize abandoned Toyota production facilities for his Tesla EV manufacturing activities in California. On this, see "Gupta plans EV plant in Australia, powered by solar and storage", by Giles Parkinson, *RenewEconomy*, Jan 222,018, at: http://reneweconomy.com.au/gupta-plans-ev-plant-australia-powered-solar-storage-94177/

completely independent of fossil fuels, insofar as hydrogen can be produced by electrolysis of water utilizing renewable sources of energy.[6]

The platform extends (propagates) via operations that link energy production and steel recycling as well as other forms of recycling such as those involving polymers (e.g. using recycled car tyres in the feedstock), as well as materials such as using fly ash from municipal incinerators in electric arc furnaces.[7] Each of these innovations reduces both the energy intensity and resource intensity of the platform – and thereby reduces the costs as well.[8] In the medium term the Green Steel platform promises to reduce its costs as renewable sources of energy become more cost favourable than traditional coal-fired electricity and coal-fired blast furnaces, and recycled steel becomes more cost-favourable than traditionally mined iron ore. Medium-term prospects for scrap steel are for a continuing fall in prices as contrasted with prices for iron ore which can be anticipated to continue to fluctuate, depending on geopolitical circumstances. In this way the green steel platform generates increasing returns (getting more for less cost) and operates at lower levels of resource and energy intensity – thus enhancing the resilience of the overall steel industry as the green steel platform propagates itself across to associated activities, in true platform fashion.

3.2 *Green food production platform*

Next consider how urban food production can shift to a paradigm where production is enclosed, under controlled conditions, utilizing renewable sources of energy and desalinated water pumped and recycled to minimize resource intensity. Take the Sundrop Farms platform as such a case of propagation of a green platform, one focused on growing clean and fresh vegetables (tomatoes, capsicum, cucumbers et al) in a hydroponic manner, in enclosed greenhouses with controlled environment. The major inputs are renewable power and desalinated water, both of which are under the operator's control. The first commercial instance of this business model is the 20-ha greenhouse-farm built at Port Augusta in South Australia, located in an

---

[6]The German steel company Thyssenkrupp announced its innovation to produce slab steel utilizing hydrogen in place of coal, in November 2019. See the announcement posted to *Clean Energy Wire*, "Thyssenkrupp tests use of hydrogen in steel production to bring down emissions", 12 Nov 2019, at: https://www.cleanenergywire.org/news/thyssenkrupp-tests-use-hydrogen-steel-production-bring-down-emissions

[7]See Yang et al. (2017), for a study of the potential for municipal fly ash to be utilized as an input in electric arc furnace steel making, where it is found that municipal incinerators could achieve zero waste by making this linkage.

[8]See Johnson et al. (2008) for a study of the energy gains in using recycled steel as input to electric arc steel furnaces in place of virgin iron ore. The results are that the operation utilizing 100% scrap steel recycling uses an energy level of 26 GJ – much lower than current operations around the world, and lower than the 79 GJ needed for 100% virgin iron ore (indeed, an energy saving of 70%).

arid area close to the Spencer Gulf. Under a 10-year supply contract with the national retail grocery chain Coles, Sundrop Farms is producing tomatoes for urban dwellers at a rate of 15,000 t per year. The energy system is based on a Concentrated Solar Power (CSP) array for power generation, while the seawater sourced from Spencer Gulf is desalinated by means of a Multiple Effect Distillation (MED) system, utilizing power supplied by the CSP system. The link is thereby established between growing vegetables in controlled conditions with supply of renewable energy and renewable water. Further, IT-enhancement is being added to the control of the mirrors and lenses of the CSP system and to the operations of the greenhouse, where water and power flow are IT-controlled to maximize efficiency and meet the target production volumes and quality standards. Individual items can be varied, while the platform can be scaled up, virtually without limit. It is this capacity to be scaled up, with diminishing costs, that is such a salient contrast with the diminishing returns of traditional agriculture (Mathews 2018).

Consider the different value chains that feed into the Sundrop Farms food production platform. There is food production itself, with its value chain encompassing seeds and horticulture supplies. There is the generation of electric power from renewable sources (solar CSP) and its associated value chain involving mirrors, lenses and service firms like Aalborg CSP that secured the contract to install the Sundrop Farms Port Augusta system in Australia. And there is the fresh water/ desalination value chain with its MED technology and associated value chain. They all creatively intersect in the Sundrop Farms clean vegetable growing operation.

Unrelated but similar initiatives have been taken in western Victoria in Australia, involving the fruit and vegetable grower Nectar Farms and wind power supplier Neoen Australia. Under an agreement announced in June 2017, Nectar plans to expand its operations to include a 30-ha greenhouse supplied with power from a 63-turbine wind farm, with a lithium-ion battery providing 20 MW or 34 MWh energy storage, allowing the facility to run day and night.[9] This is another case of protected cropping or controlled environment growing of fresh vegetables along lines that could be scaled up globally to provide fresh food for the world's cities.[10]

If we venture to call these initiatives cases of a "Controlled Environment Smart Food Production" platform then we can see it as underpinning the present operations of Sundrop Farms and Nectar Farms – as well as thousands and then millions more such urban food production operations anticipated to be set up in cities around the world. The platform can extend and propagate into other forms of food production, encompassing fruits and berries and perhaps varieties of fish aquaculture, building

[9] See the media release, "Neoen Australia, Nectar Farms and the Victorian government sign global-first partnership in power and food supply," 27 June 2017, at: https://www.neoen.com/wp-content/uploads/2017/06/Media-Release_Bulgana-MoU_June2017_UK.pdf

[10] On Sundrop Farms and its wider significance, see for example Dulaney (2017). A US example of this platform initiative is the case of Plenty, with financial backing of $200 million from the $100 billion Softbank Vision Fund, created by Japanese businessman Masayoshi Son. See the Bloomberg report at: https://www.bloomberg.com/news/articles/2017-07-19/softbank-s-vision-fund-leads-200-million-bet-on-indoor-farming

new value chains as each such extension of the platform is tried and consolidated. This is exactly how a platform is envisaged as operating.

Complementing these initiatives from the Asia-Pacific, the European Union (EU) has been actively promoting sustainable bio-platforms under the name of the Knowledge-based Bioeconomy (Birner 2018; De Lorenzo and Schmidt 2018). European research funding is being targeted at promotion of bioeconomy value chains that encompass food production, forestry, aquaculture as well as related activities in bioproduction of therapeutics. Again, IT-enabled platforms are an important aspect of such European initiatives.

3.3 The tesla EV-PV platform

The Tesla business platform is one of the first to integrate production of EVs (now extending from automobiles to commercial trucks, and encompassing the gigafactory for battery production) with household rooftop solar PV energy generation (and manufacture of rooftop solar modules) combined with battery energy storage. Thus, Tesla is threatening Schumpeterian disruption across three sectors – in vehicles, in power generation and in energy storage/battery manufacture. Tesla captures synergies across these three sectors through its EV-PV technoeconomic platform. It is vertically integrated in solar PV, producing its own PV household systems as well as installing them with the SolarCity advanced financing model whereby the home owner pays zero upfront costs. Likewise, its EV manufacture is vertically integrated, encompassing battery production in the vehicle value chain. The same batteries are used for the EV and for home energy storage –capturing powerful synergies. And the EVs themselves promise to act as a very large battery, providing power on demand to the grid (V2G). Notwithstanding the fact that Tesla has yet to make a profit, its ambitions are so large that it could end up being the dominant force in each of its chosen three sectors – transport, power generation and energy storage. In any case it provides an exemplar of green strategy at work, where each individual initiative is of significance in itself and enhances the value generated by the whole platform. There are similarly ambitious business models being pursued in China by companies such as BYD, which likewise is developing an EV-battery platform that is making substantial inroads into China's automotive, bus and commercial vehicles sectors.

What is common to these three developments, and to the many other initiatives that could be cited, is that they draw from three trends or tendencies. Let us then generalize these developments to explore the Schumpeterian economic dynamics of the emergence of smart green platforms.

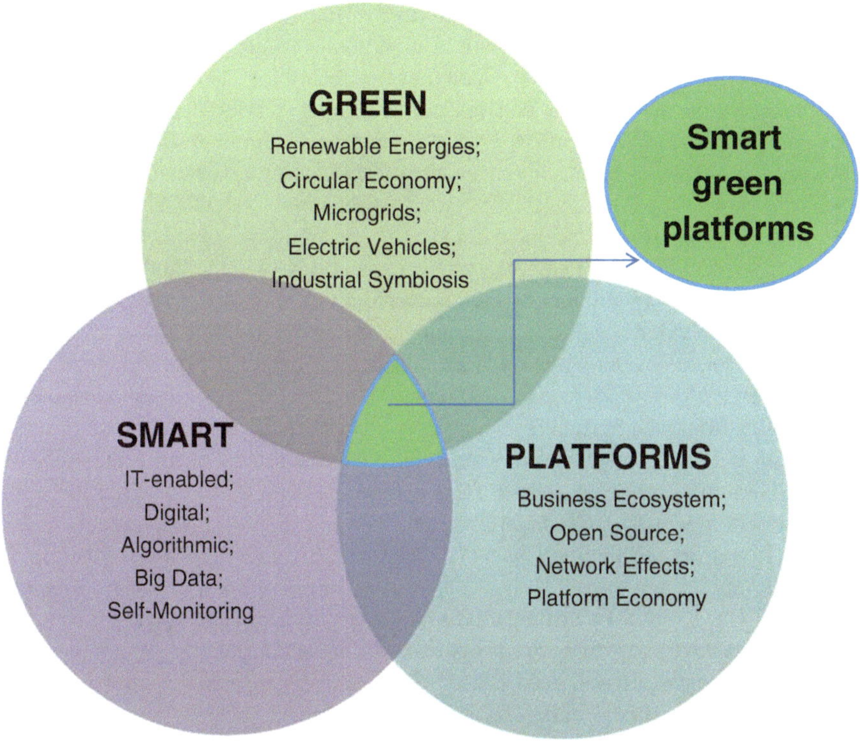

Fig. 2 Emergence of smart green platforms. Source: Author

4 Smart green platforms

The shift towards smart green platforms involves in the first place a recognition of the significance of platforms themselves -- now extending to firms being able to operate digital platforms with AI features like algorithms that collect vast quantities of data from their own IT-enhanced operations.[11] There are applications of IT as in IT-enabled or smart strategies and IT-enhanced green initiatives like EVs. And there are green initiatives themselves, as in the introduction of green renewable energy, introduction of EVs, and closing of industrial loops as in the circular economy.[12] The argument of this paper is that it is where these three trends intersect that greatest interest lies (Fig. 2).

First, the platform phenomenon represents acknowledgment that business choices and strategies are not just concerned with individual firms but with wider groups of

[11] See Kenney and Zysman (2016) as well as Zysman and Kenney (2017) for elaboration, while De Reuver et al. (2018) update the discussion with more recent findings.

[12] For a discussion of the history and current applications of the notion of the circular economy, contrasted with the resource-wasting linear economy, see Winans et al. (2017).

firms connected via complementary activities. These supra-firm phenomena that have an impact on firm strategic choices have included clusters (or industrial districts), networks, and platforms which have a technological dimension in their definition. Some networks or clusters are developed around technologies rather than geographical place – and are aptly known as (technological) platforms. As such, they can grow to be very large, as when firms strategize around the creation of platforms such as the Palm operating system for Personal Digital Assistants (PDAs), or the Symbian platform for smart phones, or the Windows platform for Personal Computers (PCs).[13] In each case, the platform can draw together thousands of firms that are linked by complementarities, such as applications developers, hardware components providers, and service providers. All these firms are inter-dependent and pursue strategies contingent on those followed by the other platform members -- albeit following the strategic lead of a network architect firm that seeks to make its platform the dominant system in the industry.[14] What is being added in the present discussion is a role to be played by green platforms that replicates the role played by those commonly recognized in the IT and other sectors. Platforms such as "controlled environment smart food production" and a combined "green steel – EV" system as well as the familiar "EV-PV" platform developed by Tesla promise to propagate rapidly and transform the economies that adopt them seriously. The key terms in this trend will be business ecosystem; network effects; open source innovation (Linux, Wikipedia); and algorithmic decision-making generating and analysing big data (all well recognized), as well as clean energy, clean food and water production, urban mining and green commodities like steel.[15]

Smart platforms Further rounds of applications of IT to familiar business processes and transactions lends them new possibilities of "smart" or "intelligent" behavior, as when an e-commerce firm offers searching services across a vast range of product or service choices. Such developments in e-commerce were the key to the rise of Amazon.com and eBay in the US and Alibaba, Tencent and Baidu in China. IT-enhancement now extends to applications of artificial intelligence (AI) as when algorithms are deployed to offer choices, and when consumer transactions generate data that is captured (and analysed as "big data") by the e-commerce firm. As noted by Zysman and Kenney (2017), the digital era, with its move to the cloud, is now characterized by the quartet: platforms, big data, algorithmic power and computation-intensive automation.[16] They argue that the changes (and opportunities) presented by this new era are comparable in scale and effect to those involved in the development of the factory, and in emergence of new firms like General Electric, in the first and second industrial revolutions. The emergence of

[13] For discussion of strategizing by firms around platforms and networks, see Gawer (2014), or McIntyre and Srinivasan (2017).

[14] For a recent exposition of the "platform leadership" concept, see Gawer and Cusumano (2014).

[15] On open innovation, see Chesbrough and Appleyard (2007).

[16] See Zysman and Kenney (2017).

specifically green platforms that add "intelligence" to food and energy production provides a powerful extension of these arguments.

The third trend that complements these platform-building and IT-enhancing trends is that of greening itself. Greening of business strategies involves firms in reducing their dependence on fossil fuels and resources dug or drilled from the earth and burnt, creating particulate pollution and longer-term less obvious effects like global warming or climate change.[17] Familiar examples include firms switching to renewable sources of energy (as when providers of IT services like Apple, Microsoft and Google swing behind their own sources of renewable power rather than drawing from the grid); or steel producers switching to green hydrogen in place of coal as reductant; or automotive firms switching to electric vehicles and fuel cell vehicles as prelude to reducing carbon emissions as electrical sources become cleaner. Likewise, firms can switch away from dependence on resources that are mined or drilled and instead rely on inputs channelled from other firms' waste – as in circular economy initiatives or "urban mining" of precious metals like copper or gold.[18] Other firms can switch to use of LEDs as an energy saving initiative, or they can offer car sharing services as a means of reducing private vehicle use and thereby carbon emissions. These trends are clearly visible but have only recently been driven by cost advantages, as when the cost of solar power falls so fast that it costs less to generate than coal-fired power, or when LEDs costs fall so fast that it is no longer sensible to install traditional incandescent bulbs. Once the changes are recognized as being driven by cost considerations, more so than by purely ethical/moral considerations or by government mandates, then the game changes. It is the business of greening that then comes into focus.

There is already abundant evidence of two-way interactions between these three processes, as in cases where desalination of water is made scalable and cost effective by being driven by solar power, or solar electricity enhances the green credentials of electric vehicles. But it is the 3-way interaction that is of greatest significance and that underpins the creative destruction potential of these green platform initiatives. What is common to these descriptions of the greening of industries is the emergence of smart green platforms (or eco-platforms) as the carriers of the shift – with all the network effects and multiple connections that are characteristic of platforms and accounting for their rise and propagation across the economy. The essential feature of these green platforms is that as they propagate, so they generate intensive growth that delivers increasing returns, best captured as green growth. Even allowing for the fact that the energy needs of expanding IT industries are also rising, their improved efficiency (e.g. the move to the cloud) delivers potential improvements in income without associated expansions in resource throughput. The smart green platform economy (SGPE) or "eco-platform economy" is emerging, in ways that graphically demonstrate the reality of circular and cumulative causation and creative

[17]Discussions of these cases can be found in Mathews (2013, 2016, 2018).

[18]Cases in China are discussed in Mathews and Tan (2014, 2016); Mathews et al. (2018); and Zeng et al. (2018).

destruction – as described by economists Arthur Young (1928) in his analysis of increasing returns, by Schumpeter (1912–1934) with his conception of creative destruction, and by Nicholas Kaldor in his happy phrase the "chain reaction" economy. These may be identified as providing the fundamental intellectual sources for the economic dynamics of the green shift – as is now to be demonstrated.

5 Business of greening: Economic drivers of the green shift

It was Young who insisted that increasing returns should be, not a marginal feature of economic analysis, but its *central concern.*[19] Young argued that how firms through their interlinkages create increasing returns should be the central feature of economic analysis. Now there is a very real prospect of this happening, because in the platform economy the central categories of economic analysis – equilibrium-based price formation – have little traction and offer minimal insights. It is increasingly recognized that the central aspects of platforms and their growth (propagation) are the increasing returns they generate – through non-equilibrium phenomena such as network effects. Algorithmic business models that feature data collection and analysis as well as production and distribution of commodities are recognized as generating increasing returns – and as such pose a problem for public policy to maintain levels of competitive interaction. While Young was ignored by mainstream economics, his insights remain valid and highly pertinent to the emergence of green eco-platforms today.

It was Schumpeter who insisted that it is not price competition that characterizes economic development (we would now say evolutionary dynamics) but innovations – as in new technologies, new production systems, new systems of logistics and distribution, new brands. New "platforms" can now be added to bring the list up to the twenty-first century. Amongst the many virtues of Schumpeter's *Capitalism, Socialism and Democracy* (Schumpeter 1942) is its Chapter 7 on "The Process of Creative Destruction". In this short six-page exposition Schumpeter lays out his famous analysis of capitalism as a restless social and economic order that never is, and never can be, a stationary system. He paints a picture of capitalism as driven by "gales of creative destruction" whereby innovation allows new players to enter markets and create new directions, financed by capitalist credit creation that puts the innovators on an equal footing with incumbents.[20]

As the innovations capture the creative dynamic of capitalism, orchestrated via entrepreneurial initiative, so they also spell doom for the incumbent firms that cannot

[19] On the power of increasing returns and how they underpin the success of mass production in the twentieth century, see Young (1928).

[20] See Schumpeter (1912/1934) for his original exposition of the sources of dynamism of the capitalist system, and Schumpeter (1928) for an exposition targeted at the economic literature, and Schumpeter, 1942 for his outline of the process of creative destruction.

or will not adapt to the new conditions. This is the "destruction" side of creative destruction – as relevant today, if not more so, as when Schumpeter was describing the process in the 1940s. Already we have witnessed extensive creative destruction as IT-based firms foment major innovations in traditional sectors – like Intel or Qualcomm or Softbank creatively destroying existing sectors such as telecommunications with their new chip-based innovations and business models. Qualcomm offered its Snapdragon chip a decade ago as a platform for the mobile internet – and this product has served as platform for countless other firms using it as a means to bring their own applications to market.[21] Greening tendencies simply enhance and reinforce trends that are already in existence – as when Tesla builds power generation and distribution features into its EV initiatives, or Thyssenkrupp injects green hydrogen into its steel-making activities.

It was Kaldor who insisted on the point that economies behave in ways that reflect or mirror suprafirm characteristics or interfirm connections, via circular and cumulative causation and "chain reactions" that propagate across the economy. It is not just large firms that create the disturbance and propagate it; it is entrepreneurial initiatives that can emanate from small and highly focused firms that maintains the endless resource recirculation within dynamic economies.[22] The neoclassical economic framework with its focus on issues of price competition at a point in time – neglecting all the features of an economy such as platform and network effects, turnover of firms as industries evolve, and creative destruction, which are the features that provide the real interest.

We may apply this constellation of ideas to our three cases of the emergence of new green platforms – the Green Steel platform, the green food production platforms, and the Tesla EV-PV platform -- to develop a sense of how the business of greening works and how green growth can be accomplished. This brings the focus directly onto the industrial dynamics of the transition, viewing it as endogenous to the wider economy rather than being imposed by some external regulatory requirement such as carbon taxes or fuel emissions standards.

6 Evolutionary economic dynamics of greening

It is worth noting that the emergence of green platforms really does result in a greener economy, evidenced by reduced dependence on fossil fuels for energy and on virgin resource flows for material consumption, as demonstrated above. Just to take the example of the Smart Food Production (SFP) platform, these greening trends are evident in both the Sundrop Farms and Nectar Farms models in the way that they offer the prospect of producing clean and fresh vegetables with reduced

[21] See "Celebrating 10 years of innovation with Snapdragon", Nov 152,017, at: https://www.qualcomm.com/news/onq/2017/11/14/celebrating-10-years-innovation-snapdragon

[22] On the original conception of circular and cumulative causation (C&CC) see Kaldor (1970).

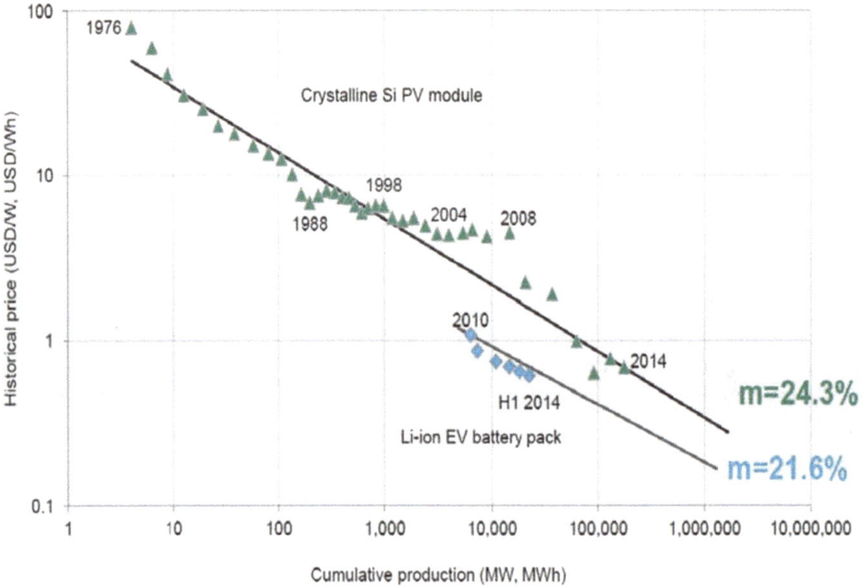

Fig. 3 Cost reductions in solar PV systems and lithium-ion batteries. Source: BNEF

water burden, reduced use of herbicides and pesticides, and reduced energy intensity from conventional thermal electric power sources. This model is scalable and extendable into diversified lines of food production (e.g. fruits, berries) to become the preferred pattern of fresh food production in cities worldwide, thereby reducing both water and energy inputs and drastically improving the efficiency and productivity of urban food production.

As their dependence on mined and drilled resources (fuels and materials) reduces, and their dependence on controlled inputs that are products of other manufacturing processes increases, so the costs of these eco-platforms will be expected to decline. This is the phenomenon of the *learning curve*, or experience curve – and it is fundamental to the cost economics of greening. As just a single example, consider the cost curve for energy sources – solar PV and lithium-ion batteries. Figure 3 reveals that the costs for solar PV have been reducing at the rate of 24% for every doubling of production – and since production globally has been doubling every two to three years, that has resulted in big drops in cost levels that are now on the verge of making solar PV cost-competitive with the energy generated by burning the cheapest and dirtiest coal. Likewise, the costs of lithium-ion battery storage have been falling at the rate of 22% for every doubling of production – making energy storage now a competitive business proposition (as captured by Tesla in its Powerwall home and factory energy storage products).

These are not cost reductions in the manner of the contingent price falls and price rises of mined and drilled commodities like coal, oil or iron ore, which rise and fall depending on local conditions, scarcities, and political reliability of the country that houses the mines or drilling operations. The uncertainties associated with these fluctuating conditions, and the wars, revolutions and terrorist actions that might accompany them, are all too well known. In stark contrast, the cost reductions associated with green platform business initiatives, derived from the learning curve or experience curve, are highly predictable. They are based on the well-known and recognized principles of cost reducing as market expands, and as the market expands so the opportunities for specialization increase. All the green platforms discussed depend for their success on recognition of these principles.

The sequence was elaborated by Young, building on Adam Smith's fundamental theorem of 1776 that the division of labor is limited by the size of the market. As Young expressed it, a price reduction triggers an expansion in demand (the size of the market) and this in turn triggers opportunities for specialization (creating entrepreneurial opportunities for small, specialized firms) which enhances productivity and cost reduction, leading to further falls in prices. This is a classic instance of what Kaldor et al. called "circular and cumulative causation."[23]

At the time that Young was describing this process, it was already being put into practice by Henry Ford with his successive models of mass produced automobiles. Between 1909 and 1916, Henry Ford reduced the price of his Model T Ford from \$950 to \$360 – a drop of 266% over just seven years. Each year, sales doubled – from just below 6000 in 1908 to over 800,000 in 1917. The same process is underway now with solar PV cells in China. In each case it is manufacturing that provides the "engine" – as the market expands, so manufacturing efficiencies are improved (via enhanced specialization) which reduces costs, and this then leads to further market expansion – and so on (subject to optimal economies of scale being reached).[24]

It is in mass production industries that entrepreneurs are able to make large investments, not because of increased demand but in anticipation of increased demand. This is what Henry Ford was doing around a century ago. This is what Chinese mass producers of solar PV cells are doing today as they build mega-factories to produce solar PV cells in huge volume – in anticipation of what the demand will be. This is what the Tesla entrepreneur Elon Musk is doing with his "gigafactory" for producing lithium-ion batteries in Nevada for his series of EVs being produced at the Fremont plant in California. At the shareholders' meeting in June 2017, Musk went on the record to state that Tesla is likely to build ten such gigafactories – in pursuit of economies of scale which will drive down costs and further expand the market for EVs. So, the greater scale of production drives cost reductions that in turn drive market expansion, and so on round and round in the process of circular and cumulative causation. The same process that described the success of Ford's Model T a century ago are today applicable to EVs, to solar PVs, to

[23] For elaboration on this point, see Mathews and Reinert (2014).

[24] For a discussion of the innovations in production achieved by Ford, and their impact on costs and market growth, see for example Abernathy and Utterback (1978).

wind power systems and to energy storage systems, all based on eco-platforms that are products of manufacturing.

Likewise, the green food production platform model is driven by the consistency of expected cost reductions generated by the control achieved over all aspects of the food growing process. As opposed to the seasonal fluctuations experienced in traditional farming, with water supplies from rainfall and sunshine the sources of greatest uncertainty, the enclosed and controlled environment of the Sundrop Farms business model, and its associated control over energy and water inputs (renewable energy production and desalination), generate accurate cost projections that are unheard of in the traditional farming sector. This is translated into the business innovation of a ten-year supply contract entered into between Sundrop and the retail grocery giant Coles – the first such long-term contract for the retail chain, spanning several seasons. Indeed, seasonality matters nothing to the Sundrop Farms model. Because of its similarity to manufacturing, the Sundrop Farms model promises to generate increasing returns rather than the diminishing returns usually associated with agriculture – a profoundly important difference.

It is the power of *increasing returns* that accounts for the success of platforms, and that helps to explain the current success of green platforms like Green Steel, Sundrop Farms and the Tesla EC-PV platform. Because of improvements in efficiency, and associated cost reductions captured as the learning curve, it is manufacturing operations that are always associated with increasing returns – and the shift in industry towards mass production. By contrast operations like mining and drilling for resources, as well as traditional agriculture, all suffer from *diminishing returns*. As one mine is exhausted another is brought on line, with lower yields. As one farm takes the best soil available, the next farm has to settle for land of inferior fertility – and so on, as explained famously by David Ricardo in the early nineteenth century. It was Arthur Young who translated these ideas from an agrarian economy into principles applicable to an industrial economy based on mass production. Now these same ideas need to be put to work to inform a twenty-first century green eco-platform economy.

Fundamentally it is these cost considerations and their predictability and expectation of costs reducing according to the learning curve, that lie at the heart of the business of greening. This is a very different perspective from the one that sees greening as a "return to nature". On the contrary, the argument developed here is that greening involves the extension of urbanization, electrification and manufacturing to further industrial sectors and to further industrializing countries. Greening, it is argued, involves transforming existing sectors like food production to the controlled environment and controlled inputs associated with manufacturing, in a way that is replicable, scalable and practicable. It is applicable at multiple levels – from that of firms linked via a green platform, to that of industrial parks (eco-industrial parks) and extending to the level of whole cities (eco-cities) and ultimately of the economy as a whole.

7 Transitional dynamics of greening

The greening of business is an emergent trend that almost all firms will eventually have to come to terms with. As described, it arises from three separate trends, namely the development of IT-enabled business models (intelligent software, smart systems); platform business models which capture open source and network effects as well as the role of complementors; and green initiatives themselves, such as investments in renewable energies and circular economy initiatives. It is when these initiatives interact, as in "smart platforms" or "digital platforms" or "smart grids" that they have most salience. It is the expansion and propagation of the green platforms that explains green growth – or growth that can be sustained without increased resource throughput. For example, the urban food production platform of Sundrop Farms can be scaled up without imposing further growth in energy, water or chemical inputs. Smart grids can embody energy-saving features when they are equipped with IT-enabled self-monitoring devices such as smart meters. As such they offer abundant opportunities for developing green energy systems that are self-aware, self-monitoring and self-repairing, that can provide platforms for the building of eco-industrial parks and ultimately (as in China) eco-cities. There are many examples now reported, such as digital platforms that underpin e-commerce like eBay and Amazon.com in the US (and now spreading globally) or Alibaba in China which started just a decade ago as a B2B platform.[25] It is the greening of such intelligent (IT-enabled) platforms that is of most interest.

So far we have discussed the supply side dynamics of greening. But of course there are demand side dynamics that generate complementary drivers of the green transition. The sharing economy, where under-utilized assets such as accommodation, transport or tools can be shared, creating new consumer markets, is a prominent example (Dyal-Chand 2015; Boecker and Meelen 2017). The sharing economy brings the focus onto IT-enabled platforms that promote resource efficiency, and thereby facilitate the green transition.

This discussion is consistent with the literature on Sociotechnical Transitions, as developed by the Multi-Level Perspective on transitions towards sustainability. This perspective emphasizes the technological and sociotechnical aspects of the transition, through a series of case studies such as the transition away from sailing ships to steam-powered ships. What the Schumpeterian perspective adds is the emphasis on the economic drivers of the transition, bringing into focus the role of increasing vs diminishing returns, circular and cumulative causation, cost reduction through mass production and market expansion, and creative destruction.[26]

---

[25] Alibaba was largely responsible for creating efficient value chains in China and now operates the largest B2B platform in the world.

[26] See Geels (2011) for a comprehensive discussion of the strengths of the MLP in characterizing sustainability transitions. And yet while mentioning evolutionary economics, this exposition offers no fundamental economic driver of the shift, and neglects to mention costs and learning curves, increasing returns, platforms and network effects, and other aspects of creative destruction.

The essence of platform growth is not growth in physical resource throughput, but growth in connections, i.e. growth in economic intensity. This is why it is reasonable to talk of "green growth" using the language of platforms and increasing returns, rather than the language of growth in physical resource throughput. The key is to see the emerging green platforms as genuine suprafirm structures to which firms wishing to make a green contribution can attach themselves, as part of multi-stranded value chains that culminate in green products and services. The criss-crossing of these multi-stranded value chains is a way of capturing the process through which an economy greens itself. The board game GO (the oldest board game in the world) captures this process in the way that players enhance their position by making connections between their groups of stones, and expanding their territory through connected formations.

8 Why is China playing such a prominent role?

One of the paradoxes of the global green shift that is under way is that China is playing such a prominent role. While everyone recognizes that China has been despoiling its own and others' environment while it pursued the same fossil-fuelled industrialization strategy as made the West wealthy, it is now recognized as well that China has emerged as a renewables superpower, dwarfing other countries in its building of renewable capacity and the speed of its transition to innovations such as electric cars, trucks and buses.[27] China is betting big on renewables, and on a circular economy, because the success of China's industrialization efforts depends on this bet. It's all about scale. China's industrialization is a process taking place at a scale without historical precedent.

The big question is: what is driving this trend? Is it a trend that is likely to continue? It seems clear that if China were to proceed with the typical industrialization strategy that all previous industrial countries pursued – based on fossil fuels and raw materials plunder – then it would face insuperable problems. These would not just be problems of shortages of resources and immediate environmental problems, but most centrally problems to do with the geopolitical limits to a fossil fuelled and virgin materials strategy. To put it bluntly, China would face entanglements in oil wars and resource wars if it were to pursue a typical fossil fuel strategy at the scale of its industrialization – not to mention the burden on its balance of payments as it sought to raise its imports of these fossil fuels. It would mean a horrendous twenty-first century – for China and for everyone else.

When one looks at the scale involved, it's clear that China really has no alternative to a green shift strategy. And in the typical no-nonsense approach of the

[27] On the greening of China, see for example Piovani (2017). On China's greening of its energy systems, see the series of studies by Mathews and Tan (2014, 2016); and on the creation of circular economy resource flows, see Mathews et al. (2018).

Chinese, their leadership has adopted this strategy with determination, and ambition. As China adopts this green shift strategy, so it drives down costs for itself and for all – and makes such a strategy more accessible to other industrializing countries like India, or Brazil, or African countries.[28] And so the green shift that is initiated by China becomes a global green shift. China's green shift in turn opens up opportunities for companies and countries that are nimble enough to take advantage of these opportunities – including companies based in the US, the EU or Japan.

9 Concluding comments

In this article the evident greening of business is taken as starting point for a discussion of the processes through which this greening is being effected. Going beyond the conventional calls that "something must be done" means engaging with the ways in which firms are building new smart green platforms and deriving advantages from their capacity to bring other firms into the new eco-systems created by the propagation of these platforms. The argument is that green growth, which delivers growth in incomes without growth in physical resource throughput, is best accounted for by growth in green platforms. Green growth, in this sense, is an immaterial process. It is one that is driven by firms making business decisions as they extend and propagate their green business platforms. A greening economy does not have to be a zero-growth economy; it can rely on *intensive growth* rather than resource-driven extensive growth. Such a perspective calls for a return to the concepts and frameworks that inform the evolutionary economic dynamics of industry – emergence of platforms and clusters with their network effects; the capture of increasing returns through the cost reductions associated with manufacturing, and the building of platforms around processes that reduce energy dependence on fossil fuels and resource dependence on virgin resources that are all products of mining and drilling rather than manufacturing. These considerations help to resolve the paradox as to why China is playing such a significant role in the green shift and is pioneering the growth of green platforms. If it is firms' business strategies that will green the planet, then it is up to business scholars to explicate these strategies and reveal why they are likely to propagate and creatively destroy the strategies of incumbents that have brought us to the present impasse. For this task, it is time to bring the insights of Schumpeter, Young, Kaldor and others into the twenty-first century.

[28] Altenburg and Assmann (2017) bring together a range of studies that address the applicability of green industrial strategies as industrialization diffuses around the world.

Compliance with ethical standards

Conflict of interest The author declares that he has no conflict of interest.

References

Abernathy WJ, Utterback JM (1978) Patterns of industrial innovation. Technol Rev 80(7):1–9

Altenburg T and Assmann C (eds) (2017) Green industrial policy: concept, policies, country experiences. UN Environment, German Development Institute, Geneva, Bonn

Birner, R 2018. Bioeconomy concepts. In I. Lewandowski (ed), *Bioeconomy: Shaping the Transition to a Sustainable, Biobased Economy*. New York: Springer.

Boecker L, Meelen T (2017) Sharing for people, planet or profit? Analysing motivations for intended sharing economy participation. Environmental Innovation and Societal Transitions 23:28–39

Chesbrough HW, Appleyard MM (2007) Open innovation and strategy. Calif Manag Rev 50 (1):57–76

Daly HE, Cobb JB (1989) *For the Common Good*. Beacon press, Boston

De Lorenzo V, Schmidt M (2018) Biological standards for the knowledge-based bioeconomy: what is at stake. New Biotechnol 40:170–180

De Reuver M, Sorensen C, Basole RC (2018) The digital platform: a research agenda. J Inf Technol 33(2):124–135

Dulaney M (2017) Waiting for the sun: Port Augusta's search for a post-coal identity. *Griffith Review* 55:22–23

Dyal-Chand R (2015) Regulating sharing: the sharing economy as an alternative capitalist system. Tulane Law Review 90(2):241–309

Gawer A (2014) Bridging differing perspectives on technological platforms: toward an integrative framework. Res Policy 43:1239–1249

Gawer A, Cusumano MA (2014) Industry platforms and ecosystem innovation. Journal of Product Development and Innovation Management 31(3):417–433

Geels FW (2002) Technological transitions as evolutionary reconfiguration processes: a multi-level perspective and a case study. Res Policy 31(8/9):1257–1274

Geels FW (2011) The multi-level perspective on sustainability transitions: responses to seven criticisms. Environmental Innovation and Societal Transitions 1:24–40

Hart SL, Milstein MB (1999) Global sustainability and the creative destruction of industries. Sloan Manag Rev 41(1):23–33

Hawken P (1993) *The Ecology of Commerce: A Declaration of Sustainability*. Harper business, New York

Hu A (2006) Green development: the inevitable choice for China (part 1). *China Dialogue* available at: http://www.chinadialogue.net/article/show/single/en/134

Johnson J, Beck BK, Graedel TE (2008) The energy benefit of stainless steel recycling. *Energy Policy* 36:181–192

Kaldor N (1970) The case for regional policies. Scottish Journal of Political Economy 17:337–348

Kenney M and Zysman J (2016) The rise of the platform economy, *Issues in Science and Technology*, (spring): 61-69

Mathews JA (2013) The renewable energies technology surge: a new techno-economic paradigm in the making? Futures 46:10–22

Mathews JA (2016) Competing principles driving energy futures: fossil fuel decarbonization vs. manufacturing learning curves. Futures 84:1–11

Mathews JA (2018) 'New wave' revolution in city-focused, closed environment food production *CAB Reviews* 13: 006, at: https://www.cabdirect.org/cabdirect/abstract/20183168248

Mathews JA, Reinert ES (2014) Renewables, manufacturing and green growth: energy strategies based on capturing increasing returns. *Futures* 61:13–22
Mathews JA and Tan H (2014) Manufacture renewables to build energy security *Nature*, 513 (10 September): 166–168,
Mathews JA and Tan H (2016) Circular Economy: Lessons from China *Nature* 331 (24 March): 440–442
Mathews JA, Tan H, Hu MC (2018) Moving to a Circular Economy in China: Transforming industrial parks into eco-industrial parks. *California Management Review* 60(3):157–181
McIntyre DP, Srinivasan A (2017) Networks, platforms, and strategy: emerging views and next steps. Strateg Manag J 38:141–160
Piovani C (2017) The 'greening' of China: Progress, limitations and contradictions. Journal of Contemporary Asia 47(1):93–115
Schumpeter JA (1912/1934) The theory of economic development: an inquiry into profits, capital, credit, interest and the business cycle. Harvard University Press, Boston
Schumpeter JA (1928) The instability of capitalism. Econ J 38(151):361–386
Schumpeter JA (1942/1950) *Capitalism, Socialism and Democracy* (with new introduction by tom Bottomore). Harper & Row, New York
Unruh GC (2002) Escaping carbon lock-in. Energy Policy 30(4):317–325
Winans K, Kendall A, Deng H (2017) The history and current applications of the circular economy concept. *Renewable and Sustainable Energy Reviews* 68:825–833
Yang GCC, Chuang TN, Huang CW (2017) Achieving zero waste of municipal incinerator fly ash by melting in electric arc furnaces while steelmaking. Waste Manag 62:160–168
Young A (1928) Increasing returns and economic progress. The Economic Journal 38 (152):527–542
Zeng XL, Mathews JA, Li JH (2018) Urban mining of e-waste is becoming more cost-effective than virgin mining. Environ Sci Technol 52(8):4835–4841
Zysman J and Kenney M (2017) The next phase in the digital revolution: platforms, automation, growth, and employment. BRIE working paper 2017-2 UC Berkeley: Berkeley roundtable on the international economy

Industrial life cycle: relevance of national markets in the development of new industries for energy technologies – the case of wind energy

Marlene O'Sullivan

Abstract About 20 years ago Klepper (1997) has shown that the life cycle theory, initially introduced for products, can also be applied to the development of industries. The industries that were examined to establish this theory were marked by relatively stable market conditions that are typically driven by innovation. However, research on the transition of the energy system has shown that markets for new energy technologies are driven by political support. As yet an analysis of the industry life cycle of an industry which has developed under politically driven market conditions has not been conducted. Therefore this paper examines the development of the global wind energy industry and the relevance of national markets in a globalized world. The study is founded on a large empirical database. A comparative analysis of various international and national developments was conducted using descriptive statistical methods. The findings show that the global development derives from the sum of individual national developments. It reveals a strong influence of national markets on the development of their respective wind energy industry. Therefore these findings provide relevant insides for the political debate on market support mechanisms in wind energy.

Keywords Industry life cycle · Wind energy industry · Relevance of national markets · Market development · Political support instruments · Market concentration

JEL codes O33 · O57

M. O'Sullivan (✉)
Department of Energy Systems Analysis, Institute of Engineering Thermodynamics, German Aerospace Center (DLR), Pfaffenwaldring 38-40, 70569 Stuttgart, Germany
e-mail: marlene.osullivan@dlr.de; http://www.dlr.de

A. Pyka, K. Lee (eds.), *Innovation, Catch-up and Sustainable Development*, Economic Complexity and Evolution, https://doi.org/10.1007/978-3-030-84931-3_15

1 Introduction

In order to meet the goals of the Paris climate agreement (United Nations 2015), the energy sector in every country has to make a transition towards an energy system with a predominant use of renewable energy sources (RES) within the coming decades (see also Teske 2019). The transition raises many questions which have to be addressed in order to help overcome the uncertainties that stand in the way of the change process. One of those uncertainties concerns the macroeconomic opportunities and risks associated with the energy transition. It raises the question which companies will provide the technology and which countries will benefit from it. To add to this debate this paper will analyze the development of the global wind energy industry. Its aim is to provide insights into the industrial development of this sector and its drivers for the discussion on the design of framework conditions.

The main theory that this paper will refer to is the industry life cycle theory (ILC) (Klepper 1997). It has been used for the empirical analysis of the development of various industries producing capital goods as well as consumer goods (see also Gort and Klepper 1982, Klepper 1996, Agarwal et al. 2002, Giachetti and Marchi 2010) and services (Menhart et al. 2004). The hypothesis that motivates the work on this paper is that the ILC of the wind energy industry might differ to the industries analyzed so far as its market creation and development have been strongly dependent on political support instruments and have therefore not been driven by innovation alone (see chapter 2). Changes in support policies for wind energy technologies due to varying political interests led to expansion paths that were unstable beyond what can be expected for capital goods markets.

Therefore, the main research question that this paper wants to address is if the development of an industry that is marked by instability in demand on national level differs to the characteristics described by Klepper (1997) in the ILC. Since this question is quite complex, it can be divided into two aspects. The first one addresses the geographic delineation, which leads to the question whether the national or the global market development was more relevant for the evolution of the wind energy industry. The other aspect is the relevance of support policies in the development of the wind industry. It raises the question if RES policies have had a significant impact on the development of the wind industry through their impact on the market development.

Looking at the evolution of wind energy for the production of electricity three different development paths can be observed. One is the utilization of small wind turbines for self-supply; another is the use of onshore wind energy with the priority to feed the electricity into the grid, and the third is the utilization of offshore wind energy. Historically the use of onshore wind for the grid has evolved from the strand of self-supply turbines. However, in the last few years a new line of turbine manufacturers has evolved which focuses on wind turbines for self-supply. Regarding the offshore wind development a similar picture can be drawn. New manufacturers appeared with the utilization of wind energy offshore alongside large incumbent onshore wind companies. The relevance of existing manufacturers in the offshore market strongly differs to the one onshore. Therefore this paper follows the view that the development of wind energy technology should be considered as the evolution of three different trajectories (Dosi 1982). The analysis in this paper will focus on the strand of onshore wind energy for the grid but will also give some insights into the offshore development.

Chapter 2 will give an introduction of the relevant theories and findings for this paper. Chapter 3 introduces the empirical data and methodology used in this paper and assesses their relevance. The results of the data analysis are presented in chapter 4. In the final chapter conclusions will be drawn and the need for further research will be indicated.

2 Theoretical foundations

The theory of industry life cycles (ILC) is derived from the concept of product life cycles (PLC) that was developed over time by a number of authors (see among others Levitt 1965, Vernon 1966). The PLC theory describes the general development of certain performance indicators of a product over its life time such as the development of turnover, profit rate as well as imports and exports. This development is typically divided and described in four phases – introduction, growth, maturity and degeneration (Levitt 1965). During the use and development of the PLC theory, certain analogies on the development of the respective industries were drawn by a number of authors (see also Wiliamson 1975; Abernathy and Utterback 1978; Clark 1985; Klepper and Graddy 1990; Jovanovic and MacDonald 1994). However, the final model on ILC is attributed to the work of Klepper (1997). Three main indicators are subject to the ILC model - the creation of technological innovation, market development, and the number of companies active in the market (see Fig. 1). Just as in the PLC theory the development of these indicators is specified in

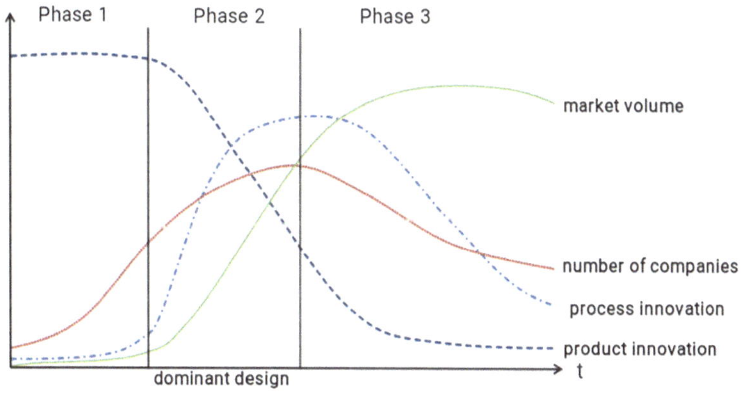

Fig. 1 Development of indicators in an industry life cycle (ILC), based on Klepper 1997

phases of industrial development. In the case of ILC there are mostly three stages that are taken into consideration neglecting the last phase, the decline of the market as described in the PLC.

Phase one refers to the early exploratory stage which is characterized by a low market volume, uncertainty regarding the technological specification required by the market, simple product design and hardly any automatization in the production process. In anticipation of future market potentials companies enter the market with different technological concepts and the volatility of market shares is high.

Phase two is specified as a growth phase with a large market expansion rate in which the dominant design emerges. As a result the number of product innovations decreases whereas process innovations and along with them automatization of the production increases (Abernathy and Utterback 1975). The number of new market entrants decreases and shake outs can be witnessed as certain technological strands have proven to be unviable.

Phase three marks the stage of maturity. Market growth slows down, innovations are less relevant and the number of companies decreases while market shares stabilize. Company shake outs that can be seen in this phase are not only driven by the inferiority of technological solutions but by consolidation to increase economic efficiency. Also results of various industry studies suggest first mover advantages with longer survival rates of early market participants (see also Klepper 2002).

Phase four, the decline of the market that is described in product life cycles so far does not play a significant role in the industry life cycle theory. One reason might be that industries that were subject to the ILC theory so far had not reached this stage. Also the decline of the market for an industry does not happen as quickly as it does for a product. Technologies as well as industries consist of a number of products. Their development could therefore be described as the sum of different product life cycles (Ford and Ryan 1981; Menhart et al. 2004). Therefore their development will only enter the phase of decline if a technology becomes dispensable for the market.

Klepper (1997) ILC theory has been established by the analysis of different industries in the US. However it does not seem to be clear which geographical boundaries have to be applied for the analysis of industries in the globalized world of today for the theory to be viable. As the ILC model has been derived from the PLC theory the international perspective and its findings in this strain of research will be taken into account.

The main findings regarding the international perspective of the PLC theory goes back to Vernon (1966, 1979). His work suggests that the production shifts over time from the country of origin – which is expected to be a developed country - to less developed countries with cost advantages. During the first phase of the PLC the advantages of the country of origin seem to be especially relevant. The theory of lead markets which was introduced much later does pick up on this aspect and widens the perspective from the higher quality of production in developed countries to the competitive advantages which are subject to such a market (see Beise 2004; Porter 1990). During the growth phase other developed countries start to produce the technology introduced by the lead market. Cost advantages become crucial in the maturation phase which leads to the shift of production to less developed countries.

Another theory that will be addressed in the course of this paper is the theory of catch-up cycles. It answers the question why it is possible for latecomer countries and firms to eventually take over the industrial leadership from incumbent companies (Lee and Malerba 2017).

Regarding the development of innovations Klepper (1997) refers to the concept introduced by Abernathy and Utterback (1975). The concept that follows the interdependency of product and process innovation in the course of the life cycle still holds true today with the restriction that it is applicable for mass products and commodities. Another concept sheds light on the development of innovations in complex products and systems (Davies 1997). This concept suggests that product innovations may maintain their importance over the product life cycle. According to this theory a complex product is characterized by a composition of defined components. The equivalent of the dominant design of a product is reached once the dominant architecture of such a product has emerged. In the course of the product life cycle product innovations take place in different components. The innovation focus therefore shifts between components over time whereas the general architecture of the complex product remains stable.

Resent research on patent publications for wind energy suggests that the creation of innovation in wind energy technology follows the characteristics of a complex product (Huenteler et al. 2016). The dominant architecture known as the Danish Design was established in the late 1980s. Up to that point different architectural concepts had been seen regarding the philosophy of tower construction (light vs. sturdy) number of blades (2–4), the orientation (horizontal vs. vertical) and the position of the rotor (upwind vs. downwind). In the end the Danish Design won the upper hand as it turned out to be the most reliable. It consists of a three bladed upwind rotor, on a horizontal axis with a sturdy tower construction (Gipe 1995; Douthwaite 2002; Maegaard et al. 2013). Even today these fundamental features are still used in nearly all wind turbines installed globally. The only component that varies depending on the manufacturer is the design of the gearbox or even the use of a gearbox at all. Innovative activity in wind turbines since the establishment of the dominant architecture has almost solely been seen in the improvement of the various components (Huenteler et al. 2016).

Coming back to the question of the relevant geographical boundaries for the ILC theory, the findings on innovation activities in wind turbines suggest that the creation of innovation in the wind energy sector is subject to a global knowledge base. This could indicate that the global perspective is predominantly relevant for the ILC of the wind industry. However a detailed analysis of market development as well as the number of companies active in the market in the context of ILC has yet to be carried out.

The formation of a market demand for new energy technologies in the course of the energy transition towards a more sustainable energy supply is subject to extensive literature. Various lock-in effects lead to inertia in the transformation of the energy system that is difficult to overcome (Unruh 2000; Seto et al. 2016). The most important one is known as the technological lock-in effect. It implies the fact that new energy technologies do not necessarily provide any new or advanced services to the consumers. Therefore a new market demand for new energy technologies cannot be created by innovation alone as implied in the technology push theory that the ILC is based on. At the same time new energy technologies are not fit to compete with incumbent technologies as they have not reached their optimal technological or economic performance at the beginning of their life cycle (Menanteau et al. 2003). The advantage of a more sustainable energy production does not create any individual economic value in itself as the external effects of incumbent energy technologies are not internalized in the energy market. This aspect in combination with increasing returns for existing technologies, form the core of path dependence. In order to overcome this inertia, political support is of essence first to provide a technological development via technology-push instruments and later to create market demand by using market-pull instruments (see also Dosi 1982; Grubb 2004; Bürer and Wüstenhagen 2009; Nemet 2009; Groba and Breitschopf 2013). As political support is strongly influenced by technological lock-in effects, institutional lock-in has been identified as an effect on its own (Seto et al. 2016). Institutional lock-in effects can result in two outcomes; they either lead to a continuation of the existing path dependence or to constantly changing political support. The relevance of political support instruments for the creation of RES markets has been identified by a number of studies (see also Kranzl et al. 2006, Kildegaard 2008, Lund 2009, Bergek and Jacobsson 2010, Haas et al. 2011, Klessmann et al. 2011, Lehmann et al. 2012, Batlle 2012, White et al. 2013, Jacobs 2014, Darmani et al. 2014). The results of these studies show that thc effectiveness to create market demand of support policies depends on two main factors; the stability of policies as well as the type and level of support.

Based on these findings the work in this paper assumes that wind energy markets were largely driven by political support systems. Therefore, the terms stable or unstable market developments or conditions used in this paper directly refer to the stability of political support in these markets. Fluctuations between individual years that lie in the nature of capital goods markets are not regarded as unstable market developments.

Another strand of innovation literature does seem to be applicable to the subject addressed in this paper. The theory on technological innovation systems (TIS) has the motivation to better understand the dynamics underlying a technological innovation (see also Carlsson and Stankiewicz 1991; Carlsson et al. 2002; Jacobsson and Bergek 2006; Hekkert et al. 2007; Bergek et al. 2008). It is widely used in the context of sustainable transitions (Markard et al. 2012) and has been applied to analyze the development of the wind energy sector in various countries or regions (see also Jacobsson and Johnson 2000; Bergek and Jacobsson 2003; Negro et al. 2012; Wieczorek et al. 2013; Darmani et al. 2014; Bento and Fontes 2015). The geographic delineation of the concept of innovation systems is not clearly addressed and subject to many discussions (Markard et al. 2015). Therefore variations of innovation systems have emerged next to TIS over time like national innovation systems (Lundvall 1992; Freeman 1995; Lundvall et al. 2002) or global innovation systems (Binz and Truffer 2017). Although there is no clear cut definition on the theory of innovation systems, there are some features that are widely accepted. Innovation systems generally consist of three elements that are intertwined with each other – actors, networks and institutions (Carlsson and Stankiewicz 1991; Jacobsson and Johnson 2000). These elements all play a role in the key system functions that have to be fulfilled in order for an innovation system to be successful. These functions slightly differ depending on the author. Seven functions that currently seem to be the essence of the development in literature are (1) entrepreneurial activities, (2) knowledge development, (3) knowledge diffusion through networks, (4) guidance of the search, (5) market formation, (6) resource mobilization, and (7) creation of legitimacy (see also Jacobsson and Bergek 2006; Hekkert et al. 2007; Bergek et al. 2008). However, the analytical framework of the TIS is not directly used in this paper as the concept in itself does not describe distinct indicators or their development over time. There are quite some publications that have applied the TIS over time (see also Bergek and Jacobsson 2003; Dewald and Truffer 2011). However, the concept that is used for the aspect of evolution is mostly the ILC with its classification of the development in phases. The TIS approach is used to explain the importance of each function in the various stages of the development. As this paper wants to look at the possible interaction between market development and the number of companies that evolve around it, the ILC theory will be in the focus of this study. However, aspects of the TIS framework are taken into consideration in the description of national developments and the interpretation of the findings.

3 Empirical data and methods

Energy security especially the supply of electricity is an area that receives a lot of attention from politics as well as the public. Therefore it is a sector that is relatively well monitored with a sound statistical basis. As the diffusion of renewable energies especially in the electricity sector was strongly dependent on political support in the past, data on the actual development was crucial to the monitoring of support instruments. The empirical basis regarding these technologies, therefore, may be even better than for conventional energy technologies. Of all renewable energies wind energy is the one with the best database in many respects.

There are a number of sources that can be used to grasp the development of wind energy globally as well as in various countries. First of all, national official energy statistics provide information regarding the wind energy production in each country. This data is collected and published by the International Energy Agency and dates back to the 1970s (IEA 2017). Secondly various governmental institutions, research institutes and industry associations gather information regarding the development of capacity expansion on national and international levels. This data has different backgrounds depending on each country. Some are derived from lists of installations such as in Denmark, others are an estimate based on data provided by market participants. The time period covered by most of these sources does not go back as far as the beginning of wind utilization in each country. Most sources provide information as of the year 2000 or later. Primarily data on cumulative wind energy

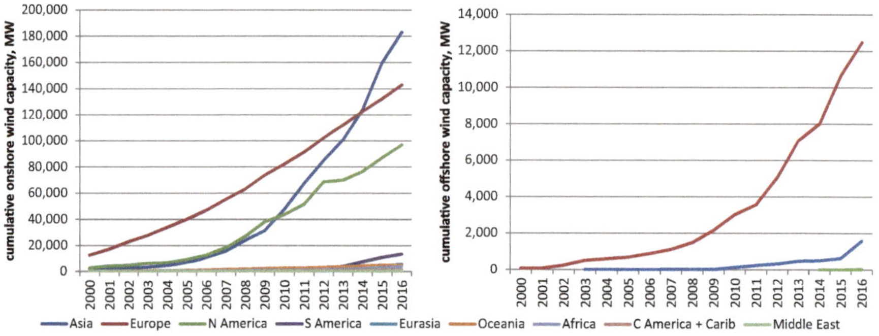

Fig. 2 Development of cumulative wind capacities in different world regions (left onshore, right offshore), MW (IRENA 2018)

capacities can be found. However, the market development can only be described by data on the newly installed capacities in each year. The source with the best information on newly installed capacities on a number of national markets as well as the global market is the Global Wind Energy Council (GWEC 2018). The period that covers global newly installed capacities goes back to 1995. National figures are available as of 2006. However, most national developments can be complemented by figures from national data sources. The global development before 1995 can be complemented by data gathered from the Earth Policy Institute as of 1981 (EPI 2018). If no information regarding the newly installed capacity is available, the development will be estimated on the basis of the cumulative development. The International Renewable Energy Agency provides such a timeline for global as well as national developments as of the year 2000 (IRENA 2018). BP provides a similar database from their statistical review of world energy that goes back to 1997 (BP 2018). The information on the diffusion of wind energy will be used for two purposes. Firstly, the data on newly installed capacities will be used as input regarding the market development of wind energy. Secondly, the cumulative capacity as well as the share of wind energy in the total energy demand will be used to select a number of countries that will be analyzed in more detail.

A first rough assessment of the development of the use of wind energy shows that three world regions have seen a considerable expansion in wind energy. Europe has been the most important world region in onshore as well as offshore development followed by Asia which took the lead in cumulative wind capacity on land in 2014. North America has played an important role in onshore development from the beginning. However, the first offshore installations have just emerged in the last few years. Regarding the development of onshore wind energy South America needs to be taken into consideration as a fourth world region. So far no offshore development has been seen here (see Fig. 2).

Regarding the choice of countries that will be presented in this paper 12 countries[1] were selected that played an outstanding role in the global wind market so far. First of all the cumulative installed capacity at the end of 2016 was used to select the nine leading countries regarding capacity expansion – China, USA, Germany, India, Spain, UK, Canada, France and Brazil. As some countries are smaller than others, the installed capacity in itself is not the only factor that displays the importance of wind energy in a market. Therefore the three leading countries regarding the share of wind energy in total energy demand –Denmark, Ireland and Portugal - were added to the table of global champions (see Table 1).

In order to gain a first impression on the individual developments of these countries the year was added in which one GW of cumulated installed capacity was achieved. The true starting point of the expansion of wind capacities is hard to pinpoint with some of these countries as official statistics do not date back that far.

As a last addition the top 10 global wind turbine manufacturers were added to Table 1. Even though most of these companies have branches in different countries they were assigned to the country where their headquarters are based. Three companies each are located in China and Germany, whereas Denmark, the US, Spain and India are home to one of the global top 10. A more detailed analysis of these companies will be conducted later in this paper. Also the analysis of individual countries in chapter 4 will start with the six countries that these companies originate in.

Regarding the development of the number of companies active in the wind energy sector over time there are a number data sources that can be taken into consideration. The most detailed and extensive one is a global database that provides information on individual wind farms. This database also includes information on the wind turbine manufacturer (The Wind Power 2018). As the data is based on hard facts and no estimations are being made regarding missing information, the market is not fully covered by this source. However, its advantage is the information it provides on all countries around the world. In order to get an impression on the coverage of the information represented in the database two comparisons will be conducted. One refers to the newly installed capacity covered in this database, the other one to the number of companies.

The newly installed capacities that are represented in the windfarm database are taken into relation to the development of newly installed capacities provided by other statistical sources (see above and Fig. 4 a)). Overall about 69% of the global capacity stated in these sources is represented in the wind farm database and 60% are linked to a turbine manufacturer. Regarding the market coverage in different countries quite a large difference can be seen. For the US the coverage equals 100% of the development referred to by other statistical sources. Denmark has coverage of 98%, Germany 53% and China reaches 28% of installed capacities that include company names. At the same time, the coverage varies between years. On the global level the

[1]The work underlying this paper has analyzed the development of 24 countries. Some of the findings from the other countries will be referred to in the conclusions.

Table 1 Global champions by selected indicators (IRENA 2018; IEA 2017; Wind Power Monthly 2017 based on figures of FTI Consulting)

country	cumulative installed capacity end of 2016, MW (global ranking)	cumulative installed onshore capacity end of 2016, MW (global ranking)	cumulative installed offshore capacity end of 2016, MW (global ranking)	share of wind energy in total electricity output in 2015 (global ranking)	Year with one GW installed	global top 10 companies 2016 (global cumulative capacity at end of 2016)
PR China (CN)	148,983 (1.)	147,503 (1.)	1480 (3.)	3.2%	2005	Goldwind (38.1 GW), United Power (16.6 GW), Envision (8.9 GW)
USA (US)	81,312 (2.)	81,828 (2.)	29 (11.)	4.5%	1985	GE (60.4 GW)
Germany (DE)	49,747 (3.)	45,639 (3.)	4108 (2.)	12.4%	1995	Enercon (44.1 GW), Nordex (21.8 GW), Senvion (15.4 GW)
India (IN)	28,875 (4.)	28,875 (4.)	–	3.1%	1999	Suzlon (16.1 GW)
Spain (ES)	22,992 (5.)	22,987 (5.)	5 (13.)	17.8%	1999	Siemens-Gamesa (74.9 GW)
UK (GB)	15,200 (6.)	10,050 (9.)	5150 (1.)	12.0%	2005	
Canada (CA)	11,900 (7.)	11,900 (6.)	–	3.9%	2006	
France (FR)	11,681 (8.)	11,681 (7.)	–	3.8%	2006	
Brazil (BR)	10,740 (9.)	10,740 (8.)	–	3.7%	2011	
Denmark (DK)	5242 (15.)	3971 (16.)	1271 (4.)	48.8% (1.)	1997	Vestas (82.9 GW)
Ireland (IE)	3046 (20.)	3021 (20.)	25 (12.)	23.4% (2.)	2008	
Portugal (PT)	5303 (14.)	5303 (14.)	–	22.6% (3.)	2005	

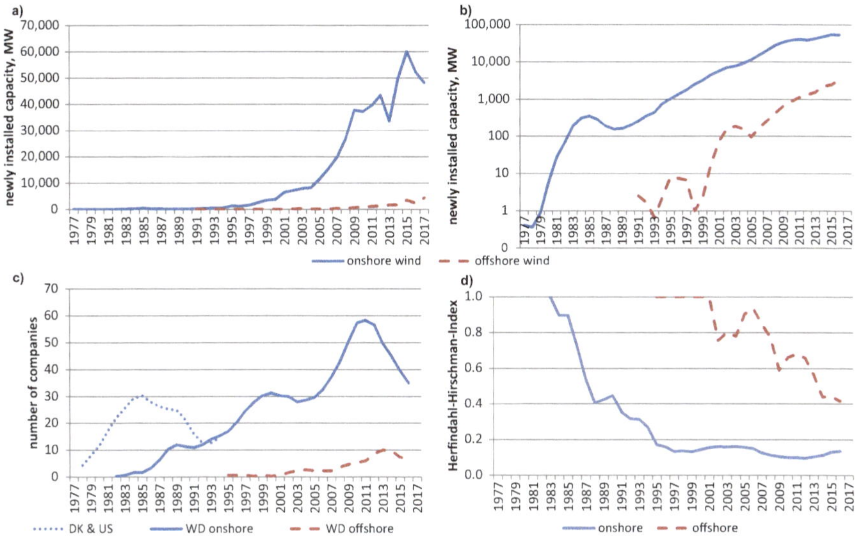

Fig. 4 **a** Development of newly installed capacity (own representation based on GWEC 2018, EPI 2018, Danish Energy Agency 2017), **b** Logarithmic representation of the development of newly installed capacity, moving average (see Fig. 4 a) **c** Development of number of companies on the global wind market, moving average (own representation based on The Wind Power 2018, Danish Energy Agency 2017, Jaeger 2013, Berkley LAB 2017), **d** Market concentration on the global wind market, moving average (own representation based on The Wind Power 2018)

market coverage of data including turbine manufacturers in a year is 42% with a maximum of 74% and a minimum of 0% in the early days of the development (1977–1991). On a national level, coverage of individual years differs with values exceeding 100% of the market stated in other statistical sources. What becomes apparent is a general problem of statistics in wind energy. Statistical sources often differ in the approach at which point in time new installations are taken into account. Some databases refer to the time when the turbine is finally erected; others consider the date of the connection to the grid. When it comes to windfarms, this problem becomes even more relevant. Wind farms can be built over time with each erected turbine counting in its year of installation, they can be considered when the farm is finally installed, or the connection to the grid can be taken as relevant. In order to reduce this problem the analysis of the development of different indicators from different sources will be conducted by using the centered moving average method over three years. Besides the advantage that this method might provide to reduce the difference in the accounting of different statistical sources, small short term fluctuations can be eliminated which puts the focus of the analysis to the long term cycles in the time series.

In order to test the relevance of the windfarm database regarding the number of companies involved in a market, various sources are taken into account that provide information on company market shares in several markets. On a global level Navigant Research (formerly BTM Research) has the longest history in this area

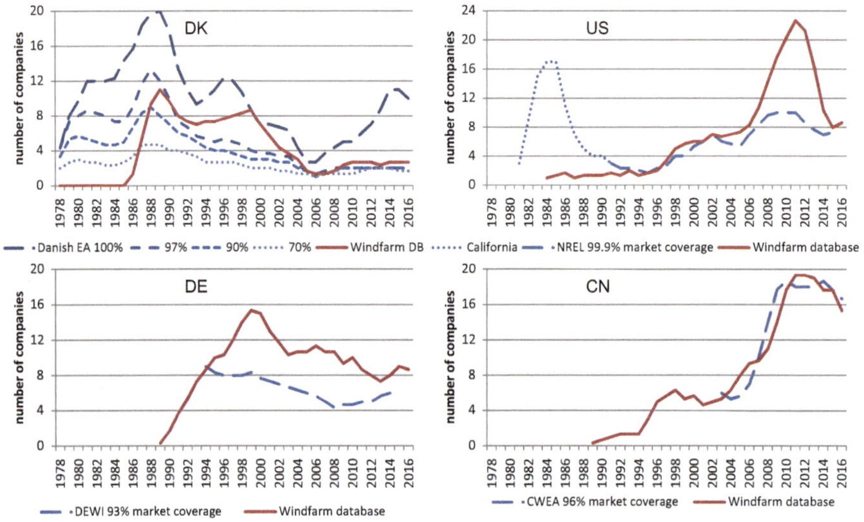

Fig. 3 Number of companies involved in the Danish (DK), US, German (DE) and Chinese (CN) wind turbine market, moving average over three years (own representation based on The Wind Power 2018, Danish Energy Agency 2017, Jaeger 2013, Berkley LAB 2017, DEWI 2017, CWEA 2017)

with data going back as far as 1994. On national levels data could be collected for four relevant markets – Denmark, the US, Germany and China - provided by governmental energy agencies (Danish Energy Agency 2017), research institutes (Berkley LAB 2017; DEWI 2017) as well as industry associations (CWEA 2017). The only source that provides information on the full wind energy market ever since its creation is the Danish Energy Agency that keeps a register of all wind turbines built in Denmark. All other sources cover a share of the total market and do not include the beginning of the market development. They provide information on the market shares of leading wind turbine manufacturers on each respective market. It can be assumed that the share of each manufacturer is collected on the basis of the companies' statements regarding their sales in the respective market and year. The market shares can be determined by putting this information in relation to the assumed market volume. This approach differs completely from the approach seen in the windfarm database that has individual wind farms in focus[2] with the information on the manufacturer being secondary. Therefore it seems to be possible that the wind farm data base can provide information on more companies than the sources on the US, German and Chinese markets even though it may cover a smaller market share (see Fig. 3).

As only the Danish registry of wind turbines provides data on the whole market the question needs to be answered whether an incomplete market representation can

[2]This also holds true for the Danish data source.

provide information on the development of the number of companies. An analysis of the Danish data in Fig. 3 shows that the general development path can be outlined by an incomplete market presentation. However, the development that cannot be captured with a reduction by only a small fraction of the market is the evolvement of manufacturers for small turbines for self-supply. As the data on Denmark is the only source including the windfarm database that provides any information on the development of small wind turbine manufacturers, the analysis in this paper will focus on the trajectories of onshore and offshore wind energy for the grid.

Regarding the relevance of the windfarm database for the development of the number of companies active in a market, the data was compared with the respective data from the above mentioned sources. The comparison shows that the general trends of the development of number of companies can be recreated by the windfarm database even though the relative height differs. The only time period that is not covered appropriately is prior to 1990. However, this shortfall can be met by including the development in Denmark and California (US) that were, at that time the most relevant markets. The Danish market can be fully represented. The market coverage of the available data on California is not clear. Jaeger (2013) offers information on 21 companies in the period between 1981 and 1991 including the top 10 of three continents; 10 from the US, 10 from Europe and one from Japan. However, he also mentions that more than 30 manufacturers were active in the Californian market at that time. Nevertheless, just like the windfarm database lacks a full coverage of the market, the relevant point in this survey is the representation of the general trend.

The methods used to analyze the data presented above are exclusively derived from the field of descriptive statistics. The graphical representation of various indicators in the form of time series provides a good overview of the course of each development and allows for the identification of the different development phases. Additionally, statistical interrelations are drawn in a regression analysis for the global as well as individual national developments. They will be performed on the individual phases of the ILC as the theory indicates differences in the potential interrelations in each phase. In combination this allows for a comparative analysis of different developments both between individual indicators and between different countries.

4 Results

4.1 Global development

To analyze the industry life cycle of the wind energy industry the global perspective will be chosen as a starting point. As mentioned before, Huenteler et al. (2016) findings on the development of innovation in wind energy seem to indicate that the global perspective is relevant for the industrial life cycle. However, analyses of the other indicators that define the ILC theory have to be conducted first in order to be able to give a definitive statement.

For the analysis of the relevant indicators four figures were created (see Fig. 4). Each figure contains two different development paths – one for onshore wind and one for offshore wind. The first figure shows the market development as it is stated by the respective sources in order to give an impression on the magnitude of the evolution (see Fig. 4 a). The second shows the same data in a logarithmic representation with the difference that short term fluctuations are reduced by applying the centered moving average method over three years (see Fig. 4 b). The third figure represents the development of the number of companies also using the moving average method (see Fig. 4 c). And the last one shows the development of the market concentration by using the moving average of the Herfindahl-Hirschman-Index (see Fig. 4 d). The onshore development will be analyzed first, followed by the offshore development.

The first thing that becomes apparent when looking at Fig. 4 a) is that the expansion of onshore wind energy covers the major share of the overall global wind energy development with 453 GW cumulative installed capacity in 2016 (IRENA 2018). The market evolution on land started in the aftermath of the international oil crisis in the mid-1970s. Import dependency became an urgent issue with regard to security of energy supply which led to the search for alternative domestic energy sources. The first market demand for onshore wind energy was created in 1977 in Denmark followed by California. The early years of the global development are easier to see in the logarithmic representation (see Fig. 4 b). It shows the short but strong expansion of wind energy in the phase of the Californian market in the first half of the 80s that ended with a market collapse in which the yearly installed capacity was reduced by almost 70% within 3 years. The global market development picked up again around 1990 with an exponential growth that could be observed until 2009, followed by a deceleration of market growth that indicates the beginning of a saturation phase. At the moment it is not yet possible to predict whether the current expansion is at a sustainable level and development will stabilize or if a decline to a lower level is to be expected in the coming years. Theoretically, it can be expected that at some point a stable expansion level should be reached. Even when the energy transition will be completed, the turbines will need to be replaced at specified intervals that are currently assumed to be every 20 years.

The two cycles which are indicated by the onshore wind market development can be further divided when looking at the evolution of the companies' active in the market (see Fig. 4 c). The data suggests that three cycles might have occurred so far. The first one from the beginning of the deployment until the early 90s with a certain amount of time lag compared to the market development. The second cycle with its peak around the year 2000 lasted until 2003 and was followed by the third wave of new companies which had its peak in 2011. It remains to be seen whether the decline in the number of companies in recent years will mark the beginning of a final phase of consolidation and maturity. However, the market development indicates that this might be the case.

A regression analysis has been conducted to see if the development in the number of onshore wind manufacturers can be statistically explained by the global market development. Looking at the development of the two indicators in the ILC theory (see Fig. 1) a strong explanatory quality would be expected for the formation phase of an industry. The shake-out phase, on the other hand, is not expected to have a good coefficient of determination.

Subsequently, the statistical analysis was conducted for different time periods. The periods were chosen according to phases of growth and consolidation of the number of companies. However, this means that the regressions are carried out with a comparatively small number of observations. This must be taken into account when interpreting the results. In the case of particularly small observation numbers, a regression will be carried out to ensure completeness. The issue will be specifically pointed out in each one of these cases. The regression tables are displayed in the Annex of this paper.

The results show an adjusted R^2 of 0.97 for the number of companies with the logarithmic representation of the global market development in the first formation phase of the industry between 1978 and 1985. The analysis of the second growth phase (1994–2000) also shows the best results with a logarithmic representation of the global market development. The adjusted R^2 amounts to 0.96. The linear regression of the third growth phase (2004–2011) shows an adjusted R^2 of 0.98. Overall, all three industry growth phases show a very high explanatory value of the global market development with a strong positive interrelation.

The three phases of consolidation that could be observed on the global level show a range of results. The first shake-out phase (1986–1993) shows an adjusted R^2 of 0.49 which does indicate some interdependency but is not sufficient. The second one (2001–2003) does not show any explanatory value of the model. The third one (2012–2016), on the other hand, provides an adjusted R^2 of 0.90 with a negative interrelation between the two indicators showing that the general market trend was positive while the number of companies was decreasing. Again, the findings of the statistical analysis have to be treated with caution as some of the periods only refer to a very small number of observations. This is especially true for the second shake-out phase.

As the appearance of a second and third cycle in the number of companies in the onshore wind market cannot be explained sufficiently by the global market development, a more detailed look into the development of companies seems necessary. Figure 5 shows the development of market shares for groups of companies from one country on the global market. The graph on the left covers the market share of onshore wind; the right one displays the offshore development. As in Table 1 companies were assigned to the country in which they have their headquarters. As the market coverage of the windfarm database differs between countries, the relative shares given in this graph have to be treated with caution. The data for the global market provided by BTM/Navigant (2017) show that the share of Chinese companies in the global onshore market was larger than indicated by Fig. 5. Especially the decreasing relevance of Chinese manufacturers in the last few years cannot be seen.

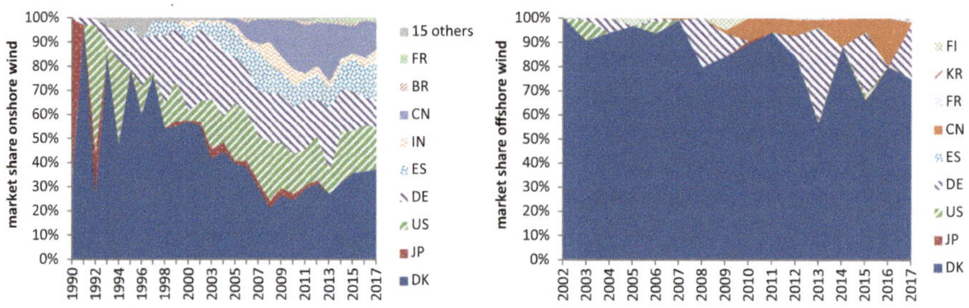

Fig. 5 Market share of companies from selected countries in the global market (own representation based on The Wind Power 2018)

However, what this graph displays is the point of entry of companies from individual countries to the wind market. For the onshore development it shows that Danish, Japanese, US and German companies were already active in the global wind market in the beginning of the 1990s. A few years later Spanish and Indian companies followed. Finally Chinese manufacturers made their appearance onto the global onshore wind market at the beginning of the 2000s, which matches the appearance of the third wave of new companies. All in all, the data indicates a relevance of national markets, which will be examined further in chapter 4.2.

Looking at the development of the market concentration in onshore wind in Fig. 4 d, the trend seems to follow the expected path. In the initial phase in which a relatively low amount of windfarms was installed in each year, market concentration was high. However, since a certain market level had been reached, competition reduced market concentration. Overall, the global onshore market appears to have been highly competitive for many years, with the result that low market concentration prevails.

The global offshore wind development is at a very different stage than the utilization of onshore wind energy with altogether 14 GW of installed capacity in 2016. The four largest offshore wind markets are the UK, Germany, China and Denmark covering 85% of the global overall installed capacity. The largest cumulative installed capacity of just over 5 GW in 2016 was located in the UK followed by Germany with just over 4 GW. China just took the third rank over Denmark in 2016 with just under 1.5 GW of overall installed capacity (IRENA 2018). The market development of offshore wind energy started in 1991 in Denmark. The development up until today as displayed in Fig. 4 a) and b) indicates that the industry is still at an early stage of market utilization. However, the development of the number of companies seems to point to a first shake out phase (see Fig. 4 c)). It has to be stressed that this impression could be deceptive, as at this stage of the development individual projects have a great influence. The impression of the offshore market still being at an early phase is also given by the high market concentration that still exists even though the trend indicates a continuous reduction.

The right graph in Fig. 5 shows the global offshore wind market shares of companies from different countries. The strong market position of Danish wind turbine manufacturers stands out as in the early days of the onshore wind development. However, it is basically one company – Siemens – that so far has provided more than 60% of the globally installed offshore wind capacity. An analysis of the industry life cycle of individual national markets for offshore wind turbines does seem interesting. However, the size of the respective national markets in combination with the size of individual offshore windfarms makes an analysis at the current point in time difficult as the number of wind farms that are installed in one year is relatively small and varies significantly between years. Therefore the analysis of national markets will focus on the onshore wind development.

4.2 National development

In simple terms, global market development can be described as the sum of national market developments. The extent to which a national market development influences the global market development depends on its share and can change over time. In order to facilitate a better overview and understanding of the national markets that will be presented in this chapter some more information is provided in Table 2 that will add to the information given in Table 1.

The information provided in Table 2 shows various indicators referring to the role of each market in the global development in the past as well as the wind onshore potential. The market potential is implied by two indicators, the total power generation which shows the current power demand of each country and the technical wind power generation potential. The data on the wind electricity generation potential was taken from an internal source. Another publication from Eurec et al. (2017) shows slightly different numbers but the overall conclusion is the same. The theoretical wind onshore generation potential does not restrict market development as it is larger than the current electricity output of each one of the countries that are analyzed in this paper.

The figures on the share of national market developments in the global market in 1995 show one of the main short comings of this study. The data provided by The Wind Power (2018) does indicate that a wind energy market existed in Spain, China, UK, Canada, France, Ireland and Portugal at that time. As market data for the early development phase could only be gathered for Denmark and the US, the first phase of the ILC can only be analyzed for these two markets.

As already mentioned, the analysis of national developments will start with the six countries hosting the global top ten wind turbine manufacturers – Denmark (DK), the US, Germany (DE), India (IN), Spain (ES) and China (CN). The analysis of each one of these markets will include a short introduction to the development of political support systems that helps to explain market developments. Also a detailed analysis regarding the wind industry active in these markets will be conducted showing the role of national based companies as well as the engagement of foreign companies. To provide some insight to the dynamics in the industry itself, detailed information regarding the origins of the top 10 global wind companies will be provided.

Table 2 Influence of selected national market developments on the global market development between 1977 and 2017 (GWEC 2018, EPI 2018, Danish Energy Agency 2017, IEA 2017, data on wind generation potential derived with the methodology described in Stetter 2014)

country	Share of global market in 1985	Share of global market in 1995	Share of global market in 2005	Share of global market in 2015	Share of global installed wind energy capacity in 2016	Wind electricity output in 2015, TWh	Total electricity output in 2015, TWh	Wind onshore generation potential, TWh
PR China (CN)	–	–	4%	48%	33%	185	5844	34,300
USA (US)	94%	3%	21%	14%	18%	193	4297	37,300
Germany (DE)	–	39%	16%	9%	10%	79	641	1800
India (IN)	–	30%	12%	4%	6%	43	1383	1400
Spain (ES)	–	–	13%	0%	5%	49	278	3100
UK (GB)	–	–	4%	2%	2%	40	336	2500
Canada (CA)	–	–	2%	2%	3%	26	671	52,500
France (FR)	–	–	3%	2%	3%	21	563	3100
Brazil (BR)	–	–	–	4%	2%	22	582	9900
Denmark (DK)	6%	6%	0.2%	0.3%	1%	14	29	400
Ireland (IE)	–	–	1%	0.4%	1%	7	28	1700
Portugal (PT)	–	–	4%	0.2%	1%	12	51	700

4.2.1 Denmark

Denmark is often referred to as the lead market of wind energy (see also Beise and Rennings 2003). With its strong energy import dependency and very good wind conditions, it was the first country to introduce wind energy for electricity production that was fed into the grid. Even though Denmark, due to its size, only has an installed wind capacity of about 4 GW onshore and another GW offshore, it is the leader in wind utilization and integration. In 2015 almost half of the electricity output of the country came from wind energy (see Table 1). Until today, the innovations that came from Denmark have shaped the use of wind energy. At the same time political support of the wind market has seen a lot of changes which makes Denmark one of the countries that has seen a high amount of instability in its market.

In Denmark wind energy has its roots in a community movement. After the oil crisis in 1973 farmers started to look for possibilities to generate electricity for self-consumption. They experimented with wind turbines that were simple, robust and reliable. This wind turbine design was gradually improved with experience from existing installations. This bottom up approach led to the creation of the Danish wind turbine design which turned out to be the dominant design up until today. The first players in the Danish wind energy movement managed to get governmental support for their request to be able to feed electricity into the grid as a private person or co-operative like society. Therefore regulation rules for guaranteed grid access were in place at a very early point in time. The first support system was a 30% subsidy on wind turbine investment in 1981 which started the Danish market development and ended in 1988. The first form of a feed in tariff with a guaranteed remuneration of wind energy which was fed into the grid was developed in 1990. Its level was set as a percentage of the retail electricity rate. When the effect on the market development was not as expected, a fixed feed in tariff was introduced in 1993 (IRENA 2012). Even though Denmark was the pioneer in all those regulative innovations that have marked the success of global wind energy deployment, the Danish wind market has seen a lot of changes in political support (Gipe 1995; Maegaard et al. 2013; Vestergaard et al. 2004; Douthwaite 2002; Karnoe and Garud 2012). The feed-in tariff system was stopped in 1999 with the introduction of renewable portfolio standards which reduced the Danish wind energy market once more. The restructuring of the energy market in 2004 was followed by the introduction of price premiums in 2009 (IRENA 2012).

Looking at the development of the national markets the effects of the history of political support can be seen (Fig. 6). Denmark currently seems to be in the third cycle since 1980 with the first cycle ending at an installation level that was more than 40% below the maximum expansion in this wave and the second one with a difference of 98%. The current cycle has seen a relatively stable market development in the last few years which might indicate a currently sustainable level of expansion.

The development of the number of companies active in the Danish market is displayed in Fig. 6 on the right. The first cycle that was seen in the development of the national market was accompanied with a complementary development of market

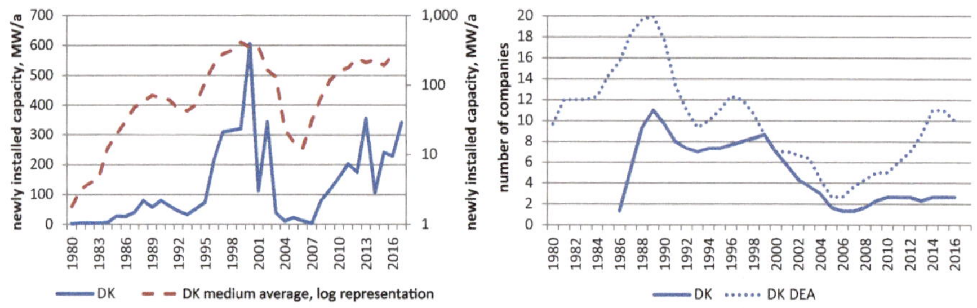

Fig. 6 left: Development of newly installed wind onshore capacity in DK (own representation based on GWEC 2018, Danish Energy Agency 2017), right: Development of number of companies in the Danish wind onshore market (own representation based on The Wind Power 2018, Danish Energy Agency 2017).

players. A regression analysis of the formation phase of the first cycle was conducted with a logarithmic representation of the national market development (see Annex). It shows that the growth in the number of companies between 1978 and 1989 can be explained by an adjusted R^2 of 0.94. A multiple regression adding the global development without the Danish market as a second independent variable increases this value to 0.96. The regression of the national market development for the short shake out phase between 1990 and 1993 has to be treated with caution due to the very small number of observations. Consequently, the significance level of this regression is not sufficient. The explanatory quality turns out to be quite high taking the theoretic assumptions into consideration (adjusted $R^2 = 0.81$). The coefficient of determination is not raised by taking the rest of the global market development into account, showing the influence of the national development. The start of the second cycle of market development in 1994 hardly increased the participants on the market for larger wind turbines. The peak of companies was reached in 1997 with 12 companies active in the Danish market. Again, the regression analysis of this short phase of another four years did not turn out with a relevant significance. It shows an adjusted R^2 of 0.67 which is increased to 0.97 with the additional consideration of the global market. The strong decline in the national market at the end of the second cycle (1998–2006) had the consequence that the number of companies has been reduced to essentially two Danish players – Vestas and Bonus that had been taken over by Siemens at the end of the second cycle. The regression analysis of this phase shows an adjusted R^2 of 0.75 with a relevant significance whereas the regression including the global market outside of Denmark did not produce a high enough significance. At the beginning of this shake out phase, market development was still ongoing indicating a shake out as it is expected in the ILC. However, the steep decline in market demand led to a relatively strong coefficient of determination for the development of the industry with a strong positive interrelation. The third development cycle in Denmark did not have any major effects on the number of companies active in the onshore market for grid applications at all. A detailed analysis of the data from the Danish Energy Agency (2017) shows that the increase in companies which can be seen in Fig. 6 can be traced back to the development of small wind turbines. The two major national players from the beginning of the development remained and as the size of the market in Denmark is not very big in terms of numbers no established companies from other countries emerged on the Danish market.

Even though the Danish market might be relatively small, it is home to two global champions (Table 1). The leading company Vestas has a history going back all the way to the beginning of wind utilization in Denmark. Its merger with NEG Micon, another reknown Danish wind turbine manufacturer with roots at the beginning of the Danish development, in 2004 needs to be mentioned (Maegaard et al. 2013). In 2014 Vestas has entered into a joint venture with Mitsubishi (JP) which concentrates exclusively on the offshore wind market. Vestas has production sites in 8 different countries on 4 continents and most of its turnover is generated outside of Denmark (Vestas 2018).

The wind business of the second largest Danish company Siemens[3] goes back to the acquisition of Bonus in 2004, another player of the early days in Denmark. In 2017 Siemens merged with Gamesa the leading wind turbine manufacturer in Spain to form Siemens-Gamesa. The headquarters of the new company are located in Spain (Siemens Gamesa 2018). The onshore wind development will be served from Spain while the Danish locations hold the headquarters for the offshore wind business. The offshore wind technology owned by Gamesa (formerly Multibrid (DE), acquired by Alstom (FR) and brought into a joint venture with Gamesa (Adwen)) will not be continued.

4.2.2 United States of America

The US wind market is currently the second largest wind energy market in the world with an installed onshore wind energy capacity of 82 GW at the end of 2016 (see Table 1). It has an enormous wind onshore generation potential of about 37 PWh that is theoretically available to provide a significant part of the electricity output (approx. 4.3 PWh) (see Table 2). Its market development so far has seen changing political support which resulted in instability.

The US was one of the leading countries in the development of wind energy. After the first oil crisis a national research program was set up led by NASA, during which several wind turbine designs were developed. However, none of these designs coming from this top-down approach managed to get the upper hand over the reliable bottom-up design of the Danish development. The national energy act of 1978 introduced the first tax credit which was not sufficient for a notable market development. California offered an additional investment tax credit in 1980 which

[3]It might seem odd to refer to Siemens as a Danish company when the Siemens group a renowned German company. However, when it comes to wind energy Siemens remained the strong bond to the Danish market by leaving its production and headquarters in Denmark. The six year time period between 2011 and 2017 in which Siemens has eventually shifted its official headquarters to Germany has not changed much of this perspective.

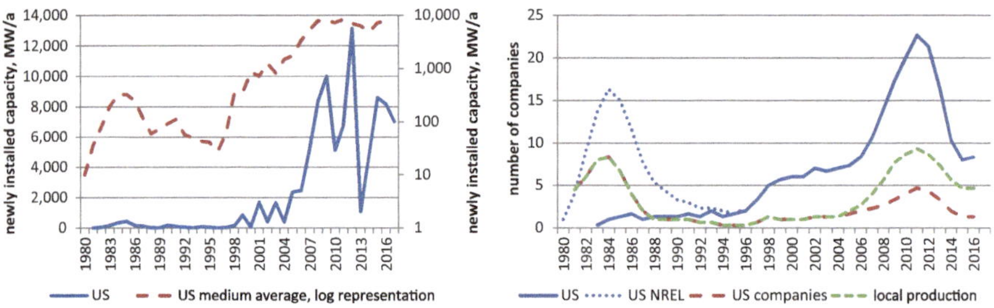

Fig. 7 left: Development of newly installed wind onshore capacity in US (own representation based on GWEC 2018, BP 2018, Berkley LAB 2017, AWEA 2018), right: Development of number of companies in the US wind onshore market; US/US NREL refer to all companies active in the US market, US companies refers to companies that are based in the US, local production refers to companies with a production site in the US (own representation based on The Wind Power 2018, Jaeger 2013, Berkley LAB 2017).

abruptly ended in 1985. This support system has been the cause for the first market cycle in the US (Fig. 7). After the high point in 1985, the market broke down by 98% until 1989. The second wave of market development that started in 1999 has been quite unsteady as many boom and bust phases could be witnessed that were the result of the short-term nature of the political support system (IRENA 2012; Gipe 1995; Maegaard et al. 2013; Vestergaard et al. 2004; Douthwaite 2002).

The development of companies in the US market has also seen the two cycles described by the market expansion path (see Fig. 7). During the first wave, a series of national based companies emerged in the Californian market within three years. The regression analysis of the national industry development with the market development for this very short time has to be treated with caution as it did not provide enough information for the regression to be significant (see Annex). The results show an adjusted R^2 of 0.90 with the logarithmic representation of the national market development. During the steep decline of the market that followed all national US companies left the market. The adjusted R^2 for the period between 1985 and 1994 is 0.95 with a very high significance and a strong positive interrelation between the two declining indicators. The explanatory value of the regression analysis is not improved by the consideration of the rest of the global market. However, it can be assumed that this shake out of national based companies from the US might have happened eventually. In this period the dominant design established which was provided by Danish companies.

During the second cycle of market growth only a few new national based companies emerged. The regression for the phase between 1995 and 2011 shows a coefficient of determination of 0.88 for the US market. Taking the rest of the global market into account R^2 is improved to 0.97 with a higher significance of the global market than the national development. Again, when looking at the national development in this period it becomes apparent that the market development between individual years was not very reliable. Therefore, it can be assumed that the global market had a stabilizing effect on the industry. The bulk of companies active in the second cycle of the US market seen in the graph are companies from other nations seeking the opportunity in one of the largest wind markets. Most of those companies started local production with the rise of the US market. It can be assumed that these decisions were primarily driven by the promises of the potential of the US wind energy market. Local production requirements were never introduced on the national level in the US. However, a number of states introduced additional incentives for companies to set up local production (OECD 2015). The regression analysis of the companies with a production in the US and the national market development shows an explanatory value of 0.94 which increases to 0.99 with the global market included.

The decline in the number of companies that was seen between 2012 and 2016 cannot be explained by the national market development. However, it does correspond to the global development in the aftermath of the financial crisis in 2009.

The one US wind company of global importance is General Electrics (GE). It is the dominant company in the US market with an average market share of 45% since 2003. GE started its engagement in wind energy technology with the acquisition of Enron (US) in 2002. Enron in turn had entered the wind market with the acquisition of Tacke (DE) and Zond (US) in 1997 which started its business in the Californian market in the early 80s. As the dominance of the Danish design became apparent Zond retreated from its own turbine production and focused on the development of wind parks in the US using Vestas turbines. In 1993 it went back to the design of its own turbines and acquired the patents of the bankrupt Kenetech (US) in 1996 (GE 2018). In the last few years GE acquired two more companies which have to be mentioned. In 2015 it took over the energy business of Alstom (FR) including all of its onshore wind activities. In 2017 GE bought LM Wind Power (DK) one of the most important wind turbine blade manufacturers that goes back to the beginning of the wind market development in Denmark.

4.2.3 Germany

Germany had an installed onshore wind capacity of about 46 GWh in 2016 and the share of wind energy output in the total electricity output amounted to over 12% in 2015 (see Table 1). The wind onshore generation potential in Germany amounts to 1.8 PWh and the current national electricity output is around 641 TWh (see Table 2). The German onshore wind energy market started slightly after the Danish and US American market. In 1995 it was the largest market in the world (see Table 2). So far it can be regarded as a relatively stable market as it was driven by feed in tariff systems throughout its development.

Germany is another country that has had a major influence on the development of wind energy technology. Just like in the US a research program was established in the mid-70s that had the goal of creating a multi-megawatt wind turbine. The “GROWIAN” was discontinued in 1987 and taken down the following year. When the challenges of large wind turbines became evident in the mid-80s the research program was opened to smaller applications. After the first demonstration

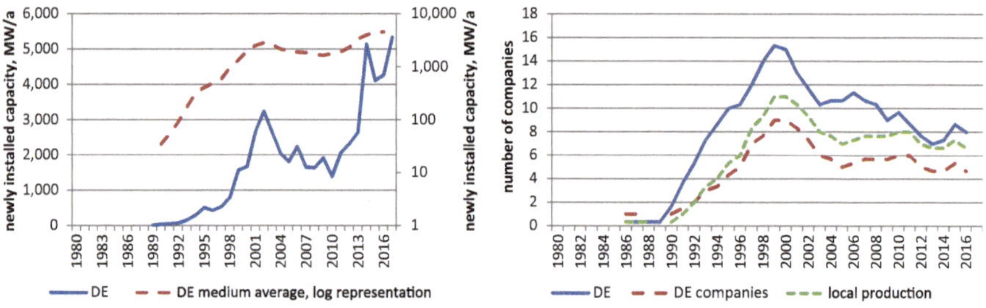

Fig. 8 left: Development of newly installed wind onshore capacity in DE (own representation based on GWEC 2018, Durstewitz et al 2001, BMWi 2018), right: Development of number of companies in the German wind onshore market; DE refers to all companies active in the German market, DE companies refers to companies that are based in Germany, local production refers to companies with a production site in Germany (own representation based on The Wind Power 2018).

projects in the 80s the "Stromeinspeisegesetz" came into effect in 1991 that complimented technology demonstration projects. This first feed-in tariff system in Germany was inspired by the Danish development and was followed by the Renewable Energy Sources Act (EEG) in 2000 with the support of all political parties (see also Hoppe-Killper 2003; IRENA 2012; Maegaard et al. 2013). This has led to a comparatively stable market development in Germany that seems to follow the path described by the classic ILC theory for industries under normal market conditions (see Fig. 8).

After a long phase of relatively constant annual capacity expansions, there has been an increase in new installations in the last few years. This can possibly be explained by the fact that a change in the support system is on its way. The fixed remunerations that had been an incremental part of the EEG, are about to run out. As of 2017 wind capacities are called for in tenders that define the compensation. The last project under the fixed remuneration can be finalized in 2018 (BMWi 2018). The effect of this system change cannot be seen in the market development yet but it can be assumed that market players were speeding up their projects to be able to realize them under the old regime (for a similar effect in the PV sector see Klein and Deissenroth 2017).

The development of the number of companies active on the German market also shows the path described by Klepper (1997) (see Fig. 8). Regarding the current status it seems like Germany has been in the phase of market maturity for quite some time now. The majority of wind turbine manufacturers active on the German market have their roots in Germany. The Danish companies that established production locations in Germany did so in the early 1990s. Even though Germany never had any local content requirements, the access to the financing of demonstration projects may have influenced those strategic decisions.

The regression analysis of the development of number of companies with the national development was conducted for two phases (see Annex). The formation phase of the German wind industry could only be analyzed between 1990 and 2000. The early years of the exploratory phase could not be considered as the data on installed capacities for Germany was not available. The results show an adjusted R^2 of 0.95 for the industry development with a logarithmic representation of the national wind market. This explanatory value could be slightly improved to 0.97 by adding the rest of the global market development. Just like in the US-American example, this shows the stabilizing role of the global market for individual years of market stagnation or decline. The analysis of the companies that were producing in Germany amounted to an adjusted R^2 of 0.94 and 0.98 respectively.

The phase of consolidation that occurred between 2001 and 2016 cannot be statistically explained by the market development. This result is in line with the ILC theory where the shake-out phase does not show an interrelation with the market development.

The early and relatively stable development of the German market has most likely been one of the reasons for the success of German wind turbine manufacturers. Three of the top 10 global wind turbine manufacturers are located in Germany (see Table 1).

Enercon was founded in 1984 as a spin-off of the University of Braunschweig that had developed a gearless wind turbine under the research program of the federal ministry of research (see also Hoppe-Killper 2003; Maegaard et al. 2013). It is the company with the highest market shares on the German market. Since 1993 the average share has been at 40% accoding to DEWI (2017). Due to a patent issue, Enercon is the only large European wind turbine manufacturer that is not active on the US market. Enercon has production facilities in 6 countries on the European continent and a subsidiary in Brazil (Wobben Windpower) (Enercon 2018).

Senvion also known under the former name RePower was founded in 2001 in the context of a merger of four German turbine manufacturers. In 2007 it was taken over by Suzlon (IN) as a subsidiary and sold to the US-investment firm Centerbridge in 2015. It is the second largest player on the German market with an average market share of 10% since 2001 (DEWI 2017).

Nordex SE was founded in 1985 in Denmark. In 1992 it started its production in Germany; in 2001 it became an incorporated company listed on the German stock exchange. In 2003 it closed down its production in Denmark. In 2016 it merged with Acciona Wind Power a renowned turbine manufacturer in Spain (Nordex 2018). Nordex is the third largest company on the German wind market with an average market share of 7% since 1993 (DEWI 2017).

4.2.4 India

India had an installed onshore wind capacity of 29 GW in 2016 with a share of 3.1% of wind power in the total electricity output (see Table 1). With a wind onshore generation potential of about 1.4 PWh it could theoretically provide its current electricity output. The market conditions in India were relatively stable after the early development phase with a mix of support schemes.

India is the first laggard country that was successful in introducing its own wind manufacturing industry. In 1982 the Indian government started its first research

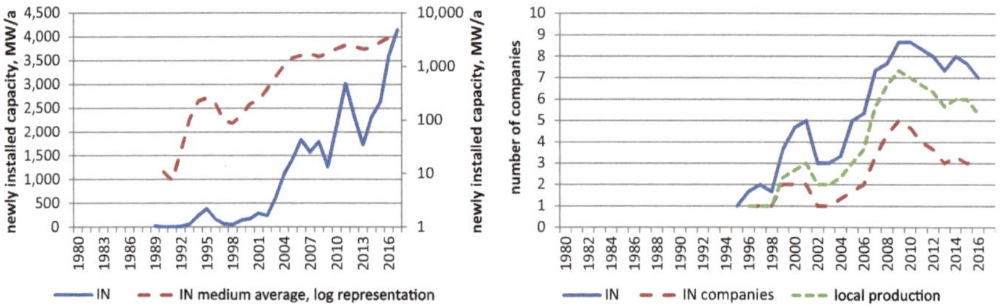

Fig. 9 left: Development of newly installed wind onshore capacity in IN (own representation based on GWEC 2018, BP 2018, Mizuno 2007), right: Development of number of companies in the Indian wind onshore market; IN refers to all companies active in the Indian market, IN companies refers to companies that are based in India, local production refers to companies with a production site in India (own representation based on The Wind Power 2018).

program followed by a demonstration program in 1985. Several investment incentives were set up in 1989 that led to the start of the Indian wind market (Mizuno 2007; Lewis 2011). The introduction of the Electricity Act of 2003 provided the first national legal framework for the promotion of renewable energies in India. It included the request for the introduction of fixed quotas to procure power by the State Electricity Regulatory Commissions. In 2009 a national feed-in tariff system was put in place (IRENA 2012). Just as in Germany, India has currently shifted this system from state-established remunerations to tenders. The market development that can be seen in Fig. 9 shows two cycles of development; a very short one at the beginning of wind utilization in India in the 90s and a relatively stable one since 1998.

The development of companies active on the Indian wind market does not reflect the two cycles of the market development as the data does not cover the first cycle (see Fig. 9). However, the initial market growth of the first development cycle resulted from a strong engagement of foreign companies on the Indian market with its large market potential. During the first cycle almost solely foreign companies were active on the Indian market mostly via subsidiaries that were created as joint ventures. The decline of the market could not harm these global players as dramatically as in the case of new national players in other wind markets as they had the possibility to sell their production in other markets that they were already active in. The development of the national players was initiated during the first cycle but had its real start at the beginning of the second cycle. Just like the US market, the potential offered by the Indian wind energy market brought a number of international companies that built production facilities in India.

The statistical analysis of the period from 1995 to 2016 did not provide a particularly good explanatory value for the industrial development in India. In the growth phase between 1995 and 2009 an adjusted R^2 of 0.46 was reached for the number of domestic companies and 0.64 for those with a production in India (see Annex). Those values were significantly higher with the rest of the global market development taken into account as another independent variable. They amounted to

0.89 and 0.92 respectively. Again the consolidation phase did not show any good coefficients of determination. The findings indicate that the global market development played a larger role in the industry development in India than in the other countries that were analyzed so far.

India has also succeeded in establishing one of the top 10 global companies. Suzlon was founded in 1995 and acquiring its technology by way of a technical collaboration with Südwind (DE). Gradually it expanded its production to all components via joint ventures with renowned companies from the US and Europe and took over Germanys RePower (later known as Senvion) in 2007 (Lewis 2011). In 2015 Suzlon sold Senvion keeping an R&D base in Germany. The company plays a dominant role in the Indian market with an average market share of about 40% according to the data of the windfarm database. Currently it has production facilities in India and China.

4.2.5 Spain

Spain had an onshore wind capacity of 23 GW in 2016 and a share of almost 18% of wind energy in total electricity output (see Table 1). Its wind onshore generation potential lies just above 3 PWh with a yearly electricity output of around 300 TWh. Due to the loss of political support, the Spanish wind energy market has collapsed in the last few years, turning it into one of the unstable markets.

Political support in Spain started with the first Renewable Energy Plan in 1986. This plan and its successor introduced targets for renewable energy production and investment that focused largely on demonstration projects. The first feed-in tariff system was introduced in 1994. However, the design of this first tariff system did not have the desired effect on the renewable energy market. As a result the Electric Power Act of 1997 introduced a number of significant changes that resulted in a relatively long phase of stable market development (IRENA 2012). This phase ended when the system was adjusted in 2010 and then ceased in 2014 after Spain was severely affected by the global financial crisis in 2009 (IEA/IRENA 2018).

Unfortunately, data for the Spanish market could not be found for the time prior to 1998. From 1998 to 2017 the Spanish market has gone through one cycle with the market falling from almost 2.5 GW in 2009 to zero in 2015. In the last couple of years the demand has picked up very slowly again indicating the beginning of a new period of potential growth (see Fig. 10).

During the market development, four Spanish wind turbine manufacturers entered the market successfully. One reason for this development of national manufacturers can be attributed to local content requirements at that time that were introduced by some Spanish regions in connection with concession tenders (OECD 2015). Those requirements in combination with the strong market development also led to the establishment of two production locations of international wind turbine manufacturers in Spain in 2005. In 2007, at the height of the Spanish market development, Alstom (FR) bought Ecotecnia. The production as well as the headquarters remained in Spain. The crash of the Spanish market in combination with the

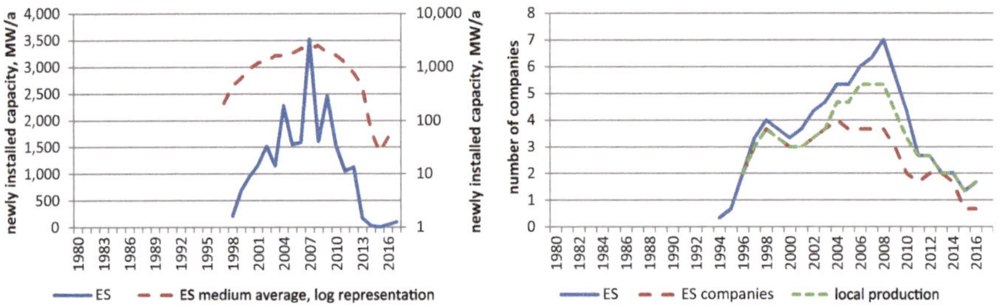

Fig. 10 left: Development of newly installed wind onshore capacity in ES (own representation based on GWEC 2018, BP 2018), right: Development of number of companies in the Spanish wind onshore market; ES refers to all companies active in the Spanish market, ES companies refers to companies that are based in Spain, local production refers to companies with a production site in Spain (own representation based on The Wind Power 2018) (Data on the market development prior to 1998 could not be determined).

global financial crisis inevitably had an influence on most of the other Spanish companies. Acciona Windpower was sold to Nordex in 2016, while Gamesa merged with Siemens in 2017.

A statistical analysis of the formative phase of the Spanish wind industry cannot be conducted as numbers on the market development were not available before 1998. By that time Spanish companies were already established. However, the shake-out phase between 2009 and 2016 was statistically analyzed (see Annex). The regression finds an adjusted R^2 of 0.54 for the Spanish market development with a positive interrelation between the two decreasing indicators. The additional consideration of the rest of the global market increases the explanatory value to 0.84. However, the interrelation of the global market development outside of Spain with the Spanish wind industry is negative. The values for the number of companies with local production are at 0.88 and 0.87 respectively. Overall, this analysis shows a considerable influence of the national market development on the consolidation of the Spanish wind industry.

The one Spanish turbine manufacturers that shows up in the top 10 of global companies is Gamesa. It was founded in 1994 at the beginning of wind utilization in Spain with Vestas being involved as technical partner holding a share of 40% of the company. This joint venture can be attributed to the local content requirements of Spanish regional energy policies at that time. It enabled Vestas to get access to the Spanish market as a whole (IRENA 2012). In 2017 Gamesa was merged with Siemens to form Siemens-Gamesa.

4.2.6 China

The Chinese wind energy market is currently by far the largest in the world. About 147 GW were installed until 2016, about one third of the global capacity. Chinas overall electricity output is also the largest in the world with about 6 PWh per year of

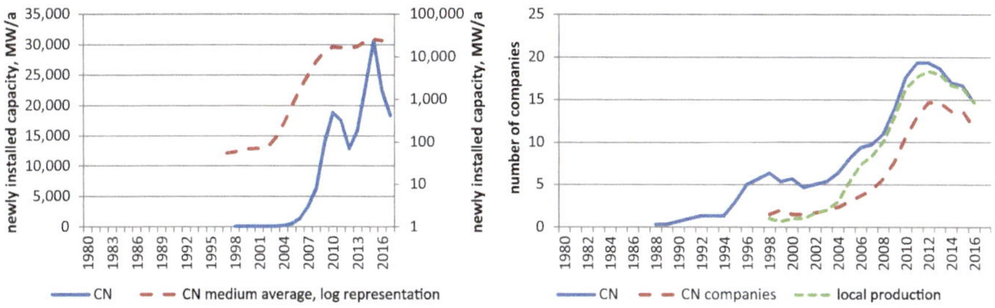

Fig. 11 left: Development of newly installed wind onshore capacity in CN (own representation based on GWEC 2018, BP 2018), right: Development of number of companies in the Chinese wind onshore market; CN refers to all companies active in the Chinese market, CN companies refers to companies that are based in China, local production refers to companies with a production site in China (own representation based on The Wind Power 2018)(Data on the market development prior to 1998 could not be determined).

which about 3.2% are provided by wind energy. The yearly wind onshore generation potential is estimated to be around 34 PWh (see Table 1 and Table 2). Up to this point, wind market conditions in China can be regarded as relatively stable.

China is often considered to be the country that successfully managed to catch-up in many technologies. This also applies for wind energy. In China the five year plans of the government are the foundation of political support. In the Ninth five year plan a first basis was set to develop a national wind energy industry by introducing an R&D program in 1996. The first market pull was initialized by the "Renewable Energy Law of the People's Republic of China" in 2005 which led to the introduction of feed-in tariffs in 2009 (Wang et al. 2012, Klagge et al. 2012).

Due to this support system the Chinese market has seen an exponential growth for a good few years with levels between 12 GW and 31 GW per year since 2009, in which the Chinese market covered more than one third of the yearly global market. The decline in installations in 2012 that can be seen in Fig. 11 can be explained by the change in approval procedures which were introduced due to grid congestions.

The number of companies active on the Chinese market has steadily risen along with the market development. The statistical analysis of the period between 1999 and 2012 provides an adjusted R^2 of 0.91 for the development of national based companies that is not improved by the integration of the rest of the world (see Annex). The development of companies with local production in China amounts to an adjusted R^2 of 0.92 which is increased to 0.97 including the rest of the world.

The development of the number of companies indicates that the Chinese market has possibly entered a phase of maturation. A consolidation of manufacturers has started that will presumably continue in the coming years (see Fig. 11). The statistical analysis of these last four years has to be treated with caution due to the low number of observations. It shows no significance or relevant coefficient of determination for the national companies or companies with local production in China.

The development of the wind industry in China follows the same pattern as in India. The beginning of market development was strongly influenced by global wind industry players followed by the rise of national companies that acquired their technologies through licenses and joint ventures (Lewis and Wiser 2007; Lewis 2011; Wang et al. 2012). Local content requirements were introduced in 2003 that led to the development of manufacturing locations of international companies in China (OECD 2015).

Regarding the development of a national industry, China has succeeded in establishing three of the top 10 global wind turbine manufacturers. The largest player on the Chinese market with an average market share of 23% since 2002 is Goldwind. It was founded in 1998 with a production agreement of a 600 kW turbine from Jacobs (DE) followed by a license to produce a 750 kW turbine of RePower. In 2003 Goldwind signed a cooperation agreement with Vensys, a wind technology developer in Germany, of which it acquired the majority in 2008 (Maegaard et al. 2013).

Next to Goldwind there are a number of Chinese wind turbine manufacturers, of which most started their business between 2006 and 2009. Many of these companies started of using technology from second or third tier wind companies from more advanced wind energy markets, often using one form or another of technology transfer mechanism. However, most of them have moved on and are developing their own technology by now even though there might be doubt that the degree of innovation is as high as it might be expected (Lewis and Wiser 2007; Lewis 2011; Wang et al. 2012; Maegaard et al. 2013; Lam et al. 2017; Quitzow et al. 2017; Sahu 2018). The two currently showing up in the top 10 are Guodian United Power which was founded in 2009 as a subsidiary of one of the largest Chinese power suppliers and Envision which started its business in 2008.

4.2.7 Comparison of national developments

The comparison of the six countries analyzed so far shows that industry life cycles can be identified on a national level. Even though all of them seem to have entered a phase of maturation they differ in the point in time when the development has started and when the third phase of maturity was reached. Also it became evident that a interdependency exists between the development of the market and its respective players. The formation phase of the national wind industries shows a particularly strong coefficient of determination with the market development for most of the analyzed countries. However, no uniform statements can be made with regard to the shake-out phase. A relevant interrelation between market development and industrial development could only be shown in those cases in which a strong market decline was observed. This leads to the conclusion that a decline of national markets reduces national players earlier and maybe even further than under stable market conditions. The early shake out of companies also seems to have a lasting effect as a renewed upturn in the market in Denmark or the US did not seem to increase the number of local companies significantly.

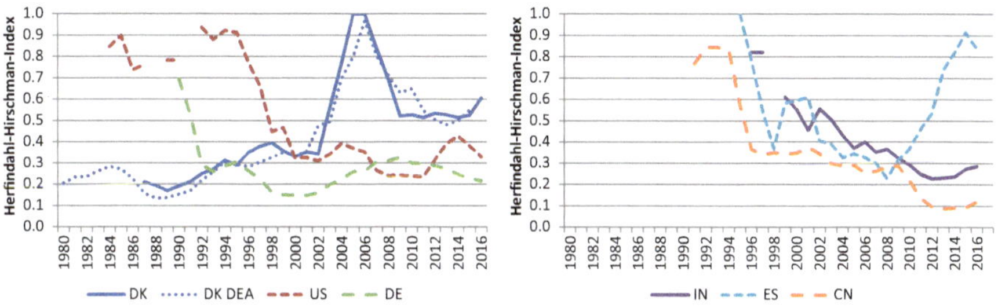

Fig. 12 Market concentration in selected wind onshore markets (own representation based on The Wind Power 2018, Danish Energy Agency 2017)

Looking at the development of market concentration on these national markets (see Fig. 12) in comparison to the market concentration on the global onshore wind market (see Fig. 4 d) it can be seen that they do not have the same level of competitiveness as the global market. Those markets with instable market developments also show higher levels of market concentration. At the same time a relatively high market concentration could be determined even in the markets with stable market development. Each one of those markets has one to two relevant national players that dominate the market they are based in. This indicates that national players have a better market position in their home market than their international competitors. This aspect will be further analyzed by looking into the other six national markets that were selected in Table 1 that are not home to one of the global top 10 companies.

Figure 13 displays the same indicators as Fig. 4. Three countries are presented together in one graph. On the left hand side the developments of the UK (GB), Canada (CA) and France (FR) are shown. Brazil (BR), Ireland (IE) and Portugal (PT) are displayed on the right hand side. The development of each of these countries is shown as of 1998 as no earlier data was available.

On the left hand side, the UK,[4] Canada[5] and France have all had a relatively stable market development and seem to have reached the phase of maturation (see Fig. 13 a) and b)). The development of the companies' active in each one of those markets also supports the observation that these countries have reached a phase of maturation (see Fig. 13 c)). Of the three countries only France has seen a small development of national wind turbine manufacturers. While Canada has tried to establish local production of onshore wind turbine manufacturers by implementing local content requirements in its political support systems, the UK and France have put their focus

[4]The strong increase of installations in the UK in 2017 can be traced back to the change in the political support system. Developers seem to have tried to meet the deadline so that their projects still have access to the old support regime. A similar effect was seen in Germany and India, as indicated above.

[5]The strong decrease in installations in Canada in 2017 cannot be explained. There is no indication that the Canadian wind market is not supported by the political regime. Therefore installations in 2018 should pick up again.

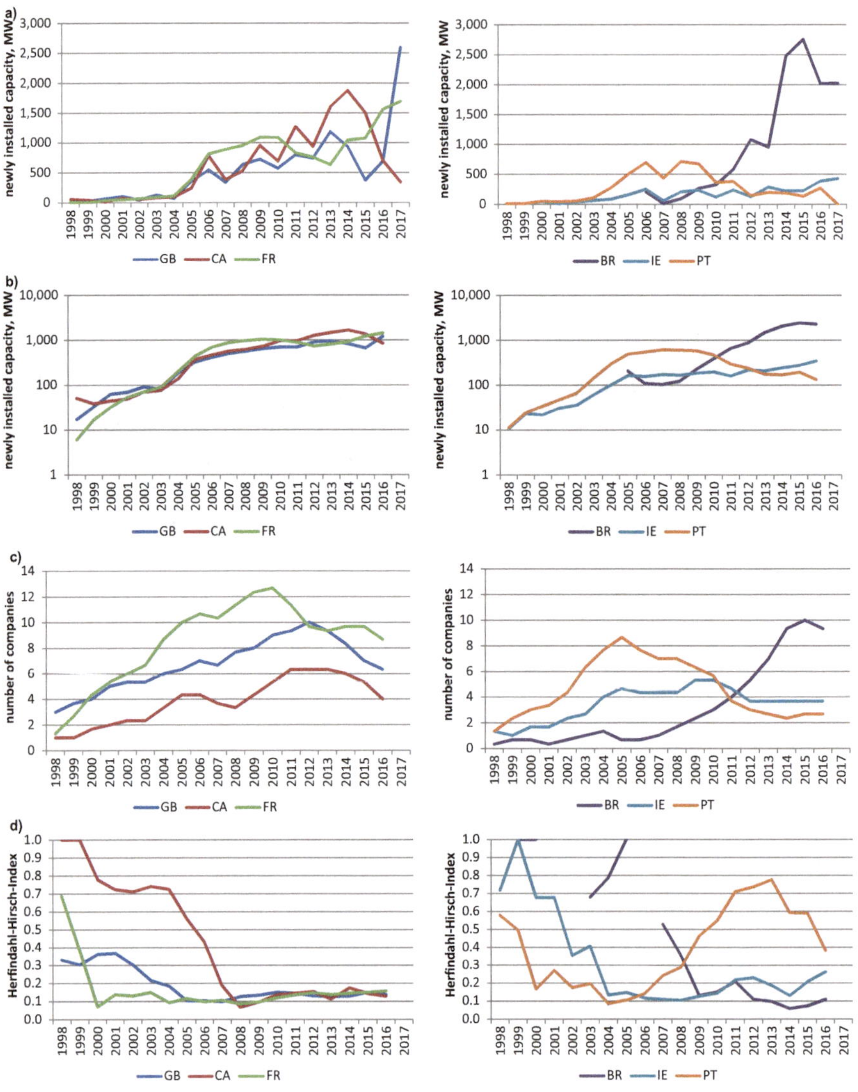

Fig. 13 **a** Development of newly installed wind onshore capacity in selected markets (own representation based on GWEC 2018, BP 2018), **b** Logarithmic representation of the development of newly installed capacity, moving average (see Fig. 6 a) **c** Development of number of companies in selected wind onshore markets (own representation based on The Wind Power 2018), **d** Market concentration in selected wind onshore markets (own representation based on The Wind Power 2018)

on the establishment of an offshore wind industry and did not introduce local content requirements for the onshore market. The results are not that different; two international wind turbine manufacturers opened manufacturing locations in Canada whereas one each established a production site in the UK and France.

On the right hand side of Fig. 13 two different types of markets are displayed. The Brazilian market has a large potential for the utilization of wind power whereas Ireland and Portugal have good wind resources but electricity demand is low. Ireland's electricity demand in 2015 was 5% that of the Brazilian market and Portugal's 9% (see Table 2).

Looking at the development of the Brazilian ILC it is not clear if Brazil is currently still in its growth phase as it shows some signs of maturation.[6] So far, all political support schemes for wind energy introduced in Brazil had very high local content requirements (IRENA 2012). Several companies have set up production facilities in Brazil and two Brazilian wind turbine manufacturers emerged, one being a subsidiary of Enercon (DE).

The markets in Ireland[7] and Portugal[8] on the other hand already entered the maturation phase in the mid-2000s. The Irish wind market is exclusively served by imported wind turbines whereas two international wind manufacturers opened production facilities in Portugal which might be attributed to local content requirements introduced in 2005.

Looking at the market concentration of the six markets displayed in Fig. 13, it can be seen that a much higher level of competition is reached in each one of those markets than in the ones displayed in Fig. 12 (see Fig. 13 d)). The market concentration in the Brazilian market has reached a similar low level as in the other three examples on the left hand side of the figure. The market concentration in Ireland and Portugal, however, seems not to be as low and stable. Looking into the data more closely it can be observed that these two markets are on a level of market size at which individual wind farms have a large influence on the overall numbers.

In order to find an explanation as of why the countries without one of the top 10 global wind turbine manufacturers seem to have a more competitive market situation than the ones with a successful global player, an analysis of the market shares of companies in each respective market was conducted.

Figure 14 shows the cumulative market shares of companies from different countries over time in different markets. The companies that are based in the country under examination are referred to as local companies and are displayed first. The countries with one of the top 10 wind turbine manufacturers are displayed in the graph on the left hand side, the ones without on the right.

What can be observed immediately is that the capacities for the markets in the left graph are largely provided by local companies. The countries in the right graph have hardly any to none local companies that supplied the markets with wind turbines. Again it needs to be stressed that this does not mean that no production sites can be

---

[6]The Brazilian wind market development is not fully represented in the graph. It started in 2002 with the introduction of a feed in tariff system that was replaced by a series of tenders in 2009.

[7]The Irish development started in 1993 with tenders that were replaced by a feed-in tariff system in 2006. Just like in Germany and India the feed-in tariff system is to be replaced by tenders, which explains the relatively strong expansion in the last two years.

[8]It cannot be explained why no onshore installations were seen in Portugal in 2017. However, Portugal has already exceeded its wind energy goals for 2020.

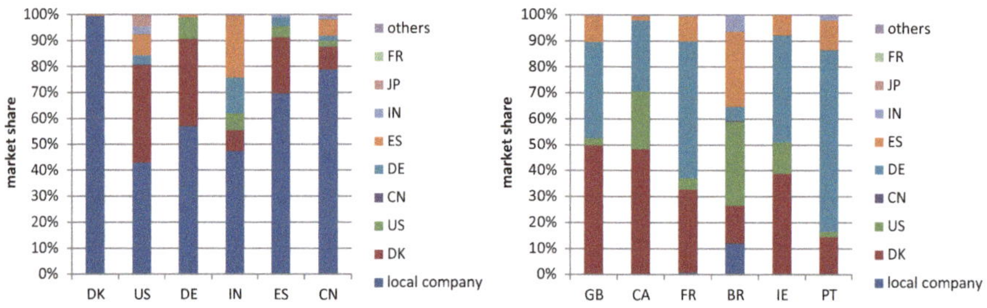

Fig. 14 Market share of companies based in different countries on selected markets (own representation based on The Wind Power 2018)

found in those countries. The difference is that these production sites are run by companies based in other countries. These results therefore show that a stronger market concentration can be expected in markets that have succeeded to establish their own companies.

Another aspect which can be seen in Fig. 8 is the role of the size of a market in the global company rankings. Chinese companies for example of which three are in the top 10 global wind turbine manufacturers are mainly active in their home market. As the Chinese wind turbine market has had extraordinary growth in the last few years, it is not surprising that the engagement of Chinese companies was limited in other national markets. However, it shows that the entrance of a large market like the Chinese, that is by far the largest in the world, can be sufficient to change the ranking of global players without the other companies losing their relevance in other national developments.

5 Conclusions

The analysis of the industry life cycle of the wind energy sector has shown that the global development of wind energy markets as well as market participants derives from the sum of individual national developments. Each national market has an influence on the development of the global market. How strong this influence is depends on the size of the national market in comparison to the global market in each year. However, the relevance of the national perspective regarding the industrial development cannot be seen in the research that focuses on the creation of innovation. The results of this research indicate that the creation of innovation is subject to a global knowledge base (Huenteler et al. 2016). Therefore, the question as to which geographical boundaries are important for the ILC in a globalized world cannot be answered unequivocally. Knowledge and the creation of innovation generally seem to be distributed globally whereas market creation and industrial development are strongly influenced by national developments.

Looking at the national level a few different findings should be pointed out. Regarding the development phases of the wind industry life cycle, it could be observed that all the countries analyzed in this paper have reached the various stages at different points in time. Regarding the development paths various insights can be gained. First of all there were national wind markets with relatively stable market conditions. The development of these markets as well as the development of the number of companies active on these markets did follow the path described by Klepper's (1997) ILC theory. Other national markets did not have the same stability in political support which resulted in an unstable demand for wind turbines. Especially changes in effective support systems created an escalating demand followed by a strong reduction in the market. The development of those markets followed a number of cycles that included all four phases described by the PLC theory (see Levitt 1965). What is particularly noteworthy is the relevance of the forth development phase in this context. Usually it is only relevant for industries and their technologies that disappear from a market. In the case of the wind industry the relevance of the technology for the energy market remains high. However, the consequences of market decline for the industry providing the technology were extensive. Those countries that had been able to establish their own wind turbine manufacturers saw an early consolidation of their firms that reduced national players dramatically. This led to a higher concentration on the respective markets. Even though the market concentration was reduced in later phases of market expansion once again, the dominating role of the few companies that remained after the initial shakeout phase persisted. Also, once a national market had seen a severe consolidation of its local market players, new company formations in later cycles never even closely reached the level of the first cycle again. Another interesting aspect is the dominance of home based companies. Those countries that succeed in establishing domestic wind turbine manufacturers did see a higher market concentration than those without. This is the case for all countries, regardless of the stability of their respective market development.

Looking at the establishment of companies quite a few different insights could be gained. After the initial introduction of wind energy technology in the lead market Denmark around 1980, the potential of each respective market and its stable development seem to have been a very important factor in the success to establish national based companies. The importance of this factor appears to be growing as companies from other countries get established on the global market. The Spanish market for example was able to provide enough potential for its own industry to develop in the mid-90s whereas ten years later similar market developments in countries like Italy, France, UK, South Africa, Chile or Mexico did not initiate the same dynamic. The Chinese market on the other hand was able to create its own industry around that time. The sheer size of the Chinese market even made it possible that companies that are basically only active in their home market show up in the top ranking of global players. The aspect of national market size therefore seems to be an issue that needs to be addressed in further research regarding catch-up cycles in industrial leadership.

Another factor that seems to influence the ability to establish a local value chain is the proximity to countries that already have succeeded in their efforts. As the number of countries active in a technology is growing this factor gains importance. After the successful establishment of Danish, German and Spanish companies no other European country has succeeded in establishing its own wind companies. The same goes for Canada which does have a relatively large market potential but is located in close vicinity to the already established US wind market. Another example is South Korea. Five large international Korean based technology companies tried to enter the wind turbine market around 2010, so far none of them succeeded as the Chinese market and its established value chain dominates the industrial development in this region.

Policy approaches to establish a home based wind turbine industry are essentially based on the creation of a national market with the help of different support mechanisms often combined with direct or indirect local content requirements. Most of these approaches are focused on the onshore wind market but some countries have started to focus on the establishment of companies and value chains in the new offshore wind trajectory. This can especially be seen in Europe where the onshore wind value chain is already established and market dynamics do not seem to leave much room for further expansion. The question of the effects of local content requirements on the industrial development is too large to be answered in this paper. However, the findings do indicate that local content requirements only had a secondary effect on the establishment of wind turbine manufacturers. The two aspects of market potential and the proximity to markets with established value chains do seem to have a larger influence on the strategic location decisions of companies.

Another aspect that can be added to the findings are the approaches of companies to either gain access to the wind energy technology in the catch-up process or on the flipside the approaches of companies to gain excess to new markets. The historic development of various companies described in this paper shows that technological knowledge was widely acquired from the knowledge base of already existent markets due to collaborations, licensing production or company acquisition. The acquisition of already established companies was especially chosen by large technology groups. As wind energy was introduced by a bottom up approach large technology groups entered the market at a later point in time, mostly when their home markets showed a relatively reliable market development. The role of the technology introduced by Vestas in the creation of many companies stands out especially. The very open approach to share the knowledge regarding their technology derives from the background this company originated in. It could be argued that this open approach contributed to the successful introduction of wind energy technology on a global level by helping to avoid potential obstacles that might have had a negative effect on the acceptance and therefore would have slowed down the diffusion. The reasons for companies to cooperate or hand out licenses for the production of their technologies can be explained by strategic considerations. The wind turbine industry in its beginning consisted of small to medium enterprises that tried to enter new arising markets and at the same time limit the risks that come with those expansions. Collaborations were the initial approach to enter new markets beyond exports, often initiated by local content requirements. As successful turbine manufacturers started to set up their own production facilities in other countries their need for collaborations was reduced. However, second or third tier wind companies from more advanced wind energy markets continued to provide technological collaborations for companies in other countries that were interested in investing in wind energy technology. Another strand of companies that evolved in the aftermath of the initial establishment of wind energy production in some established countries were engineering companies that often had strong links to research institutions. These companies develop and design wind turbines to sell licenses for production. For the most part these licenses were not bought by national wind turbine manufacturers as they already had their own technology at hand. Also, no new wind turbine manufacturers tried to enter those markets as laggards had difficulties to establish in their home markets that were dominated by already established national companies. Therefore, the licenses were mainly sold to companies in emerging markets.

Regarding the relocation of production to countries with cost advantages in later stages of ILCs as mentioned in literature (Vernon 1966, 1979), no such development could be observed in wind energy so far. The proximity to the respective national markets that set of an industry development does seem to remain important even in the maturity phase of the ILC. One reason might be the market position local companies have in their home countries; another might be the innovation base of those countries. One circumstance that supports this thesis is that Suzlon maintained an R&D location in Germany even after leaving the German market by selling Senvion.

It cannot be answered so far if the findings in this paper hold true for other technologies and their industries with changing political support that results in unstable market conditions. This question will have to be subject to further research.

Also, it should be stressed that this paper does not try to argue that industrial development solely depends on market development. As Porter (1990) has shown in his diamond model there are many more factors that influence the success of a nations industry.

However, the paper shows that fundamental changes in political support for wind energy not only had an effect on the market development, as discussed in literature, but also on the national based industry that provides the technology. This aspect should be taken into consideration in the further development of policy frameworks for wind energy.

Publisher's note Springer Nature remains neutral with regard to jurisdictional claims in published maps and institutional affiliations.

Funding information Open Access funding provided by Projekt DEAL.

Compliance with ethical standards The work was carried out within the framework of two research projects: a) "Network analysis and simulation of innovation dynamics of new key technologies in the energy sector" (03ET4032B) funded by the German Federal Ministry of Economic Affairs and Energy within the scope of the 6th Energy Research Programme of the Federal Government; b) "The 'System integration' Kopernikus project: Energiewende navigation system" (03ET4032B) funded by the German Federal Ministry of Education and Research.

Annex

Regression Statistics

Global

	1978–1985⁺	1986–1993	1994-2000⁺	2001-2003	2004-2011	2012-2016
	I	*II*	*III*	*IV*	*V*	*VI*
R^2	0.98	0.56	0.97	0.15	0.99	0.93
Adjusted R^2	0.97	0.49	0.96	−0.70	0.98	0.90
Standard Error	1.63	4.32	0.82	1.09	1.45	2.51
Observations (n)	8	8	7	3	8	5
Coefficients						
Intercept	7.1501446	32.4083155	−29.4901785	27.4819094	14.4185171	97.1406868
global MW/a	3.65433***	−0.04468*	6.63432***	−0.00033	0.00096***	−0.00117**

⁺ln(MW/a)
***$p < 0.001$ **$p < 0.01$ *$p < 0.05$.$p < 0.1$

Denmark

Domestic companies.

	1978–1989⁺	1990–1993	1994-1997	1998-2006	2007–2016
	I	*II*	*III*	*IV*	*V*
R^2	0.95	0.87	0.78	0.78	0.83
Adjusted R^2	0.94	0.81	0.67	0.75	0.81
Standard Error	1.11	1.59	0.60	1.72	0.20
Observations (n)	12	4	4	9	10
Coefficients					
Intercept	7.7706191	−3.2016369	9.8155185	1.0315811	1.2720830
DK MW/a	2.65148***	0.29747.	0.00940	0.01862**	0.00526**

⁺ln(MW/a)
***$p < 0.001$ **$p < 0.01$ *$p < 0.05$.$p < 0.1$

	1978–1989⁺	1990–1993	1994–1997	1998–2006	2007–2016
	I	*II*	*III*	*IV*	*V*
R^2	0.97	0.92	0.99	0.85	0.95
Adjusted R^2	0.96	0.75	0.97	0.80	0.94
Standard Error	0.92	1.81	0.17	1.51	0.11
Observations (n)	12	4	4	9	10
Coefficients					
Intercept	8.1987535	19.6636503	20.3982751	6.6702630	0.6923504
DK MW/a	3.13822***	0.00913	0.08060	0.00750	0.00181
global w/o DK MW/a	−0.42306*	−0.02847	−0.02077	−0.00048	0.00003**

⁺ln(MW/a)
***$p < 0.001$ **$p < 0.01$ *$p < 0.05$.$p < 0.1$

United States of America

Domestic companies.

	1982–1984⁺	1985–1994	1995-2011	2012-2016
	I	*II*	*III*	*IV*
R^2	0.95	0.96	0.89	0.02
Adjusted R^2	0.90	0.95	0.88	−0.31
Standard Error	0.41	0.42	0.44	1.52
Observations (n)	3	10	17	5
Coefficients				
Intercept	−1.4984664	−0.5957625	0.6492829	3.4918708
US MW/a	1.73805	0.02048***	0.00038***	−0.00015

⁺ln(MW/a)
***p < 0.001 **p < 0.01 *p < 0.05 .p < 0.1

	1982–1984⁺	1985–1994	1995–2011	2012–2016
	I	*II*	*III*	*IV*
R^2	1.00	0.96	0.98	0.99
Adjusted R^2	65,535.00	0.95	0.97	0.99
Standard Error	0.00	0.45	0.20	0.15
Observations (n)	3	10	17	5
Coefficients				
Intercept	−3.3166250	−0.6684231	0.3794422	10.8225960
US MW/a	2.39867	0.02073***	−0.00005	−0.00001
global w/o US MW/a	−0.88424	0.00021	0.00014***	−0.00020**

⁺ln(MW/a)
***p < 0.001 **p < 0.01 *p < 0.05 .p < 0.1

Companies with local production.

	1982–1984⁺	1985–1994	1995-2011	2012-2016
	I	*II*	*III*	*IV*
R^2	0.95	0.96	0.95	0.02
Adjusted R^2	0.90	0.95	0.94	−0.31
Standard Error	0.41	0.42	0.78	2.34
Observations (n)	3	10	17	5
Coefficients				
Intercept	−1.4984664	−0.5957625	0.2147455	8.2019536
US MW/a	1.73805	0.02048***	0.00101***	−0.00022

⁺ln(MW/a)
***p < 0.001 **p < 0.01 *p < 0.05 .p < 0.1

	1982–1984⁺	1985–1994	1995–2011	2012–2016
	I	*II*	*III*	*IV*
R^2	1.00	0.96	0.99	0.99
Adjusted R^2	65,535.00	0.95	0.99	0.98
Standard Error	0.00	0.45	0.40	0.27
Observations (n)	3	10	17	5
Coefficients				
Intercept	−3.3166250	−0.6684231	−0.2529145	19.5261266
US MW/a	2.39867	0.02073***	0.00025.	0.000004
global w/o US MW/a	−0.88424	0.00021	0.00024***	−0.00032**

⁺ln(MW/a)
***$p < 0.001$ **$p < 0.01$ *$p < 0.05$.$p < 0.1$

Germany

Domestic companies.

	1990–2000⁺		2001–2016	
	I	*II*	*III*	*IV*
R^2	0.95	0.97	0.16	0.38
Adjusted R^2	0.95	0.97	0.10	0.28
Standard Error	0.64	0.49	0.70	0.62
Observations (n)	11	11	16	16
Coefficients				
Intercept	−7.3283847	−11.8280241	6.3553076	6.4290006
DE MW/a	2.04183***	0.67033	−0.00030	−0.00009
global w/o DE MW/a		1.92694*		−0.00002*

⁺ln(MW/a)
***$p < 0.001$ **$p < 0.01$ *$p < 0.05$.$p < 0.1$

Companies with local production.

	1990–2000⁺		2001–2016	
	I	*II*	*III*	*IV*
R^2	0.95	0.98	0.12	0.35
Adjusted R^2	0.94	0.98	0.06	0.25
Standard Error	0.84	0.56	0.69	0.62
Observations (n)	11	11	16	16
Coefficients				
Intercept	−9.8408745	−16.5093094	8.2586761	8.3303722
DE MW/a	2.65364***	0.62109	−0.00025	−0.00005
global w/o DE MW/a		2.85570**		−0.00002.

⁺ln(MW/a)
***$p < 0.001$ **$p < 0.01$ *$p < 0.05$.$p < 0.1$

India

Domestic companies.

	1995–2009		2010–2016	
	I	*II*	*III*	*IV*
R^2	0.50	0.90	0.22	0.58
Adjusted R^2	0.46	0.89	0.07	0.37
Standard Error	0.98	0.45	0.61	0.50
Observations (n)	15	15	7	7
Coefficients				
Intercept	0.8442831	0.7871978	5.0804225	6.6257236
IN MW/a	0.00140**	−0.00070.	−0.00062	0.00019
global w/o IN MW/a		0.00018***		−0.00008

***$p < 0.001$ **$p < 0.01$ *$p < 0.05$.$p < 0.1$

Companies with local production.

	1995–2009		2010–2016	
	I	*II*	*III*	*IV*
R^2	0.67	0.93	0.32	0.52
Adjusted R^2	0.64	0.92	0.19	0.29
Standard Error	1.27	0.60	0.52	0.48
Observations (n)	15	15	7	7
Coefficients				
Intercept	0.9633491	0.8900610	7.8375969	8.8880006
IN MW/a	0.00256***	−0.00014	−0.00067	−0.00012
global w/o IN MW/a		0.00022***		−0.00006

***$p < 0.001$ **$p < 0.01$ *$p < 0.05$.$p < 0.1$

Spain

Domestic companies.

	2009–2016	
	I	*II*
R^2	0.61	0.89
Adjusted R^2	0.54	0.84
Standard Error	0.52	0.30
Observations (n)	8	8
Coefficients		
Intercept	1.0961985	7.2266962
ES MW/a	0.00080*	−0.00040
global w/o ES MW/a		−0.00012*

***$p < 0.001$ **$p < 0.01$ *$p < 0.05$.$p < 0.1$

Companies with local production.

	2009–2016	
	I	*II*
R^2	0.89	0.91
Adjusted R^2	0.88	0.87
Standard Error	0.34	0.35
Observations (n)	8	8
Coefficients		
Intercept	1.553632	3.369052
ES MW/a	0.00124***	0.00088.
global w/o ES MW/a		−0.00004

***p < 0.001 **p < 0.01 *p < 0.05 .p < 0.1

China

Domestic companies.

	1999–2012		2013–2016	
	I	*II*	*III*	*IV*
R^2	0.92	0.92	0.34	0.61
Adjusted R^2	0.91	0.91	0.02	−0.17
Standard Error	1.40	1.39	1.25	1.36
Observations (n)	14	14	4	4
Coefficients				
Intercept	1.594155	0.439332	18.107248	23.467314
CN MW/a	0.00064***	0.00050**	−0.00021	−0.00007
global w/o CN MW/a		0.00014		−0.00032

***p < 0.001 **p < 0.01 *p < 0.05 .p < 0.1

Companies with local production.

	1999–2012		2013–2016	
	I	*II*	*III*	*IV*
R^2	0.93	0.97	0.59	0.77
Adjusted R^2	0.92	0.97	0.38	0.30
Standard Error	1.86	1.18	1.18	1.26
Observations (n)	14	14	4	4
Coefficients				
Intercept	2.662406	−1.056491	23.829339	29.048575
CN MW/a	0.00093***	0.00048**	−0.00033	−0.00019
global w/o CN MW/a		0.00046**		−0.00031

***p < 0.001 **p < 0.01 *p < 0.05 .p < 0.1

References

Abernathy WJ, Utterback JM (1975) A dynamic model of process and product innovation. OMEGA, The international Journal of Management Science 3(6):639–656

Abernathy WJ, Utterback JM (1978) Patterns of industrial innovation. Technol Rev 80(7):40–47

Agarwal R, Echambadi R, Sarkar MB (2002) The conditioning effect of time on firm survival: a life cycle approach. Acad Manag J 45(8):971–994

Batlle C, Pérez-Arriaga IJ, Zambrano-Barragán P (2012) Regulatory design for RES-E support mechanisms: learning curves, market structure, and burden-sharing. Energy Policy 41 (2012):212–220

Beise M (2004) Lead markets: country-specific drivers of the global diffusion of innovations. Res Policy 33(6–7):997–1018

Beise, M, Rennings, K (2003): Lead markets of environmental innovations: a framework for innovation and environmental economics. ZEW discussion paper no. 03-01, Mannheim

Bento N, Fontes M (2015) The construction of a new technological innovation system in a follower country: wind energy in Portugal. Technological Forecasting and Social Change, Volume 99:197–2010

Bergek A, Jacobsson S (2003) The emergence of a growth industry: a comparative analysis of the German, Dutch and Swedish wind turbine industries. In: Metcalfe JS, Cantner U (eds) Change, transformation and development. Physica, Heidelberg

Bergek A, Jacobsson S (2010) Are tradeable green certificates a cost-efficient policy driving technical change or a rent-generating machine? Lessons from Sweden 2003-2008. Energy Policy 38(2010):1255–1271

Bergek A, Jacobsson S, Carlsson B, Lindmark S, Rickne A (2008) Analyzing the functional dynamics of technological innovation systems: a scheme of analysis. Res Policy 37:407–429

Berkley LAB (2017): Annual U.S. Turbine Installation Capacity by Original Equipment Manufacturer (OEM) 1990-2016. Based on wind technologies market report, personal information from mark Bolinger, Lawrence Berkeley National Laboratory, 21.12.2017

Binz C, Truffer B (2017) Global innovation systems – a conceptual framework for innovation dynamics in transnational contexts. Res Policy 46(2017):1284–1298

BMWi (2018) Time series for the development of renewable energy sources in Germany – based on statistical data from the Working Group on Renewable Energy- Statistics (AGEE-Stat). Federal Ministry for Economic Affairs and Energy, https://www.erneuerbareenergien.de/EE/Navigation/DE/Service/Erneuerbare_Energien_in_Zahlen/Zeitreihen/zeitreihen.html

BP (2018): Statistical review of world energy. https://www.bp.com/en/global/corporate/energy-economics/statistical-review-of-world-energy.html

BTM/Navigant (2017): World Wind Energy Market Updates. https://www.navigantresearch.com/research/world-wind-energy-market-update-2017

Bürer MJ, Wüstenhagen R (2009) Which renewable energy policy is a venture capitalist's best friend? Empirical evidence from a survey of international cleantech inventors. Energy Policy 37 (2009):4997–5006

Carlsson B, Stankiewicz R (1991) On the nature, function and composition of technological systems. Evol Econ 1:93–118

Carlsson B, Jacobsson S, Holmén M, Rickne A (2002) Innovation systems: analytical and methodological issues. Res Policy 31:233–245

Clark KB (1985) The Interaction of Design Hierarchies and Market Concepts in Technological Evolution. Risomb Policy 14:235–251

CWEA (2017): Annual report of China wind power installed capacity statistics (2002-2016). Chinese wind energy association (CWEA)

Danish Energy Agency (2017): Stamdataregister for vindkraftanlæg, ultimo september 2017, https://ens.dk/service/statistik-data-noegletal-og-kort/data-oversigt-over-energisektoren

Darmani A, Arvidsson N, Hidalgo A, Albors J (2014) What drives the development of renewable energy technologies? Toward a typology for the systemic drivers. Renew Sust Energ Rev 38 (2014):834–847

Davies A (1997) The life cycle of a complex product. Int J Innov Manag 1(3):229–256

Dewald U, Truffer B (2011) Market formation in technological innovation systems-diffusion of photovoltaic applications in Germany. Ind Innovation 18:285–300

DEWI (2017) Wind energy use in Germany 1992–2016. Deutsches Windenergie Institut https://industries.ul.com/energy/wind

Dosi G (1982) Technological paradigms and technological trajectories – a suggested interpretation of the determinants and directions of technical change. Res Policy 11(1982):147–162

Douthwaite B (2002) Enabling innovation – a practical guide to understanding and fostering technological change. Zed Books Ltd.

Durstewitz M, Ensslin C, Hahn B, Hoppe-Klipper M, Rohrig, K (2001) Wind energy report Germany 1999/2000. Annual evaluation of WMEP; Windenergie Report Deutschland 1999/2000. Jahresauswertung des WMEP. Germany

Enercon (2018): Historie von Enercon. https://www.enercon.de/unternehmen/historie/

EPI (2018) The great transition: shifting from fossil fuels to solar and wind energy. Earth Policy Institute http://www.earth-policy.org/?/data_center/C23/

Eurec K, Sullivan P, Gleason M, Hettinger D, Heimiller D, Lopez A (2017) An improved global wind resource estimate for integrated assessment models. Energy Econ 64:552–567

Ford D, Ryan C (1981) Taking technology to market. Harv Bus Rev 59:117–126

Freeman C (1995) The ‚national system of innovation' in historical perspective. Camb J Econ 19:5–24

GE (2018) Geschichte. GE Renewable Energy https://www.gerenewableenergy.com/de/unternehmen/uber-uns

Giachetti C, Marchi G (2010) Evolution of firms' product strategy over the life cycle of technology-based industries: A case study of the global mobile phone industry, 1980–2009. Bus Hist 52 (7):1123–1150

Gipe, P (1995): Wind energy comes of age. John Wiley & Sons, Inc, ISBN 0-471-10924-X

Gort M, Klepper S (1982) Time Paths in the Diffusion of Product Innovations. Econ J 92(367):630

Groba, F and Breitschopf, B (2013): Impact of renewable energy policy and use on innovation – a literature review. DIW discussion paper, 1318

Grubb M (2004) Technology innovation and climate change policy: an overview of issues and options. Keio Economic Studies 41(2):103–132

GWEC (2018) Global wind report 2006–2017. Global Wind Energy Council http://gwec.net/publications/global-wind-report-2/

Haas R, Panzer C, Resch G, Ragwith M, Reece G, Held A (2011) A historical review of promotion strategies for electricity from renewable energy sources in EU countries. Renewable and Sustainable Energy Review 15(2011):1003–1034

Hekkert M, Suurs RAA, Negro S, Kuhlmann S, Smits R (2007) Functions of innovation systems: a new approach for analysing technological change. Technol Forecasting Soc Change 74:413–432

Hoppe-Killper, M. (2003): Entwicklung der Windenergietechnik in Deutschland und der Einfluss staatlicher Förderpolitik-Technikentwicklung in den 90er Jahren zwischen Markt und Forschungsförderung. Dissertation, university Kassel, 2003

Huenteler J, Schmidt TS, Ossenbrink J, Hoffmann VH (2016) Technology life-cycles in the energy sector-technological characteristics and the role of deployment for innovation. In: Technological Forecasting and Social Change, Volume 104:2016

IEA (2017) World energy balances (2017 edition). In *IEA energy statistics (Beyond 20/20)*. International Energy Agency, Paris

IEA/IRENA (2018): IEA/IRENA Joint Policies and Measures database. https://www.iea.org/policiesandmeasures/renewableenergy/

IRENA (2012) 30 years of policies for wind energy – lessons from 12 wind energy markets. International Renewable Energy Agency
IRENA (2018): Renewable capacity statistics. International renewable energy agency, march 2018, ISBN: 978-92-9260-05-0
Jacobs D (2014) Policy invention as evolutionary tinkering and codification: the emergence of feed-in tariffs for renewable electricity. Environmental Politics 23(5):755–773
Jacobsson S, Bergek A (2006) A framework for guiding policy-makers intervening in emerging innovation systems in 'catching-up' countries. Eur J Dev Res 18:687–707
Jacobsson S, Johnson A (2000) The diffusion of renewable energy technology: an analytical framework and key issues for research. Energy Policy 28(2000):625–640
Jaeger, A (2013): California: wind farms retrospective. In: Maegaard, P., Krenz, A., Palz, W. (2013): wind power for the world: the rise of modern wind energy. Pan Standford series on renewable energy volume 2, Taylor & Francis Group, LLC
Jovanovic B, MacDonald GM (1994) The life cycle of a competitive industry. Journal of Political Economy 102:322–347
Karnoe P, Garud R (2012) Path-creation of Heterogeneous Ressources in the Emergence of the Danish Wind Turbine Cluster. European Planning Studies Vol. 20, No. 5, May 2012.Klagge, B., Liu, Z. and Campos Silva, P. (2012): Constructing China's wind energy innovation system. Energy Policy 50(2012):370–382
Kildegaard A (2008) Green certificate markets, the risk of over-investment, and the role of long-term contracts. Energy Policy 36(2008):3413–3421
Klein, M and Deissenroth, M (2017): When do households invest in solar photovoltaics? - An application of prospect theory. Energy policy, 109, Seiten 270-278
Klepper S (1996) Entry, exit, growth and innovation over theproduct life cycle. Am Econ Rev 86:562–583
Klepper S (1997) Industry life cycles. Ind Corp Chang 6(1):145–182
Klepper S (2002) Firm survival and the evolution of oligopoly. Rand Journal of Economics 33 (1):37–61
Klepper S, Graddy E (1990) The evolution of new industries and the determinants of market structure. RAND J Econ 21(1):27–44
Klessmann C, Held A, Rathmann M, Ragwitz M (2011) Status and perspectives of renewable energy policy and deployment in the European Union – what is needed to reach the 2020 targets? Energy Policy 39(2011):7637–7657
Kranzl L, Stadler M, Huber C, Haas R, Ragwitz M, Brakhage A, Gula A, Figorski A (2006) Deriving efficient policy portfolios promoting sustainable energy systems—Case studies applying Invert simulation tool. Renewable Energy 31(15):2393–2410
Lam LT, Branstetter L, Azevedo IML (2017) China's wind industry: leading in deployment, lagging in innovation. Energy Policy 106(2017):588–599
Lee K, Malerba F (2017) Catch-up cycles and changes in industrial leadership: windows of opportunity and responses of firms and countries in the evolution of sectoral systems. Res Policy 46(2017):338–351
Lehmann P, Creutzig F, Ehlers M-H, Friedrichsen N, Heuson C, Hith L, Pietzcker R (2012) Carbon lock-out: advancing renewable energy policy in Europe. Energies 5:323–354
Levitt T (1965) Exploit the product life cycle. Harvard Business Review, November 1965:81–94
Lewis JI (2011) Building a national wind turbine industry: experiences from China, India and South Korea. Int. J. Technology and globalisation 5(3/4):281–305
Lewis JI, Wiser RH (2007) Fostering a renewable energy technology industry: an international comparison of wind industry policy support mechanisms. Energy Policy 35(2007):1844–1857
Lund PD (2009) Effects of energy policies on industry expansion in renewable energy. Renewable Energy 34(1):53–64
Lundvall B-A (ed) (1992) National Systems of innovation: towards a theory of innovation and interactive learning. Pinter, London

Lundvall B-A, Johnson B, Andersen ES, Dalum B (2002) National systems of production, innovation and competence building. Res Policy 31(2002):213–231
Maegaard, P, Krenz, A, Palz, W (2013): Wind power for the world: the rise of modern wind energy. Pan Standford series on renewable energy volume 2, Taylor & Francis Group, LLC
Markard J, Raven R, Truffer B (2012) Sustainability transitions: an emerging field of research and its prospects. Res Policy 41:955–967
Markard J, Hekkert M, Jacobsson S (2015) The technological innovation systems framework: response to six criticisms. Environmental Innovation and Societal Transitions 16(2015):76–86
Menanteau P, Finon D, Lamy M-L (2003) Prices versus quantities: choosing policies for promoting the development of renewable energy. Energy Policy 31(2003):799–812
Menhart M, Pyka A, Ebersberger B, Hanusch H (2004) Product innovation and population dynamics in the German insurance market. Zeitschrift für die gesamte Versicherungswissenschaft 93(3):477–519
Mizuno, E (2007): Cross-border Transfer of Climate Change Mitigation Technologies: The Case of Wind Energy from Denmark and Germany to India. Dissertation, 2007 Massachusetts Institute of Technology
Negro SO, Alkemade F, Hekkert MP (2012) Why does renewable energy diffuse so slowly? A review of innovation system problems. Renew Sust Energ Rev 16(2012):3836–3846
Nemet GF (2009) Demand-pull, technology-push, and government-led incentives for non-incremental technical change. Res Policy 38(2009):700–709
Nordex (2018): 25 years of Nordex – A pionier and trailblazer in the wind industry. https://www.enercon.de/unternehmen/historie/
OECD (2015) Overcoming barriers to International Investment in Clean Energy: local-content requirements in the solar- and wind-energy global value chains. Green Finance and Investment, OECD Publishing, Paris. https://doi.org/10.1787/9789264227064-en
Porter ME (1990) The competitive advantage of nations. Free Press, New York
Quitzow R, Huenteler J, Asmussen H (2017) Development trajectories in China's wind and solar energy industries: how technology-related differences shape the dynamics of industry localization and catching up. J Clean Prod 158(2017):122–133
Sahu BK (2018) Wind energy developments and policies in China: a short review. Renewable and Sustainable Energy Revies 81(2018):1393–1405
Seto KC, Davis SJU, Mitchell RB, Stokes EC, Unruh G, ürge-Vorsatz D (2016) Carbon lock-in: types, causes, and policy implications. Annu Rev Environ Resour 41:425–452
Siemens Gamesa (2018): History. https://www.siemensgamesa.com/en-int/about-us/company-history
Stetter, D (2014). Enhancement of the REMix energy system model: global renewable energy potentials, optimized power plant siting and scenario validation
Teske S (ed) (2019) achieving the Paris climate agreement goals – global and regional 100% renewable energy scenarios with non-energy GHG pathways for +1.5°C and +2°C. Springer https://www.springer.com/la/book/9783030058425
The Wind Power (2018) Wind farm database. Status 3:2018 https://www.thewindpower.net/index.php
United Nations (2015): Paris Agreement. http://unfccc.int/paris_agreement/items/9485.php
Unruh GC (2000) Understanding carbon lock-in. Energy Policy 28(2000):817–830
Vernon R (1966) International investment and international trade in the product cycle. Q J Econ 80:190–207
Vernon R (1979) The product cycle hypothesis in the new international environment. Oxf Bull Econ Stat 41:255–267
Vestas (2018): https://www.vestas.com/en
Vestergaard, J, Brandstrup, L, Goddard, RD (2004): Industry formation and state intervention: the case of the wind turbine industry in Denmark and the United States. Published in the academy of international business (Southeast USA chapter) conference proceedings, November 2004, pp. 329-340

Wang Z, Qin H, Lewis JI (2012) China's wind power industry: policy support, technological achievements, and emerging challenges. Energy Policy 51(2012):80–88

White, W, Lunnan, A, Nybakk, E, Kulisic, B (2013): The role of governments in renewable energy: the importance of policy consistency. Biomass Bioenergy

Wieczorek AJ, Negro SO, Harmsen R, Heimeriks GJ, Luo L, Hekkert MP (2013) A review of the European offshore wind innovation system. Renew Sust Energ Rev 26(2013):294–306

Wiliamson OE (1975) Markets and Hirarchies: analysis and antitrust implications. Free Press, New York

Wind Power Monthly (2017): Top ten turbine makers of 2017. https://www.windpowermonthly.com/article/1445638/top-ten-turbine-makers-2017

On application of the precautionary principle to ban GMVs: an evolutionary model of new seed technology integration

Shyama V. Ramani and Mhamed-Ali El-Aroui

Abstract Since the 1990s, agri-biotech multinationals have introduced a radical innovation in the form of seeds derived from genetically modified plant varieties or GMVs. However, on the basis of the 'precautionary principle' that advocates ensuring a higher environmental protection through preventative decision-taking, many countries have banned the cultivation of GMVs within their territories. Thus, the objective of the present paper is to attempt to explore the rationale for application of the precautionary principle. This is done through development of an evolutionary model of farmers' technology choice incorporating intrinsic features of agriculture such as the technological obsolescence of seed varieties, impact of environmental degradation engendered by new seed technology adoption and farmers' compliance choice vis-à-vis sustainability guidelines. Further, instead of a unique representative farmer, two types of farmers are considered. The first type is driven by short term profit maximization, while the second type aims to be sustainable, by maximizing profit over the life time of the technology. Integrating the above elements and considering two possible rules for application of the precautionary principle, the paper explores the conditions under which the precautionary principle can be implemented. It demonstrates that, even under complete and perfect information the need to exercise such caution depends principally on four factors: the economic gains from GMVs, the possibilities for sustaining the production of the conventional variety in the post-GMV period via compliance, the distribution of farmers over types and the compliance-contamination burden.

Keywords GMV seed · Farmer heterogeneity · Technology obsolescence · Irreversibility · Evolutionary model · Precautionary principle · Ecology

---

S. V. Ramani (✉)
UNU-MERIT, Boschstraat 24, 6211 AX Maastricht, Netherlands
e-mail: ramani@merit.unu.edu

M.-A. El-Aroui
Rabat Business School, International University of Rabat, Technopolis, Sala-al-Jadida, 11000 Rabat, Morocco
e-mail: mhamed-ali.elaroui@uir.ac.ma

A. Pyka, K. Lee (eds.), *Innovation, Catch-up and Sustainable Development*,
Economic Complexity and Evolution, https://doi.org/10.1007/978-3-030-84931-3_16

JEL classification K32 · O30 · Q12 · Q15 · Q16

1 Introduction

Worldwide, farmers are burdened with an ever-pressing need to increase productivity. This often drives them to apply more chemical inputs such as fertilizers and pesticides, which in turn lead to substantial environmental degradation and lower soil fertility. In response, since the 1990s, agri-biotech multinationals such as Monsanto, Dupont and Syngenta have introduced a radical innovation in the form of seeds derived from genetically modified plant varieties or GMVs. With desirable traits such as pest resistance, GMVs reduce the need for agrochemicals and lessen soil and water contamination. However, many countries, notably in Europe, have banned the cultivation of GMVs within their territories on the basis of the 'precautionary principle' that advocates taking preventative measures to tackle potential threats to society. In this setting, the objective of the present paper is to attempt to explore the rationale for application of the precautionary principle to ban the diffusion of innovations such as GMVs.

The precautionary principle, which forms a part of Article 191 of the Treaty on the Functioning of the European Union, is to enable a policy response to economic activity that can pose a possible danger to human, animal or plant health, or the environment. It advocates that whenever scientific data does not permit a complete evaluation of risk, the precautionary principle may be applied as a preventive measure to curb the concerned economic activity. In other words, if an objective evaluation of a phenomenon, product or process indicates that it may pose a threat to living beings and/or the environment, the scientific uncertainty is high and/or the evaluated risk is elevated, then the precautionary principle can be evoked to address the concerned challenge.

While the precautionary principle in general is accepted worldwide, it is interpreted differently in different countries. For instance, with respect to new crop plant varieties, Europe follows a process based regulatory framework wherein the techniques used to create the innovation also determine the form of regulation, in contrast to a product-based regulatory framework, followed in the USA and Canada, which focuses only on the inherent risk of the final product. The precautionary principle can also be reinterpreted as investment in monitoring and generating knowledge about a new technology that can have unintended consequences (Miller and Engemann 2019). However, such a tailored and rationalized application assumes the existence of monitoring, regulatory and scientific capabilities, which are inadequate in many countries, especially developing ones (Adenle et al. 2018). Such diverse policy stances stem from differing scientific capabilities, regulatory prowess and societal concerns over the medium term and/or long term returns and risks of GMV.

It is important to review the precautionary principle discourse anew with respect to agriculture, because the agri-biotechnology revolution is scaling new heights with gene editing. New genome editing techniques such as 'zinc finger nucleases', 'TALENS' and 'CRISPR Cas9' allow scientists to change, delete or replace DNA more easily than ever before. It is expected that they would revolutionize agriculture and enable increases in yield, nutritive value and pest resistance, while making plants more robust to deteriorating agroecological conditions and climate change (Voytas and Gao 2014). While the final product may be even closer to the original due to gene editing, the risks of unpredictable consequences related to the process of new plant variety creation through gene editing remain similar (Caplan et al. 2015).

Presently, the European stance is supported by studies confirming that diffusion of GMVs has led to genetic contamination of conventional plants and the emergence of super weeds with increased resistance to herbicides (Gilbert 2013). It takes the perspective of Weaver and Morris (2005) who explain that while such risks of genetic contamination are present with conventional varieties also, it is essentially the process of creation of GMVs that increases the risk of unpredictable consequences. They point out that genetic modification is often to enable the targeted plant to produce proteins that they would not otherwise produce, but this creates a risk that the GMVs may also produce proteins that were not intended, and such effects may be manifested with a time lag longer than that required for safety tests.

In sum, the application of the precautionary principle to ban a new technology is founded upon the threats posed by its possible but uncertain and irreversible impact (Sandin 1999). We aim to make a contribution to this discourse in the context of GMVs by demonstrating that even in the absence of informational constraints, the precautionary principle may be called upon under certain conditions pertaining to the economic gains opened up by the new technology versus its ecological impact. For this, we develop an evolutionary model of farmer behavior. There are two types of farmers, differentiated by their criteria for new technology adoption. The first type is driven by short term profit maximization, while the second type aims to maximize profit over the life time of the technology. Further, agriculture specific features that are under examined in innovation studies are integrated. These include the natural built-in technological obsolescence of seeds, the environmental degradation engendered by new seed technology adoption, and farmer choice vis-à-vis compliance with sustainability guidelines. Then the rationale for the application of the precautionary principle is explored.

The present paper makes a twofold contribution to the existing literature. First, it provides an explanation for why some countries have opted for GMVs, whereas others have refused them. At present, while the literature provides justification for one or the other stance, there is no unifying theoretical framework that demarcates the contexts under which each stance can be rationalized. The model developed in this paper is an attempt to fill this gap. It incorporates agriculture specific features such as possibilities for contamination and irreversibility, the role of science, compliance burden, farmer types and farmer choices, in order to highlight the nature of their influence on the applicability of the precautionary principle. It demonstrates that even if uncertainty were to be absent, the nature of the context-specific trade-offs between the economic opportunities and ecological impact may justify the implementation of the precautionary principle in the corresponding regions.

Second, this work also adds to the literature on new technology adoption in agriculture by introducing farmer heterogeneity and studying the consequences of technology-compliance choices on Nature. By Nature, we refer to the local ecological conditions or "the state of ecological systems, which includes their physical, chemical, and biological characteristics and the processes and interactions that connect them.... An 'ecological system' (ecosystem) is a biological community consisting of all the living organisms (including humans) in a particular area and the nonliving components, such as air, water, and mineral soil, with which the organisms interact." (https://www.epa.gov/report-environment/ecological-condition). This approach is distinct from the majority of papers on agricultural innovations, which consider a unique representative farmer and focus on the impact of new technology introduction on total factor productivity.

The remainder of this paper is organized as follows. Section 2 presents a brief survey of prominent findings of the relevant literature. Section 3 contains the evolutionary model. Section 4 presents its results and Section 5 discusses them in the light of the rationale of the precautionary principle. Section 6 concludes.

2 Precautionary principle, new technology integration in agriculture and Nature

There is an extensive literature on the rationale for application of the precautionary principle. Starting with Henry (1974) and Arrow and Fisher (1974), it has been demonstrated that even for risk neutral agents, if there is a possibility of negative irreversible outcomes, then it is worthwhile to wait to gain more information about the outcomes. A decision takes on the characteristics of irreversibility to the extent that it shrinks the space of available options in present or future. In other words, an irreversible decision is one which, if taken, results in not being able to exercise (for a long time or forever) some option that was available earlier. Henry (1974) put forward the link between irreversibility, uncertainty and information explicitly in a proposition called the 'irreversibility effect'. This states that an irreversible decision that yields better payoffs as compared to a reversible decision under a particular situation, may with more information (and under the same situation) yield lower payoffs than the reversible decision. 'More information' here connotes an increased capability to anticipate with greater accuracy and precision the state of the world tomorrow. Through different analyses these authors arrived at the same normative conclusion, that in the face of anticipated increases in information, it might be better to take a reversible rather than an irreversible decision (Gollier et al. 2000). For instance, the precaution exercised against GMVs stems from the possible irreversible nature of their introduction into the ecology.

At the same time, it is recognized that the existence of ecological hazards per se cannot be used as a reason to stop innovations altogether (Giampietro 2002). For example, in addition to irreversibility, the future strategic flexibility provided by an option must be examined, and if the gain from expected flexibility can compensate for the expected losses, then an irreversible decision might be welfare enhancing (Ramani and Richard 1993). Firms whose innovations pose environmental risk can be nudged to acquire more information and voluntarily take measures to limit potential damages (Orset 2014). Given the diversity of contexts, applying the precautionary principle in a one size fits all approach may not be efficient and stand in the way of welfare enhancing initiatives (Immordino 2003).

The application of the precautionary principle to the European risk regulation of genetically modified crops has led to a better understanding of the diverse cognitive framing of the relevant uncertainties corresponding to different framing visions for agriculture (Levidow 2001). As such, researching the ecological basis for sustainable agriculture wherein the needs of the present vis-à-vis agriculture are met without compromising the ability of future generations to meet their own needs is a recent phenomenon (Gliessman 1990). It has been fuelled by the realization of the negative impact of the Green Revolution,[1] which while saving many developing countries from famine, also led to degradation of the soil and groundwater resources, given its water intensive and chemicals intensive production technology (Murgai et al. 2001) and caused a significant loss of bio-diversity (Shiva 1989). Moreover, recent 'accidents' such as 'Starlink', in 2000, whereby many food products containing genetically modified corn that had not yet been approved for human consumption were recalled, seem to be nudging policy makers to hold a more cautious view (Prakash and Kollman 2003). In developing countries also, controversies about GMVs are centered on these possible negative ecological consequences rather than immediate economic effects (Ramani and Thutupalli 2015). Scholars note that effective systemic dialogue with all societal stakeholders about the impact of new technology will help to minimize the risk of applying the precautionary principal wrongly, thereby foregoing valuable opportunities that may be opened with application of the new technology (Ishii 2018; Bogner and Torgersen 2018; Pant 2019).

Such controversies have also led to the recognition of farmer heterogeneity in terms of preferences for ecological sustainability that have been corroborated by empirical studies in the form of choice-experiments, in different parts of the world and for different solution packages. Innovation for the agriculture sector can take the form of a combination of improved inputs such as seeds, fertilizers or pesticides or mechanical equipment or new routines i.e. novel agro-ecological practices. With respect to new technology adoption in agriculture, there is a very extensive literature on the determinants of their economic impact in terms of higher profits and/or improved factor productivity (e.g. Sunding and Zilberman 2001; Feder and Umali 1993). The relationships between the nature and magnitude of innovation rent and systemic features such as actor-strategy, policy design and contextual factors (Klerkx et al. 2012), the nature of markets (David 1975), farmer and farm characteristics (Feder et al. 1985), public investment (Hayami and Ruttan 1971) and a

[1]The Green Revolution was a technology package involving improved quality seeds, controlled irrigation and measured doses of fertilizers. Created by the agricultural scientist Norman Borlaug, these modern variety seeds were a new dwarf variety of wheat, with "short legs" that could support a greater amount of wheat grains on any stalk. The hybrid dwarf variety clearly yielded more than the conventional varieties of wheat of that time. While the Green Revolution heralded a veritable increase in yields with respect to cereals, and saved developing countries, especially India, from famine, it led to very intensified use of water and application of agro-chemicals causing soil degradation and groundwater depletion.

combination of the above (Szirmai 2005) have been highlighted. That said, starting from the seminal work of Griliches (1957), most scholars assume that for farmers, the main driver of adoption of new technology in agriculture is the expectation of higher profit it carries in its wake.

In the existing literature on new technology adoption in agriculture, what is striking is that barring exceptions, Nature or ecology is taken as given. Turning to these exceptions, there are a few articles that highlight how Nature is impacted by farmer technology choices. Noailly (2008) develops a model where farmers in a region choose their pesticide dosage, which in turn determines the evolution of resistance to the pesticide in the pest. Farmers can choose between a low or high level of pesticide, the higher the sum of the pesticides use in the region, the higher is the resistance of the pest to the same. When pests develop resistance to the pesticide, their population grows and lowers the revenues of all farmers. Noailly (2008) shows that there can be many initial configurations under which the pesticide use can converge to its maximal level, while a lower use could yield higher incomes for all farmers. Thus, as a policy recommendation, they invoke the precautionary principle whereby the natural environment is exploited less than it could be.

It would seem that the main reason for the non-inclusion of Nature as an actor in the innovation system is because unlike economic actors who are driven by objectives set by self-interest, Nature's strategy is not governed by standard economic rationale, but by biophysical laws as responses to the strategies of other economic players, especially farmers. Nature does not seek to optimize, i.e. to maximize self-payoffs vis-à-vis the moves of other players, but it responds with passive actions of self-organization (or changes to itself) as dictated by universal biophysical laws to the strategies of economic players. However, given the complexity of the ecological system, Nature's responses constitute uncertainty for the economic actors. While the short run responses of Nature can be forecast using the existing scientific knowledge base to some extent, there is real scientific uncertainty about the long term consequences of adoption of new techniques in agriculture. That said, the evolutionary response of Nature to achieve biophysical efficiency is analogous to the evolutionary behavior of economic actors trying to achieve economic efficiency. We thus propose that Nature must also be considered as a non-economic actor in the agriculture innovation system.

Incorporating Nature, we further integrate the evolutionary and systemic features associated with agriculture. We take into account the fact that farming practices such as application of agrochemicals and utilization of water impact Nature. For instance, farmers can decide whether or not to invest in preserving Nature by preserving soil fertility, minimizing water contamination, nurturing bio-diversity etc. In most countries, farmers receive guidance from a variety of agriculture extension services on how this can be achieved. The mission of the latter is to transfer useful knowledge generated by public and private research to farmers and educate and accompany them to improve their livelihoods. While it is well known that national agriculture extension services were responsible for the success of the Green Revolution, with the acceptance of economic liberalization, there is a sea of change. Worldwide, public sector extension services are increasingly being supported or replaced by public-private partnerships or private providers (Anderson and Feder 2004).

In the context of GMV production, farmers also come under regulators' purview. For instance, there are GM crops, called Bt crops, containing genes from the bacterium *Bacillus thuringiensis*, which express a toxin that kills insect pests popularly known as bollworms. When bollworm pests attack a Bt crop, they are killed by the toxin. As acreage under Bt crops increases, there is a risk that bollworms might develop resistance to the toxin. To minimize this, farmers are requested to plan a refuge of non-Bt crop around Bt crop fields to ensure the survival and maintenance of susceptible insect populations on the non-Bt crop. To date, there has been regulatory swings vis-à-vis refuge. In the USA, for example, planting of refuges around Bt corn was initially voluntary and then mandatory, with clear definitions of accountability of farmer and seed company (Huang et al. 2011). In developing countries such as India, on the other hand, planting of refuges around Bt cotton is voluntary and it has been noted that there is mainly non-compliance (Singla et al. 2013). By and large, worldwide, for farmers, compliance to sustainability guidelines is voluntary rather than mandatory.

We now turn to the model.

3 Farmer technology and compliance choices: a model

3.1 Systemic setting

Three main actor-groups are considered, namely farmers, Nature and the regulator. Both the regulator and Nature are taken to be non-strategic in the sense that they do not align their strategies to maximize personal payoffs.

At the start, all farmers have access to only conventional variety seeds. Then a new genetically modified variety or GMV seed is submitted to the regulator for possible introduction into the market. The GMV is an innovation proposed in the system. The GMV comes along with a set of compliance measures to contain environmental degradation once cultivated. Input and output prices are the same for both seed varieties. Finally, all actors, farmers and the regulator have perfect and complete information.

Farmer types and strategy space The region contains farmers who can be one of two types: type 1, who is 'short term profit driven' or type 2, who is 'sustainability driven'. They start with the same amount and quality of endowments. At every time period t, type 1 farmer strives to maximize profit at time t, while type 2 farmer seeks to maximize profit over the lifetime of possible technological choices starting from time t. Let the technology or seed choice of farmer i at time t be given by $s_i^t = \{0, 1\}$ such that, if $s_i^t = 1$, it implies that the GMV seed has been chosen for cultivation; and if $s_i^t = 0$, the conventional variety has been picked by farmer i. At every planting season t, each farmer i also decides on the allocation of his land between two seed technologies, the conventional variety and the GMV. If a farmer i opts for GMV at time t, then he has to decide whether or not to comply with sustainability guidelines, i.e. choose between $c_i^t = 1$ and $c_i^t = 0$. Whatever properties are specified for farmer i hold similarly for farmer j and so we drop the farmer index j whenever possible.

The above framing reflects heterogeneous farmer preferences that have been observed vis-à-vis land management practices to preserve the quality of local water sources in the UK (Beharry-Borg et al. 2013), subsidy schemes for pesticide-free buffer zones in Denmark (Christensen et al. 2011), design of agri-environment schemes in UK (Aslam et al. 2017) and across Europe, (Ruto and Garrod 2009) and crop rotation to preserve soil fertility in Malawi (Ortega et al. 2016) etc.

Another way of understanding the difference between the two farmer types is in terms of their rate of discount d of future payoffs. The profit driven farmer discounts future payoffs very highly, at $d = 1$; while the sustainability driven farmer does not discount future payoffs, at $d = 0$. Considering d to be either 0 or 1 also permits analytical tractability, which would not be possible otherwise.

Compliance-contamination burden To preserve the state of Nature or local ecological conditions, the GMV comes with voluntary compliance measures that involve a fixed cost. In keeping with the discussion of the previous section, compliance refers to costly agro-ecological practices that maintain soil fertility over the long run. Let the compliance burden per unit of land cultivated with GMV be given by B.

Furthermore, whenever a farmer adopts GMV and does not comply, he might decrease the profit of the neighboring farmer through contamination. While, in reality, contamination would depend on individual farmer type and the number and type of his neighbors, in order to construct a tractable analytical model, we consider each farmer to be affected only by one neighbor. Thus, in what follows, we consider two neighboring farmers i and j who might be both of type 1 (i.e. profit driven) or both of type 2 (i.e. sustainability driven) or mixed (i.e. one profit driven, one sustainability driven).

Let the additional contamination burden to farmer i at time t by his neighbor j be given by $s_j^t B\theta\left(1 - c_j^t\delta\right)$, where θ is the degree of contamination and δ is the efficiency of existing science to preserve the original state of Nature through compliance. Let $\theta \in [0, 1]$ and $\delta \in]0, 1[$. For example, if the neighbor cultivates GMV without complying then there is an additional loss in profit due to contamination given by $B\theta$. On the other hand, if the neighbor complies then the profit loss due to contamination is less at $B\theta(1 - \delta)$, with the decrease depending on the efficiency of science δ.

Then, the compliance-contamination burden per unit of land of farmer i at time t, $B_i^t = B_i\left(s_i^t, c_i^t, s_j^t, c_j^t, \theta, \delta\right)$, is given by Eq. (1) and illustrated in Table 1.

Table 1 Compliance-contamination cost burden matrix

Farmer i, Farmer j	$s_j = 1 = \text{gmv}$; $c_j = 0 = \text{non-compliance}$	$s_j = 1 = \text{gmv}$; $c_j = 1 = \text{compliance}$	$s_j = 0 = \text{conventional}$
$s_i = 1 = \text{gmv}$; $c_i = 0 = \text{non-compliance}$	$-\theta B, -\theta B$	$-B\theta(1-\delta), -B(1+\theta)$	$0, -\theta B$
$s_i = 1 = \text{gmv}$; $c_i = 1 = \text{compliance}$	$-B(1+\theta), -B\theta(1-\delta)$	$-B(1+\theta(1-\delta)), -B(1+\theta(1-\delta))$	$-B, -B\theta(1-\delta)$
$s_i = 0 = \text{conventional}$	$-\theta B, 0$	$-B\theta(1-\delta), -B$	$0, 0$

$$B_i^t = B_i\left(s_i^t, c_i^t, s_j^t, c_j^t, \theta\delta\right) = B\left(s_i^t c_i + \theta s_j^t (1 - c_j \delta)\right). \tag{1}$$

For ease of notation, in what follows we will refer to the compliance-contamination burden for farmer i when he adopts GMV without compliance at time t as $B_i\left(1, 0, s_j^t, c_j^t, \theta, \delta\right) = B_i^{gm}(t)$. Similarly, the burden for GMV adoption with compliance will be given by $B_i\left(1, 1, s_j^t, c_j^t, \theta, \delta\right) = \widehat{B}_i^{gm}(t)$ and the burden for farmer i when he does not adopt GMV is given by $B_i\left(0, 0, s_j^t, c_j^t, \theta, \delta\right) = B_i(t)$. This short hand will be used only whenever possible.

Ecological impact The state of Nature is given by the ecology index, which captures the fit of the seed to the ecological conditions at time t and determines farmland productivity. At the start $t = 1$, the ecology index is the same for all farmers, being ξ. But, over time, it evolves differently for each farmer according to his seed and compliance choices. The evolution of the ecology index of farmer i over time, $\xi_i(t)$, is determined by the interaction between the seed and compliance choices of the farmer and Nature as:

$$\xi_i(t) = \xi_i(t-1)\psi(t)^{\left(s_i^{t-1}\right)\left((1-\delta)^{c_i^{t-1}}\right)}. \tag{2}$$

Let $\psi(t) \in]0, 1[$ represent the yearly degradation of the ecology index due to the use of GMV such that the resulting function $\xi_i(t)$ is a downward sloping concave function. Recall that whenever compliance is observed with GMV cultivation, δ indicates the efficiency of science to preserve the state of Nature. According to Eq. (2), if farmer i cultivates the conventional variety (i.e $s_i^{t-1} = 0$) or observes compliance when cultivating a GMV ($s_i^{t-1} = 1$ and $c_i^{t-1} = 1$) and science is very effective, i.e. $\delta \to 1$, then there is practically no degradation of the ecological conditions.

This is in keeping with acknowledged findings that the 'vigor' of the seed falls regularly and over a span of years, the plant also becomes vulnerable to new pests and pathogens, leading to diminishing returns in yield (Peng et al. 1999; Swanson 2002; Peng et al. 2010). Nature also responds to the agro-ecological practices of the farmers in terms of their technology and compliance choices according to bio-physical and bio-chemical laws in a cumulative manner (Van der Werf and Petit 2002). Finally, as Tisdell (2010) explains, GMVs designed by human ingenuity independently of natural environmental forces are more fragile than conventional varieties and are likely to lose their ecological fitness at a faster rate. Thus, by Eq. (2), whenever GMVs are cultivated, the ecology index falls, while conventional variety cultivation does not lower it.

Irreversibility of ecological impact via GMV One of the issues raised with respect to GMVs is the possible irreversible impact they may engender. Hence, we consider a reversibility index $\gamma \in [0, 1]$ where $\gamma = 0$ indicates total irreversibility and any $\gamma > 0$ means some degree of reversibility to move back to cultivation of the conventional variety after the GMV has been adopted. Let $\overline{s}^t$ be an indicator of the past cultivation of GMV i.e. $\overline{s}^t$ is either 1 or 0. Then, at time t, if $\overline{s}^t = 1$, i.e. the farmer has cultivated GMV prior to time t and he switches back to the conventional variety, then he will get only γ of the profit associated with cultivation of the conventional variety. We detail this further in the next section.

Role of the regulator Let the time period 0 to T be the lifetime of a conventional seed. Similarly, let the time periods from 0 to $\widehat{T}^{gm}$ and T^{gm} be the lifetime of GMV with and without compliance, with $\overline{T} = Max\left(T^{gm}, \widehat{T}^{gm}, T\right)$. With respect to the regulator, the focus is on his choice as to whether or not allow the commercialization of GMV at $t = 1$. The objective of the regulator is to safeguard of livelihoods of the farming community.

3.2 *Properties of profit functions (net of production costs)*

We start by defining the profit functions of farmers net of production costs and distinguish these from farmer payoffs obtained by further subtracting their compliance-contamination burden.

For a configuration $s_i^t, c_i^t, s_j^t, c_j^t, \xi_i^t, \delta, \theta, \gamma, \overline{s}_i^t$ let the yield maximizing inputs combination for farmer i at time t be x_i. Let the input prices and output price be the same for both the varieties and unchanging over time, being given by w and p, respectively. Let the production or yield function for the GMV be given by f^{gm} and, for the conventional variety, by f. They are common to both farmers as they are assumed to have the same knowledge base. The agricultural yield functions is assumed to be strictly concave over inputs x_i, and, as mentioned earlier, increase with ecology index ξ_i. Then the profit net of production costs of farmer i at time t for GMV or conventional variety cultivation is given respectively by:

$$
\begin{aligned}
&pf^{gm}(x_i^{gm}(t), \xi_i(t)) - wx_i^{gm};\\
&pf(x_i(t), \xi_i(t)) - wx_i.
\end{aligned} \tag{3}
$$

The yields f^{gm} and f depend on the state of ecology, $\xi_i(t)$ which in turn depends on the farmer's history of technology and compliance choices. For any configuration, $s_i^t, c_i^t, s_j^t, c_j^t, \xi_i^t, \delta, \theta, \gamma, \bar{s}_i^t$ let the profit function per unit land of farmer i at time t on land allocated to conventional variety and GMV be $\pi_i(t)$, $\pi_i^{gm}(c_i, t)$ respectively. For notational convenience, let $\pi_i^{gm}(0, t) = \pi_i^{gm}$ refer to GMV cultivation without compliance and let $\pi_i^{gm}(1, t) = \widehat{\pi}_i^{gm}(t)$ refer to GMV cultivation with compliance. By construction all these profit functions are downward sloping and concave over time. Let the total quantity of land be normalized to 1. Then from the definition of $\xi_i(t)$ two properties of the profit functions (given by Eqs. (4) and (5)), which are independent of the strategies of neighboring farmer, can be noted.

Advantages from compliance are directly proportional to the prior time period over which compliance has been practiced. Let $\widehat{\pi}_i^{gm}(t|t_{start} = \widetilde{t})$represents the profit of a late complier who begins adopting guidelines at time $\widetilde{t} > 0$. Then:

$$
\widehat{\pi}_i^{gm}(t|t_{start} = \widetilde{t}) > \widehat{\pi}_i^{gm}(t|t_{start} = \bar{t}) for\ \widetilde{t} < \bar{t} \leq t. \tag{4}
$$

If the GMV engenders significant environmental degradation such that its yields fall as compared to those of the conventional technology, then with prior compliance this would occur at a later time; or:

$$
\text{If at time } T*,\ \pi_i^{gm}(T*) = \pi_i(T*) \Rightarrow \widehat{\pi}_i^{gm}(T*|t_{start} = \bar{t}) > \pi_i(T*) for\ \bar{t} < T*. \tag{5}
$$

3.3 *Properties of payoff functions*

Now, as GMVs come with a compliance-contamination burden, this value has to be deducted from the production profit to arrive at payoffs. Thus, the payoff of farmer i at time t when he cultivates GMV without compliance is $\pi_i^{gm}(t) - B_i^{gm}(t)$; with compliance it is $\widehat{\pi}_i^{gm}(t) - \widehat{B}_i^{gm}(t)$and, for conventional variety cultivation, it is $\pi_i(t) - B_i(t)$. Then, given a compliance burden, B, a rate of contamination, θ, the efficiency of science, δ, a reversibility index γ and prior cultivation of GMVs, s_i^t, the payoffs to farmer i at time t will be given by:

$$\left(s_i^t.\left(\pi_i^{gm}(c_i^t,t) - B_i\left(1,c_i^t,s_j^t,c_j^t,\theta,\delta\right)\right)\right) + \left((1-s_i^t).\left(\pi_i(t)\left(\gamma\bar{s}_i^t + (1-\bar{s}_i^t)\right)\right.\right.$$
$$\left.\left. -B_i\left(0,0,s_j^t,c_j^t,\theta,\delta\right)\right)\right). \quad (6)$$

The first term models returns from GMV. The second term indicates that once the GMV is adopted, the profit from cultivation of conventional variety also depends on the degree of reversibility. For instance, if $\bar{s}_i^t = 1$, i.e. the land had been used to cultivate GMV in a previous time period, then the returns to the conventional variety from the next period onwards will be $\gamma(\pi_i - B_i)$, where γ is the index of reversibility. This payoff structure is further illustrated in Table 2.

Three assumptions, A1-A3 based upon the findings of the literature further define the properties of the payoff functions[2].

A1: When a GMV seed is introduced, it is a viable alternative to the conventional one with or without compliance. The GMV yields high enough yields to bear any own compliance burden and any imposed through contamination from a neighboring farm:

$$\pi_i^{gm}(t) - B_i^{gm}(t) > \pi_i(t) - B_i(t) \text{ and } \widehat{\pi}_i^{gm}(t) - \widehat{B}_i^{gm}(t) > \pi_i(t) - B_i(t) \text{ at } t = 1. \quad (7)$$

Empirical studies on the economic impact of GMVs (Areal et al. 2013; Carpenter 2010) confirm its higher profit as the main reason for its commercial success and this is also confirmed by reports on the 'Global Status of Commercialized Biotech/GM Crops' (ISAAA 2018).

A2: However, for GMV seeds, sustainability guidelines ensure higher cumulative payoffs for farmer i when he practices compliance from the start rather than from time $\tilde{t} > 1$whatever the strategies chosen by the neighboring farmer:

$$\sum_{t=1}^{T^{gm}}\left(\widehat{\pi}_i^{gm}(t) - \widehat{B}_i^{gm}(t)\right) > \left(\sum_{t=1}^{\tilde{t}-1}\pi_i^{gm}(t) - B_i^{gm}(t) + \sum_{t=\tilde{t}}^{T^{gm}}\left(\widehat{\pi}_i^{gm}(t) - \widehat{B}_i^{gm}(t)\right)\right). \quad (8)$$

A3: For farmer i, compliance lowers returns at the start, as it involves a fixed cost. Then as ecology gets less damaged, it yields higher returns, implying there exists a time T_1 beyond which returns from compliance are higher, for all farmer j's strategy profile histories:

[2]Interested readers can obtain examples of precise functional forms of the profit and payoff functions that satisfy these properties from the authors.

Table 2 Payoff matrix of farmers at time t

Farmer i, Farmer j	$s_j = 1 = \text{gmv}$; $c_j = 0 = \text{non-compliance}$	$s_j = 1 = \text{gmv}$; $c_j = 1 = \text{compliance}$	$s_j = 0 = \text{conventional}$;
$s_i = 1$ $c_i = 0$	$\pi_i^{gm}(t) - B\theta$, $\pi_j^{gm}(t) - B\theta$	$\pi_i^{gm}(t) - B\theta(1-\delta)$, $\widehat{\pi}_j^{gm}(t) - B(1+\theta)$	$\pi_i^{gm}(t)$, $\gamma \overline{s}_j^t \pi_j(t) + \left(1 - \overline{s}_j^t\right)\pi_j(t) - \theta B$
$s_i = 1$ $c_i = 1$	$\widehat{\pi}_i^{gm}(t) - B(1+\theta)$, $\pi_j^{gm}(t) - B\theta(1-\delta)$	$\widehat{\pi}_i^{gm}(t) - B(1+\theta(1-\delta))$, $\widehat{\pi}_j^{gm}(t) - B(1+\theta(1-\delta))$	$\widehat{\pi}_i^{gm}(t) - B$, $\gamma \overline{s}_j^t \pi_j(t) + \left(1 - \overline{s}_j^t\right)\pi_j(t) - B\theta(1-\delta)$
$s_i = 0$	$\gamma \overline{s}_i^t \pi_i(t) + \left(1 - \overline{s}_i^t\right)\pi_i(t) - \theta B$,$\pi_j^{gm}(t)$	$\gamma \overline{s}_i^t \pi_i(t) + \left(1 - \overline{s}_i^t\right)\pi_i(t) - \theta B(1-\delta)$, $\widehat{\pi}_j^{gm}(t) - B$	$\gamma \overline{s}_i^t \pi_i(t) + \left(1 - \overline{s}_i^t\right)\pi_i(t)$, $\gamma \overline{s}_j^t \pi_j(t) + \left(1 - \overline{s}_j^t\right)\pi_j(t)$

$$\pi_i^{gm}(t) - B_i^{gm}(t) > \widehat{\pi}_i^{gm}(t) - \widehat{B}_i^{gm}(t) \text{ for } t < T_1; \\ \text{but } \pi_i^{gm}(t) - B_i^{gm}(t) < \widehat{\pi}_i^{gm}(t) - \widehat{B}_i^{gm}(t) \text{ for } t > T_1. \tag{9}$$

Identification of contamination by GMVs, its measurement and its containment are subjects of scholarly enquiry (Ceddia et al. 2007, 2009; Belcher et al. 2005; Friesen et al. 2003). Further, the impact of cultivation of GMV and contamination depends on soil conditions of farmlands, ecological conditions, plant variety, spatial arrangements of lands, their sizes etc.

Assumptions 2 and 3 reflect the scientific rationale of compliance measures such as planting a refuge around a field of GMVs (Reisig and Kurtz 2018; Tabashnik and Carrière 2017; Jin et al. 2015; Catarino et al. 2015; Tabashnik et al. 2008). The purpose of refuges is twofold. First, it is to delay build-up of resistance in the GMVs. Second, it is to prevent the emergence of insect species that are not susceptible to the expressed toxin, which can develop into secondary pests (Lu et al. 2010). Field outcomes documented by scholars confirm that refuge strategy, namely a generous border of non-GMV host plants around GMV fields can substantially address the above risks, and yield better performance in the long run (Anderson et al. 2019). Thus, we assume that complying with guidelines will protect farmers' livelihoods over the lifetime of the technology.

3.4 Game setting

Starting from time $t = 1$, farmers have to decide between GMV or conventional variety and, in the case of the former, also choose whether or not to comply. Recall that $\overline{s}^t$ is simply an indicator function of past cultivation of GMV. Suppose $\prod_{i=profit}^t(\cdot)$ is the payoff of a type 1 profit driven farmer i at time t. Then, his objective at time t is to maximize immediate profit as given below:

$$\underset{s_i^t, c_i^t}{Max} \prod\nolimits_{i=profit}^t \left(s_i^t, c_i^t, s_j^t, c_j^t, \theta, \delta, \overline{s}_i^t\right) \text{ where}$$

$$\prod\nolimits_{i=profit}^t(\cdot) \\ = \left[\left(s_i^t \cdot \left(\pi_i^{gm}(c_i^t, t) - B_i\left(1, c_i^t, s_j^t, c_j^t, \theta, \delta\right)\right) + \left((1 - s_i^t) \cdot \left(\pi_i(t)\left(\gamma \overline{s}_i^t + (1 - \overline{s}_i^t)\right)\right)\right.\right. \\ \left.\left.\left. - B_i\left(0, 0, s_j^t, c_j^t, \theta, \delta\right)\right)\right)\right] \tag{10}$$

Let $\prod_{i=sust}^t(\cdot)$ be the payoff of a type 2 sustainability driven farmer i at time t. In this case, the farmer's objective at time t is to maximize profit over the lifetime $\overline{T} = Max\left\{T, T^{gm}, \widehat{T}^{gm}\right\}$ by choosing the optimal sequence s_i^z, c_i^z for $z = t, t+1, \ldots, \overline{T}$; i.e.:

$$\underset{s_i^z c_i^z \text{ for } z=t,t+1,\ldots,\overline{T}}{Max} \prod_{i==sust}^{t} \left(s_i^t, c_i^t, s_j^t, c_j^t, \theta, \delta, \overline{s}_i^t\right); \text{where}$$

$$\prod_{i=sust}^{t} \left(s_i^t, c_i^t\right)$$
$$= \sum_{z=t}^{\overline{T}} \left[s_i^z \cdot \left(\pi_i^{gm}(z) - B_i\left(1, c_i^z, s_j^z, c_j^z, \theta, \delta\right)\right) + \left(\left(1 - s_i^z\right) \cdot \left(\pi_i(z)\left(\gamma \overline{s}_i^z + \left(1 - \overline{s}_i^z\right)\right)\right.\right.\right.$$
$$\left.\left.\left. - B_i\left(0, 0, s_j^z, c_j^z, \theta, \delta\right)\right)\right)\right] \tag{11}$$

A Nash equilibrium of the above dynamic game is an evolutionary trajectory of strategy profiles of farmer pairs i and j or $\left(S_i^t, C_i^t, S_j^t, C_j^t\right)$ for every t where $1 \leq t \leq \overline{T}$ such that for every farmer i the Nash equilibrium strategy profile $\left(S_i^t, C_i^t, S_j^t, C_j^t\right)$ satisfies:

$$\prod_{i=profit}^{t} \left(S_i^t, C_i^t | S_j^t, C_j^t\right) \geq \prod_{i=profit}^{t} \left(S_i^t, c_i^t | S_j^t, C_j^t\right) \text{ for all possible } \left(s_i^t, c_i^t\right) \text{ at time } t;$$
$$\prod_{i=sust}^{t} \left(S_i^t, C_i^t | S_j^t, C_j^t\right) \geq \prod_{i=sust}^{t} \left(S_i^t, c_i^t | S_j^t, C_j^t\right) \text{ for all possible } \left(s_i^t, c_i^t\right) \text{ at time } t.$$

Similarly for farmer j. Do such Nash equilibrium strategies exist? We attempt to answer this question in the next section.

4 Co-evolutionary dynamics: Discussion of results

We start with an observation on compliance choices.

Result 1: On compliance choices

1.1 Whenever a profit driven farmer adopts GMV, his dominant strategy is to start without compliance and then comply after a time, say T_1.
1.2 Whenever a sustainability driven farmer adopts GMV, his dominant strategy is to comply from the start.

Proof: 1.1. From Table 1, for any farmer, the contamination-compliance burden is greater when compliance is observed than not, whatever his neighbor's strategies. By assumption 3, a profit driven farmer i would start without observing compliance, and beyond time period T_1, as the ecological conditions get eroded, he would begin complying. By Table 2, clearly the time he starts complying will be later if his neighbor is a sustainability driven farmer as his compliance-contamination burden will be less then. □.

1.2. Suppose the sustainability driven farmer i adopts GMV at $t = 1$. By assumption A3 (or Eq. 9) on this land, compliance yields higher payoff each period beyond time T_1. As the life time of the GMV cannot decrease with compliance, i.e. $\widehat{T}^{gm} \geq T^{gm}$, assumption 3 assures that after T_1, a sustainability driven farmer will always comply:

$$\sum_{t'=T_1+1}^{\widehat{T}^{gm}} \left(\widehat{\pi}_i^{gm}(t) - \widehat{B}_i^{gm}(t)\right) > \sum_{t'=T_1+1}^{\widehat{T}^{gm}} \left(\pi_i^{gm}(t) - B_i^{gm}(t)\right). \tag{12}$$

Then what about the time before T_1 when payoff without compliance is higher? We prove the result by contradiction. Consider a time $t' < T_1$. As the objective of the sustainability driven farmer i is to maximize payoffs over the horizon $t = 1$ until $\overline{T}$, he will not comply at $t' < T_1$ if:

$$\sum_{t=t'}^{\widehat{T}^{gm}} \left(\widehat{\pi}_i^{gm}(t) - \widehat{B}_i^{gm}(t)\right) < \sum_{t=t'}^{\widehat{T}^{gm}} \left(\pi_i^{gm}(t) - B_i^{gm}(t)\right) \text{ for } \widehat{T}^{gm} \geq T_1 > t' \geq 1 \tag{13}$$

Now let us add $\sum_{t=1}^{t'-1} \left(\widehat{\pi}_i^{gm}(t) - \widehat{B}_i^{gm}(t)\right)$ where $1 \leq t' < T_1$ to both sides of Eq. (13) to get:

$$\sum_{t=1}^{\widehat{T}^{gm}} \left(\widehat{\pi}_i^{gm}(t) - \widehat{B}_i^{gm}(t)\right) < \sum_{t=t'}^{\widehat{T}^{gm}} \left(\pi_i^{gm}(t) - B_i^{gm}(t)\right) + \sum_{t=1}^{t'-1} \left(\widehat{\pi}_i^{gm}(t) - \widehat{B}_i^{gm}(t)\right). \tag{14}$$

Splitting the first term on the right hand side of Eq. (14) we can write:

$$\begin{aligned}\sum_{t=1}^{\widehat{T}^{gm}} \left(\widehat{\pi}_i^{gm}(t) - \widehat{B}_i^{gm}(t)\right) &< \sum_{t=t'}^{T_1} \left(\pi_i^{gm}(t) - B_i^{gm}(t)\right) + \sum_{t=T_1+1}^{\widehat{T}^{gm}} \left(\pi_i^{gm}(t) - B_i^{gm}(t)\right) \\ &\quad + \sum_{t=1}^{t'-1} \left(\widehat{\pi}_i^{gm}(t) - \widehat{B}_i^{gm}(t)\right).\end{aligned} \tag{15}$$

Now according to assumption (3):

$$\begin{aligned}\sum_{t'=T_1+1}^{\widehat{T}^{gm}} \left(\pi_i^{gm}(t) - B_i^{gm}(t)\right) &< \sum_{t'=T_1+1}^{\widehat{T}^{gm}} \left(\widehat{\pi}_i^{gm}(t) - \widehat{B}_i^{gm}(t)\right) \text{ and } \sum_{t=1}^{t'-1} \left(\widehat{\pi}_i^{gm}(t) - \widehat{B}_i^{gm}(t)\right) \\ &< \sum_{t=1}^{t'-1} \left(\pi_i^{gm}(t) - B_i^{gm}(t)\right).\end{aligned}$$

Substituting the above terms into (15), we can re-write it as:

$$\sum_{t=1}^{\widehat{T}^{gm}} \left(\widehat{\pi}_i^{gm}(t) - \widehat{B}_i^{gm}(t)\right) < \sum_{t=t'}^{T_1} (\pi_i^{gm}(t) - B_i^{gm}(t)) + \sum_{t'=T_1+1}^{\widehat{T}^{gm}} \left(\widehat{\pi}_i^{gm}(t) - \widehat{B}_i^{gm}(t)\right) + \sum_{t=1}^{t'-1} \times (\pi_i^{gm}(t) - B_i^{gm}(t)).$$

Or

$$\sum_{t=1}^{\widehat{T}^{gm}} \left(\widehat{\pi}_i^{gm}(t) - \widehat{B}_i^{gm}(t)\right) < \sum_{t=1}^{T_1} (\pi_i^{gm}(t) - B_i^{gm}(t)) + \sum_{t'=T_1+1}^{\widehat{T}^{gm}} \times \left(\widehat{\pi}_i^{gm}(t) - \widehat{B}_i^{gm}(t)\right). \tag{16}$$

But Eq. (16) contradicts assumption 2 that sustainability guidelines ensure higher payoffs for farmer i when compliance is practiced from the start at $t = 1$ over the life time T^{gm} rather than from time $T_1 > 1$whatever the strategies chosen by the neighboring farmer.

It suffices to note here that our model accords an inbuilt 'bonus' to sustainability driven farmers. The returns to GMV for a sustainability driven farmer will fall more slowly over time than for a profit driven farmer because the ecology deteriorates less due to compliance observance. Hence, result 1.2 is proved.□.

Without detailing the functional forms of the profit trajectories, it is impossible to identify the optimal sequence of strategies s_i^t for $t = 1, 2, \ldots, \overline{T}$ for a sustainability driven farmer that explain when he would adopt the GMV or the best time for switching to conventional post-adoption. However, we can identify the necessary and sufficient conditions for repeated adoption of GMV by the two farmer types.

Result 2: On GMV adoption by a sustainability driven farmer: Whenever $\widehat{\pi}_i^{gm}(t) - B > \pi_i(t)\ \forall t$ the dominant strategy of the sustainability driven farmer is to adopt the GMV at the start.

Proof: At the outset, note that if a sustainability driven farmer i does not adopt the GMV at the start, he will not adopt it thereafter. However, the opposite is not true. The argument can be proved as follows. By assumption 1, the payoff from GMV is higher than from conventional varieties even with compliance, i.e. $\widehat{\pi}_i^{gm}(1) - \widehat{B}_i^{gm}(1) > \pi_i(1) - B_i(1)$. A sustainability driven farmer adopts GMV at the start, $t = 1$, if the area under the payoffs function to GMVs is greater than that from conventional variety (taking into account his neighbor's type and strategy sequences). As the profit functions are downward sloping and concave, the difference in the areas under the payoff function to GMVs and conventional varieties will decrease over time. Thus, if the area under the GMV payoff function is not greater to start with, it cannot become so over time. In other words, if a sustainability driven farmer opts for the conventional variety at $t = 1$, he will continue with it thereafter.

Now, from Table 2, whatever the neighbor type, for a complying sustainability driven farmer, the strategy of GMV adoption and cultivation at every time period (i.e. $s_i^t = 1 \quad \forall t$) would yield higher payoffs than from the conventional variety (i.e. $s_i^t = 0 \quad \forall t$) if:

$$\sum_{t=1}^{\overline{T}} \left(\widehat{\pi}_i^{gm}(t) - B\right) > \sum_{t=1}^{\overline{T}} \pi_i(t) \tag{17}$$

Thus, if $\widehat{\pi}_i^{gm}(t) - B > \pi_i(t)\forall t$, Eq. (17) holds and the sustainability driven farmer would adopt GMV at $t = 1$. □.

Result 3: On repeated adoption of GMV by both farmer types: Let T_1 be the time when complying yields higher payoff than non-complying for a profit driven farmer i as a function of neighbor type j. If the following conditions hold, then the dominant strategy of the profit driven farmer and the sustainability driven farmer is to adopt the GMV repeatedly from the start:

(i) $\widehat{\pi}_i^{gm}(t) - B > \pi_i(t)\forall t$; and,
(ii) $\widehat{\pi}_i^{gm}(t|t_{start} = T_1) - B(1 + \theta(1 - \delta)) > \gamma\pi_i(t)$ for all $t \geq T_1 > 1$.

The Nash equilibrium is then $\left(S_{i=1}^t = 1, C_{i=1}^t = 0, S_{i=2}^t = 1, C_{i=2}^t = 1\right)$ for $1 \leq t < T_1$ and $\left(S_{i=1}^t = 1, C_{i=1}^t = 1, S_{i=2}^t = 1, C_{i=2}^t = 1\right)$ for $t \geq T_1$.

Proof: For a profit driven farmer i, by assumption 1, the GMV yields higher payoff than the conventional seed with or without compliance. Hence, the profit driven farmer will adopt the GMV, without observing compliance, whatever his neighbor type.

By assumption 3, payoff from compliance becomes higher than that without compliance after time T_1. As the sustainability driven farmer always complies (by result 1), whatever the neighbor type, the profit driven farmer will now get $\widehat{\pi}_i^{gm}(t|t_{start} = T_1) - B(1 + \theta(1 - \delta))$ from GMV cultivation. Thus, if this remains above what he would get from conventional variety cultivation, namely $\gamma\pi(t)$, then he will continue to cultivate GMV.

Let us now turn to a sustainability farmer i. By result 2, given $\widehat{\pi}_i^{gm}(t) - B > \pi_i(t)\forall t$, he can adopt GMV at $t = 1$. But what about thereafter? He would opt for repeated adoption only if the returns from GMV cultivation exceed the stream from conventional, which would be $\gamma\pi_i(t)$ during each period.

After $t > T_1$ we know that $\widehat{\pi}_i^{gm}(t|t_{start} = T_1) - B(1 + \theta(1 - \delta) > \gamma\pi_i(t)$ for all $t \geq T_1$. By advantages of compliance (Eqs. 4 and 5) we have $\widehat{\pi}_i^{gm}(t) > \widehat{\pi}_i^{gm}(t|t_{start} = T_1)$ for all $t > T_1$. Thus, whatever the neighbor type, the dominant strategy for a sustainability driven farmer is repeated adoption after $t > T_1$ (also confirmable by a look at payoffs Table 2).

Then, what about the optimal strategy during $t < T_1$? Consider a time, z, where $z < T_1$. Under this scenario, a profit driven farmer adopts the GMV at the start and continues to cultivate it until the end complying from time $t > T_1$, or $\pi_i^{gm}(t) > \pi_i(t)$ for $t < T_1$ and $\widehat{\pi}_i^{gm}(t|t_{start} = T_1) - B(1 + \theta(1 - \delta) > \gamma\pi_i(t)$ for all $t \geq T_1$. So we can write:

$$\left(\sum_{t=z}^{T_1-1}(\pi_i^{gm}(z)-B)+\sum_{z=T_1}^{\overline{T}}(\widehat{\pi}_i^{gm}(z)-B(1+\theta(1-\delta)))\right)>\sum_{t=z}^{\overline{T}}\pi_i(t)\gamma. \tag{18}$$

By result 1, we know that the sustainability farmer complies from the start and by assumption 2, we can write:

$$\sum_{t=z}^{\overline{T}}\left(\widehat{\pi}_i^{gm}(t)-\widehat{B}_i^{gm}(t)\right)>\left(\sum_{t=z}^{T_1-1}(\pi_i^{gm}(z)-B_i^{gm}(z))+\sum_{z=T_1}^{\overline{T}}\left(\widehat{\pi}_i^{gm}(z)-\widehat{B}_i^{gm}(z)\right)\right)$$
$$>\sum_{t=z}^{\overline{T}}\pi_i(t)\gamma.$$

Therefore, at $t=z<T_1$, whatever the neighbor type, adoption with compliance from the start is the dominant strategy for the sustainability driven farmer. Hence, the Nash equilibrium. □.

Result 4: On repeated adoption of GMV by the sustainability driven farmer but not the profit driven farmer: The profit driven farmer will start by adopting GMV without compliance, continue to cultivate the GMV with compliance but switch to the conventional after a period of time and, the sustainability farmer will comply from the start and adopt the GMV repeatedly throughout its lifetime if:

(i) $\widehat{\pi}_i^{gm}(t)-B(1+\theta(1-\delta))>\gamma\pi_i(t)\forall t;$
(ii) $\widehat{\pi}_i^{gm}(t|t_{start}=T_1)-B(1+\theta(1-\delta))<\gamma\pi_i(t)$ for all $t\geq T_2>T_1>1$.

In other words, the Nash equilibrium is $(S_{i=1}^t=1, C_{i=1}^t=0, S_{i=2}^t=1, C_{i=2}^t=1)$ for $1\leq t<T_1$, $\left(S_{i=1}^t=1, C_{i=1}^t=1, S_{i=2}^t=1, C_{i=2}^t=1\right)$ for $T_1\leq t\leq T_2$, and $\left(S_{i=1}^t=0, C_{i=1}^t=0, S_{i=2}^t=1, C_{i=2}^t=1\right)$ for $T_2\leq t\leq\overline{T}$:

Proof: Note that whatever the neighbor type, once he starts complying profit maximizing farmer will get $\widehat{\pi}_i^{gm}(t|t_{start}=T_1)-B(1+\theta(1-\delta))$. Thus, by condition (ii) he will stop cultivating the GMV after T_2 .

By condition (i) and result 2 the dominant strategy of the sustainability driven farmer is to adopt the GMV at the start. By the same argument as in result 3, we can show that for all time periods $t<T_1$, the sustainability driven farmer will adopt the GMV. From T_1 onwards his payoff is $\widehat{\pi}_i^{gm}(t)-B(1+\theta(1-\delta))$and, as this is greater than $\gamma\pi(t)$, by condition (i) he will continue to cultivate GMV. □.

5 Policy reflection: so what about the precautionary principle?

Consider the following thought experiment of a policy maker, who has two identical villages of farmers to administer. The farms are organized in neighboring pairs, comprised of two profit driven farmers, two sustainability driven farmers or one of each type. He has to take a decision on allowing the commercialization of a GMV in the region. To do this, he supposes that he will introduce the GMV in one village, keeping the other village as a control with only the conventional variety to cultivate. He considers two possible rules for application of the precautionary principle. Either he can take a survey at the end of every season to evaluate the livelihoods or payoffs generated for the farmers, or he can conduct a survey at the end of the lifetime of the GMV to assess how the two villages have fared. The former calls for a more stringent application than the latter. Let us refer to the two evaluation routines as rule 1 and rule 2. By farmer livelihoods' in the GMV village, we refer to the sum of the payoffs of all farmers from playing their Nash equilibrium strategies. Similarly, farmer livelihoods' in the non-GMV village is the sum of production profit from cultivating the conventional variety.

The model and results developed in the preceding sections for evaluation of new technology in agriculture lead us to the following inference:

Result 5: On application of the precautionary principle.

5.1. The precautionary principle may be applicable even in the absence of informational constraints and be uninfluenced by the degree of irreversibility under both rule 1 and rule 2

5.2. The likelihood of application would decrease with greater gains from the new technology, lower detrimental ecological impact, lower contamination possibilities, higher effectiveness of science, lower compliance burden, lower irreversibility burden and a greater proportion of sustainability driven farmers. This effect would be greater under rule 1 than rule 2.

Proof: 5.1. Consider the best possible case, wherein the village has only sustainability driven farmers and where the Nash equilibrium is repeated adoption as in results 3 and 4. Then according to payoff matrix of Table 2, at time t every farmer would be earning $\widehat{\pi}_j^{gm}(t) - B(1+\theta(1-\delta))$ in the GMV village and $\pi_i(t)$ in the conventional variety village (or just conventional village henceforth). Then the precautionary principle would not be applied if:

$$\left\{\begin{array}{r} \widehat{\pi}_j^{gm}(t) - B(1+\theta(1-\delta)) \geq \pi_i(t)\ \textit{for any } t \textit{ where } 1 \leq t \leq \overline{T} \textit{ under rule } 1. \\ \sum_{t=1}^{\overline{T}} \widehat{\pi}_j^{gm}(t) - B(1+\theta(1-\delta)) \geq \sum_{t=1}^{\overline{T}} \pi_i(t) \quad \textit{under rule } 2. \end{array}\right\} \tag{19}$$

Now from results 3 and 4, the necessary condition for repeated adoption of GMV by a sustainability driven farmer is $\widehat{\pi}_i^{gm}(t) - B > \pi_i(t) \forall t$ and the sufficient condition is $\widehat{\pi}_i^{gm}(t) - B(1 + \theta(1 - \delta)) > \gamma\pi_i(t) \forall t$. Putting these together we have two possibilities:

$$\widehat{\pi}_i^{gm}(t) - B > \pi_i(t) > \widehat{\pi}_i^{gm}(t) - B(1 + \theta(1 - \delta)) \tag{20}$$

$$\widehat{\pi}_i^{gm}(t) - B > \widehat{\pi}_i^{gm}(t) - B(1 + \theta(1 - \delta)) > \pi_i(t) \tag{21}$$

The precautionary principle would then be applied under the situation given by Eq. (20) but not (21). Clearly the value of γ does not influence the application of the precautionary principle when the community contains only sustainability driven farmers. This could be because this factor has already been taken into account in their cultivation division. □.

5.2. The case of the GMV village also serves to prove the second part. Clearly, Eq. (20) is more likely to hold, when the value of B or θ is higher and the value of δ is lower. Similarly, the higher is the difference between the ecology indices due to continuous cultivation of GMV even with compliance, $\xi_i(t, s_i^t = 1, c_i^t = 1) - \xi_i(t, s_i^t = 0, c_i^t = 0)$, the greater is the difference $\pi_i^{gm}(t) - \pi_i(t)$.

To understand the role of irreversibility, let us consider the same context, but with one major difference. Let the village be full of profit driven farmers. According to result 3, farmers will adopt GMV without compliance first, then comply from time T_1 onwards. Here, the necessary and sufficient for GMV cultivation at every time period is: $\widehat{\pi}_i^{gm}(t|t_{start} = T_1) - B(1 + \theta(1 - \delta)) > \gamma\pi_i(t)$.

The policy maker would not call for the precautionary principle if Eq. (22) hold. However, unless reversibility is perfect, i.e. $\gamma = 1$, the required condition would not hold for rule 2 or for rule 1 after time T_1. Hence, the precautionary principle will be applied.

$$\left\{ \begin{array}{l} \pi_j^{gm}(t) - B\theta \geq \pi_i(t)\ for\ t \leq T_1\ and\ \widehat{\pi}_i^{gm}(t|t_{start} = T_1) - B(1 + \theta(1 - \delta)) \\ > \pi_i(t)\ for\ t > T_1 under\ rule\ 1. \\ \sum_{t=1}^{T_1} \pi_i^{gm}(t_1) - B\theta + \sum_{t=T_1}^{\overline{T}} \widehat{\pi}_i^{gm}(t|t_{start} = T_1) - B(1 + \theta(1 - \delta)) \\ > \sum_{t=1}^{\overline{T}} \pi_i(t)\ under\ rule\ 2. \end{array} \right\} \tag{22}$$

Interestingly from *5.1.* we know that if Eq. (20) holds, then for the same context if the village was full of sustainability driven farmers instead of profit driven ones, then the precautionary principle would not be applied. Hence, heterogeneity of farmer type in population matters. □.

6 Concluding remarks

The precautionary principle is a policy response in the context of risk management to any activity that poses a threat to society. It corresponds to an action in the decision-making phase to ban the activity, based on the evaluation of possible irreversible adverse effects, the effectiveness of the present scientific knowledge base to contain them and the extent of scientific uncertainty on both. This has been exemplified, particularly in the European risk regulation of genetically modified crops. In this regard, the present paper sought to develop a framework that would permit a better understanding of the role of different factors specific to new technology introduction in agriculture. An evolutionary model of new seed technology adoption was formulated incorporating novel elements such as farmer heterogeneity, technology obsolescence, ecological impacts, compliance and contamination burdens and the efficiency of the present scientific knowledge base to redress any possible negative effects of new technology adoption. Under assumptions based upon the findings of the literature, the evolutionary model then identified the conditions for repeated GMV adoption and compliance vis-à-vis sustainability guidelines by profit driven and sustainability driven farmers.

Five main results were obtained by solving for the Nash equilibria of the game. Results 1–4 pertained to individual farmer behavior in terms of technology and compliance choices. According to result 1, a sustainability driven farmer would always comply if he adopted GMV, whereas a profit driven farmer would comply only if and when it became necessary. Furthermore, the likelihood of a sustainability driven farmer adopting GMV, result 2 showed, depends on the magnitude of the compliance burden. Only if the burden were sufficiently small so as to make it financially manageable would he adopt GMV, as he would be complying from the start. On the other hand, the profit driven farmer would always adopt GMV by result 3. Thereafter, results 3 and 4 demonstrated that the repeated adoption of GMV would depend on a multiplicity of factors and their interactions such as the ecological impact, the contamination engendered, the compliance and irreversibility burdens and the effectiveness of science as embedded in the compliance routines to counter any possible negative effects. Whatever be the case, result 4 showed that if a sustainability driven farmer adopted GMV, then the duration of his repeated adoption of GMV would be longer than that of a profit driven farmer because he would have protected Nature and soil fertility by being compliant.

The present discourse on application of the precautionary principle rests primarily on scientific uncertainty and irreversibility of possible deleterious impact of an activity. Our exploration at the macro, policy level demonstrated that it could be rationalized even under weaker conditions. To show this, two possible policy rules were considered, one being more stringent than the other, with respect to the application of the precautionary principle. Under the former, the precautionary principle would be applied if cultivation of GMV yielded lower collective farmer payoffs at any harvesting season, while under the latter, it would be evoked only if livelihoods were lower over the lifetime of the GMV – the benchmark being payoffs obtainable from growing the conventional variety. Integrating the above elements and considering these two possible policy rules, result 5 proved that the precautionary principle may be applicable even in the absence of informational constraints and remain uninfluenced by the degree of irreversibility. Result 5 indicated that the likelihood of application of the precautionary principle should increase with lower gains from the new technology, higher detrimental ecological impact, higher contamination possibilities, lower effectiveness of science, higher compliance burden and a lower proportion of sustainability driven farmers.

With this insight, do present patterns of positioning of countries vis-à-vis GMVs seem rational? Since worldwide, the majority of farmers are considered to be profit driven, the application of the precautionary principle would hinge on pessimistic perceptions about the potential for present scientific knowledge to be encapsulated into protocols that can address possible forms of environmental degradation in the future and/or the ability of the regulatory system to nudge or enforce farmers to integrate them into their production systems. Moreover, as regulatory systems are highly developed in both Europe and North America, the difference in their stance towards GMVs seems to lie in their confidence about science being always able to provide solutions to problems, the former being less optimistic than the latter.

A paradox that contradicts the above inference, however, is that at present, GMVs are cultivated more in countries that do not have the scientific, technological and regulatory capabilities of the Western world. Presently, 19 low and middle income[3] countries account for about 53% of the global area devoted to biotech crops (ISAAA 2018). The only way to explain the non-application of the precautionary principle in these countries given a retarding in both technology and regulatory capabilities is that they trust the multinational agribiotech companies to be able to churn out solutions to any major problem that could arise in the future.

Lastly, our model was constrained by its assumptions that had been framed for analytical tractability. We suggest that future research explore how outcomes would change under less restrictive settings. We note several possibilities for future research.

First, using simulation techniques and the existing findings of agricultural scientists, different scenarios for externalities generation from GMVs adoption can be modelled. Externalities generation is likely to depend on the total number of farmers, the composition of farmer types, and their spatial configuration. Impact of technology choice for a farmer would then depend on his own technology and compliance choice as well as those of his neighbors. That said, even at present, there is real uncertainty on the forms of the profit trajectories from different seed technologies, due to a combination of scientific and market uncertainty. Analytical and numerical simulations could be also considered with standard functional forms for profit, to explore the impact of varying the rate of discount among farmer types between 0 and 1, rather than considering only 0 and 1. Finally, monitoring and incentivization

[3] Following the World Bank Country Classification by Income https://datahelpdesk.worldbank.org/knowledgebase/articles/906519-world-bank-country-and-lending-groups

schemes can be introduced to arrive at farmer compliance through cooperation and coordination.

Second, our model considered an artificial two farmer world where both are perfectly rational with perfect and complete information for analytical tractability. Multiple farmer types can be introduced and a population of farmers can be considered so that the regional impact is mapped as a function of the size and composition of the population used agent-based modelling techniques. Informational problems can also be introduced in keeping with the reality. The attitudes of different stakeholders such as the regulator, producing agents and consumers can also be integrated in deciding about the implementation of the precautionary principle.

Third, the integration of the ideas developed in this paper can be explored in other contexts where the implementation of the precautionary principle is still being debated such as in medical practices (Gorlin 2019), artificial intelligence (Castro and McLaughlin 2019), international trade negotiations (Cai and Kim 2019) and representations of rationality (Christiansen 2019).

These signal the many avenues for extensions of our model.

Publisher's note Springer Nature remains neutral with regard to jurisdictional claims in published maps and institutional affiliations.

Acknowledgements We would like to thank the editor and the anonymous referees enormously for their useful comments and patience, which have greatly contributed to the improvement of this paper.

Compliance with ethical standards

The present paper did not require any interaction or experimentation that demands ethical compliance.

Conflict of interest The authors declare that they have no conflict of interest.

References

Adenle AA, Morris EJ, Murphy DJ, Phillips PW, Trigo E, Kearns P et al (2018) Rationalizing governance of genetically modified products in developing countries. Nat Biotechnol 36(2):137

Anderson JR, Feder G (2004) Agricultural extension: good intentions and hard realities. World Bank Res Obs 19(1):41–60

Anderson JA, Ellsworth PC, Faria JC, Head GP, Owen MD, Pilcher CD et al (2019) Genetically engineered crops: importance of diversified integrated pest management for agricultural sustainability. Frontiers in Bioengineering and Biotechnology 7:24

Areal F, Riesgo L, Rodriguez-Cerezo E (2013) Economic and agronomic impact of commercialized GM crops: a meta-analysis. J Agric Sci 151(1):7–33

Arrow KJ, Fisher AC (1974) Environmental preservation, uncertainty, and irreversibility. Q J Econ 88:187–191

Aslam U, Termansen M, Fleskens L (2017) Investigating farmers' preferences for alternative PES schemes for carbon sequestration in UK agroecosystems. Ecosystem Services 27:103–112
Beharry-Borg N, Smart JC, Termansen M, Hubacek K (2013) Evaluating farmers' likely participation in a payment programme for water quality protection in the UK uplands. Reg Environ Chang 13(3):633–647
Belcher K, Nolan J, Phillips PW (2005) Genetically modified crops and agricultural landscapes: spatial patterns of contamination. Ecol Econ 53(3):387–401
Bogner A, Torgersen H (2018) Precaution, responsible innovation and beyond—in search of a sustainable agricultural biotechnology policy. Frontiers in Plant Science 9:1884
Cai Y, Kim E (2019) Sustainable development in world trade law: application of the precautionary principle in Korea-radionuclides. Sustainability 11(7):1942
Caplan AL, Parent B, Shen M, Plunkett C (2015) No time to waste—the ethical challenges created by CRISPR. EMBO Rep 16(11):1421–1426
Carpenter JE (2010) Peer-reviewed surveys indicate positive impact of commercialized GM crops. Nat Biotechnol 28(4):319
Castro D, McLaughlin M (2019) Ten ways the precautionary principle undermines progress in artificial intelligence. Retrieved from https://itif.org/publications/2019/02/04/ten-ways-precautionary-principle-undermines-progress-artificial-intelligence
Catarino R, Ceddia G, Areal FJ, Park J (2015) The impact of secondary pests on Bacillus thuringiensis (Bt) crops. Plant Biotechnol J 13(5):601–612
Ceddia MG, Bartlett M, Perrings C (2007) Landscape gene flow, coexistence and threshold effect: the case of genetically modified herbicide tolerant oilseed rape (Brassica napus). Ecol Model 205(1–2):169–180
Ceddia MG, Bartlett M, Perrings C (2009) Quantifying the effect of buffer zones, crop areas and spatial aggregation on the externalities of genetically modified crops at landscape level. Agric Ecosyst Environ 129(1–3):65–72
Christensen T, Pedersen AB, Nielsen HO, Mørkbak MR, Hasler B, Denver S (2011) Determinants of farmers' willingness to participate in subsidy schemes for pesticide-free buffer zones—a choice experiment study. Ecol Econ 70(8):1558–1564
Christiansen A (2019) Rationality, expected utility theory and the precautionary principle. Ethics Policy Environ 1–18
David PA (1975) Technical choice innovation and economic growth: essays on American and British experience in the nineteenth century. Cambridge University Press, New York
Feder G, Umali DL (1993) The adoption of agricultural innovations: a review. Technol Forecast Soc Chang 43(3–4):215–239
Feder G, Just RE, Zilberman D (1985) Adoption of agricultural innovations in developing countries: a survey. Econ Dev Cult Chang 33(2):255–298
Friesen LF, Nelson AG, Van Acker RC (2003) Evidence of contamination of pedigreed canola (Brassica napus) seedlots in western Canada with genetically engineered herbicide resistance traits. Agron J 95(5):1342–1347
Giampietro M (2002) The precautionary principle and ecological hazards of genetically modified organisms. Ambio 31(6):466–470
Gilbert N (2013) A hard look at GM crops. Nature. 497:24–26
Gliessman SR (1990) Agroecology: researching the ecological basis for sustainable agriculture. Springer, New York
Gollier C, Jullien B, Treich N (2000) Scientific progress and irreversibility: an economic interpretation of the 'precautionary principle'. J Public Econ 75(2):229–253
Gorlin JB (2019) Iron replacement: precautionary principle versus risk-based decision making. Transfusion 59(5):1613–1615
Griliches Z (1957) Hybrid corn: an exploration in the economics of technological change. Econometrica 25:501–522
Hayami Y, Ruttan VW (1971) Agricultural development: an international perspective. The Johns Hopkins Press, Baltimore

Henry C (1974) Investment decisions under uncertainty: the "irreversibility effect". Am Econ Rev 64(6):1006–1012
Huang F, Andow DA, Buschman LL (2011) Success of the high-dose/refuge resistance management strategy after 15 years of Bt crop use in North America. Entomol Exp Appl 140(1):1–16
Immordino G (2003) Looking for a guide to protect the environment: the development of the precautionary principle. J Econ Surv 17(5):629–644
ISAAA (2018) Global status of commercialized biotech/GM crops: 2018. ISAAA Brief No. 54. ISAAA. Ithaca, NY
Ishii T (2018) Crop gene-editing: should we bypass or apply existing GMO policy? Trends Plant Sci 23(11):947–950
Jin L, Zhang H, Lu Y, Yang Y, Wu K, Tabashnik BE et al (2015) Large-scale test of the natural refuge strategy for delaying insect resistance to transgenic Bt crops. Nat Biotechnol 33(2):169
Klerkx L, Van Mierlo B, Leeuwis C (2012) Evolution of systems approaches to agricultural innovation: concepts, analysis and interventions. Springer, Dordrecht
Levidow L (2001) Precautionary uncertainty: regulating GM crops in Europe. Soc Stud Sci 31 (6):842–874
Lu Y, Wu K, Jiang Y, Xia B, Li P, Feng H et al (2010) Mirid bug outbreaks in multiple crops correlated with wide-scale adoption of Bt cotton in China. Science 328(5982):1151–1154
Miller HE, Engemann KJ (2019) The precautionary principle and unintended consequences. Kybernetes 48(2):265–286
Murgai R, Ali M, Byerlee D (2001) Productivity growth and sustainability in post-green revolution agriculture: the case for the Indian and Pakistan Punjabs. World Bank Res Obs 16:199–218
Noailly J (2008) Coevolution of economic and ecological systems. J Evol Econ 18(1):1–29
Orset C (2014) Innovation and the precautionary principle. Econ Innov New Technol 23 (8):780–801
Ortega DL, Waldman KB, Richardson RB, Clay DC, Snapp S (2016) Sustainable intensification and farmer preferences for crop system attributes: evidence from Malawi's central and southern regions. World Dev 87:139–151
Pant LP (2019) Responsible innovation through conscious contestation at the interface of agricultural science, policy, and civil society. Agric Hum Values 1–15
Peng S, Cassman KG, Virmani S, Sheehy J, Khush GS (1999) Yield potential trends of tropical rice since the release of IR8 and the challenge of increasing rice yield potential. Crop Sci 39:1552–1559
Peng S, Huang J, Cassman KG, Laza RC, Visperas RM, Khush GS (2010) The importance of maintenance breeding: a case study of the first miracle rice variety-IR8. Field Crop Res 119 (2):342–347
Prakash A, Kollman KL (2003) Biopolitics in the EU and the US: a race to the bottom or convergence to the top? Int Stud Q 47(4):617–641
Ramani SV, Richard A (1993) Decision, irreversibility and flexibility: the irreversibility effect re-examined. Theor Decis 35(3):259–276
Ramani SV, Thutupalli A (2015) Emergence of controversy in technology transitions: green revolution and Bt cotton in India. Technol Forecast Soc Chang 100:198–212
Reisig DD, Kurtz R (2018) Bt resistance implications for Helicoverpa zea (Lepidoptera: Noctuidae) insecticide resistance management in the United States. Environ Entomol 47(6):1357–1364
Ruto E, Garrod G (2009) Investigating farmers' preferences for the design of agri-environment schemes: a choice experiment approach. J Environ Plan Manag 52(5):631–647
Sandin P (1999) Dimensions of the precautionary principle. Hum Ecol Risk Assess 5(5):889–907
Shiva V (1989) The violence of the green revolution—ecological degradation and political conflict in Punjab. Natraj Publisher, Dehra Dun
Singla R, Johnson P, Misra S (2013) Examination of regional-level efficient refuge requirements for Bt cotton in India. AgBioForum. 15(3):303–314
Sunding D, Zilberman D (2001) The agricultural innovation process: research and technology adoption in a changing agricultural sector. Handb Agric Econ 1:207–261

Swanson TM (2002) Biotechnology, agriculture and the developing world: the distributional implications of technological change. Edward Elgar Publishing Ltd., Northampton
Szirmai A (2005) The dynamics of socio-economic development: an introduction. Cambridge University Press, Cambridge
Tabashnik BE, Carrière Y (2017) Surge in insect resistance to transgenic crops and prospects for sustainability. Nat Biotechnol 35(10):926
Tabashnik BE, Gassmann AJ, Crowder DW, Carrière Y (2008) Insect resistance to Bt crops: evidence versus theory. Nat Biotechnol 26(2):199
Tisdell C (2010) The precautionary principle revisited: its interpretations and their conservation consequences. Singap Econ Rev 55(02):335–352
Van der Werf HM, Petit J (2002) Evaluation of the environmental impact of agriculture at the farm level: a comparison and analysis of 12 indicator-based methods. Agric Ecosyst Environ 93 (1–3):131–145
Voytas DF, Gao C (2014) Precision genome engineering and agriculture: opportunities and regulatory challenges. PLoS Biol 12(6):e1001877
Weaver SA, Morris MC (2005) Risks associated with genetic modification:–an annotated bibliography of peer reviewed natural science publications. J Agric Environ Ethics 18(2):157–189